Presented to Purchase College
by
Gary Waller, PhD Cambridge

State University of New York
Distinguished Professor

Professor
of Literature & Cultural
Studies, and Theatre &
Performance, 1995-2019
Provost 1995-2004

OXFORD HISTORY OF
ENGLISH LITERATURE

Edited by
F. P. WILSON *and* BONAMY DOBRÉE

THE OXFORD HISTORY OF
ENGLISH LITERATURE

Edited by

F. P. WILSON AND BONAMY DOBRÉE

ENGLISH LITERATURE
IN THE
EARLIER SEVENTEENTH
CENTURY
1600–1660

BY

DOUGLAS BUSH

Second edition, revised

OXFORD
AT THE CLARENDON PRESS
1962

Oxford University Press, Amen House, London E.C.4

GLASGOW NEW YOUK TORONTO MELBOURNE WELLINGTON
BOMBAY CALCUTTA MADRAS KARACHI LAHORE DACCA
CAPE TOWN SALISBURY NAIROBI IBADAN ACCRA
KUALA LUMPUR HONG KONG

FIRST PUBLISHED 1945
REPRINTED 1946, 1948, 1952, 1959
SECOND EDITION, REVISED, 1962

PRINTED IN GREAT BRITAIN
AT THE UNIVERSITY PRESS, OXFORD
BY VIVIAN RIDLER
PRINTER TO THE UNIVERSITY

PREFACE TO THE SECOND EDITION

SINCE this history was published in 1945, books, articles, and essays have multiplied in such numbers that the bibliographies, those at least for general topics and all but minor writers, have increasingly lost their utility. The Clarendon Press graciously granted *carte blanche* for total revision. The bibliography has been overhauled and brought up to date—that is, through 1961 and often beyond—as well as the author's knowledge and judgement and the limits of space allowed. As for the text, while accounts of the greater writers could seldom be expanded, a good many sections have been rewritten, and many small changes have been made all along the way. Advancing knowledge has also corrected some matters of fact.

I am obliged to a number of persons who answered queries or volunteered information: officers of five University Presses, Harvard, Oxford (New York), Rutgers, Washington, and Yale; Mmes. C. S. S. Higham, Joan Rees, Joan Varley; Sir Geoffrey Keynes; Messrs. William Addison and J. M. Osborn; Dr. Ronald Berman and Dr. Louis B. Wright; Professors R. C. Bald, J. Frank, V. B. Heltzel, D. Novarr, F. S. Siebert, and especially Professors W. A. Jackson, S. Schoenbaum, and E. Weismiller and the general editors, Professors Bonamy Dobrée and F. P. Wilson. Professor Wilson above all has been, as before, indefatigably helpful.

I return thanks to the American Council of Learned Societies for an award which enabled me to take a term off duty and start on this work. I am grateful, as always, to the staff of the Harvard libraries and, for summer privileges, to the Dartmouth College Library; and to the staff of the Clarendon Press for their general care and their patient acceptance of late additions to the bibliography.

D. B.

PREFACE TO THE FIRST EDITION

THIS volume is (or was supposed to be) limited to about 150,000 words of text, and many things, as Purchas said of Sir Anthony Sherley's travels, 'are left out not for want of worth, but of roome'. Particular problems of inclusion and proportion are complicated by the necessary effort to maintain a balance between the contemporary and the modern scale of values. In regard to authors who straddle 1600, my normal rule has been to mention but not discuss works written before that date, since these will be treated in the volume on the sixteenth century. Doubtless many readers would prefer to have chapters grouped around men rather than around types of writing and modes of thought, but it is hoped that the present arrangement, though it requires the slicing up of some authors, may contribute to a more philosophic unity; it is at least a continual reminder that most great prose of the period was didactic and utilitarian. It is hoped also, since there is continual occasion for doubt or debate, that the apparent assurance of brevity may not 'sound arrogantly unto present Ears in this strict enquiring Age, wherein, for the most part, Probably, and Perhaps, will hardly serve to mollify the Spirit of captious Contradictors'. As for more fundamental complaints, the author can only admit the general impeachment lodged by Hobbes against the Oxford mathematicians: 'There is within you some special cause of intenebration which you should do well to look to.'

Texts are normally quoted from first or authoritative early editions with no change except that italics are not retained, that contractions are expanded, and that *i, j, u, v,* and *w* are made to conform with modern usage. Titles are given in their original form in the bibliography and modernized in the text and chronological tables.

I must record my gratitude for assistance of various kinds: to the President and Fellows of Harvard College for grants from the Clark Bequest; to the Army Medical Library, the Boston Public Library, the Library of Congress, the Newberry Library, the libraries of the University of Chicago, Columbia University, Cornell University, the University of Illinois, Yale University and Divinity School, and the Harvard Divinity School and

School of Business Administration, for the loan of books; to the Boston Public Library and the libraries of the Harvard Law School and the Union Theological Seminary, for the privilege of consulting books; and to the staff of the Widener and Houghton libraries for their untiring help over a long time. The University of Toronto Press and the Cornell University Press have willingly allowed me to use bits of two small volumes of mine, *The Renaissance and English Humanism* (1939) and *Paradise Lost in Our Time* (1945).

President Wilbur K. Jordan of Radcliffe College, Professors J. Milton French of Rutgers University, William A. Jackson, George W. Sherburn, and A. P. Usher of Harvard, F. A. Patterson of Columbia, and John W. Spargo of Northwestern University, Dr. Louis B. Wright of the Huntington Library, and Dr. C. William Miller of the University of Virginia, have been good enough to answer queries. For amiable and valuable criticism of parts of the manuscript I am indebted to friends and colleagues of Harvard University, Professor Jackson again and Professors Charles H. McIlwain, James B. Munn, Kenneth B. Murdock, Hyder E. Rollins, and Theodore Spencer, and to my friends Professors Warner G. Rice of the University of Michigan and Arthur S. P. Woodhouse of the University of Toronto. This large sum of scholarly insurance does not of course exempt the insured from the common lot of man. Professor F. P. Wilson has been from beginning to end not only a patient and helpful adviser but an active co-worker to a degree quite beyond what might be expected of a general editor, and in matters of critical opinion both he and Professor Dobrée have shown a tolerant magnanimity. It would be superfluous if not impertinent to pay tribute to the Clarendon Press, but I must acknowledge its noble indulgence of my bibliographical excesses—though a large portion of my wild oats has had to be ploughed under. Finally, my wife has listened to many pages and many groans, and has done much to prevent the multiplication of both.

D. B.

Harvard University

CONTENTS

I

THE BACKGROUND OF THE AGE

WHILE all ages are ages of transition, there are some in
which disruptive and creative forces reach maturity and
combine to speed up the normal process of change. In the
history of England, as in that of Europe at large, the seventeenth
century is probably the most conspicuous modern example, unless we except our own age, of such acceleration. In 1600 the
educated Englishman's mind and world were more than half
medieval; by 1660 they were more than half modern. The
character and causes of such a transformation are far too complex to be summed up in a formula, but something of its breadth
and scope may be suggested by such labels as democracy and
imperialism, industrialism and capitalism, the advance of pure
and applied science and the gospel of progress, the spread of the
scientific, secular, and anti-authoritarian spirit through other
domains of thought and action.

But this process of change did not begin or end in the years
1600–60, and it took place against a background of continuity
and compromise. We encounter the clash and the fusion of old
and new on every side, in science and religion, politics and
economics, law and literature, music and architecture. It is the
impact of modernism upon medievalism that gives the age its
peculiar character. Yet the forces of 'modernism' were themselves generally as old as the forces of conservative tradition,
and it was in the name of conservative tradition that the great
rebellion in politics and religion was conducted. As the quarrel
between 'ancients' and 'moderns' developed, champions of
modern superiority could appeal to the telescope and the microscope, but otherwise there was hardly any new idea of the
century, from the motion of the earth to the motion of the atom,
from democracy to absolutism, from the theory of ethics to the
theory of prose style, of which the germ at least was not to be
found in ancient Greece and Rome. In other spheres, such as
the religious, social, and economic, the elements of change had
been operating since the Middle Ages. What distinguished the
seventeenth century from the sixteenth was not so much the

arrival of new ideas and forces as the accumulated and irresistible pressure of old and new ones in potent combination and interaction. Even the belief in a rigorous order of nature, which lies behind 'classical' mechanistic thought, may be regarded as in some sense an unconscious heritage from theology. And the period which transformed scholastic and Calvinistic determinism into a scientific counterpart was also the period of mercantilism and mysticism. Surveying the age and its representative minds, in 1660 as well as in 1600, we may say that normality consists in incongruity.

There were, of course, whole-hearted conservatives and whole-hearted modernists, but even they were aware of a changing world, and a multitude who belonged to neither category were disturbed by violent contrasts and divided loyalties. From Donne to Dryden thoughtful men ask 'What do I know?' Sharing the critical spirit, yet conscious of its destructive results, they seek some valid authority, some standing-ground more firm than that which had served their fathers. Is the edifice of knowledge built by ancient genius the modern man's permanent home or is it his prison? In his view of the universe and God and man, shall he hold by the Bible, Aristotle, and Ptolemy, or by one of the confusing new theories? Or, since very few men were troubled by science, what is the final authority in religious doctrine and discipline, the Church of Rome, the Church of England, the Bible, individual reason, or the supra-rational inner light? In the tremendous matter of the salvation or damnation of souls, can those who possess the truth tolerate the propagation of error? Should Protestants worship God according to a prescribed ritual borrowed from the Scarlet Woman or with austere and spontaneous simplicity? What is the divinely appointed form of church government, episcopal, synodical, or congregational? Are Church and State united or separate, and which is superior? Where does supreme political and constitutional authority reside, in the king, the judges of the common law, or Parliament? Does the tyranny of the sovereign justify armed resistance? Does the tyranny of Parliament justify forcible purging and military rule? Is society an organism actuated by religious motives or an aggregate of individuals actuated by economic self-interest? Is morality founded on right reason and divine precept, or on the current law of the land?

Such a catalogue might be prolonged indefinitely, but these far from theoretical questions will serve to illustrate the permanently unsettled state of the seventeenth-century man's inner and outer world. It is not unnatural that melancholy has been taken as a conspicuous, even a dominant, characteristic of late Elizabethan and Jacobean literature. Its manifestations are infinitely various in kind and degree—Jaques, Hamlet, and Thersites are three out of many dramatic voices—and the causes assigned range from introspection to indigestion, from Puritanism to the plague. Certainly we find much disgust with men and society, much vague bitterness against a world that seems out of joint, against the apparent futility of life. Many young men might have uttered, with a difference, the later judgement of Margaret of Newcastle that there was no employment for heroic spirits under so wise a king as James. The young Sir William Cornwallis and the elder statesman Fulke Greville, to cite only two witnesses, see about them nothing but the corruptions of a sick time. Ancient heroes, Cornwallis declares in his essay on 'Fame', searched for substance, modern men chase shadows: 'we are walking Ghostes'. We of the present, who have had our generation of hollow men, our literature of defeatism, are perhaps especially qualified to understand one side of the early seventeenth century, yet we should be unwise in seeking too much affinity between it and the recent past, since selective and plausible parallels can be and have been drawn between our time and every notable period from Chaucer's to the Victorian.

Jacobean pessimism, like the modern, is commonly taken as a reaction against the optimism of the preceding age, although the writers who have held forth on that text seem to regard the name of Marlowe as sufficient evidence of Elizabethan optimism. In fact, Elizabethan literature, like Victorian literature, was pessimistic enough, and it is permissible to think that 'Jacobean melancholy' has been exaggerated. Against the 'Jacobean pessimism' of Shakespeare's partly Elizabethan tragedies and problem comedies may be set the 'Jacobean optimism' of his dramatic romances. 'There never was a merry World', said Selden, 'since the Faries left Dancing, and the Parson left Conjuring.' But in all ages 'Merry England' has been both a living reality and a nostalgic fiction. Much Jacobean melancholy, like that of our own day, was the fashionable exploitation of what in some men was authentic, and while young intellectuals were nourishing one another's disillusionment, many happy extraverts were singing the madrigals and ballets of Thomas Morley and his fellows. The meditations on the brevity of life, so numerous and so rich throughout our sixty years, are not the rhetorical funguses of an age of decay; they are the seventeenth-century version of the Dance of Death, and they tell rather of immense vitality contemplating its inevitable extinction. If Calvinistic religion had its dark and terrifying side, it also raised the humblest of the elect above the lords of the earth. If astronomical discoveries and speculations bewildered and dismayed some philosophical minds, for others they enhanced the glory of God; and applied science promised the conquest of all nature for the use and benefit of man. If some writers were troubled by the belief that they were living near the end of the world, in a time of general deterioration, the mass of men, from politicians, merchants, and colonizers down to ploughmen, were far too busy to be melancholy. They would have shared the retrospective verdict not of the romantic duchess but of Fuller: 'Indeed all the Reigne of King James was better for one to live under, than to write of, consisting of a Champian of constant tranquility, without any tumours of trouble to entertain posterity with.' And if the latter half of our period was one of war and continued discord, the rebellion and the Commonwealth were the culmination of intense zeal for the establishment of a new era. Altogether, one could make out a strong argument for the Elizabethan age as one of pessimistic gloom and the earlier seventeenth century as one of optimistic recovery.

However, granting the whole period its fair share, and no more, of the melancholy that runs through all English literature, we may illustrate some of its special features and causes in a brief sketch of the changing background. The general political, religious, and economic causes, even the philosophic ones, were all alive in the time of Elizabeth. Political and religious strife was brought to a head by the clear-cut Stuart theory of State and Church, partly because the sovereign's conception of sovereignty had become more rigidly legalistic, and still more because the structure of society and the temper of the nation and Parliament had changed. The Tudors were skilful in avoiding both doctrinaire theory and open conflict, and were lucky in not having to face the ultimate consequences of active problems, though even Elizabeth in 1601 bowed to a refractory Parliament. Anxiety about the succession and the various other troubles of her last years—among them the execution of Essex, the patron and the national hope of many young literary men—contributed to make the welcome given to James much more than empty adulation. The king, however, always remained a stranger in England, and he was quite incapable of inspiring patriotic devotion to himself and the Crown. His outlook, and that of his son, were dynastic rather than national. Men who recalled the days of the Armada did not feel proud over James's unwearied appeasement of Spain and his sacrifice of the Palatinate, Bohemia, and continental Protestantism—the theme of the bitter 'Tom Tell-Truth' (c. 1622) and of the potent *Vox Populi* (1620) by the prolific Rev. Thomas Scott. Yet others could justly rejoice because he had kept the country out of futile and unnecessary war. The domestic problems he inherited were far beyond the grasp of a dogmatic academic theorist, however erratically shrewd he might be, and through a long series of arbitrary acts he contrived to alarm or antagonize almost all the substantial groups in the nation except the orthodox clergy. All classes alike resented the king's extravagance, his attachment to unworthy favourites, and the moral and financial corruption of the court circle. In fairness we should remember that the increasing friction between James (and Charles) and Parliament was caused in part by quite inadequate governmental revenue. And James was wiser than Parliament in his desire for union with Scotland and for more liberal treatment of Catholics, perhaps also in his pacific foreign policy.

It is more difficult to find any evidence of Charles's wisdom. Yet, when Parliament was exasperated beyond endurance, invincible respect for the Lord's Anointed was still shown in the honest efforts to dissociate abuses from the king and fasten them upon his advisers. Even in 1640, when the Long Parliament began to take over royal powers, its aim was to curb the prerogative, not to assert the sovereignty of Parliament. Up to the last the parliamentarians were too instinctively monarchical to contemplate revolution; only step by step were they driven into it. For the most part they did not consider themselves pioneer democrats, they were patriotic—and propertied—Englishmen who appealed to Magna Carta and Bracton in defence of their traditional rights and the traditional supremacy of law. And whatever the modern world owes to the creators of parliamentary government, from the passionate Eliot to the sober Pym and the rest, the conflict cannot be regarded in terms of black and white. We may perhaps set aside the personal appeal which the royal martyr and sainted cavalier has always made, but we should not forget that all along he had had a large share of legality, if not of equity, honesty, and intelligence, on his side. And the king lacked not only revenue but a national civil service, a solid framework of royal authority, apart from uncertain local gentry. On the other hand, we cannot, as even Milton discovered, idealize the Long Parliament as an assembly of political Galahads, and the behaviour of the victorious army, however strong the provocation, was scarcely in accord with the doctrine of the supremacy of law for which they had fought. When war came, it divided individual souls as well as families and districts. Many men on both sides were happy in seeing only one course before them, but many also had a hard decision to make. It was with broken hearts that the chivalrous Sir Edmund Verney and the philosophic Falkland followed their liege lord.

As events showed, the nation was not prepared for a republic, and it did not get one. If Cromwell had had a free hand, the protectorate would have been a happier era than it was, and in spite of the pressure of conflicting factions he succeeded to a remarkable degree, in a few years, in commanding a new respect abroad and creating order at home. But his foreign policy, based on a mixture of commercial, religious, and imperialistic motives, was expensive, if nothing worse, and domestic order was partly artificial. No amount of beneficent and liberal reform, and there was a good deal, could obscure the fact that the government was not a free republic but a military dictatorship. The greatest of republicans betrayed his anxiety even in eulogizing the Protector. What had been thinly disguised became very clear with the inquisitorial jurisdiction of the regional major-generals. Altogether, experience of the iron hand, the repressive severity of Puritan legislation on manners and morals, the political chaos that attended and followed the brief reign of Richard Cromwell, and the extremities of economic depression, were enough to inspire London itself, the former stronghold of Puritan resistance, with an ardent longing for the return of king, Parliament, prosperity, and the open use of the *Book of Common Prayer*.

During these sixty years religious and ecclesiastical questions were increasingly bound up with politics, and they directly touched larger numbers of people and kindled passions which constitutional issues might leave cool. The Elizabethan compromise from the first had failed to draw in the more resolute Catholics and Protestants. James's tolerant inclinations were frustrated by alarm over Catholic conspiracies and the multiplication of recusants, and the re-enforcement of the penal laws resulted in the Gunpowder Plot, which was to remain in the popular imagination an inflammatory warning of the political dangers of popery. The oath of allegiance (1606), James said in his *Apology*, was a test of civil obedience and, though the oath went beyond the merely civil, it might, but for papal *breves* and Parliament, have been a virtual instrument of toleration. Later years brought comparative relief to English Catholics, and under Charles's French queen Catholicism raised its head at court and won some notable converts. In the eyes of Puritans who dreaded the grim wolf with privy paw, Laud's High Church was Roman in all but name. And in 1641 Lord Falkland, who was no Puritan, declared in Parliament that some bishops were so absolutely, directly, and cordially papists that it was all that £1,500 a year could do to keep them from confessing it.

But Catholicism proved a much less formidable force than Puritanism, which grew from a drop of dissent to an angry flood. At the beginning of 1644 John Greene wrote in his diary that 'now 'tis made a warre almost merely for religion, which I feared'. To intensely serious people, learned and unlearned, who demanded apostolic simplicity, the Church of England with its Romish ritual and hierarchy appeared a very imperfect fulfilment of Reformation ideals. The word 'Puritan' came to mean many things, so that modern like early usage is often loose and misleading, but in the individual sphere it increasingly stressed conversion, rebirth in Christ; as a general movement towards the holy community, Puritanism carried on its initial principle of firm adherence to the Bible as the sole and sufficient authority in all matters of ecclesiastical government and ceremony as well as of belief and conduct. The Bible and the congregation were for the religious republican or democrat what the common law and Parliament were for his political counterpart, and both effected a revolution by appealing to a remote and somewhat nebulous past against a corrupted present. Theologically, there was for generations little or no difference between Anglicans and Puritans, since the Church of England until the early seventeenth century was largely Calvinistic. The advance of Arminian theology and its association with High Church principles were registered in George Morley's famous answer to the question 'What the Arminians held?'—that they held all the best bishoprics and deaneries in England. Indeed, though Laud was liberal in his theological outlook, through his rigorous insistence on external uniformity and his far-reaching interference in all departments of life, Arminianism was identified with the doctrine of divine right, royal and episcopal, and with the whole Stuart régime. Mrs. Hutchinson was not unwarranted in saying, as the Grand Remonstrance had said, that if any gentleman maintained the good laws of the land, or stood up for any public interest, he was called a Puritan. The union of prelacy and monarchy brought about the union of religious and political nonconformity which finally overthrew both Church and State. But before condemning the motives and methods of Bancroft and Laud and their sovereigns in enforcing conformity, we should remember that our religious tolerance has been largely the by-product of religious apathy, and that the Church, in the conviction of many good men, could not afford to be tolerant when its very survival as a national institution was in danger. As Laud said, in dedicating the *Conference with Fisher* (1639) to the king, the Church of England—which we think of as a serene *via media*—was ground between two millstones, Romanist and Puritan. We must not forget, moreover, the Tudor legacy of disorder, ignorance, inefficiency, and poverty among the mass of the clergy.

During Elizabeth's reign the growing body of Puritans were mostly content to form the left wing of the Church, but in the seventeenth century that position became less and less tenable. At the Hampton Court Conference (1604) James enunciated Stuart policy with a mixture of short-sighted violence and prophetic penetration. His promise to harry Nonconformists out of the land bore immediate fruit in the ejection of perhaps ninety Puritan clergymen. The sectarian exodus from the Church had begun much earlier—Sir Andrew Aguecheek hated a Brownist—and some people moved to Holland, but the most impressive portents were the voyage of the *Mayflower* (1620) and the 'great migration' of 1630 and subsequent years. The religious origins of Massachusetts illustrate the mingled loyalty and ingenuity of the emigrants and the invincible instinct for unity and uniformity which was a general heritage. Across the wide ocean, in 'the savage deserts of America', faithful Englishmen and Christians could maintain the paradox of non-separating Congregationalism with much less trouble than at home; they were only separating from the corruptions of the Church. In England Puritan antagonism to prelacy, which had long been seething, boiled over in 1640–1. In addition to some detached and more or less secular Erastians, there appeared among the warring Puritans three main parties or groups of parties. The Solemn League and Covenant (1643) signalized a Presbyterian predominance which was to last for four or five years. The English Presbyterians wanted a national Presbyterian Church, controlled by the State, with no toleration for dissent; what emerged, however, was only the shell of a Presbyterian system. Reactionary and *bourgeois* Presbyterianism gave way before the liberal and flexible Independents, who stood for toleration and feared parliamentary absolutism, and whose strength was centred in Cromwell's army. They were able in 1648–9 to purge the House of Presbyterians and execute the king. The third and much more miscellaneous group comprised the sects and parties which were being born every month, with varying religious, political, or economic creeds and often with lunatic fringes. In his *Gangraena* (1646) the Presbyterian Thomas Edwards listed sixteen recognizable groups and over two hundred 'errors, heresies, blasphemies' (including the innocent three of Sir Thomas Browne's 'greener studies') which had developed in recent years. This burgeoning of sects was of course the logical outcome of Protestant individualism, and the centrifugal impulse was stimulated by more immediate causes, the flourishing of old and new abuses in the Church, the royal and episcopal campaign for High Church uniformity, and some experience of what promised to be the equally tyrannous uniformity of Presbyterianism. There was, too, the positive desire, sometimes partly spurious and fanatical, sometimes deep and real, for a kind of illumination which the Establishment did not seem to give. An example of the one kind would be the Fifth Monarchy men, who were looking—as Milton could look—for the second coming of Christ. The finest example of the other was the Society of Friends, which grew so rapidly under the compelling leadership of the itinerant mystic, George Fox.

If the fusion and the variety of political and religious problems made an insoluble tangle, a further important element of complication was the economic. As Peter Chamberlen said, in *The Poor Man's Advocate* (1649), 'None more fond of a King then the English, yet they departed from him to ease their purses, and their Consciences.' The complaints of men of property against arbitrary taxation and other evils were uttered in a succession of stormy Parliaments and, after 1629, were kept alive by such individuals as Hampden. The middle and poorer classes, if they did not win satisfactory relief, at least made their grievances audible through local petitions and through union in secular or religious groups. The Levellers, headed by the brave, much-enduring, and difficult John Lilburne, aimed at political democracy. The communistic Diggers, who represented a more extreme demand for economic and social justice, and other older bodies like the Anabaptists and Family of Love, revived the radical-mystical movement of the Middle Ages. In the seventeenth century, especially after 1640, the breaking-down of things established seemed to open the way for the rebuilding of society, for the realization of perennial dreams of Christian communism. To the eyes of authority the inner light had always looked decidedly red.

While the economic causes of discontent were greatly aggravated by the war and its aftermath, most of them were much older than our period. Apart from such acts of God as the recurring plague and bad crops, the seventeenth century inherited the related evils of enclosures, evictions, unemployment, pauperism, and vagrancy. Behind these and other particular troubles was the general fact of accelerated change in the economic structure of society, both rural and urban. The corpuscular life of the Middle Ages was becoming the fortuitous collision of atoms that we know. There was still the medieval pattern of the small agricultural unit, the self-contained and stable manorial community with its unwritten but powerful law of 'custom'. In the towns the craft guilds were parallel units of corporate life, with authority and traditions which were economic, fraternal, and paternal. But both systems were declining, or at any rate changing, before the advance of capitalistic enterprise and large-scale production (in farming as well as in industry) with their division of labour and division between employer and employed. The result was economic confusion, depressions, much occupational and social disturbance, and widespread distress. Monopolies, which bulk so large in the period, affected everyone from the sovereign or government and actual or would-be monopolists and 'projectors' down to the great body of helpless workers and consumers; one achievement of the interregnum was the virtual abolition of that particular evil. Masses of people were increasingly dependent on the fluctuations of national and international trade. As usual, the poor grew poorer and the rich richer. Economic along with religious motives took emigrants to America. While some men, from Dekker to Winstanley, had a feeling for the poor, economic writers were more concerned with improving the methods of production, with the problems of big business, of a self-sufficient national economy and the balance of trade. If the first forty years of the century can be called relatively prosperous, the decade of the civil war almost ruined agriculture and business, and the decade of the Commonwealth, which brought a measure of recovery, ended amid cries of despair from London and the counties. The problems of unemployment and poor relief were often more than the notable statutes of 1597–1601 and later efforts could cope with. It can be said at least that poverty, even more than education, attracted charitable bequests; apart from the impressive statistics, there is some evidence in the exhortations and the funeral eulogies delivered by clergymen, especially Puritans, and in such books as Stow's *Survey of London* and Fuller's *Worthies*. And thoughtful pamphleteers, among them Samuel Hartlib, studied causes and remedies.

The long years of comparative peace under Elizabeth and James, and the dynamic effect of the bullion acquired from America and Spain, made possible the transformation of a country which had lived mainly at the subsistence level into a financial power. The formation of the great trading companies, the expansion of foreign commerce, not merely on the Continent but in the Far East, and the exploration and colonizing of America were both causes and results of the accumulation of capital. The development of woollen and other textile manufactures, and of mining, coal-mining in particular, required capital, credit, technological inventions, and a national and foreign market. During the sixteenth and seventeenth centuries prices rose much faster than rents and wages, and the royal exchequer and the mass of the population suffered alike. But there were vast profits for the capitalist. One obvious indication was the rapid spread of luxury. The Plugsons and Bounderbys might rejoice in progress and prosperity; many others saw greed for money, sinful usury, competitive commercialism, speculative gambling, and reckless extravagance poisoning good old ways. A modern theory has identified the growth of individualistic capitalism with Puritanism, with the illiberal, ascetic, and acquisitive devotion to business and thrift which merits and receives divine approbation. This theory, though congenial to the many who are inclined to believe anything ill of Puritans, has been considerably modified by more recent economic historians, and even the layman can discern large flaws in the equation. At any rate, what had been an agricultural country of self-sufficing local units was beginning to turn into the workshop of the world. While the nobility, gentry, and yeomen were, in their several ways, attached to the land, much of the new money was concentrated in the towns, above all in London. The capital, with somewhat less than 250,000 people in 1600 and somewhat more than 400,000 in 1660, was the one real city—'second to none beyond Seas, a noble Mart', said Robert Burton—and its public and private opulence impressed foreign visitors. But though at the beginning of the century London had almost a monopoly of business, the provincial towns, especially the seaports, were increasing in population and economic importance.

The rise of the commercial and industrial middle class is such a standard feature of every modern century that we may well hestitate to claim it for any one, yet it is in the late sixteenth and the early seventeenth century that we first encounter a solid array of merchants, manufacturers, entrepreneurs, bankers, shipowners, and tradesmen enjoying the prosperity and the consciousness of economic and political power which the war fully revealed—and which Henry Robinson philosophized. From the relatively small number of merchants came nearly half of the very large sums given to charity. The definite emergence of a substantial *bourgeoisie* had of course the most varied social and literary consequences. Men of business bought estates and added new blood and new money, often without the old conception of duties, to the squirearchy; and it was difficult to avoid the stream of titles that flowed so insistently from the royal fountain of honour. On the other hand, the prejudice of the landed classes against commercial connexions relaxed under the most persuasive of arguments. Shares of stock and middle-class dowries were exciting if speculative lures. Younger sons might start better game in the City or abroad than on the paternal and perhaps mortgaged acres. The distinctions of degree had lost much of their rigidity, and economic class-distinctions had not yet hardened, so that there was, in scientific language, a good deal of osmosis. The heralds, if not the moralists, were disposed to see a gentleman in any well-to-do male. Literature is full of complaints about upstarts. All of these social changes, which had begun ages before and were quickened by the growth of industry and commerce, were still further quickened by the war and the mainly middle-class victory.

These changes are mirrored in drama and satire, treatise and sermon, petition and remonstrance, and yet pictures of change are less deeply registered in our memories than the milkmaid and franklin of the Overbury characters, the bovine content of Earle's plain country fellow, and the unchanged countryside of 'L'Allegro', the *Hesperides*, and *The Complete Angler*. The rural world was still so largely feudal that much depended on the character of the landlord and his wife. Many of the nobility and gentry were seduced by the attractions of London, and both James and Charles tried, in vain, to compel them to stay at home; yet many also continued to practise the beneficent doctrine of *noblesse oblige*, to dispense hospitality, charity, and educational and literary patronage. After the Restoration they are found, as before, administering local government and upholding the *mores* of their communities. The evolution of the impersonal economic order, or disorder, did not extinguish the expression at least of the medieval sense of human and ethical considerations and of the principle of subordinating private gain to public good. Governmental paternalism worked in the old spirit in its constant struggles with the problems created by economic individualism. And if that individualism was partly Puritan, the Puritan principle of the 'calling', in alliance with the old and universal principle of 'degree', was a conservative force. The ambitious might seek to rise in the world and share class privileges, but only antinomian radicals thought of class war.

The universities and schools were not immune from these

various kinds of disturbance. In some ways it was good for the country that the proportion of students and graduates should have been so high. The other side of the picture appears in Bacon's repeated objections to the increasing number of schools and the breeding of more scholars and clerics than 'Preferments can take off', which means the breeding of seditious discontent and an inadequate supply of manual workers. Similar views were expressed in 1656 by the thoroughly practical Francis Osborn. Less tough-minded observers, like Robert Burton, lamented the economic plight and social humiliations of many teachers, tutors, and clergymen. Then, while alarms and controversies were frequent in the first four decades, the war brought university education almost to a standstill. Oxford, the king's headquarters, combined the atmosphere of a court with that of a garrison. Much college plate went to the royal mint, and pious hands destroyed many relics of idolatry. During and after the war parliamentary visitations caused wholesale evictions of scholars, among them a number of our authors.

Further, the political, religious, economic, and social revolution was paralleled by a movement for educational reform, although in this sphere, happily, some radical ideas did not get translated into practice. The standard-bearers of secondary education were of course the public and free schools inherited from earlier times, Winchester, Eton, St. Paul's, and the rest. Harrow, chartered in 1571, commenced its activity in 1608, and in 1609–11 Thomas Sutton was granted letters patent for the Charterhouse. While the sixteenth century had been active in founding schools, the huge and sudden rise in benefactions during two decades, 1611–30, evokes from the latest authority, W. K. Jordan, the statement: 'It is not too much to say that the basic structure of English secondary education as it was to exist for a very long time was literally created in the early Stuart period.' Gifts for scholarships and for the universities also multiplied. In the seventeenth century the British Isles possessed what was to be for a very long time their full complement of universities: Oxford, Cambridge, St. Andrews, Glasgow, Aberdeen, Edinburgh, and Trinity College, Dublin. There was much building and rebuilding, but the one new college added to an old foundation was Wadham (1610). Matthew Sutcliffe's 'Spirituall Garrison', 'King James his Colledge in Chelsey' (1610), was scarcely born, and the college established at Durham (1657), in response to pressure from the north, died after a brief but lusty infancy, 'an orphan scarce bound up in its swaddling cloaths'. Since a growing portion of England lay across the sea, we may notice the founding of the Boston Latin School (1635) and of Harvard College (1636); most of Harvard's founders were Cambridge men, and of the early university emigrants to New England a high proportion had belonged to Emmanuel. A survey of the English educational scene should not omit the Inns of Court, which Ben Jonson saluted as 'the Noblest Nourceries of Humanity, and Liberty, in the Kingdome'. They not only fostered the law—and the drama—but provided a finishing school and club for courtiers and the heirs of country gentlemen.

The operation of the classical curriculum in school is described by two ardent and enlightened provincial schoolmasters. John Brinsley's *Ludus Literarius* (1612) and Charles Hoole's *New Discovery of the Old Art of Teaching School* (1660) are both built on the tradition of Renaissance humanism, the ideal of learned piety. Although Hoole had just translated, with a sympathetic preface, the famous *Orbis Sensualium Pictus* of Comenius, he was little of a Comenian in his major work, and the differences between him and Brinsley are mainly the result of advancing classical scholarship. Both men, like many contemporaries, prescribe Hebrew. The immediate object of secondary education was complete mastery of Latin as a spoken and written medium, and that of course involved close study of the literature. The character of school life may be indicated by a summary of the routine at Westminster in the sixteen-twenties, as an alumnus described it. From a quarter-past five, when the boys were roused by a monitor's *Surgite!* for Latin prayers and ablutions, until supper at five, they were almost continuously occupied in repeating rules of Latin and Greek grammar, writing prose and verse in Latin or Greek, translating from one form or language into the other, and analysing the grammatical and rhetorical figures of classical texts. After supper a master might have senior boys in his rooms for the study of extra-curricular things like maps or, in the case of Lancelot Andrewes, for Greek and Hebrew. On Friday the week's lessons were reviewed. On Saturday declamations were held. On Sunday the King's Scholars construed the Greek Testament and wrote verses on the morning sermon. At all times, even on the playing-field, monitors took care that the boys spoke only Latin. The curriculum Milton proposed, which shocks the degenerate modern, becomes much less shocking when judged by contemporary standards of what constituted work, and also by contemporary faith in the efficacy of right methods.

Among many things which temper our impression of educational rigour we should not forget one of supreme importance. Both schools and colleges possessed as masters and dons a remarkable number of personalities, intellectual or temperamental, men like Richard Mulcaster, Thomas Farnaby, John Hales, Sir Henry Savile, Sir Henry Wotton, John Earle, John Wilkins, and the Dr. Kettell whose eccentricities Aubrey reported. Against Bacon's assertion that university students learned nothing but to believe may be set such a tutor as Joseph Mead, who was wont to greet his charges with 'Quid dubitas? What Doubts have you met in your studies to-day?' Lancelot Andrewes, said Bishop Hacket, frequently took a hand in teaching, and 'never walk'd to Cheswick for his Recreation, without a brace of this young Fry; and in that way-faring Leisure, had a singular dexterity to fill those narrow Vessels with a Funnel'. A later Westminster figure had another kind of dexterity as well; Dr. Busby left his mark upon many distinguished minds and bodies, including Dryden's. And unusual talents might be found in provincial schools—Philemon Holland at Coventry and at Warwick John Owen, whose European fame as an epigrammatist would hardly be inferred from Jonson's description, 'a pure Pedantique Schoolmaster sweeping his living from the Posteriors of litle children'.

University students enjoyed more freedom than schoolboys, though less than they have nowadays; of course they were commonly younger. At Cambridge, in Milton's time, the day began with chapel at five. Breakfast was followed by some six hours (with time out for dinner) of attendance at tutorial sessions, lectures, and disputations. There was leisure for talk, reading, writing, music, and the less innocent recreations that the 'Lady' of Christ's hit out against. The same critic later denounced theological students' participation in the dramatic performances that were a traditional feature of academic life, especially on the occasion of royal visits. The herd of undergraduate loafers have generic representatives in Richard Brathwait's Law of Drinking and in John Earle's 'A young Gentleman of the University', and particular ones in Christopher Guise and his 'ingeniouse' fellow tipplers at Oxford. And we may remember Thomas Randolph's appeal to a Cambridge landlord to rebuild the fallen Mitre at the students' expense—'We drank like Freshmen all before, But now wee'll drink like Doctors'. Then, as Guise said (and Brathwait amply indicated), *Post vinum Venus*. Dissipation at the universities was one article of faith on which Puritans and Chancellor Laud could agree.

The intellectual and the social patterns of Oxford and Cambridge carried on the sixteenth-century process of transition from the medieval to the modern. They had begun and continued, in the words of Anthony Wood, 'to noe other end but to propagate religion and good manners and supply the nation with persons cheifly professing the three famous faculties of Divinity, Law, and Phisick'. The traditional dominance of Aristotle and theology was reinforced by the Laudian statutes for Oxford. The prime purpose was still, in theory if much less fully in fact, the education of clerics; and the founders of Harvard, while seeking to avoid the ecclesiasticism of Oxford and Cambridge, were moved by the fear of leaving 'an illiterate Ministery to the Churches, when our present Ministers shall lie in the Dust'. Rhetoric and logic were still, ostensibly, a practical and professional rather than a vaguely cultural discipline. But behind the medieval façade changes were going on, at the pace prescribed or allowed by academic conservatism and the English instinct for compromise. In the seventeenth as in the sixteenth century Oxford and Cambridge increasingly attracted sons of the nobility and gentry, and many of these, and many middle-class students also, left with (or without) the bachelor's degree to pursue a secular career. Medieval scholasticism was increasingly leavened by Renaissance humanism, and the liberalizing process advanced through the growing importance and freedom of individual tutors. Along with larger study of the classics went reading in modern books of history, philosophy, and science. Chairs of history were established at both universities in the 1620's. The Laudian code fixed the statutes for the Savilian chairs in geometry and astronomy and required Greek (after the second year of residence); Laud also founded a chair in Arabic. And the parliamentary committee in 1649 insisted, no less urgently than Laud, on the old rule that only Latin or Greek should be spoken.

If the final test of an educational method is the quality of the minds and characters it produces, then the programme and teaching in school and college, whatever their deficiencies, can hold their own with any before or since. At all times students were masticating tough food. If there was more concern with grammar and flagellation than with ideals of spontaneity and self-expression, the later careers of the many illustrious victims reveal few traces of cramped intelligence and originality. If accounts of classical teaching sometimes suggest aesthetic and humane deficiencies, the literature of the age amply proves that the classics were an abiding joy, stay, and stimulus to educated readers and writers. And their dynamic power was manifested on a larger stage, in the upholding of both liberty and order in politics and religion.

With this glance at educational orthodoxy, we may turn to the current of modernism that accompanied the Puritan ascendancy (though it would have come without any Puritan impetus). The greatest mathematician of the period, John Wallis (1616–1703), recalled his early days at Cambridge (1632–40) as a time when 'Mathematicks . . . were scarce looked upon as Academical Studies, but rather Mechanical'. In 1661 Isaac Barrow, Professor of Greek at Cambridge, complained in a humorous speech that he sat lonesome as an Attic owl cut off from all companionship with other birds—and in 1663 he became the first Lucasian Professor of Mathematics. Probably both men exaggerated their isolation, but they bear witness to a real shift in academic interests. The humanistic tradition of the Renaissance had not been invariably indifferent or opposed to science, and in the seventeenth century the rising tide trickled, if it did not quite flood, into the citadels of learning. Sir Francis Kynaston, in his account (1636) of his new academy for young noblemen and gentlemen before they went abroad, provided for the sciences as well as for languages and courtly accomplishments, and for teaching 'by Demonstration and Experiment'. Sir Balthazar Gerbier's academy (1649) also included 'experimentall naturall philosophy'. Lord Herbert prescribed for a gentleman, along with the usual subjects, the serious study of geography, medicine, anatomy, and botany. Francis Osborn (1593–1659), in his *Advice to a Son* (1656–8), dismissed most academic learning as 'but Lumber and Formes' and extolled mathematics and medicine. Recalling the slender science possessed by the Oxford of his day, and its popular repute, Osborn said that 'Not a few of our then foolish Gentry' refused 'to send their Sons thither, lest they should be smutted with the Black Art'. But scientists had been multiplying, without much official encouragement, in response to the demands of practical technology. Gresham College, opened near the end of the six-teenth century, was a home of science, and in 1619 Oxford received the stimulus of the Savilian chairs. In 1621, the year in which the Sedleian lectureship in natural philosophy (Aris-totle's) was inaugurated, Nathanael Carpenter published his anti-Aristotelian *Philosophia Libera*. From 1626 at least, Oxford medical students were expected to acquire some knowledge of anatomy; the Tomlins lectureship in that subject (1624) may have revealed a gap.

From about 1640 there was a vigorous campaign for the over-hauling of both universities and schools. One significant event was the visit (1641–2) of the great Czech educator, John Amos Comenius (1592–1670). The Ramist movement had given a general impulse to empirical thought and educational reform, Bacon had shown the direction it should take, and the Puritan middle class was eager for constructive action. Comenius had devoted himself, partly as an educational reformer and partly as a builder of international religious amity, to universal ele-mentary, vocational education, on a simplified, realistic, gradu-ated, encyclopaedic, and of course religious plan, a plan distinctly lacking humane and liberal ideals. His mission in England, the organizing—presumably under parliamentary auspices—of a pansophic college, was frustrated by public disturbances, the Irish rising in particular, but the breadth of its appeal is indi-cated by the names of such patrons as Bishop John Williams (who had been a friend of Bacon), Archbishop Ussher, Lord Brooke, Pym, Selden, and Sir Cheney Colepeper. Comenius's visit was engineered chiefly by a man who had for some time been propagating his ideas, that indefatigable humanitarian 'projector', Samuel Hartlib (*c.* 1596/1600–62), the friend of Milton and, at least a few years later, of Dr. Wallis and other members of the group of scientists which began to meet about 1645 and later became the Royal Society. Another admirer and ally of Comenius was John Dury (1596–1680), a friend of Hartlib and Milton and a zealous worker for the unification of the evangelical churches of Europe. While the great aim of

Comenius and the English Comenians was not the experimental research of Wallis's group, the educational and scientific lines of thought and activity met in a preoccupation with 'things', in a return to nature, observation, and experience. Another bond of affinity was the moderate Puritanism of some of the scientists and of Comenius's backers and disciples.

During the last third of our period Puritan and especially radical antinomian dislike of the traditional academic curriculum in school and university erupted in vehement and voluminous debate. One motive, a logical if extreme development of Protestantism, was hostility to theological, scholastic, and classical learning as the corrupter of the simple Gospel and the religion of the spirit. That note, heard sometimes from the learned Milton and Roger Williams, is more characteristic in the blasts of William Dell (who became master of Caius College in 1649), John Saltmarsh, Gerrard Winstanley, George Fox, and others against a 'Hireling Ministry', a 'Carnal and Antichristian Clergie'. Traditional education and learning, as a symbol of class privilege, authority, and intolerance, could be attacked also from the political and social standpoint by the Levellers Walwyn and Overton. Another aim was practical and scientific education on a broad basis. Hartlib published works by Comenius in 1637 and following years and several tracts by Dury in 1642, 1649, and 1650(?). His friend Hezekiah Woodward issued some Baconian and Comenian pieces in 1640–1. Milton's *Of Education* (1644) and William Petty's *Advice* (1648) were both addressed to Hartlib, who could not have altogether relished the former. Modernist reforms were urged by John Hall (1649), who was a sort of Cambridge agent for Hartlib, by George Snell (1649), and John Webster (1654). Noah Biggs (1651) and the quack George Starkey (1657) denounced the tyranny of Aristotle and Galen in medicine. Dury, Dell, and others, including James Harrington (1656) and Milton (1659–60), pleaded for popular education as a duty of the State. In partial harmony with Puritan strictures were the anti-academic utterances of Hobbes in *Leviathan* (1651) and of Hobbes's friend, Francis Osborn (1656–8). And we might end with a less polemical item, Cowley's *Proposition for the Advancement of Experimental Philosophy* (1661).

Whether or not all the writers were directly influenced by Bacon or Comenius (who was himself somewhat indebted to

Bacon), a new spirit was in the air; it would have come without Bacon, but his name helps to define it. In general, Bacon's separation of religion and knowledge, his hostility to the scholastic and humanistic traditions, his positive scientific, empirical, utilitarian, and humanitarian ideals, were translated into practical and pedagogical terms. The strongly Puritan middle class, learned or unlearned, felt a natural impulse to replace the old, abstract, aristocratic, and 'useless' studies with the modern, concrete, popular, and useful. Their watchword was 'the public good', the union of progress and piety. Petty concerned himself narrowly with 'Reall Learning'; Dury, an Anglican clergyman, prescribed Hebrew (for the sake of the Bible) and the Latin and Greek languages, but these only as keys to the useful sciences and moral philosophy, not to literature. In Milton's tract, of course, the Baconian by no means submerged the Renaissance humanist; and John Hall, the minor poet and essayist, though his *Advancement of Learning* was urgently Baconian and progressive, was not illiberal. The hard-headed John Webster, in his *Academiarum Examen*, summed up the Baconian complaints of his time and class with philistine religiosity, and with a scientific and utilitarian zeal which did not forbid the glorifying of astrology and Robert Fludd—a joint in his armour not missed by Seth Ward and John Wilkins in their *Vindiciae Academiarum* (1654). The two Oxonians, though they could not but share some of Webster's views, easily showed that he and Hobbes had overlooked the recent progress of science at Oxford. There were other defences of the universities on traditional lines. Surveying the whole educational controversy, we can see prejudice and wisdom on both sides. In the popularizing of the Baconian gospel, shorn of its original grandiosity, is heard the gritty voice of Mr. Gradgrind and his numerous modern descendants; the human spirit is to be nourished in technical schools. On the other hand, whatever England and Europe owed, and still owe, to the scholastic and humanistic traditions (and most of this volume is a record of their fruits during two generations), they did not provide a satisfactory framework for popular and scientific education, and the claims of the middle class in a commercial and technological world had become insistent. The Puritan and progressive movement had some effect but, like many other advanced ideas of the time, this one was not fulfilled until the nineteenth century.

The reforming impulse was directed also to practical and domestic training for girls, though the private schools of our period, like Mrs. Salmon's at Hackney, which Katherine Fowler (later Philips) and her friend Mary Aubrey (John's cousin) attended, seem to have been devoted more to fashionable accomplishments than to household science. The Reformation had cut off one of the two careers open to gentlewomen, the monastic—Mary Ward's Catholic community (1638–42) and what a pamphlet of 1641 called the 'Arminian Nunnery' of Little Gidding were *sui generis*—and had left only the marital. One matrimonial lure, said Burton, was music, so that a gentlewoman learned that art before she could 'say her *Pater Noster*, or ten Commandements'. Yet the multitude of women who, like Mrs. Donne, 'had yearly a child'—and every other year a death —were more than decorative. In an age when households great and small were relatively self-contained, the wife and mother, like Mrs. Donne's sister, Lady Oglander, or Magdalen Herbert or Lady Mildmay, was perforce a busy and capable manager. In addition to supervising her servants, her family, and any girls who might be committed to her charge, a lady of the manor was likely to combine the functions of estate bailiff, Lady Bountiful, and Mrs. Grundy, and the 'skill in Chirurgery' of Burton's mother. The continual exercise of biological fortitude and of a wide range of practical talents left the average married woman, however intelligent, no great freedom or energy for intellectual culture; and normally she was married when young.

About feminine attainments on the literary and academic side it is difficult to generalize, because the means of education were so varied and uneven and because, from the nature of the case, evidence is somewhat meagre. The ideal woman of Erasmus, More, Ascham, and Sir Anthony Cooke had such representatives in the seventeenth century as Elizabeth Jane Weston (1582–1612), Elizabeth Lady Falkland (1585?–1639), Lady Anne Clifford (1590–1676), who according to Donne could 'Discourse of all things, from Predestination to Slea Silk', and Lady Conway and Lady Pakington, who enjoyed the friendship and admiration of many eminent divines. But in the feminine as well as in other spheres there was a change from aristocratic to middle-class standards, a change by no means peculiar to Puritans. For the common masculine view, which women held also, of the limited furnishings desirable for the female mind we have not merely Milton's attitude towards his daughters but, in addition to books of conduct and courtesy, such documents as Overbury's popular poem, *A Wife* (1614), and Sir Ralph Verney's famous letter (1652) to his god-daughter who had announced her intention of learning Hebrew, Greek, and Latin: 'Good sweet hart bee not soe covitous; beleeve me a Bible (with the Common prayer) and a good plaine cattichisme in your Mother Tongue being well read and practised, is well worth all the rest and much more sutable to your sex.' If Sir Ralph's precept, however golden, might fail to produce mates 'sutable' for cavalier husbands, either of the literary or the hunting type (though he did recommend French), a broader kind of cultivation was increasingly provided for the girls of well-to-do families. Lucy Apsley, better known as Mrs. Hutchinson, when she was about seven had eight tutors in languages, music, dancing, writing, and needlework. And Sir Ralph's letter reminds us that it would be wrong to infer too much from the epistolary spelling of such women as Lady Harley and Dorothy Browne, since both sexes and all classes enjoyed a pleasant orthographic freedom. In general, feminine reading was expected to be pious and elegant rather than classical and solid, and one prominent part of it comprised books of devotion. On another level we think of such charming devotees of French romance as Dorothy Osborne and Mary North.

In the realm of letters the great patronesses, Lady Pembroke and Lady Bedford, had no worthy successors, but the number of female authors multiplied. Sidney's sister had done her writing before 1600. His daughter, the Countess of Rutland, was a poet, Jonson told Drummond, 'nothing inferior to her Father'. Sidney's niece, Lady Wroth, published an Arcadian romance. Lady Falkland wrote a juvenile play or two, translations, and perhaps a history of Edward II. Elizabeth Countess of Kent may have contributed indirectly to the production of literature — at least to the nourishment of two men under her roof, Selden and Samuel Butler—through a popular cookery-book. We acknowledge, if we do not quite understand, the fame of the matchless Orinda, but we prefer to read the letters of Dorothy Osborne, who never dreamed that she would be the best-loved woman writer of the age. If it was natural for women to turn to *belles lettres*, some of them held their own with men in more popular writing. Elizabeth Grymeston's posthumous

Miscellanea had four editions from 1604 to about 1618; for this
pious manual of advice to her son the compiler might have used
the title Dorothy Leigh gave to her far more popular book, *The
Mother's Blessing* (1616). In 1641 the Amazonian Katherine
Chidley published a vigorous justification of Independency
in answer to the gangrenous Presbyterian, Thomas Edwards.
And finally there appears the Duchess of Newcastle, voyaging
through strange seas of Thought, alone.

During our period the lower layers of the reading public were
enlarged, and political, religious, social, and cultural lines of
cleavage grew sharper than they had been. A shifting of the
centre of gravity had results parallel to those that became more
obvious in the reign of Anne. The new gentry and the commercial class needed instruction and were prepared to receive
what they could absorb of their Renaissance heritage, along
with more modern and useful matter. Besides, many men, like
Robert Burton, deplored the intellectual and moral decline of
the aristocracy and, though such nostalgic lamentations were
not new, there was always need to rekindle dying ideals of
gentillesse. We have abundant evidence of these facts and sentiments in the continued production of books of conduct and
courtesy (with such allies as the essay), and in the alterations
of scope and tone that reflect a changing society. One large
branch of the genre took the form of 'advice to a son', a form
exemplified in the brief, Polonian, and popular counsels of Lord
Burghley and Ralegh, posthumously printed in 1616–17 and
1632, and in Francis Osborn's pungently independent book
(1656–8). Two interesting treatises have been made available in
recent years. One, written partly in the Tower in 1609, was by
Ralegh's scientific friend, Henry Percy, ninth Earl of Northumberland. The other (1651) was the work of a more gracious lover
of religion and his family, Richard Vaughan, the second Earl
of Carbery, Jeremy Taylor's patron; it illustrates a stage in the
transition from learned humanism towards the gentlemanly
ideal. And we should add such cousins of the 'advice' family as
the autobiographies of Lord Herbert and others.

Advice to a son was likely to have the more personal and
realistic character of a private testament than manuals addressed
to the public. The moral, civic, and cultural handbook had an
illustrious pedigree, from many ancients down through Italian,
Spanish, French, and English writers, and it filled the gap

between the universities and the world. While the hundreds of courtesy books of the Renaissance represented some diversity of aim and emphasis, the central tradition, the tradition most congenial to Englishmen, embodied the solid objects of Christian humanism, the training of young men of the governing class for active public life. One practical and initially private example was King James's *Basilikon Doron* (1599, 1603). A lesser Scot, James Cleland, in *The Institution of a Young Noble Man* (1607), carried on the old ideal, with an infusion from Bacon. The best-known work of our period, the *Complete Gentleman* (1622, 1634) of Henry Peacham (1578?–1642?), is often taken as the ideal picture of the cavalier, and it evidently continued to please the gentry; but, apart from its modern style, a large portion of the book might have been written generations earlier. In fact Peacham owes something to Elyot's *Governor* (1531), and even when he may not be borrowing his outlook is very similar; in his survey of poetry, moreover, he draws upon Scaliger and Puttenham. Peacham's emphasis on religion and virtue united with good letters and knightly exercises, his fusion of aristocratic and amateur with utilitarian standards and motives, his constant appeal to classical precept and example, even the idealist's inevitable strain of pessimism about the present, all this and more is thoroughly in the spirit of Tudor humanism. But while the book takes its place in the long line of treatises on the education of a Christian prince, there are, of course, marks of a later age and of the author's own varied interests. His hero is on the way to becoming not so much a statesman or courtier as a public-spirited country gentleman with cultivated tastes and hobbies. Classical literature, especially Latin (and neo-Latin), and the Bible form the literary, ethical, and religious foundation; but Peacham calls the lengthening roll of English authors—outside of the drama—and rejoices in the lustre of his native tongue. He takes account of science, and names Copernicus, though his outline of cosmology is Ptolemaic. Whatever his particular debts, he writes with first-hand authority on many subjects—teaching, writing, music, travel, heraldry (he was a worthy contemporary of 'Master Guillim'), and fishing. If not a first-hand authority on noble birth, he is as stout an upholder of degree as Elyot; but nobility, as usual, belongs to merit, not merely to rank. As the author of a book on drawing, and also as a follower of Castiglione, Peacham can discourse expertly on art and antiquities, and he incorporates sketches of many Italian painters (derived, ultimately, from the fuller accounts in Vasari). Altogether Peacham shows himself an intelligent conservative, a cosmopolitan patriot, a man of zest and flavour. A generation later the hard-boiled Francis Osborn, rewriting Bacon's *Essays*, as it were, for the sceptical age of Hobbes and Butler, repudiated this humanistic ideal in the interest of practical experience, mundane utility and success, and Chesterfieldian *savoir-faire*.

Meanwhile another change in the character of the tradition had been recorded in a whole swarm of books like the *English Gentleman* and *English Gentlewoman* (1630–1) of the prolific Richard Brathwait (1588?–1673). This royalist country gentleman also slighted aristocratic culture, but in order to emphasize pietistic goodness and well-doing. Peacham, Brathwait, and Osborn show in varying degrees the adaptation or adulteration of Renaissance humanism for the benefit of a solidifying squirearchy and middle class. In many other works the stress is on the pious activities of every day, and in the poetic book of conduct there is the significant change from *The Fairy Queen* to *Paradise Lost*. On a lower plane we have—not to mention the cynical satire of Thomas Powell's *Tom of All Trades. Or the Plain Pathway to Preferment* (1631)—such a *vade mecum* for the virtuous apprentice as *An Essay of Drapery: or, the Complete Citizen* (1635) by William Scott, an early Rotarian, and books on common life and family relations which range from William Gouge's earnest and prolix *Of Domestical Duties* (1622) to the well-known works of Fuller and Jeremy Taylor. In such treatises there is more of unexciting good sense, of piety and prudence, sometimes in unctuous excess, than of magnanimous ardour and many-sided culture. But more or less Puritan pictures of the family as a religious commonwealth of busy bees, if they lack the aristocratic virtues, exalt some others—an ideal of marriage, for instance—not always found among their betters. And such families did not live merely on paper, they were the backbone of the nation—though the reader of literature may feel moved to ask, as a modern essayist asked in a parallel connexion, if the backbone should be exposed.

The broad extension of the reading public meant the final establishment of English as the medium not only for popular books, which of course had always been written in that tongue, but for those addressed to the educated. Latin was still the international language of scholarship and thought; without it English science and philosophy would have been much the poorer, and continental workers would have missed the writings of Gilbert and Harvey, Bacon and Hobbes. Bacon's attitude towards 'these modern languages' is familiar. The Latin epigrams and miscellaneous verse of Campion, John Owen, George Herbert, Crashaw, Milton, and many other men, and the works of John Barclay, are evidence of the vitality of the literary tradition. Sir Francis Kynaston tried to make Chaucer readable at home and abroad by translating part of *Troilus and Criseyde* (1635). The *Religio Medici* won its first continental repute in a Latin version, and foreign visitors who called on the aged Milton were seeking the annihilator of Salmasius rather than the English poet. To write in the mother tongue, as Milton said of his own resolution, was to forgo European fame and be 'content with these British Ilands as my world'. Yet the tide had long set in the modern direction. From the early sixteenth century even most scientific books had been done in English. Fynes Moryson wrote his big *Itinerary* in Latin but published his translation (1617). The stationers would not hear of a psychological treatise in Latin, so that Burton was compelled to prostitute his muse in English; we might say that she remained a *demi-vierge*. Browne intended to offer the *Pseudodoxia Epidemica* 'unto the Latine republique and equal Judges of Europe' but shifted, happily, to English.

Although the omnivorous Burton groaned over the multiplication of books, the figures look very small in modern eyes. During the period 1500–1630 the annual production of books of all kinds rose from about 45 to about 460, and in what may be loosely classified as 'literature' there was a corresponding advance from a dozen to about 115; of the literary items perhaps a fifth would be broadside ballads. By 1640 the total figure was approaching 600, and works of 'literature' numbered over 150. In the twenty troubled years that followed the number of books of course greatly increased. For various reasons statistics are somewhat uncertain; these are drawn from a tabular survey made in 1938 at the Huntington Library.

All books printed in England, except those issued by the presses of Oxford and Cambridge, were produced by the master-printers in London who belonged to the Stationers' Company, a modern guild called into being, in 1557, by a modern trade.

The company controlled, or tried to control, every phase of the business, from the number of apprentices to the number of copies in an impression. Among insoluble problems were surreptitious and piratical printing and monopolies of profitable books. The problem most familiar to the modern reader was the enforcement of censorship. Under the governmental regulations of 1586, books legally published had to be approved by the Archbishop of Canterbury or the Bishop of London (that is, by their chaplains); a little later a panel was set up. The licensing of plays for performance and (from 1607) for press was handled by the Master of the Revels and his Deputy. Even in normal times the law was constantly ignored, and with Parliament's abolition of the Star Chamber in 1641 the flood of pamphlets poured forth unchecked. The reviving of controls in 1643 by the Stationers' Company and Parliament gave the occasion for Milton's grand defence of liberty.

In 1637 the number of printers in London was limited to twenty, but this, like many other regulations, proved ineffectual, and by 1650 there were about forty. The centre of publishing and bookselling remained St. Paul's churchyard, though shops began to spread along Holborn and the Strand. From the first, English printers had rarely approached the standard of scholarship, taste, and technical execution set by the great continental printers, and if in the seventeenth century continental work declined, English printing hardly advanced—mainly because of Company control embodied in the so-called 'English Stock'. Most printers were men of business without much interest in literature and without very exacting ideals in mechanical matters. Among exceptions the most notable was Humphrey Moseley, who published many of the chief authors of the period and whose preface to Milton's volume of 1645, for instance, attests his literary zeal and discernment. English printers were still backward in the publishing of classical and especially Greek authors, apart from the common texts; but one illustrious achievement was Sir Henry Savile's edition of Chrysostom in eight folio volumes, which was done at Eton in 1610-13 by the king's printer.

We hear much more about publishing from the author's standpoint. Outside of such staple commodities as Latin grammars, almanacs, and devotional works, the market was usually small and uncertain, and the author suffered accordingly.

Everyone knows of the £18 paid for *Paradise Lost* late in the century, and it sold pretty well. There was no royalty system, and rates of payment were low, so that few men could think of living by writing. Gervase Markham's repetitious efforts resulted in his capitulation (1617) and a promise to write no more books on the diseases of cattle. The thrifty Shakespeare gained a competence chiefly from the dividends of his theatrical stock, but the ordinary dramatist received only the price of his plays. A hand-to-mouth playwright like Dekker could supplement his earnings by producing pamphlets perhaps at £3 or £4; a lesser author might be paid £2 or less. However much these sums are multiplied to approximate modern values (and figures on that point have little real meaning), it was not easy for the most industrious free-lance writer, impelled by what Samuel Sheppard called 'a mercenary dizzinesse', to keep far ahead of the catchpole. John Taylor the Water-Poet published his books on travel by subscription; once a host of his 'mongrel' patrons refused to pay and thereby occasioned another pamphlet. A not very reliable hope in the struggle for existence lay in the generosity of more exalted patrons, whose bounty might range from a present in return for a dedication to substantial annuities or such prolonged hospitality as Jonson and Donne received. Literature owed much to Prince Henry, the Earls of Pembroke and Southampton, the Countesses of Pembroke and Bedford, Fulke Greville, Sir Robert Cotton, Endymion Porter, and others, but the new wealth engendered few Maecenases, and the number of needy authors increased. Indeed, our period witnessed a gradual shift from the aristocratic tradition of private patronage towards modern ways. King Charles was the last English sovereign who was a real patron of letters. A large proportion of authors, to be sure, had other means of subsistence and wrote with no serious thought of profit; and of course the gentleman of quality seldom breathed the tainted air of Grub Street. Before we leave this general topic, one speculative consideration may be allowed. When we remember that the population of England was about five million and then look at the list of books produced in the years 1600–60, we may be inclined to transfer the quarrel over the ancients and moderns to the seventeenth and twentieth centuries. We may think of the two hundred and fifty million people nowadays whose language is English, and compile a list of the books written in the last sixty years which, according to the best light we have (a dim light, it is granted), seem destined to be alive three centuries hence, and we may wonder if the list would be much longer than the early one, if the best of it would equal the best work of the earlier seventeenth century in quantity or quality.

One explanation of the realistic strength of seventeenth-century literature is the fact that few of its makers were merely men of letters. From King James down to John Taylor most of them led active lives in the workaday world and shared the experience of non-literary men. A multitude of authors held posts in the public service or at court, or were members of Parliament. Many men from Jonson to Bunyan had experience in arms. The civil war and the Puritan ascendancy left hardly any writers undisturbed. Even that man of peace, Izaak Walton, found himself transmitting the royal 'George' after the battle of Worcester. Most literary men of course were on the king's side and, led chronologically by the timorous Hobbes, a number of them crossed over to the Continent, to become royalist agents, to travel, and to pick up French ideas and tastes. The wholesale expulsions and replacements in the universities involved literary losses and some scientific gains. Among non-academic church-men who lost their preferments were Earle, Fuller, Herrick, and Bishop Hall. Fuller, Chillingworth, John Pearson, and Jeremy Taylor spent some time with royalist armies. William Dell and John Webster, whose educational tracts we have noticed, and John Saltmarsh and Richard Baxter were chaplains on the opposing side. But apart from the dislocations and dangers of war, which are not unknown to modern authors, the literary life was subject to other mutations; for instance, some fifty more or less prominent writers—half a dozen of them clerics—suffered imprisonment, civil or political.

If on the one hand literature was close to life and action, on the other it was wedded to learning. One reminder of that fact is the medieval 'clerkly' predominance that clergymen still re-tained. 'All Confess there never was a more Learned Clergy', said the anti-clerical and immensely learned Selden, and their writings were by no means confined to the religious and scholarly but included much of the best poetry of the time. There were clerical mathematicians and scientists like Wil-liam Barlow, William Oughtred, John Wallis, Jeremiah Hor-rocks, and, to represent another area, Thomas Vaughan the alchemist. There was a whole galaxy of literary, scholarly, and scientific bishops—Andrewes, Bramhall, Corbett, Earle, Gauden, Godwin, Goodman, Hall, King, Morley, Pearson, Sanderson, Taylor, Ussher, Brian Walton, Ward, and Wilkins. The three most popular writers on astronomy were clerics, Nathanael Carpenter, John Swan, and John Wilkins. The chief geographers of several generations were relatively untravelled clergymen, Hakluyt and Purchas, George Abbot (later Archbishop of Canterbury), Carpenter again, and Heylyn.

These lists suggest other facts of broad significance. For one thing, relatively little prose can be classified as *belles lettres*. Nearly all the works that we now read as 'literature' were written as contributions to religion, ethics, politics, science, travel, and the other fields of inquiry and instruction. Prose fiction, which bulks so large in the modern output, was represented by a meagre bunch of minor authors; its place, to be sure, was partly filled by innumerable plays, social pamphlets, character-books, and 'Providence' books.

Another broad fact, another legacy from the Renaissance, is the extraordinary versatility of an extraordinary number of men, whatever qualifications we make concerning the amount of knowledge to be compassed at that time. The most obvious Renaissance types are Bacon and Ralegh. And if Ralegh belongs to heroic drama, Sir Kenelm Digby may be called the Ralegh of light opera. Henry Peacham, who pronounced Digby a 'noble and absolutely compleat Gentleman', was himself not only an author of varied parts but a painter, composer, mathematician, and heraldic expert. A somewhat startling footnote to Sir John Harington's undoubted versatility is his solicitation of the archbishopric of Dublin. Joseph Mead, one of many learned college dons, was master of half a dozen sciences and of Egyptian and Semitic lore. Selden's varied learning was proverbial. Among physicians who were not enslaved by what one of them termed 'the fruitless importunity of Uroscopy' were William Gilbert, Mark Ridley, Thomas Lodge, Philemon Holland, Campion, Matthew Gwinne, Henry Vaughan, Sir Thomas Browne, John Collop, Walter Charleton, Martin Lluelyn, Richard Whitlock, and William Chamberlayne. Browne's medical studies and practice did not hinder his exploration of religion, morals, and metaphysics, science and antiquities, and many languages, including Old English. Versatility was almost

a condition, or a result, of membership in what became the
Royal Society. John Wilkins we shall meet later. Sir William
Petty, the founder of political economy, and Sir Christopher
Wren live by virtue of the work they did after 1660, but before
that date Petty was an Oxford professor of anatomy and the
first scientific surveyor of the land of Ireland, and Wren was
professor of astronomy at Gresham College and a figure in
anatomical and other scientific investigations. What is of more
immediate concern to us, there has never been a period in
which there were so many good minor poets (in addition to the
major ones), so many men of varied pursuits who could turn off
good poems.

These few random names remind us that the inevitable but
disastrous division of labour had not yet pulverized the learned
world into a mass of mutually repellent particles. The various
sciences were still 'natural philosophy' and, before 1660, anyone of scientific interests pursued several at once. Moreover,
almost all authors, scientists like other men, had had a thorough
classical training, and the classical tradition was a unifying and
humanizing force. Although the old antagonism between the
humanities and science deepened considerably, it was that fine
humanist, Sir Henry Savile, the translator of Tacitus and editor
of Chrysostom, who founded two important scientific chairs
at Oxford; and Hobbes, the scientific materialist and foe of
classical libertarianism, began and ended his career with translations from the Greek. Thanks to the humanistic ideal of
universality, educated authors—and that means nearly all the
authors we read, except pot-poets and the like—could not
follow one road in hostile ignorance of other roads. It was
difficult for the seventeenth-century writer to be insular, since
his reading was likely to be more European than English. He
was an intellectual citizen of the world, the child of the whole
past as well as of the present. And whatever the rift between
science and the humanities, there was little or none between
scholarship and literature. It is not merely a coincidence that
the earlier seventeenth century is the Golden Age of both learning and literature—and of most other arts and sciences from
music to law. From one point of view it appears as a spring-time
of ploughing and sowing, from another as the autumnal harvest
of the Renaissance and Reformation.

Both aspects receive illustration in every chapter of this book.

Here we may record some concrete facts in the cultural background. One landmark is the Bodleian Library, which was opened, with more than 2,000 volumes, in 1602. Sir Thomas Bodley (1545–1613), the quondam pupil of Calvin and Beza, collected much massy divinity but would have no such 'riffe raffe' as contemporary plays and pamphlets; however, new books were soon brought in through the agreement with the Stationers' Company (1610). Bodley's watchful care over every detail is revealed in his statutes and in his letters to the first Keeper, Thomas James; he was grievously disappointed by the matrimonial desires of that able officer, who had seemed 'alienissimus from any suche cogitation'. Bodley was zealous both in giving and in begging. Among the library's multitudinous benefactors were Sir Robert Cotton, Ralegh, Sir Francis Vere, William Herbert, Earl of Pembroke, Sir Thomas Roe, Sir Kenelm Digby, Laud, Robert Burton, Cromwell, and Selden. The catalogue printed in 1605 was apparently the second general catalogue issued by a European public library. Of nearly 6,000 volumes only 36 were in English and only 3 belonged to English literature—Chaucer's works, Lydgate's *Fall of Princes*, and Puttenham's *Art of English Poesy*. A religious zeal similar to Bodley's, on the middle-class level, animated the Manchester clothier and private banker, Humphrey Chetham (1580–1653), who, says Fuller, had 'signally improved himself in piety and outward prosperity'. His bequests included money for a public library and for the purchase of 'godly English Bookes . . . proper for the edificacion of the common people', to be chained in the local parish churches. The library at Lambeth and one opened in 1631 at Sion College were of course ecclesiastical. The fine collection started by Archbishop Bancroft passed to Cambridge in 1646–7. Archbishop Ussher's library became the property of Trinity College, Dublin. The most famous of private libraries, that of Sir Robert Cotton (1571–1631), was at once a symptom and an instrument of the antiquarian and Anglo-Saxon studies which were being carried on in all directions. And we must not omit a man to whom scholars are grateful, the London bookseller and friend of Milton, George Thomason, who assembled and dated over 22,000 pamphlets, newspapers, and books issued during the years 1640–61.

The zeal for collecting ranged far beyond books, from the

coins that Laud gave to Oxford (along with manuscripts and money) to the heterogeneous curiosities of Sir Thomas Browne. The virtuosity that Restoration wits were to satirize was not of course altogether critical, and the collector's itch became a kind of polite aristocratic disease. The many collectors of rarities were overshadowed by the *magnifico* of the century, Thomas Howard, second Earl of Arundel (1585–1646). His friendship and patronage extended from Inigo Jones, Van Dyck, and Rubens to the antiquarian set; Francis Junius was his librarian. Personally and through agents Arundel gathered artistic treasures such as England had not seen before. The marbles, many of which were given to Oxford in 1667, were described in Selden's *Marmora Arundelliana* (1628). A connoisseur and patron still more illustrious was King Charles, from whose accession Horace Walpole dated the first era of real taste in England. It is not unfitting that we always see him, comely and calm, on the canvas of Van Dyck, the painter whom he was able to attract to his court. Two of the king's most notable acquisitions were Mantegna's *Triumphs of Caesar* and Raphael's cartoons.

These various libraries and antiquarian, scientific, and artistic collections are evidence of cultural breadth and maturity, of the desire and the means to preserve and study the past. If in painting (apart from miniatures) and sculpture original achievement lagged far behind that of the Continent, the more necessary art of building was, like literature, in active transition from the medieval to the neoclassical and displayed a similar hybrid character. The new movement, which drew its inspiration from Vitruvius and the Italians, had had an early Elizabethan pioneer in John Shute, and it reached its first culmination with the learned architect and stage-designer, Inigo Jones (1573–1652)—'Vitruvius Hoop' the estranged Jonson called him. Though Jones's work and influence, like Wren's, were far-reaching, we identify him with the Banqueting House at Whitehall (1619–22) as we identify his successor with St. Paul's. In domestic architecture Tudor peace and prosperity had inaugurated a change from the baronial castle or fortress to mansions like Theobalds and Holdenby House, and many less palatial manors, planned for spacious dignity and comfort. In his essay of 1625 Bacon has such stately homes in mind, and his ideas on building are a mixture of old and new; for example, he retains the quadrangular form with the great hall, although that semi-public centre of household life was shrinking into the modern vestibule. The altered conditions and purposes of domestic architecture were reinforced by Palladian taste—Jones's state room at Wilton is a famous specimen of interior design—and Elizabethan irregularities were somewhat curbed and co-ordinated without, as yet, the loss of picturesque vitality. With a changing style of life and building came a refinement and luxuriousness of furnishing which made Tudor ways seem primitive. These benefits were not entirely confined to the nobility and gentry; the old timbered houses of London citizens might contain an impressive array of plate and panelling. In literature neoclassical discipline did not readily impose itself upon a vigorous native tradition, but in architecture the native tradition had no exponents who could rival the masterful genius of Jones. The general evolution is illustrated in the Gothic towers and 'high embowed Roof' of 'L'Allegro' and 'Il Penseroso' and the neoclassical palace of Pandemonium which is akin to St. Peter's. Yet the exotic style was, before 1660, the ideal of the few like Wotton and Evelyn; most people preferred English variety to Palladian uniformity. The Englishman's conservatism was manifested likewise in regard to that most personal possession, his garden, and in the more or less unsophisticated manuals of Sir Hugh Platt, Gervase Markham, William Lawson, John Parkinson, Sir Thomas Hanmer, and others. Continental influence was beginning, but only beginning, to extend architectural symmetry and axial design into the formal garden. According to Aubrey, Italian taste was first displayed by Sir John Danvers, the young husband of Magdalen Herbert. Sylvester's Eden, for one early example, is dressed 'In true-love-knots, tri-angles, lozenges', yet patterns did not extinguish simple delight in floral profusion, and natural prospects were more satisfying than artificial vistas.

This chapter has outdone the variety of an English garden, but it cannot end without a brief reminder of some intellectual and spiritual attitudes which are fundamental in most authors of the earlier seventeenth century and are alien to most modern minds. The working philosophy inherited by those authors was the Christian humanism which during the Middle Ages and the Renaissance had fused Christian faith and pagan reason into a stable framework of religious, ethical, political, economic, and cultural thought. That tradition, the main European tradition,

comes from Plato and Cicero down through Erasmus and others
to such men as Spenser, Hooker, Daniel, Chapman, and Jonson
—and, though less obviously, Shakespeare. Its central religious
and philosophic doctrine is order, order in the individual soul,
in society, and in the cosmos. To mention two large elements of
that doctrine which we meet everywhere in the seventeenth
century, one is the concept of 'right reason', the eternal and
harmonious law of God and nature written in every human
mind and heart; the other is that of the great chain of being, the
hierarchical order which descends from God through angels
and men to plants and stones, which at once distinguishes and
unites all levels of existence. This orthodox ideology was the
foundation of most reflective and imaginative writing up to
the Restoration. As we move from 1600 to 1660, however, that
traditional orthodoxy is more and more undermined by changing economic and social conditions, by the causes and effects of
civil war, by political and scientific thought, and by various
individual rebels of the two kinds especially feared by Henry
More, enthusiasts and atheists. At the same time the old religious and humanistic verities are reaffirmed, stoutly or subtly, by
such diverse champions as the schoolmasters Brinsley and Hoole,
the Cambridge Platonists and Bishop Bramhall, and Milton. If
the phrase 'Christian humanism' recurs in this book with what
is for some readers damnable iteration, it is because there seems
to be no better name for the central, traditional orthodoxy, the
total outlook, which was a common inheritance and possession
(and which was held, of course, on varying levels of philosophic
sophistication).

Modern readers and writers, who prefer the brandy of bold
rebellion to the brown bread of orthodoxy, resent the endless
classical commonplaces to which even Montaigne appeals, but
they fail to understand that for the humanist such moral plati-
tudes could be living realities. There is, after all, no unbridge-
able gulf between the Polonian creed and the Apollonian.
Especially to Englishmen who looked back upon continual war,
change, and confusion, peace, order, and conformity were
precious things. Shakespeare as well as lesser men clings to the
humanistic principles of order. He stands in the centre, not on
or beyond the margins of the normal and ethical. On the other
hand, he does not share that untroubled confidence in the
goodness and greatness of man which we are so often told was

fostered by the Renaissance. That confidence was one element in Christian humanism, but it was kept in check by a religious sense of man's littleness and sinful frailty. Shakespeare and the rest know, as Pico had said, that man may sink to the brute or rise to the divine. With a simultaneous double vision they see man as both a god and a beast. That double vision is, to be sure, the mark of the greatest writers of all ages, especially the ancients; but the Christian religion intensified the paradox by exalting man's sense of his divinity and deepening his sense of bestiality. There is a vast difference between that humanistic view and the unchecked optimism of the romantic who does not believe in the fall of man, or the unchecked pessimism of the realist who is a romantic on all fours. And both of these extremes, the impulse to see either the god or the beast to the exclusion of the other, are largely the result of the scientific movement which in the early seventeenth century began to inspire such grandiose dreams of the conquest of external nature as the goal of mankind.

While this religious and ethical view of man and society was a possession by no means confined to scholarly writers, a still more universal possession was its macrocosmic complement. Not merely the soul of individual man but the whole world is the battle-ground between God and Satan. For nearly all men, simple or sophisticated, the universe and human life constitute a divine order with a divine purpose, not an ordered or a haphazard mechanism. Shakespeare may have been withdrawn far enough from religion to see the natural man acting in a natural world, yet he is not so far withdrawn, in time or in temperament, that medieval religious concepts have lost their imaginative and emotional power over him. And what is plain enough in Shakespeare is much plainer in the host of writers more explicitly religious and philosophical. The modern reader who would understand seventeenth-century literature must shake off his habit of believing only what he sees and must try to realize a world in which man's every thought and act are of vital concern to God and to his own eternal state, a world interpenetrated by spiritual potencies.

> Millions of spiritual Creatures walk the Earth
> Unseen, both when we wake, and when we sleep.

Of course men could think and act, then as now, in entire

forgetfulness or disregard of divine omniscience and the judgement day, but very few would have denied the major premiss
itself. The consciousness of the immediate presence and active
intervention of God in all the affairs of life and the universe was
even stronger in the seventeenth century than in the sixteenth;
it was heightened by Puritanism and by various forms of more
or less mystical thought. This ultra-religious view of the world
entailed, to be sure, a belief in witchcraft, and the practical
consequences of that belief were horrible; yet one could hardly
accept God and His angels without accepting Satan and his.
At any rate literature—above the level of such books as Thomas
Beard's horrific *Theatre of God's Judgements*—was infinitely the
gainer from a conception which was religious, imaginative, and
poetical, which enlarged the human stage beyond that of merely
naturalistic motives. Whatever the general and particular problems and pains felt by writers as by other people, all that they
needed, as writers, was there. Everyday life was bound up with
the order of the seasons and the Church calendar and with
divine visitations from storms to the plague, with the passions
of the flesh and the assured immortality of the soul; it was at
once primitive and civilized, mundane and miraculous.

Some peculiar and fundamental characteristics of seventeenth-
century literature arise from the simultaneous embracing of
different planes of knowledge and experience or the habit of
immediate and almost unconscious transition from one to another. That is, in brief, the medieval allegorical instinct. Ultimately it springs from the religious belief in the divine unity of
all things physical and spiritual, a universal network of analogy
and correspondence. But in the seventeenth century that belief
operates in an enlarged terrestrial and celestial world, against
a developing background of philosophic and scientific scepticism, so that the allegorical mode of thought and feeling now
appears less instinctive and normal, more eccentric and 'quaint',
than it did when its basic assumptions were unquestioned,
when the realm of knowledge had not been separated from the
realm of faith. The result is 'metaphysical' poetry and prose.
As one of the greatest metaphysical writers said, 'thus is man
that great and true *Amphibium*, whose nature is disposed to live
not onely like other creatures in divers elements, but in divided
and distinguished worlds; for though there bee but one world to
sense, there are two to reason, the one visible, the other invisible'.

II

POPULAR LITERATURE AND TRANSLATIONS

1. *Popular Literature*

THE vague term 'Popular' is used here rather than the still more vague 'Miscellaneous' to cover a body of prose and verse that does not belong in other chapters. By far the most popular of all books of course was the Bible, while much fiction in English as well as Latin was certainly not popular in the same sense. But a large proportion of the writing to be surveyed here did mirror the everyday world of the middle and lower classes, and a very large proportion of this popular literature, like the money its authors usually lacked, was concentrated in London.

The walled, mile-square city that Shakespeare knew was in most respects still medieval. Only a few of the buildings that he saw survived (up to 1939), such as the Tower, the Inns of Court, and 8 of the 114 parish churches. Chaucer would have missed—not very keenly—the crowd of monks and friars, whose two dozen houses had been torn down or put to other uses, and he might have admired the coaches groaning through the narrow, dirty, dark, and ill-paved streets, but he would have been surprised by little except the city's growth in population. Between 1600 and 1660 the population apparently doubled, though the data on which modern estimates are based are uncertain. Throughout that time governmental and civic authorities, unable to cope with the aggravated problems of population and traffic, tried repeatedly and vainly to check the spread of building. There was nothing like city-planning until the great fire gave an opportunity, an opportunity also for replacing timber with brick. The distribution of the inhabitants was in general the reverse of that which, thanks to improved means of transport, prevails in modern cities. The court circle and the well-to-do were likely to live within the city or in Westminster, while the poor and disreputable multiplied in the districts outside the walls and outside of effective control, districts which

were the recognized nurseries of vice, crime, and the plague.
What is now London was a wide expanse of country containing
the 'Twin-sister-Cities' (in Heywood's phrase) of London and
Westminster, with suburbs sprawling in every direction, isolated
villages, and the beginnings of the modern 'ribbon' development. Within as well as without the walls public services were
lacking and conditions were fairly primitive, but at least no one
was very far from green grass and trees and flowers, and Moor-
fields was early laid out as a park. The river not only united
London with Westminster and with the theatres and bear-
gardens of Southwark but was still the main thoroughfare of the
city. However, the livelihood of the army of watermen was more
and more threatened, as John Taylor urgently protested, by the
popularity of 'hackney hell carts'. Another kind of rivalry is
indicated in Henry Peacham's *Coach and Sedan* (1636).

While the variegated pageant of London life is displayed
most fully by the army of playwrights, there are vivid supplements in the writings of the journalists. The best of these,
Thomas Dekker (1572?–1632), was of course himself a playwright by vocation, but he found pamphleteering a useful side-
line, especially when the theatres were closed. Like Dr. Johnson's
luckless acquaintance, Dekker 'lived in London, and hung
loose upon society', and being—to echo Nashe—subject to debt
if not to deadly sin, he spent a long time (1613–19) in prison.
That experience gave authenticity to his prison 'characters' in
the fifth edition of *Lanthorn and Candlelight*, called *Villainies
Discovered* (1616). In general, the vicissitudes of a precarious
existence bore fruit in an extensive and peculiar knowledge of
London and, without souring his zest for life, deepened his
feeling for the submerged nine-tenths. He had the full-blooded
toughness of his age and a tenderness of his own.

One large segment of Dekker's work comprises his pamphlets
on the recurring plague, *The Wonderful Year* (1603), the roughly
impressive poem *News from Graves-end* (1604), *The Meeting of
Gallants* (1604), *A Rod for Runaways* (1625), *London Look Back*
(1630), and *The Black Rod* (1630). Only the first and fourth were
claimed by him, but the others seem to bear his hall-mark. To
think of accounts of the plague is to think of Defoe, but while
Defoe writes as a social historian, marshalling his facts and
statistics into a sober analysis, Dekker is a reporter, humorist,
and poet who, with a mixture of personal emotion and artistic

detachment, seizes upon whatever has immediate human interest. Both writers accept the plague as a divine punishment for sin, but the later *bourgeois* moralist does not ring such poetic changes upon the eternal contrasts between health and disease, exuberant vitality and sudden extinction, the marriage-bed and the grave. Dekker is much closer to the medieval and pictorial tradition of the Dance of Death; *The Meeting of Gallants* carries us back, in its setting if not in its quality, to the *Pardoner's Tale*. Dekker's Jacobean imagination is kindled into macabre intensity by the lurid horrors of wholesale mortality and corruption, yet even the plague does not check his flow of robust humour and racy slang and puns. In *The Wonderful Year*, after visions of the charnel house and crawling worms, come the *fabliau* of the cobbler's wife who made a death-bed confession of her affairs with neighbouring husbands and then recovered, and the anecdote, told with such dramatic verve, of the bold tinker who came sounding through a country town and, to his great profit, buried the Londoner's corpse which the villagers were afraid to approach. In a very different key Dekker speaks out against the people of London who have had the means and the will to escape from the trials of their fellow citizens and have carried the pestilence into the country.

The journalist and the poet appear, in varying proportions, almost everywhere in Dekker's prose. In *The Seven Deadly Sins of London* (1606) the pattern and the fervour of a medieval sermon permit an urban vignette of carts and coaches thundering, people jostling at every corner, hammers beating, tubs hooping, pots clinking, water-tankards running at tilt, porters sweating under burdens, merchants' men bearing bags of money, chapmen skipping out of one shop into another. . . . But the lover of the city from whose womb he received his being, from whose breasts his nourishment, brings no less spontaneity to such a biblical apostrophe as this:

O London, thou art great in glory, and envied for thy greatnes: thy Towers, thy Temples, and thy Pinnacles stand upon thy head like borders of fine gold, thy waters like frindges of silver hang at the hemmes of thy garments. Thou art the goodliest of thy neighbors, but the prowdest; the welthiest, but the most wanton. Thou hast all things in thee to make thee fairest, and all things in thee to make thee foulest; for thou art attir'de like a Bride, drawing all that looke upon thee, to be in love with thee, but there is much harlot in thine eyes. Thou sitst in thy Gates heated with Wines, and in thy Chambers with lust.

Such a passage may lessen our surprise at Dekker's producing a piece of devotional literature, *Four Birds of Noah's Ark*, an attractive distillation of sincere religious feeling, unspoiled innocence of soul, and instinctive sympathy with forgotten men like prisoners and miners. He rarely slips, as authors of prayers may, into unctuousness, and his language reflects without effort the rhythmical simplicity of the Bible and the liturgy.

In the same year, 1609, Dekker published his very different *Gull's Hornbook*. Dedekind's *Grobianus* (1549) had been translated as *The School of Slovenry* by one R. F. in 1605, and Dekker himself had rendered a good deal of it, but, 'not greatly liking the Subject, I altred the Shape, and of a Dutchman, fashioned a meere Englishman'. Although, as he says, his own book tastes strongly of Grobianism in the beginning, his ironical guide to etiquette owes little to the crude Latin poem. Dekker's gull is not a mere nasty boor but an ignorantly pretentious young man from the country who wants to cut a dash as a sophisticated man about town, and whose behaviour is inspired by the one motive of attracting attention to himself. He is at least a cousin of Master Stephen, though Dekker suffers a fool more gladly than Jonson. The London scene is sketched with satirical liveliness in the chapters on Paul's walk, ordinaries, a playhouse, a tavern, and the street. The account of the audience in a theatre, the most detailed and vivid we have, releases the emotions of a much-enduring dramatist. What is now the best known of Dekker's prose works was never reprinted until 1812, though it was revamped for the Restoration world by Samuel Vincent as *The Young Gallant's Academy* (1674).

A journalist on the alert for timely topics could not overlook the 'coney-catching' tribe whose felonious little plans Greene had so profitably exploited. *The Bellman of London* and *Lanthorn and Candlelight*, both of 1608, were and remain popular, for the literature of roguery is always fascinating, and Dekker, if he lacks his customary anecdotal gusto, seldom lacks the unexpected fancy and phrase. He was original, too, in his exposure of literary cozenage and in his sketches of prison life. But he probably had no very expert knowledge of the criminal underworld, and in borrowing, like his contemporaries, from Harman, Greene, and others, he gave a picture less true of

Jacobean than of Elizabethan conditions. It is more important that these pamphlets on social cankers spring partly from a serious impulse which runs through Dekker's hastiest concoctions. A man who abhorred bear-baiting was not likely to be unmoved by the poverty and suffering of his fellow creatures; here certainly he had expert knowledge. Many of the ills of a changing economy, which successive statutes had been trying to cure, find illustration in Dekker's pages; even the gull has his social significance. Dekker is very serious in *Work for Armourers* (1609), which lives up to its motto, 'God helpe the Poore, The rich can shift'. He denounces all kinds of greed and corruption, but, though a townsman, he is especially vehement in regard to enclosures and evictions, and he does not cherish sentimental illusions about rural virtues. He found country life (in the *Bellman*)

ful of care, and full of craft; full of labour, and yet full of penurie; I saw the poore husbandman made a slave to the rich farmour; the farmour racked by his landlord: I saw that covetousnesse made deere yeares when she had fullest barnes; and to curse plentie for being liberal of her blessings. I had heard of no sinne in the Cittie, but I met it in the village; nor any Vice in the tradesman, which was not in the ploughman.

Like Dickens, Dekker is a middle-class humanitarian, not a radical economic theorist. He sees and hates the rapacious Bounderbys and Merdles, the 'yea-and-by-nay Cheaters', landlords, courtiers, and lawyers, who suck the blood of others. He is not unlike Dickens also in having no remedy, unless it is in uprightness and benevolence, and no economic ideal except security within the existing frame of things, whether the sweet content and golden slumbers of the poor or the modest affluence of jolly Simon Eyre and his busy little kingdom. To redress the injustice of this world he can only call in the next, hell as well as heaven.

Samuel Rowlands, whose conjectural dates are 1570–1628/30, is, biographically, little more than a name, though he may be identical with a cooper and churchwarden of East Smithfield who lived from 1565 to 1627. At any rate he was a prolific writer. His first and last and two middle works (1598, 1605, 1618, 1628) were religious and were doubtless inspired both by current fashion and by the *bourgeois* ideals of virtue which underlie his satires. In *A Terrible Battle between Time and Death*

(1606), a great traditional theme, very real in a plague-stricken age, raised a hack-poet above his common level. A fluent version of the old tale of Guy of Warwick (1608) remained, like the best comic pieces, a favourite for generations. But Rowlands's main body of work, which gives him his small niche as a painter of manners, is a great mass of satirical epigrams, characters, jests, and anecdotal skits, and a few titles are better than description—*The Letting of Humour's Blood in the Head Vein* (1600), *'Tis Merry when Gossips Meet* (1602), *Look to It, for I'll Stab Ye* (1604), *Humour's Looking Glass* (1600–8), *Democritus* (1607; later *Doctor Merryman*), *Diogenes' Lanthorn* (1607), and a series of 'Knave' volumes (1600?–19/20). Among the later pieces are *The Melancholy Knight* (1615), a burlesque survey of a corrupt age by a man who is at once a Quixotic lover of medieval romance and a far from virtuous malcontent, and *The Bride* (1617), a pleasant defence of marriage. Though his writing is almost wholly in verse, Rowlands's talent is a prose talent, suited for the re-creation of a world of knaves, gulls, fools, and shrews. His topics and jests, vices and 'humours', however old, are given a contemporary London costume, rich in detail if not very rich in variety. If he has what Saintsbury would have called a diploma piece, it might be *'Tis Merry*, an alcoholic discussion of marriage by a widow, a wife, and a maid which is more amusing than Sir John Davies's courtly *Contention* of a few months later, and which is somewhere between the earthy prodigality of Skelton and the dramatic economy of the parallel scene incorporated by the translator in *The Bachelor's Banquet* (1603).

Although literary history generally associates 'popular literature' with London, both logic and the Englishman's traditional attachment to the country warrant a wider view. It might strain logic to take account of such exotic, not to say occult, things as Topsell's *History of Four-footed Beasts* (1607) and *History of Serpents* (1608), but we may notice four writers who have at least one foot in the country, Markham, Breton, John Taylor, and Brathwait. The industrious hack, Gervase Markham (1568?–1637), has perhaps only one toe in literature (by virtue of some miscellaneous writings), since he is identified with numerous manuals for horse-breeders, gardeners, housewives, and other practical readers, manuals which grew, like popular ballads, by incremental repetition. Yet his useful books were reprinted unceasingly throughout the century and even later (witness Diana

Vernon's horror at Frank Osbaldistone's ignorance); they tell or imply a great deal about rural life, and their author deserves mention if only for one enchanting title, *Country Contentments* (1615).

Nicholas Breton (1555?–*c*. 1626), a stepson of George Gascoigne, combined gentility with professional writing. His several dozen volumes of verse and prose were spread over forty-odd years and ranged from romantic fiction to religion and satire. His euphuistic fluency is sometimes vitalized by religious feeling, a love of nature, a quiet relish for life and character, and a sincere attachment to good old ways. These qualities, the qualities of an amiable essayist, may also soften the edge of his social observations. Breton followed up his successful satire in verse, *Pasquil's Madcap* (1600), with a rapid series in the same vein, but he could never snarl and his indictments of the age were quite general and innocuous. The prose tale, *Grimello's Fortunes* (1604), might have been a serious treatment of the problem of the educated and honest gentleman's finding employment, but Breton is content to apply a soothing salve to what Burton and others regarded as a dangerous sore. The *Merry Dialogue betwixt the Taker and Mistaker* of 1603 (in 1635 called *A Mad World, my Masters*) is an anecdotal exposure of hypocritical selfishness and knavery, but the author is no Timon, and in his dedication to Florio he says: 'The Dialogue is not tedious, nor the matter so serious, but it may passe the musters of a merry humor.' Breton's fondness for the dialogue, by the way, illustrates the effect of that form in retarding the growth of the essay. In general we forget Breton's little sermons and toothless satire and enjoy the pictures of manners and such lively tales as that of the eel and the magpie in *Grimello's Fortunes*. In the realistic, critical, and cynical Jacobean age he irradiated the simple idealism of the age of Lyly—unlike his contemporary, Barnabe Rich (1542–1617), who turned during these years to sour and angry social pamphlets. Breton is at his lyrical best in *Fantastics* (which was entered in the Stationers' Register and presumably published in 1604) and *The Court and Country* (1618), when he celebrates with loving detail the timeless world of Chaucer's franklin, *The Complete Angler*, and Hardy's Wessex.

A more robustious spirit inhabited the active body of John Taylor the Water-Poet (1578?–1653). The son of a Gloucester

'Chirurgian', he found work in London as one of the tribe of watermen, of whose rights he remained a loyal defender. In 1596–7 he went on the Cadiz and 'Islands' expeditions. In 1612 he published his first book, *The Sculler*, which carried tokens of friendship with Jonson, Breton, and Rowlands; one epigram started a feud with Coryate which Taylor followed up with relentless pugnacity. The first of a number of 'stunts' which made him a well-known character was his 'pennyles pilgrimage' to Edinburgh in 1618, an enterprise not altogether relished by Jonson. For pleasure and profit Taylor made two short visits to Germany and numerous trips, often by water, about England, and, in the absence of Sunday newspapers, printed pamphlets about them. Besides the gossip of travel, and due recording of hospitalities received from provincial knights and mayors, he called attention to the neglect of inland waterways. After many years of life in Southwark, in 1643 Taylor took refuge, like some greater authors, in Oxford. In 1640 he had opened fire, on behalf of King and Church, against Roundheads and 'Amster-damnable opinions', and in 1645 he broke an old friendship by denouncing Wither as a 'Juggling Rebell'. Taylor's *Works* had been collected in a folio in 1630, and he produced an even greater number of tracts after that date. He may be said to have carried the prose of his admired Nashe into the age of Cromwell, but verse was his favourite medium. For his countless miscellaneous pieces any catch-penny subject would do. He wrote on religion, the plague, the oldest man in England (Thomas Parr of Shropshire), the death of King James, Bishop Andrewes, and other notables, on tobacco, sea-fights, beggars, jails, murder, clean linen, the history of English kings and English drinks. In general he is a *bourgeois* satirist, ready to assail anything from pride to prostitution. We may exclaim, in his own semi-Shakespearian phrase, 'Here's a sweet deale of scimble scamble stuffe', or, to borrow from his abuse of William Fennor,

> Thou art the Rump, the taile, or basest part
> Of Poetry, thou art the dung of Art.

And yet, though Taylor is a man of earth (if his sobriquet allows the term), his voluminous pages reflect a buoyant zest in their author as well as a panorama of the middle and lower levels of English society. He proclaims that he knows 'no forreigne speach', that he is 'an artlesse creature' with 'no learning but

the booke of Nature', but he can be as mythological as other
self-taught men of the age, and he even mentions Copernicus.
He has read ancients and moderns in translation, from Homer
and Ovid to Du Bartas and Montaigne, and he praises Philemon Holland. He knows Don Quixote and 'our English sir
John Falstaff'. More than once he celebrates the great line of
native poets from Chaucer to Shakespeare, Donne, and the rest,
and we find him, in 1622, quoting Peter Quince's prologue.
The general public might, as Jonson scornfully declared, have
voted for 'the Water-rimers workes' in preference to Spenser's
(or Ben's), but our picture of the age owes something to the
'home-spun medley of my mottley braines'. Robert Burton
possessed fourteen of Taylor's tracts.

A rival to Taylor in slipshod productivity, on a more cultivated plane, was the country gentleman Richard Brathwait
(1588?–1673). Though his courtesy-books retain some social
interest, his acknowledged works have all been eclipsed by
the pseudonymous *Barnabae Itinerarium*, of which two parts, in
Latin, were printed about 1636 and the four parts, in parallel
Latin and English, in 1638. The doggerel poem (like Hobbes's
translation of Homer) lives chiefly in one quotation:

> Where I saw a Puritane-one,
> Hanging of his Cat on Monday,
> For killing of a Mouse on Sonday.

But there are many amusing bits (heightened in the Latin by
a sonorous ironical gravity which is often lost in the English),
for in his perambulation of provincial England the normally
moralistic author becomes an irresponsible and jovial Bacchus,
and every other public-house has a casual Ariadne. The jog-
ging journal is better than any of Taylor's travelogues—and a
world away from *Poly-Olbion*.

While the first half of our period yielded a large crop of
popular tracts from many more or less well-known hack-
writers, in the latter half pamphleteering naturally grew more
serious and controversial, and much of it belongs to political
and religious thought. But one sturdy veteran cannot be overlooked. Henry Peacham (1578?–1642?) is associated with an
early book on art and with epigrams and emblems, above all
with *The Complete Gentleman* (1622), but in his later years he
produced semi-popular essays, some royalist tracts, and several

lively pieces on London life. *Coach and Sedan* (1636) has already been mentioned. *The Worth of a Penny, or a Caution to Keep Money* (1641?) had seven more editions in the years 1664–1704. The civilized and serious Renaissance humanist was now old and poor, but he brought unimpaired good humour and vitality to his anecdotal survey of Lady Pecunia's everyday domain. Though he has plenty of classical tags (translated in 1664), he is addressing the middle-class reader, and his quiet colloquial manner represents a step towards the next age. Peacham tapped this vein again in *The Art of Living in London* (1642).

As in the Elizabethan age, the functions of the modern magazine of fiction and the tabloid newspaper were discharged by the broadside ballad. Shakespeare's picture of Autolycus and Earle's character of the pot-poet relieve the historian from a vain effort to describe a vast amount of heterogeneous material, though a lively and instructive chapter might be made of a mere list of titles. 'More solid things do not shew the Complexion of the times so well, as Ballads and Libels', said Selden, whose collection of ballads gave Pepys his start. On the whole ballads changed less in character from age to age than other forms of literature, but there was a steady widening of the gulf between balladist and poet which had developed in the later years of Elizabeth; and with the rapid rise of the newsbooks the proportion of political ballads rose too. Although, as the collections of Pepys and Anthony Wood indicate, the output continued, the Golden Age of the ballad may be said to have ended, like that of the drama, with the beginning of the civil war, or perhaps one should say with the death of the popular laureate (and tavern-keeper), Martin Parker (c. 1600–52). For many years, as contemporary allusions prove, Parker ruled as he thought fit the universal monarchy of ballad wit. 'For a peny', said Peacham in 1641, 'you may have all the Newes in England, of Murders, Flouds, Witches, Fires, Tempests, and what not, in one of Martin Parkers Ballads.' Parker could be sensational or didactic, but he was often at his best in humorous songs of wives, husbands, and hussies. And, along with his tuneful and topical genius for popular song, he had a strain of manly poetry in him. He celebrated the worthies of English legend, and one sound-hearted ballad, 'Sailors for my Money', after some sea-changes inspired Campbell's 'Ye Mariners of England'. About 1638 Parker's muse became outspokenly royalist and he was named in the Root and Branch Petition of December 1640 as one of the authors of 'lascivious, idle and unprofitable Books'. He and his friend John Taylor were attacked as 'Papisticall, Atheisticall Ballad makers'. Parker's great contribution to the Stuart and Jacobite cause was 'When the King Enjoys His Own Again' (1643), which Ritson pronounced 'the most famous and popular air ever heard of in this country'. The decline of the old ballad tradition was furthered by parliamentary hostility, and in 1647 Parker transferred his energies to journalism in prose. (The poet received a posthumous accolade when two of his ballads were quoted in *The Complete Angler*.) In spite of vigorous censorship many humble authors like Parker made the ballad a political force during the war and the interregnum. And a sort of trinitarian attachment to King Charles, Venus, and Bacchus was nourished also by the very popular verse of such sophisticated cavaliers as Cleveland, Denham, Sir John Mennes, James Smith, and Alexander Brome.

During the winter of 1620–1, when English interest in continental affairs was especially keen, the regular weekly 'coranto' of foreign news came into being, at Amsterdam. It was the quite natural child of the topical broadside, the occasional news-pamphlet, and the various kinds of official or unofficial dispatches and private letters such as Sir Dudley Carleton, the English ambassador, received from John Hales at Dort or John Chamberlain in London. From 1621 to 1641, with an interval of suppression in 1632–8, corantos confined to foreign news were issued in London; the pioneer publishers were Nathaniel Butter, Nicholas Bourne, and Thomas Archer. Near the end of 1641 the mounting public fever and the collapse of censorship brought the first reports of domestic politics. In the next fifteen years there were over 300 periodicals, of which a fourth appeared but once and only a tenth lasted for more than a year. The first royalist newsbook, issued from Oxford and London, was *Mercurius Aulicus* (1643–5). The three 'grand mercuries', also royalist, were *Mercurius Melancholicus* (1647–9), which was quickly taken over by Martin Parker and later employed John Taylor; *Mercurius Pragmaticus* (1647–50), in which Samuel Sheppard, Marchamont Needham, and probably John Cleveland were the chief figures; and *Mercurius Elencticus* (1647–9), with which the mercurial Sheppard was especially associated. It may perhaps be said—and on better authority than Cleveland's 'characters' of a diurnal-maker and a London diurnal—that the parliamentary newsbooks were on the whole less scurrilous and less clever than the royalist. The first opponent of the *Aulicus* was *Mercurius Britanicus* (1643-6); Needham, in his first parliamentary phase, was its editor in 1644-6. Abler opposition was furnished by the *Spy* (1644) of Durant Hotham, son of the defender of Hull and biographer of Boehme. We may mention also George Wither's *Mercurius Rusticus*, which achieved one number in October 1643, and the *London Post* (1644-5, 1646-7) of John Rushworth, a licenser of the press for a time, whose *Historical Collections* remain useful. The censorship exercised by Parliament and the Stationers' Company from 1643 onward was sometimes vigorous, sometimes ineffectual. After an ordinance of 1649 exterminating newsbooks, only a few official and semi-official journals were allowed; the best known of the former class, *Mercurius Politicus* (1650-60), was edited by Needham, once again a Commonwealth man, who in 1651 had Milton as his supervisor or associate. A new Act of 1653 centralized control of printing in the Council of State, but this too failed, and in 1655 Cromwell suppressed all newsbooks except two edited by Needham.

While that indispensable manual, the almanac, had no more literary claims than its modern descendants, there were, as there had been since Geoffrey of Monmouth's 'Prophecies of Merlin', great numbers of prognostications related in character to the political ballad and pamphlet. Whether based upon private revelation, astrology, or common sense, whether bona fide or propagandist, these prophecies could affect as well as indicate the climate of popular opinion. King Charles and Laud were disturbed by the ominous success of Lady Eleanor Davies (one of whose judges, after the sibyl's own anagrammatic fashion, turned 'Dame Eleanor Davies' into 'Never so mad a ladie'). In William Lilly's prognostications, 1645-60, the stars consistently favoured the parliamentary side. In quite innocuous ways, moreover, the prophetic habit left its mark upon literature. Breton's *Fantastics* was a 'perpetuall prognostication'. And the mock-prognostication, a type which carries us down to Swift and Partridge, ranged from the social satire of the fool's speech in *King Lear* to that of Dekker's *Raven's Almanac* (1609).

The general astrological colouring of literature and language is more familiar. The occult vagaries of judicial or prophetic

astrology, which was opposed for appropriate reasons by Church
and State and true science, must be distinguished from a limited
belief in the influence of the stars as well as from genuinely
astronomical prediction. But distinction can be difficult; the
learned almanac-makers, Edward Gresham and Thomas Bretnor, were among early Copernicans. In any case we cannot feel
superior, since astrologers still flourish. For various reasons there
was much less scepticism about witchcraft. It is represented
chiefly by Sir Robert Filmer and, most fittingly, by the 'atheist'
Hobbes. As late as 1677, in *The Displaying of Supposed Witchcraft*,
John Webster, the educational iconoclast (and believer in astrology), displayed, like the Elizabethan Reginald Scot, a limited
and peripheral scepticism not directed against the central dogma
of evil spirits. Among thorough believers flourishing after 1660
were Jeremy Taylor, Browne, Sir Matthew Hale, Meric Casaubon, Glanvill, More, Cudworth, Isaac Barrow, and Robert
Boyle. We cannot go into the literature of witchcraft, much less
the painful record of trials and executions, but three statements
may be made: that King James's odious repute as a witch-
hunter is largely undeserved; that, as James Howell (a believer)
noticed, the civil war brought a recrudescence of witchcraft or
prosecution; and that, as most of the names just cited indicate,
there was no essential connexion between witch-hunting and
Puritanism.

A public conscience which accepted as a matter of course
the punishment of witches was shrilly divided on the 'art of
whiffing' that Ralegh had helped to make fashionable. Tobacco
gave birth to a whole controversial literature of its own and to
countless allusions in the satirists, dramatists (with the exception of Shakespeare), and other writers. Some gentlemen,
snorted King James in his *Counterblast to Tobacco* (1604), bestowed three or four hundred pounds a year 'upon this precious
stinke'. The king used his pen to more effect in raising the duty
enormously, but in vain. Barnabe Rich, whose persistent antipathy gave him a multiplying eye, declared in 1614 that London had upwards of 7,000 tobacco shops. Brathwait's *Smoking
Age* (1617) contains an illustration of a shop—'the Randevous
of spitting', in Earle's phrase—and its puffing gallants; Jonson's Dame Ursula charged the high price of threepence a
pipeful, and for adulterated tobacco at that. While we might
expect Josuah Sylvester to write *Tobacco Battered*, it seems odd,

whatever we allow for some efforts to win royal favour, that popular authors like Rich, Breton, Dekker, Rowlands, and Taylor should cry out against 'Tobacco's stillified stink'. Among the well-known men who showed a recreational or medicinal interest in the subject were Sir John Beaumont, Bacon, Burton, Howell, whose encomium includes the savoury anecdote of King James in a pigsty, and the young William Temple, who stands with the enemy. And one must quote a late and poignant item from the diary of the Puritan divine, Henry Newcome: 'My base heart is but too much concerned with this tobacco.'

One lively legacy from the past was satire on women and marriage, and the best contribution, *The Bachelor's Banquet* (1603), was a rendering, probably by Robert Tofte (1561/2–1619/20), of the fifteenth-century satire, *Les Quinze Joies de Mariage*. The book was very popular in its century and the enraptured Swinburne took it, as well he might, for an original composition. With inspired ease and freedom the author turned the old text, which was good, into something better which was completely and racily English. On a much lower level was Joseph Swetnam's *Arraignment of Lewd, Idle, Froward, and Unconstant Women* (1615), which revived the everlasting *querelle des femmes*; much ink was shed in a prolonged battle. To mention one witness to feminine virtues, the humanistic tradition dignified Thomas Heywood's historical compilations about famous women (1624, 1640). Brathwait's bolster lecture, *Art Asleep, Husband?* (1640), is half jestbook and provides a transition to that very popular type of popular literature.

The material in jestbooks was of three principal kinds: detached jests, practical and verbal jokes ascribed to one hero, and comic short stories or *novelle*. Among the collections of detached jests, not to speak of older books that still flourished, were Robert Armin's *Fool upon Fool* of 1600 (enlarged in 1608 as *A Nest of Ninnies*), in which the jests were grouped around half a dozen characters; *Jests to Make You Merry* (1607), by Dekker and George Wilkins; and several compilations (1628–38) by John Taylor. Clever repartee might belong to the alehouse or the humanistic tradition or to both; and some jests and some subjects, such as women, the clergy, and national characteristics, are ageless, though they may change their costume. In the second or 'biographical' class, among the progeny of such crude ancestors as *Eulenspiegel* ('Howleglas') and some English works, are *The Merry Conceited Jests of George Peele* (1607) and pieces of rural waggery or *diablerie* like *The Merry Devil of Edmonton* (1608) of Thomas Brewer, *The Pleasant History of Friar Rush* (1620), *Robin Goodfellow, His Mad Pranks and Merry Jests* (1628), and the excellent *Pinder of Wakefield* (1632). Some of these titles and dates only represent, as it were, one of the heroes' nine lives. The prime example of the third class is *Westward for Smelts*, a collection of *novelle* published in 1620 and possibly in 1603; one tale provides an analogue to the wager in *Cymbeline*. The comic *novella* and the biographical jestbook are fused in *Dobson's Dry Bobs* (1607), which, if its racy pictures of provincial and university life had a better basis than practical jokes, would hold a high place in the early history of the picaresque novel.

Some of these jestbooks, various social tracts, books of characters, and such things as *The Bachelor's Banquet* and Breton's *Post with a Mad Packet of Letters*, bring us to the threshold of the realistic middle-class novel. One effort to cross it was *Penny-Wise, Pound-Foolish* (1631), in which Dekker gave a happy ending to a tale of a dissolute Bristol merchant reclaimed by his devoted wife. But the realistic-romantic Deloney had no worthy successor. Nor did the promise of picaresque fiction bear fruit, though a fresh impulse was provided by James Mabbe, who translated in 1622 Mateo Alemán's *The Rogue* (which is cited in *The Religion of Protestants!*), *The Spanish Bawd* (1631), from De Rojas's old *Celestina*, and the *Exemplary Novels* (1640) of Cervantes. The dominant tradition was that of the chivalric, courtly, or pastoral romance, a pattern which combined all the intricate and fantastic loves and adventures that Greek, medieval, and Renaissance authors had evolved. Heliodorus (this in verse), Achilles Tatius, and Longus were translated afresh by William Lisle, Anthony Hodges, and George Thornley respectively, in 1631, 1638, and 1657. 'What Schole-boy,' exclaimed Joseph Hall in 1620, anticipating Macaulay, 'what apprentice knows not Heliodorus?' Caxton's version of Lefevre's courtly tale of Troy, revamped, had at least eight editions in the century and reached its so-called eighteenth in 1738. Foreign romances and those of Greene and Sidney—the *Arcadia* of course was much more than a romance—remained very popular and had many unoriginal imitators: Breton, Emanuel Ford, whose work survived into the eighteenth century, Gervase Markham,

Lady Mary Wroth, Sidney's niece, and others. The old British and English heroes, and such newer recruits as Tom a Lincoln (1599–1607) and Tom Thumb (1621)—these last the offspring of Richard Johnson, author of the long-lived *Seven Champions of Christendom*—rubbed shoulders with Palmerin and his sons and Amadis de Gaule, who were naturalized by Anthony Munday between 1581 and 1618. For a symbol of the state of English fiction we might take the title of Brathwait's novel of 1640, *The Two Lancashire Lovers: or The Excellent History of Philocles and Doriclea*; in the tale itself an instinct for native realism is not quite submerged by romantic convention.

While the old romance was dying, or passing into the euthanasia of the chapbook, a new pattern was being woven into the complex web. The arrival of modern French romance is registered in the comments of readers like Dorothy Osborne, in the allusive preciosities of Katherine Philips and her circle, and, more concretely, in translations. In 1620 appeared the first part of the *Astrea* of 'the great and incomparable Urfé, . . . the Painter of the soul'; the work had been entered in 1611. Later comes a series which includes Gombauld's *Endimion* (1639), Gomberville's *Polexander* (1647), La Calprenède's *Cassandra* (1652) and *Cléopâtre* (*Hymen's Praeludia*, 1652–9), Georges and Madeleine de Scudéry's *Ibrahim* (1652), *Artamenes or the Grand Cyrus* (1653–5), and *Clelia* (1655–61), and, in 1657–8, the complete *Astrea* of D'Urfé—not to mention such signs of reaction as Sorel's *Extravagant Shepherd* (1653). At the head of English imitations may stand Sir Kenelm Digby's autobiographical romance written in 1628. In 1648–50 Dorothy Osborne's serious young lover wrote, though he did not print, adaptations from Rosset's *Histoires Tragiques*. But French romance bore its first famous fruit—apart from *Argenis*—in Roger Boyle's *Parthenissa* (1651–69), which is more often named than read and which disappointed even the omnivorous Dorothy. A minor specimen of another kind of fruit, which in the Restoration was to flourish along with pseudo-heroic idealism, was Walter Charleton's anti-Platonic, anti-Puritan, and of course partly Petronian piece, *The Ephesian Matron* (1659).

French romance had owed something to the Scotsman John Barclay (1582–1621). Barclay's chief works in prose were *Euphormionis Satyricon* (1603–7), a Petronian mixture of episodic adventure, satire, and learned discourses; *Icon Animorum* (1614), a series of essays on national and temperamental types which Thomas May translated as *The Mirror of Minds* (1631); and the extraordinarily celebrated *Argenis* (1621), which was translated in 1625 and again in 1628 (Ben Jonson's version, entered in 1623, was one of Vulcan's victims). As a scholar and, by virtue of his continental birth and background, a man of the world, and as the son of a noted champion of monarchy, Barclay was well fitted to write a book which combined the attractions of a courtly romance with those of a political and didactic *roman à clef*. Owen Felltham expressed the sentiments of the European public, if not ours, when he declared that he read *Argenis* for pleasure and for its 'Wisdome, with Worth, and State-Philosophy'. Barclay's influence in England was shown in James Howell's *Dodona's Grove* (1640), Samuel Gott's *Nova Solyma* (1648), Brathwait's *Panthalia* (1659), and Sir George Mackenzie's *Aretina* (1660).

The use of Latin and a degree of European fame link Barclay with Joseph Hall (1574–1656). In *Mundus Alter et Idem* (1605?), which was to draw Milton's gibes, Hall utilized the timeless device of the imaginary country that Renaissance exploration had reanimated. Among his many and various antecedents were Plato and Lucian, Marco Polo and 'Sir John Mandeville', Sir Thomas More, Rabelais, and Hakluyt. The picture of an Antarctic land of Cockaigne is a burlesque of credulous travellers and encyclopaedists and ideal commonwealths, and a general satire, in the words of Heylyn, on 'the Vices, Passions, Humours, and ill Affections' of mankind (and womankind); and, finally, the hero's travels form an allegory of the individual life. In Healey's translation, *The Discovery of a New World* (1609?), Hall's ironic restraint gives place to the lusty lingo of Nashe.

One last kind of writing, destined to be a notable phenomenon of the seventeenth and eighteenth centuries, dealt with the imaginary voyage that was not merely terrestrial. The Jules Verne or H. G. Wells who inaugurated the scientific romance was the historian and bishop, Francis Godwin (1562–1633); his *Man in the Moon* appeared in 1638, the year of John Wilkins's lunar treatise. The date of its composition is uncertain, but not its popularity; by 1768 it had gone through some twenty-five editions in four languages, and its range of influence embraced Cyrano de Bergerac. The moon had had earlier visitors, from those of Lucian (whose *True History* and *Icaromenippus* were included in Hickes's translation of 1634) to Ariosto's Astolfo, but it acquired a new face and a new actuality through Galileo and Kepler. Godwin's Spanish hero, after many adventures, finds himself on St. Helena; he is carried—here we have an idea Bacon had touched—by a brigade of trained swans to the moon, sojourns in that utopian climate and society, and returns to earth in China. The scientific amateur is further revealed in discussions of such topics as the diurnal rotation of the earth and magnetic force.

Bishop Godwin, however interesting, scarcely counts as a novelist (though he has a strain of Defoe and, according to Lady Harley, of 'Donqueshot'), and fiction in our sense of the word was only coming to birth in the seventeenth century. Both elegant and popular tales were, to be sure, thumbed by multitudes of readers, from noble ladies down to young John Bunyan. But the Duchess of Newcastle could affirm in 1656 that she had 'never read a Romancy Book' through and had scorned such 'foolish Amorosities, and desperate Follies'. And if the Duchess was individual in this as in other things, there is the solid negative evidence of William London. In his *Catalogue of the most Vendible Books* (1657-8), London warned gentlemen against sitting down idly with *Sir John Mandeville* or *Bevis of Southampton*, and he gave romances, poems, and plays four and a half pages, less than half the space accorded 'physick' or law and very little compared with the twenty-seven pages of history and the seventy-five of divinity.

But fiction, mainly romantic, had its best-sellers, some of which were or became chapbooks. In descending order of popularity (so far as editions, in this period, are an approximate gauge), the leaders in the century were: Bernard's *Isle of Man*, which, with nineteen editions, was second only to *Pilgrim's Progress*; Greene's *Pandosto*; *Gesta Romanorum*; Ford's *Parismus*; Johnson's *Seven Champions*; Deloney's *Jack of Newbery* and *The Gentle Craft*; *The Seven Wise Masters of Rome*; *Valentine and Orson*; Sidney's *Arcadia*; the Faust book; Ford's *Montelyon*; *Mandeville*; and, with ten editions each, *Euphues*, *Friar Bacon*, *Reynard the Fox*, and Dr. John Reynolds's *Triumphs of God's Revenge* (this last first published in parts, 1621-35). Nearly all of these appeared before, some long before, 1600.

2. *Translations*

Translations may well be joined with popular literature, if we allow the adjective an elastic meaning. From the beginning of English history the translation of ancient and modern books had been a main agent in the development of religious and secular culture and of literary style. To mention only one kind of writing, of the nearly 500 seventeenth-century books that can be included in the literature of conduct and courtesy, over 100 were translated. The sixteenth century, with patriotic zeal for the enrichment of the English mind and the English language, had produced an immense and heterogeneous body of translation from the classical and modern languages, but its work had not all been on the level of North's *Plutarch*, and there was constant need of more modern or more direct and accurate versions. There were, too, conspicuous gaps; Plato and Greek drama and Dante remained, and were long to remain, almost untouched. The whole *Decameron* first appeared in 1620, in a version—perhaps by Florio—of more decorum than fidelity. Machiavelli's two chief works, the *Discourses* and the *Prince*, were first printed in English, very belatedly, in 1636 and 1640, and Patericke's version of Gentillet (1602) might be called belated also, since Machiavelli had been a bogyman for generations. However, our sixty years produced more great and still living translations than any other period in English literary history, and for that very reason we must largely ignore a crowd of notable minor writers and salute a few giants.

By virtue of scholarship, bulk and variety of performance, and nobility of style Philemon Holland (1552–1637) stands at the head of the list as 'the Translator Generall in his Age', although he has, unfortunately, been less reprinted and read than his fellows. After nearly two decades of teaching in Coventry, Holland took a medical degree at Cambridge (1597) and began to practise, but in 1608 he resumed teaching, as a humble usher in the Coventry Free School. His weighty volumes, which drew a groan from Pope, made, as Fuller said, a competent library of historians for a country gentleman— Livy (1600), Pliny's *Natural History* (1601), Plutarch's *Morals* (1603), Suetonius (1606), Ammianus Marcellinus (1609), Camden's *Britannia* (1610), and Xenophon's *Cyropaedia* (1632). Along with the patriotic aims of an Englishman and a literary voyager

Holland has a theory of his art, though only hints of it are given in his prefaces. What he calls his 'meane and popular stile' might be taken as a generic representative of the best early seventeenth-century writing. Holland's unusual learning and care chastened his prose without robbing it of colloquial energy, concrete amplitude, and metaphorical colour. His slight but frequent additions are made in the interest of complete and vivid clarity and emotional effect. And the whole tone of his work reflects his Elizabethan veneration for, and sense of contemporaneous intimacy with, the great men and events and the ethical wisdom of antiquity. Pliny's philosophy gave him some qualms, but these were satisfactorily quieted. In his life and in his work Holland was a fine example of the Christian humanist.

Modern literature, including neo-Latin, was not of course a closed account and it yielded a growing harvest. In addition to many able and attractive works, such as James Mabbe's, we have the three supreme translations of John Florio, Thomas Shelton, and Sir Thomas Urquhart (1611–60). Shelton's *Don Quixote* (1612–20) is by far the happiest version of the great book which he so quickly made available (though popular appreciation did not come quickly); in robust ease, grace, and verve he stands between the restrained Holland and the extravagant Florio and Urquhart. This last, we might say, was born to naturalize in England the exploits of Gargantua and Pantagruel, though his work (1653, 1693) had to be finished by Motteux. The Scottish royalist had many adventures and troubles, and a mind full of learned quirks and quiddities; one notorious achievement was the tracing of his pedigree to Adam. For most English readers Rabelais has taken the very form and pressure of his eccentric, full-blooded translator, and doubtless he would have smiled upon the joyous excess to which Urquhart, with the aid of Cotgrave's lustily Rabelaisian *Dictionary* (1611), carried his verbal gymnastics. Since, however, we can touch only one of this gallant triumvirate of translators, that one must be Florio, partly because of his literary prominence in his day and partly because of his more radical alteration of his author.[1]

---

[1] John Florio (1553–1625?) was born in London, the son of an Italian Protestant refugee, but his youth was spent abroad. He returned to England to become a teacher of Italian and published his first lively textbook in 1578. About 1580 he married Daniel's sister; he married again in 1617. In 1583 he began to work at the French embassy and by 1594 he was in the 'paie and patronage' of the Earl of Southampton. In 1604 he entered the service of Queen Anne. Florio had numerous

Florio's translation of Montaigne, which seems to have been urged upon him by the Countess of Bedford, was entered in 1600 and apparently circulated in manuscript before it was published in 1603. He has in full measure the common sins of the Elizabethan translator, frequent inaccuracy and the habit of rendering single words by two or three. He takes both an Elizabethan and a pedagogical delight in words and compounds, picturesque and dramatic metaphors and proverbs. To adapt a phrase from the text, the 'volubility' of his 'loose-capring minde' ('la volubilité de nostre esprit detraqué') gives an embroidered exuberance and artifice to the informal simplicity of Montaigne. His expansions, rhetorical or explanatory, not only have a somewhat coarsening effect but may embody personal convictions of the 'resolute' malcontent who in life rubbed many men the wrong way. Such a refracting medium, or re-creation, obviously will not serve the student of Montaigne. Yet Florio's translation surpasses all others, from Cotton's to those of our time, in energy, gusto, and native flavour. Like North and the rest, he passes easily from slang to poetry. At one pole we have 'certaine verball wilie-beguilies, whereat I shake mine eares: but I let them runne at hab or nab' ('certaines finesses verbales, dequoy je secoue les oreilles; mais je les laisse courir à l'avanture'). At the other pole we have a rendering, inspired in diction and rhythm, of Montaigne's fine phrase about the death of Socrates, 'à souffrir l'engourdissement des riches allures de son esprit'—'to endure the benumming of his spirits richest pace'. Florio made the *Essais* a rich and racy English book, and the miracle appears all the greater when we remember that neither French nor English was his native tongue. Large claims have been made for Shakespeare's debt to Montaigne and to Florio, but the wide currency of moral commonplaces warrants some scepticism; Florio, by the way, seems to have borrowed from Shakespeare when he turned *un lievre* into 'a seelie dew-bedabled hare'.

All these men and many lesser ones are akin in their robust

feuds and friendships. Among his literary acquaintances, besides Daniel, were Hakluyt, Giordano Bruno, Jonson, Breton, John Healey, and Matthew Gwinne, who helped him with Montaigne's quotations. Another helper was Theodore Diodati, the father of Milton's friend. Florio's importance in the propagation of Italian culture and in the enrichment of the English vocabulary was signalized by his *World of Words* (1598; much enlarged, 1611). He came to poverty and died of the plague.

virtues and faults. Like their fellows of the theatre, they instinctively put ancients and moderns into contemporary English dress. If their authors in consequence lost something of their individual character, they had the infinite compensation of quickened vitality and relevance. For the translators were not dilettantes of leisure but Renaissance humanists with a mission. Then they illustrate, perhaps more clearly than original writers, the linguistic felicity of their age and the lessons that translation helped to teach. Modern English prose is in its first fresh maturity; youthful intoxication with words and ideas is just beginning to receive wholesome discipline (the discipline of Euphuism had not been altogether wholesome). From Caxton and Berners onward there is a frequent and marked contrast between the rhetorical extravagance of translators' prefaces, in which they are striving, on their own, for ornate dignity, and the degree of restraint imposed by their texts. But Elizabethan force and concreteness and figurative prodigality have not been subdued into elegant and abstract flatness. No rigorous canons of propriety have divided the language of prose from the idiom of the street on the one hand or from that of poetry on the other.

What has been said of translations in prose is largely true of those in the other medium, at least for the first third of the century. The qualities of Holland and Florio are fused and intensified in the greatest of poetic translators, George Chapman (1559?–1634).[1] Chapman's *Iliad* (completed in 1611) and *Odyssey* (1614–15) are among the great heroic poems in the English tongue. Everyone knows of Keats's rapturous discovery, and almost everyone of Arnold's less rapturous verdict on

[1] Chapman was the son of a yeoman of Hitchin (Herts.); 'his youth was initiate' in the service of Sir Ralph Sadler (d. 1587), who had houses there and in London. He probably did not attend Oxford (as Wood says he did), though he might have left without a degree. He was abroad, probably as a volunteer in the Low Countries in 1591–2, and perhaps earlier. His first book, *The Shadow of Night*, appeared in 1594. Chapman was associated with the circle of Marlowe, Ralegh, Harriot, and Matthew Roydon; he was a relative, friend, and literary debtor of the historical translator, Edward Grimeston (q.v.). By 1598 he was well enough known as a playwright to be mentioned by Francis Meres. He was in prison in 1600 (and 1613) for debt, in 1605 on account of *Eastward Ho* (along with Jonson and Marston). In 1603–4 he entered the service of Prince Henry (d. 1612); his next patron, the Earl of Somerset, soon fell from power. During 1614–19 Chapman was probably living with his older and prosperous brother at Hitchin to avoid arrest (in 1617 he was reported as 'of mean or poor estate' and as living 'in remote places and . . . hard to be founde'). He returned to London in 1619, but doubtless found it impossible to pick up dramatic work again. Apart from publications, the facts of his later life are obscure.

Chapman's Elizabethan fantasticality. Arnold found the translator's diction and syntactical structure appropriate, and recognized his fresh vigour and, with qualifications, his rapidity, but
dwelt chiefly on the figurative and intellectual sophistication
of a nobly plain original. While Chapman's lack of simplicity
and sobriety is obvious, Arnold missed the essential character
and causes of his treatment of Homer. Modern scholarship,
in partly shifting Chapman's intellectual roots from ancient
to Renaissance sources, may have damaged his title to large
original erudition (though even Jonson shares whatever kind of
guilt is involved), yet it has only confirmed his standing as a
Christian humanist who drew philosophic nourishment from
Ficino and Erasmus as well as from Plutarch and Epictetus. And
he was not a mere transmitter but an individual force. In poetry
and drama he carried on a crusade for the humanistic tradition,
its aristocratic learning and ethical wisdom, the control of the
rebellious passions by the reason and will, the ideal of Stoic
strength and completeness. Approaching with religious and
medieval fervour the supreme teacher (one who had suffered,
moreover, from the 'soule-blind' Scaliger's elevation of Virgil!),
Chapman could not but translate Homer into the spirit and
language of the creed he held with such strenuous intensity. For
him as for Sidney, Spenser, and the rest, the ancient heroes are
moral *exempla*. In the noble dedication of the *Iliad* to Prince
Henry and, more quotably, in the preface to the *Odyssey*, Chapman sums up his—and Poliziano's—conception of the two epics
which begin so significantly with the words μῆνιν and ἄνδρα:

In one, Predominant Perturbation; in the other, over-ruling Wisedome: in one, the Bodies fervour and fashion of outward Fortitude,
to all possible height of Heroicall Action; in the other, the Minds
inward, constant, and unconquerd Empire; unbroken, unalterd,
with any most insolent, and tyrannous infliction.

But Odysseus, Chapman's ideal hero, was not initially ideal;
Chapman sees him as a man of unruly affections who learns
self-control and wisdom in his allegorical journey towards 'the
proper and onely true naturall countrie of every worthy man,
whose haven is heaven and the next life, to which this life is but
a sea in continuall æsture and vexation'. Such views lead to much
rephrasing and many expansions of the text; and some ethical
as well as much scholarly aid was furnished by the lexicon of
Scapula and the commentary of Spondanus. From the quarrel

between Agamemnon (who is subject to irrational passions) and
Achilles (who is moved to just anger) to Odysseus's slaying of
the wooers, Athene explicitly ministers to the human reason and
will by infusing the divine knowledge of virtue. In the simple
speech of Nausicaa to her maidens Chapman interpolates eight
lines, suggested in part by Scapula, on the man who

> is truly manly, wise, and staid;
> In soule more rich; the more to sense decaid.

After Odysseus and his men have set foot on Circe's island,
the hero's brief expression of despair becomes a homily on the
limitations of human knowledge and the need of using one's
best powers with trust in the wisdom of God. Thus Chapman
is not content with Homer's objectivity but constantly incorporates ethical glosses in the text, a method which extends to
the conscious modification of character.

Of course many small additions are metrical, explanatory,
and rhetorical, yet even Chapman's figurative conceits may
represent something more than normal Elizabethan taste. He
carries over into 'our sacred Homer' his high and esoteric conception of divine poetry and its essentially difficult symbolism.
He despises 'word-for-word traductions' and defends the expansiveness incurred in making a foreign author English.
(Jonson, whose hostile marginalia survive in his copy of the
Whole Works of Homer of 1616, may have been one of the critics.)
Chapman avowedly had Latin and French versions before him,
like other translators, and he made increasing if arbitrary use of
Scapula, but charges of inadequate Greek he disposed of in his
notes with his usual confidence in his unique understanding of
Homer. Although he did the last twelve books of the *Iliad* in
fifteen weeks, he was conscientious in revising or rewriting the
parts he had already published, and he tried to meet criticism
by making an effort towards greater fidelity, simplicity, and
smoothness. Many faults remained, and conceits were added,
yet Chapman could justly affirm: 'I have rendred all things of
importance, with answerable life and height to my Authour,
(though with some periphrasis, without which no man can
worthilie translate anie worthie Poet).' And later, when he had
translated the minor poems attributed to Homer and furled 'the
proud full saile of his great verse' (if the phrase may be used
without implications), he could proclaim, in words of more

than common significance: 'The Worke that I was borne to doe, is done.'

In Augustan days Dryden and Pope did not share the 'incredible Pleasure and extreme Transport' that Chapman aroused in 'the Earl of Mulgrave and Mr. Waller, two of the best Judges of our Age', although in his own small ventures Dryden sometimes followed Chapman when Chapman did not follow Homer, as Pope (who followed Dryden and others in the same way) pointed out. Chapman's revival came with the romantic age, but even Coleridge did not better Pope's final word on the 'daring fiery spirit that animates his translation, which is something like what one might imagine Homer himself would have writ before he arrived at years of discretion'. If Homer could return from Elysium to read all the English renderings, he would surely find in Chapman his truest son, a man who has fed on lions' marrow; he would rejoice in such phrases as 'The sea had soakt his heart through', and he might not disapprove of Chapman's moral emphasis. For, one may repeat, it is not merely Chapman's poetical genius that gives his erratic versions what Swinburne called their 'indefatigable strength and inextinguishable fire', but the ethical and religious passion that inspires his conception of the 'Promethean facultie', of Homer, and of himself.

Of the lesser translators, some turned to such comparatively neglected classics as Lucan, Persius, Juvenal, and Martial, but the perennial favourites were still Virgil and Ovid. In Virginia, George Sandys (1578–1644), treasurer of the Company and brother of one of its chief backers, continued his Ovidian labours, with Drayton's friendly encouragement. The complete *Metamorphoses* appeared in 1626. Dryden relied rather too much on his boyish impressions in condemning 'the so-much-admired Sandys' for unpoetical literalness. We may say of his style and tone what can be said, *mutatis mutandis*, of most other translators of the period, that he is about halfway between the fresh colour and freedom of Golding and the conventional correctness of the Augustans. Metrically, Sandys is one of the notable early builders of the closed and balanced couplet. In a commentary, added in 1632, he summed up a venerable allegorical tradition which was soon to be driven underground by critical rationalism, but both the tradition and his book emerged in the romantic age to attract Leigh Hunt and Keats.

In the field of modern literature we encounter, in 1600, a work that no subsequent translator has rivalled, Edward Fairfax's version of the *Gerusalemme Liberata*. Even the *ottava rima* tends to run into distinct couplets. Dryden named Spenser and Fairfax as great masters in our language, and—the supreme tribute!—reported Waller's assertion 'that he derived the harmony of his numbers from *Godfrey of Bulloign*'. The work of the literary ambassador, Sir Richard Fanshawe (1608-66), is less familiar. In addition to graceful versions of Guarini's *Pastor Fido* (1647) and selections from Horace (1652), Fanshawe translated the fourth *Aeneid* (1647) in Spenserian stanzas and made it a warmly passionate poem. His pioneer rendering of the *Lusiad* (1655) displays his vagaries on a large scale but, like his other work, it displays also, as Sir Richard Burton said, the gallant energy of a gentleman, a scholar, and a soldier. From the half-Elizabethan cavalier we may turn to the chief of a group of more elegant translators, Thomas Stanley (1625-78), the historian of philosophy and editor of Aeschylus. Stanley (a pupil of Fairfax's son) wrote some original poems, but the bulk of his work (1647-51) consists of translations from Anacreon, Bion, Moschus, and other small ancients, and from many moderns like Johannes Secundus and Marino. The choice of such authors, and Stanley's 'smooth and genteel' manner, illustrate the changing motives of translators, the dwindling of humanistic and patriotic seriousness into the cultivation of a polite accomplishment.

Such changing motives only stimulated theorizing about the right method of translation. The next age might forget Chapman's protests against literalness but not those of Sir John Denham (1615-69). Denham applauded Fanshawe's rejection of the 'servile path', and in the preface to his Virgilian *Destruction of Troy* (written in 1636, revised and published in 1656) he urged sympathetic and truly poetical freedom. Although, as Dryden said, Denham advised more liberty than he took himself, he did much to mould the theory and practice of translation. Dryden's dislike of Chapman's eccentricity and of Sandys's fidelity we have seen. Jonson's literal rendering of Horace's *Ars Poetica* Dryden labelled metaphrase (and Swinburne violently damned). For an example of 'Paraphrase, or Translation with Latitude', Dryden named the version of the fourth *Aeneid* (1658) which Waller completed after it had been begun by Sidney Godolphin. These translations, moreover, had a significant effect upon prosody. The evolution of the closed couplet had already been forwarded by translators of the ancient elegiac distich like Marlowe and Heywood, by Drayton in his imitation of Ovid's *Heroides*, and by other translators such as Fairfax and Chapman in his *Odyssey*. In the work of Sandys, Jonson, Denham, Godolphin, and Waller we can follow the further development of the Augustan manner in both metre and diction.

The briefest catalogue of religious and philosophic translations illustrates the 'amphibian' character of the period. On the one hand we have Lodge's *Flowers of Lodowick of Granada* (1601), representing a Catholic writer very popular in England; the *Introduction to a Devout Life* (1613) of St. Francis of Sales; the *Boethius* (1609) of 'I.T.', probably a Jesuit, Michael Walpole; Healey's *City of God* (1610) and St. Augustine's *Confessions* by the Catholic Sir Tobie Matthew (1620) and the Protestant William Watts (1631); five or six new or revised versions of the *Imitation of Christ*, the latest (1654) by John Worthington; Nicholas Ferrar's *Hundred and Ten Considerations* (1638), from Juan de Valdés; a rapid series (1645–62) of the works of Jacob Boehme, chiefly by John Sparrow and John Ellistone; the translations (1644–53) from 'Hermes Trismegistus' and Nicholas of Cusa, the *Theologia Germanica* and other mystical writings, by two popular and earnest preachers, John Everard and Giles Randall, who were obnoxious to both the Court of High Commission and Presbyterians; and, finally, *The Mount of Olives* and *Flores Solitudinis* (1652, 1654) by Henry Vaughan. These translations, and many more, are representative of the widespread European effort, in the face of institutional dogma, strife, and worldliness, to kindle a truly spiritual religion. On the other hand, in addition to Florio's *Montaigne* and Holland's *Pliny* and *Plutarch*, there are such signs of the naturalizing of Stoic or sceptical thought as Lennard's version of Charron's *De la Sagesse* (1607–12?), Healey's *Epictetus* (1610), Lodge's fine translation of Seneca's prose works (1614), Meric Casaubon's *Marcus Aurelius* (1634), the second and third English renderings of Lipsius's *De Constantia* (1653, 1654), and the first translations of Descartes (1649, 1650) and of Hobbes's Latin works (1651, 1656). Some of these names will come up again, but this section must be given mainly to 'the noblest monument of English prose', the great moulder of English literature and life, the Bible unofficially authorized by King James in 1611.

The project of a new translation was the one happy result of the Hampton Court Conference (1604), and the proposal, made by John Reynolds, President of Corpus Christi College, was the one Puritan idea that the king warmly endorsed and carried into effect. Nowadays we are accustomed to co-operation in scholarship and science, but we do not associate great literary work with committees. The Bible, however, was produced by an organization worthy of Salomon's House. The preliminary labour occupied several years. It was divided among nearly fifty translators, who worked in six groups; two met at Westminster and two at each of the universities. To the Westminster committees, whose most illustrious figure was Lancelot Andrewes, were allotted the section from Genesis to Kings and the Epistles of the New Testament. The Cambridge groups were given the section from Chronicles to the Song of Solomon, and the Apocrypha. Edward Lively, Regius Professor of Hebrew, died before the work really began; other members were John Bois, Andrew Downes, Regius Professor of Greek, and two eminent Puritans, Laurence Chaderton, Master of Emmanuel College, and Samuel Ward, who in 1610 became Master of Sidney Sussex College. The Oxford groups had charge of the Old Testament from Isaiah to Malachi and of the Gospels, Acts, and Revelation. Among the Oxonians were John Reynolds, who died in 1607, Sir Henry Savile, Miles Smith, and George Abbot, who became Archbishop of Canterbury in 1611. After the first drafts had been circulated for mutual criticism, a central committee carried out a prolonged revision; but we do not know how completely the machinery operated, and there was some unevenness in the work of the various groups. The translators did not tie themselves 'to an uniformitie of phrasing, or to an identitie of words, as some peradventure would wish', and as some modern scholars have wished; such scruples, they thought, would 'savour more of curiositie then wisedome' and rather 'breed scorne in the Atheist, then bring profite to the godly Reader'. Miles Smith and Thomas Bilson did the final editing and saw the folio through the press, and to them are attributed the dedication, preface, and chapter headings. In spite of all this careful labour, the text was twice revised during the next generation.

The new version was 'more exact' as well as more beautiful because, though Tyndale and the Genevan group had been conspicuously learned, the Jacobean translators had at hand a richer store of oriental and classical scholarship (and fifty years later Brian Walton's learned band produced the Polyglot Bible). Then, like the secular translators, they were working at a singularly propitious season in the history of the language and of prose style; to appreciate that fact one has only to look into modern revisions and translations. With a few exceptions, the translators were not men of literary genius and do not belong to literature by virtue of their original works. But they had, so to speak, a collective ear and taste and, above all, they had intense and reverent zeal. For the Bible is the grand proof in English that in the greatest writing literary beauty is not a main object but a by-product. Of course the translators, like their predecessors, wished to render the book of books in a style worthy of its Author and His purpose, but the fundamental fact for them and their readers was the infinite importance to every individual soul of God's revelation of the way of life and salvation. 'It is a fearefull thing to fall into the hands of the living God', says the preface, in the one passage that touches eloquence; 'but a blessed thing it is, and will bring us to everlasting blessednes in the end, when God speaketh unto us, to hearken; when he setteth his word before us, to reade it; when hee stretcheth out his hand and calleth, to answere, Here am I; here we are to doe thy will, O God.' Like earlier translators, these men were raised above themselves by the consciousness of their responsibility for making the divine Word clear and persuasive to 'the very vulgar'.

Their aim was not to create a new translation 'but to make a good one better, or out of many good ones, one principal good one, not justly to be excepted against'. As a basic English text they took the official Bishops' Bible (1568; revised in 1572). They were to consult the versions of Tyndale and Coverdale; the Matthew Bible (1537), which had combined the work of the two pioneers; the Great Bible of 1539–40 (Coverdale's revision of the Matthew Bible), which Archbishop Parker and his co-adjutors had taken as the basis for the Bishops' Bible; and the Geneva Bible (1560). One special contribution which this last made to the Authorized Version, in addition to many miscellaneous changes, was the correcting of Hebrew names. The

Geneva Bible, the first with roman type and verse divisions, had been, and for a generation or more after 1611 continued to be, the popular and the Puritan text, thanks to its size and price and the Puritan colour of its ecclesiastical terms and marginal notes. The Jacobean translators avowedly shunned invidious words associated with both the Puritan and the Catholic traditions. The Catholic version of the New Testament (1582), which had kept fairly close to the Protestant texts, was not prescribed (in fact some of its language was expressly censured), but many traces of its learned diction show that it was read. The Catholic Old Testament (1609–10) came out too late to be used. And along with all these and foreign translations, and the original Hebrew and Greek, we must remember the language and rhythms of the traditional Vulgate.

The main texture of the Authorized Version was the English of Tyndale and Coverdale. Of the New Testament about nine-tenths remained in the words or the pattern of Tyndale, and he had translated parts of the Old Testament and set the style for the whole. In his fervent desire to 'stablysh the laye people' Tyndale had stressed Saxon simplicity, even to occasional bluntness, though he was capable of both tender feeling and grandeur. Coverdale the preacher inclined to make the rhythms more full and flowing. Thus Tyndale writes (Matthew xxv.21):

> Then his master sayde unto him: well good servaunt and faithfull. Thou hast bene faithfull in lytell, I will make the ruler over moche; entre in into thy masters joye.

The Great Bible brings us almost to the familiar version:

> His lorde saide unto him: well thou good and faithfull servaunt. Thou hast bene faythfull over few thinges, I will make the ruler over many thinges: entre thou in to the joye of thy lorde.

On the whole the Jacobean revisers, while eclectic, may be said, like the Bishops, to have carried Coverdale's refinement and elevation of phrase and rhythm to its consummation without losing the plain strength of Tyndale. The partial classicizing of biblical diction had been going on steadily from the Great Bible through the Geneva and the Bishops' Bible, and of course the Catholic New Testament. For instance, from the Bishops' Bible the 1611 version retained, to the improvement of the rhythm if not of the sense, the word 'charity' in the thirteenth chapter of

1 Corinthians; it had been in the Wycliffe translation and was in the Rheims (the Vulgate word was *caritas*), but Tyndale and his successors had used 'love', which returned to the text in 1881.

A few parallels will suggest, however inadequately, both the nature of the changes made and the basic preservation of older readings. It is impossible to illustrate the various kinds and levels of writing represented in the Bible, but there is room for some phrases from the New Testament and one prose poem from the Old. Tyndale renders Matthew v.13 thus: 'Ye are the salt of the erthe: but and yf the salt have lost hir saltnes, what can be salted ther with?' The Great Bible has: 'Ye are the salt of the erthe: But yf the salt have lost the saltnes, what shalbe seasoned therwith?' The Geneva version, which was followed in 1611, is this: 'Ye are the salte of the earth: but if the salte have lost his savour, wherewith shal it be salted?' Tyndale's rendering of Matthew vi. 34 is typically plain: 'For the daye present hath ever ynough of his awne trouble.' The Great Bible approaches the familiar reading: 'Sufficient unto the daye, is the travayle therof.' The Geneva reverts toward Tyndale: 'The day hathe ynough with his owne grief.' The final form appears in the Bishops' Bible: 'Sufficient unto the day, is the evyl therof.' Tyndale's phrase in Luke xx. 17, 'The stone that the bylders refused', is kept in the Great Bible and the Geneva; the Bishops' text has 'disalowed', while the Rheims and the King James versions have 'rejected'. In Romans viii. 30, Tyndale and the Great Bible have 'appoynted before'; the Geneva, Bishops', Rheims, and 1611 texts use 'predestinate'. In 1 Corinthians ii. 10 the phrase of Tyndale and the Great Bible is 'the bottome of Goddes secretes'; the Geneva and the Bishops' Bibles, which were followed in 1611, change to the more literal, sonorous, and emotional expression, 'the deepe thinges of God'.

The reader may make his own inferences from such items, and also from these versions of one of the greatest of meditations on mortality. This is the Great Bible:

Remember thy maker in thy youth, or ever the dayes of adversytie come, and or the yeares drawe nye, when thou shalt saye: I have not pleasure in them: before the sunne, the lyght, the moone and starres be darckened, and or the cloudes turne agayne after the rayne, when the kepers of the house shall tremble, and when the stronge men shal bowe them selves: when the myllers stande styll, because they be so few, and when the syght of the wyndowes shall waxe dymme: when the dores in the stretes shalbe shutt, and when the voyce of the myller shalbe layed downe: when men shall ryse up at the voyce of the byrde, and when all the daughters of musike shalbe brought lowe: when men shall feare in hye places, and be afrayed in the stretes: when the Almonde tree shall florysh and be laden with the greshoper, and when all lust shall passe (because when man goeth to hys longe home, and the mourners go aboute the stretes.) Or ever the sylver lace be taken a waye, and or the golden bande be broken: Or the pot be broken at the well, and the whele upon the cysterne: Then shall the dust be turned agayne unto earth from whence it came, and the sprete shal returne unto God, which gave it. All is but vanite (sayth the Preacher) all is but playne vanyte.

This is the Geneva version:

Remember now thy Creator in the daies of thy youth, whiles the evil daies come not, nor the yeres approche, wherein thou shalt say, I have no pleasure in them:

Whiles the sunne is not darke, nor the light, nor the moone, nor the starres, nor the cloudes returne after the raine:

When the kepers of the house shal tremble, and the strong men shal bowe them selves, and the grinders shal cease, because thei are fewe, and they waxe darke that loke out by the windowes:

And the dores shal be shut without by the base sounde of the grinding, and he shal rise up at the voice of the birde: and all the daughters of singing shalbe abased.

Also thei shalbe afraied of the hie thing, and feare shalbe in the way, and the almonde tre shal florish and the grashopper shalbe a burden, and concupiscence shalbe driven away: for man goeth to the house of his age, and the mourners go about in the strete.

Whiles the silver corde is not lengthened, nor the golden ewer broken, nor the pitcher broken at the well, nor the whele broken at the cisterne:

And dust returne to the earth as it was, and the spirit returne to God that gave it.

Vanitie of vanities, saith the Preacher, all is vanitie.

Many phrases carried over from the Geneva version into the Authorized did not appear in the Bishops' (1572 edition):

Remember thy maker the sooner in thy youth, or ever the dayes of adversitie comme, and or the yeeres drawe nye when thou shalt say, I have not pleasure in them.

Before the sunne, the lyght, the moone, and starres be darkened, and or the cloudes turne agayne after the rayne:

When the kepers of the house shal tremble, and when the strong menne shal bow them selves, when the milners stande styl because they be so few, and when the sight of the windowes shal waxe dimme:

When the doores in the streetes shalbe shut, and when the voyce of the mylner shalbe layde downe, when menne shal ryse up at the voyce of the bryde, and when al the daughters of musicke shalbe brought lowe:

When menne shal feare in hie places, and be afrayde in the streetes, when the Almonde tree shal floryshe, and be laden with the grashopper, and when al lust shal passe: because man goeth to his long home, and the mourners goe about the streetes:

Or ever the silver lace be taken away, and or the golden wel be broken: Or the pot be broken at the wel, and the wheele broken upon the cesterne.

Then shal the dust be turned agayne unto earth from whence it came, and the spirite shal returne unto God who gave it.

Al is but vanitie (sayth the preacher) al is but playne vanitie.

It will perhaps be more convenient than impertinent to add the version of 1611:

Remember now thy Creatour in the dayes of thy youth, while the evil daies come not, nor the yeeres drawe nigh, when thou shalt say, I have no pleasure in them:

While the Sunne, or the light, or the Moone, or the Starres bee not darkened, nor the cloudes returne after the raine:

In the day when the keepers of the house shall tremble, and the strong men shall bowe themselves, and the grinders cease, because they are fewe, and those that looke out of the windowes be darkened:

And the doores shal be shut in the streets, when the sound of the grinding is low, and he shall rise up at the voyce of the bird, and all the daughters of musicke shall be brought low.

Also when they shalbe afraid of that which is high, and feares shall bee in the way, and the Almond tree shall flourish, and the grashopper shall be a burden, and desire shall faile: because man goeth to his long home, and the mourners goe about the streets:

Or ever the silver corde be loosed, or the golden bowle be broken, or the pitcher be broken at the fountaine, or the wheele broken at the cisterne.

Then shall the dust returne to the earth as it was: and the spirit shall returne unto God who gave it.

Vanitie of vanities (saith the preacher) all is vanitie.

Unlike their secular contemporaries, the translators of the Bible erred at times on the side of literalness; Selden, while he pronounced it the best translation in the world, anticipated some future complaints in saying that the Bible was translated rather into English words than into English phrase. Another and more especially modern complaint is that the vocabulary of relatively central words is small in comparison, say, with that of Shakespeare. Then, since the Authorized Version was not in the main a new thing, its language was already somewhat archaic in 1611, and with the lapse of 350 years the significance of many words has altered or grown dim. Finally, when we recall that the first ancient manuscript of the Greek Testament arrived in England in 1628, we realize that the deep but limited learning of the translators, and the century-long effort after clarity and dignity, could not suffice to prevent mistakes and obscurities; and even these have become hallowed, if not intelligible, through immemorial association. But whatever the shortcomings of the old version, it may be doubted if modern accuracy has led more souls to heaven. The history of the English Bible has been parallel to that of its great ally, the classics; critical scholarship rose as the spiritual and moral fire of the Middle Ages and the Renaissance died down. Like translations from the classics, the Bible became a Tudor and Stuart book, and in being so thoroughly assimilated to the English genius it inevitably lost—again like classical litera- ture—a good deal of its original character and the individual qualities of its various authors; in other words, it was alive. From the opposite standpoint the effect of the Bible upon English writing has sometimes been deplored because, it is said, its spiritual ardours and florid oriental imagery have from the beginning heightened an imaginative, emotional, and pictorial exuberance always in need of restraint. No doubt the Bible has appealed to the non-rational and 'poetical' elements in the English temper, yet it could be made English, as it could be made German, because it was universal; and its concreteness both of spiritual idea and of expression happened to be especi- ally close to the age of Shakespeare. As for exotic and emotional excess, one might point to men from Bunyan to Lincoln whose saturation in the Bible fostered the beauty of simple strength. But to attempt here a formal discussion of the religious and literary influence of the Bible, as of the book itself, would be a predestinate absurdity—*Si monumentum requiris, circumspice*. The all-embracing power of the Bible was of course at its height in the seventeenth century, but that power lasted well through the nineteenth (about the twentieth one hesitates to generalize). In the sixteenth and seventeenth centuries the Bible was, moreover, a radical and revolutionary book; for leftist writers it and the classics had to do in the absence of Marx.

From the Bible we descend for a moment to a chain of foot-hills, or an ant-hill, which cannot be altogether ignored. Unquenchable zeal went into the effort to provide a national psalter for congregational and domestic singing which would be more satisfactory than that of Sternhold and Hopkins; and the first book printed in the American colonies was the Bay Psalm Book of 1640. The widespread impulse to paraphrase the psalms, which had touched poets like Marot, Wyatt, Surrey, Buchanan, and Sidney, was greatly stimulated by the growth of Puritanism and the influx of Protestant refugees. The psalm-singing weaver was not loved by Falstaff and Sir Toby Belch. In the first half of the seventeenth century there was an overwhelming flood of metrical versions of the complete psalter or of selected psalms. In the long list we find such various men as Bacon, Carew, Denham, Joseph Hall, George Herbert, King James (with Sir William Alexander), Henry King, Milton, Sir Edwin Sandys, and especially George Wither and George Sandys. In all this activity, public and private and religious and literary motives might be mixed; Wither objected to the rhetorical trimming of 'easy and Passionate Psalmes'. Of this mass of writing it can only be said that all service ranks the same with God—though critics have been analysing the distinctive and partly 'metaphysical' character and possible influence of the Sidney Psalter.

Milton's earliest attempts at psalmody revealed the influence of a religious translator whose work his own epic was destined to supplant. Josuah Sylvester (1563–1618) is only on the edge of our period, since his translation of Du Bartas had begun to appear in 1591–2 (and his minor writings done after 1600 do not invite comment), but the first collected edition of the *Divine Weeks and Works* was published in 1605, and in the seventeenth-century landscape it stands as a kind of Albert Memorial of encyclopaedic fundamentalism.[1] *La Semaine, ou Création du Monde* (1578) is the largest and, after *Paradise Lost*,

---

[1] At Southampton Sylvester learned French under Hadrian à Saravia (who later had some part in the compiling of the King James Bible), and passed early 'From Arts, to Marts (and Miseries among)'. By 1591 he could subscribe himself 'Marchant-adventurer'. At some time he appears to have been a steward to the Essex family. About 1606 he became a groom of the chamber to Prince Henry; on

probably the best-known relic of the great body of hexaemeral literature of the Middle Ages and Renaissance. In a long but unfinished sequel (1584 ff.) Du Bartas essayed to carry on the history of mankind. The poetical leviathan may be said to have had its ultimate descendants in the numerous sub-literary books of the nineteenth century which provided for an edifying 'Sunday at Home'. The amplified story of the Creation and youth of the world hit exactly the taste of the mass of people who had more interest in the material than in poetry. Yet the Huguenot poet, a disciple of the Pléiade, captured sophisticated taste as well, and the roll of his French and foreign admirers was commensurate with the bulk of his poem. In England there were Sidney, Spenser, Florio, and countless other writers, including King James, a personal and literary friend of Du Bartas. The energetic and grandiose poem was full of picturesque description and narrative, geography and popular science (much of it from Pliny), sound moralizing, and ardently optimistic pietism. The Christian Lucretius rhapsodized about the beneficent harmony of God's creation and, with all the appearance of learned scientific modernity, took a firmly traditional and reassuring stand on the problems of cosmology. His conception of the divine nature and function of poetry sustained him and contributed greatly to the exaltation of the Christian and Platonic Muse. Although many men made partial translations, and many had read or could read the French, it was Sylvester who established Du Bartas for half a century or more as an English classic. While generally faithful to the letter and the spirit of the poem, Sylvester made it more vigorously Protestant. His work became a quarry for poets but, since almost any idea in it may be assumed, *ipso facto*, to be a commonplace, we may be on our guard about the specific indebtedness of Donne, Milton, and lesser authors. Probably one main reason for the poem's eventual eclipse was what had been a main reason for its prestige, the religious medievalism of its scientific substance. Intellectuals did not remain content along the shore with sails of Faith to coast, 'Their Star the Bible; Steer-man th'Holy-Ghost.'

the Prince's death he published an elegiac volume, *Lachrymae Lachrymarum* (1612). Sylvester was then appointed secretary to the Merchant Adventurers and removed to Middelburg, where he died in 1618, 'having had', according to Henry Peacham, 'very little or no reward at all, either for his paines or Dedication'.

Another reason is indicated in Dryden's famous verdict on the 'abominable fustian' which had rapt him into an ecstasy in his uncritical youth. But Dryden was unwittingly biting the hand that had fed him. Sylvester, through his popularity and his influence on poets from Drayton and Browne onward, had a large effect upon the language of poetry. While his inventive boldness, good or bad, went beyond his original and fostered the taste for what Florio calls 'high-swelling and heaven-disimbowelling words', he carried on (from Spenser?) the process which was to culminate, though not to end, in Pope's *Iliad*, namely, the creating of 'poetic diction'. The ultimate and immediate source of the common devices—Latin idioms and syntax, participial adjectives, generalized descriptive phrases, the use of Latin derivatives in their literal sense, and the like—was, of course, the Roman poets. And it was Sandys who in his *Ovid*, seeking literalness and compression more than ornament, purged, refined, and canalized the variegated effects of Sylvester. Thus the translators are the clearest index not only of the development of neoclassical versification but of the development of neoclassical poetic diction—which includes the standardizing of much simple English too. Sylvester uses the plainest words like 'fishes' (even 'slippery Fishes') and 'sheep', but the idea of man's sovereignty suggests 'the scaly Nation' and a pretty shepherdess may well drive her 'bleating happiness'. (We may be less sure of William Browne's 'fleecy traine' and 'bleating charge', though Browne can be concrete also.) Sandys likewise has plenty of homely diction but, in harmony with a metaphorical idea, the sea may become 'the wavy Monarchie' or 'that liquid Plain'. Milton in *Comus* uses the Spenserian 'finny drove' because he wants us to see fins moving in the moonlight. Benlowes, among his many echoes of Milton, takes over the phrase because it fits into a compressed catalogue, 'The wing'd, hoof'd, finnie Droves'. Conventional censures of such poetic diction, based on the merely stilted and 'elegant' use of it in late and bad writers (or in early bad writers like Sir William Alexander) are as idle as wholesale condemnations of metaphysical poetry because of its decadent excesses. Indeed, these methods of compression, the generalizing or humanizing references to creatures and things, the literal use of such words as 'obvious', 'error', 'horrid', and the like, these devices might have, originally, the kind of neat precision and surprise achieved by metaphysical wit.

III

THE SUCCESSORS OF SPENSER:
SONG-BOOKS AND MISCELLANIES

I

THE first half of this chapter embraces both disciples and congeners of Spenser and some other conservative poets who are not sealed of any particular tribe. Since modern devotees of Donne have seldom grasped the breadth and depth of Spenser himself, they may not be inclined to recognize the claims of generally voluminous inheritors of a divided legacy. Indeed, our first group of poetic friends, of which Drayton came to be the acknowledged head, seem to constitute, in their patriotic and popular principles, a nucleus of conscious or half-conscious opposition to the matter and manner of the intellectuals of their day. But if these poets and others were somewhat old-fashioned in their own time, their best work outlives the whirligigs of taste; and Daniel and Chapman and Greville have philosophic as well as poetic importance.

Michael Drayton (1563–1631) was not merely the chief heir of Spenser but a younger contemporary of original force who was moulded by the same age and who, without ceasing to grow, remained a stout-hearted Elizabethan. He was born in Warwickshire of yeoman stock and spent many years in the service of Thomas Goodere and of his brother Sir Henry, whose daughter Anne, later Lady Rainsford, was the 'Idea' of the sonnets and the object of Drayton's continued devotion. (Sir Henry was the uncle and father-in-law of Donne's Sir Henry.) Drayton's life was divided between the country and London. His biography is largely the record of his writings (of the two dozen plays in which he collaborated all but one are lost), and of his relations with patrons, the Gooderes, the Countess of Bedford, Sir Walter Aston, and Edward, fourth Earl of Dorset. Among his literary acquaintances or friends were Jonson (after a fashion), Shakespeare (who was said to have had the fatally 'merry meeting' with Drayton and Jonson), Chapman, John Stow, Camden, Selden, Izaak Walton, Wither, Davies of

Hereford, and especially Alexander, Drummond, 'the two Beaumounts' (Sir John and Francis), Browne, George Sandys, and Henry Reynolds. In the survey of English poets in Drayton's epistle to Reynolds (1627), 'Grave morrall Spencer' is pre-eminent, but six lines of the poem are the finest distillation of Marlowe's 'brave translunary' genius ever written; and poetic autobiography has no more winning picture than that of Drayton's boyish appeal to his tutor to make him a poet. In an age when, said Francis Meres in Falstaffian language, 'there is nothing but rogery in villanous man', Drayton stood out as an example of 'vertuous disposition, honest conversation, and wel governed cariage.'

Like Shakespeare, he was always a man of Warwickshire and of England, not one of a sophisticated London coterie. Native endowment, an ideal of 'noble Poesie', and a devoted craftsmanship which led to both persevering revision and happy experiment, these combined to produce a large body of verse of distinctive flavour and of frequent and varied beauty; many inferior poets have been more readily credited with genius. Drayton was bitterly disappointed by his failure to win James's patronage and, though he had an eye to current fashions and enjoyed great popularity during his lifetime, he came more and more to feel, like some fellow Spenserians, that modern barbarism was deaf to heroic numbers, that 'the worlds coldnesse', as he said in 1619, 'had nipt our flowery Tempe'. We think of Drayton's flavour and beauty as Elizabethan, but actually of course nearly all of his work that we read was Jacobean and Caroline. And in the main it stands as a sweet and wholesome and (to use his own favourite epithet) 'brave' antidote to Jacobean melancholy—or to the common dogma about it. The chief satirical exceptions are *The Owl* (1604) and 'The Moon-Calf' (1627), in which Drayton's anger against public and private corruption fuses the spirit of *Mother Hubberd's Tale* with that of other and older things; and the puzzling 'Shepherd's Sirena' of 1627. Partly satirical, too, was 'The Man in the Moon' (1606), the unfortunate recast of the freshly pastoral and Platonic *Endymion and Phoebe* of 1595. Du Bartas (that is, Sylvester), who had had a finger or two in those mythological poems, may be debited with Drayton's biblical tales, though even these contain some pastoral attractions, and they confirm the abundant evidence of his sober piety.

In the new sonnets of 1602 (eighteen), 1605 (seven), and 1619 (ten), as in some amatory odes of 1619, Drayton carried on the anti-romantic, ironic, and colloquial strain which had shown itself in 1599. In the famous 'Since ther's no helpe, Come let us kisse and part' (1619), manly dignity achieves dramatic tension and dramatic plainness of speech, of a kind nearer to Wyatt than to Donne, and if drama is a little blurred by the abstract personifications that follow, these enlarge our sense of the high power of love, and of the trembling balance, so as to make the final couplet an inevitable surprise.

Drayton was much more prolific as a lover of his country than as the lover of 'Idea', and for us, if not for his own age, the historian is less inviting than the pastoral poet. The most successful of all his works was *England's Heroical Epistles* (1597–9), in which the Ovidian distich had a marked effect in shaping closed and often antithetical couplets. One of Drayton's later biographical and historical narratives, the *Legend of Great Cromwell* (1607), proclaimed its ancestry by finding a place in the last edition of the *Mirror for Magistrates* (1610), although the poet was here turning from the conventions of the tragical complaint to present, not John Foxe's Protestant hero, but a doubtful, and timely, 'Example of a new Mans fortune'. The relatively epical *Mortimeriados* (1596) he rewrote as *The Barons' Wars* (1603). Since he would not wish, as he said of Daniel, 'To be too much Historian in verse', he was not too rigorous in pruning descriptive luxuriance, but, with recent anxieties about civil dissension in mind, he did essay a more historical and epical technique and tone, and changed from rhyme royal to the *ottava rima* of Daniel's *Civil Wars* for the sake of 'Majestie, Perfection, and Solidity'. In 1627 came his most completely epic tale, 'The Battle of Agincourt', which may have been inspired by preparations for the relief of Rochelle. Though it has its moments, the narrative has never competed with the early ode.

In the group of odes—twelve in 1606 and eight more, chiefly amatory, in 1619—Drayton was indebted to Horace, Skelton, Ronsard, and the Anacreontic tradition, and he was aware of Pindar, Soowthern's poor adaptations of Ronsard, and more popular things, but he was thoroughly English in his virtual creation of what had been a loosely lyrical genre. The two great odes, 'To the Virginian Voyage' and the 'Ballad of Agincourt',

both of 1606 and revised of course, were based on Hakluyt and
Holinshed, and in

> Holding one stately height,
> In so brave measure,

the poet was giving an Elizabethan version of the heroic songs
of 'Th'old British Bards, upon their Harpes'. His simple, buoyant patriotic fervour, which becomes epic in the mere proper
names of 'Agincourt', is as far from Marvell's 'Bermudas' and
'Horatian Ode' as 'To his Coy Love' is from 'To his Coy Mistress'.

The *Fairy Queen*, the *Principal Navigations*, and Camden's
Britannia (Drayton's chief guide) have a not unworthy companion in

*Poly-Olbion. Or a Chorographical Description of Tracts, Rivers, Mountains,
Forests, and other Parts of this Renowned Isle of Great Britain, with Inter-
mixture of the most Remarkable Stories, Antiquities, Wonders, Rarities,
Pleasures, and Commodities of the same.*

In this vast heroic and panoramic poem the national and local
patriot, the scholar, and the pastoral writer had full scope. As
for the metaphysical poet all experience is one, so for the sturdy
extravert all things British make up a rich and variegated
whole—sheep, birds, country games, saints, and heroes from
Brute and Arthur to Essex and Ralegh. The best translation of
the title is simply 'Merry England'. But the great work, which
had been planned before 1600, found in 1612 and 1622 a public
which was outgrowing chorography and lusty river-nymphs.
In his prefaces Drayton defended his 'true native Muse' against
chamber-poets and public lethargy, and in commending the
second part his friends Browne and Wither saluted the happy
pen which in unheroic times upheld Elizabethan virtue. In the
nineteenth and twentieth centuries at least, *Poly-Olbion* has not
always 'met with barbarous Ignorance, and base Detraction'.

Drayton had commenced pastoral writing with *The Shepherd's Garland* (1593), which contained the partly Chaucerian
ballad of Dowsabell, and in the revised eclogues of 1606
'Rowland' was still the pupil of 'learned Colin', 'the prime
Pastoralist of England'. In the thirteenth song of *Poly-Olbion* he
had turned from the sottish world to glorify a hermitage, and
if his pastorals became poetry of escape, no escapist was ever
more healthy. 'The Shepherd's Sirena' appeared in 1627 but

seems to have chronological and other affinities with Browne's
Shepherd's Pipe (1614) and Wither's *Shepherd's Hunting* (1615),
and to reflect troubles and resentments; these do not, however,
cloud the central lyric in praise of Sirena, 'Neare to the Silver
Trent'. 'The Quest of Cynthia' (1627), like 'The Description
of Elysium' (1630), celebrates the sequestered paradise of poetry
and nature, in Drayton's own way, through a loving catalogue
of observed beauties, but with a simplicity chastened and
condensed. The supernatural is still more concrete in the very
different 'Nymphidia' (1627). This always popular poem is
linked by debt or affinity with Chaucer, Shakespeare, Browne
(the first song of the third book), and Herrick, but Drayton's
robust fancy and carefree mock-heroic gusto are his own.

Though the poet of the Golden Age had become increasingly
conscious of living in an iron age, *The Muses' Elysium* (1630)
was his happiest work, in both senses of the word. It was indeed
something of a miracle that the veteran of sixty-seven, in spite
of his long-proved stamina and flexibility, should display such
fertile vigour and such added lightness and grace. Drayton
was not, to be sure, a Herrick or a young Milton; his fresh
effects were gained rather by the page than by the phrase. But
his ripened assimilation of literature old and new had steadily
refined his own clear vein of bucolic and poetic enjoyment, and
now homely English realism and classical artifice are mingled
with more civilized delicacy. In this 'Poets Paradice', this
elysium of eternal youth and beauty and song, Drayton possesses
his soul. The serene exhilaration of his old age becomes a kind
of spiritual vision, a triumph over the ugly world. He died, poor,
in the next year, the year of Donne's death (and of Dryden's
birth), when rising poets were intent upon ideas and 'strong
lines'. In 1637 the man of many collected editions had what was
to be his last one until 1748. One wishes that he could have
foreseen the noble edition of our day.

Probably no one except the author of *Britannia's Pastorals*
(1613, 1616) ever had more than a hazy notion of the doings of
his nymphs and swains, of Walla and Tavy, Thetis and Pan,
and Riot and Truth and Limos.[1] There is a degree of literary,

---

[1] William Browne (1590/1?–1643/5?) was educated at Exeter College, Oxford,
and the Inns of Court. He joined with several friends in *The Shepherd's Pipe* (1614);
his *Inner Temple Masque*, performed in January 1615, was not printed until 1772.
In 1624 Browne returned to Oxford and then, according to Wood, took service with

romantic, and exotic tinsel in Browne's pastoral matter and style, derived in part from Guarini, Tasso (and Fairfax), and especially Sannazaro; but he gives us a larger view than Herrick of Devonshire, that blessed plot 'Whose equall all the world affordeth not!' And affectionate observation may beget simple pictures of fields, valleys, rocks, and streams, flowers, singing birds, bees, snails, squirrels (and badgers with the inequality of legs to be rejected by Sir Thomas Browne), maypoles and other rustic festivals, milkmaids, ploughmen, blacksmiths, fishermen, ballad-mongers, the games of children and of fairies. In the seasonal round of work and play, pastoral realism and idealism are mixed. Some shepherds' boys may, like Shakespeare's Dick, blow their nails for cold; another 'lovely' one, taken no doubt from Sidney's *Arcadia*, sits piping on a hill as if his joy would still endure. Naturally the singer of country contentments is something of a primitivist (and in his most elaborate eulogy of the Golden Age he apparently uses Chaucer and Cervantes), yet his vision can be disturbed by thoughts of a decayed navy, of enclosures, rack-rents, and 'The Prelate in pluralities asleepe'.

Like most of the Spenserians, Browne inherited only a slender portion of the master's poetic and humanistic legacy, but he was a literary scholar. While we might take for granted his wide range of classical reading, we might not expect, even in an increasingly antiquarian age, citations from Bede, Geoffrey of Monmouth, Joseph of Exeter, and others; and we may remember his hope of editing Occleve. Browne formally reviews the poets of Italy and France and patriotically winds up with tributes to Sidney, 'Well-languag'd Danyel', and his friends Chapman, Drayton, Jonson, Christopher Brooke, Davies of Hereford, and Wither. Spenser in general seems to occupy a special pedestal. Such poets as Marlowe and John Fletcher are echoed but not named. Like the young Keats, the young Browne was in love not only with nature but with the idea of poetry. As everyone knows, Keats may have recalled the shepherd's boy from the *Arcadia*, the maiden undressing (a passage in the Arcadian style), and, among other things, one of the few lines in Browne in which rhythm counts—'Let no Bird sing!' But the endless flow of loose pastoral couplets, and the miscellaneous verse, hardly prepare us for the famous poem on the

the Earl of Pembroke, to whom he had dedicated the second book of *Britannia's Pastorals*. He seems to have spent his later years near Dorking.

Countess of Pembroke, which has perhaps received sufficient praise in being long attributed to Jonson. Yet Browne is altogether himself in a briefer and more touching epitaph dated in May 1614:

> May! Be thou never grac'd with birds that sing,
> Nor Flora's pride!
> In thee all flowers & Roses spring,
> Mine onely died.

George Wither (1588–1667), that 'most profuse pourer forth of English Rhime', changed, about 1619, from a sort of Browne into a sort of combination of John Taylor and Quarles, and he was popular in all his roles, satirical, pastoral, and didactic.[1] Most of his great mass of religious and journalistic verse and prose, such as the long jeremiad on the plague, *Britain's Remembrancer* (1628), has now only an historical interest, if any, but in his own egoistic and irritating way Wither was a zealous champion of righteousness, liberty, and moderation, a latitudinarian (and anti-Calvinist) Anglican opposed to both Arminian and Puritan dogmatism and intolerance. Though in 1635 he could dedicate his *Emblems* to Charles and the queen, the civil war found him in the other camp. 'Honest George Withers', said Baxter in 1681, 'though a Rustick Poet, hath been very acceptable as to some for his Prophecies, so to others for his plain Country-honesty.' It is the 'Rustick Poet' whose 'homely heartiness of manner' (in Lamb's phrase) appeals to us in his early pastorals, *The Shepherd's Hunting* (1615), written in prison, *Fidelia* (1615)—which included the famous 'Shall I wasting in Dispaire?'—and the belatedly published *Fair Virtue* (1622). Especially in his easy septasyllabics there is simple and pleasant praise of love, the country, poetry, and virtuous independence and content, and it is not out of keeping with the genre and the character of 'Philarete' that he should seek 'How on each object

---

[1] Wither (or Withers), scion of an old and well-to-do Hampshire family, was at Oxford (? 1603 ff.) and had his first terms in prison in 1614 and 1621–2, on account of *Abuses Stript and Whipt* (1613) and *Wither's Motto* (1621). *Hymns and Songs of the Church* (1623), which was authorized by royal patent for insertion in all metrical Psalm-books, led to a prolonged quarrel with the stationers. Wither was in prison in 1624–5, perhaps because of his attack on the Stationers' Company in *The Scholar's Purgatory*. He became an active officer in the parliamentary army and held minor posts under the Commonwealth; he wearied Parliament with his efforts to repair his damaged fortunes. He was imprisoned in 1646–7 for libel and in 1660–3 for his unpublished poem *Vox Vulgi*. He wrote busily to the last.

I may moralize'. In later works, as he grew old-fashioned and more didactic, Wither defended his 'lowly stile' and useful matter against the taste for 'Strong-lines' and 'Verball Conceites'.

Another friend of Browne, and perhaps of Wither, William Basse (1580?–1654) occupies a tiny but secure niche through his 'Elegy on Shakespeare', to which Jonson alluded in his lines of 1623 (and which was first printed in Donne's *Poems* in 1633), and through Walton's quoting 'The Angler's Song' 'that was lately made at my request by Mr. William Basse, one that has made the choice Songs of the *Hunter in his careere*, and of *Tom of Bedlam*, and many others of note'. Basse's early 'Urania. The Woman in the Moon' was a mythological satire on women, more mildly humorous than Drayton's 'Man in the Moon', which perhaps inspired it. In his eclogues Basse achieved nothing of distinction, but he gave a picture of a cheerful, stable, rural world, a picture almost untouched by the public problems which had clouded the pastorals of his admired Spenser. As a member of the household of Sir Richard (later Lord) Wenman in Oxfordshire, Basse had a genuine knowledge and love of the country, and his homely flavour is not killed by literary convention and moralizing.

The golden book of Elizabethan pastoral lyrics, *England's Helicon* (1600, 1614), belongs to the age preceding ours, but some of its better-known pieces, 'In the merry moneth of May' and other love-makings of Phillida and Coridon, are happy reminders of the eternal youth of Nicholas Breton (1555?– c. 1626), a sort of 'Georgian' who could greet the new century with buoyant as well as melancholic humours. In his *Passionate Shepherd* (1604), as in his prose *Fantastics* (1604?), Arcadian idealism and artifice admit authentic, though pleasant, rural realism. The wooer of Aglaia, drawing the conventional contrast between court and country, records the familiar sights of the merry country lad, the fox sneaking through the hedge, the little black-haired cony sitting in the sun to wash her face with her forefeet. The Renaissance pastoral, though it yielded much lovely verse of peculiar fragrance, was always in danger of inanition, but it was not promptly killed by the rational realism of Donne and Jonson. Jonson himself ended his career with the English and Theocritean *Sad Shepherd*, and even Carew's 'Rapture' started from the first chorus of Tasso's *Aminta*. In the Caroline age the old conventions were quickened by fresh feeling in Drayton and Milton and others. If *Comus* and 'Lycidas' stand apart, the cause is not only Milton's genius but his reviving of the pastoral's concern with great themes, public or private. In Quarles's *The Shepherd's Oracles* (1644–6) that revival was rather a journalistic than a poetical success. On the other hand, the country is the real country in the charming ode to Anthony Stafford by the author of *Amyntas*, Thomas Randolph, and in the less familiar but also charming 'Ode upon occasion of His Majesty's Proclamation in the Year 1630. Commanding the Gentry to reside upon their Estates in the Country', by the translator of *Pastor Fido*, Sir Richard Fanshawe.

We may pause here to look at the chief of Scottish writers, who was in some degree isolated in body and spirit from current English poetry. Like his friend Alexander, William Drummond of Hawthornden (1585–1649) gave his English allegiance to the author of the *Arcadia* and *Astrophel and Stella*, but he may be counted with the Spenserians by virtue of his smooth fluidity of movement (a movement delicately varied and restrained by the irregularities of the *canzone*) and his pictorial and mythological texture of clear and often vivid colour.[1] As his library and his verse testify, Drummond had a knowledge of French, Spanish, and especially Italian *belles lettres* probably unrivalled in England in the second decade of the century. His special admirations included not only such familiar authors as Ronsard and Desportes, Tasso and Guarini, but the less familiar, like Garcilaso and Marino, and he read many others. When about 1614–15 Drummond characterized the English poets of love (the first four were Sidney, Alexander, Daniel, and Donne), his criterion was Petrarch. His own verses, Jonson told him, 'smelled too much of the schooles and were not after the Fancie of the tyme'. But if he was in part a Jacobean—or half-Elizabethan—Stanley, a bookish artist whom we identify with graceful translation and imitation, his borrowings from diverse

---

[1] Drummond attended Edinburgh University (M.A., 1605), spent several years abroad in study and travel, and in 1610 became laird of Hawthornden. He settled down to a retired life of reading, writing, and, on the side, mechanical invention; he conceived, among other things, of machine-guns and tanks. His chief literary friends were Alexander, Drayton (by letter only), and Jonson, who visited him in the winter of 1618–19. Drummond's first fiancée died in 1614/15; he married in 1632. From 1635 onward he wrote a number of tracts on public affairs, inspired mainly by his royalism and love of peace. His history of Scotland from 1423 to 1542 was printed in 1655. His best piece of prose, *A Cypress Grove* (1623), is noticed in Chapter X.

poets did receive the transforming and unifying impress of his own lucid decorative instinct, reflective melancholy, and melodious rhythms.

Drummond's first publication, the lament for Prince Henry, indicated his attachment to continental models of pastoral elegy and to Sidney (the *Arcadia*). In the panegyric on King James, *Forth Feasting* (1617), he remembered Virgil's eclogues and Ronsard's *Le Bocage Royal*. Both poems show skill in regular couplets. Drummond's best work was in the amatory *Poems* of 1616 and the religious *Flowers of Sion* (1623, 1630). The former has such pure literary beauties as the radiant madrigal, 'Like the Idalian Queene', and the *canzone*, 'Phoebus arise'; if we are surprised by an image of unwonted violence,

> Night like a Drunkard reeles
> Beyond the Hills to shunne his flaming Wheeles,

we find that it comes from *Romeo and Juliet* (and Isaiah xxiv. 20). The ecstasies and pangs of the lover, rather more sensuous than Petrarchan, yield in the second part of the *Poems* to grief for the death of the beloved. 'It Autumne was' embodies the Stoic, Neoplatonic, and Christian *contemptus mundi*, the Neoplatonic vision of the heaven of eternal life and love and beauty, which were expressed in the prose of *A Midnight's Trance* (1619), the first version of *A Cypress Grove*. One line, 'O leave that Love which reacheth but to Dust', illustrates both Drummond's Platonism and his use, even in sorrow, of other poets. His desire to live 'Farre from the madding Worldlings hoarse Discords', his philosophic and religious sense of earthly vanity—instincts heightened by his serious illness of 1620—explain the relative originality and depth of *Flowers of Sion*. When, for instance, he rewrites Ronsard's 'Hymne de l'Eternité' as the 'Hymn of the Fairest Fair', he changes Ronsard's half-Epicurean thought into a picture of the Creator and Creation which accords with his own Christian Platonism. In 'The woefull Marie', adapted from Marino's *Stabat Mater*, the baroque strain is much subdued, as it is in the fine 'Hymn of the Ascension' and other purely religious poems.

Before we come to the chief heirs of Spenser's religious and moral allegory (and without lingering over the fluent products of Breton's sacred muse), we must give a paragraph to John Davies of Hereford (1565?–1618). Davies, the most famous penman of his day, had pedagogical and literary connexions with many members of the great families, and in *The Scourge of Folly* (1610?) he addressed complimentary epigrams to some two dozen authors, including Shakespeare and Donne. He was associated with Browne, Wither, and Brooke in *The Shepherd's Pipe* (1614). Davies's rough satirical epigrams belong to the semi-popular rather than the classical section of the very large and drab body of verse of that kind. But his main effort went into a series of religious, moral, and psychological treatises or sermons in verse, *Mirum in Modum* (1602), *Microcosmos* (1603), *Summa Totalis* (1607), *The Holy Rood* (1609), and other things. Among his sources were De la Primaudaye's *French Academy*, Mornay's *Trueness of the Christian Religion*, and Agrippa's *De Incertitudine*; and he has some small interest for the historian of ideas. In manner Davies was a sort of scholastic Sylvester; one example of eccentric taste is the anatomical mysticism of 'Formosity' in *Wit's Pilgrimage* (1605?). He could achieve the raw material of poetry in describing the plague, in *Humour's Heaven on Earth* (1609), and his 'Picture of an Happy Man' in *The Muse's Sacrifice* (1612) is a respectable religious pendant to Wotton's Horatian poem, but the master (in Fuller's words) of fast, fair, close, and various handwriting was as a poet slow, laborious, diffuse, and flat. There is no answer to his query:

> Busie Invention, whie art thou so dull
> And yet still doing?

Giles Fletcher's *Christ's Victory and Triumph* (1610) is, apart from some things of Donne, the chief example of baroque devotional poetry between Southwell and the young Milton and Crashaw.[1] Although Fletcher crowned his prefatory list of 'divine and heroical' poets with those 'two blessed Soules', Du Bartas and Spenser (and King James), he did not seek to embrace

---

[1] Giles Fletcher (1585/6–1623) and Phineas (1582–1650) were the sons of Giles Fletcher, M.P., diplomat, and author, who died in 1611, and cousins of John Fletcher the dramatist. Giles was educated at Trinity College, Cambridge (B.A., 1606; B.D., 1619), and became Reader in Greek in 1615. In 1617 he received from Bacon a living which in 1619 he exchanged for another in Bacon's gift, that of Alderton in Suffolk, which he held until 1623—a change made unhappy, says Fuller, by the intractable character of his parishioners. Phineas Fletcher went to Eton and King's College (B.A., 1604; M.A., 1608) and was ordained in 1611. In 1615 he became chaplain to Sir Henry Willoughby and married. In 1621 his patron presented him to the living of Hilgay in Norfolk, which was his home for the rest of his life.

their large poetic domain but centred his four cantos around the birth, temptation, crucifixion, and resurrection of Christ. His Spenserianism shows itself in his metrical movement (though his stanza is not Spenser's), in narrative and allegorical imitations like the Bower of Vain-delight, in the borrowing and echoing of lines, phrases, and diction, in the fusing of biblical and pagan story, and in the lusciously Italianate embellishment of heroic virtue. The picture of Mercy suggests Ovid, the Hero of Marlowe and Chapman, Spenser's Belphoebe and Mercilla, and, by anticipation, the Theophila of Phineas Fletcher's friend, Edward Benlowes. It has been suggested that the two Fletchers and Benlowes all reflect the 'baroque' influence of the early Christian Latin poets whom Giles named in his preface. Milton, who in his younger days owed something to the Fletchers, may have remembered Giles's handling of the temptation even in the late and austere *Paradise Regained*, but the earlier Christ in the wilderness is modelled on the lover in the Song of Solomon; he has black hair in small curls, 'cheekes as snowie apples, sop't in wine', and (like Belphoebe also) 'two white marble pillars' for legs. He is, moreover, the true Orpheus who conquered hell, and he ascends to heaven like Ganymede. But while Fletcher has not the 'voice of steel' that he craves, his tendency towards soft excess is checked by antithetical 'wit'. His opening stanza is only the first of many series of those paradoxes which are at the centre of baroque—as of traditional—Christianity:

> The birth of him that no beginning knewe,
> Yet gives beginning to all that are borne,
> And how the Infinite farre greater grewe,
> By growing lesse, and how the rising Morne,
> That shot from heav'n, did backe to heaven retourne,
>   The obsequies of him that could not die,
>   And death of life, ende of eternitie,
> How worthily he died, that died unworthily.

Further, especially in the latter half of the poem, sincere if 'naïve' devotion and homely directness triumph over allegory as Christ triumphs over death, and though Giles leaves to his brother the composing of a divine epithalamium, his own 'beatificall' vision inspires a finer ecstasy than Phineas attained at the end of *The Purple Island*.

Phineas Fletcher has his moments of sensuous charm and beauty, but he is perhaps at his best and simplest in the

late and private verses of *A Father's Testament*. On the whole
he is of coarser grain and less pure spirituality than Giles.
His favourite model, in addition to Spenser, was Du Bartas
or rather Sylvester, to whom Giles owed little or nothing.
Among his models we should perhaps include himself, for he
was thriftily repetitious as well as diffuse. Most of his verse was
written during the years 1607–12, though published later.

Locustae vel Pietas Jesuitica and the larger English version,
The Locusts, or Apollyonists (1627), include Satan, an infernal
council, and Sin, but in poetical quality and anti-Romanism
are closer to Milton's small 'epic' on the Gunpowder Plot, *In
quintum Novembris* (1626), than to *Paradise Lost* (though *Locustae*
had been written long before 1627, it seems unlikely that the
young Milton saw a manuscript). *Venus and Anchises* was printed
in 1628 as *Britain's Ida* and as a work of Spenser's. Even in an
age which allowed some latitude to the clerical muse it might
have been awkward to acknowledge a voluptuous addition to
the Elizabethan series of Ovidian and Italianate narratives,
though Fletcher's warmth is mitigated by touches of humour.
With that poem may be placed the unprinted 'Epithalamium'
discovered in 1923, which has perhaps more than a family
resemblance to the 'Epithalamium' of Johannes Secundus. In
1631 appeared *Sicelides, a Piscatory*, which had been acted at
King's College in 1615. The piscatory eclogues in *The Purple
Island* (1633) were praised by Walton as the excellent work of
an excellent angler, but they are for the most part dull imitations of the pastorals of Spenser and Sannazaro. *The Purple
Island* itself has a pastoral background. On a first encounter with
the text and gloss of this notorious poem one may exclaim, like
H. G. Wells's Kipps when he first beheld an anatomical chart,
'Chubes! Chubes!' The medieval theme of 'the castle of the body',
which had been grotesque enough in Du Bartas and in Spenser,
becomes still more grotesque in becoming more laboriously
scientific. Fletcher may be called the Jacobean or Caroline
Erasmus Darwin. Since the poem was apparently begun about
the same time as *Christ's Victory and Triumph*, we cannot blame
the author for versifying Vesalian anatomy and Galenic rather
than Harveian physiology. Fletcher's zeal was of course religious
and ethical as well as scientific—his book was dedicated to
Benlowes and received high tributes from Benlowes and
Quarles—and if we survive the anatomy (which attracted

James Joyce), we reach a catalogue and a battle of the vices and virtues. It is, however, a static mixture of decorative abstraction and satirical realism. While Spenser at his best can vitalize ethical and religious ideas in his characters and action, Fletcher can only describe emblematic figures.

We turn to several religious poets who cannot be readily classified, though a Spenserian affinity sometimes appears. Sir John Beaumont (1583?–1627), the elder brother of the dramatist, was a friend and partial disciple of Drayton and Jonson and in 1606 he was indicted for recusancy soon after Jonson and Lodge. His modest position in the history of the heroic couplet was consolidated by the classical 'good sense' of his verse-essay, 'To his late Majesty, concerning the True Form of English Poetry', though he said little that had not been said, as he suggests, by King James, or by Jonson (or by Puttenham, who gave sanction for various later phenomena, from half-Hobbesian rationalism to poems shaped like lozenges). Beaumont's metrical importance has been somewhat diminished by modern recognition of the large number of men who were moulding the couplet, but he did display unusual regularity and smoothness. Nearly all of his verse was written in that form, the mythological and mock-heroic *Metamorphosis of Tobacco* (1602), *Bosworth-Field* (1629), a narrative of the kind cultivated by Drayton and Daniel, most of his classical translations, and sacred and occasional poems. Some of these pieces, such as 'Of True Liberty' and the elegy on his son, are the work of a poet and bear out Anthony Wood's report of him as 'a Person of great knowledge, gravity and worth'. Beaumont is here placed in a religious group because of his most elaborate work—in twelve books—the unpublished *Crown of Thorns*, which he was apparently writing from about 1607 until his last years. It is a poem of devotional meditation, both Catholic and Platonic, on Christ as God, man, and Saviour, symbolic and paradoxical in plan and texture.

Francis Quarles (1592–1644) cannot have had many readers since Lamb, Browning, and Thoreau, but his *Emblems* (1635) was the most popular book of verse of the seventeenth century and his *Enchiridion* (1640–1) the most popular book of aphorisms, and other works were frequently reprinted too.[1] In Horace

---

[1] Quarles was the son of a surveyor-general of victualling for the Navy. He was educated at Cambridge (B.A., 1609) and Lincoln's Inn. In 1613 he went abroad

Walpole's phrase, Milton was forced to wait till the world had
done admiring Quarles. Cowley in 1656 censured his biblical
narratives and Edward Phillips in 1675 called him 'the darling
of our Plebeian Judgments', but less sophisticated comments
help to explain his hold on the public. Samuel Sheppard, in
The Times Displayed (1646), ranked him 'next to Bartas'; according to Fuller, he drank of Jordan instead of Helicon; and
Baxter in 1681 said that he 'out-went' Wither in 'mixing competent Wit with Piety'. Such popular fame might, in a later
age, have been the reward of facile optimism, but Quarles's
first book was *A Feast for Worms* (1620), and he seldom came
nearer optimism than in the assertion 'Tis glorious misery to
be borne a Man'. His life and outlook were of Puritanical
sobriety, though his 'Genius jumpt with' that of his admired
friend Phineas Fletcher to the length of one 'vain amatorious
poem', *Argalus and Parthenia*. A believer in established order
and uniformity, a zealous defender of divine right and 'a true
sonne of the Church of England', Quarles nevertheless was not
blind to Anglican errors and, holding by the authority of the
individual conscience and reason, he could not be intolerant.

We need not then be surprised by the mingled Puritan and
Catholic religiosity of Quarles's *Divine Fancies* (1632), *Emblems*
(1635), and *Hieroglyphics of the Life of Man* (1638). The emblem,
a symbolic picture with a motto and an exposition, had become
one of the last European manifestations of a medieval habit of
mind. It was born, or reborn, in 1531 with Alciati's collection,
drawn largely from the Greek Anthology and other ancient
sources. The first English collection was in the Dutch Van der
Noot's *Theatre for Worldlings* (1569), to which the young Spenser
contributed; the second was Geoffrey Whitney's *Choice of
Emblems* (1586). Among the later men interested in emblems
were Peacham, Wither, Christopher Harvey, John Hall, and
Bunyan. Hoole spoke of the use of emblems in schools. More
important was the significance of the emblem in poetry and
literature generally, notably in Donne, George Herbert, and

in the train of the Earl of Arundel, who was one of the newly married Princess
Elizabeth's escorts. He was abroad again, 1615–17, and married in 1618. From
about 1626 to 1629–30 Quarles was in Ireland as secretary to Archbishop Ussher.
By 1633 he had retired to his native Essex. In 1640 he was appointed chronologer
to the city of London. In that year he wrote *The Virgin Widow* (printed in 1649),
an allegorical play about the Church of England. His last four years were given
mainly to prose. His widow was left in poverty with nine of their eighteen children.

Crashaw, and the emblem poet *par excellence* was Quarles. His plates were taken from two Jesuit emblem books and his verses sometimes echoed theirs. In the preface of *Argalus and Parthenia* (1629) he repudiated 'the tyranny of *strong lines*, . . . the meere itch of wit', but the emblem was an essentially 'metaphysical' device, at once epigrammatic, metaphorical, and concrete. 'Before the knowledge of letters', says Quarles, 'God was knowne by Hierogliphicks; And, indeed, what are the Heavens, the Earth, nay every Creature, but Hierogliphicks and Emblemes of His Glory?' In his penitential dialogues with God, in his carnest *contemptus mundi*, in his dark vision of puny, lustful, and restless man, Quarles is something of an inferior Herbert, a less jerky and vehement Benlowes. The latter, his friend and patron, must have studied him. Both, by the way, see man as a magnetic needle trembling until he comes to rest in God (an image handled by a finer artist, Jeremy Taylor, in his sermon on Bramhall), and both, as poets, have the uncertainty of the needle. Likening death to a long sleep in bed, Quarles asks, 'And why not Wormes as well as Fleas?'

If Quarles did not attempt allegory on a large scale, two later poets, Henry More (1614–87) and Joseph Beaumont (1616–99), outdid Spenser in philosophic and narrative complexity. (Benlowes belongs rather with the metaphysical poets.) More is a metaphysical poet in the general sense of the word. The nature and evolution of his thought are indicated in the tenth chapter, and the reader cannot hope here for a compendious account of 'Psychozoia, or the Life of the Soul', 'Psychathanasia, or the Immortality of the Soul', 'Antipsychopannychia, or the Confutation of the Sleep of the Soul', and 'Antimonopsychia, or Confutation of the Unity of Souls', all published together as *Psychodia Platonica* (1642), and of *Democritus Platonissans, or an Essay upon the Infinity of Worlds out of Platonic Principles* (1646). These and other pieces were collected in *Philosophical Poems* (1647). As a child More had thought *The Fairy Queen* 'a Poem as richly fraught with divine Morality as Phansy', and his debt embraced the *Four Hymns* and other things. However, even the sage and serious and 'Platonic' Spenser might not have recognized as his poetic children such complex and abstract efforts to expound a rational and ethical Christian Neoplatonism and defend it against materialism old and new. The most Spenserian and most attractive of these poems is the earliest,

'Psychozoia', which has the first spontaneous glow of the satisfying revelation the author's passionately hungry soul had
sought and found. Here, too, in the course of a pilgrim's progress,
and in a mood both earnest and genial, More gives satirical
sketches (much enlarged in 1647) of erroneous and spurious
types of religion, the self-sufficient humanist, the scholastic
rationalist, the Calvinistic bibliolater, the sectarian enthusiast,
the greasy ecclesiastical authoritarian, Corvino ('Most like
methought to a Cathedrall Dean'), and Pico, the High Church
ritualist. Prominent models for this last were the late Archbishop and Bishop Wren.

To More, Joseph Beaumont—who was Wren's protégé—
might have seemed a ritualist, and to Beaumont, who was later
to attack More's *Grand Mystery of Godliness*, More may already
have appeared as a dangerously latitudinarian individualist.
Beaumont was ejected from his Cambridge fellowship in 1643–
4, along with his friend Crashaw and others, and though he
remained an Anglican or Anglo-Catholic, he had a close spiritual
affinity with the more intense Crashaw. In his shorter and more
inviting poems Crashaw's influence predominates. Beaumont's
mystical instincts received full expression in *Psyche, or Love's
Mystery* (1648), a vast allegory of the soul's pilgrimage through
earthly trials to heavenly felicity. Such a work, in the Spenserian
and Fletcherian tradition, bears some general resemblance to
the poems of More, but Beaumont is rather a pallid reflection
of conventional mystical thought than a spiritual genius like
More (or even Benlowes), and his style is oppressively Marinistic.

2

We turn back to some poets who cannot be called Spenserian,
although the first three of them were more nearly akin to
Spenser in moral temper than most of the writers who bear the
label. The first is Samuel Daniel (1563?–1619).[1] His early

---

[1] Daniel was born in Somerset. In 1581 he entered Magdalen Hall, Oxford,
where he studied under his brother-in-law, John Florio. In 1586 he was employed
by the English embassy in Paris. In 1585 he had dedicated his translation of Paulus
Jovius's tract on *imprese* to Sir Edward Dymoke, and he was still attached to
Dymoke in 1592; the pair had travelled in Italy, probably in 1590–1, and visited
Guarini. Daniel became tutor to William Herbert, third Earl of Pembroke, and a
member of the Countess of Pembroke's literary circle. Before 1599 he became tutor
to Lady Anne Clifford and was associated with her mother, the Countess of Cumberland, and with the Countess of Bedford, through whom he entered the service
of Queen Anne. In 1604–5 he licensed plays for the Children of the Queen's Revels.

poems lie outside our limits. *The Civil Wars* (1595; revised and
enlarged, though not completed, 1599–1609) was a contribution to 'the Tudor myth' which earned for its author the title of
the English Lucan. Apparently it affected Shakespeare, who in
turn affected some of Daniel's revisions. Daniel's epic and
philosophic seriousness allowed the classical and modern
'licence, of framing speaches', but excluded 'fictions, fantasies'
(an exception, in book vi, is the Nemesis–Pandora myth about the
invention of artillery). Concrete language and imagery, inconspicuous enough at first, were increasingly overlaid by the
general and abstract. Daniel has battles, but his concern is
with war. Most modern readers, except Coleridge, have shared
Drayton's judgement that Daniel was 'too much Historian in
verse'. He suffers partly because we have Shakespeare in our
heads. Though the poem can make an impression, the author's
sober earnestness perhaps shows to better advantage in his
prose *History*, which does not evoke Shakespearian comparisons.

Daniel indeed stands out among the men of letters of his
time for his philosophic sense of history. This is the critical
mainspring of his urbane *Defence of Rhyme* (1603). To Daniel,
Campion's plea for classical metres meant the dead hand, not
the living spirit, of antiquity. With full reverence for Greece and
Rome, he rejoiced in the Middle Ages and above all in 'the
wonderfull Architecture of this state of England, . . . continually
in all ages furnisht with spirites fitte to maintaine the majestie
of her owne greatnes. . .'. And though his concern is practical,
he sees the literary problem *sub specie aeternitatis*: 'and we must
heerein be content to submit our selves to the law of time, which
in few yeeres wil make al that, for which we now contend,
Nothing.' Daniel's appeal to custom, nature, and judgement,
his sense of historical relativity, may reflect both Fulke Greville
and Montaigne; he echoed the latter in the *Defence* and in his
epistle to Sir Thomas Egerton and commended him in commending Florio's translation.

Daniel steps outside himself into the current of Renaissance
naturalism in such lyrical pieces as the eulogy of the Golden

He got into trouble over his own play, *Philotas* (1605), because of its supposed
reference to the Earl of Essex. During 1604–14 he wrote two masques and two
pastoral plays for the court. He was apparently still in the queen's service in 1619,
since he was a mourner at her funeral in that year, the year of his own death.
Daniel's early poems are treated by C. S. Lewis in vol. iii, his plays and masques
by F. P. Wilson in vol. v.

Age (1601) taken from Tasso's *Aminta*, and the 'Description of Beauty' (1623) rendered, in no Marinistic fashion, from Marino. Daniel's historical sense is bound up with the ethical ideals of the humanistic tradition, which he shares with Spenser, Jonson, Chapman, and the more pessimistic Greville, his patron and friend, 'the right worthie and judicious favourer of Virtue'. For good or ill, the past is one with the present and future; they are parts of a continuous whole. The simple fact that 'Man is a creature of the same dimension he was' is the sobering and inspiring text of *The Civil Wars* and the *History of England*, *Musophilus* and the *Defence of Rhyme*, the tragedies, and the noble series of Horatian epistles of 1603. (With these last may be grouped the poem of 1601 to Sir Thomas Bodley and the 'Funeral Poem' of 1606 on the Earl of Devonshire.) The epistles are signal proofs that it does not ill beseem 'The function of a Poem, to discourse'. Other writers might have saluted Sir Thomas Bodley, who had conquered time by assembling 'The glorious reliques of the best of men'; but only Daniel perhaps could have addressed to the Lord Keeper Egerton, who has won the glory that does not end 'with our breath', a stately poem on the difference between inflexible Law and Equity, 'the soule of Law'. (The poem owes some ideas to Montaigne's 'Of Experience'.) The young Lady Anne Clifford, if she would fulfil the responsibilities of her noble mind and descent, must, like the planets, 'keep the certaine course Of order'. In the more famous epistles to the Countesses of Bedford and Cumberland, Daniel achieves the perfect statement of his Christian Stoicism. He knows, to quote lines Wordsworth quoted,

> that unlesse above himselfe he can
> Erect himselfe, how poore a thing is man!

He is translating a Senecan phrase which Jonson also translated, in *Cynthia's Revels*, and which the naturalistic Montaigne cited to reject. The same humanistic idealism inspires 'Ulysses and the Siren' (1605), and here too, along with the lyrical movement, the effect is created, not by surprises or subtleties, but by straightforward rightness of thought and feeling and style and tone. Daniel's celebrations of order and right reason assuredly do not provide the concrete poetic excitements of the *Songs and Sonnets* (in many parts of which the young Donne turned those ideals upside down); but Daniel's best poetry is

an Arnoldian criticism of life. In *Musophilus* and the epistles the
dominant metaphor is of a building, an inward citadel, and
this is not an ivory tower. After one has been stirred afresh by
these poems, one does not hesitate to endorse the modest and
manly claim offered 'To the Reader' in 1607:

> I know I shalbe read, among the rest
> So long as men speake english, and so long
> As verse and vertue shalbe in request,
> Or grace to honest industry belong.

Contemporary, like most modern, references to Daniel stress
honest industry and pure diction more than higher qualities,
and he saw himself as old-fashioned. But with some few readers
in every generation he is 'in request'. If there are persons who
agree with C. S. Lewis that 'there is more poetry in one of
Campion's *Airs* than in all Daniel's epic and epistles', there are
others for whom his grave ethical passion and his faith in the
immortal life of culture, poetry, and the English tongue do
kindle poetic fire.

There is a hotter fire, sometimes attended with dense smoke,
in two poets akin to Daniel in their ethical urgency but
tougher in sensibility and mode of utterance, George Chapman
(1559?–1634) and Fulke Greville (1554–1628). In our time
Chapman has been linked with Donne as a pioneer metaphysical
poet, and, like many men, he did share in that general movement; yet the texture of his verse as well as his humanistic
creed may warrant his having a place apart. The reading of
Chapman confirms Anthony Wood's description, 'a Person of
most reverend aspect, religious and temperate, qualities rarely
meeting in a Poet'. The character of his Renaissance humanism
has been already observed in connexion with his translations of
Homer. In his first dedication Chapman began to set forth the
conception of poetry—as philosophic, 'prophetic', and inevitably
obscure—that he pursued with religious and solitary devotion
to the end of his ill-rewarded life. Parts of his philosophy of
order were expounded (if the word is not too euphemistic) in a
series of difficult and—to the uninstructed reader—disorderly
poems, *The Shadow of Night* (1594), *Ovid's Banquet of Sense* (1595),
a radical departure from the Ovidianism of *Venus and Adonis*,
and the continuation of Marlowe's *Hero and Leander* (1598),
an elaborately symbolic exaltation of marriage and 'ceremony'.

The most central and lucid exposition is *Euthymiae Raptus, or The Tears of Peace*, which Chapman dedicated to his patron Prince Henry in 1609. *Andromeda Liberata* (1614) was an unfortunate attempt to link Neoplatonic doctrines of love with the marriage of the Earl and Countess of Somerset—published, we may remember, before their trial (though Chapman remained a loyal believer in the Earl's innocence). There were other miscellaneous poems and translations.

In poems as well as plays the Christian Platonist and Stoic glorified truth and wisdom and the complete and heroic soul of the 'Senecall man' that rules over perturbation and passion and is proof alike against the corruptions and the assaults of the world. As a Christian humanist, with a prophetic and mystical fervour of his own, Chapman stands, not with Donne, but in the line of poets less occult than himself, Spenser, Daniel, Jonson, and Milton. Swinburne pronounced Chapman, among other things, a Theognis rather than a Homer not yet come to years of discretion; he might have discerned something Pindaric or Aeschylean. In Chapman the ethical and didactic gospel of Renaissance humanism was heightened and strengthened, and darkened, by an avowed and passionate belief in the learned and esoteric obscurity of divine (and nocturnal) inspiration. In the nature of his revolt against conventional Elizabethan style Chapman was less close to Jonson than to Greville and Donne. The impression he leaves is best conveyed in his own words, from the fine epistle to his friend Thomas Harriot (1598):

> O had your perfect eye Organs to pierce
> Into that Chaos whence this stiffled verse
> By violence breakes: where Gloweworme like doth shine
> In nights of sorrow, this hid soule of mine:
> And how her genuine formes struggle for birth,
> Under the clawes of this fowle Panther earth.

While Chapman has a lucid gnomic strain, his characteristic texture is tough and knotted with emblematic images and symbols sought for their philosophical and functional expressiveness, and, as in many poets of our own day, these tend to become a semi-private code. Yet Chapman works in a great tradition and his symbols are not merely personal and miscellaneous, nor are they, like Donne's, largely realistic, scholastic, and scientific; much of his imagery comes, along with his ethical ideas, from such favourite authors as Plutarch, Epictetus, Ficino, Erasmus, and the allegorical mythographer Natalis Comes.

In *The Tears of Peace*, which is indebted to Erasmus's *Querela Pacis* and the Hermetic *Poimander* (in Ficino's translation), Chapman is less muscle-bound than usual, though he is far from the straightforward clarity of Daniel's *Musophilus*. In the induction the spirit of Homer presents the lady Peace mourning over the strife and chaos that prevail among men who prize outward more than inward worth, and the body of the poem is a dialogue on that text between Peace and the poet. Contemplating a blind and sordid world of ambitious men of action, ignorant idlers, and self-seeking intellectuals, Chapman passionately urges the claims of divine learning, not the erudition of 'a walking dictionarie' but 'the rich crowne of ould Humanitie', the sovereign empire of the soul over 'the bodies mutinous Realme'. The soul works on the body as the sculptor (a Plotinian image) reveals in shapeless stone the true God-like man by cutting away the impure and 'redundant matter'. The soul is not mere reason but is from God and should aspire to its true sphere 'Where burns the fire, eternall, and sincere'. This metaphor reminds us that in Chapman generally flashes of pure fire often break through the blanket of the dark in unforgettable phrases, from 'The downward-burning flame, Of her rich hayre' in *Ovid's Banquet of Sense* to the celebration ('A Hymn to our Saviour on the Cross') of the Redeemer and condemnation of the soul which

for nothing takes
The beauties that for her love, thou putst on;
In torments rarefied farre past the Sunne.

There was a gulf between the poor and inconspicuous playwright-poet and the rich and prominent statesman, Fulke Greville, first Lord Brooke (1554–1628),[1] but there was a partial

---

[1] Greville's friendship with Sidney began at Shrewsbury School and they entered upon court life together, with similar political and literary interests. In 1584 Greville entertained Giordano Bruno. Except in his efforts to get abroad, he enjoyed the special favour of Elizabeth. His public career, which involved at least the usual amount of subservience, came mostly after Sidney's death (1586). Greville represented Warwickshire in Parliament, held various minor posts, was Treasurer of the Navy from 1598 to 1604, and Chancellor of the Exchequer from

affinity in their philosophic and religious outlook and earnestness and in their poetic manner. Greville can also be obscure, though he does not deal in Chapman's mythological and other symbols. What Edward Phillips called his 'close, mysterious and sentencious way of writing' is nearer the metaphysical than the Spenserian manner, yet Greville shows, in his *Treaty of Human Learning*, a Hobbesian distrust of metaphor, and his normal utterance is of a massive realistic plainness fitted for the sober and penetrating thought that is his main concern. In parts of *Caelica*, which was begun under Sidney's inspiration, he wreathed iron pokers into true-love knots, and although, according to Naunton, he 'lived, and dyed, a constant Courtier of the Ladies', no series of love poems was ever less amorous. For all the Petrarchan and Sidneian fancies, and the omnipresence of Cupid, Caelica, Myra, and Cynthia are something less than shadows, and towards the end they fade away altogether behind religious and philosophical reflection.

The last part of *Caelica* was apparently written late, in the period of the 'treaties' on *Wars, Fame and Honour, Human Learning*, and *Religion*. The plays—completed about 1600–1 and later revised—were also treatises, cast in the form of Senecan dramas; the treatises were in fact, Greville tells us, overgrown choruses, and the earliest, *Monarchy*, has a close affinity with the plays. The closet dramatist, in handling 'the high waies of ambitious Governours', was not merely a closet philosopher. He burned a play on Antony and Cleopatra (1600–1?) because it revealed too clearly his reaction to the disgrace of his kinsman the Earl of Essex; and many lines in *Mustapha* and *Alaham* might have been given a topical application. Thus Greville's poetic material— and with it his *Life* of Sidney—was preponderantly political. A natural royalist, a devoted admirer of Elizabeth, now a close observer of both active conflicts and the conflicting doctrines of Bodin, George Buchanan, and others, Greville, a public man

1614 to 1622. He received a knighthood in 1603 and a peerage in 1621. He became a wealthy landowner and rebuilt Warwick Castle. He remained loyal to Essex, and his attachment to Bacon, though less warm, survived Bacon's fall. Greville befriended a number of literary men, Daniel, Speed, Camden, and young William Davenant, and he helped to procure the deanery of Westminster for Andrewes. In 1628, a few days after the murder of Buckingham, he was stabbed by a servant (for whom he had provided an annuity) and died some weeks later. Apart from an unauthorized edition of *Mustapha* (1609), all of Greville's longer works, which he assiduously revised, were published after his death. The *Life of Sidney* is discussed in Chapter VII.

and a thinker, grappled with the problems of sovereignty, resistance, natural and positive law, and the rest. But we must neglect the complications of his political thought for the work that best reveals his central motives and questionings, the *Treaty of Human Learning*.

In this as in the other philosophical poems Greville often treads on the margin of poetry. But for the strong tradition of the didactic poem, indeed, he might have made prose the medium for his essays and counsels, civil and moral, as he did in his 'Letter to an Honourable Lady' on the duties of marriage. While his outlook sometimes suggests Bacon's *Essays* and *Advancement of Learning*, or Daniel and Chapman at the opposite pole, Greville does not share either kind of relative optimism. Having the realistic tough-mindedness of a courtier and states- man, and a starkly Calvinistic conviction of human depravity, he is too experienced, philosophical, and sceptical to rest in either cynical expediency or humanistic idealism (though he has his Stoic supports and is, in his world, a kind of modern Seneca). The contradictions Greville sees in the nature and destiny of man are unresolvable. To quote the *locus classicus*, from *Mustapha*:

> Oh wearisome Condition of Humanity!
> Borne under one Law, to another bound:
> Vainely begot, and yet forbidden vanity,
> Created sicke, commanded to be sound:
> What meaneth Nature by these diverse Lawes?
> Passion and Reason, selfe-division cause.

'I know the world and believe in God', he wrote in 1613, and the much-quoted phrase is a partial clue. As he says in his *Life* of Sidney, Greville found his 'creeping Genius more fixed upon the Images of Life, than the Images of Wit', and he addressed 'those only, that are weather-beaten in the Sea of this World, such as having lost the sight of their Gardens, and groves, study to saile on a right course among Rocks, and quick-sands'. All about him he sees change, chaos, and corruption. For him, as for Donne in the *Anniversaries*, science is mainly an example of intellectual vanity. Learned ignorance and blind presumption, disguised by the specious diversity of modern verbal knowledge, have obscured and blighted man's sense of the divine and of the true ends of life. Self-will, the lust for power, has set up false gods.

And, like so many Christian humanists before him, Greville seeks to recall men from sinful 'pride of minde' to humility and obedience, to re-establish the sovereignty of religion, reason, and order in the individual soul and in society. But whereas Calvin and Machiavelli, starting, one might say, from similar premisses, had moved confidently along widely divergent roads, it is Greville's difficulty, and the source of his gloomy strength, that he has a good deal of the one along with something of the other. And while Daniel and Chapman can take a more or less confident stand on humane culture, or culture and religion, Greville's position is nearer the disillusioned fundamentalism of the early Cornelius Agrippa or the contemporary Donne.

A bolder courtier who lacked Greville's capacity for self-preservation, and whose career is too familiar to need an outline, was Sir Walter Ralegh (1552? 1554?–1618). So much of Ralegh's verse was written before 1600, the canon is so uncertain, and his concentrated and poignantly individual poems are so famous, that we may limit ourselves to a few bald facts about a few of the pieces printed after 1600. 'Conceipt begotten by the eyes', published in the *Poetical Rhapsody* of 1602, begins in the manner of the song sung to Bassanio but passes into Ralegh's characteristic brooding on the vanity and mutability of man and the world. That direct and bitter blast on the same theme, 'The Lie', appeared in the 1608 edition of the same anthology. 'What is our life? a play of passion', which, like 'The Lie', has been attributed to several authors, embodies the theme again, in the favourite Elizabethan image of a stage-play; this real epigram Orlando Gibbons made into one of the greatest of madrigals (1612). 'Give me my Scallop shell of quiet' was printed first in Anthony Scoloker's *Daiphantus* (1604) and later in Ralegh's *Remains*; it seems to be charged with the writer's fierce feeling about his trial and death-sentence of 1603, and some odd conceits which grow out of the thematic metaphor scarcely mar its powerful intensity. The still more familiar 'Even such is time' is enveloped in complications, partly because the first six lines (with small variants) are a last and appropriate stanza in the manuscript text of a love poem of six stanzas beginning 'Nature that washt her hands in milke'; but there is good reason to accept the well-authenticated tradition and suppose that on his last night Ralegh remembered lines he had written before and added the concluding prayer.

3

The Golden Age of English music and song is so rich, especially after 1600, that the historian is lucky in having one pre-eminent representative of the united arts in Thomas Campion (1567–1620) who, unlike his fellow composers generally, wrote his own words.[1] Apart from the masques, his principal works were the *Poemata* of 1595 (enlarged in 1619); *A Book of Airs* (1601), edited by his friend Philip Rosseter, who composed the music and apparently the words of the second half of the volume; *Observations in the Art of English Poesy* (1602); *Two Books of Airs* (1613–15?); *Third and Fourth Book of Airs* (1617?); and *A New Way of Making Four Parts in Counterpoint* (c. 1618?). Campion's early poetic evolution gives a special significance to the prefatory words in the first *Book of Airs*: 'What Epigrams are in Poetrie, the same are Ayres in musicke, then in their chiefe perfection when they are short and well seasoned.'

Campion has been commonly held guilty of a belated and unfortunate aberration in his supposed plea for classical metres. Daniel was the first of many critics who did not altogether understand Campion's not altogether lucid argument, and his great reply, happily enough, was not always strictly relevant. Campion, though he got himself into awkward corners, was not viewing the problem with quite the confused simplicity of some earlier classicists. (That is not a reference to 'the Areopagus', since no amount of scholarly reiteration can create a literary club out of Harvey's and Spenser's ironical allusions to Sidney and Dyer.) While modern English verse was still in its uncertain infancy, there had been extremists who wished to take over classical metrics *in toto*, and moderates like Harvey and Puttenham who were looking for an English and accentual equivalent

---

[1] Campion was born in London, of well-to-do parents who died when he was a boy. He proceeded from Peterhouse to Gray's Inn and, if his Latin poems are reliable evidence, he led a free life about town. In 1591–2 he seems to have been with Essex's expeditionary force in France, probably in the troop of Robert Carey (the autobiographer). Campion's first printed poems appeared, like Daniel's, in the surreptitious edition of *Astrophel and Stella* (1591). He received a medical degree at the University of Caen in 1605 and thereafter practised in London. At some time between 1595 and 1619 he appears to have become a Catholic. In 1607 he wrote a masque for the wedding of Lord Hay (or Hayes) and in 1613 three masques, one for the queen, and two for the weddings of the Princess Elizabeth and the Countess of Essex. Campion had a small and apparently innocent part in the intrigues which resulted in Overbury's death.

of the quantitative system. Campion was a more sophisticated moderate and a poet. He did not want English hexameters, which had had such 'passing pitifull successe', but, in place of reliance on syllable-counting and rhyme as the principles of verse, he urged more exact handling of iambic and trochaic feet and various substitutions. And although he shared the Renaissance scholar's contempt for unlettered scribblers, he wrote rather as a musician than as a neoclassicist, and was moved less by classical authority than by a technician's desire to achieve a flexible and fruitful compromise between quantitative discipline and the accentual genius of the English language. It was that desire which led him in his songs, nearly always with felicitous results, to couple his 'Words and Notes lovingly together'. When we read his verse all through, our pleasure may in the end be clouded by some sense of thinness and monotony, for his amatory world is small (though he also wrote some fine religious lyrics), but it must be remembered that the reader gets less than half of the poet-composer's effect. When we read Shakespeare's lyrics we do not have their original music in mind, it is true, but we do have the whole background of the plays.

If Campion's quantitative experiments yielded only one triumph, 'Rose-cheekt Lawra, come', the pragmatic value of his theories, as of Bridges's, consisted in the tuning of his own ear and others' to more delicate and subtle devices of lyrical artistry. We prefer the emotional and imaginative wealth, the natural magic, and the apparent spontaneity of Shakespeare, but there is still room for 'When to her lute Corinna sings', 'Follow your Saint, follow with accents sweet', and many other jewels of pure art or artifice which carry no trace of the everyday world (and Shakespeare has his share of artifice too). Yet Campion owes much to the popular tradition; it appears in varying degrees of refinement from 'Jacke and Jone they thinke no ill' to 'There is a Garden in her face'. On the classical side, Campion has such Horatian echoes as 'The man of life upright', but he gave his chief study to Catullus and Martial. Like Jonson, and like Herrick and Carew, Campion may be at his best when romantic and classical inspirations are fused and evoke an atmosphere of contrived but potent magic. 'The fayry queen Proserpina' of the early 'Harke, al you ladies that do sleep' is a sister of Titania and of Chaucer's 'Proserpina, and al hire fayerye'. The passions of the Roman lyrists are subdued and altered in Campion's ideal dream-world of love. His most obvious and familiar paraphrase of Catullus is the first stanza of 'My sweetest Lesbia let us live and love', and the rest of the poem is developed from Propertius (II. xv, &c.), but the whole loses the intensity of both originals and becomes detached, reflective, almost serene. Propertius apparently suggested one of Campion's finest openings:

> When thou must home to shades of under ground,
>   and there ariv'd a newe admired guest,
> The beauteous spirits do ingirt thee round,
>   white Iope, blith Hellen, and the rest,

but the richly mythological and emotional vision, the contrast between radiant love and vitality and the darkness of death (a classicist's parallel to 'A bracelet of bright haire about the bone'), this dwindles, as Propertius himself can dwindle, into the conventional hyperbole of a sonneteer.

While Campion the poet cannot be separated from Campion the musician, the former ranks higher among lyrists than the latter among composers. As a maker of graceful tunes within a fairly narrow range, he is not to be numbered with the great galaxy, Byrd, Wilbye, Morley, Dowland, Weelkes, Gibbons, and many other men; indeed, the plenitude of English musical genius within one generation is probably unmatched in the history of music. Campion exploited that one of the several chief forms of lyrical composition which gave most prominence to the words, namely, the 'ayre'. This form, inaugurated by Dowland in 1597, was quickly established by Dowland himself, Morley, and Robert Jones, and by Campion and Rosseter, in their books of 1600–1. It was in 1601 that the older madrigal reached its climax in *The Triumphs of Oriana* which Morley edited. The madrigal was 'a composition for two or more unaccompanied voices singing in combination, all the voice parts being of equal interest and mainly designed from the same melodic material'. The themes and moods of the madrigal ranged from the grave to the merry, its structure from the intricacy of Byrd's 'Though Amaryllis dance in green' to the air-like simplicity of Gibbons's 'The Silver Swan'. The madrigal, with its normal complexities of fugal succession and repetition, could hardly be carried beyond a single stanza or be followed by hearers intent upon the words. The air, on the other hand, was a melody for one voice, usually accompanied by the lute, but sometimes by the bass-viol or by other voices, and the same melody was repeated for each stanza. The ballet was a composition for combined voices which was less complex than the madrigal and kept much of the clear-cut regularity of dance music; its obvious characteristic was the 'fa-la' refrain. There were of course many other forms, from Byrd's majestic liturgical music to catches like that of Sir Toby Belch. But this paragraph is only the briefest reminder of the manifold relations between music and lyrical poetry and of the place of music in English life throughout our period. To ignore the great mass of music in manuscript circulation, there were printed, in the forty years before 1630, about ninety collections of madrigals, airs, canzonets, and ballets; of madrigals alone there were nearly a thousand. We do not need the evidence of Morley and Peacham and others to prove that the glory of English composition was accompanied by a knowledge of music more widespread than it has ever been since. And if the lyric ever had a bird-like note, the Elizabethan and Jacobean lyric had. 'For Poetry (like honesty and olde Souldiers)', said Dekker in *News from Hell*, 'goes upon lame feete, unlesse there bee musicke in her.' But in later lyricism, even in Herrick, the intimate relation between song and music did not survive in its old full-throated ease.

Those useful scapegoats, the Puritans, have traditionally been made responsible for extinguishing music along with the other joys of Merry England, but in recent decades the charge has at least been modified. Puritans did frown upon church music that savoured of popish profaneness; they would have agreed with Bacon that 'the curiositie of division and reports, and other figures of Musick, have no affinitie with the reasonable service of God, but were added in the more pompous times'. The Puritans' real crime against music was their abolition of the liturgy and the ecclesiastical establishments which were the great nurseries of the art. In the cultivation of secular music many Puritans, from the elder Milton (who contributed to *The Triumphs of Oriana*) and his illustrious son down to the obscure, took their full share. Even William Prynne, Edwards's chief rival as the voice of Presbyterian rigour, commenced his harangue, in *Histriomastix*, against 'lascivious, amorous, effeminate, voluptuous Musicke' with the assertion: 'That Musicke of it selfe is lawfull, usefull, and commendable; no man, no Christian dares denie, since the Scriptures, Fathers, and generally all

Christian, all Pagan Authors extant, doe with one consent averre it.' We may (with due regard for Purcell) ascribe the general decline of music during the century in part to such various causes as helped to blight lyrical verse, from national disunity and economic and social change to the growth of science and satire. But one cause was the internal evolution of music itself—the shift of emphasis from the vocal to the instrumental by which the English genius was largely shorn of its strength; the shift, encouraged by Puritanism, from religious to secular music; the development of operatic recitative; and so on. There was in general a movement away from bold imaginative freedom towards regularity which was roughly parallel to the movement in verse associated with Waller and Denham; one representative of the new tendencies was Henry Lawes.

The sketch of Campion must serve to suggest the kind of lyrics, amatory, pastoral, religious, and miscellaneous, that fill the long array of song-books, and we may turn for a moment to the miscellanies which, while they may contain songs for music, belong to literature proper. During the period 1601–60 there were some thirty-five volumes of English verse which can be called miscellanies, and about seventy-five wholly or mainly in Latin and other foreign languages. The connexion between the academic muse and the Crown is indicated by the fact that sixty-five of these learned effusions appeared before 1642, five in the years 1643–59, and five in 1660; one humbler volume which obscures all the rest is the *Justa Edouardo King* (1638). The mainly or wholly English collections included the elegiac volumes in honour of Jonson (1638) and Lord Hastings (1649); several books, like Cotgrave's *Wit's Interpreter* (1655), offered as guides to amorous and courtly expression; the unique *Annalia Dubrensia. Upon the Yearly Celebration of Mr. Robert Dover's Olympic Games upon Cotswold Hills* (1636), which had among its contributors Drayton, Randolph, Jonson, Felltham, Basse, Mennes, Marmion, and Heywood; and the volumes of unkind satires upon *Gondibert* published by Denham and others.

Apart from their varying intrinsic worth, the more general anthologies provide an index of changing taste. Davison's *Poetical Rhapsody* (1602), which reached a final edition in 1621, was the last predominantly Petrarchan and pastoral collection; it has many lyrics from the song-books, and a number of poems reveal a crystallizing conception of the ode. In 1640 we come to *Wit's Recreations*, the first of a long line of anthologies which owed their success to a mixture of poetry, ribaldry, and royalism, and of which the chief fathers, or grandfathers, were Sir John Mennes and the Reverend James Smith. The stationer assured the readers of *Musarum Deliciae* (1655) that 'Plain Poetry is now disesteem'd, it must be Drollery or it will not please'. Among further fruits of Puritan domination were *Choice Drollery* (1656), *Wit and Drollery* (1656), *Wit Restored* (1658), *J. Cleaveland Revived* (1659), and, in 1660, more patent broadside reminders of political change in *Rats Rhymed to Death* and its second edition, *The Rump*. Along with these things may be mentioned the 'Sack-inspired Songs', first collected in 1661, of 'the English Anacreon', Alexander Brome (1620–66). A less slipshod anti-Puritan nostalgia animated the Reverend Abraham Wright, who put together the partly clerical *Parnassus Biceps . . . Composed by the best Wits that were in both the Universities before their Dissolution* (1656). Most of the well-known poets included, Donne, Jonson, Wotton, Herrick, Randolph, Corbett, Cartwright, King, and others, did not appear at their best or in good texts, but the book is an attractive and representative collection of amatory, elegiac, royalist, and miscellaneous verse. If *Parnassus Biceps* was transitional in a retrospective way, Joshua Poole's *English Parnassus* (1657) is a small landmark in the development of Augustan neoclassicism. In a short prefatory discourse on poetry, one 'J. D.' (possibly Dryden), who knows Sidney and Campion and especially Puttenham and Daniel, lays down general and particular rules for attaining regularity and correctness in versification and style. On the whole the Restoration and the eighteenth century did not cherish the religious or—apart from drollery—the secular verse of the earlier seventeenth century, though a number of things survived. For instance, Jacob Tonson, in re-editing Dryden's *Miscellany* in 1716, included about a hundred poems by Drayton, Wither, Donne, Jonson, Corbett, Carew, Suckling, and Marvell, and broadside and popular ballads, drawn from *Parnassus Biceps* and other anthologies and from less obvious sources. But while some twenty-five of the pieces—mainly not those of the poets named—were reprinted in other books of the earlier eighteenth century, the old material does not seem to have made an appeal in 1716. We have, however, leaped far beyond our period and must turn back to survey the exponents of 'modernist' poetry, classical and metaphysical.

IV

JONSON, DONNE, AND THEIR SUCCESSORS

WITH a heterogeneous crowd of poets behind us, we arrive at the traditional division of the rest into the schools of Jonson and Donne, cavalier and meta-physical. The dichotomy is sound enough to be useful, and false enough to be troublesome, since lines and planes which at times seem quite divergent do in fact often meet. The impossibility of a clear-cut grouping is epitomized at the start in the much-discussed question whether three elegies were written by Jonson or by Donne; and their contemporaries and successors, indifferent to posterity's need of distinct labels, drew in varying proportions from both masters. On this point it may be said once for all that the names of Jonson and Donne stand not only for their actual and demonstrable influence but for the whole set of traditions and conditions which worked upon their fellows as well as upon themselves. Both poets rebelled, in their generally different ways, against pictorial fluidity, decorative rhetorical patterns, and half-medieval idealism, and both, by their individual and selective exploitation of established doctrines and practices, created new techniques, a new realism of style (or new rhetoric), sharp, condensed, and muscular, fitted for the intellectual and critical realism of their thought. But while Donne—'Wit's forge and fire-blast, meaning's press and screw', in Coleridgean phrase—hammered out an irregular personal instrument, it was typical of Jonson that he should, among other things, have had a large share in the development of the regular heroic couplet, 'the bravest sort of Verses'.

I

Jonson, the first great English theorist and practitioner of neoclassicism, the first really direct, learned, deliberate, and single-hearted heir of antiquity, gave poetry a new charter through his dynamic assimilation of the main tradition of the past.[1] His non-dramatic verse, bulky and varied though it is, we may regard as a minor part of a dramatist's output, but he apparently did not. Nearly all Jonson's poems, apart from the songs in plays and masques, were occasional, and for the purpose of this sketch may be divided into three groups: epigrams, lyrics, and reflective pieces. Nowadays we are perhaps inclined to skip the main body of epigrams, in spite of the author's pronouncing

[1] Benjamin Jonson (1572/3–1637) was the grandson of a gentleman of the Scottish border and the son of a clergyman who died in 1572. His mother married a master bricklayer of Westminster. Jonson had a few years (until about 1589) at Westminster School and always remained devoted to his master, Camden. Some experience in bricklaying and in service in Flanders, and his marriage in 1594— his wife was to receive intermittent devotion—bring him to the stage; his first role was that of actor. In 1598 he was listed by Francis Meres among tragic dramatists, but his first great extant play, of that year, was *Every Man in his Humour*, in which Shakespeare acted. In 1598 also Jonson was tried for killing an actor; he pleaded self-defence and claimed benefit of clergy. While in prison he was converted and 'therafter he was 12 yeares a Papist'; but he assisted official inquiries into the Gunpowder Plot and did not suffer when charged with recusancy (1606). In 1600–1 he exchanged dramatic blows with Marston and Dekker in the 'war of the theatres'. With the accession of James began Jonson's career as purveyor-in-chief of masques and entertainments for the court, and *Sejanus* (1603) inaugurated a great series of plays, *Volpone* (1606), *Epicoene* (1609), *The Alchemist* (1610), *Catiline* (1611), and *Bartholomew Fair* (1614). In 1605 Jonson was in trouble, along with Chapman and Marston, over the anti-Scottish satire in *Eastward Ho*. In 1612–13 he was abroad as tutor to young Walter Ralegh. Jonson collected his plays, masques, epigrams, and *The Forest*, his best writings up to 1612, in the folio *Works* of 1616. For a decade after 1616 he wrote no plays. In 1618–19 he made his pedestrian journey to Scotland. His dignity as a scholarly artist was confirmed by Scottish tributes, an honorary degree from Oxford (1619), and perhaps a deputy professorship of rhetoric at Gresham College (1619 ff.). In his later years he had various troubles— a fire (1623) which destroyed many of his books, notes, and unpublished manuscripts; poverty, ill health, and, in 1628, a paralytic stroke; the failure of *The New Inn* (1629) and most of his other dramatic 'dotages'; the sporadic character of King Charles's favour; and an old feud with Inigo Jones which culminated in 1631. But Jonson could always study and he had, as always, many more friends than enemies. There were, or had been, people of rank like the Countess of Bedford, Lord d'Aubigny (with whom he lived for some years), the Earl of Pembroke and other men and women of the Sidney connexion, and the Earl of Newcastle; men of learning and affairs like Bacon, Camden, Cotton, Hoskyns, Edward Hyde, and Selden; and men of letters from Shakespeare, Donne, Chapman, and Beaumont and Fletcher to Herrick, Carew, Suckling, Sir Kenelm Digby, Richard Brome, and others. Gatherings at the Mermaid tavern were succeeded by those at the Devil, 'the Sun, The Dog, the triple Tunne' (in Herrick's phrase), and, later still, in Ben's sick-room. He was the privileged dictator and oracle of a whole tribe of younger writers who were proud to be called his 'sons'. Jonson was buried in the Abbey. Among the contributors to *Jonsonus Virbius* (1638), a volume of thirty-three elegies, were Lord Falkland, Sir John Beaumont, Henry King, Thomas May, Habington, Waller, James Howell, Sidney Godolphin, Jasper Mayne, Cartwright, Felltham, Marmion, and John Ford. A third volume of *Works* (1641) contained later plays, masques, and non-dramatic verse, and *Timber* and *The English Grammar* (see Greg's *Bibliography of English Printed Drama*, iii, 1957).

them 'the ripest of my studies'. The epigram was one of the favourite genres of the European Renaissance, and in Elizabethan and Jacobean England it had such exponents as Campion and John Owen in Latin, Sir John Davies, Guilpin, Bastard, Harington, Weever, Donne, Peacham, Parrot, Davies of Hereford, Rowlands, and Jonson's despised Heath. In most of these writers the epigram inclined more or less towards social satire and a popular manner. Certainly none was so serious, complete, artistic, and original a disciple of Martial as Jonson, and none was such a Roman epigrammatist in temper, for Jonson the playwright and even Jonson the lyrist may be said to see and think and feel in terms of the epigram. His satirical epigrams, like those of his contemporaries, are interesting chiefly as acrid pictures of manners. They show what they helped to train, their author's caustic eye, tough vigour of language, and rhetorical resource and economy, but they are less distinguishable from other men's work, and less attractive to most readers, than the addresses and compliments to titled and literary patrons and friends. And much better still, in their masculine tenderness, are the epitaphs on his daughter and son and on the child actor, Salomon Pavy, which enshrine the most felicitous of all Jonson's adaptations of Martial.

A reader fresh from *Timber* may well expect to find in Jonson less of the ardent lover than of the confident and competent artist for whom love is a part of his *métier*. A strong, not to say cynical, head and a firm hand rule his heart and his senses. 'All extremes I would have bard', he says in his prescription for the ideal mistress, a prescription based on Martial and on the idea of love as a courtly game 'Neither too easie, nor too hard'. ' 'Twas an ingeniose remarque of my lady Hoskins', says Aubrey, 'that B. J. never writes of love, or if he does, does it not naturally.' The moral of 'Still to be neat, still to be drest' (a version of a post-classical epigram first printed by Scaliger in 1572) is only half-true of Jonson's amatory verse. Yet artistic feeling, if not love, refined and ordered in a pattern of delicate strength, gives to his best lyrics a cool, assured poise, an idealism at once artificial and rational, hardly less compelling in its way than emotional intensity. The most familiar example, 'Drinke to me, onely, with thine eyes', is one of those perfect poems which somehow seem to have always existed, but the geometrical conceit is woven out of scattered threads in the Greek prose of

Philostratus. Similarly, in the songs derived from Catullus, 'Come my Celia' and 'Kisse me, sweet', there is more courtliness than passion, and no hint of the metaphysical fourth dimension. In Jonson's code of urbane gallantry the lady (if not a patroness) is something below a Petrarchan divinity, and her lover is decidedly not a worm. And impersonal detachment enables the poet, despite 'My mountaine belly, and my rockie face', to grow old gracefully. 'A Celebration of Charis' is in the main *vers de société* of mingled artifice, elegance, and plainness, though the fourth part is an ecstatic vision which recalls Lodge's 'Rosalind' and Spenser's *Prothalamion*:

> See the Chariot at hand here of Love,
> Wherein my Lady rideth!

The triumphal divinity of the first stanza has the power of the Anacreontic Cupid; the praise of her sensuous beauties in the last may start from the very differently motivated set of hyperboles in Martial's lament for Erotion. The ardent idealism of this fourth part is somewhat cooled and complicated, though not nullified, by the lyrics that precede and follow, lyrics which blend courtly devotion with ironic awareness of the human and earthy limitations of lover and lady and the business and language of love. If the reader of *Timber* is prepared for the classical qualities of Jonson's amatory art, the reader of the *Conversations* may not be prepared for the metaphysical treatment of love, either in the broad or the special meaning of the term. Yet it is not the Roman poets but Lucian, Macrobius, and many allegorical mythographers who furnish the conception of love in the 'Epode' as 'a golden chaine let downe from heaven'. Nor is it mere fancy that glows in the conventional decorative setting of the Haddington masque:

> At his sight, the sunne hath turned,
> Neptune in the waters, burned;
> Hell hath felt a greater heate:
> Jove himselfe forsooke his seate:
> From the center, to the skie,
> Are his trophæes reared hie.

When love as a cosmic force, or as viewed against a cosmic background, is described in 'witty' and intellectual images and argument, the 'metaphysical' result is more obvious. That kind of writing Jonson at least approaches, notably in the three

amatory elegies (*Underwood*, xxxviii, xl, xli) which he probably
wrote when inspired by Donne's 'The Expostulation'. But Jonson's strength of judgement normally keeps his 'wits great over-
plus' within mundane bounds ('Metaphors farfet hinder to be
understood, and affected, lose their grace'); and when he uses
the figure of the compass, it is to suggest Selden's circle 'Of
generall knowledge'.

Of those three 'metaphysical' elegies which can safely be
ascribed to Jonson, the first, ' 'Tis true, I'm broke!', is largely
a mosaic drawn from Seneca's *De Clementia*. Even Ben's con-
versational censures of Drayton, Du Bartas, and Beaumont took
the form of phrases from Quintilian. To a man saturated in
ancient and especially Latin prose and verse, modern continental literature meant correspondingly little, apart from
humanistic neo-Latin, handbooks of mythology, and the like.
It was to be expected that Jonson should rank as the first great
disciple of Catullus in England, though he was, or thought he
was, much better qualified for discipleship to Horace, Horace
the satirist, moralist, lyrist, and critic; the *Ars Poetica*, which he
so baldly translated, and commented upon, was part of his
being. Ben's assimilation of Martial has been noticed already.
But it would need a volume to cite his borrowings from the
classics and, when he has learned the lessons of their wisdom
and craftsmanship, he remains their peer and contemporary,
not a tame 'classicist' but his own very English self. With even
more than the serious Renaissance poet's usual reverence for
learning and scorn for half-educated writers and their public,
Jonson insists that the ancients are 'Guides, not Commanders'.
The artist, the imitator of normal nature, must bring critical
independence to the integration of ancient and modern experience, as, in his diction, he should fuse 'the eldest of the present,
and newest of the past Language'. Reacting against Elizabethan
vagaries of matter, form, and style, Jonson demanded, and
unceasingly strove for, the ageless classical virtues of clarity,
unity, symmetry, and proportion; in short, the control of the
rational intelligence. His poems are wholes, not erratic displays
of verbal fireworks, and false taste always pronounces such
writing 'barren, dull, leane'. The curt phrase, 'Shaksperr
wanted Arte', which only bardolaters have resented, is probably
nearer Ben's considered judgement than the lapidary generosity
of his noble tribute in verse. We are hardly surprised to hear

that he wrote all his poems 'first in prose, for so his master Cambden had Learned him'. If the fact symbolizes and partly explains the prosaic element in most of Jonson's poetry, it suggests too his colloquial tone and idiom and clear, tough intellectual fibre. As the most influential of recent classicists has said, 'to have the virtues of good prose is the first and minimum requirement of good poetry'. That does not mean that one could readily summarize the prose content of such lyrics—more Elizabethan than Jonsonian—as those two in *Cynthia's Revels*, the silvery 'Queene, and Huntresse, chaste, and faire', and the exquisitely modulated song of Echo, 'Slow, slow, fresh fount, keepe time with my salt teares'. And while Jonson is no bird-like songster, the classicist who would write as he drinks, 'In flowing measure, fill'd with flame, and spright', can also warble such native wood-notes wild as 'The faery beame upon you' and 'The owle is abroad, the bat, and the toad'.

But Jonson's classicism was far too deep and genuine to expend itself on mere technique. His broadest and noblest statement of the ethical and didactic function of poetry is given, with special reference of course to the stage, in the dedication of *Volpone* to 'the Two Famous Universities'. Recalling the ideal poet of Strabo and Horace, and the ideal orator of Cicero and Quintilian, Jonson affirms 'the impossibility of any mans being the good Poet, without first being a good man', and if he falls short of Milton in religious fervour of utterance, he is wholly sincere. He goes on, in words which link him with Milton, Spenser, and Sidney and a host of other men, to elaborate the Renaissance ideal of the poet as the supreme instructor of youth and age, 'the interpreter, and arbiter of nature, a teacher of things divine, no lesse then humane, a master in manners', who 'can alone (or with a few) effect the businesse of man-kind'.

Such words, amplified in many passages from ancient and modern humanists in *Timber*, express the solid and positive essence of Jonson's classicism. And his ethical view of poetry, which on the one hand supports his satire, on the other animates a great deal of soberly reflective verse. The hundred and first epigram, a genial and gracious invitation to supper, leads up, as it were, to what is a kind of apostolic consecration, 'An Epistle answering to one that asked to be Sealed of the Tribe of Ben'. Such bread-and-butter epistles as 'To Penshurst' and 'To Sir Robert Wroth' bring weight and dignity—and Martial and

Virgil's second *Georgic* and Horace's second *Epode* (which Jonson translated)—to the celebration not only of the country but of the good old ways of feudal life and pure religion breathing household laws. Seneca furnishes a large part of the epistle to Sir Edward Sackville. As we might expect from Jonson's devotion to Seneca, his central creed is rooted in Stoic magnanimity and inward order, the virtuous strength 'Here in my bosome, and at home' which preserves the individual soul among

> such as blow away their lives,
> And never will redeeme a day,
> Enamor'd of their golden gyves.

And with these Arnoldian lines 'To the World' may be placed the manly and beautiful epitaph on Vincent Corbet (a modern parallel to the younger Pliny's philosopher Euphrates), who exemplified 'A life that knew nor noise, nor strife'. Jonson is nowhere more explicitly didactic, and seldom more truly poetical, than in the early 'Epode', or in one strophe of the Senecan ode of a generation later which inaugurated the strictly Pindaric form in English (or at least made Pindar neoclassical):

> It is not growing like a tree
> In bulke, doth make man better bee;
> Or standing long an Oake, three hundred yeare,
> To fall a logge at last, dry, bald, and seare:
> A Lillie of a Day,
> Is fairer farre, in May,
> Although it fall, and die that night;
> It was the Plant, and flowre of light.
> In small proportions, we just beautie see:
> And in short measures, life may perfect bee.

And yet, finally, Jonson's serious thought and feeling do not always move on the plane of Stoic ethics. The modern reader, when confronted, in writers of the Renaissance tradition, with pieces of salty wit alongside devotional poems, is given to assuming that the latter are only the conventional pietisms of essentially emancipated minds. But the Renaissance mind did not run on a single track, and we should have a mistaken view of Jonson—and of many other poets—if we ignored rare but authentic moments of confessional humility, faith, and aspiration:

> Good, and great God, can I not thinke of thee,
> But it must, straight, my melancholy bee?

The 'great lover and praiser of himself' and 'contemner and Scorner of others' can pray, like Herbert, 'Use still thy rod'. The lover of sack and canary, who had nocturnal visions of Tartars and Turks, Romans and Carthaginians, fighting about his great toe, could also entreat 'My Maker, Saviour, and my Sanctifier' that he might be truly glorified 'Among thy Saints'.

Swinburne, in whose critical vocabulary 'gods' and 'giants' were roughly equivalent to 'Apollonian' and 'Dionysian', gave to Ben the supremacy among English giants that Shakespeare held among English gods—and 'No giant ever came so near to the ranks of the gods'. With all his fervent praise, Swinburne (who of course was assessing the whole body of Jonson's work) represents the main line of nineteenth-century romantic criticism. The flowers of Jonson's growing 'have colour, form, variety, fertility, vigour: the one thing they want is fragrance'. In recent decades critical noses have been in great indignation at the thought of poetical fragrance, and of magic and wonder and mystery, and Jonson has risen on the wave of the anti-romantic reaction. We still praise the rational virtues Swinburne praised, but with a less easy assurance that they are of an inferior kind; Jonson himself would probably have snorted that the plain style is the hardest of all styles to achieve. Our increasing respect for his classical art is doubtless a mark of increasing sanity. Yet our dislike of romantic excesses, our preference for dry over damp poetry, still leaves unharmed the greater poetry of Jonson's own and slightly later days, from 'Full fathom five' to 'Lycidas', and of those worlds the clear-eyed, robust, concrete Jonson has at most partial glimpses. His achievement is a strong, massive, and symmetrical pyramid, if not 'a Star-ypointing' one; and we may perhaps cancel the qualification when we return to his individual and enduring beauties, or think, with Swinburne, of the 'something heroic and magnificent in his lifelong dedication of all his gifts and all his powers to the service of the art he had elected as the business of all his life and the aim of all his aspiration'.

Among all Jonson's disciples the nearest heir of his Renaissance humanism, the ethical and scholarly solidity of his art, was the young Milton. The rest, in their various ways and degrees, and with varying responsiveness to the metaphysical fashion, cultivated such patches of the Jonsonian garden as amatory, complimentary, elegiac, and epigrammatic verse. The most versatile and, in a limited sense, the most classical was Robert Herrick (1591–1674).[1] While Herrick praised very few English poets, he bestowed a number of tributes upon Jonson. A large proportion of his verse, as of Jonson's, belongs to the genre of the epigram, and he has some moralizing epistles on country contentment in the vein of Jonson (and of Horace, Tibullus, and Martial). But in general the bricklayer has, so to speak, given place to the goldsmith's apprentice, the master of filigree. In Herrick Renaissance neo-pagan and belated Elizabethan united to form a pure artist, who would rather see his book dead than not perfected, whose poetic creed is to love beauty, live merrily, and trust to good verses, and who in a troubled age is largely content to create a timeless Arcadia. Apart from the serious Jonsonian realms which the disciple scarcely enters, there is a difference as well as a likeness between Ben's lyrics of manly gallantry and courtly idealism and Herrick's 'Carkanet' of more richly artificial fancies offered to a bright but indistinct procession of dainty mistresses. We may remember, by the way, his classical apology: 'Jocond his Muse was; but his Life was chast.' Like Jonson and others, Herrick could print devotional poems—a whole collection—along with 'unbaptized Rhimes'; a genre was a genre, and, as we observed before, a poet could be sincere in both wantonness and piety.

Herrick refines his commonplaces with a loving and individual subtlety in the use of words and rhythms. An amorous trifle can be almost transcendentalized by one startling, half-metaphysical, and triumphant phrase, 'That liquefaction of her clothes'. Jonson's 'Still to be neat, still to be drest', with its plainness of generalized statement, makes its impression as a well-turned whole. Herrick's 'Delight in Disorder' has the feminine particularity of a dressmaker, and the phrases are a

---

[1] Herrick's father, a London goldsmith, died in 1592. In 1607 the boy entered upon a ten-year apprenticeship with his wealthy uncle, Sir William Herrick, a goldsmith also. But in 1613 he went up, at a late age, to Cambridge (B.A., 1617; M.A., 1620). He was ordained in 1623. Between 1617 and 1629 he may have lived more or less in London, associating with Jonson and the other wits and with such courtiers as Endymion Porter and Mildmay Fane. By 1625 he was well known as a poet, though he had published nothing. In 1627 he went with the expedition to the Isle of Rhé, as chaplain to the Duke of Buckingham. In 1629–30 he became vicar of Dean Prior in the diocese of Exeter. He was ejected in 1647 and returned in 1660; he seems to have spent the intervening years chiefly in London. A volume of his poems had been entered in 1640, but it was not until 1648 that *Hesperides* (with *Noble Numbers*) appeared; he wrote hardly anything thereafter. Herrick died in the same year as Milton and Traherne.

succession of delicate or delicately mock-heroic paradoxes which
turn a woman into a dainty rogue in porcelain, and one whose
roguishness is not limited to her costume. (It is pleasant to find
that Herrick's earnest bishop, Joseph Hall, had spoken in a
sermon of 'a loose lock erring wantonly over her shoulders'.)
Among the countless sensuous or sensual conceits and metrical
experiments that the cool-hearted poet lays on the altar of love,
there are a few poems to which consummate art gives the
semblance of passion, poems which enshrine the ideal attitude
of the cavalier. In

> Bid me to live, and I will live
> Thy Protestant to be,

formal symmetry and firm texture may recall Jonson, but the
inspired wit of 'Protestant' is Herrick's (even if, like many
details in his verse, this came from a hint in Burton's *Anatomy*).
And in the novel setting, at once rich and homely, of 'The
Night-piece, to Julia'—which has metrical and other affinities
with Ben's 'The faery beame upon you'—Julia is not the mere
possessor of lacteal breasts and hairless legs but a divinity of
nature whom glow-worm and moon are alike happy to serve.

When Herrick rings the changes on that universal Renaissance theme, the brevity of youth and beauty and love, and
when he tells us of himself and his pride in his craft, he is conscious of course of his descent from Anacreon, Catullus, Horace,
Tibullus, Propertius, Ovid, and Martial, though his thumb-nail
painting on ivory owes much of its tone to modern continental
imitators of the ancients and to Jonson. What is most obvious
in Herrick's classicism is not the mythological symbols (which
dwindle in stature without quite losing their ideal quality), nor
the technical discipline that has won him such urbane simplicity,
but a degree of saturation in the atmosphere of Roman life
which has no comparable parallel unless in the purple eloquence
nourished at Golden Grove. If we read him as he wished to be
read, 'When Laurell spirts 'ith fire', we see the incumbent of
Dean Prior (who looked like a Roman emperor) 'Drinking
wine, & crown'd with flowres', performing or prophetically
receiving the ancient rites of burial, pouring libations to his
household gods, promising a cock to Aesculapius on behalf of
his maid Prue. All this and much more is not merely escape from
'lothed Devonshire' into neo-pagan hedonism; Herrick's attitude is refined and deepened by his instinct for ceremonial, in

life and in art. The artifice of eternity is one defence man can raise against the flux of time and death.

The genuineness of this ceremonial instinct and atmosphere is attested by Herrick's fusion of classical and native lore, a fusion happily proclaimed in the title *Hesperides*. The 'free-born Roman' is also 'Robin Herrick'. The Anglican clergyman worships his Lares while he trolls a bowl of North-down ale and crickets sing on the hearth. The priest of Cupid and Bacchus inhabits a country vicarage with his faithful Prue, his cock, hen, goose, lamb, cat, and spaniel (he does not mention the pig he taught to drink out of a tankard), and he can enjoy, or at least praise, the frugal diet of 'Pea, or Bean, or Wort, or Beet'. The Theocritean, Ovidian, and Marlovian invitation 'To Phillis, to love, and live with him' is purely English. 'To the Maids to walk abroad' mingles mythological tales with wedding-smocks, posies, gloves, and ribbons. In the epithalamia we have Hymen's torch, Juno, and filleted door-posts along with the bride's garters, the bridegroom's points, and the sack-posset. Classicism has a homely base; and it is not always festive. In the noble numbers on his brother's death, addressed to Endymion Porter, Herrick is closer to Catullus than in his amatory verse:

> Sunk is my sight; set is my Sun;
> And all the loome of life undone:
> The staffe, the Elme, the prop, the shelt'ring wall
> Whereon my Vine did crawle,
> Now, now, blowne downe; needs must the old stock fall.

At times Herrick abhors the currish people about him and impales luckless individuals in epigrams, and he exults in returning to London after his 'long and irksome banishment' in 'the dull confines of the drooping West'; but he gained enduring fame in his parish, and real affection for 'the Countries sweet simplicity' went to the making of his half-English, half-classical pictures of the seasonal round of work and play. Herrick's volume of 1648 was no more remote from public affairs than the works of other poets published about that time, but none offered such an open challenge to the spirit of civil war:

> I sing of Brooks, of Blossomes, Birds, and Bowers:
> Of April, May, of June, and July-Flowers.
> I sing of May-poles, Hock-carts, Wassails, Wakes,
> Of Bride-grooms, Brides, and of their Bridall-cakes. . . .

So, 'in time of "the breaking of nations" ', we have what goes onward the same though dynasties pass, the sports of Christmas and Twelfth Night, the 'tough labours, and rough hands' of Devon harvesters ('the Lords of Wine and Oile'!), and the glorified Maying of that 'sweet-Slug-a-bed', Corinna.

In the middle of the seventeenth century Herrick's poems probably seemed old-fashioned to devotees of 'strong lines', though a number were reprinted (as a rule anonymously) in miscellanies and song-books. His volume was not reissued as a whole until 1823. The poet himself did not begin to emerge from obscurity until the end of the eighteenth century, and did not win real fame until the later nineteenth. But he went under a cloud again with the metaphysical revival of our time; intellectual readers, having been weaned on a pickle, were not inclined to suck 'on countrey pleasures, childishly'. That Herrick is a lyrist of civilized grace is obvious. That he is a 'serious' poet is not so obvious and has needed, and received, demonstration. In our day classical art on any level may be underestimated because its smooth surface is deceptive; we suspect lack of stress and depth if there is no huffing and puffing. But Herrick's best poems have a vein of seriousness that is more than pagan, and in this vein we find his emotional and artistic complexity and strength. Though the case for his religious consciousness in *Hesperides* can be overstated, he has the unified vision that was the common inheritance of his age, the vision that embraces God and the book of creatures in a divine whole. In Herrick, with his earthly and sensuous concreteness, that vision is present chiefly in suggestion and overtone. His place is somewhere between Spenser and Marvell; or, like a sort of incomplete Milton, to interpose a little ease he dallies with false—yet not wholly false—surmise. 'The Argument of his Book' is an ordered and inclusive sequence, from the observed beauties of nature in spring and summer through seasonal rituals and humanity and youth and love to 'Times trans-shifting', the twilight fairyland of fantasy, and the ultimate mysteries of hell and heaven. 'Gather ye Rose-buds while ye may' (perhaps the most popular lyric of the latter half of the century) may be called simply pagan in both its lightness and its gravity. But critics have required pages to analyse the subtleties and ambiguities of 'Corinna's going a Maying'. Here one can only signalize the unobtrusive and felicitous 'wit', the joyous and sober interweaving of rustic and pagan and Christian elements, of nature and myth and ritual, of May-time greenness and youthful senses; and if the poet's final picture of the human condition is pagan—

> So when or you or I are made
> A fable, song, or fleeting shade;
> All love, all liking, all delight
> Lies drown'd with us in endlesse night—

it gains some of its poignancy from his awareness that this world of natural beauty and natural feeling is partly divine reality and partly idyllic illusion. There is tension in Herrick, but it is seldom overt; for it is resolved, up to a point, in the perpetual renewal of life in his semi-Spenserian 'Garden of Adonis'. In *Noble Numbers* the Christian's sense of sin is not very acute, and Herrick can 'chant Gods praise with cheerfulnesse'.

Thomas Carew (1594/5–1640) has a narrower range than Jonson or Herrick and his courtly, impersonal, fastidious elegance of form and texture is still closer to pure art.[1] In him as in other men the influence of Jonson and Donne is merged. Carew's double allegiance, and his individuality, may be seen in the lucid, logical, and tender conceits developed in the epitaphs on Maria Wentworth and Lady Mary Villiers. At the Jonsonian end of the spectrum are—along with Carew's one masque—those pleasant pictures of country-house life, 'To Saxham' and 'To my friend G. N. from Wrest', which are especially welcome from a poet of Whitehall; at the other end is the very Donnian 'Elegy' on Donne, the most precise and significant critique of a poet the age produced, and one of Carew's few impassioned utterances. Perhaps we may say, in spite of his judicial admiration for Father Ben and the fervent tribute to Donne's anti-classicist originality (in which Donne is hailed as a priest of Apollo with Promethean breath), that

---

[1] Carew, son of the Cornish Sir Matthew Carew, Master in Chancery, graduated from Merton College, Oxford, in 1611. After a sojourn at the Middle Temple he held a secretaryship under Sir Dudley Carleton (a relative by marriage) in Italy (1613–15?) and at The Hague (1616); he was dismissed for slandering Sir Dudley and Lady Carleton. He went to France in 1619 in the train of Sir Edward (later Lord) Herbert. In 1630 he received a post at court. Among his literary friends were Edward Hyde, James Howell, Suckling, and the men to whom he addressed verse-epistles: Jonson, Aurelian Townshend, Walter Montagu, Thomas May, George Sandys, and Davenant. Carew was with the king's forces in the first Bishops' War (1639). His masque, *Coelum Britannicum*, was presented at Whitehall and printed in 1634. His *Poems* were published shortly after his death in 1640.

without Donne Carew would have been poorer but that without Jonson he would not have been a poet at all.

These major influences—to which has been added the lush wit of Marino—are, of course, most pervasive in the love poems that make up two-thirds of Carew's output. He could echo Donne's words and ideas, and sometimes give the poetry of love a half-metaphysical dimension, but he had few traces of the real Donne. 'The Oracle of Love' in his day was essentially—and mainly at second-hand, through Jonson—a classical amorist. His lyrics, like Jonson's, exist as even, rounded wholes, with hardly any of Herrick's inspired phrases. To Carew as to his fellows, Jonson the humanist is quite alien, and the qualities of Jonson's love poetry become in transmission less robust and more precious. No Elizabethan sonneteer praised, persuaded, or chided a mistress with more ingenuity, and Carew's amatory artifice is most enjoyable in small draughts. Passion is controlled, or the want of it almost supplied, by sophisticated gallantry, poise, and grace, by structural symmetry, urbanity of tone, and smooth variations of rhythm; both the woman and the poet-lover disappear behind the miniature work of art. Whereas Donne might draw into one poem the most heterogeneous ideas and images, Carew, in his usually short songs or song-like pieces, is given to working out a single metaphor—fire in 'Eternity of Love Protested', a military siege in 'A Deposition from Love'. 'Ask Me No More' is his most perfect, though not his most typical, lyric because conventional images, here varied, are ordered and exalted by Jonsonian discipline and rhythm and metaphysical wit, so that one man's eulogy of one woman becomes a cosmic hymn to transcendent beauty. Even 'The Complement' is raised above luscious Marinism through being firmly moulded. Since Carew is not a poet of ideas, it may be observed that in the notorious and probably early 'Rapture' he followed Tasso and Donne in upholding 'Nature' against 'Honour'; but even here, where he abandons his usual courtly reserve for ultra-Ovidianism, he creates—in contrast with the immediacy of Donne's 'Elegy xix'—a degree of aesthetic distance through mythological, pastoral, and pictorial images, and while Donne reports a unique, self-contained experience, Carew's poem takes its place in a philosophical and literary tradition. No doubt there is a gulf between the stately 'Song' and 'A Rapture', and no doubt most of Carew's amatory verse was closer in spirit to the latter, but the 'Song' and some other things enable us to accept the possibility that at moments the libertine courtier might become aware of his

> restlesse soule, tyr'de with persuit
> Of mortall beautie, seeking without fruit
> Contentment there.

We remember also the story of his summoning John Hales once too often for a death-bed repentance and absolution, and we may perhaps include a pious along with a poetic and musical impulse behind his quota of Psalms.

In contrast with Carew, whose 'Muse was hard bound', the author of that phrase, Millamant's 'Natural, casy Suckling', was the first of 'The Mob of Gentlemen who wrote with Ease'.[1] In 'A Sessions of the Poets' (which may have taken its start from Boccalini's *Ragguagli di Parnaso*), he is complacently conscious of his amateur status:

> He loved not the Muses so well as his sport;
> And prized black eyes, or a lucky hit
> At bowls, above all the Trophies of wit.

And it is that Suckling whose lucky hits at verse we prize, 'Why so pale and wan fond Lover?', ' 'Tis now since I sate down before That foolish Fort, a heart', 'Out upon it, I have lov'd Three whole days together', and above all, of course, the daintily robust 'Ballad: Upon a Wedding', which was written probably for the marriage of Lord Lovelace and Lady Anne Wentworth on 11 July 1638. Suckling's poetical bent is partly indicated in his allusions to Jonson's vanity and laboriously learned brain and to Donne as the unrivalled lord of wit. The one clear imitation of Ben—'Hast thou seen the Down in the Air . . .?'—turns the ecstatic praise of Charis into satire, while the pervasive spirit

---

[1] Sir John Suckling (1609–42), a scion of an old Norfolk family and son of a government official, left Cambridge apparently without a degree, had a few weeks at Gray's Inn, and was freed by his father's death for adventures abroad (the Isle of Rhé, 1627; the Netherlands, 1629–30; Sir Henry Vane's embassage to Gustavus Adolphus, 1631–2). At home Suckling became, says Aubrey, 'the greatest gallant of his time, and the greatest gamester, both for bowling and cards, so that no shop-keeper would trust him for 6*d*.' He was said to have invented cribbage. Much of his writing was done in 1637–8. He drew some gibes with the gorgeous costuming of both his play *Aglaura* (1637–8) and the troop he led to Scotland in the first Bishops' War (1639); he also served in the second. In 1641 he was involved in the 'first army plot', escaped to France, and died there—by suicide, Davenant told Aubrey. His *Fragmenta Aurea* appeared in 1646.

of Donne goes beyond such obvious echoes as 'Oh! for some honest Lovers ghost'. It is chiefly the cynical strain of the young Donne that Suckling carries on, with a lighter flippancy and with some notes suggestive of the French *libertins*—though the friend of Hales and Falkland, and the author, whatever his motives, of *An Account of Religion by Reason* (and some private letters as well) was not merely the frivolous or sensual man about town who wrote most of the verse. But when Suckling chooses to think in verse, he seldom rises above the simple, lucid, and witty exposition of conventional naturalism; he feels no need of reconciling soul and body, love and desire. He writes repeatedly 'against fruition' not because the conqueror of Bridget and of Nell subscribes (unless in his plays) to the fashionable 'Platonics', which in fact he ridicules, but because the chase is a titillating refinement of ultimate pleasure.

For us, to think of the cavalier spirit is to think first of Richard Lovelace (1618–56/57), and it is hard to believe that his two most familiar lyrics were rescued from oblivion by Bishop Percy and that Scott, misquoting the shorter one, assigned it to Montrose.[1] As soldier, courtier, lover, poet, scholar, musician, and connoisseur of painting, the 'extraordinary handsome' Lovelace exemplified the tradition of Sidney and Castiglione. His poems display the extreme unevenness of a gentleman amateur, and fame has rightly fixed upon the few lyrics in which he struck a simple, sincere, and perfect attitude; in these, with pure and exalted idealism, he enshrined the cavalier trinity, beauty, love, and loyal honour. 'To Lucasta, Going to the Wars', which states a chivalric theme far older than its century, is Jonsonian in its logical brevity and completeness; we may remember, by the way, that Lovelace was the first literal translator of the terse Catullus (to use Herrick's epithet). 'To Althea, from Prison' (which perhaps owes a hint to Voiture's 'Dans la prison', though 'prison philosophy' was a cavalier convention) might almost be called a royalist broad-

---

[1] Lovelace, the son of a Kentish knight and soldier, was educated at the Charterhouse, where Crashaw was his contemporary, and at Oxford (M.A., 1636). His life as courtier and country gentleman was interrupted in 1639–40 by the Bishops' Wars, and in 1642, when he presented the Kentish Petition to the Commons, by a brief imprisonment. He spent much of the years 1643–6 abroad. In 1648 he was again imprisoned, for ten months. *Lucasta* appeared in 1649; the identity of the lady has not been established. Lovelace passed his remaining years in obscurity, though probably not in the extreme penury reported by Aubrey and Wood. Another volume was issued after his death.

side, refined and ennobled but retaining the air of masculine spontaneity. The cavalier spirit and the quiet hermitage of the mind receive a more complex and more moving celebration in 'The Grasshopper'; here, starting from Anacreon and taking in Horace (especially *Epode* xiii), Lovelace depicts the winter of royalists bereft of their king and the inward, eternal summer they can create for themselves. Plainer and more directly topical is 'To Lucasta, from Prison', in which, with sober and selfless dignity, Lovelace views the disruption of the established order. In the bulk of his verse, he represents courtly lyricism, modern continental fashions, and the influence of Donne. He has a wider range of theme and tone and image than Carew and Suckling; as a craftsman he is nearer the former than the latter, though his art, like Carew's, is not always rewarding. He has energy and originality, but, along with some other poets of his time (including his kinsman Stanley), he often illustrates the pernicious anaemia of the secular metaphysical muse, the dwindling from cosmic audacities into laboured and eccentric artifice. The radiant Elizabethan vision of Gratiana dancing hovers between inspired *naïveté* and fantastic sophistication. With much that is simply dull, Lovelace offers some miscellaneous and incidental attractions, but his achievement remains a handful of poems.

A modern addition to the roll of cavalier poets is Sidney Godolphin (1610–43), Suckling's 'little Sid', the admired friend of Falkland, Hyde, and Hobbes. Though retired, bookish, and 'melancholique', 'of so nice and tender a composition' that he would turn back from a ride if the wind were against him, Godolphin was a member of Parliament and, like Falkland, one of the first volunteers and early victims of the war. Like Falkland, too, he wrote elegies on both Jonson and Donne, and in the distinctive manner of each; the compressed and critical tribute to Jonson, 'The Muses fairest light in no darke time', was long ascribed to Cleveland. Such lyrics as 'Or love mee lesse, or love mee more' combine fastidious clarity of style and sound with a strain of metaphysical pregnancy and paradox, the 'strong' quality that Suckling reproved. Godolphin's grave thoughtfulness is illustrated on another plane in 'Lord when the wise men came from Farr', or in the celebration of Donne not as the wit and rebel but as the 'Pious dissector' of hearts and sins who gave 'a religious tincture to our feares'.

The poetical claims of such sons and heirs of Jonson as Richard Brome, James Howell, and Jasper Mayne are not very urgent, and Lord Falkland's poems are of interest chiefly as personal and metrical documents. Some other men cannot be overlooked. The most familiar poem of the dramatist Francis Beaumont (1584?–1616) is one of his two epistles to Jonson from the country, about the convivial gatherings at the Mermaid; if he wrote the long *Salmacis and Hermaphroditus* (1602), he added an unusual degree of humour to the luxuriant Ovidian convention. The pastoral, erotic, and festive verse of the short-lived and much-praised Thomas Randolph (1605–35) was rather too facile and unoriginal for the convenience of either the anthologist or the historian; among the courtly and metaphysical poets he remained the precocious undergraduate, though we can still feel his genuine delight in the country. Bishop Corbett (1582–1635), who, if not quite the Friar Tuck of Aubrey's sketch, lacked the Stoic sobriety Jonson honoured in his father, is for ever identified with 'Farewell, Rewards & Faeries', that robustly nostalgic lament for a Catholic Merry England blighted by Puritanism. And Corbett's chaplain, William Strode (1602–45), is also virtually a man of one poem, the gracious little conceit 'I saw faire Cloris walke alone', though he has a few other attractive pieces, such as 'On Westwell Downs', in which he is a sort of metaphysical Georgian.

Strode's *Floating Island*, produced at Oxford in 1636 in honour of the king and queen, may be said to have sunk, though it employed the talents of Inigo Jones and Henry Lawes, but the next night's play, *The Royal Slave*, staged by the same pair, was a resounding success. Its author, William Cartwright (1611–43), like Corbett and Strode was a Christ Church man, and 'the most florid and seraphical Preacher in the University', a scholar and wit beloved by a multitude of men from King Charles down. But the poet disappoints expectations aroused by Jonson's unwonted encomium, 'My Son Cartwright writes all like a Man'. His lustre, indeed, grew dim after 1660. A disciple of Jonson and, in a lesser degree, of Donne, he seldom rose above smooth and skilful imitation, whether in his courtly compliments and elegies or in his amatory ardours. One Platonic stanza of 'To Chloe who wish'd her self young enough for me' attracted Coleridge. Cartwright's commendatory poems are somewhat more critical than the mass of their kind (such as the

fanfare which accompanied his own volume of 1651), and, if
he exalts John Fletcher's sophisticated art at the expense of
Shakespeare's 'Old fashion'd wit', he is taking a step towards
Dryden, or one of several Drydens.

2

Most of the courtly lyrists, major as well as minor, live chiefly
and on the whole not undeservedly in anthology pieces, and
these perhaps give a stronger impression of family resemblance
than of the individual flavour which even the slighter poets may
possess. The endless problems of authorship that envelop
fatherless or many-fathered poems supply concrete evidence for
a degree of homogeneity among the writers who went to school
to Jonson or Donne or both. At the same time, the cultivation
of wit made for less obvious homogeneity than had characterized the choir of Elizabethan singers. So far we have been concerned with Jonsonian cavalier poets, and the frequency with
which the name of Donne and the word 'metaphysical' have
occurred illustrates the impossibility of any clear-cut distinction
between two 'schools'. Indeed, one sometimes thinks of grouping the lyrical poets, and some others, as disciples of Donne who
felt the influence of Jonson and disciples of Donne who did not.
Yet even that suggestion reminds us that the influence of Jonson
was by its very nature less palpable as well as less seductive.
Before we come to the major metaphysical poets—and partly
by way of avoiding a prolonged anticlimax at the end of this
chapter—we may notice a reasonable number of small poets
who are mostly nearer to Donne than to Jonson or who cannot
be given any very precise label.

These remarks make an odd prelude to the name of Shakespeare, though the word 'notice' is prudentially appropriate for
a reference to that fascinating enigma (treated by C. S. Lewis in
his volume of the Oxford History), 'The Phoenix and the Turtle',
which was printed in Robert Chester's Love's Martyr (1601),
along with poems on the same theme by 'Ignoto', Marston,
Chapman, and Jonson (who was represented by the 'Epode'
and its appendages). Lesser mysteries of another kind, now
cleared up, have obscured the fame of the lawyer, scholar, and
wit, John Hoskyns (1566–1638). For nearly three centuries portions of his tract on rhetoric lay unrecognized in Jonson's Timber
and some later textbooks, and his 'Absence, heare thou my

Protestation', a poem printed anonymously in Davison's *Poetical Rhapsody* (1602), was assigned to Donne; Saintsbury was almost ready to go to the stake for Donne's authorship. Sir Henry Wotton (1568–1639), the friend of Donne and Walton and the eulogist of *Comus*, wrote like a greater Dyer in one famous poem, the Horatian 'Character of a Happy Life', which Jonson had by heart, and like a lesser Carew in his other famous piece, the lyric on the Queen of Bohemia, 'You meaner Beauties of the Night'. One of Wotton's unsuccessful rivals for the provostship of Eton, Sir Robert Aytoun (1570–1638), the cultivated courtier and friend of Jonson, Hobbes, and 'all the witts', was the first notable Scotsman to use English. The sober dignity of his amorous complaints can be quickened by neat wit and occasional humour, and Dryden pronounced them 'some of the best of that age'.

In the next generation we have such definitely metaphysical lyrists as the 'poore & pocky' Aurelian Townshend (1583?–1651?), who for a time travelled with Lord Herbert, and Sir Francis Kynaston (1587–1642), whom we have met before as an educational 'projector'. Townshend produced two masques in 1632, but he lives in a handful of lyrics like 'Victorious beauty', and 'Though regions farr devided', in which manly gallantry and wit are wedded to manly music. Kynaston is less restrained and less musical; but once at least, though avowedly heartwhole, he is touched by the authentic spark and rivals Carew in symmetry if not in finish:

> Do not conceale thy radiant eyes,
> The starre-light of serenest skies,
> Least wanting of their heavenly light,
> They turne to Chaos endlesse night.

The soaring fire which in this age was distributed with such pentecostal generosity seldom kindled William Habington (1605–54), author of the popular *Castara* (1634). This Catholic poet hardly belongs to any school, as his concentration on the sonnet indicates, and his sincere glorifying of chaste love (and rural retirement) separates him from both 'Platonic' and more candid amorists. However, his self-consciously edifying muse was inclined to be dull, if not sublunary (to echo the phrase of Donne that he borrowed), and less attractive than what he deplored, 'loose coppies of lust happily exprest'. But his soul could spread her wings in such religious poems as *Nox nocti indicat Scientiam*.

Sir William Davenant (1606–68), though hailed by Suckling as Donne's successor, does not reveal any special allegiance. His famous song, 'The Lark now leaves his watry Nest', is a compliment more cavalier and Elizabethan than metaphysical. Still less metaphysical is the very different *aubade*, 'O Thou that sleep'st like Pigg in Straw, Thou Lady dear, arise'. But Davenant at his best has both a large masculine energy of imagination, as in 'Wake all the dead! what hoa! what hoa!' (in *The Law Against Lovers*), and a distinctive vein of thoughtful sobriety. He was, or was to be, a signal actor and sufferer in the royalist cause, yet in 'The Soldier going to the Field' he strikes more than the conventional notes:

> And, for the sport of Kings, encrease
> The number of the Dead.

In such things as the 'Song. Endymion Porter and Olivia' and 'The Philosopher and the Lover to a Mistress Dying' the time-worn theme of love and death becomes metaphysical, though the grave dignity of tone and movement belong rather to the poet of *Gondibert* than to the metaphysical manner.

A greater cavalier than Davenant, or than Lovelace, was James Graham, Marquis of Montrose (1612–50), whose famous 'My dear and only Love' may have been merely amatory, though it has been commonly taken as a fervent expression of patriotic devotion, 'the song [in John Buchan's words] of a man who has at last found assurance, the confession of a soul which has a vision of a noble purpose, and holds no risk too high in its attainment':

> He either fears his Fate too much,
>   Or his Deserts are small,
> That puts it not unto the Touch,
>   To win or lose it all.

From the gallant and glamorous man of action we turn for a moment to an attractive man of books, Thomas Stanley (1625–78). His few original lyrics show a tinge of Donne through the predominant graceful artifice of foreign models and cavalier convention. Though himself rather a moon than a sun, Stanley had a number of poetical satellites, kinsmen, and friends. One relative was William Hammond (1614–55?), whose *Poems* (1655) are not distinctive. One friend was the vigorous and versatile John Hall (1627–56), author of a precocious volume of essays, *Horae Vacivae* (1646), *Poems* (1647), a tract on the reformation of the universities (1649), the first English translation of Longinus (1652), and other things. Herrick and Lovelace saluted the young Apollo and Cicero, and Henry More commended at length his 'Satyrick Flail'. Hobbes, who esteemed Hall's talents, might have welcomed an 'Epicurean Ode' linking metaphysical passion with atomism, and Traherne might have liked his 'Pastoral Hymn'. What Saintsbury calls the poet's 'Gold *dust* only . . . but *gold* dust' may be assayed, too, in 'The Call' and 'The Lure', which bring fresh feeling to the theme of love and passing time.

The older James Shirley (1596–1666), whose plays over-shadow his other work, was praised by Stanley as 'dearest Friend', and he in turn praised the high yet clear and terse and innocent muse of Stanley. Shirley the lyrist was a smooth Jon-sonian cavalier with some touches of wit, a sort of Carew with-out Carew's genius. His long *Narcissus*, which had been entered and presumably published in 1618, was, in his *Poems* of 1646, one of the last facile products of Elizabethan Ovidianism. But Shirley was the last of the Elizabethans in a stronger way. In that noble dirge in *The Contention of Ajax and Ulysses* (1659) the greatest of medieval and Renaissance commonplaces is treated with an unabashed exaltation of traditional metaphor and statement in which we just hear the Augustan note:

> The glories of our blood and state,
>   are shadows, not substantial things,
> There is no armour against fate,
>   Death lays his icy hand on Kings. . . .

Many small voices are not inaudible. The clergyman Thomas Pestell (1585–1667) especially imitated Sir John Beaumont and praised Donne as the 'Prince of Wits' and 'The late Copernicus in Poëtrie'. Ralph Knevet (1602–72), in *A Gallery to the Temple*, was something more than an imitator of Herbert. Thomas Beedome (1613–40/41?) in *Poems Divine and Human* (1641), Thomas Philipott (*c.* 1616–82) in *Poems* (1646), and the physi-cian John Collop (1625–*post* 1676) in *Poesis Rediviva* (1656), could on religious themes strike genuine sparks of metaphysical fire; Collop's wit took in medical as well as amatory and conventional subjects, and he was fervent in praise of Harvey, Dr. Browne, and others. Martin Lluelyn (1616–82), Oxonian, cavalier, and later physician, in *Men-Miracles* (1646) displayed fanciful humour and rural realism along with metaphysical wit, and real intensity of thought and feeling in his Anglican and royalist carols. Mildmay Fane, Earl of Westmorland (1602–66), a relative of Marvell's Lord Fairfax, in his musing 'on Natures Book' in *Otia Sacra* (1648) was more preoccupied than Marvell or his friend Herrick with religious 'Mysterie'; he could also, as an Anglican and royalist, write satire. Robert Heath's miscellaneous and amatory *Clarastella* (1650) was respectable but not distinguished; Edward Phillips in 1675 ranked him and Herrick together.

We may end this catalogue of a few out of many minor or sub-minor poets with a respectful bow to two illustrious women. The Duchess of Newcastle (1623–74) had, like Petulant, a pretty deal of an odd sort of a small wit and, like Petulant, she relied altogether on her parts. What tribute can be paid to her, however, may be better bestowed upon her *Life* of the Duke than upon such scientific, metaphysical, and moral effusions as her *Poems and Fancies* and *Philosophical Fancies* (1653). The other and less eccentric woman was a poetic disciple of William Cartwright and the first real English poetess, Katherine Philips (1632–64). The matchless Orinda's circle of admired and admiring literary friends, intimate or remote, included— besides Cartwright, the 'Prince of Phansie', who died in 1643— Cowley, Henry Vaughan, Jeremy Taylor, Sir Charles Cotterell (translator of La Calprenède), and the Earls of Roscommon and Orrery. Thanks largely to Gosse's imagination, we have a mental picture of Mrs. Philips as something between Madame de Rambouillet and Mrs. Leo Hunter. There is no evidence for a salon, or for anything more than a sincere portion of the fashionable Platonism which turned good friends like Mary Aubrey and Mrs. Owen into Rosania and Lucasia, and enveloped Mr. Philips and other men in similar celestial hues. Orinda's Platonism, if somewhat Frenchified, was particularly a heritage from Cartwright. As Keats perceived, she has her poetic moments; the most familiar example is 'To my Excellent Lucasia, on our Friendship'. But we recognize Orinda's individuality and her blameless renown more willingly than we read her verse.

3

The revival of Donne and other 'metaphysical' poets has of course been a main movement of our time; quickening in the 1890's and proceeding slowly, it came to a rather sudden peak in the third decade of this century, the period after the First World War. It not only brought a relatively neglected body of writing into active life but strongly affected modern poetry and criticism and indeed altered the whole contour map of English poetry of the last three centuries and a half. Metaphysical poetry, or simply Donne, became for a time the virtual criterion of all good poetry. The circumstances of this revival also brought into active life a number of dogmas about the nature and causes of metaphysical poetry which, though valuable as aids to modern perception, might not have been understood by the metaphysicals themselves. One major circumstance was the parallel felt between the metaphysical 'revolt' and the revolt of Pound, Eliot, and the later Yeats (in which Donne's influence was a factor) against the moribund romantic tradition. The parallel should not lead us, as it has led a number of people, to the assumption that Elizabethan orthodoxy, as represented by Spenser, was effete, since Spenser, however little read or understood, remains a greater poet than Donne.

In the earlier seventeenth century, when writers got along for the most part without formal criticism, the metaphysical manner in both verse and prose was loosely referred to as 'wit' or 'strong lines'. William Drummond, whose tastes were conservative and continental, complained about 1625–30 of new 'Metaphysical Ideas and Scholastical Quiddities', perhaps chiefly those of Donne (though he had admired and echoed Donne). Dryden was a main agent in giving currency to the label—he was, apropos of Donne, remarking that amatory verse and the minds of women readers should not be ruffled by abstruse ideas. In the first full critique ('Cowley'), Dr. Johnson stressed the violent yoking of discordant ideas and images and the straining after novelty, particularity, intellectual subtlety, and recondite learning, though he found some compensating virtues. In the modern view, Johnson's sane but limited neoclassical insight was focused largely upon degenerate extravagances and missed the essentials of the metaphysical genius. These would be, to attempt a brief summary of modern

definitions: a philosophic consciousness as the matrix of amatory, religious, and other poetry; the concentrated, pregnant
fusion of thought and feeling, of argumentative logic and passion; the assimilation by an active and unified sensibility of
widely different ideas and kinds of experience; the questioning
exploration of the individual poet's complex impulses and
attitudes in dramatic tension and conflict, rather than the presentation of an assured, preconceived result—a special kind of
private rather than public poetry; a texture and tone not in
one key but of mingled seriousness and ironic wit, of contrast
and surprise; the homely and realistic or the erudite rather than
the fanciful or mythological image, and the intellectual, organic,
and functional rather than the decorative or illustrative use of
it; the language and rhythms of speech, of expressive dissonance,
instead of the smoothly 'poetical'.

While these ideas have degrees of validity or value, they are
ex post facto. Some of the doctrines and phrases that had most
influence in the metaphysical revival were a restatement of
nineteenth-century reactions (though put forth in a much more
auspicious climate), the reactions, that is, of critics nurtured in
the romantic tradition and not at home in the earlier period;
and Dr. Johnson and his age had lost touch with the religio-
philosophic beliefs and presuppositions of the earlier seventeenth century, so that he lacked the essential key. Historical
criticism would consider the summary description in the preceding paragraph as too much of a modern reinterpretation and
would add important correctives: that central elements of
sensibility and technique, while exploited by the metaphysical
poets with distinctively original results, were present in orthodox
theory and practice; that definitions based largely on Donne do
not apply very well to other so-called metaphysicals; that such
definitions somewhat distort Donne himself by seeing only
psychological and technical novelties and neglecting the current
rules of decorum governing the various poetic genres; that
Donne's unified sensibility was really multiple and decidedly
not philosophical, although he used philosophical ideas; that
much of what is now taken to be peculiarly metaphysical or at
least Donnian learning, from alchemy to religious iconography,
was in its own day more or less common property; that supposedly unrelated ideas and images were less startling in an
age that accepted the great chain of being and the divine unity

and correspondence of all parts of creation. This last conception, it may be observed, is likely to retain its philosophic wholeness in religious poetry (if not always in Donne's), while in secular verse it may become a flickering ghost of its old self, a mental habit or technique cut loose from philosophic totality and applied in tangential ways.

Approached from another direction, metaphysical poetry appears as the complement of the anti-Ciceronian movement in prose. That movement (characterized a little less briefly in later pages) may in retrospect, and again with due regard to decorum, be summed up as a revolt against the flowing oratorical period and the established verities which it commonly expressed, and an attempt to create a medium fitted to render the realistic questionings, complexities, and diversities of private experience in a world of changing values. The qualities that developed in the usually short metaphysical poem developed also to some degree in the prose essay—though they developed also in public sermons, notably those of Andrewes and Donne. Both poets and men of prose knew, to give an enlarged sense to George Herbert's advice on preaching, that 'particulars ever touch, and awake more then generalls'.

It would doubtless be a good thing if the term 'metaphysical' had never become established, since it is in itself quite misleading, since it has been conventionally applied to a school or group of poets who were not a school or a group and who for the most part had little in common except that they wrote in the earlier seventeenth century, and since it does in fact apply more or less to nearly all poets of the period. However, the adjective is less cumbrous than 'earlier-seventeenth-century' and it suggests some kind of 'wit'; there is even less significant and settled meaning in the increasingly popular word 'baroque'.

George Chapman began to publish his tough, difficult, 'metaphysical' poems when Donne began to write, in the early 1590's, but Chapman's conservative humanistic doctrine links him more closely with Davies, Daniel, and Greville. It was the young Donne who gave utterance to the discontents and libertine consolations of the intellectuals who had outgrown the old verities and ideals.[1] Donne had had the same kind of education in logic,

[1] John Donne (1572–1631) was the son of a prosperous London ironmonger, John Donne (d. 1576). His mother was the daughter of John Heywood and the granddaughter of Sir Thomas More's sister, Elizabeth Rastell; his uncle, Jasper

rhetoric, and literary 'decorum' as most other Elizabethan poets, but he effected a revolution by manipulating—with transforming genius—current conventions of attitude and style. Into amatory verse, the realm of Petrarchan and pastoral idealism and mellifluous language and rhythm, Donne carried over the realistic outlook, the dramatic immediacy and particularity, the masculine wit, the irony, the rough colloquial language and staccato rhythms that were the established mode of Elizabethan satire—as his own satires indicate. In celebrating

Heywood, was a Jesuit and his brother died in 1593 in Newgate, where he had been put for harbouring a priest. Thus Donne had his 'first breeding and conversation with men of a suppressed and afflicted Religion, accustomed to the despite of death, and hungry of an imagin'd Martyrdome' (*Biathanatos*). After some years of study at Oxford (1584 ff.) and Cambridge, he seems to have travelled abroad (1591?). He was a member of Thavies Inn (1591) and Lincoln's Inn (1592–4); he combined reading and writing with the life of a young man about town. His satires and many amatory poems were evidently written during the 1590's. Donne took part in Essex's Spanish expeditions of 1596 and 1597. In 1597–8 he was made secretary to Sir Thomas Egerton, the Lord Keeper (and hence must have become by this time, if not by the time of the third 'Satire', at least a nominal Anglican). What promised to be a brilliant career was blasted by a secret marriage (December 1601) with Lady Egerton's niece, Ann More; her father, Sir George More, procured Donne's imprisonment and dismissal. Thenceforth Donne and his increasing family were more or less dependent upon relatives and patrons; difficulties were eased after 1608, when Sir George began to pay a dowry. According to A. Jessopp's biography (1897), Donne may (c. 1605–7?) have assisted Thomas Morton (who became Dean of Gloucester in 1606) in his anti-Romanist polemics, though evidence seems to be lacking. During this middle part of his life Donne wrote some prose works: *Biathanatos* (pub. 1646), *Pseudo-Martyr* (pub. 1610), *Ignatius his Conclave* (pub. 1611), and *Essays in Divinity* (pub. 1651): and some of the *Songs and Sonnets*, probably most of the 'Holy Sonnets' (1609–10), and the two *Anniversaries* (pub. 1611, 1612). He was abroad in 1605 and, with a new patron, Sir Robert Drury, in 1611–12; during 1612–21 he and his family lived in London, in a house beside Drury House. Donne was a member of Parliament in 1601 and 1614. In 1615, when all secular doors seemed to be closed, he was ordained; in 1616 he was presented to two country livings, one of which, Sevenoaks in Kent, he held to the end of his life. During 1616–22 he was Reader in Divinity to the Benchers of Lincoln's Inn. His wife, who had borne twelve children and lost five, died in 1617. A good part of 1619 Donne spent with Viscount Doncaster's embassy to Germany. In 1621 he was nominated Dean of St. Paul's by King James. A serious illness in 1623 gave birth to *Devotions* (pub. 1624). In 1624 Donne became vicar of St. Dunstan's-in-the-West, where he had Izaak Walton as a parishioner. During the plague of 1625 Donne lived in Chelsea with his old friend Magdalen Herbert, who had married Sir John Danvers in 1609. The death of Donne's wife had been a lasting grief, and the first half of 1627 brought three deaths—Lucy, his oldest unmarried daughter, Lady Danvers, and his former patroness, the Countess of Bedford. On 25 February 1631 Donne left his sick-bed to preach his last sermon, *Death's Duel*, and returned home to make his elaborate preparations for his end (31 March). Most of Donne's poems were first printed posthumously in 1633 and later years. The earlier poetry is treated by C. S. Lewis in the *OHEL*, vol. iii; the prose works and sermons are discussed below in Chapter x.

love as the supreme, the only, thing in the world, he did not disown Petrarch but went beyond him to new, twisted kinds of hyperbole. He did not disown Ovid, but, while other Elizabethans exploited the mythological and pictorial, Donne exploited Ovid's amatory casuistry and wit. The heterogeneous elements in his pregnant pot, from scholastic philosophy and theology to alchemy, from everyday London life to preternatural folk-lore, were in his best poems or passages fused in moments of passionate, complex intensity. Though we cannot assume that all the most serious and exalted tributes to love were addressed to his wife, a few of the best certainly or probably were. Donne's major themes were woman and God, or perhaps one should say himself in relation to each, and the relation of his mind and soul to his body. Marriage polarized his affections on one level, ordination on another; and, as he said in the sonnet on his dead wife, his love for her 'did whett To seeke thee God'.

The preceding paragraph was a brief and over-simplified reminder of some commonplaces, because chronology excludes from this volume the definitely early poems and logic puts with them the rest of the short poems concerned with women and love, including those clearly or possibly written after 1600. These we have in our minds in reading Donne's other works and the works of his successors, but our direct interest is limited to *The Progress of the Soul*, the divine poems, and the *Anniversaries*. We do not need to linger with the 'Epicedes and Obsequies' and the 'Letters to Several Personages', in which complimentary ingenuity is seldom fused with strong feeling and which are at any rate much inferior to the religious poems.

The Progress of the Soul, Donne's longest satire (though it was left unfinished), is dated 16 August 1601. Six months previously the Earl of Essex, his former commander, who for some time in 1599–1600 had been confined at York House, the Lord Keeper's residence, had attempted the rising that brought him to the scaffold, and many people, especially of the younger generation, forgot the earl's criminal folly and saw only a relentless old queen extinguishing the brightest hope of a brave new world. But that, if it counts, is only one of many facts and feelings behind Donne's 'sullen Writ, Which just so much courts thee, as thou dost it'. The brief summary Jonson gave Drummond—that the soul of Eve's apple was to be carried through the bodies

of heretics from Cain to Calvin—does not fit the long fragment
we have: heresy as such does not come into it; in over 500 lines
Donne does not move far towards Calvin; and in stanza vii he
seems to say that he will end with Elizabeth. The clearest statement in the whole poem, the entire relativity of good and evil,
is made in the abrupt conclusion, but that is not the idea Donne
has been developing. One initial impression, of nature red in
tooth and claw, is submerged in a brutal sexuality we might not
expect from a young man who in a few months was to lose all for
love. However, his bitter mood may have arisen in part from the
problems of marriage along with his perennial questioning of
the relations of man and woman and soul and body. According
to a novel argument, Donne—with hints from such Pythagorean-
Platonic allegorizers as Philo Judaeus—was showing how, in a
world of original sin and destiny (God's 'Commissary') and
inexorable law, the soul of the apple, or the 'power of moral
choice', has its successive mansions (the creatures it dwells in)
ruined by the corruption of fallen nature; the various incarna-
tions illustrate problems of sex, problems of survival in a savage
world, and, finally, the two together. Against and above the
world of evil is set the Redeemer (whose Cross—here as in
Donne's late 'Hymn'—stands in the same place as Adam's tree).
While this interpretation, too complex for an epitome, makes
sense as abstract theory, the poet's vision of good, like that of
many modern novelists, is obscured by his preoccupation with
ugliness and evil and by an excess of particularity. The poem as
a whole may be thought a rather dull extravaganza, though De
Quincey found in it 'thoughts and descriptions which have the
fervent and gloomy sublimity of Ezekiel or Æschylus'.

Donne's early concern with religion, manifest in the third
'Satire', did not become a dominant poetic motive until years
later. 'A Litany' (1608?) is at once obviously liturgical and
characteristic of the secular poet in its colloquial language,
rough rhythms, and a paradoxical wit not confined to the central Christian mysteries; and the whole is an earnest, muscular
plea for 'evennesse', for a middle way of life in the world, for
deliverance from pernicious extremes. 'La Corona', which was
written probably late in 1608 or early in 1609, a little before the
more famous sonnets, observes the decorum of meditations in
the tradition of the rosary. This 'crown of prayer and praise',
in seven linked sonnets, touches the life of Christ from the

Annunciation to the Ascension; the prominence the Virgin Mary has in Catholic devotions is reduced. The sonnets state the Christian paradoxes with a degree of Donnian density, but, in comparison with the series that followed, they are quiet, smooth, and impersonal—until the personal note emerges, the effort of a 'dry soule' to conquer death and win salvation through Christ's blood.

In the 'Holy Sonnets' the Donnian characteristics appear with the fullest dramatic violence, in the very personal expression of anguished guilt and fear and appeals or demands for divine grace and mercy—all this within a year or two of 'La Corona' and the 'Litany'. Our view of Donne's religious and poetic evolution has been radically altered by Helen Gardner's arguments, bibliographical and theological, which nullified the traditional assumption that these nineteen sonnets were all written after Mrs. Donne's death (1617). To summarize the results, without the complex evidence, sixteen of the sonnets were not isolated utterances but were composed in several groups: twelve (including most of the famous ones) which make two sequences, six on death and judgement and six, less closely linked, on God's love for man and the love man owes to God and his neighbour; and a group of four 'penitential' sonnets (among them 'I am a little world made cunningly'). A further conclusion is that the twelve sonnets were written in the first half of 1609, the last four between the latter half of 1609 and the composition of the *First Anniversary* in the first half of 1611. The three remaining sonnets are isolated 'ejaculations' and two at least come much later: the sonnet that relates Donne's dead wife to his own religious condition (15 August 1617–19?), and 'Show me deare Christ, thy spouse'. The latter is convincingly read as a 'contrast between the Church promised in Scripture and the Church as it appears in the world and throughout history', and as prompted by the defeat of the Elector Palatine and the Protestant cause in October 1620. While the new dating seems to stand firm, grouping of the sonnets by themes—though there is also bibliographical evidence—involves some fine-spun distinctions, and it has been argued that all nineteen sonnets form a unified sequence concerned with the Anglican discipline of contrition. However that may be, the progress of Donne's soul, and of his poetry, is now seen in a changed perspective.

The structure of individual sonnets, especially the first six, shows Donne's awareness of the systematic devotional meditation, yet explosive personal feeling—'Despaire behind, and death before doth cast Such terrour'—strains even a method that prescribed the use of the imagination and the deliberate confronting of sinful impulse. One might expect these sonnets to have preceded rather than followed the comparative serenity of 'La Corona', the comparative rationality of the 'Litany', but reason is not an actor—though logic is—on this tempestuous microcosmic stage. Like the love poems, the sonnets render, *in extremis* as it were, the immediacy of experience, with a texture and bold, harsh rhythms that are pure Donne. The sonnet form and the iambic line are both strained by urgency of utterance; yet we hardly think of technical matters in overhearing these colloquies or battles carried on by the poet with himself and God. It is not questioning the dramatic force and originality of the poems to remark that none of them would ever make a sinner more conscious of his sins—as many of Herbert's do.

Having won the friendship and patronage of Sir Robert Drury with an elegy on his fourteen-year-old daughter, who died in December 1610 and whom he had never seen, Donne went on to compose the two so-called *Anniversaries*, *An Anatomy of the World* (1611) and *Of the Progress of the Soul* (1612). Ben Jonson's comments to Drummond indicate a feeling apparently shared by the Countess of Bedford and others who did not grasp Donne's real theme:

that Dones Anniversarie was profane and full of Blasphemies
that he told Mr Donne, if it had been written of the Virgin Marie it had been something to which he answered that he described the Idea of a Woman and not as she was.

Elizabeth Drury is a symbol of all the vitality, goodness, order, and proportion of the childhood of the world, and her death is a symbol of all the corruption and disorder, external and internal, that have grown to a head in the old age of nature and the race—'the breaking of the circle' of perfection. However, even if the girl was such a symbol, and carried overtones of the Virgin Mary, Christ, and Astraea, for Donne's purpose of self-analysis, of spiritual stock-taking, she was, at least in the

First Anniversary, perhaps more of an encumbrance than an integrating inspiration.

A few paragraphs on such long and complex works cannot do more than indicate the direction of modern criticism. Behind the two poems is the tradition, especially familiar to the ex-Catholic Donne, of the formal devotional meditation which had been notably codified in the *Spiritual Exercises* of Ignatius Loyola and had been widely adapted in less rigorous forms. The method had shown itself, with variations, in Donne's 'Holy Sonnets' and is elaborately developed in the *Anniversaries*. Thus (to follow Louis Martz), the *First Anniversary* comprises an introduction (1–90); five sections (91–190, 191–246, 247–338, 339–76, 377–434), each containing a meditation, a eulogy, and a refrain and moral; and a general conclusion (435–74). The *Second Anniversary* is less rigid in its divisions and a more successful whole. It is more compelling, too, in its impassioned treatment of a more positive theme, the repairing of the broken circle, the soul's deliverance from the world and the flesh and its attaining the knowledge of God that is man's true end and salvation. While such words approximate the way and the goal of traditional mysticism, this is not, unless at moments, a mystical poem, but rather a preparative towards the journey. Moreover, thinking of Donne's temperament and subsequent active life as a clergyman, one might suggest that rejection of the world, however old a solution for the troubled soul, was not a possible solution for him, and was indeed the kind of extreme he had deplored in the 'Litany'.

Some passages have been lifted from their context and given undue or distorted emphasis. The signal example is 'And new Philosophy calls all in doubt . . .'. While Donne was at this time unusually well read in Kepler and Galileo, he was no scientific modernist either in the sense of a progressive Baconian or in the sense of a confident Copernican who put the old world-view behind him; least of all was he a modern intellectual lost in a meaningless universe. A passage in the *Second Anniversary* (254 ff.), which corresponds to the *locus classicus* of the *First*, is a recital of man's scientific ignorance of his body, a reminder of his more fatal ignorance of himself; in both passages nature's decay is related to sinful man's intellectual pride and confusion, and both are arguments for turning to the pure and unshakeable truth of religion—the thesis of Greville's *Human Learning* and of

Godfrey Goodman's treatise, *The Fall of Man* (1616). The minor place of science in Donne's mind is further indicated by his indiscriminate use of the new science, old science, pseudo-science, and fable, as these suit his varying purposes. (In point of fact, or probability, Donne seems, like many other informed men, to have accepted the Tychonic system; and in his poems and sermons he normally assumes a geocentric world as a matter of course.) If we read the *Anniversaries* as pictures of the Jacobean mind's sense of intellectual and religious crisis, they may be thought far more off-centre, far less alive and relevant, than Chapman's *Tears of Peace* or even Greville's work. And if we read them simply as personal poems, much of the texture is still a network of now meaningless particulars in prose of staccato energy, with some passages and bits of great poetry.

Two short poems may be mentioned chiefly on their own account but also as examples of the occasional meditation; one is wholly religious, the other becomes so, indirectly. 'Good Friday, 1613. Riding Westward' develops out of the paradoxical fact that Donne's body is being carried towards the West while his 'Soules forme bends toward the East'. Almost every line or couplet that follows is a paradoxical variation on the power and the fate of Christ, the miracle of God's death and His love for man. The theme is of the commonest; the arresting quality, as usual, is in the imaginative realization of concrete particulars. The very different 'Nocturnal upon St. Lucy's Day' is arresting for the same reason, though here many particulars require a knowledge of Paracelsian doctrines. The poem expresses almost inexpressible despair, utter annihilation by grief; according to a plausible surmise, it could not have had a lesser occasion than the actual or imagined death of Donne's wife. She—at any rate the woman of the poem—is now a saint in heaven, and in the religious service of the 'Nocturnal' or 'Vigill' he would 'prepare towards her'. Whoever she was, the poem is one of overwhelming immediacy. In the sonnet that is certainly on his wife, 'Since she whome I lovd', the fact of her death gives place to God's way of turning his loss into good.

This idea of God's loving stratagems is more elaborately handled, with emblematic images of the sea, in 'A Hymn to Christ, at the Author's Last Going into Germany', written in May or April 1619. Donne's three late 'Hymns', along with *Devotions*, are reminders that the man whose sermons give a normal impression of personal security was haunted by personal fears. His fear and hope in the first 'Hymn' would have been much the same even if he had not been going on a journey from which he did not expect to return; but the assurance of divine love predominates in the rhythm as well as in the words. The two latest 'Hymns' are both characteristic, both direct, prayerful, intense, and 'witty' appeals to God. 'A Hymn to God the Father' has an urgent tautness in its questions and replies; in 'A Hymn to God, my God, in my Sickness' geographical metaphors are elaborated in a relaxed, quietly exultant, almost posthumous meditation. Scholars accept Walton's associating of the former with Donne's illness of 1623, but they have been divided in regard to the latter; Sir Julius Caesar dated his copy December 1623 and Walton in 1658 assigned the poem precisely to 23 March 1631, eight days before Donne's death. The arguments are too complicated for summary, but one may think that internal evidence at least supports Walton. (*Devotions* can be cited on both sides.) In Donne the sense of guilt and fear do not necessarily imply any near prospect of death, and 'A Hymn to God the Father' implies on the contrary that he hopes and expects to go on living an active life. But the other 'Hymn' reads like an integral part of his solemn ceremonial preparations for his end; his thoughts of sin have almost vanished, and he stands, or rather lies, with serene confidence on the threshold of heaven.

The religious experience revealed in Donne's chief poems is equally intense and limited. While his modern revival has been based especially on his love poems, the highest claims have been made for the religious poetry also, and by critics not much concerned with religion *per se*. Yet the quality and range of a poet's religious experience comes into literary judgement no less than the quality and range of any secular poet's general experience, and on both counts Donne falls short of the highest. No one can fail to recognize his genuine spirituality and his extraordinary expressive power, the power of the 'naked thinking heart'—or perhaps more often the naked feeling heart. At the same time his virtues have their obverse side. The 'Holy Sonnets' and the 'Hymns' are focused, like the love poems, on a particular moment and situation, on John Donne, and the rest of life and the world is blacked out, does not exist. Then the religious experience itself is so narrowly and concretely fundamentalist that it can hardly be translated into larger, more comprehensive terms; all questions are dissolved in Christ's blood. For both reasons a modern reader may not find enough of the common ground needed for full imaginative participation; he may well be moved, but it is by the torments of a human being in another and alien world—whereas one cannot help sharing the spiritual vicissitudes of George Herbert, whose religious experience, though founded on the same creed, is so broadly and deeply human. If Donne helped to kindle the religious poets who came after him, he kindled poetry that embodied central religious elements largely wanting in his own, from the difficult practice of the Christian life to contemplative vision (for the latter heading would surely have to be strained to admit the *Anniversaries*).

Although Jonson represented critical theory as well as poetic creation, his influence, as we have seen, is seldom found 'pure', and the strongly individual followers of a more infectious and dangerous example were even less likely to be homogeneous. Moreover, Donne was merely the most compelling exponent of a sensibility and technique which would have appeared if he had never been born. That is not to minimize his potent influence (his poems circulated widely in manuscript): it is only to say that the degree of unlikeness among the poets who are rightly or wrongly called metaphysical—Lord Herbert, George Herbert, Crashaw, Vaughan, King, Cowley, Marvell, Cleveland, Benlowes, and others—forbids our defining metaphysical poetry simply in terms of Donne. All but one of his chief successors were religious poets, and neither spiritually nor technically are Herbert, Crashaw, and Vaughan much like their supposed progenitor. But all three were accustomed, in their several ways, to religious meditation.

4

No one turned so completely away from human to divine love as the author of *The Temple* (1633).[1] Herbert does not electrify

[1] George Herbert (1593–1633), the fifth son of Richard and Magdalen Herbert, and the younger brother of Lord Herbert of Cherbury, sprang from an ancient, distinguished, and martial family of the Welsh border. His father died in 1596 and he grew up under the watchful eye of his gifted mother, the friend of Donne; she married Sir John Danvers in 1609 and died in 1627. Herbert won distinction at Westminster School and at Trinity College, Cambridge (B.A., 1613; M.A., 1616). He became a fellow, a Reader in Rhetoric (1618), and during 1620–7 was Public

the nerves so often or so startlingly as Donne, but, instead of
Donne's fevered preoccupation with death and judgement, he
has a far more truly religious preoccupation with everyday
fulfilment of the divine will here and now; the quiet Herbert is
also a more subtle artist than the explosive Donne. If the modern
reader sees inner tension as a prime essential of metaphysical
poetry, no writer has more than the man whose manuscript
was 'a picture of the many spiritual Conflicts that have past
betwixt God and my Soul, before I could subject mine to the
will of Jesus my Master: in whose service I have now found perfect freedom'. By his mother's wish and his own, Herbert had
been early dedicated to the Church, but his university career
and his experience as Public Orator strengthened worldly
ambition in a young man not unnaturally disposed, in Izaak
Walton's words, to put 'too great a value on his parts and
Parentage'. So 'he enjoyed his gentile humor for cloaths, and
Court-like company, and seldom look'd towards Cambridge,
unless the King were there, but then he never fail'd'. The death
of King James and other patrons, Herbert's own inward wrestlings, his mother's counsel and probably Donne's, brought him
back to 'Divinity'—which, indeed, he had never given up,
though he had thought for a time that he could combine it
with civil employment. However, the years following his dia-
conal ordination did not apparently bring the peace of single-
hearted assurance. Possibly there were doubts over the step
taken; certainly there were deeper causes, ill health, a sense of
inadequacy and unworthiness, the continual effort of a proud
and passionate Herbert to comprehend the nature of God's love
for man and of man's love for God. That comprehension and
fulfilment did come, and so irradiated his brief and humble
pastorate at Bemerton that the life as well as the works of 'Holy
Mr. Herbert' remained an inspiration for his century. There
are poems, like 'The Odour' and 'The Call', which express profound serenity; and a happy sense of vocation fills the prose
'character' of the country parson, *A Priest to the Temple*. Yet even

Orator to the University. He was elected M.P. for Montgomery in 1624 and again
in 1625. In or before 1626 he was ordained deacon and for some time he lived with
relatives and friends, unsettled in mind and more or less ill in body. In 1629 he
married Jane Danvers. In 1630 he was appointed rector of Bemerton, near Salisbury, and was ordained priest. His English poems, which had circulated in manuscript, he sent, just before his death, to his friend Nicholas Ferrar, to be either
printed or burned.

at Bemerton, where he wrote perhaps the larger half of *The Temple*, Herbert was afflicted by thoughts of unfitness and futility, by apprehensions of a 'shrivel'd heart' and 'Thy distance from me'. Thus in part Herbert's experience and career resembled Donne's; but a closer parallel would be with his other friend, Nicholas Ferrar, who in 1625 turned his back upon the world to fulfil his deepest desires by establishing a religious community at Little Gidding.

This short and simple outline has taken roughly chronological form, but one cannot impose chronology or any logical pattern upon the variable and recurrent moods of a sensitive soul. As Aldous Huxley has said, Herbert is the poet of 'inner weather', in the full English sense of the metaphor. That is one element in his peculiar intimacy and honesty. With all his sophisticated art, he seems unaware of an audience, so that we rather over-hear him than read him. The Puritan Baxter said in 1681: 'Herbert speaks to God like one that really believeth a God, and whose business in the world is most with God.' He is less than himself when he addresses others, in the homespun gnomic counsels of 'The Church-Porch', which reminds us of the *Outlandish Proverbs*, and in the historical panorama of 'The Church Militant', though these poems have their organic place in the architecture of *The Temple*.

We may partly distinguish two poets in Herbert. There is, first, the parish priest of early seventeenth-century England who revered his Church as a chaste mother neither 'painted' nor 'undrest'; who deplored the worm of schism eating away the English rose and (to the disturbance of the Cambridge licenser in 1633) saw Religion standing

> on tip-toe in our land,
> Readie to passe to the American strand;

who celebrated with loving particularity and complete security of belief the meaning of God's temple and worship. It is this poet who can be fully appreciated, in Coleridge's words, only by 'an affectionate and dutiful child of the Church'; and it is to Herbert's writings and life that we owe much of our picture of the order, strength, and beauty of seventeenth-century Anglicanism at its best. But church-bells are heard beyond the stars, and the Anglican parish priest merges with the greater poet, with the very human saint who gives fresh and moving

utterance to the aspirations, failures, and victories of the
spiritual life, and whose experience the non-religious reader can
largely share. This is the Herbert we know through 'Affliction
(I)', 'Discipline', 'The Collar', 'The Pulley', and many other
poems in which he strives to subdue the wilful or kindle the
apathetic self. (We should not forget that meditative self-
examination is likely to exaggerate the sins it would ward off.)
We share no less in Herbert's gleams of humour and his human
and religious happiness:

> And now in age I bud again,
> After so many deaths I live and write;
> I once more smell the dew and rain,
> And relish versing: O my onely light,
>   It cannot be
>   That I am he
> On whom thy tempests fell all night.

Herbert's main themes are those 'two vast, spacious things . . .
Sinne and Love', and both are realities within himself—'My
stuffe is flesh, not brasse; my senses live, . . . Yet I love thee.'
But he can make divine love a reality too. And there is nothing
soft in the poet who would engrave that love in steel, and who
ends a catalogue of gratuitous, untempered, short-lived sweets
with the magnificent contrast (the image perhaps developed
from Ovid's *Ars Amatoria*, ii. 111 ff.!):

> Onely a sweet and vertuous soul,
> Like season'd timber, never gives;
> But though the whole world turn to coal,
>   Then chiefly lives.

As the Anglican merges with the larger vision, so the 'quaint'
writer merges with the sophisticated and timeless artist. Herbert
had his share of the age's passion for anagrams and the like,
and he stimulated the vogue of visually shaped or 'pattern'
poems, the kind of thing condemned by Addison as 'false Wit';
but 'The Altar' and 'Easter Wings' rose far above other poems
of the sort in turning what might seem naïve artifice to structural and expressive account. 'Aaron', though not a shaped
poem, is a piece of intricate and completely validated artifice.
Farther below the surface are the effects attained in 'Church-
Monuments', in which (to quote Joseph Summers) 'The dissolution of the body and the monuments is paralleled by the

dissolution of the sentences and the stanzas'. It is in keeping with Herbert's habit of mind and that of his age that the title and the organization of his volume carry symbolic suggestions of the body and spirit of both the Church and the individual Christian, and that many of his poems are allegorical anecdotes, transfigured 'emblems'.

The friend and admirer of Donne (and of Bacon) did not cultivate intellectual diction or imagery. The Bible and the liturgy, nature and everyday life were his chief sources, and, though some of these had been Donne's sources also, the results were very different. Herbert's most serious dealings with God can employ the language of business, law, even games. The highest truth, as he said more than once, must be plainly dressed. But his clean simplicity of language is not bareness; whereas Donne's words commonly have great immediate, local force but carry little aura, Herbert's evoke suggestive associations. We may catch biblical and liturgical overtones, but we are, unless instructed, likely to miss traditions of religious iconography and typology. Herbert moves from this world to the next, from the Old Testament to the New, 'As from one room t'another', or dwells simultaneously in all, since all are embraced by the sacramental vision.

If at times art flags along with inspiration, in the mass of his poetry Herbert has a highly functional sense of form and metre and rhythm. The poet whose stanzaic and metrical experimentation is statistically and artistically astonishing was also, we remember, a skilled and devoted musician. The movement of his verse, taut or relaxed, can suggest all his fluctuating moods, from self-will or weakness to glad surrender and renewed strength. In 'Love bade me welcome'—an 'emblem' of the Eucharist or of the soul's reception into heaven, or both—the dramatic contrast between humble human guilt and divine grace is active in the rhythm as well as in the words—on the one side hovering diffidence, on the other quick, all-powerful love.

Though Herbert wrote Latin and Greek verse, his material and instincts excluded any surface classicism; but he had the elements of a deeper classicism, if we care to use the term— muscular density, precision, deceptive simplicity, a concern for subordinating details to an evolving, unified whole. One possible model or at any rate predecessor who displayed some of Herbert's prime qualities of structure, language, tone, and metrical diversity was Sir Philip Sidney, in his sonnets and especially in his versification of the Psalms. Herbert loves, and enriches, the word 'neat'. His great effects are the greater for rising as a rule out of a homely, colloquial quietness of tone, and he is a master of quiet endings, of ironic and pregnant understatement: 'something understood'; 'banquetting the poore, And among those his soul'; 'So I did sit and eat'. In 'The Collar' the unwonted violence of rebellion is real, but, artistically, the disorder is controlled; the picture of it is a tissue of ambiguities which are perceived as such only when they are resolved in the final 'And I reply'd, *My Lord*'.

In contrast with the English and untravelled Herbert, who moved only from Cambridge to Bemerton, outward circumstance and inward compulsion made the physical and spiritual life of Richard Crashaw a pilgrimage to Loreto.[1] His father, the Rev. William Crashaw, a notable clergyman from Yorkshire who became preacher at the Temple, was a disciple of Perkins and a friend of Selden and Ussher. Although the Protestantism of the young Crashaw's poems on the Gunpowder Plot approached the young Milton's, by 1634 he had become a thorough High Churchman, and in 1635 he was rebuking both Puritanism and the kind of anti-papal hostility upheld by his father (who had died in 1626) and even by his friend Nicholas Ferrar. Possibly, if he had not been uprooted and exiled by the war, Crashaw might have remained an Anglo-Catholic like Ferrar, and like Joseph Beaumont and a fellow-exile, Dr. Cosin, the Master of Peterhouse, who were uprooted at the same time.

---

[1] Richard Crashaw (1612/13–49) was born in London and educated at the Charterhouse (1629–31) and Pembroke College, Cambridge (B.A., 1634); in 1635 he became a fellow of Peterhouse. Both were High-Church colleges. Along with teaching he pursued his favourite avocations, poetry, music, and painting. His poetic friends were Cowley and Joseph Beaumont. Crashaw may have been the 'R. C.' who contributed a Latin poem to the volume of elegies on Edward King (1638). He was a frequent participant in the religious life of Little Gidding. By 1639 he must have been ordained; he was described as a poetic and ravishing preacher. He quitted Cambridge in January 1643, before being formally ejected by the Puritans. He was in Holland in 1644, and perhaps at Oxford. In 1645, apparently, he entered the Roman communion. In 1645–6 he lived in Paris, in association with Cowley and other exiles, including the Countess of Denbigh and Queen Henrietta. Crashaw journeyed to Rome, where he suffered from poverty, ill health, and, in spite of the queen's patronage, from neglect. In 1647 he was in the service of Cardinal Pallotta, who in 1649 gave him a post at Loreto. Here he died. *Steps to the Temple* had appeared in 1646 and been much enlarged in 1648. Among the additions in *Carmen Deo Nostro* (Paris, 1652) were ll. 85–108 of 'The Flaming Heart'.

Yet the Italianate and Spanish intensities and excesses of Crashaw's poetry suggest a temperament which could not have found full 'Catholick contentation' in the *via media*, even on its High level. It was characteristic of his intellectually simple faith that, when in Paris he wrote the relatively muscular poem urging the Countess of Denbigh to become a Catholic, the problem appeared merely as one of 'Resolution in Religion', 'Twixt life & death, twixt in & out'.

Crashaw holds a place between Herbert and Vaughan mainly because of chronology and convenience. If the chief stigmata of the metaphysical poet, according to modern definitions, are inward conflict and tension, philosophic and analytic complexity of mind, and a colloquial, realistic, and non-pictorial manner and texture, Crashaw was something else; his 'wit', though both emblematic and individual, was rather in line with the ordinary Elizabethan conceit. It is hard to see any real affinity with Donne, and, apart from the title *Steps to the Temple*, echoes of Herbert are too much modified by their setting to be readily recognizable. Whatever the influence of continental poets (and Marino's has been questioned), Crashaw is the one conspicuous English incarnation of the 'baroque sensibility'. The religio-aesthetic creed and culture of the Counter-Reformation affected all the arts, and indeed aimed at mixing and transcending them, in its effort to make the five senses portals to heaven. The elements of the revival most stimulating to the artistic imagination were the clash and fusion of extremes in the human and divine, the pictorial and the abstract, in the joys and agonies, the spiritual splendour and the mean estate, of Christ, the Virgin, and the pantheon of saints and martyrs. Poetry took on a new and bizarre intricacy of sensuous decoration and symbolic metaphor, a kind of form—or formlessness—which sought a unity deeper and higher than the classical through emotional and impressionistic multiplicity. Aestheticians and literary critics have pursued the elusive concept of baroque as Browne pursued the quincunx, often with equally spacious and elliptical logic, but the simplest definition is 'poetry like Crashaw's'. Its motto might be 'Over-ripeness is all'. Crashaw's abundant revision always led to further elaboration and rarely to improvement.

In the *Epigrammatum Sacrorum Liber* of 1634 Crashaw expressly turned away from the traditions of the genre (though not from

classical myth) to follow chiefly the Jesuit epigrammatists in
treating religious themes while restricting himself to the New
Testament. The completely religious character of the volume
was only the most obvious sign of the direction its author was to
take. We find, not a theologian or thinker, or a troubled soul
like Donne or Herbert, but a secure, single-hearted worshipper
whose feeling for the central paradoxes of faith does not lessen
his sense of the human values in the story of the Son of Mary.
And, in spite of the general hard and 'witty' brevity imposed by
the form, there are not a few hints of sensuous fancy, the association of gold and purple and roses with the new-born or the
crucified Christ, the endless variations on tears, and a version
of the popular conceit on the water changed to wine—*Nympha
pudica Deum vidit, & erubuit.*

Among the early secular poems in *Steps to the Temple* are
sober, half-Jonsonian epitaphs and the more artificial 'Wishes.
To his (supposed) Mistress' and 'Love's Horoscope', in which
idealism takes a half-cavalier or half-Donnian form. Among
translated pieces we might expect two Psalms, if not the *Dies
Irae*, to be near Crashaw's heart, and his dilution of such great
originals is not altogether insignificant. For all his skill in Latin
and Greek verse Crashaw is one of the most unclassical, and
erratic, of English poets. The nature of his artistic roots is partly
suggested by two re-creations. One is 'Music's Duel' (*ante*
1634?), the uniquely expressionistic and technical elaboration
of the Jesuit Strada's popular Latin poem; Crashaw adds
religious and symbolic significance to the contrast between the
bird's music and the man's. The other, 'Sospetto d'Herode'
(1637?), is a highly charged rendering of the first book of
Marino's epic on the Slaughter of the Innocents which carries
Crashaw's own emphasis on the Christian paradoxes. The
Jesuits and perhaps Marino contribute to the famous or
notorious 'Weeper' (*ante* 1634?), which offers a severe though
not a final test for appreciation of Crashaw and baroque
religiosity. A central theme, penitential progress from sin to
spiritual perfection, can be extracted, but with difficulty, from
the profuse and largely unfocused images. The subject was
familiar, even in English, and for the contemporary reader who
knew Sidney's *Arcadia* and the sonneteers, Southwell and Giles
Fletcher and the emblem-books, there would be little surprise
in the individual conceits; but no English poet had produced

such a concatenation, or perhaps such grotesque extravagances as some of them—even if playful—are.

Crashaw went far beyond Marinism in power of vision and symbol, yet even in his greater poems he generally hovered between the ideal organic unity of baroque inspiration and a dazzling spray of associated images, and the reader who lacks a special temperament and a knowledge of the symbolic code may be more repelled than attracted. Crashaw's words and details are not vague as modern romantic poetry can be, nor even esoteric, since they grow out of the concrete creed of European Catholicism, but we may be unable to find or follow the controlling motive, and at times the poet himself may have lost it. At times, too, he is capable of relatively simple beauty like the opening of 'On the Assumption' or that couplet in 'The Weeper':

> Nowhere but heere did ever meet
> Sweetnesse so sad, sadnes so sweete.

There is some resemblance in 'naïve' conceits between Milton's most Italianate poem, the 'Nativity', and Crashaw's 'Hymn' on the same theme, though their responses to the wonder of the Incarnation are characteristically different; this is one poem of Crashaw's that gained in unity and depth from revision. 'The Glorious Epiphany' is nearer to Milton in part of its substance; here, in a manner very different from the 'Hymn' and of course from Milton, Crashaw develops a threefold contrast, physical, historical, and spiritual, between natural and supernatural light. Another of Crashaw's irregular odes or ecstasies, 'To the Name Above Every Name, the Name of Jesus', is not unlike the 'Epiphany' in symphonic multiplicity, but its devotional passion, 'the witt of love', is more central and typical; and its structure, as Louis Martz has shown, seems to have profited from an ordered model of meditation.

Those who read Crashaw perhaps come back most often to the strong and simple 'Hymn' to St. Teresa, and to the sequel, 'The Flaming Heart', in which cool ingenuity becomes incandescent. The author of the preface of 1646 spoke truly of 'the Quintessence of Phantasie and discourse center'd in Heaven . . . the very Outgoings of the soule'. The 'Poet and Saint' of ascetic life and luxuriant imagination, who seeks fulfilment in the pain and joy of divine annihilation, and freedom from years in Eternity, has little to do with this earth and common experience. He is

> Drest in the glorious madnesse of a Muse,
> Whose feet can walke the milky way;

a beautiful angel beating his luminous wings in a richly coloured Catholic heaven. His nests and spices and wounds and blood, whether we like them or not, have along with their Latin warmth a degree of ritualistic remoteness and abstractness. But the 'strong wine of Love' is a heady drink which, to put to illegitimate use another phrase from the preface, may give birth to the 'prodigious issue of tumorous heats and flashes'. It is almost inevitable that a poet striving to express the inexpressible should seem, at least, not to know the difference between gold and gilt, between spiritual vision and verbal intoxication. One who can soar and burn can also sink and melt. And not merely the uninformed or unsympathetic reader may be embarrassed by the kind of religious emotion that hails the Virgin as 'rosy princesse' and St. Teresa as 'My Rosy Love'. The feeling may not entirely vanish even when, so to speak, Murillo gives way to El Greco:

> By all thy brim-fill'd Bowles of feirce desire
> By thy last Morning's draught of liquid fire;
> By the full kingdome of that finall kisse
> That seiz'd thy parting Soul, & seal'd thee his. . . .

(While the mystic's instinct for erotic imagery has a long tradition behind it, we may be startled to learn that lines 63–117 of 'On a prayer booke sent to Mrs. M. R.' employ a number of images from Carew's 'A Rapture'.) The question whether an indisputable poet is also an indisputable mystic cannot be settled by rule of thumb, and perhaps does not need to be settled. As for the poet, the ordinary reader may feel uneasy when the authentic motives of adoration and self-surrender issue in an undisciplined fervour which has never been rational and never ceases to be sensuous and excited; and he may think that larger and clearer glimpses of the One were granted to the quiet Vaughan.

While Crashaw's short life was an ascent, by way of Rome, to the rosy heaven of Christ, the Virgin, and the saints, the soul of Henry Vaughan, during much of his long sojourn on earth, was meditating, to borrow Crashaw's language,

her immortall way
Home to the originall sourse of Light & intellectual Day.[1]

There is perhaps no more signal example than Vaughan of spiritual and poetical rebirth. The *Poems* of 1646, which opened with a tribute to Jonson and Randolph and reflected the influence of Donne and especially Habington, were mainly the efforts of a 'weak striver' in fashionable modes. *Olor Iscanus* (1651) included commendation of the 'dark shades of deep Allegorie' in Gombauld's *Endymion*, of John Fletcher, William Cartwright, Mrs. Philips, and Davenant's *Gondibert*, and showed more gravity of substance and tone, notably in elegies on friends killed in the war and in translations from Boethius. Both volumes carried hints of the author of *Silex Scintillans* (1650) in 'metaphysical' elements of structure, style, and imagery. But he had already largely forsaken his secular muse, which had nourished little of his mature quality, and by 1654, when he wrote the preface to the second part of *Silex*, he had come to look upon 'idle verse' as the fruit of vanity and spiritual sickness. Vaughan's so-called 'conversion' was evidently not any sudden event but a gradual process of deepening seriousness and illumination. Some apparent causes were the personal and public distresses of prolonged civil and religious strife and its aftermath, the death of his brother William in 1648, and new and intent study of the Bible, which showed him the pearl he had sought elsewhere; and to these were added—after the appearance of the

[1] Henry Vaughan (1621/2–95) came of an old Welsh family of Breconshire, a county once inhabited by the Silures; hence the appellation 'Silurist' on most of his title-pages. He went to Oxford, probably to Jesus College, in 1638, along with his twin brother Thomas. After two years he was sent to London to study law but was called home when war began. He was secretary to a Welsh judge for some time during 1642–5, and served with royalist troops at least in 1645. The period of his medical study may have come about 1655. He practised in his native district on the Usk. He was twice married. His late years were troubled by family disputes. His kinsman John Aubrey extracted some valuable letters.

Half of Vaughan's first volume (1646) was filled by a rendering of Juvenal's tenth satire. *Olor Iscanus* ('The Swan of Usk'), published in 1651 with a preface dated 1647, contained original verse (some of it later than 1647), translations from Ovid, Ausonius, Boethius, and the Polish Casimir, and prose essays from Plutarch and others. Vaughan's great poetry appeared in 1650 and 1655 in the two parts of *Silex Scintillans* ('Sparkling Flint'). An inferior volume of verse, *Thalia Rediviva*, was printed in 1678. Of Vaughan's compilations of religious prose, mainly translated, the most original parts were the meditations in *The Mount of Olives* (1652) and 'Primitive Holiness', a life of St. Paulinus of Nola, in *Flores Solitudinis* (1654). He also translated two works by Henricus Nollius, *Hermetical Physic* (1655) and *The Chemist's Key* (1657).

first part of *Silex*—a severe illness of his own and the death of his wife. The special agent of spiritual and poetical quickening to whom Vaughan avowed his great debt was 'The first, that with any effectual success attempted a diversion' of worldly and licentious poetry into the religious channel, 'the blessed man, Mr. George Herbert, whose holy life and verse gained many pious Converts, (of whom I am the least) . . .'.

In such a case 'influence' is an inadequate term. Herbert sometimes suggests the theme, spirit, and form of whole poems; more often he supplies single words, phrases, and ideas, many of which are embedded in quite different contexts. But, whether taken over or transformed, these things are, as Dowden said, less an appropriation than an inheritance. On the artistic side, Vaughan could follow his master in developing his own intimate, reflective colloquialism, though he more seldom attained to Herbert's technical mastery of structure and rhythm. The inward affinity is more important. As Herbert contains in himself two poets, the Anglican priest and the spiritual struggler, so in Vaughan there are the Herbertian religious poet and the timeless (but no less Christian) Neoplatonist. Since it is the latter and larger Vaughan that we cherish, his generally inferior expressions of evangelical experience are likely to be neglected. Yet the very high proportion of these, the author's view of all his 'Sacred Poems' as a body of 'ordinary Instructions for a regular life', his echoing not only of Herbert but of Felltham's *Resolves*, and his considerable devotional prose, all this testifies to an everyday religious effort which explains, not the magic, but the strength and centrality of his richest intuitions of the invisible. The God of 'deep, but dazling darkness' is also God the Father. Over and over Vaughan celebrates the redeeming love of Christ; still more constantly—and even in his epitaph— he laments his sinful or frozen heart and prays for a regenerating breath of divine grace. 'Certaine Divine Raies breake out of the Soul in adversity, like sparks of fire out of the afflicted flint.' Vaughan's consciousness of spiritual failure is not so specific and dramatic as Herbert's, but it is none the less real in a poet who strives for 'a true, practick piety', 'for perfection and true holiness, that a door may be opened to him in heaven'.

Vaughan's great poems are those in which the door is opened—'Regeneration', 'The Retreat', 'The Morning-watch', 'Peace', 'And do they so?', 'The Dawning', 'The World',

'Ascension-Hymn', 'They are all gone into the world of light', 'The Bird', 'The Seed Growing Secretly', 'The Night', 'The Waterfall', 'Quickness', and others. Part of Vaughan's theme, expressed in the familiar though untypical 'Retreat', we have met in Donne's *Second Anniversary* and shall meet again, since it was recurrent in religious writing from Plato and Cicero to Calvin and was especially congenial to the seventeenth century: that is, the exiled soul's longing to return to its heavenly home, the 'sea of light'. That longing was not merely *contemptus mundi* or nostalgia for a lost Eden; it could, as in Vaughan, become an overmastering desire to apprehend God and divine unity in and beyond the flux of life. Though imprisoned in the flesh, and in the darkness of earth, the soul, in its 'little inch of time in this life', may enter into the kingdom of heaven, in the true sense of Christ's words, by regaining the unsullied vision of 'Angell-infancy', by re-creating, so to speak, God's primal intention, by recognizing His immanence in all things, the 'prolusions and strong proofs of our restoration laid out in nature, besides the promise of the God of nature'. As Thomas Vaughan put it, 'There is nothing on earth—though never so simple, so vile and abject in the sight of man—but it bears witness of God, even to that abstruse mystery, His Unity and Trinity'; and a similar conviction was held by others, from Sir Thomas Browne to the naturalist John Ray. It is a main article in the creed of Henry Vaughan. Even in such an ostensible imitation of Herbert's 'The Church-Porch' as 'Rules and Lessons', Vaughan's voice is clear:

> There's not a Spring,
> Or Leafe but hath his Morning-hymn; Each Bush
> And Oak doth know I AM . . .
> Thou canst not misse his Praise; Each tree, herb, flowre
> Are shadows of his wisedome, and his Pow'r.

Flowers and fallen timber, blades of grass and the 'poor highway herb', stones and stars that 'nod, and sleepe', singing birds and crowing cocks, the 'gilded Cloud' and the waterfall, dew and rain and the seed growing secretly, all the letters of the divine alphabet proclaim 'The great Chime And Symphony of nature'. For the regenerate soul, life is 'A knowing Joy' in ordered harmony, 'A quickness, which my God hath kist', and death is only a rebirth in the fullness of knowledge and joy.

To think of nature and intimations of immortality is to think of Wordsworth (who apparently never met Vaughan's poems) and of other nineteenth-century poets, but the fundamental difference has already been emphasized. While Vaughan can see childhood, like the childhood of the race, as nearer to God than adult or modern man, his conception is rooted in a religious and moral concern with sin; it is not romantic primitivism. As for a major preoccupation, Vaughan is thoroughly orthodox in studying God in the secondary book of His works as well as in His word. Nature, like man, suffered through the Fall (and will have its renewal), and yet, lacking man's sinful will, it is not so far removed from God. (On the other hand, nature cannot share regenerate man's conscious sense of God— though Vaughan can envy the inferior creatures' instinctive, sinless constancy of participation in divinity.) Thus nature can be a partial agent of insight and purification. Vaughan is not a close aesthetic or scientific observer; he sees God's creation as the great symbol of relative purity and goodness, the great source of image and analogy; his two favourite epithets, 'green' and 'white', are not opposed but linked together. Yet Vaughan's thought and feeling are always centred in God and man's relation to Him, and his religious awareness of the Many gives reality and positive direction to his quest of the One; 'That *One*' who 'made all these lesser lights' is also, for erring man, the 'one, who never changes, Thy God, thy life, thy Cure'. 'The World', which begins with such casual sublimity, as one might say 'I saw John Brown the other night', and which is encircled by 'the Ring', is for the most part a melancholy picture of earth-bound, deluded man. Vaughan's understanding of human waywardness and weakness, his orthodox faith and moral effort, do not dull his feeling for the mystery and wonder of life but do prevent his losing himself in either soft idealism or naturalism; his moments of intense contemplative vision are not moments of auto-intoxication or escape. Much modern criticism has tried to make Vaughan a Hermeticist (and some of his poetry can be illustrated by Hermetic glosses), but he was drawing on a rich and multiform tradition that fed such contemporaries as Browne and John Smith and, in his Platonic poems, Henry More. And the Neoplatonic radiance that is distinctive in some of his best pieces would not be what it is if it were not fused with a Pauline and Augustinian conviction of sin, with evangelical faith and practical piety.

Whatever his spiritual and poetical debt to Herbert and others, Vaughan had in some sense to create his own way of writing. A poet of his creed, temperament, and experience was virtually committed to the emblematic mode, whether in the form of a single pure emblem ('The Waterfall') or a generally allegorical or symbolic theme and texture. This mode, conspicuous in Herbert, was of course very attractive to the earlier seventeenth century—though it did not make Vaughan popular. His great subject is exalted but not, in its main lines, abstruse. Mystical language and metaphor can harbour apparent contradictions (usually resolved, however, by the context): thus God is both white light and dazzling darkness, and both light and darkness may be associated with the trivial busyness or positive evil of life and also with divine illumination. The most pervasive and important element in Vaughan is biblical allusion and symbol, and these, in our day, are often not readily grasped. The reader is confronted at the outset by what is perhaps Vaughan's only difficult poem, 'Regeneration', a poem which has affinities with writers so diverse as St. John of the Cross and Wither and Quarles. The main drift, Christian rebirth, is clear enough; less clear, to the uninstructed, are the several stages of the pilgrim's progress from sin to full and sanctified reception of grace. But some of the specific difficulties are in biblical images: for instance, the bright stones, which have occasioned some wild guesses, are the regenerate souls of John iii. 5 and 1 Peter ii. 5. Then, as we have seen, next to the Bible Vaughan's great source of image and symbol is nature, nature as sacramental and hieroglyphic. While Herbert's use of nature is rare and incidental (and Donne's rarer still), it is central in Vaughan, and it adds a degree of concreteness to poetry of vision which is inevitably imprecise and must employ analogy. Even a less unequal workman than Vaughan could hardly sustain the themes of immanence and transcendence at the ecstatic pitch, and Vaughan can not only sink, he can be flat, diffuse, and slipshod in form and style. But although relatively few poems are perfect wholes (like 'The Morning-watch' or 'The Night'), in these and in many lines and passages, the vital gold shot from an unthrift sun, Vaughan is a unique voice. And, while he shares colloquial speech and rhythm with Herbert and others, unlike them—and like his own hills and valleys—he can 'into singing break'.

Thomas Traherne (1637–74) is in some ways very nearly akin to Vaughan, although in one essential he is quite remote.[1] Most of his important writings in verse and prose were first printed in 1903 and 1908. Those who think that his fame has shone somewhat the brighter for being belated would not deny his authentic lustre and significance. Traherne has all the excited urgency of a man who has been vouchsafed a spiritual revelation which he must share. The gradual process of his discovery, or rediscovery, of the true way of life is vividly set forth in the autobiographical third *Century*. His whole quest and message are comprised in 'felicity', of which he had found the magical secret in himself and in nature, in the Bible and in philosophy. Childlike innocence, love, and joy are man's natural endowment, but if that 'first Light' is lost, as in the unnatural course of common life it well may be, it can be regained. Man can recover his primal, God-like state by shunning the false aims and values of the world and by cleaving to the simple, universal, incorruptible things, the goodness and glory of God, mankind, and all creation, the 'illimited feild of Varietie and Beauty' in earth and sky and sea, flowers and grains of sand, 'Orient and Immortal Wheat', and 'Especialy Ones self', the whole outer and inner world in which God is daily revealed to those who love and seek Him. Thus reborn in love and 'the Highest Reason', man ceases to be a distracted, futile creature and is filled with beatific power, peace, and happiness. Through his soul and his senses he reigns in communion with God, and his life here and now links Eden with eternity.

The *Centuries of Meditations* are generally ranked above the poems, since it is the poet who is chiefly given to prosaic stumbling and incoherent diffuseness, but the two portions of his work are as like in substance and manner as prose and verse can be. Both prose and verse are all 'News', a series of mainly lyrical variations on Traherne's one great theme. The briefest account of it may suggest close kinship with Vaughan, and the

[1] Traherne, the son of a Hereford shoemaker, was educated, probably by a well-to-do relative, at Brasenose College, Oxford (B.A., 1656; M.A., 1661; B.D., 1669). In 1657 he was presented to the living of Credenhill in Herefordshire but was not instituted until 1661. During 1669–74, years of active writing, he was chaplain to Sir Orlando Bridgeman, who was Lord Keeper from 1667 to 1672 and who retired to his house at Teddington (near Hampton Court), where Traherne died. Manuscripts of the poems and *Centuries* first turned up in a London bookstall in 1896–7 and were printed in modernized form by Bertram Dobell, who discovered their authorship.

two have some instincts in common, though the list of essential differences is on the whole a list of Traherne's defects. His normal prose is less angular and muscular than Vaughan's and has a winning candour and simplicity; in its higher flights it often reminds one of the florid rhapsodist Peter Sterry. Traherne's poetry is, artistically, like a bright fountain crossed with bars of shadow. In verse a concern for direct expression, a deliberate avoidance of 'curling Metaphors' and 'painted Eloquence' was not enough, and far less often than Vaughan was Traherne able to roll all his sweetness up into one ball.

The undisciplined quality of his verse reflects the undisciplined quality of his temperament and his religious experience. Vaughan, though here and there he touches men like his brother and Boehme, stops short of 'enthusiasm'. Traherne does not. He is 'all Light and Life and Love' and, instead of being a sad and sober alien, he exuberantly possesses the glorious earth. When we dip into Traherne we find pure refreshment, even inspiration, in his ardent love of God and goodness, his exaltation of the divinity of man, his unspoiled faculty of wonder and joy, his eager and sensitive apprehension of common and unregarded beauty, and perhaps we should be grateful for that and not ask for more. The trouble is, for some readers, that even these positive qualities lose something of their virtue in the absence of others.

Traherne was of course a devout Christian and Anglican and he did not apparently perceive how far the Christian centre of gravity could shift in himself. He writes, in all sincerity, about sin, but one does not feel that evil to him is a reality, an inescapable fact of life and religion. And that blind spot in his 'Infant-Ey' explains both the strength and the weakness of his work. Whatever spiritual trials Traherne had gone through before he won felicity, in his ecstatic writings he seems to be far removed from the inward struggles of the troubled Donne, the passionate and choleric Herbert, the 'proud and humorous' Vaughan, even the supposedly serene Browne who has Lucifer and the battle of Lepanto raging within him—or we might think of the ardours and torments of Gerard Manley Hopkins. Traherne enjoys 'the Hony even without the Stings'. He was a master of philosophical learning, and in his *Roman Forgeries* and much richer *Christian Ethics* he showed an awareness of the world

of men (in the latter book of Hobbes), yet in the poems and
Centuries his mind and nature seem to have little edge or toughness. Neither as Christian nor as philosopher does Traherne
seem quite mature; he hardly graduates from songs of innocence
to songs of experience. There is a great difference between him
and the Cambridge Platonists with whom he is often linked;
they are predominantly rational and ethical and have a sober
sense of sin. Behind Traherne's very genuine spiritual (and
sensuous) fervour we may feel a degree of poverty and monotony, a lack of true religious humility, a large element of facile,
expansive, emotional optimism, the kind of optimism which in
the next generations passed easily into deistic sentimentalism
and vague aspiration towards infinity.

We drop back, chronologically and poetically, to take account
of Edward Benlowes (1602–76).[1] Although *Theophila* (1652), as
a 'Heroick Poem' of 'Spiritual Warfare', belongs with the works
of Joseph Beaumont and Henry More, it represents metaphysical
religious poetry *in excelsis* and *in extremis*. In style Benlowes is the
Cleveland—or the Urquhart—of 'divine and Christian Poesie'.
Oppressed by the sway of atheism and sin 'in this Dotage of the
World' and by national strife, he sought to awaken man's sense
of himself as 'the Image of his Maker', above the beasts and
just below the angels. His poem pictures the soul's ascent to
God 'By Humilitie, by Zeal, by Contemplation', by the three
mystical ways, 'Purgative, Illuminative, and Unitive'. Benlowes
can be very moving in his religious and philosophic vision of
life as a point between eternities of space and time and between
Nature and Grace, of the soul's triumph over 'the World, Hell,
and her own Corruptions' and of her ecstatic union with the
One. But the poetic eagle whom Davenant saluted flies too near
the sun:

---

[1] Benlowes, the heir of a wealthy Catholic family, went from Cambridge to
Lincoln's Inn. By 1627 he had turned Protestant. After a grand tour of two years
(1627–9) he settled on his Essex estate as squire and cultivator of poetry and the
arts. He encouraged or helped such writers as Phineas Fletcher, Quarles, Alexander
Ross, James Howell, and Fuller; another poet-friend was Mildmay Fane, and
Theophila was praised by two other small poets whom we met above, Pestell and
Philipot. Benlowes's various benefactions, heavy parliamentary fines (before and
especially after his slight share in the second civil war, 1648), the burning of his
house in 1653, and prolonged litigation (1657–67), reduced him by degrees to
poverty. But in his last years of reading and writing at Oxford 'the most helpless
creature in the world' (as Dr. John Fell described him) was not altogether
unhappy.

> Heav'ns Paths are traceless, by Excess of Light;
> O're-fulgent Beams daz'd Eyes benight.
> Say Ephata, and Clay's Collyrium for my Sight!

Though Benlowes as a captain of horse was said (by Samuel
Butler, to be sure) to have given allegorical names to his
accoutrements, he can affirm partly Hobbesian principles:

> Now 'tis Judgement begets the Strength, Invention the Ornaments
> of a Poem; both These joyn'd form Wit, which is the Agility of
> Spirits: Vivacity of Fancie in a florid Style disposeth Light and
> Life to a Poem, wherein the Masculine and refined Pleasures
> of the Understanding transcend the feminine and sensual of the Eye:
> From the Excellencie of Fancie proceed grateful Similies, apt Meta-
> phors, &c.

The alarming hints in this are more than borne out in the text.
Benlowes has all the metaphysical qualities, homely realism
and far-fetched learning, general and scientific, indubitable
'wit', intensity of thought and feeling; but with a basic texture
resembling that of Donne's *Anniversaries* are blended such other
elements as emblematic epigrams, the excited staccato of traditional satire, and something of Crashaw's baroque lusciousness.
He becomes grotesque because of his peculiar vocabulary and
syntax ('Poets have Legislative Pow'r of making Words'), his
constant, sudden, and violent juxtaposition of images, and his
complete lack of 'Judgement'. There is hardly a stanza in the
long poem that is not vivid, hardly one that is not more or less
odd, and the reader who finishes the soul's quest of grace and
glory feels as if he had been riding on the rims over an endless
timber bridge. Granting the difficulties of the mystic who 'doth
Inexpressibles expresse', we may say, with appropriate exaggeration, that Benlowes is every other inch a poet. As a sample of
his non-mystical best, this might be set beside Nashe and
Marvell:

> Deaths Serjeant soon thy courted Helens must
>   Attach, whose Eyes, now Orbs of Lust,
> The Worms shall feed on, till they crumble into Dust.

One of Benlowes's marked characteristics is the 'conveying',
with little or no change, of phrases and longer bits from other
writers. It is not perhaps a surprise that he borrows from
Jonson and Randolph and Quarles, from Donne's 'Hymn to

Christ', *Second Anniversary*, and sermons, from Cleveland(among other things the first line of 'To Fuscara'), and that, in drawing upon Sylvester, he uses twice the notorious image of the peri-wigged woods; but it is a surprise, in this poem and at this date, to find some forty echoes of Milton, nearly half of these from *Comus*, the rest chiefly from the 'Nativity', 'L'Allegro', 'Il Penseroso', 'On Time', and 'Lycidas'. Benlowes also lifted phrases from the English translation (1646) of 'the Polish Horace', the Jesuit Casimir, and imitated his themes.

5

As George Herbert stands at the head of the metaphysical religious poets, so his eldest brother, Lord Herbert of Cherbury (1582–1648), is the first disciple of Donne on the secular side.[1] In his elegy on Donne, where he falls far short of the critical discernment of his friend, 'my witty Carew', he testifies his admiration for his master's pregnant originality. In general, Herbert is scornful of the sensuous clichés of the 'old Poetry' of 'Our vulgar wits', and he partly reveals his own instinct when he intellectualizes traditional forms like the sonnet and madri-gal, when—unlike Carew in 'The Complement'—he turns the Italianate catalogue of the female body into a series of cosmic images, or when he adds to the chorus of lamentation for Prince Henry the elegy that led Donne to write 'Looke to mee faith' in order 'to match Sir Ed: Herbert in obscurenesse'. On the other hand, Herbert has little of Donne's personal intimacy, glancing wit, everyday realism, recondite learning, verbal and metrical power, and dramatic force. He rarely raises his voice

[1] Edward Herbert was at Oxford from 1596 to 1600 and while there married his cousin. In the following years he was a member of Parliament for Merionethshire and, in 1604–5, sheriff of his own county of Montgomery. He also frequented the court and the society of the London wits, and travelled abroad; at all times he was a student as well as man of the world. In 1619 he went to France as ambassador (with Thomas Carew in his train), and he held that post, with an interval, until 1624. He had been one of James's early flock of knights, and in 1629 he was created Baron Herbert of Cherbury. His later years were rendered unhappy by the war and ill health. He tried to keep neutral but had to surrender Montgomery Castle in 1644, and in 1645 he submitted to Parliament and received a pension. If not one of the most admirable characters of the age, he was certainly one of the most energetic, versatile, and complex. In later chapters of this volume Herbert appears as his-torian, autobiographer, and in his major role as philosopher. His poems circulated chiefly in manuscript and were not published until 1665. One defiance of the times is dated 1644, and there are other late pieces, mainly Latin, but nearly all of the English verse seems to have been written between 1608 and 1631.

above a studied and almost prosaic quietness, and his diction is
so simple that one is surprised at the effort of comprehension his
close and sometimes knotted texture requires. All these nega-
tives indicate that Herbert is not an immediately compelling
poet, in the ordinary meaning of the term. Whereas Carew's
perfectly moulded and generalized 'Ask me no more' casts such
an hypnotic spell that we hardly observe what the words mean,
the 'Elegy over a Tomb', one of Herbert's best and simplest
pieces, has the true metaphysical effect of 'unfinality', of insist-
ing that it be understood.

Herbert was unique among the metaphysical poets in being a
figure of real importance in the history of philosophy. He could
philosophize the age's sense of passing time and mortality, or
work out a satire on kingship and aristocracy with complex
boldness of thought, but most of his poetical thinking revolved
around love. Like Donne, he outdoes the Petrarchans in glorifying love and his mistress with argumentative hyperbole, but, as
we might expect of the philosopher if not of the autobiographer,
he is far more of a Platonist. Three poems called 'Platonic Love'
and one called 'The Idea' (this last written at Alnwick during
the first Bishops' War!) are only the most obvious marks of a
serious and abstract analysis of love as an avenue to knowledge,
liberty, unity, and eternity, a light in darkness, a religion, and
a mysterious magnetic force. The most elaborate and most
famous proof that there is feeling blended with Herbert's dry
cerebration is the 'Ode upon a Question Moved, Whether Love
Should Continue For Ever?', a contribution to the pastoral-
Platonic casuistry of love (a convention opposed in such anti-
Platonic 'pastorals' as those of Randolph and Carew). Donne in
'The Ecstasy' urges that love, however exalted, must express
itself by descending to the level of the body. Herbert's lover,
when his mistress fears the extinction of love in death, argues,
with Sidney's Pamela, that 'eternall causes' cannot 'bring forth
chaunceable effects', that love must transcend the limitations of
earth and time; similar ideas are philosophized in Herbert's
De Veritate. In this poem if anywhere Herbert achieves felicity
of phrase and rhythm, and his concluding image of the stars
may be mentioned along with 'Else a great Prince in prison lies'.

Henry King (1592–1669), son of the bishop who ordained
Donne, was himself the executor of his 'most dear and incomparable Friend' and wrote an elegy on that 'Rich Soul of wit

and language'.[1] He also paid elegiac tribute to Ben Jonson. One layer of King's verse includes mainly Donneish amatory wit, in both lyrical and couplet form. Another is best represented by 'Tell me no more how fair she is', in which artifice gains a Jonsonian neatness, dignity, and grace. At the top are those poems, such as 'The Legacy' and 'The Surrender', in which death or destiny inspires moods and images with something of 'that awful fire' that once burned in Donne's 'clear brain'. Of these last the great example, one of the few great elegies that are elegies, is of course 'The Exequy', on the poet's young wife. Reading his other obituary poems, which make up two-fifths of his work, we should never guess that he was quite capable of this. Donne's name is linked with it merely as a shorthand description of the poetical medium, the realistic blend of emotion and poignant wit, that was available. But it is Henry King whose love and Christian faith find utterance here. Though Donne might have conceived such a phrase as

> And a fierce Feaver must calcine
> The body of this world like thine,

it may be doubted if he could have written an elegy of such selfless devotion, such simple and suggestive clarity, such unified progression through diverse clusters of images, and such a magnificent movement:

> But heark! My Pulse like a soft Drum
> Beats my approch, tells Thee I come;
> And slow howere my marches be,
> I shall at last sit down by Thee.

The contemporary fame of John Cleveland (1613–58) was much greater even than Cowley's, and it has shrunk even more.[2]

---

[1] King was educated at Westminster and at Christ Church, Oxford (B.A., 1611; M.A., 1614). He rose through a series of preferments to the bishopric of Chichester (1642). In 1643 he was ejected and led a migratory life, in dependence on various friends, until the Restoration restored him to his see. About 1617–18 he had married Anne Berkeley, who became the mother of six children and died, 'scarce' twenty-four, about 1624. King's poems were first collected in 1657.

[2] Cleveland was the son of a Yorkshire clergyman who had moved to Leicestershire. He was a contemporary of Milton and Henry More at Christ's College, Cambridge (B.A., 1631; M.A., 1635). He became a fellow of St. John's (1634) and a Reader in Rhetoric. In 1640 he opposed the election of Cromwell as M.P. for Cambridge. In 1643, apparently, he retired to Oxford, though not formally ejected from his fellowship until 1645. As judge-advocate at Newark (1645–6), he held that town against the Scots. For some years thereafter he moved about in dependence

His name now calls up the bee that

> tipples Palmestry, and dines
> On all her Fortune-telling Lines,

the doom of a Scottish Cain, and perhaps several characters in prose, two of them on London 'diurnals', which mark the adaptation of a popular genre to political uses. In the seventeenth century there was a large audience not merely for the author of the dazzling 'Fuscara' and the genial 'Mark Antony' but for the royalist wit and satirist *par excellence*, the gadfly of Presbyterians and shirtless Scots. While the poetry of Milton, Crashaw, Vaughan, King, and even Lovelace failed to sell, Cleveland received an almost unanimous chorus of eulogy and went through some twenty editions, editions often swollen with that final kind of tribute, the products of other men's 'Clevelandism'. The war, in raising Cleveland's royalist fervour and satirical ferocity to boiling-point, gave him as a poet one deep emotion. He would scarcely have been heard of if he had only continued the serious extravagance of the elegy on Edward King. In his amatory verse, apart from the subdued piquancy and fresh charm of 'Upon Phillis', Cleveland surpassed all strong-lined men in weaving complex tissues of the prettily or boisterously fantastic. 'His Epithetes', says Fuller in 1662, in one of his few useful summaries of critical opinion,

were pregnant with Metaphors, carrying in them a difficult plainness, difficult at the hearing, plain at the considering thereof. His lofty Fancy may seem to stride from the top of one Mountain to the top of another, so making to it self a constant Level and Champian of continued Elevations.

Cleveland has no feeling but the joy of the game and, as *l'homme moyen sensuel*, he can turn the hose of common sense or mockery upon the idealistic sparks of the cavalier and metaphysical tradition. His far-fetched and twisted wit might be condemned by Dryden, but his robust levity and irreverence helped to form the spirit of the Restoration, most obviously of course through his friend and disciple, Samuel Butler.

on friends. During 1647–9 he apparently had a hand in *Mercurius Pragmaticus* and perhaps in other journals. In 1655–6 he suffered a short imprisonment at Yarmouth, on vague charges, and was released after a manly appeal to Cromwell. He died at Gray's Inn. The first edition of his poems appeared in 1647.

The metaphysical impulse might seem to have had its death-throes in Cleveland, but it had a euthanasia in Abraham Cowley (1618–67), who carried his personal charm and fame into the fairly congenial age of the Restoration.[1] Yet after 1700 Cowley's great lustre somewhat faded among the critical, and he was foreordained to hold an eminence both bad and good at the head of Johnson's *Lives of the Poets*. He was one of the few men who felt all three of the major influences in poetry, Spenser, Jonson, and Donne. *Poetical Blossoms* (1633) was the work of a boy who had been enchanted by Spenser and knew other Elizabethans (including Golding); this astonishingly precocious volume was enlarged and reached a third edition in 1637. At Cambridge Cowley wrote three plays, a pastoral he had begun at school, a Latin comedy, and *The Guardian* (1642), which was revamped as *Cutter of Coleman Street*. In 1643 he discharged a vigorous broadside, *The Puritan and the Papist*. He paid part of his tribute to Donne in *The Mistress* (1647). The *Poems* of 1656 contained 'Miscellanies' (among these were 'Of Wit', the elegies on Hervey and Crashaw, the gay 'Chronicle' of mistresses, and the Anacreontics), *The Mistress*, the Pindaric odes, and the unfinished religious epic *Davideis*, which provided a main text for the important preface. Some more verse and the familiar essays appeared in 1663 and 1668.

The essays have been enjoyed since the early eighteenth century, and in recent decades Cowley the poet has, at a distance, followed the great metaphysicals back into favour. He

[1] Cowley, a middle-class Londoner, was educated at Westminster (1628?–36) and Trinity College, Cambridge (1636–43). He became a fellow in 1640. Among his Cambridge friends were Crashaw, whom he later assisted in Paris, and especially William Hervey (d. 1642). Like Crashaw, Cowley anticipated his ejection and early in 1643 repaired to the court at Oxford. During 1644?–54 he was in France as secretary to Jermyn and the queen and he went on several missions as a royalist agent. He returned to England in 1654, was imprisoned in 1655, and on his release took up the study of medicine (M.D., Oxford, 1657). The preface to his *Poems* of 1656 contained some words on submission to authority which were not to be forgotten, and it remains uncertain whether, as Sprat said, Cowley had been masking continued royalist activity or had been really convinced of the necessity and wisdom of accepting the Cromwellian régime. In 1659–60 he was again in France. After the Restoration he was reinstated in his fellowship and given land by Queen Henrietta, a reward possibly commensurate with what seemed his dubious loyalty but not with his hopes. Henceforth he led a retired life at Barn Elms and Chertsey, busy with books and botany and writing his familiar essays. He had been one of the first men nominated for the Royal Society but, though interested in its work, he did not become a fellow. Cowley's funeral was more splendid than any mere man of letters had received before.

deserves critical respect, for he was a very clever, versatile, learned, self-conscious, and serious artist, a mirror, if not a profound interpreter, of the new rationalism of the English and the European mind. It is characteristic of both his nature and his position that in him the Christian humanist was not extinguished by the scientific modernist, nor metaphysical wit by neoclassical good sense. He remains a writer of more interest to the student of intellectual and literary history than to the reader of poetry. Much of his work suffers from lack of intensity, from both prosaic flatness and oratorical magniloquence, and from the incessant play of unfelt and uncontrolled wit, wit that is more tangential and coolly analytical than dynamic and passionate. As we go through the eighty-four poems of *The Mistress* we may admire the endless ingenuity employed to embroider the prescribed themes of metaphysical and cavalier lovers, but we seldom have any other reaction. Donne's fever of the bone has become a case of measles. If any poem makes an impression, it is 'Against Hope', and that is not mainly amatory. Unlike most other men of the age, Cowley offers no inevitable pieces to the anthologist. Roman influence is stronger in him than in any of the metaphysical amorists, though Ovid may only have encouraged rhetoric and antithetical conceits. But when Cowley 'Translated Paraphrastically' some Anacreontic poems, his wit was restrained by his model and his want of depth was an advantage, so that he produced charming cameos of vivacious neatness. In later paraphrases of Martial and others the same quality appeared, with some dilution. In temper, of course, Cowley was supremely Horatian.

The innocently and happily epicurean poet had an itch to be 'the Muses Hannibal'; the Alps of the religious epic he essayed in *Davideis*, but that can best be treated along with other things of its kind. The odes, Pindaric and miscellaneous, constitute the most impressive portion of Cowley's work. Beginning with free translation of Pindar, he went on to imitation; though not the first English imitator, he created the genre for the next hundred years and more. Cowley was much too good a scholar to be ignorant of the Pindaric structure, but he wished to develop a looser form suited to the English genius, and he recognized, more clearly than many turgid followers, that the 'Pindarique Pegasus' 'flings Writer and Reader too that sits not sure'. The interest of the odes varies between the topical and the

poetical. 'Brutus', which could not fail to be related to Cromwell, was not quite cancelled out by the *Vision* of 1661. The
celebration of Hobbes's overthrow of the Stagirite is a poem,
since Cowley can be stirred by ideas, and the ode is one obvious
clue to his absorption, however incomplete his grasp, of recent
thought. 'Life' begins on the Hobbesian level but rises higher.
Determinism appears in 'Destiny'. Cowley was destined to
celebrate the Royal Society, and his last grandiose ode is an
historical document that lives chiefly in the image of Bacon as
the Moses of the new science denied admission to the promised
land, an image, by the way, which the poet had earlier applied
to 'Reason. The Use of It in Divine Matters'. In these and other
more or less ambitious odes there are bits of noble thinking and
writing, yet hardly any poem stands out as compelling or completely good. The once admiring Dryden came to see that
Cowley 'cou'd never forgive any Conceit which came in his
way; but swept like a Drag-net, great and small'. Here, as in
most of his work, 'nimble-footed Wit' is joined with 'smooth-
pac'ed Eloquence', but 'strong Judgment' is not always in command of 'unruly Phansie'. For one of many illustrations there is
the fantastic and prolonged mythological conceit which opens
the ode 'Upon Dr. Harvey', though the poem settles down into
a sober eulogy of science. The elegies on William Hervey and
Crashaw have the exaltation of the odes, or rather more than
that, thanks to the unwonted strength of deep feeling. The
poet's mind is almost purged of artifice as he recalls the high
soul of his 'dearest Friend' and their days and nights of intellectual companionship. The elegy on Crashaw, after the fine
and famous beginning, lapses—if it is a lapse—into literary
criticism akin to the preface of 1656, but soon soars up again
in an impassioned Anglican tribute to the Catholic poet and
saint. There is emotion also, of a different kind, in the late
'Hymn. To Light'. Cowley is not, like Vaughan, contemplating
the white radiance of eternity so much as the dome of many-
coloured glass. As country gentleman and as virtuoso, and in
a mood both serious and happy, he enjoys 'All the Worlds
bravery that delights our Eyes'.

  Two odes, 'The Muse' and 'Of Wit', are critical essays in
verse which almost epitomize the poetical evolution of Cowley's
age, the shrinking of a large, deep, and lofty vision of poetry
and life into an ideal of rational congruity and decorum. And

Cowley himself reflects part of the process. In real metaphysical poetry wit and feeling were fused by the heat and pressure of inner tension; they remained separate and relatively shallow and narrow in Cowley, whose cool critical temper was still further cooled by Hobbesian rationalism. The poet was an essayist in more than his essays. He was not born for exile and secret service but for a time of moderation and security; and in spite of his troubles and his constitutional melancholy—'When all's done, Life is an Incurable Disease'—one would hardly guess from a cursory glance at his writings that he had ever been driven from an academic retreat. Instead of being a poet who wrestled with experience Cowley was a man of letters who produced 'literature' for a social group. In most of his mature work he was both the enfeebled grandson of Donne and the enfeebled grandfather of Dryden. 'Not being of God, he could not stand.'

While the great religious poets, after Herbert, were not strictly heirs of Donne, and secular wit ran more or less to seed in Cleveland and Cowley, the finest flower of secular and serious metaphysical poetry was Andrew Marvell (1621–78).[1] Marvell developed such a variety of gifts and attitudes that it is not easy to say which of several poets he chiefly is. He combines a fresh, muscular, agile, subtle, and ironic metaphysical wit and the disciplined rationality, clarity, impersonality, economy, and structural and stylistic sense of a classical artist, the cultured, easy grace of a cavalier and the religious and moral earnestness of a Puritan Platonist, a feeling for nature both spontaneous and

---

[1] Marvell's father was a clergyman, 'facetious, yet Calvinistical', who in 1624 became preacher and master of the alms-house at Hull and was drowned in 1641; his devoted life received the praise of Fuller. From 1633 to 1641, as undergraduate and then as Scholar of Trinity, Marvell was at Cambridge, the Cambridge of Cowley and Crashaw, John Sherman and Whichcote. He had a brief Catholic phase and was recalled to Anglicanism by his father. From 1642 to 1646 he travelled abroad, perhaps as a tutor. During 1651–2 he was tutor to Lord Fairfax's daughter at Nun Appleton House in Yorkshire, where much of his best poetry was presumably written. He had sympathized with the king and the king's cause, but he passed from acceptance to admiration of Cromwell. In 1653 he became tutor to a ward of Cromwell's; this post took him to Eton—in 1656 to France—and led to a valued acquaintance with Hales. During 1657–9 he was a colleague of Milton (now much less active as Secretary for Foreign Tongues to the Council of State), who had strongly recommended him in 1653. According to Edward Phillips it was Marvell who protected Milton at the Restoration. As member for Hull, Marvell served in Parliament, with exemplary zeal and probity, from 1659 until his death. His political satire of this period lies beyond our limits. None of Marvell's important early poems was printed in his lifetime. The first collection was published in 1681, ostensibly by his widow, though she was a legal fiction.

philosophic and a high tragic intensity in poems of love; and to all themes and moods he brings a simple but flexibly expressive suppleness of rhythm, in the short couplet and in other forms. In some of these qualities, and in his response to the claims of both contemplative solitude and public affairs, Marvell, though much more detached, has a degree of affinity with his friend Milton, whose early poems he was among the first to echo and to whose epic he paid homage in 1674. We assume a general debt to Donne and Donne's disciples, though actual resemblances are few, and perhaps a small and partly negative one to such poets of *solitude* and *jouissance* as Saint-Amant; other tinctures in his elixir are implied in his praise of Lovelace and Jonson. Spenser is one representative of some larger affinities, of religious and Neoplatonic attitudes towards nature and art, flux and order—and possibly he affected particulars (e.g. 'the three fork'd Lightning' of the 'Horatian Ode' and *The Fairy Queen*, i. viii. 9). The general elements, classical and metaphysical, continental and English, epicurean and Puritan, civilized and simple, are mingled in varying proportions in Marvell's poems and are not necessarily harmonized, unless in his style—and even that varies with his themes. The Christian and the Platonist are not very close to the passionate lover, nor the poet of gardens to the political commentator; and 'The Coronet', with its quietly interwoven antitheses between thorns and poetic garlands, divine humility and human pride, is a religious sacrifice of all poetry. But to speak of unharmonized attitudes is only one way of recognizing the balanced, impersonal complexity of mind that distinguishes individual poems. Also, perhaps even more than most poets of his age, Marvell is actively and obviously aware of the different demands of different genres—which is not a reflection upon his sincerity.

The 'Horatian Ode upon Cromwell's Return from Ireland' (1650) stands apart from the body of early lyrical pieces. Like all Marvell's major poems, this has been much analysed of late years, and disagreements about the poet's view of Cromwell would seem to attest that balanced complexity of mind just referred to. In 1681, when the poems were printed, there was no problem; the ode was too much of a tribute to the regicide to be included. Some points may be thought indisputable: that Marvell, sharing his period's providential conception of history, sees Cromwell as an austere patriot of the early Roman breed, a Cincinnatus, who becomes the irresistible instrument of 'angry Heaven' for the renewal of the nation; that the man of power and destiny must go on to subdue alien enemies of the new republic; that, at the same time, his casting of 'the Kingdome old Into another Mold' involved violent if unavoidable breaks with a hallowed past; and that, set over against the man of action, 'the Royal Actor' played his last scene with royal dignity. But while there can be no doubt concerning Marvell's support here (as in later poems) of Cromwell as a heaven-sent leader, a bald summary cannot show how his suggestive phrases weigh opposed causes, motives, and acts. Still less can a brief comment show that this is the only English poem, except some of Milton's sonnets, in which the tone of Horace's heroic odes is recaptured with original strength, sinewy Latin conciseness being quickened by 'wit'; or how significant in the total effect is the maintaining of Roman decorum. Marvell's pictures of both Cromwell and Charles are coloured by Lucan's accounts of Caesar and Pompey, especially in the translation by the Tom May on whose death (1650) he wrote a satire.

'A Dialogue between the Resolved Soul and Created Pleasure' and 'A Dialogue between the Soul and the Body' have long traditions behind them. The former, a miniature oratorio, recalls the ancient fable of Hercules, Pleasure, and Virtue, and many Renaissance writings, from the second book of *The Fairy Queen* and Daniel's 'Ulysses and the Siren' to *Comus* and Cowley's 'The Soul'. Of the second 'Dialogue' the famous predecessor is the Middle-English 'Debate'; a more obscure one is *Querela . . . The Complaint or Dialogue, Betwixt The Soule and the Bodie of a damned man; Each laying the fault upon the other* (1616), translated by Rev. William Crashaw, Richard's father. Marvell's 'Resolved Soul', like Spenser's Red Cross Knight, has the armour of a Christian soldier (Ephesians vi) and easily repels the allurements of the five senses (the points of attack in Spenser's House of Alma—and in 'Upon Appleton House', xxxvi). More fully characteristic of Marvell are the concentrated paradoxes and ironies exchanged between the flesh-imprisoned soul and the soul-ridden body; the body's claims, if tacitly denied, are presented with full force, and it has the last word. The poem might be called Marvell's version of the antinomies of the human condition summed up in Fulke Greville's much-quoted lines. 'On a Drop of Dew' treats a kindred theme, though almost wholly from one side, and with lyrical delicacy of phrase and hovering variations of rhythm. This is in structure and substance a clear-cut 'emblem', somewhat like Vaughan's less sophisticated 'Waterfall': as the drop of dew, poised insecurely on the flower, is absorbed by the sun, the soul, 'that Ray Of the clear Fountain of Eternal Day', 'recollecting its own Light', maintains its purity until it is drawn back to its heavenly home. Here the corruptions of the world are represented chiefly by 'sweat leaves and blossoms green', and the phrase leads us into the group of poems in which nature is more or less central and is seen in more than one aspect, sensuous, ethical, or emblematic; it is commonly an image of ideal innocent perfection or order, or both.

We may look first at the long, perhaps over-long, 'Upon Appleton House', which stands in contrast with the neoclassical sobriety of *Cooper's Hill* of a decade earlier. Both poets make topography a vehicle for historical and philosophical reflection, but Marvell takes up other themes as well and has, of course, a livelier perceptiveness and a wider range of particular reference, from 'The hatching Thrastles shining Eye' to 'The Circle in the Quadrature' and *Gondibert*. The Fairfax estate, once the home of nuns, is now identified with the retired life of the parliamentary general—who himself translated Saint-Amant's *La Solitude*—and his young daughter, the poet's tutorial charge. This island of pastoral peace and cultivation is a microcosmic symbol of pre-war England, 'The Garden of the World ere while', and Mary Fairfax becomes more of a symbolic figure than a little girl. Marvell's wit plays, with mingled lightness and seriousness, upon the ways of man and, in a happy passage that parallels 'The Garden', upon his own secure and easy intimacy with birds and trees. His reading 'in Natures mystick Book' stops well on this side of Vaughan and Traherne and Sir Thomas Browne, but he has his own version of the traditional concept of nature as the art of God.

Marvell's concern with nature, and his poetic art, are distilled in 'Bermudas', the 'Mower' poems, 'The Picture of little T. C. in a Prospect of Flowers', and above all in 'The Garden'. In 'Bermudas' the tropical luxuriance of an island paradise is rendered with such clean yet magical strokes—God Himself was the provider and decorative artist—that it becomes a fit Puritan temple 'where to sound his Name', the very home of primitive

Christianity, and the music of 'An holy and a chearful Note' is as simple as the chime of the falling oars. (In addition to Psalm civ, Marvell may have re-created items from the chromatograph at the beginning of Waller's 'Battle of the Summer Islands', or from Captain John Smith's *General History of Virginia*, or he may have drawn upon the Bermudan memories of his Eton host, John Oxenbridge, or he may have got hints from a source mentioned in the next chapter.) In the 'Mower' poems Marvell's feelings are not deeply engaged, and his wit is more playful than plaintive, but he touches a serious theme: man's mind, which once reflected the harmonious unity of nature, has been divided and disturbed by love, and his quest of artificial luxury has corrupted nature's 'wild and fragrant Innocence'. The Mower with his scythe, who replaces the pastoral shepherd, is himself a destroyer, and a symbol of time and death. In the 'Picture of little T. C.', complex *vers de société* in a floral setting, the carefree child, a 'Nimph' who is at home in the nature she seems to rule (though she cannot make it ideally perfect), will grow up to conquer that part of nature represented by man and love—or she may not grow up, if nature should turn cruel.

'The Garden', for all its speed and air of lyric slightness, carries rich implications (not to speak of those foisted into it by critics); it is much less simple than Marvell's Latin version *Hortus*. The poem is linked in different ways with at least two current European traditions, the especially Horatian praise of rural solitude and content, and the libertine celebration of sexual license as an element of a primitive, pastoral Golden Age (examples of the latter are Daniel's translation from Tasso and Carew's 'A Rapture'). Marvell's poem far transcends the often tame conventionalities of the first tradition and implicitly and explicitly repudiates the conventional immorality of the second; and his detached, ironic intelligence is in full control of an argument to which his heart is committed. He turns away from worldly ambitions to glorify the quiet and innocence of the garden, a heaven on earth; from love and sex to nature and the sublimation of desire in art; and from merely voluptuous delight in abundant fruits to the greater happiness of the contemplative and creative mind,

> Annihilating all that's made
> To a green Thought in a green Shade.

In the climactic stage or metamorphosis, his disembodied soul
glides like a bird into a tree,

> And, till prepar'd for longer flight,
> Waves in its Plumes the various Light.

Then he returns, by way of Eden, to the actual garden, but with
a new acceptance of time and earthly life as more fully understood in a rational, imaginative, and religious perspective. The
theme and the evolution of the poem invite a comparison with
Keats's 'Ode to a Nightingale' that would reveal much about
two poets and two ages. Here one can only say that 'The
Garden' displays the perfect blending of the classical artist and
the metaphysical wit. The two couplets quoted are examples:
in the first, Virgil's pastoral *viridi umbra* is translated into metaphysical dimensions; in the second, the contrast between heaven
and earth is rendered in spare but recognizably Christian-
Platonic terms (examples range from *Phaedrus* 249D onward).

'The Nymph Complaining for the Death of her Fawn', though
quite distinctive in tone and story, has the relatively soft pathos
and diffuseness associated with the pastoral genre, and has partial affinities with many things from Virgil (an episode in
Aeneid vii) and other ancients to William Browne's *Britannia's
Pastorals*. The poem is related to themes already encountered—
the innocence of nature and girlhood, the corruption of man—
and may be left at that; implications of religious allegory, discerned by some critics in some passages, have been increasingly
rejected in favour of a literal (though not simple) reading.

Other aspects of nature and love appear in two very different
poems. 'The Definition of Love' might have started, though
Marvell's antitheses of steel are his own, from Cowley's 'Impossibilities', or from the complaint of Sidney's love-stricken Philo-
clea, who appeals to the influence of the stars and laments that,
whereas in others hope kindles love, 'in me despaire should be
the bellowes of my affection; and of all despaires the most
miserable, which is drawen from impossibilitie'. On Marvell's
as on other metaphysical lovers 'Loves whole World . . . doth
wheel', and the paradoxical argument utilizes precise cosmic
images which, welded and ordered with classical symmetry,
attain something like grandeur. The fusion of the two modes is
exemplified in the joining of the philosophical paradox, 'my
extended Soul' (Cartesian dualism distinguished *res cogitans* from

res extensa), with Horace's iron wedges of Fate (an image used by a number of poets of Marvell's age). This is Marvell's only major lyric that reminds us of Donne, and it is not very Donne-like in its taut structure and high abstract tone.

'To his Coy Mistress' proclaims its origin in one of the most familiar of classical and Renaissance traditions, that of *carpe diem*, but Marvell's re-creation would provide a fair definition of metaphysical poetry. In the great body of Petrarchan sonnets, and in the lyrics from Anacreon and Theocritus down to Marlowe and Jonson and Herrick, Carew and Cleveland and Cowley (whose 'My Diet', with its tracts of years and 'vast Eternity', may have been in Marvell's mind), the 'persuasion to love', whether sober or sportive, generally moved on one plane. But when seriousness has gone as far as it can, it can be both heightened and restrained by self-mocking irony. In Marvell's first paragraph emotion is so interpenetrated with apparent levity that hyperbole, being hypothetical, becomes rational. More concretely and gaily than in the sombre 'Definition of Love', the poet sees the whole world of space and time as the setting for two lovers. But wit cannot sustain the pretence that youth and beauty and love are immortal, and with a quick change of tone—like Catullus's *nobis cum semel occidit brevis lux* or Horace's *sed Timor et Minae*—the theme of time and death is developed with serious and soaring directness, until wit takes over to weave its antitheses of macabre irony. (Among many variations on his ancient text, one wonders if Marvell remembered Herbert's 'Church-Monuments'—'How tame these ashes are, how free from lust'.) In the third paragraph traditional directness soon gives way again to bold metaphysical images, expressive now of consummated love's triumph over time. Throughout, the most complex reverberations are set up by simple words in a simple pattern and a simple tune, a tune carried, to be sure, with Marvell's peculiar *brio*. And throughout the syllogistic argument, emotional intensity and ironic wit are under such control that the lyric possesses a cavalier elegance and poise, beyond the cavalier level.

Marvell's unique quality and his chronological position—his best poems seem to have been mostly written in 1650-3—might appear to contradict what the names of Cleveland and Cowley imply, and might suggest that metaphysical poetry could have had a second birth. But the poet's own career is itself proof of

the radical change in the climate which had nourished the
metaphysical genius; the nature of the change is partly indicated in the rest of this chapter and in the later chapters on
science and religion and heroic verse. Marvell's satirical instinct
had appeared, not very happily, at the very beginning—his first
victim was that *corpus vile*, Richard Flecknoe—and it ultimately
extinguished the metaphysical. The heir of Donne became, as
political satirist, the chief heir of Cleveland, the admirer of
Rochester, and, in spite of mutual dislike, the father of Dryden.

6

This chapter has been concerned with two of the three principal currents in poetry, and of these two the more conspicuous
was the metaphysical. It is of course far more distinct to us
than it was in the seventeenth century, when many men were
loosely credited with wit and learning or 'strong lines'. Even
Dryden's later censures took in only Donne and the notorious
Cowley and Cleveland. Carew, and Crashaw's English poems,
had only one edition after 1660; Herbert's popularity was more
pious than poetical; Vaughan was almost, and Traherne quite,
unknown; and Marvell's early poems, when printed in 1681,
were overshadowed by his satires. Apart from Carew's early
elegy on Donne, there was not much critical appreciation of the
qualities we prize. On the other hand, increasing distaste for
extravagance was coupled with increasing esteem for the virtues
represented by the mediocre pair who happened to lead the
return to the main tradition of European neoclassicism, 'those
Standard-bearers of Wit and Judgment, Denham and Waller',
in the phrase of Alexander Brome. If Milton's full poetic fruition
had not been postponed, he might have been the standard-
bearer. As it was, the classicism of Waller and Denham was
only the ghost of Jonson's. Yet Dryden, himself a true heir of
Renaissance humanism, often and generously acknowledged
his age's debt to the Dioscuri:

But the Excellence and Dignity of it [rhyme], were never fully
known till Mr. Waller taught it; He first made Writing easily an
Art: First shew'd us to conclude the Sense, most commonly, in
Distichs; which in the Verse of those before him, runs on for so many
Lines together, that the Reader is out of Breath to overtake it. This
sweetness of Mr. Wallers Lyrick Poesie was afterwards follow'd in
the Epick by Sir John Denham, in his Coopers-Hill: a Poem which

your Lordship knows for the Majesty of the Style, is, and ever will be the exact Standard of good Writing.

Dryden and others were not wholly unaware that the smoothing process had begun before Waller and Denham, and Waller himself, Dryden recorded, looked back to Fairfax as his master. In addition to Fairfax a crowd of poets contributed more or less to the development of the closed and balanced couplet, for instance, Marlowe, Sylvester, Heywood, Drayton, Hall, Sir John Beaumont, Drummond, Jonson, George Sandys, Henry King, who praised Sandys and could sound an Augustan note himself, Lord Falkland, Godolphin, Cartwright, and others. As some of these names suggest, much reflective, occasional, and commendatory verse took this form. Many of the names represent translation, especially from Latin and from the elegiac distich; something was said in Chapter II of that chain of stylistic and prosodic evolution. Translation was one link between Waller and Denham, and between them and their precursors and successors. Over half of Denham's non-dramatic verse was in that kind, much of it from Virgil; and Waller had a share in Godolphin's version of the fourth *Aeneid*. Of Denham's Virgilian paraphrases, done in 1636, the two revised portions which were printed show freer treatment of the original along with a stricter handling of the couplet. One sample of antithetical neatness is 'Darkness our Guide, Despair our Leader was', which Dryden sharpened into 'Night was our Friend, our Leader was Despair'. There are, incidentally, bits from Virgil in *Cooper's Hill*.

No poetical reputation of the seventeenth century has been so completely and irreparably eclipsed as that of Edmund Waller (1606–87).[1] Whereas Cowley and Cleveland can still give

[1] Waller, the son of a country gentleman of wealth and ancient name, attended Eton, had a brief sojourn at Cambridge, and seems to have commenced his parliamentary career at sixteen. In 1631 he married an heiress, apparently for love; she died in 1634. During 1636–9 Waller paid poetical homage to Lady Dorothy Sidney ('Sacharissa'), who married Lord Spencer in 1639. Waller was, like Cromwell, a cousin of John Hampden, but in politics he held in the main to the constitutional royalism of which his friend Falkland was the finest representative. 'Waller's Plot', supposedly a scheme to seize London for the king, was exposed in 1643. Waller, who did not play a noble part (though he was less base than Clarendon made out), escaped with banishment and a heavy fine. He married again and spent seven years abroad, with Evelyn and with the English exiles in Paris. His early verse, which had circulated in manuscript, was first collected in 1645, the year of Milton's first volume. In 1651 Waller was pardoned by Parliament and

pleasure, Waller's name calls up scarcely more than two lyrics of attenuated cavalier grace, 'On a Girdle' and 'Go lovely Rose', and a dim memory of much complimentary and occasional verse. He had, like Samuel Rogers, the prestige of wealth, culture, and wit, but Rogers was never celebrated as the standard-bearer of a new poetical movement. Probably the most significant crystallization of all the tributes paid to Waller was the equating of his name, in the Soame-Dryden 'translation' of Boileau (1683), with that of Malherbe (which was, by the way, rather more logical than the substitution, for Villon, Marot, and Ronsard, of Fairfax, Spenser, and Davenant). And assuredly the most succinct was Thomas Rymer's heading: 'Chaucer refin'd our English. Which in perfection by Waller.' Francis Atterbury, in his preface to the *Second Part of Mr. Waller's Poems* (1690), praised the poet's avoidance of monosyllabic excess like Donne's and of run-on lines, his making pauses in sense and metre coincide, his good and new rhymes, in short, the harmonious 'dance of words' which we associate with the balanced and antithetical half-lines of the closed couplet. Even in this preface, by the way, Atterbury appealed to Roscommon, Dryden, and Milton as men who had resented or broken the tyranny of rhyme, and in later years he turned highly critical of Waller.

Apart from his importance in the history of style and technique, and half a dozen slight amatory pieces, there is little attraction in Waller. Any public or private occasion could release a stream of his lucid rhetoric and, seen through that medium, all occasions appear about equally significant, whether 'Of a War with Spain, and a Fight at Sea' or 'Of Tea, Commended by her Majesty'. In the former we have a couplet about Cromwell as Jove transferred from an earlier poem 'To the King, on his Navy'. Classical myth, which had been and in Milton was still to be a rich inspiration, is everywhere, and everywhere is of the true Augustan coinage, smooth, polite, and pallid. And though, as a member of the Royal Society, Waller took a modest interest in the habits of toads and the generation of insects as well as in the improvement of the English language,

allowed to return home. The poetical superiority of his panegyric on Cromwell (1655) over his welcome of Charles II occasioned a famous display of his ready wit. In 1661 he joined the Royal Society and returned to Parliament, where he made frequent pleas for religious toleration. His tombstone at Beaconsfield proclaimed him *inter poetas sui temporis facile princeps*.

the scientific ideas in his verse do not go very far; they, like his mythology, dwindle into material for courtly gallantry. (Since there is so little to put to Waller's credit, perhaps we should remember that he greatly enjoyed Chapman's *Homer*.) Of the last verses of Waller's old age one couplet remains famous, a sombre version of a conceit he had once used in addressing the sick Amoret:

> The Soul's dark Cottage, batter'd and decay'd,
> Let's in new Light thrô chinks that time has made.

He may have remembered the phrase in Fuller's 'Life of Monica', 'her soul saw a glimpse of happinesse through the chincks of her sicknesse-broken body' (or perhaps a passage in Sylvester's 'Sixth Day of the First Week'); at any rate comparison with Fuller suggests the loss involved in the whole poetical mode that Waller stood for. For us he remains a fluent trifler, the rhymer of a court gazette. But we need not deny that 'he added something to our elegance of diction, and something to our propriety of thought'.

Waller and Denham may have met as early as 1635–6; they admired each other's work and Denham in particular supplies evidence of imitation as well.[1] The critical decision, said Dr. Johnson, following Dryden and Pope, had identified Waller with sweetness and Denham with strength, strength, as Johnson explained, in the sense of conciseness. Denham resembled Davenant, whose *Gondibert* he burlesqued, in being a cavalier of irregular life with an instinct for regular verse and moral reflection which made him a harbinger of the new era. He had ribald affinities with Sir John Mennes and Thomas Killigrew, but his

---

[1] Sir John Denham (1615–69) was born in Ireland, where his father was Chief Baron of the Exchequer. He spent several years (1631–4) at Oxford, but gave more time to dice, cards, and dreaming than to study. He entered Lincoln's Inn in 1634 and was called to the Bar in 1639. He won fame with his play *The Sophy* (1641) and especially with *Cooper's Hill*, which was piratically published in 1642. Denham fought on the king's side and lost some of his property to George Wither, whose life he was said to have saved later by a stroke of wit. Both abroad, during 1648–52, and afterwards at home, he worked for the royalist cause. In 1660 he became Surveyor of Works; among the results of his tenure of office were Burlington House, Greenwich Palace, and improved pavements in London. He was knighted (1661) and received grants of land and money. In 1661 he was elected M.P. and in 1663 a member of the Royal Society. He married again in 1665. For a time he lost his mind; the cause was probably his own early excesses rather than, as contemporaries thought, his young wife's becoming the Duke of York's mistress. He recovered enough to write a fine elegy on Cowley and to pay the first tribute to *Paradise Lost*. He was buried in the Abbey beside Cowley.

historical significance rests on his graver work. One minor piece, 'The Progress of Learning', is a sober historical survey, a world removed from Fanshawe's mythological and allegorical canto on the same subject (1647), which opens with an appeal to 'Spencers Ghost', or from George Herbert's witty 'Church Militant'. Yet Denham can feel the great question of his age:

> Through Seas of knowledg, we our course advance,
> Discovering still new worlds of Ignorance.

And a philosophic consciousness animates and unifies *Cooper's Hill* (1642), an early example of the topographical-reflective genre which was to drag its slow length through the eighteenth century. The topics are not unskilfully articulated and the texture, with all its antitheses and 'turns', has a massive plainness and economy; Denham's couplets are bolder and less monotonous than Waller's. Recent criticism has enriched our understanding of his ideas, his emotional stress, and his artistry, and has thereby given *Cooper's Hill* a distinctive place among, or rather apart from, most poems of its kind. The scenes described are not merely excuses for incidental reflection but, in the vision of a moderate and not uncritical royalist, become historical metaphors for age-old attitudes and the political and religious conflicts that broke out into war in the year of the poem. If the additions of 1655 modify or blur some things—such as the apparent association of the hunted stag with Strafford— the general structure and outlook remain firm. Against the background of the traditional concept of *concordia discors*, Denham sees the danger of extremes in English history, the union of strength and beauty in Charles and his queen, right and wrong relations between king and church and king and subjects, ordered stability and continuity in Windsor and the Thames, and much besides. The famous quatrain on the Thames, an addition of 1655—which may owe something to Cartwright's elegy on Jonson and to a poem Denham echoed elsewhere in *Cooper's Hill*, Randolph's tribute to Owen Felltham (quoted below in Chapter VI)—sums up not only a classical ideal of style but a civic and religious ideal, the harmony of opposites:

> O could I flow like thee, and make thy stream
> My great example, as it is my theme!
> Though deep, yet clear, though gentle, yet not dull,
> Strong without rage, without ore-flowing full.

These smoothly controlled—and long admired—antitheses are far from the harmony of opposites embodied in the river of Kubla Khan, and they reflect the Augustan temper; the daring and questioning 'wit' of the earlier seventeenth century is subject to the moderating 'judgement'.

Metaphysical poetry, if we ignore its rich results, may be said to have only held back for a time the wave of European neoclassicism that had reached its first crest in Jonson. And though Denham and Waller deserved some of the credit they received for curbing eccentricity and moulding versification, they were but heralds of a larger movement. That movement was far from being merely literary and neoclassical, for its dynamic—and desiccating—symbols are the names of Descartes and Hobbes. Nor is it altogether paradoxical, after mentioning one of those names at least, to say that the slow rise of the closed couplet to dominance implied in some measure the rise of a collective sense of political, social, and philosophic order. In literature that sense of security was attained partly by turning from troubled explorations of the individual soul to the accepted sentibusness of public occasions, general experience, and judicious compromise.

V

THE LITERATURE OF TRAVEL

IN the early seventeenth century people travelled, according to their means and station, in their own carriages, on horseback, and on foot. As literary representatives of these several classes we might think of Bacon stopping his coach to stuff the notorious hen with snow, of Fuller loading his saddle-bags with antiquarian notes, and of Ben Jonson and John Taylor the Water-Poet walking up to Scotland. Stage-wagons had been on the road in Elizabeth's time, but stage-coaches did not come into use until the reign of Charles I. Though roads and conveyances slowly improved, a long journey required a good reason, a stout heart, and a resilient frame. Business kept many people in motion, from royalty to beggars and highwaymen, but travel in Britain for the sake of travel was relatively rare and its literary fruit still rarer. However, there was a marked increase of books on county antiquities, topography, and resources, and ample evidence of affection for the English scene appears in such poems as *Britannia's Pastorals* and the encyclopaedic *Poly-Olbion*. In the course of thirty-five years John Taylor made many journeys by land or water, chiefly around England, and published pamphlets about them from 1617 onward. A unique item in the literature of travel and of 'Merry England' is Will Kemp's infectious account (1600) of his dancing a morris from London to Norwich. But our attention must be given to a few of the numerous travellers who recorded their observations of the Continent, the Near and the Far East, and America. As one of them says, 'the nature of man, by an inward inclination, is alwaies inquisitive of forraine newes; yea, and much more affecteth the sight and knowledge of strange, and unfrequented kingdomes, such is the instinct of his naturall affection'.

Throughout the Middle Ages the motives of pilgrim, ecclesiastic, scholar, business-man, diplomat, soldier, and mere tourist had led multitudes to surmount the difficulties and dangers of foreign travel. For Protestant Englishmen of the sixteenth and seventeenth centuries all these motives except the first were operating with greater urgency than ever. The political and commercial conditions of Europe, combined with the ideals of Renaissance humanism, gave a new importance to study of the history, policy, language, and manners of foreign countries as a preparation for public service and international trade. Many a young man, as Wood says of Overbury, 'travelled for a time, and returned a most accomplished Person'. Sometimes a tutor like Ben Jonson or Hobbes went along. A Polonian letter of advice from an elder was a frequent preliminary, and a frequent sequel was the writing of a report, which might serve as an informal equivalent of a modern Civil Service examination. While the grand tour developed as a privilege or obligation of sons of the nobility and gentry, such as Evelyn, it was shared— thanks to patron or parent—by such others as Inigo Jones and Milton. These names remind us that Italy was still attractive for antiquities, architecture, art, and music, and the liberal University of Padua enjoyed scientific and legal renown among transalpine students; but the sun of Italian humanism had set. From the early seventeenth century onward, as travellers' manuals and the royalist migrations testify, France was more and more recognized by Englishmen as the centre of thought, business, fashion, accomplishments, and vice. Another country of growing interest to Englishmen, through religious and military ties and commercial rivalry, was the Netherlands.

Variety of motives meant variety of literary reactions. On the one hand, the affected traveller who picked up his clothes and his behaviour everywhere was a stock figure for satire, and the Elizabethan fear of moral and religious contagion was still a reality, a somewhat lurid reality in Joseph Hall's *Quo Vadis?* (1617). Moreover, if at home a traveller's physical safety was not a matter of course, still less was it so for a Protestant Englishman in many parts of Europe. On the other hand, in the minds of philosophic travellers and essayists from Robert Johnson and Dallington and Bacon to Peacham and Howell and Harrington, the cultural advantages of travel far outweighed the dangers. Serious travellers kept journals and, if ambitious too, wrote them up when they returned to England, where they could buttress their first-hand observations with solid borrowings from foreign works, ancient and modern, of history and cosmography. While the great mass of travel literature was a by-product of trade, exploration, and colonizing, three of the best-known books were written by independent and disinterested globe-trotters, and our brief survey may begin with them.

Fynes Moryson (1566–1630) was a Cambridge man, Thomas Coryate (1577?–1617) an Oxonian, and William Lithgow (1582?–1645?) was, as patriot and stylist, a worthy fellow-countryman of Sir Thomas Urquhart's. (Scotland, says Lithgow, is 120 miles longer than England; he paced out the distance.) When we contemplate a map of Europe and the Orient not yet embraced by the paternal arms of Thomas Cook, it quickens the pulse to think of these resolute travellers who let no toil or danger subdue their desire to see the world, and whose peripatetic economy reveals such a mixture of romantic wanderlust, pedagogic zeal, and *bourgeois* thrift. Fynes Moryson's journeys were made in the last decade of the sixteenth century. His *Itinerary* (1617) combines lyrical praise of travel with sage practical advice and, along with substantial information on the serious subjects every gentleman should know, gives especially full details about life and manners in various countries (including Ireland). But the modern reader relishes most the more personal items. When French highwaymen rob Moryson they miss the money he has cannily hidden in a box of ointment and a ball of thread. Sober and prudent as he is, curiosity leads him into tight places for the pleasure of getting out of them— which he does, through his skill in disguise and in foreign tongues. Posing as a Frenchman he visits Bellarmine at the Jesuit College in Rome; as a German he inspects a Spanish fort. He preserves the purity of his faith by dodging the Holy Stairs, he flits about Italy to escape the sacramentary census at Easter, and in Jerusalem he avoids attendance at Mass by feigning illness. On such occasions we share the narrator's modest pride in his own ingenuity.

Moryson's normal warmth of anti-Catholic feeling becomes incandescence in William Lithgow. His title, *Rare Adventures and Painful Peregrinations* (1632), gives the reader a foretaste of an aureate style which often soars into passages of execrable verse. Yet there is also much straightforward narrative and description of frequently vivid intensity. Lithgow has a dour nature, embittered by Spanish tortures, and he takes his joys as well as his sufferings rather grimly. But dogged determination and 'ambitious curiosity' drove on his 'paynefull feet' and 'fatigated corps' for nineteen years over 36,000 miles, exclusive of journeys by water. Historically, Lithgow's chief claim to attention is the fact that he was the first Briton to give a first-hand if inadequate report of Greece and the Aegean.

A happier gusto inspired the wanderings of 'the Hierosolymitan Syrian-Mesopotamian-Armenian-Median-Parthian-Persian-India-Legge-strecher of Odcomb in Somerset, Thomas Coryate'. He traversed a good part of the Continent in 1608 and walked home from Venice; before setting off for India in 1612 he hung up his well-worn shoes in his father's parish church. From the court of the Great Mogul at Ajmere Coryate wrote home to his old friends of the Mermaid tavern, 'Right Generous, Joviall, and Mercuriall Sirenaicks'. But his 'pancraticall and athleticall' health did not survive his continued exertions, and at Surat in 1617 English merchants 'laid his rambling Brains at Rest'. Coryate's 'sesquippledan verboojuice' (to quote another ink-hornist wanderer, Mr. Polly) is not, like Lithgow's, chronic and gritty, it is the occasional and oratorical effervescence of vitality. He had been a notable Grecian at Oxford and he mastered a number of oriental languages. Not only did he honour the Mogul (and embarrass Sir Thomas Roe) with a speech in Persian but, a more remarkable feat, worsted a termagant Indian laundress in a duel of Hindustani Billingsgate. What has survived of Coryate's eastern journal shows a pioneer interest in antiquities of the Levant, including the ruins of Troy. *Coryate's Crudities*, an account of his earlier European travels, appeared in 1611, with a prolonged salvo of mock-commendatory poems from dozens of the wits, whose jocosity was mixed with affectionate admiration for the 'single-soled, single-souled, and single-shirted Observer'. Coryate gobbled up a good deal in his five months' travel. The gibe provoked by his zeal in copying inscriptions, that he was 'a tombe-stone traveller', he disdained, but he promised to pay more attention to affairs of state in his next book. Along with careful descriptions of the conventional sights he records such Italian devices as 'wooden flaps' for use against flies, umbrellas for use against the sun, and those implements unique in Europe, table forks. One of the glories of Venice, which his predecessors have not described, Coryate investigates with scientific innocence, namely, the courtesans who are truly if oddly said to be 'famoused over all Christendome'. These elegant sirens, by the way, rarely have children, as 'the best carpenters make the fewest chips'. But Coryate is interested in higher things, buildings and books and scholarship, and his comments, like those of other English travellers, display a mixture of cosmopolite and patriot. He would gladly spend his old age in lovely Mantua if the Italians were not idolaters and—this is an echo of Lucian— if the very smoke of Odcombe in Somerset were not dearer than the fire of all other places under the sun.

The East was visited by more sober and affluent tourists. George Sandys's *Relation of a Journey* (1615), a richly illustrated and popular book which was of use to authors like Bacon, Milton, and Browne, combined first-hand and second-hand information about the present and past of the Graeco-Roman East. In 1628–9 Thomas Herbert (who in his old age was to write a memoir of his attendance upon the captive King Charles) traversed Persia in the suite of the English ambassador. His graphic picture of the land and its people (1634) was in later editions increasingly submerged under bookish erudition. Sir Henry Blount's *Voyage into the Levant* (1636) showed unusual appreciation of Turkish virtues. Thus the multiplication of visitors and residents and books of travel gradually reduced oriental legend to fact, but without dispelling the glamour that still remains for us. Knolles's opening phrase proclaimed a great reality, 'the glorious Empire of the Turkes, the present terrour of the world', an exotic, splendid, sensual, and barbaric civilization united by a crude and powerful religion against divided Christendom. There was the Holy Land, from which sacred relics had once been transported to Italy by angels, and there was the whole classical Orient, from which antique marbles were now being transported to England by agents of the Earl of Arundel. The romantic and realistic attractions of eastern geography, history, and ethnology are attested not only by travellers' narratives but by such books as Fuller's *Holy War* (1639) and *Pisgah-Sight of Palestine* (1650), not to mention *Paradise Lost* and *Paradise Regained*.

Then 'the wealth of Ormus and of Ind' had opened up a more prosaic but even more potent vision of the East as an unlimited field for commercial enterprise, a vision translated into actuality by the formation of the great trading companies. Thomas Mun, economist and champion of eastern trade, was not concerned with history or manners but with drugs, spices, raw silk, indigo, and calicoes. Indeed, the silk trade was the occasion of the ambassadorial journey in which Thomas Herbert took part. Romance and realism are mingled in the strange careers of the brothers Sherley—'Quæ regio in terris', exclaims Purchas, 'Sherlii non plena laboris?'—and of the numberless traders who turn up in Syria, India and the Indies, and Russia, bargaining as shrewdly though not so securely as if they were in Cheapside. They faced not only the normal dangers of travel but, to condense one of Purchas's spacious headings, Turkish treachery, Portugal hostility, Moorish and ethnic perfidy, Dutch malignity, ignorant and malicious calumny. Abundant information about all aspects of the East was contained in the narratives and reports of diplomats like Sir Thomas Roe, chaplains like William Biddulph and Edward Terry, and many sailors and business-men who could write vivid descriptions of what they saw and did. Roe's journal and correspondence give a clear impression of his vigorous character and ability and of the difficulties he overcame as the first English ambassador at the court of the Great Mogul (1615–19). Although he shares with Sir James Lancaster the title of founder of British India, Roe urged the East India Company to confine itself to trade and avoid military entanglements.

But the greatest of eastern travellers, perhaps the ideal traveller of the whole period, was that middle-class man of business, the astonishing Peter Mundy (1596?–1667?). From 1608 until 1656 Mundy was in almost perpetual motion, and in 1647, when he did not know he was to make a third voyage to India, he reckoned that he had covered more than a hundred thousand miles and had been preserved from a thousand dangers. Mundy always hated 'waistinge of meanes' at home and always 'had a Mind to see Farther First'. He never gratified his desire to go round the world, but he saw or lived in most parts of Europe and Asia and adjacent islands. His huge journal, copiously illustrated with drawings, was begun in 1620, when he returned overland from Constantinople, and broken off in 1667. It first reached print, in six volumes, in the present century. Though mainly in the form of disconnected notes and almost completely impersonal, the record displays a rare combination of gifts, laconic prose, a scientific concern for accuracy, invincible fortitude and good humour, and an alert and insatiable curiosity about every aspect of the world. Mundy is interested in geography and the stars (he cherished a telescope); books of travel, philosophy, and science; birds, fish, animals, and people; clothes, scenery, and wholesome 'chucculatte'; religious rites and grisly executions (in the East and in Restoration London); the building of the Taj Mahal and of 'Pel Mel'; trade and languages; music in the Cathedral of Seville and at feasts at Agra. Did ever any other traveller's ears, when his eyes were on dancing girls, record that Indian music seems to lack thirds and fifths? And in farthest Asia the tireless nomad recalls England, which excels all countries in the world 'both For conveniency and delightt', and all English counties, we feel, give place to Cornwall.

East and West meet in the pages of Purchas, and voyages in both directions were made with partly similar motives, sometimes by the same navigators. (Davis and Baffin, whose names are perpetuated on the map of northern Canada, were both killed in the East.) It was of course the commercial desire for a shorter route to the East which sent ship after ship and 'many of the best sort of men' in search of a North-West Passage. In the exploring of the American coast early dreams of a waterway to the Pacific did not vanish with the acquisition of such tangible commodities as tobacco, whale-oil, fish, and furs. But while the East encouraged the establishment of nothing more than trading posts, the virgin spaces of America invited colonization. The vision of Hakluyt and Ralegh inspired others, and during the seventeenth century hundreds and then thousands of people left England—not to mention undesirables who were sent—to obtain land and security or religious and political freedom, or to achieve 'the Conversion of Salvages to Christianytie'. 'The first and last thing therefore in this Virginian argument considerable, is God; that is, whether we have Commission from him to plant, and whether the Plantation may bring glory to him.' Because of the large and novel issues involved from the beginning, and the ultimate results, the story of early colonizing in America is by far the most important branch of the heterogeneous literature of travel. But that story of dissension and failure, of perseverance and courage, of miseries and triumphs, needs no recounting here.

In the nature of the case America did not attract cosmopolitan tourists, though one whom we have met already, George Sandys, combined official and Ovidian labours in Virginia.

Mere wanderlust did not send Ralegh to the Orinoco or drive men into strange seas where 'The ice did split with a thunderfit', or even to face the discomforts and dangers of Virginia and New England. Early reports on America, written for London backers and prospective settlers, were highly practical, even in their eulogies of natural resources, but accounts of exploration, of Indian manners, and of the colonists' struggle to survive, could never be dull. One happily dramatic incident is the arrival of Lord De la Warr bringing salvation to the despairing remnant of Jamestown settlers who had just embarked for home. Some narratives have an accidental importance, like the several concerning the storm that cast Sir George Somers and Sir Thomas Gates upon 'the Ile of Divels', otherwise 'the still-vex'd Bermoothes'. Apart from storms, Bermuda appears in the accounts of Strachey and Jourdain as an earthly paradise, with fruits ripening in a continual spring and with a supply of ambergris; and another story, that of Richard More's party landing in Bermuda in 1612, contains, along with a similar picture of the islands, the description of men rowing and the singing of a Psalm of thankfulness—all of which carries us forward from *The Tempest* to Marvell's lovely lyric. For contrast we might transport ourselves to the frozen north described by Luke Fox, Thomas James, and others; and to think of the north is to think of that darkly vivid narrative of Hudson and his loyal followers being set adrift by mutineers.

But since we can notice only one writer on America, we must take the one whose commonplace name might stand as a symbol of English enterprise in all parts of the globe, and who has long enjoyed popular fame by reason of his extraordinary career, his vigorous personality, and his unwearied labours in person and in print on behalf of Virginia and New England, Captain John Smith (1579/80–1631). Scholarship seems now less sceptical than it once was concerning Smith's romantic autobiography, and the reader of literature may take untroubled pleasure in the tale of the Lincolnshire apprentice who ran away to seek adventures and found plenty in soldiering on the Continent; whose three single and victorious combats with Turkish heroes won a royal reward; who escaped from captivity with the aid of a pasha's wife, the first of four ministering angels in the life of an attractive bachelor; who was made a slave, killed his master, and after long wanderings returned to England, a veteran of twenty-four. During 1607–9 he was active in Virginia, as both administrator and explorer. Comparison of his narratives with other evidence indicates a degree of masterful ambition and jealousy, yet Smith did much to carry Jamestown through the first distresses caused by inexperience, factions, famine, disease, and Indians. We have no good ground for doubting the story that he was saved from death, when captured by the Indians, through the intercession of Pocahontas. A less celebrated but unforgettable item in the expansion of Britain is the picture of Captain Smith as guest of honour at an Indian banquet, with thirty naked damsels dancing before him—a sort of analogue to Sir Calidore and the Graces, except that the Indian nymphs, after vanishing, returned to swarm upon the Captain crying 'Love you not mee?'

In 1614 Smith made a successful voyage to New England; a second attempt (1615) was frustrated by storms and pirates and ended in another of his difficult escapes. Though he had much less actual experience of New England than of Virginia, he was during his retirement even more zealous in advertising the northerly region; it was he who established its name. The Pilgrims preferred Smith's helpful books to his company. Much of his own and others' earlier writings was gathered up in his *General History of Virginia, New England, and the Summer Isles* (1624). In 1626 he published a manual for seamen. In 1630 appeared the *True Travels, Adventures, and Observations of Captain John Smith, in Europe, Asia, Africa, and America,* and in the year of his death the indefatigable champion of colonization issued his last appeal to 'men that have great spirits and small meanes', *Advertisements for the Unexperienced Planters of New England, or Anywhere.* Whatever discounting may be done, Smith's career, like that of not a few contemporaries, is an astonishing mixture of the romantic and the prosaic. If he had been cast up on an island he would have been Robinson Crusoe. And along with practical knowledge, sagacity, and energy, Smith had devotion to a cause. We could not ask for a sturdier piece of eloquence than this declaration concerning the American settlements:

By that acquaintance I have with them, I may call them my children, for they have bin my wife, my hawks, my hounds, my cards, my dice, and in totall my best content, as indifferent to my heart as my left hand to my right; and notwithstanding all those miracles of disasters have crossed both them & me, yet were there not one English man remaining (as God be thanked there is some thousands) I would yet begin againe with as small meanes as I did at the first.

(One wishes that the gallant Captain could have known that in 1960 a statue of him would be unveiled by the Queen Mother outside the Church of St. Mary-le-Bow.) Smith was an explorer-promoter from England. Among the many early documents two outstanding ones illustrate the growing American consciousness of established settlers, Governor William Bradford's *Of Plymouth Plantation* (1620–47) and Governor John Winthrop's *Journal* (1630–49).

This chapter, brief as it is, cannot end without a paragraph in honour of the toiler who first printed many of these narratives. Samuel Purchas (1577–1626)—his name was pronounced 'Purkas'—never travelled 200 miles from his birthplace in Essex, but a lifelong passion for geography made him a master of the globe. His first book, *Purchas his Pilgrimage* (1613), appealed to its generation by virtue of its main design as a survey of the peoples and religions of the world, and also as an encyclopaedia of geography and history. Its success enlarged the compiler's circle of learned or travelled acquaintances, and the friendly offices of Hakluyt, Ralegh, Sir Dudley Digges, Sir Thomas Smith, and others contributed to the enlarging of the work. For the first edition Purchas drew upon 700 authors; in the end the list was nearly doubled. If King James's delight in the book is a dubious recommendation for modern readers, we may remember that the *Pilgrimage* (along with related items in the *Pilgrims*) kindled Coleridge's dreams of Xanadu, and that bits of it passed into the accounts of eastern religions in the fourth book of *The Excursion*. Purchas's next plan—to pass by the long jeremiad, *Purchas his Pilgrim* (1619)—was nothing less than a history of the world as it was contained in the whole body of the literature of travel, and he laboured almost single-handed, in the face of domestic sorrows and physical and pecuniary disabilities. The result was the largest English work yet printed in England; the four folios of *Hakluytus Posthumus or Purchas his Pilgrims* (1625) occupy twenty volumes in the modern reprint. Among the editor's countless sources were his own *Pilgrimage* and his manuscript collections, the papers left by Hakluyt, and the archives of the East India Company; some narratives that came in late were added to the fourth edition

(1626) of the *Pilgrimage*. The *Pilgrims* inevitably fell short of its grandiose scheme. It was neither a well-edited series of documents, like Hakluyt's, nor a coherent history. The reproduction of much printed matter necessitated the abridging, often injudicious, of many new and valuable narratives, and the compiler's verbose rhetoric and obtrusive pietism remain a liability. Thus Purchas suffers in comparison with his great predecessor, yet he has hardly received just praise for the gathering and preserving of materials which would otherwise have been lost. And while he was not, like Hakluyt, an active patriot and promoter of voyages, he had something of Hakluyt's vision; he arranged the story of earlier exploration as a prologue to the swelling act of the imperial theme, the colonizing of America.

Although this survey has given only hints of the mass and variety of the literature of travel, a few general observations may be made. In the first place, if at times we incline to regard the early seventeenth century as wholly absorbed in introspection, we should think of the multitude of robust extraverts, merchants, sailors, and travellers, who were going about their lawful or unlawful occasions all over the seven seas. It is their narratives which compose the island epic. We find, too, the conscious or unconscious beginnings of imperialism (if the word may be used with little or nothing of the meaning it has for modern liberals). Along with the large dreams of such men as Hakluyt, Purchas, and Captain John Smith may be mentioned one small item: Thomas Gage's *New Survey of the West Indies* (1648) was used by Cromwell and later by Colbert to mould public opinion in favour of their West Indian policy. Then, if we incline to regard this period as one of rhetorical and poetic prose, we should remember that the authors of records of travel were mostly plain men with utilitarian aims who produced a great deal of good plain prose without knowing it. Further, in a more immediate and popular way than the scientists, and in frequent co-operation with them, travellers helped to enlarge the known world and actual knowledge and to emancipate their age from legend. As in the past, the spirit of travel and maritime discovery continued to affect every kind of imaginative and reflective literature, from drama and epic to sermon, but our period shows a marked advance upon the sixteenth century in geographical range and accuracy. Finally, although travel for general scientific purposes was not really organized until after 1660, the possibilities of such work were made manifest by the achievements of the earlier independent travellers and commercial explorers.

VI

ESSAYS AND CHARACTERS

1. *Essays*

SINCE the essayists as a group reveal an early and deliberate concern with style, we may take a preliminary glance at the nature of prose in general. Literary history has given currency to the notion that prose writing before 1660 was largely ornate and poetical, and that a plain, workaday, modern style was first inaugurated after the Restoration, chiefly through the efforts of the Royal Society to develop this along with other elements of its Baconian heritage. To correct that vulgar error we have only to think of the vast bulk of plain writing in books of travel, history, biography, politics, economics, science, education, religion, and much popular literature. Plain prose was the natural medium for most kinds of utilitarian writing, and most writing was utilitarian. That old and vigorous tradition was steadily reinforced, moreover, by the needs and demands of a rapidly expanding public. We may grant, to be sure, that the prose of the Restoration achieved a more coherent form and texture, a more civilized ease and urbanity, but we must acknowledge that Dryden and his fellows represented a culmination rather than a beginning. We must acknowledge, too, that the civilizing process, in prose as well as in poetry, was a levelling process which gained some virtues at the cost of some others, and we may be glad that it was not completed in our period.

Such a movement was necessary because Elizabethan prose, while it encouraged both poetic elevation and homely raciness, had not become a tempered and reliable instrument. Along with the general circumstances and purposes that nourished plain prose in the seventeenth century, one special and self-conscious motive, which came over from the Continent, left few intellectual writers untouched. Although by 1600 English prose, even in Hooker, had scarcely attained Ciceronian maturity, there ensued a repetition of the phenomenon that had taken place in imperial Rome, a reaction against the rotund, balanced, oratorical period and in favour of a concise, flexible, semi-colloquial style. If the ultimate theoretical sanction was derived from Aristotle, the stylistic models were Seneca and Tacitus and the editor of both, the chief reviver of Stoic thought, Justus Lipsius. The 'Attic' style of the anti-Ciceronians was not of course uniform; it ranged from the 'libertine' naturalness of Montaigne or Burton to the weighty condensation of Bacon and Jonson or the clipped, pointed sententiousness of Hall or Felltham. But with all its theoretical and individual differences the movement as a whole implied the recognition of a changing world in which the accepted verities were less secure than they had been, and it embodied a philosophic desire for a more realistic, arresting, and subtle expression of both general ideas and private experience. Hence the simplicity of the new style or styles was not always simple. Like the parallel manifestation in verse, the Senecan style had its 'metaphysical' tricks of antithetical and epigrammatic patterns, abrupt surprises, and ingenious images, and it did not meet with unanimous approval. Breton's *Characters upon Essays* was commended for its 'Lipsian stile, terse Phrase', but Earle—though he later deleted a remark that did not leave his own withers unwrung—censured his 'selfe-conceited Man' as one who preferred 'Lipsius his hopping stile, before either Tully or Quintilian'. And Milton jeered at Hall for making 'sentences by the Statute, as if all above three inches long were confiscat'. Dr. Kettell's judgement of Seneca's style, recorded by Aubrey, was more critical than quotable. Senecan or Lipsian prose, loose or curt or a mixture of both, was frequently wedded to Stoic thought, and among the offspring of the marriage were the English essayists, whose moral didacticism and studied informality made them the natural exponents of the new modes.

We think of the essay as one of the late courses in the banquet of literature. It presupposes a class of readers who possess economic and social security and who can appreciate rational reflection upon civilized manners and morals. While Plato and Cicero and Horace have contributed to the spirit and sometimes to the form of the modern essay, the classical prototypes are the moral works of Seneca and Plutarch. Seneca's *Epistles to Lucilius*, as Bacon observed, 'are but Essaies,—That is dispersed Meditacons, thoughe conveyed in the forme of Epistles'. The essay absorbed many other tributaries, the formal treatises and often formal letters of medieval and Renaissance humanists and the academic exercises of generations of students, the private commonplace books that almost all serious readers kept, and the published collections, ancient and modern, of anecdotes, aphorisms, and didactic discourses. And behind all these things was the inexhaustible treasury of classical literature as a whole. Then although the essay tended in its very nature to be secular in tone, it long bore traces of the religious homily and devotional meditation. These various kinds of writing were themselves being carried on in our period, so that a working definition of the essay must be both comprehensive and arbitrary. The genre was at any rate a natural expression of the heightened self-consciousness of the seventeenth-century mind.

The essay was born when Montaigne retired to his tower to take stock of himself and thereby of all human experience, and the evolution of his essays epitomizes the general evolution of the form from the commonplace book to independent reflection. Bacon's went through a partly parallel development, though he never approached nor apparently wished to approach the spacious freedom and intimate personal candour of the first and greatest of modern essayists.[1] While the two men

---

[1] The life of Bacon (1561–1626) is both too full and too familiar to be summarized. As the younger son of Elizabeth's first Lord Keeper and of one of the learned daughters of Sir Anthony Cooke, he had, except in the pecuniary way, a fortunate heritage and background. At Trinity College, Cambridge, he first rebelled against the tyranny of Aristotle. He was attached to the embassy in France (1576–9), became an 'utter barrister' in 1582, and entered Parliament in 1584. He soon established a solid reputation in the House and in committees, and through his letters of advice on state affairs. Bacon's opposition to the court (1593) won him the queen's ill will, which, with the coolness of his uncle and cousin, the two Cecils, long delayed his legitimate advancement. He took an active share in the prosecution of Essex, who had been his friend and over-zealous patron. This episode has, rightly or wrongly, told against Bacon's character perhaps even more than his later judicial disgrace; but Bacon had early conceived both a personal and a sincerely patriotic distrust of the earl's violent ways, and the two had fallen apart. After many disappointments he got his foot on the official ladder; he became Solicitor-General in 1607, Attorney-General in 1613, Lord Keeper in 1617, and Lord Chancellor in 1618. In 1603 he had been knighted, 'gregarious in a troop', and he received the title of Baron Verulam in 1618, of Viscount St. Alban in 1621. (At no time was he 'Lord Bacon'.) In the year of his last honour the prosecutor of Essex and Somerset and Ralegh, and the rival of Coke, became himself the scapegoat of a lax judicial system and of parliamentary hostility to the government. Bacon admitted the accepting of presents but defended the justice of his decisions, apparently with reason, since few if any seem to have been reversed. Apart from the question of moral obtuseness in this matter, Bacon ranks among the greatest minds in English legal history. After his fall he retired to his estate of Gorhambury and

naturally had some common roots, they were far apart in
temperament and outlook, and Bacon, after borrowing Montaigne's title, seems to have gone his own way. To the general
recognition of the tentative character of the essay Bacon added
his special belief in the suggestive virtues of the aphoristic style.
The ten 'Essays' of 1597 were merely groups of related apoph-
thegms transcribed from the commonplace book. That Bacon
was aware of a more fluid form is sufficiently indicated by other
early writings, and when his own and the public's interest in
his book led to extensive revision and enlargement he inclined to
the looser, more 'methodical' and persuasive style which he had
brought to maturity in the *Advancement of Learning* and which was
nearer to the established manner of the essay. Although in their
final state (1625) his essays remained strongly aphoristic in texture, the discontinuity and abstract severity of the early *sententiae*
had been increasingly unified and relieved by expatiation and
by interpolated examples and quotations, and enriched by
metaphor and cadence. There was, however, only a little re-
laxing of Bacon's cool objectivity. That, while partly inherited
from his chosen models and the commonplace book, represents
also the attitude of the scientific analyst who does not gossip and
ramble, whose mind is a dry light. Even in his reflections on
adversity the fallen Lord Chancellor's pen betrays no momen-
tary quiver; the essay might have been written by a cloistered
sage. It is Bacon's impersonality and Tacitean brevity, rather
than grandiloquence, that make his style seem less familiar than
it is. Though his name suggests full-dress stateliness, he was the
theoretical and practical leader of the anti-Ciceronian movement in England, and the groundwork of his prose is reinforced
homespun. And along with his genius for pithy and proverbial
expression goes a full share of the 'wit' of his age; many of his
opening phrases remain as arresting as those of Donne's poems.

Of the fifty-eight essays in the final edition, more than half
deal with public life or public affairs, and the statesman or

courtier has at least a finger in many others, including such
varied pieces as those on truth, marriage, love, and friendship.
Bacon reveals to us the interests, problems, and modes of thought
of the ruling class of his age, but the artist who is wedded to the
mundane and temporal has given hostages to fortune. We are,
to be sure, vaguely aware of some wholly admirable counsels of
moral wisdom and public and private virtue (especially in the
volume of 1612), but we are much more strongly impressed by
an atmosphere of 'business', of cold-blooded expediency, and
sometimes of unscrupulous self-interest. While Montaigne's chief
concern is in man sitting upon his 'owne taile', Bacon's is in man
sitting in an office chair. Obvious reasons for a degree of moral
obtuseness are at hand in the facts of his own world and career
and in the influence of his favourite authors. But a more fundamental explanation of Bacon's choice and treatment of themes
appears in the second book of the *Advancement of Learning*. There
he deplores philosophers' preoccupation with abstract ethics
and their neglect of the basic material of morality and policy,
that is, ordinary human nature as it operates in the various
circumstances of the active life. The several lists of particular
desiderata which he proceeds to give make a fair table of contents for the *Essays*. In spite of Bacon's disclaimer, in a dedica-
tory epistle to Andrewes, the essays were not merely the casual
recreation of a busy life, they were to a great extent an integral
part of the *Instauratio Magna*, an appendix—as innumerable
borrowings remind us—to the *Advancement*. Bacon wished to
fill a gap in practical psychology and ethics, to contribute to
that realistic knowledge of the genus *homo* without which the
individual cannot prescribe for his own needs nor the statesman for the needs of society.

Thus it is not simply the limitations of the essayist's mind and
heart that lead him to see life so much in terms of tangible
success and failure. Even when he reveals a Jonsonian world
of politic knaves and gulls he can claim a philosophic purpose.
In the *Advancement* he notes the lack of serious studies of professional frauds and vices, a kind of knowledge which is 'one
of the best fortifications for honesty and vertue that can be
planted', and he pays tribute to 'Macciavell & others that
write what men doe and not what they ought to do'. At the
same time, in his expert dissection of human egoism, Bacon
may forget the ends of honesty and virtue, and the essays are,

morally, something of a jumble. The two elements that appear in harmonious innocence in the title *Essays or Counsels, Civil and Moral* appear in Machiavellian or Hobbesian nakedness in the distinction made in the *Advancement*: 'Againe, morrall Philosophye propoundeth to it selfe the framing of Internall goodnesse: But civile knowledge requireth onelye an Externall goodnesse: for that as to societye sufficeth.' These psychological and utilitarian motives keep Bacon's *Essays* in the category of admired books rather than among the well-thumbed and beloved. Everyone has read them, but no one is ever found reading them. Yet, if he is less generous and companionable than the other great essayists, we should remember what he was and was not trying to do. And we rejoice all the more when Machiavelli, or a Machiavellian Samuel Smiles, gives way to the Jacobean lover of beauty or royal magnificence in the loving particularity of the essays on gardens, building, or masques and triumphs, and much more still when flashes of poetic phrase and intuition light up Truth and Death and other noble themes. For all his narrowness or obliquity of vision, his tense, athletic prose reflects his unquenchable vitality and his eager curiosity about the earthly doings and experience of man.

Before we leave Bacon a less familiar collection of short discourses must be mentioned. His interest in allegorical mythology is patent to every reader of the *Essays* and the *Advancement of Learning*, and it received full expression in the popular *De Sapientia Veterum* (1609), which Sir Arthur Gorges translated as *The Wisdom of the Ancients* (1619). Here Bacon, not without a note of apology, allows his philosophic mind and poetic fancy to play around some thirty characters of classic myth. In part he takes over the methods and materials of the mythographers, but his interpretations, whether new or old, are adapted to his own special view of science and civil and moral knowledge. It is easy to guess what the herald of modern science makes of Prometheus or of Oedipus unriddling the Sphinx (Cupid is less obvious as the natural motion of the atom), or what the statesman makes of Cassandra and Typhon. Thus if *The Wisdom of the Ancients* represents Bacon's less modern side (though he was by no means the last exponent of allegory), it is, except in the character of its initial texts, a twin volume to the *Essays*, and also a partial link between the *Advancement* and the *Novum Organum*.

From the standpoint of general fame the early history of the essay is a picture of a whale followed by a school of sober porpoises, but before Bacon published the genuine essays of his second edition the form had been more or less ably handled by a number of men, such as the Baconian Robert Johnson and Daniel Tuvill. We can take account of only one, the first exponent of the more personal and informal essay, Sir William Cornwallis (1579?–1614).[1] Cornwallis's *Essays* (1600–1) were published when he was only a little past twenty and, if it were not for references to his youth, we might think so sage a moralist, so disillusioned a critic of society, was a lean and slippered pantaloon. He has got beyond adolescent follies but he is still only crawling through the darkness of 'Opinion' towards 'the Land of light'. 'I write therefore to my selfe, and my selfe profits by my writing.' In a decayed and corrupt world men must seek guidance and strength from within. To himself and others Cornwallis preaches a Stoicism which is really, if not very explicitly, Christian. But Stoic rigour is modified by compromises between abstract and practical morals, by the attitudes of an Elizabethan Englishman, and by the inconsistency of youth. How, for instance, is ambition to be shunned by a young man of his time, how is the contemplative life to be reconciled with the duty of public service? 'I must choose the active course, my birth commands me to that.'

The sources of Cornwallis's wisdom are largely classical. Plato (read in Latin) is the supreme philosopher, and he sometimes inspires flights above the Stoic level. But Cornwallis owes most to Seneca and Plutarch, and of their disciple Montaigne he had acquired some knowledge in a translation (probably Florio's unpublished manuscript). It is not the sceptical or naturalistic Montaigne who attracts him, but the man, the nobleman, who makes moral philosophy doff its gown and speak courageously, who puts 'Pedanticall Schollerisme' out of countenance and shows that 'learning mingled with Nobilitie,

---

[1] Cornwallis may have been privately educated. He married early (1595) and rivalled his friend Donne in fathering children (eleven); debts also multiplied. He took part in Essex's Irish campaign (1599) and received one of the earl's overgenerous knighthoods. In Scotland (1601 or 1602) he met Sir Thomas Overbury. In 1604 (and again in 1614) he was a member of Parliament. When his father, Sir Charles, became ambassador to Spain (1605), he carried dispatches back to England. The father regarded him as an 'unthrifty and unfortunate sonne', who cost him large sums and was one of those 'that are Philosophers in their wordes and fooles in their works'. Sir Charles inherited his son's family.

shines most clearly'. Along with aristocratic morality Cornwallis upholds aristocratic standards of culture, the amateur
ideal of Montaigne and Renaissance courtesy books. And,
though he is chiefly concerned with individual man, he expounds the traditional view of 'degree' as the frame of the
social fabric. But he is aware that gentlemen's bodies may
contain slavish minds and, standing between Diogenes and
Carlyle, the apologist of order can imagine a naked assemblage
from which pre-eminence has vanished with clothes.

Like other early practitioners Cornwallis has a critical consciousness in regard to the scope and spirit of the essay. Ancient
writers of short discourses and even Montaigne, he thinks, went
beyond the proper limits of the genre. He himself avoids both
schematic and unduly loose writing and aims at the familiar
level—'Montania and my selfe . . . doe sometimes mention our
selves'. Though he respects Cicero the moralist he dislikes the
tradition of Ciceronian rhetoric. In spite, however, of his attachment to the concise Tacitus and Seneca, he inclines to the
discursive manner of Montaigne. His normal style is a colloquial but dignified 'plainencssc' (his own word), with occasional
touches of both solemnity and journalism.

Cornwallis's two posthumous volumes, *Essays or Rather
Encomions* and *Essays of Certain Paradoxes* (1616), represent a
different genre. The facetious or ironical encomium was a
classical device, analogous to the mock-epic, which the Renaissance revived, notably in Erasmus's *Praise of Folly*. This kind of
encomium was related to the paradox, which also had a long
and varied pedigree. A form sanctioned by Cicero was made
witty and lively by Ortensio Lando, whose *Paradossi* (1543) were
everywhere imitated. The paradox could not fail to attract
men brought up on academic disputations and touched by the
current of scepticism. It might be called the *enfant terrible* of the
essay family. The author takes a holiday from truth and moral
responsibility in order to amuse and stimulate his readers by a
display of dialectical ingenuity and rhetorical wit in the proof
of any thesis, however contrary to reason or convention. The
paradox was especially alluring to disillusioned young intellectuals, in the grey time around 1600, as a counterpart in prose to
the overworked satire and epigram. The brilliant exponent of
the paradox and the somewhat similar 'problem' was Donne,
whose chief activity in this field belongs to the years 1598–1602.

His pieces, circulating in manuscript, were treasured by Wotton and other friends, though they were not published until 1633, after his death. The paradox was a weapon made to Donne's hand. His half-playful, half-serious questioning of accepted ideas about man and woman, society and the universe, is a link between the 'cynical' poet and the troubled preacher. Cornwallis knew Lando's work, and acquaintance with Donne, which probably began about 1600, may have stirred him to emulation of his more learned, acute, intense, and speculative friend. Though his *Essays* proper include some *jeux d'esprit*, Cornwallis lacks the light touch and edged wit that irony demands, and he cannot readily divest himself of his sober moral principles. Whereas Donne attacks some articles of the Stoic creed, Cornwallis's 'Prayse of Sadnesse' (that is, 'Seriousness') becomes another exposition of the Stoic ethical ideal; and his eulogy of debt—despite his painful experience—rises, with eloquence more restrained than that of Panurge, to contemplation of the ordered system of nature. Some of his paradoxical material was borrowed from abroad.

Possibly the paradox, and certainly the developing 'character', did something to relieve and diversify the gravity and abstractness of the moral essay. Some authors who used both forms, like John Stephens (1615) and Geffray Mynshul (1618), distinguished between the decorous plainness of the essay and the mannered wit of the character; others, like Nicholas Breton and Sir William Cavendish—the pupil of Hobbes and friend of Bacon—in his *Horae Subsecivae* (1620), made a conscious or unconscious fusion of the two. In Breton's *Fantastics* (1604?) the 'characters' of the seasons, months, and hours, for all their balanced itemizing, resemble the 'Nows' of Leigh Hunt. And Breton's *Characters upon Essays, Moral and Divine* (1615), though dedicated to Bacon, treat wisdom, learning, and similar themes in the pattern and pointed style of the character. Such variations, however, did not carry the essay very far towards informal flexibility. The *Horae Vacivae* (1646) of the young John Hall (1627–56), which received unusual commendations from the literary, was largely in the Baconian tradition. If any writer before 1660 fulfils our notion of the familiar essayist, it is that versatile ex-schoolmaster, Henry Peacham (1578?–1642?), in *The Truth of our Times: Revealed out of one Man's Experience, by way of Essay* (1638). Peacham has of course an eye to the good of the commonwealth, from manners to agriculture, and he is a preacher of moderation, but he writes to please himself. Whether his theme is God's providence or fashions in dress, schools or authorship or liberty or travel, he sets forth his serious convictions with easy, intimate discursiveness and with a store of reminiscence and anecdote—a Holborn sempster's report of the fantastic price of neck-bands, a boyhood memory of Tarlton's acting, the capture of a continental town. A 'character' of a plain country fellow reminds us of Earle's, but Peacham's farmer, in 1638, grudges the payment of ship-money. We are not reminded of Bacon's essay on friendship when we read of those acquaintances who, on a chance encounter, exclaim, 'Good Lord, are you alive yet?' The familiar essayist's capital is personality and style, and Peacham has something of both. His industrious and unprosperous career has given a touch of disillusionment to his wide experience and sturdy good sense. He is 'living in the last age of the world, wherein all iniquity and vice doth abound'. But Peacham's interest in life is not dulled by pessimism and is quickened by some special antipathies, for Nonconformists in particular. His book is a small landmark in the history of the essay and it remains enjoyable on its own account.

The didactic motives of so much secular prose make it hard to distinguish the essay from kindred forms, and it is almost impossible to separate the religious essay from its congeners. Even within fairly strict limits we find such various names as Breton and Brathwait, Joseph Hall and Fuller, and Drummond and Browne, but here we may pass by these men of many books for a less prolific author. If the essays of Cornwallis partake of the 'resolve', Owen Felltham's *Resolves, Divine, Moral, Political* (1623?) often approach the pure essay.[1] Like Cornwallis and the rest, Felltham upholds wisdom and the amateur ideal of culture against mere knowledge and pedantry. He defends the practice Burton censured, quoting without naming one's authors; to

---

[1] The facts of Felltham's life (1602?–68) are obscure. He was the son of a man of some property in Suffolk. He visited the Low Countries probably before 1627; the literary result appeared much later. He was acquainted with the London wits and contributed poems to Long's translation of Barclay's *Argenis* (1625), *Annalia Dubrensia* (1636), Randolph's *Poems* (1638), and other books. Before 1641, perhaps about the time of his father's death (1632), Felltham took service with the Earl of Thomond at Great Billing, Northamptonshire, and spent the rest of his life as steward of the estate. He died in London. Some details about the enlargements of the *Resolves* are given in the bibliography.

do otherwise would be 'for a Gentleman . . . a little pedanticall', especially in an essay, 'which of all writing, is the neerest to a running Discourse'. Books are Felltham's delight and recreation, not his trade. His praise of poetry has an intimate warmth which reminds us that he was a poet in his own right. (Of late years he has regained his title to a lyric long ascribed to Suckling, 'When, Dearest, I but think on thee'.) As a devout Anglican and royalist, who could look back on Charles the First as 'Christ the Second', Felltham was a man of piety but not a pietist. His essay on Puritans illustrates his fundamental reverence for 'the beauty of order' in the Church, in society, and in the individual. Although he seeks the *via media* in all things—except the love of God and hatred of evil—and although the commonplaces of religion and morals are his staple article, he can, more than most didactic essayists, make virtue sound exciting and moderation adventurous. Felltham's harmony of Christianity and Stoicism is tempered and sweetened by a love of life and literature, by philosophic charity and undogmatic good sense. His moralizings on death and mutability and vain-glory, as well as his Christian Stoicism, carry us forward, if not to *Urn Burial*, at least to *Christian Morals*. Thomas Randolph in his eulogy summed up the qualities of thought and style which the age increasingly admired:

> I mean the stile, being pure, and strong, and round,
> Not long but Pythy: being short breath'd, but sound.
> Such as the grave, acute, wise Seneca sings,
> That best of Tutours to the worst of Kings.
> Not long and empty; lofty but not proud;
> Subtile but sweet, high but without a cloud,
> Well setled, full of nerves, in briefe 'tis such
> That in a little hath comprized much.

But the pointed style does not exclude homeliness or metaphysical wit. 'A bounded mirth, is a Pattent adding time and happinesse to the crazed life of Man.' 'When the Husband and the Wife are together, the World is contracted in a Bed.' And with Felltham's Christian faith and pagan reason is blended a strain of the Platonism that we encounter everywhere in the period. Earthly music awakens thoughts of 'a higher Diapason'. For Felltham as for Marvell and others the soul is 'manacled' by the flesh. We are not surprised to find that

Vaughan often echoed him, and it was the poet in Felltham who saw 'Eternities Ring' and the soul as 'a shoot of everlastingnesse'.

While the infant essay was taking its first uncertain steps in various directions, its parents, the aphorism and the commonplace book, were still moving along the familiar paths. The tradition of Machiavelli, Guicciardini, and Bacon was carried on in Sir Robert Dallington's *Aphorisms Civil and Military* (1613) and Ralegh's posthumous *The Prince, or Maxims of State* (1642); the moral tradition of humanism in the *Aphorisms of Education* (1654) of Sir Henry Wotton (1568–1639); and both 'Piety and Policy' in the very popular *Enchiridion* (1640–1) of Francis Quarles, who borrowed a good deal from Bacon and Machiavelli. The aphorism usually remained impersonal but was handled somewhat loosely, perhaps because few men had Bacon's or Jonson's gift for massive compression. It was such a natural outgrowth of the commonplace book (or vice versa), entered so largely into the texture of the essay, and was itself treated in such various ways, that it can scarcely be distinguished as a special type of writing.

The commonplace book *par excellence* is Jonson's *Timber: or Discoveries*, which was posthumously published in the folio of 1640–1 'edited' by Sir Kenelm Digby. The collection was apparently made in Jonson's later years, since the fire of 1623 had destroyed 'twice-twelve-yeares stor'd up humanitie, With humble Gleanings in Divinitie'. He seems to have contemplated publication, though he—or others—did not arrange the material very clearly. The longer pieces of the latter part constitute a sort of draft for a treatise on the art of writing and on types of literature. The first part is a much less homogeneous body of observations which range from isolated *sententiae* to miniature essays and which deal mainly with such aspects of life, thought, and learning as we find in the essayists—though Jonson damns that tribe, 'even their Master Mountaigne', for rushing into print with undigested reading. Thus *Timber* is a visible link between the commonplace book and the essay. It is also a link between a learned poet's reading and his method of poetic composition.

A commonplace book was not as a rule an original product, and the title-page of *Timber* indicated its character. Modern scholarship has traced nearly all of the material to its sources. Jonson's chief creditors were the two Senecas and Quintilian (with Heinsius for a good deal of literary theory), but he drew more or less from other ancients and from such moderns as Vives, Erasmus, Machiavelli, Lipsius, John Hoskyns, and Bacon. The moving eulogy of the fallen Lord Chancellor apparently came almost verbatim from Hobbes's manuscript translation of the letters of the Italian scholar, Fulgenzio Micanzio, to the second Earl of Devonshire (formerly Sir William Cavendish the essayist). Of the four passages on life and conduct cited in the standard edition of Jonson in proof of his sterling honesty and fearlessness, his searching insight and fine economy of words, three and a half are borrowed. Even ostensibly personal bits may be translated. Yet such facts by no means contradict such praise. Jonson's choice of authors and items reveals hardly less of his mind and temper than if the book were wholly original. 'He invades Authours like a Monarch, and what would be theft in other Poets, is onely victory in him.' Then, while there is much translation and para-phrase, there is also much recasting and condensed analysis, with comments and illustrations from Jonson's own store of experience. 'And such his Wit,' as Falkland said in *Jonsonus Virbius*, 'He writ past what he quotes.' Finally, apart from occa-sional traces of Latin diction or idiom, Jonson's prose is no less masculine and pithy, and more naturally crisp and colloquial, than Bacon's. The writers he borrowed from had borrowed from others, and they often lacked the pregnant force that makes his moral reflections arresting.

The book may, therefore, be justly accepted as a portrait of the compiler, a man too independent and too sincere to put down what he has not weighed or does not believe. If, for instance, the wise remarks on the right attitude towards the ancients are derived from Vives, or those on 'Custome of speech' and good style from Quintilian, they none the less repre-sent Jonson's own fundamental faith and practice. The tribute to Bacon's oratory, or the censure of Shakespeare's facility, gains rather than loses when we read the originals in Seneca, for we realize that Jonson's scale of values is not set by personal prejudice or by fashion, that he speaks with the authority of a central and living tradition. Everywhere we see the critical inheritor and the active exponent of the aristocratic and prac-tical wisdom of Renaissance humanism, the poet who is not merely an artist but a philosophic citizen vitally concerned with questions of private and public conduct, with education and government, with the whole range of moral and cultural ideas. Jonson's moral utterances are less well known than his literary dicta, but the latter, with all their judicious breadth and good sense, were recorded by the neoclassical theorist, the former by the man and the strongly Stoic humanist. If the one group of observations explains the disciplined art of his poems and plays, the other explains their rational sobriety and weight.

To this heterogeneous but far from exhaustive survey of the essay family one important member is still to be added. From antiquity to the present the letter has been an elder sister, if not a twin, of the essay. During the Middle Ages and the Renaissance the art of letter-writing was assiduously cultivated as a branch of rhetoric. Writers in the vernaculars, like Guevara and Pasquier, inherited from the humanistic tradition a didactic aim and a rhetorical method. In England in the early seventeenth century the literary epistle, like the essay itself, was breaking away from didactic formalism and approaching the genuine familiar letter. Joseph Hall (1574–1656) invited Prince Henry to observe that his *Epistles in Six Decades* (1608–11) inaugurated 'a new fashion of discourse, by Epistles; new to our language, usuall to others'. But we cannot give heed to his clerical, anti-Romish, and Senecan exhortations when livelier authors are frisking before us.

Nicholas Breton's *Post with a Mad Packet of Letters*, published in 1602 and later enlarged, went through many editions. Breton was aware of 'Latine, French, Italian, and Spanish, Bookes of Epistles'—indeed he imitated one of Guevara's letters—and presumably also of the popular middle-class formularies of William Fulwood and Angel Day, but he changed 'the complete letter-writer' into literature. In his compound of moralizing, satire, and romantic love, and his euphuism, he was a sort of lighter and less didactic Lyly. But to these conventional elements Breton adds novel situations and motives and fresh bits of humorous realism in background, characterization, and expression. In fact, though he treats essay themes, from education and travel to love and marriage, he comes closer to epistolary fiction than to the essay. And, unlike the aristocratic and philosophic essayists, Breton makes a distinct appeal to the moral and mercantile interests of the middle-class reader. As late as 1678 and 1685, when for a generation French preciosity had dominated the English letter-book, there were editions of the *Post*.

The supreme epistolizer of the age was James Howell (1593?–1666). He 'came tumbling out into the World a pure Cadet, a true Cosmopolite; not born to Land, Lease, House or Office'. Both as a man of business, in connexion with Sir Robert Mansell's glass factory, and as a minor diplomatic envoy, Howell enjoyed—the word is not colourless—extensive travel; he became an expert linguist and an authority on foreign countries. He had a wide acquaintance among literary and public men, including Sir Kenelm Digby, who claimed to have cured him of a wound by his powder of sympathy. In 1626 he became secretary to Lord Scrope, Lord President of the North, and in 1627 a member of Parliament. Shortly after being sworn Clerk of the Council in August 1642, Howell was arrested by parliamentary order, probably because of royalist activity during the previous decade. The eight years of incarceration (1642–50) were, until his appointment as Historiographer Royal in 1661, the most settled period of his career and turned him into a professional author. He had already published a political allegory, *Dodona's Grove* (1640; enlarged later), and *Instructions for Foreign Travel* (1642). There followed dozens of political pamphlets and miscellaneous and philological works. Howell lives, of course, in the *Epistolae Ho-Elianae*, the four books of which appeared in 1645, 1647, 1650, and 1655. Whether or not he used actual letters, the necessitous and thrifty author drew freely upon his own and other men's works, and especially no doubt upon his note-books, for the more solid portions of his masterpiece, such as the virtual articles or essays on the religions, wines, and languages of the world, the unity of creation, and the theory of the habitable moon. Howell's Oxford education had never been 'any burden or encumbrance' to him, and the chances and changes of his life had provided him with one kind of capital, a fund of varied experience and observation.

The first letter, originally prefixed to the second book, indicates his knowledge of epistolary authors and manuals, and his dislike of neo-Latin commonplaces and French affectation and emptiness. The true familiar letter, he says (after Seneca), should have the naturalness of talk but should not lack sub-

stance and ideas. Howell's letters live up to his theory. Like
Leigh Hunt, he was a tricksy sprite for whom stone walls did
not a prison make. The bulk of his work deals with the course of
English and continental affairs and with the life and manners
of continental countries and cities. There are few names, events,
or topics that do not come in somewhere and do not give an
impression of immediacy. Howell's eager curiosity embraces
ship-money, Platonic love at court, and the disease of witty
preaching; Spinola and Galileo; the siege of Rochelle and the
glories of Venice. Whatever charges of inaccuracy or shallowness the historian may lodge against him, it is to Howell that
we owe our most vivid pictures of the Overbury trial, of Gondomar stalking in to King James to ejaculate 'Pyrats, Pyrats,
Pyrats', of Prince Charles's difficult courtship of the Infanta,
of Buckingham rising on the fatal day and cutting a caper or
two—these and many other incidents great and small are
sketched with the dramatic instinct of a journalist. We see
Ben Jonson at the supper table betraying his 'Roman infirmity'
of self-praise, or Lord Leicester bearing up stoutly through
thirty-five healths at a Danish banquet and departing, unlike his
royal host, on his own legs. Something is always putting Howell
in mind of a good anecdote, like the Earl of Kildare's ingenuous
explanation that he would not have burned a church if he had
not thought the bishop was in it. Then there are some famous
and more serious tales, of the anchorite, the pied piper of
Hamelin, and the white-breasted bird of the Oxenhams.

Like all good essayists, Howell reveals his own character.
Our true cosmopolite is glad to return 'to the sweet bosom of
England' and breathe again the smoke of London. His mer-
curial spirit has its saturnine moods, but misfortunes cannot
submerge a man so interested in life—one who, moreover,
looks back to that illustrious Armorican dynasty of the Howells.
Mercurial and mundane gusto is carried, quite sincerely, into
his religion, even if his devotional schedule does not suggest
Celtic kinship with Henry Vaughan; he can address his Maker
every day in a different language 'and upon Sunday in seven'.
With Sir Thomas Browne Howell rather pities than hates
Turk or infidel. If he hates any, it is those schismatics 'that
puzzle the sweet peace of our Church, so that I could bee
content to see an Anabaptist go to Hell on a Brownists
back'.

2. *Characters*

It was not an accident that the birth or rebirth of character-writing coincided with that of the essay, since both forms were engendered by the same social and cultural conditions. The character, like the essay, appeared late in antiquity. Theophrastus was an elder contemporary and probably a teacher of Menander; in other words, his *Characters* were written when Athens was shrinking from a state into a cultured suburb, when the new comedy was devoting itself to the realistic portrayal of urban manners and types of character. In the second place Theophrastus was the pupil of Aristotle and his successor at the Lyceum. His characters, in part the diversions of a philosopher and scientist, in part dramatic footnotes to his serious works, might serve as illustrations of Peripatetic ethics. The vices that he pictures, flattery, surliness, arrogance, and the like, constitute lapses from the rational standards of civilized behaviour. (If Theophrastus wrote characters of virtues they are not extant.) The formal pattern is simple. It is a paragraph which begins with a brief definition of a vice, proceeds with a series of descriptive and narrative items that show a representative of it in his everyday conduct, and ends when the author chooses to stop. In manner, as Richard Flecknoe said in his *Enigmatical Characters* (1658), 'tis more Seneca than Cicero, and speaks rather the language of Oracles than Orators'.

Of course informal sketches of individuals or types are as old as literature and were produced in our period as in every other, for instance in social pamphlets and in epigrams; and the long line of character books may perhaps be said to have been inaugurated by Breton's very un-Theophrastian *Fantastics*, if it was first published in 1604. But the Theophrastian *descriptio* itself had been a traditional branch of rhetoric and education and hence of writing generally, so that seventeenth-century characters were new chiefly in being exploited in a more standardized and wholesale way. Besides these living traditions of the usually isolated character, many other factors combined to give a fresh welcome to the Greek pattern after Casaubon brought out his edition and translation of Theophrastus in 1592 (to this, the first nearly complete text, five more characters were added in 1599). General attachment to classical models, particularly in satire and epigram; the Horatian precepts regarding fixed dramatic types and the familiar examples in Terence and Plautus; the persistence of the classifying habit of mind, of allegorical and typical modes of conceiving character and of medieval forms of social satire; the medieval and continuing use of character-sketches as *exempla* in sermons (such as Thomas Adams's); the growth of psychological studies and the medical, psychological, and dramatic doctrine of 'humours'; the love of aphorisms, proverbs, and paradoxes; the instinct for realistic treatment of actual life and manners, which had achieved fuller expression in social pamphlets, satires, and plays than in the modern medium of prose fiction; the eagerness to apply a simple formula that could be both didactic and entertaining; and perhaps one may add literary men's consciousness of aristocratic cultural standards and of the disturbing pressure of commercial, professional, and religious groups—these were some main reasons for the enormous vogue of character-writing in the seventeenth century.

The formal introduction or revival of the Theophrastian character had been accomplished before the appearance in 1616 of John Healey's translation of Theophrastus, and, for such an imitable kind of writing, the Greek model was not essential. Some writers echoed Theophrastus, but not a great deal, partly because they were concerned with a different world and partly because they soon outgrew his deceptively simple technique and style. Indeed, the first seventeenth-century characters have already left Theophrastus behind. More than one of the conditions listed in the preceding paragraph would suggest that the genre ought to have been introduced by Ben Jonson, and in some sense it was. In the sketches of the dramatis personae prefixed to *Every Man out of his Humour* (1600), and in some fullfledged portraits in *Cynthia's Revels* (1601), we have objective catalogues of particular habits, though without an abstract definition and without a clearly unifying moral idea, and plain statement mostly gives way to satirical and figurative wit. The subjects, moreover, are social rather than ethical types. Jonson was no doubt conscious of his favourite Martial, and of recent satire and epigram, as well as of Theophrastus.

The first formal collection, *Characters of Virtues and Vices* (1608), was the work of that inevitable pioneer, Joseph Hall.[1]

---

[1] Joseph Hall (1574–1656), after a distinguished career at Emmanuel College, Cambridge, was given (1601) a meagre living in Suffolk by the Drurys (Donne's

The most obvious resemblance to Theophrastus is that of Hall's twenty-six (originally twenty-four) characters all but one or two deal with ethical types. In his choice of some identical subjects and in a number of details Hall evidently has Theophrastus in mind. In method he is only partly Theophrastian. The Greek characters are brief, bare, and lively photographic reports; Hall, in his longer and solider pieces, can use the external, local, and specific, but much of his realism is of the generalized kind excogitated in the study. And with dramatic objectivity he continually mingles comment and interpretation, so that his vices are not free from abstraction and his virtues are almost wholly abstract. In treating virtues Hall would get no help from Theophrastus, though he had some English predecessors. Finally, Hall does not adhere to Theophrastian plainness of expression. 'Our English Seneca' is always a conscious stylist, and especially in the characters of vices he strives for epigrammatic and antithetical wit and point, the 'lesse grave, more Satyricall' manner apologized for in the proem. Hall urges that Christians may learn good lessons from heathen wisdom and pays tribute to 'that ancient Master of Morality' (Theophrastus) whom he follows 'with an higher & wider step'. But in his exposition of true peace and tranquillity he follows much more closely in the steps of Seneca (who is, of course, only a partial guide). Hall's moral and religious aim— we may remember that he counts among the casuists of the age—contributes to both his relative heaviness and his subtlety of delineation. His characters, especially of virtues, are, apart from their form, a natural sequel to his Christian-Senecan

patrons). In 1608 he became a chaplain to Prince Henry and moved to a better cure at Waltham Holy Cross in Essex, which he held for twenty-one years. In 1616, while in France with Lord Doncaster's embassy, he was made Dean of Worcester. He was one of the king's representatives at the Synod of Dort (1618). Hall became Bishop of Exeter in 1627 and of Norwich in 1641. In 1640–1 the moderate Low Churchman wrote pamphlets in defence of episcopacy which brought on controversy with the Smectymnuans and Milton. He was one of the thirteen bishops imprisoned by parliament during the earlier part of 1642, and in 1643 he was forced into retirement by sequestration. Hall had known Donne well enough to be remembered in his will, and in his later days he had some association with Sir Thomas Browne. He wrote numerous books of meditative and practical piety as well as sermons and miscellaneous things, and was an important exemplar of Christian Stoicism and Senecan prose. He was, in fact, one of the most versatile and experimental of literary clerics: witness his notable satires, *Virgidemiarum* (1597–8), the 'utopian' prose satire, *Mundus Alter et Idem* (1605?), which was noticed in Chapter II, and the *Epistles* and *Characters*.

Meditations and Vows (1605) and *Heaven upon Earth* (1606). In the depiction of vices Hall, though still earnest, could pretty well hold his own with the wits, and his phrases, unlike theirs, do not cry out for footnotes. The author of *Virgidemiarum* here wields the scourge or the scalpel with an occasional forgetfulness of his didactic purpose which the reader willingly condones. Hall's *Characters*—and the other prose works just mentioned—soon received the unusual honour of foreign translations.

When so sincere a moralist as Hall could yield to the satirical allurements of the form, it was to be expected that young men of letters would go farther. One 'W.M.' put a set of characters into a framework in *The Man in the Moon* (1609). But the witty character was definitely established by Sir Thomas Overbury and 'other learned Gentlemen his Friendes'.[1] The first bunch of twenty-one characters, by Overbury and others, was added to his poem *A Wife* (1614), and the number was rapidly enlarged, mainly, it would seem, by the work of professional authors rather than 'gentlemen'. The chief names are John Webster, the dramatist, who on good grounds is now assigned thirty-two of the characters added to the sixth edition (1615); Dekker, who is thought to have done the six pieces on a debtors' prison added to the ninth edition (1616); and John Donne, whose character of a dunce and 'Essay of Valour' were the last pieces added (1622). The final total was eighty-two. There were several reasons for the great popularity of the book—the characters, the much-praised and much-imitated poem (itself a sort of character), and, when the news broke, the tragic scandal of Overbury's death, which was the theme of many broadsides.

The Overbury group had cleverness and variety of matter, they made the character thoroughly English, and set the standard for that kind of writing, but they brought little to the genre that was actually new. Both their technique and their subjects

---

[1] Sir Thomas Overbury (1581–1613) was an able and ambitious courtier of literary tastes. The first chapter of his life included Oxford and the Middle Temple. He became the friend and adviser of Robert Carr, later Earl of Somerset, and for some years he forwarded and shared his patron's prosperity at court. When he opposed Carr's marriage with Frances Howard, Countess of Essex, the combined hostility of the countess, the Howards, and the king brought him to the Tower, where he was poisoned. The story leaked out and a trial followed (1615–16). The earl and countess were convicted but their lives were saved by the king; the lesser flies, as Howell calls them, were executed. The case has as many dubious as unsavoury elements. Overbury's poem, *A Wife*, was entered in December 1613, a few months after his death.

represent a selective exploitation of existing elements. They largely avoid Hall's didacticism and generalized satire, but they carry on his mingling of fact with comment and carry much further his epigrammatic and conceited wit. In other words their method was very close to that of Jonson, a friend of Overbury's, who to all these negative and positive qualities had added a notable amount of pungent observation. Indeed in most of their work the Overbury group may be called lighter and more flippant Jonsons. In subject-matter they much prefer the English social types of Jonson to the ethical types of Hall and Theophrastus, and the idealistic portraits which furnish such an attractive wing in the Overbury gallery have precedents in Jonson as well as in Hall. Of course all these elements from native realism to puns were familiar in the less formal and more popular character-sketches of pamphleteers and preachers.

To say this is not to detract from the writers' real originality in re-creating their instrument and playing so many lively tunes upon it. Our chief interest in their work is in the broad cross-section it gives of early Jacobean society, male and female, high and low, bad and sometimes good. The point of view is mainly satirical, because young men about town and men of letters seldom look amiably upon the academic, professional, and commercial *bourgeoisie* or upon Puritans. Yet the writers do not spare their own class; if university pedants have too much learning, the courtier, the 'Inns of Court man', and the gentleman of town and country may have too little. As a rule, however, the authors' intellectual and social attitude is not very seriously philosophic. They take their world as they find it and are more concerned with discovering victims for their wit than with diagnosing social ills. One exception is the prison characters probably written by Dekker and written within the walls he knew so well. While these too keep up a rattle of witty musketry, they have besides touches of the poignant realism and human sympathy that distinguish Dekker from many of his contemporaries.

One principle of the early character is summed up in the nursery tag: when he is good he is very, very good, and when he is bad he is horrid. The painter, unless he happens to be John Earle, does not mix black and white but lays on each colour with single-hearted gusto. There are in the Overbury collection a dozen idealistic characters, and seven of them, including the best ones, are among those assigned to Webster. 'An Excellent Actor', a reply to John Stephens's 'A Common Player', is a gracious and dignified portrait possibly drawn from Burbage. The famous prose lyric, 'A Fair and Happy Milkmaid', which Walton so happily remembered, may, like Elizabethan pastoral verse, be too Arcadian for some tastes—bits of it are in fact taken from Sidney's book—but that fault, if it be one, cannot be charged against 'A Franklin', a sturdy pillar of a paternal rural economy.

From 1614 onward every warbler had the tune by heart and only a few names can be mentioned here. One, which attests more clearly than Hall's the mutual debt of character and sermon, is that of the great Puritan preacher, Thomas Adams. Earlier in this chapter the mingling and the merging of the character and the essay were illustrated by reference to such men as Breton, Stephens, and Mynshul, and other developments will be noticed as we go on. But the best of all character-books, Earle's *Microcosmography* (1628–9), does not owe its primacy to formal innovations; in some outward and inward ways it is more Theophrastian than any of its kind.[1] To a mode of writing that encouraged the brittle and flashy, Earle, without loss (and with better control) of wit and satirical edge, added the element of quiet contemplation, so that his best pieces, which are numerous, become essays; though impersonal, they reveal the mind and heart that charmed his friends. Like Felltham, and like his associates at Great Tew, Earle is a liberal and cultivated divine who loves the beauty of order in the individual and in Church and State. He condemns the irrational eccentricity of the blunt man and the sceptic, and the

---

[1] As one of the younger lights of Oxford, John Earle (1600?–65) was a member of the choice company which forgathered at Great Tew. In 1641 he became tutor to Prince Charles and the attachment lasted till his death. As a 'malignant' he was soon deprived of his preferments and he lived abroad for sixteen years. In exile he translated the *Ecclesiastical Polity* and the *Eikon Basilike* into Latin; the unfinished manuscript of the former was accidentally destroyed but the latter was published. At the Restoration Earle was made Dean of Westminster, then Bishop of Worcester and later of Salisbury. His personal character and his efforts on behalf of persecuted Nonconformity won the admiration of such men as Baxter.

Unlike his 'staid man', Earle wrote some verse in his younger days. The first edition of *Microcosmography* (1628) contained fifty-four characters; twenty-three were added in the fifth edition (1629) and one in 1633. The seventeenth-century editions were anonymous, though the authorship was early known. The book reached its 'eighth edition' in 1664, the year when the Overbury collection attained its seventeenth. Two unnumbered editions of Earle had been issued in 1650.

irrational conformity of the vulgar-spirited man and the mere formal man; and he contrasts the shallowness of the 'Young Raw Preacher' with the humane solidity of the 'Grave Divine', who 'is a Protestant out of judgement, not faction'.

A number of Earle's characters are more or less direct replies to those of the Overbury group, and comparison shows at once the difference between shooting at a haystack target and critical and sympathetic analysing of actions and motives. The Overburian 'Old Man' is merely a tedious, stubborn, offensive nuisance. Earle's 'Good Old Man' is not a sentimental idealization, but he has wisdom and dignity along with his Polonian defects. In the 'Mere Scholar' the man of the world is only scoring points and produces a conventional caricature. Earle, a don who excels in academic satire, presents in his downright scholar a worthy ancestor of Dominie Sampson; his manners are not those of a courtier, but 'his fault is onely this, that his mind is somewhat too much taken up with his minde'. The melancholy man, though an unwontedly philosophic figure in the Overbury collection, is a catalogue of symptoms. Earle defines a discontented man in an arresting phrase, 'one that is falne out with the world, and will bee revenged on himselfe', and cuts immediately to 'The roote of his disease . . . a selfe-humouring pride'. Whether praising or blaming, Earle is not content to report what a character does or is, he asks why.

Earle unites all the virtues of the tradition, the dramatic observation and ethical reason of Theophrastus, the moral and religious seriousness and interpretative habit of Hall, the epigrammatic wit and English realism of the Overburian writers. And these qualities are broadened and deepened by insight, wisdom, kindliness, and humour, especially remarkable in a young man. Like Theophrastus's boor, the 'Plain Country Fellow' stands dumb and astonished in contemplation of a good fat cow, yet Earle brings humorous truth and sympathy to the picture of an immortal Hodge, a brother of Tennyson's northern farmer—but not of the peasant of modern fiction, since he has 'reason enough to doe his businesse, and not enough to be idle or melancholy'. Earle's book lives up to its title; it is a miniature human comedy. And, like his own contemplative man, 'Hee looks not upon a thing as a yawning stranger at novelties; but his search is more mysterious and inward, and hee spels Heaven out of earth'. Earle's child, a charming addition to the normal range of subjects, is a child of tears and laughter who is not made unreal either by a hint of Neoplatonism or by Shakespearian irony: 'his Drums, Rattles and Hobby-horses' are 'but the Emblems, & mocking of mens businesse'. It is indeed Earle's enveloping irony that gives even slight sketches and trivial items a philosophic largeness of suggestion. A 'Pot-Poet' is not merely a bibulous and ridiculous balladmonger; it is scarcely hyperbole to say that the whole tragicomic contrast between what man is and what man would be is implicit in the phrase, 'sitting in a Bawdy-house, hee writes Gods Judgements'.

The English character had begun with a wide extension of the Theophrastian range and method, and our survey may end with a work that unites character, aphorism, injunction, essay, and biography in what is essentially a comprehensive conduct-book, Fuller's *The Holy State* (1642).[1] The first, second, and fourth books deal in the main with family relationships, occupations, and the governing class respectively, and the fifth with 'the profane state' from the harlot and witch to the traitor and tyrant. The formal division between sheep and goats had precedents in Hall and in Breton's *The Good and the Bad* (1616), but Fuller's entire and practical didacticism sets him apart from the normal Theophrastian tradition and compels abandonment of the Theophrastian pattern. The essays or 'General Rules' of his third section, in themselves a book of conduct and courtesy, consist of strings of maxims elaborated in comment and anecdote, and the same method is used in the characters, so that dramatic realism and satirical analysis give way to good counsel. The addition of numerous separate *exempla* is prompted by Fuller's interest in biography and by the instinct of a popular-izer. Altogether *The Holy State* answers the plea made in the *Advancement of Learning* for studies of 'the proper duty, vertue,

---

[1] Thomas Fuller (1608–61) was the son of a clergyman and the nephew of two prominent ecclesiastics. He was at Cambridge in the period of George Herbert, Taylor, and Milton. His actual or nominal connexion with his University, of which he published a *History* in 1655, covered seventeen years. A successful ministerial career, which brought him to the Savoy Chapel, was interrupted by the war. In 1643 he took refuge in Oxford, then served as chaplain with Hopton's army, and stayed a while at Exeter, where he printed the first volume of his popular *Good Thoughts* (1645). After some years of wandering Fuller found peace in the curacy of Waltham Abbey (1649), and was allowed to do a good deal of preaching in London. With one of his patrons he went to The Hague to welcome Charles II— his sole foreign travel. He became a royal chaplain and regained old preferments but did not enjoy them long. Fuller's chief works in biography and history are noticed in the following chapter.

challenge, and right, of every severall vocation, profession, and place', and much of its inspiration comes from Bacon, the thinker and essayist who had translated abstract philosophy into terms of modern utility, and from William Perkins, the theologian who had taught family and social duties and ministered to the individual conscience. And, of course, Fuller is never far from the Bible.

To those whose affection for him is solidly based on Lamb and choice extracts it may seem blasphemous to say that *The Holy State*, read as a whole, is extremely dull. But it is of great interest as a literary and social document. We noticed in the first chapter how the aristocratic courtesy book adapted itself to the needs of the country gentry and prosperous commercial class; and Fuller, like Brathwait (whom he frequently echoes), is a conspicuous exemplar of classical and Christian humanism reduced to the plane of philistine common sense and rather pedestrian obligations and virtues. For one aspect of the matter there is his view of 'degree' as the framework of society. From the king, 'a mortall God' embodied to perfection in Charles, down to the household servant, all creatures, including the lay patron with livings in his gift, have their place and duties. This traditional theory, most familiar to us in the speech of Shakespeare's Ulysses, is a law of nature more readily appreciated by the upper than by the lower classes. Fuller, accepting the divine and feudal scheme without question, labours to heighten his readers' sense of responsibility to God and especially to man, but he points out, with a characteristic mixture of piety and worldly wisdom, the chances of an individual's overleaping the bars of caste. A younger brother, though divinely ordained to be a younger brother, may with divine help win fame and fortune in war, in business, at court, or by marriage. The sturdy yeoman, by thrift and enterprise, may become a gentleman. While the contemporary scene cast some dark shadows over his buoyant pages and particularly over his preface, in 1640–2 Fuller saw only dimly that his static, comfortable world of mutual obligation and trust, of pure and unenthusiastic religion breathing household laws, had long been changing from a fact, if it ever was a fact, into an ideal; and it was soon to be shaken so violently that Clarendon, a not unprejudiced witness to be sure, was to trace the corruptions of the next age to the break-up of family ties and traditional *mores* in the civil war.

In general, there is a large difference in tone between the magnanimous *sententiae* hallowed by humanistic tradition and the proverbial wisdom of Fuller. 'Knowing that knotty timber is unfit to build with, he edifies people with easie and profitable matter.' Never a man's thought in the world keeps the roadway better than his, but fertility in platitude is equalled by the fertility of fancy that turns platitude into epigram. At his best Fuller crystallizes common sense in unforgettable phrases: 'They that marry where they do not love, will love where they do not marry'; 'one is not bound to believe [of the controversial divine] that all the water is deep that is muddy'. Coleridge's dictum, that wit was the stuff and substance of Fuller's intellect, has often been used to set him as an amiable gargoyle in an isolated niche of quaint eccentricity. But no small share of his writing is quite plain and direct and, moreover, wit was a quality of mind and style almost universal in his time, not least among preachers, though Fuller's wit was perhaps more homely and spontaneous, and certainly was less integral, penetrating, and serious, than that of many contemporaries. Magistrates and ministers, Fuller says, should be 'metamorphos'd from all lightnesse to Gravity', but in his case the process was never completed. George Fox would, not without reason, have called him a great lump of earth, and Fuller would, not without reason, have pronounced Fox an arrogant trouble-maker. But Fuller's writings as a whole leave us in no more doubt of his fundamental earnestness than of his fundamental limitations. If in guiding his readers to heaven he was fascinated by many good things along the road, at any rate he did not get too far in advance, and as a preacher a child of this world is sometimes more effective than the children of light.

While some more or less readable writers had continued to play the standard tunes, others struck out original variations. One highly original book—even if it owed something to Breton's *Fantastics*—was *A Strange Metamorphosis of Man, Transformed into a Wilderness* (1634). The anonymous author deals with the natural world, from the stag and the horse and less familiar beasts down to the snail and the gnat (and he includes trees and shrubs, the lake and the coal-pit); his fresh and fanciful awareness of creatures and things is fused with a wise knowledge of man, but, as his period and his brisk, witty, 'Lipsian' style guarantee, he has no trace of sentimentality. In general, the early writers started a number of hares which produced large and doubtfully legitimate families. Early characters of Puritans led on to the religious and political invectives of the civil war and the interregnum. Early sketches of places developed into such extended but lively things as Felltham's *Brief Character of the Low Countries* (1652), Marvell's 'Character of Holland' (1653) in verse, and Evelyn's *Character of England* (1659). But we have met the chief representatives of the genre before 1660 and must be content with microcosmography.

In the course of this chapter we have, inevitably, seen almost as much of the essay's parents and aunts and uncles as of the growing child. One title of Francis Osborn's partly indicates the variety of kinship—*A Miscellany of Sundry Essays, Paradoxes, and Problematical Discourses, Letters and Characters* (1659). While the numerous writers would yield a respectable anthology of familiar essays, the definite emergence of the pure type comes after 1660, with Cowley. The old traditions of the impersonal religious homily and the impersonal humanistic discourse did not encourage the essayist to speak freely of his own experience and of the small matters of everyday life. If the great French essayist had done so, the great English one had not. Montaigne was widely read, but his actual influence is hard to estimate; it is fairly clear, for instance, in the young Cornwallis and in the early unpublished essays (1652–3) of Sir William Temple. We cannot ascribe all the qualities of the essayist's temper, which many Englishmen of our period possessed, to the study of Montaigne, but certainly he would support the writers who preached rational moderation and urbane, gentlemanly culture, and who aimed at a colloquial, personal manner.

Since the early essay springs so directly from Renaissance humanism it is more seriously and solidly didactic and ethical, more aristocratic and masculine in its appeal, than the papers of Steele and Addison. Our essayists are always striving to re-express, chiefly for the educated ruling class, the eternal verities of moral and civil wisdom as these had been laid down by the ancients. They teach Stoic control of the passions rather than the solution of domestic problems, the management of a state rather than of a fan, the knowledge of man rather than of London. But if most essayists of the age carried heavier guns than most of their successors, their readers did too. And didactic seriousness was more or less mitigated by touches of personal reminiscence, wit, humour, satire, and a frequent vein of poetry. Unlike Montaigne, the early essayists rarely scrutinize the fundamentals of orthodox religion and morality. Following the Tudor humanists, they take these as fixed and labour to uphold tradition, order, and authority—as, to be sure, Montaigne did also, in his own way. But at the end of the period we have such a significant portent as Francis Osborn, that disillusioned rationalist who was akin to Samuel Butler. (In that, while 'wanting the Engines of Learning', he endeavoured 'to shake the Pillars of the Schooles', Osborn was akin to the Victorian Butler as well.) Another sceptic, of greater moral earnestness than Osborn, but a disciple of Bacon, Montaigne, and especially Charron, was Richard Whitlock, author of *Zootomia* (1654), a combination of 'anatomy', essays, and characters.

The vast popularity of the character, wit's descant on the plainsong of the essay, did a good deal to check the growth of the more learned and contemplative form. The evolution of the two was roughly parallel and we have observed their tendency to merge. Both widened their scope to take in almost any kind of writing, and in both the original preponderance of *utile* over *dulce* diminished. The essay and the character alike embodied ideals of rational, civilized behaviour and culture. These ideals were a traditional and international inheritance, yet in England they continued to be nourished by a vigorous and heterogeneous individualism. In contemporary France the same ideals and the same literary forms suffered from the dominance of a standardized and overcivilized minority. Montaigne had no worthy successors; the genuine essayist could hardly live in the close air of the *salon*. And while the English character-writers painted the rich variety of street and farm, study and tavern, La Bruyère, though he began by translating Theophrastus, analysed members of the *beau monde*.

VII

HISTORY AND BIOGRAPHY

HISTORY, said Cicero, in words often repeated—and with emblematic elaboration in the frontispiece to Ralegh's *History of the World*—is 'testis temporum, lux veritatis, vita memoriae, magistra vitae, nuntia vetustatis'. These oracular phrases, understood in diverse but distinctly forward-looking ways, might cover the several broad conceptions of history and historiography that constituted the inheritance of writers of our period. There was, first, the religious and teleological view, which had an early exemplar in Augustine's *City of God*, and which in time embraced many variations, unilinear and cyclical, deteriorationist and progressive, scripturally prophetic and scientifically prophetic (we may think of the currents of ideas represented by the philosophic clerics, Godfrey Goodman and George Hakewill). In the Tudor chronicles and their successors the religious and providential conception could merge with the humanistic and ethical view of history as philosophy teaching by examples, examples of both states and men reaching greatness through virtue and wisdom and brought low by wickedness and folly. A third and in its way no less didactic view, derived, like that of orthodox humanism, from the classics, was the realistic analysis of the actual motives and workings of statecraft, power politics; the great ancient model here was Tacitus, the great modern exponents were Machiavelli and Guicciardini. The English historians of our period, while they moved on different lines and levels, could not help sharing these established aims and principles.

In the long list of English translations from the classics in the sixteenth and early seventeenth centuries the works of ancient historians and moralists together far outweigh other kinds of literature. By 1600 many minor historians and some major ones had been turned into English, and in that year Philemon Holland's *Livy* announced a translator who combined nobility of style with a new standard of scholarship. Among his later translations were Suetonius (1606) and Camden's great antiquarian work, *Britannia* (1610). Heywood translated Sallust in

1608, with a preface taken from Bodin's *Methodus ad Facilem Historiarum Cognitionem*. The industrious Edward Grimeston rendered many modern works and, in 1633, Polybius. In 1629 Hobbes commenced his literary and anti-democratic career with a version of Thucydides, a version more faithful to the author's style than the smooth periods of Jowett. Tacitus had been done in the late years of Elizabeth, and his high prestige both as a stylist and, in Donne's phrase, as 'the Patriarch, and Oracle of States-men' is attested by such admirers as Bacon (who pointed out to Elizabeth Sir John Hayward's Tacitean 'felony'), Jonson, and the essayists Cornwallis, Robert Johnson, and Daniel Tuvill. The names of Hayward and Tacitus remind us that historians suffered from royal and official fear of propaganda and that in 1627–8 the first incumbent of Fulke Greville's chair of history at Cambridge was silenced because his lectures on the *Annals* seemed to have a contemporary bearing. Oxford, by the way, already had the professorship of history founded by Camden (1622) and probably inspired by Sir Henry Savile's two scientific chairs.

The classical historians, along with such moderns as Comines, Sir Thomas More, Polydore Vergil, Edward Hall, Machiavelli, Guicciardini, Bodin, and Sarpi, contributed to raise the level of English historiography. A new era may be said to begin with Hayward. The simple method of the average Tudor chronicler had been to start with Brute, or Noah, or the Creation, and come down with increasing patriotic fervour through English history. We have links between old and new in the chronicles of the two tailors, the plain-sewing of the not very critical John Stow (1525–1605) and the stylistic embroidery of the more critical John Speed (1552?–1629); the latter received help from such men as Greville, Camden, and Cotton. Some old ways died hard. Even the scholarly Camden and the late and less scholarly Fuller clung to the annalistic method. The *Chronicle of the Kings of England* (1643) by Sir Richard Baker, that unfortunate old knight who commenced author in the Fleet prison, was eyed askance by scholars, but it continued, with many enlargements, to satisfy generations of country gentlemen like Sir Roger de Coverley. For us the persistence of medievalism (which was partly classical too) is more of a virtue than a defect. Clio was still in possession of her throne. The historian was a man, often a man of action, with a temperament, not a cloistered and impersonal card-index. The conception of history as epic story and drama, of individual men rather than social and economic forces as the causes of events, of God working out His will in human and especially English affairs, all this—though it included more and more of realistic diagnosis—meant that history had not yet been entirely robbed of its traditional poetry, that the Tudor historians could be distilled, and outdone, by Shakespeare. At the same time the record of the past was a guide to the present and future.

Our brief survey may begin with a glance at one general topic that touches many authors and illustrates the background of politics as well as the rise of the critical spirit in historiography. That is the slow death of the matter of Brute, New Troy, and Arthur. In the Middle Ages Geoffrey of Monmouth's 'lies' about Arthur might be attacked, but for the most part the Trojan dynasty stood firm. The later scepticism of the Italian Polydore Vergil drew protests from generations of patriotic chroniclers. The strength of traditional feeling is seen in the discretion with which Camden, the pioneer of historical criticism, indicated his doubts concerning Brute. Speed, in his review of the long controversy, declared that a renowned Christian nation should follow other countries in repudiating descent from 'Venus that lascivious Adulteresse'. The less emotional Selden, annotating *Poly-Olbion*, could argue for Brute 'but as an Advocat for the Muse' and speak of 'the Arcadian deduction of our British Monarchy'. Critical acid ate steadily into the roots of romantic legend, though poets were loath to relinquish stories that had lived so long in the hearts of Englishmen, stories that now, said Drayton, 'the envious world doth slander for a dreame'. Thus, apart from a few late and unimportant items, our period witnessed—to echo an excited phrase about Polydore from Edmund Howes (the continuator of Stow)—the cashiering of three-score princes, the definite separation of legend and history. Henceforth the story of Britain was to begin with Julius Caesar, a more substantial descendant of Venus than Brute. But Oxford, the home of lost causes, did not drop Brute from its Almanack until 1675.

The tradition involved more than literary sentiment. During the Middle Ages the tale of Arthur's empire and prophecies of his return had had political significance, and that they were made a part of Henry VII's dynastic propaganda we are reminded by the name given to his eldest son. In the latter part of the sixteenth century imperialistic, commercial, and antiquarian zeal revived the idea of the Tudor house as the true Arthurian line—an idea writ large in *The Fairy Queen*. After the prolonged anxiety about the succession, the union of England and Scotland evoked a fresh outburst of salutations in pageantry and in books to the second Arthur and second Brute. Shakespeare, Bacon, Jonson, Warner, Campion, Alexander, Drayton, Drummond, and other men of letters celebrated the sovereign who was, in Speed's phrase, the 'Inlarger and Uniter of the British Empire; Restorer of the British Name'.

We may digress from British history to take account of two works of grandiose sweep and sometimes epic power in which the medieval spirit works along with the modern. One is Richard Knolles's *General History of the Turks* (1603). The provincial schoolmaster was inevitably a compiler from secondary sources, but he had a fiery vision of God using the might of Islam to punish the sins of Christendom. We are arrested on the threshold by 'The glorious Empire of the Turkes, the present terrour of the world'. Knolles's fame in his own century was confirmed by the praise of Dr. Johnson, Southey, and Byron, and he would receive more than honourable mention here if this volume were, like his, a folio of 1,200 pages.

Sir Walter Ralegh's *History of the World* (1614), the huge fragment of a work which, like the *Instauratio Magna* or *The Fairy Queen*, only Elizabethan energy could conceive, was written by a man who had been a soldier, sailor, colonizer, statesman, courtier, and chemist, as well as an author of poetry and prose, a man now prematurely old and broken, confined in the Tower under suspended sentence of death. Ralegh was not a scholar but he had always been, as Naunton said, an indefatigable reader whether by sea or land, and in this task he had some helpers, Robert Burhill the orientalist (according to Aubrey), and Ben Jonson for 'a peice . . . of the punick warre' (according to Jonson); and tradition includes other names. There were also the usual short cuts; the first four chapters on the Creation were indebted to commentaries on Genesis like that of Benedict Pererius. Even so the book is a monument of Ralegh's own labour and learning and literary power. Its vast scope grew out of its kinship with the medieval encyclopaedia or 'mirror' and the literature *de casibus virorum illustrium*, and the book of advice to princes. All these motives were unified by Ralegh's desire to show the working of Providence from the beginning of the world down—and not too far down—through British history; his emblematic frontispiece, already referred to, has at the top a great eye labelled 'Providentia'. But the death of his young patron, Prince Henry, and no doubt his increasing restlessness of soul and body, led him to break off in the second century B.C. Prudential flattery of James proved vain. Ralegh's daring to publish a book when 'civilly dead', his saucy censuring of princes, and his anti-Spanish feeling only roused his captor's animosity. But the *History* was popular from the first and was esteemed by such various persons as Elizabeth of Bohemia and Ussher, Cromwell and Montrose, Milton and Joseph Hall, and even the exacting Peter Heylyn.

Ralegh's long preface was the most comprehensive and eloquent discussion of historiography so far given by an Englishman. It included a philosophized survey of English history from Edward II to Henry VIII which links him with Hayward and Daniel and Shakespeare; and his general conception of history as a cyclical pattern, though not a novel one, is a special link with Daniel. As for the earliest part of the text proper, Ralegh's speculations on the waters above the firmament and the site of Paradise led Matthew Arnold to contrast him with the critical modernity of Thucydides. However, within the limits set by his entire acceptance of Scripture, Ralegh brings critical reason to the scrutiny of all human authority, historical, Aristotelian, patristic, and scholastic, and his mind works more freely when he leaves the Bible and the chosen people for profane history. In comparing Roman with English soldiers or showing the advantages of control of the sea he writes with the plain force and sagacity of an experienced commander, and his admiration for the great generals of old is mingled with a quite natural and contemporaneous sense of professional kinship. Thus Ralegh unites, in more even balance than his contemporaries, the realistic and the religious traditions of historiography; but it is probably the religious, medieval, and poetic strain that predominates in our memories. In the great drama of the rise and fall of kings and empires the head of the 'school of atheism' sees everywhere the hand of God, who casts down the mighty from their seats. The grand panorama of God's judgements especially commended the *History* to Puritans and republicans in the seventeenth century, though the general belief in Providence in history was shared by such realists as Lord Herbert and Clarendon—and has its adherents in our own day. Allied with that is the conception of mutability in the lives of nations and of men, and Ralegh touches the great theme with spontaneous and masculine beauty of phrase and rhythm. The gallant man of action is haunted by thoughts of time and age and death,

towards which we alwayes travaile both sleeping and waking: neither have those beloved companions of honour and riches any power at all, to hold us any one day, by the promises of glorious entertainments; but by what crooked path so ever wee walke, the same leadeth on directly to the house of death: whose doores lie open at all houres, and to all persons. For this tide of mans life, after it once turneth and declineth, ever runneth with a perpetuall ebbe and falling streame, but never floweth againe: our leafe once fallen, springeth no more, neither doth the Sunne or the Summer adorne us againe, with the garments of new leaves and flowers.

It is not the new science, for all Ralegh's knowledge, that darkens his broodings over the frailty and brevity of life. Such words are in the spirit of Homer and Catullus and Ovid, still more of *Everyman* and the Dance of Death and 'To-morrow, and to-morrow, and to-morrow. . .'. And what gives these common-places their special poignancy is that Ralegh is sincere but not secure in his *contemptus mundi*. We read knowing that he was to make one last effort to regain honour and riches and taste 'the false and durelesse pleasures of this stage-play world', knowing too how soon his pride, cruelty, and ambition were to be covered all over with those two narrow words, *Hic iacet*.

While Ralegh writes history as an amateur, Sir John Hayward (1564?–1627)[1] and Samuel Daniel (1563?–1619) have a semi-professional air. Both exemplify the mixed inheritance of Tudor historiography, on a new plane of philosophic and artistic syn-thesis and prose style; both, too, look forward to Clarendon. They have the full humanistic faith in the political and ethical

---

[1] On leaving Cambridge (B.A., 1581; LL.D., 1591), Hayward combined legal practice with writing. *Henry IV* (1599), with its account of Richard's deposition and its dedication to Essex, led to the author's imprisonment (1600–1/3?). Hay-ward became historiographer of Chelsea College (1610), a Master in Chancery (1616), was knighted (1619), and was on the Court of High Commission (1620, 1626) and in Parliament. His minor writings include a reply to Robert Parsons the Jesuit concerning the succession (1603), which owed much to Bodin's *République*, and devotional works, of which one, *The Sanctuary of a Troubled Soul* (1601?–7) was more popular than the histories.

value of history, along with full awareness of the historian's
problems. Hayward's first book, *Henry IV* (1599), is well known,
if rarely read; it was more concerned with the reign, dethrone-
ment, and death of Richard than with its ostensible subject,
Henry's first year. He also wrote *Lives of the III Normans* (1613),
Edward VI (1630), and an unfinished book which covered the
first four years of Elizabeth. He has been said to deal with
history precisely as Shakespeare did. *Henry IV* showed him as
already a conscious reformer of English historical writing and
as a pioneer of the Tacitean-Machiavellian school, a realistic
interpreter of political events, the sequence of cause and effect,
in terms of men's character and behaviour. At the same time,
as we might expect from the author of devotional books, Hayward makes moral judgements and can appeal to the divine
nemesis, to what, in his account of William the Conqueror, he
calls 'the secret working and will of God, which is the cause of
all causes'.

Daniel's *History of England* was to have come from the beginning through the Tudor age, but the two parts published (1612;
1618?) got no farther than 1377. A promised appendix of documents did not appear, though the promise of such a thing was
significant; and the text included a number of letters ('which
are the best peeces of History in the world'). This work, having
a much longer span than Daniel's poem, *The Civil Wars*, required scrutiny of much more diverse sources. He dropped the
whole mass of legendary history and began with Julius Caesar;
but he was less ready than the strongly Protestant Milton to
discount monastic chroniclers. One example of his critical sense
is his affirming that the 'maine streame' of the common law,
which Coke held to be of immemorial antiquity, came in with
the Normans: 'it is the equity, and not the antiquity of lawes,
that makes them venerable' (a phrase that recalls the epistle to
Egerton). Daniel's broad scope, and perhaps also lack of inclination, do not encourage the dramatic incidents that give imaginative immediacy to Hayward's work. He takes in 'all varietie
of accidents fit for example, and instruction' and regards 'in-
tegritie' as 'the chiefest duty of a Writer'. Like Hayward, he
analyses mundane motive and cause and effect and delivers
moral verdicts. In half a dozen places (one of them his last
sentence) he appeals with conviction to God's judgements and
providence. These attitudes coalesce with the philosophic and

ethical sense of history that is conspicuous in Daniel's other writings, with the doctrine, here stated at the beginning, that, while circumstances change, the virtues and vices of men and nations are the same in all ages.

Only mention can be made of a book which a modern scholar (J. G. A. Pocock) has called 'perhaps the most outstanding piece of historical writing achieved by an Englishman in James I's reign', namely Sir John Davies's *Discovery of the True Causes Why Ireland Was Never Entirely Subdued . . . until the Beginning of his Majesty's Happy Reign* (1612). Certainly—granted its premisses— Davies's work is a statesmanlike and remarkably lucid analysis of the defects of English military and civil policy in Ireland from the first attempts at conquest.

Of the various accounts of English sovereigns this period produced the only one that is now read is Bacon's *History of the Reign of Henry VII* (1622), a work which, though stripped of its authority, still commands the admiration of historical specialists. This book, the first fruit of enforced leisure after his fall, was Bacon's own partial and hasty fulfilment of a larger design, a history of the Tudor age, which in the *Advancement of Learning* he had held out to other writers as a worthy enterprise (and which Daniel fell short of). He had in fact written a fragment which Speed was able to quote in discussing Henry in his *History of Great Britain* (1611). The groundwork of Bacon's book was furnished by Polydore Vergil, through the medium of Edward Hall. To Cotton's manuscript collections he was indebted for supplementary materials, from Fabyan's 'London Chronicle', Bernard André's account of Henry, and various documents; and he made full use of the Rolls of Parliament. Selden praised him, with Camden, for going to such records. Bacon added his considered theory of history, his political and legal experience and insight, his imagination (especially in speeches on the classical model), and his style. His concentration on kingcraft may now appear somewhat narrow, and he has erroneous and fanciful details, yet he far excels most of his predecessors in his artistic and coherent picture of events and still more in his analysis of Henry's policy. As 'a perfect and peremptory royalist' and as a fallen Chancellor, Bacon wished to gratify James, but he said truly that he had not flattered his subject, and his sensitive master could hardly have relished some of the facts and comments. The Henry of modern research is a less Machiavellian

ruler than Bacon saw; in that altered light, however, the book
only reveals the more of its author. While Bacon occasionally
refers to God's providence, his political didacticism is in the
tradition of Tacitean realism, not religious teleology. Perhaps
the chief influence on his conception and method of historiography was Guicciardini.

We noted the wave of 'British' feeling that greeted King
James's accession. That wave ebbed, or rather flowed strongly
into a deeper channel, as his reign wore on and loyalties became
divided between king and Parliament. There appeared the
beginnings of the 'Whig' view of English history. Against the
theory of divine right champions of Parliament and the common law could maintain that these institutions were much older
than the Norman conquest and, with more validity, could cite
Magna Carta. Such appeals to a remote if sometimes nebulous
past had been made possible by the researches of many scholars
into all phases of early and especially Saxon history, legal, political, ecclesiastical, archaeological, and linguistic. Though the
Society of Antiquaries did not survive James's antagonism, the
library of Sir Robert Cotton might be called the Trojan horse
from which emerged the men who overthrew, or provided the
means of overthrowing, the walls of prerogative. Such students
of legal history as Coke (who was more uncritical than others
in his notions of pre-Conquest history), Cotton, Selden, and
Sir Henry Spelman (the interpreter of feudalism) were, indeed
had to be, readers and collectors of manuscripts. And, to revert
to a matter noticed above, 'Saxon' sentiment, allied as it largely
was with the rising opposition to the Crown, hastened the death
of British legend, while royalist sentiment helped to prolong its
life. In a non-political area one may mention the definite arrival
of a new standard of antiquarianism in the first volume (1655)
of the *Monasticon Anglicanum* compiled by Roger Dodsworth and
Sir William Dugdale, and of a new type of county history in
Dugdale's *Antiquities of Warwickshire* (1656).

Milton had reason to feel more keenly than most men the
pressure of conflicting claims, and his view of English origins, as
of more urgent problems, underwent changes. He gave up the
long-meditated Arthurian epic, but he cherished much old lore
in his imagination. In the *History of Britain* Milton was sympathetic towards Brute and early 'poetic' fable but quite sceptical about the historical Arthur. Writing in the decade after

1646—though the *History* was not published until 1670—with his eye on his own times, Milton found both British and Saxons incapable of maintaining true liberty; what virtues the latter had they lost, the former never had any, and God punished a sinful and servile nation with successive conquests. In general Milton combined a feeling for romantic story (if not monkish) with critical use of both the standard chroniclers and original sources. Incidentally, his effort at condensed narrative and characterization of persons confirms his expressed preference for Sallust over all the Latin historians.

The great monument of historical memoirs, Clarendon's, was begun in our period but belongs to the next. Some lesser examples are the attractive sketches of Elizabethan courtiers and statesmen that make up Sir Robert Naunton's *Fragmenta Regalia* (written about 1630 and published in 1641); Sir Anthony Weldon's account (1650–1), according to Heylyn and others a libellous account, of the courts of James and Charles; and the product of Thomas May's political conversion, *The History of the Parliament* (1647). The formidable mass of miscellaneous records we must pass by, though some of them will come into the discussion of autobiography.

The form and spirit of early biography, as of almost every kind of literature, were born of the marriage of classical and Christian traditions. Plutarch supplied the most winning ancient model for the handling of material and, what was even more attractive to the Renaissance humanist, a conception of biography based, like the 'character', on ethical principles. Then there were the motives and methods inherited from the vast body of medieval lives of saints, ecclesiastics, and exemplary rulers; when the main object was to glorify an illustrious servant of God and show readers what heights a human soul could attain, classical rationality might give place to credulous *naïveté* and an individual portrait to an ideal pattern. Medieval biography yielded many notable exceptions, however, and a vivid modern one was Roper's *Sir Thomas More*, written about 1556 and first printed at St. Omer in 1626. A typical 'saint's life' composed in our period was John Duncon's *Lady Falkland* (1648). One is at a loss to classify Urquhart's unique panegyric of the admirable Crichton. Another important biographical tradition was that represented by the long succession of works in verse deriving from Boccaccio's *De Casibus Virorum Illustrium*, which mirrored the lives of great sinners struck down by the hand of God, and great men brought low by the turn of Fortune's wheel or through a defect of character. An example of that dramatic conception was Cavendish's *Thomas Wolsey*, which, though finished in 1558 and circulated in manuscript, was first published as a whole in 1641, in garbled form, as a timely anti-episcopal tract.

In the *Advancement* Bacon lamented the deficiency of lives, and the century grew active in filling the gap; but during our period biography, like the essay, was only detaching itself from related forms and much of it was 'impure'. Since we must fix upon writers who still are or ought to be generally read, we can only mention a work which, if judged by its positive effect, might rank as one of the greatest books ever written in English, the *Eikon Basilike* (1649), the portrait of the royal martyr apparently completed from his papers by Dr. John Gauden and revised by Charles himself. And our general criterion must be strained at the outset, since not many people have read a famous piece of what Bacon would call 'Ruminated History', the *Life of Sir Philip Sidney* by Fulke Greville, Lord Brooke. This was written probably about 1610–14, perhaps revised later, and published in 1652. Greville was writing not a 'Life' but a 'Dedication', a partly autobiographical grand testament, to be prefixed to his own works, the exercises of his youth which owed much to Sidney's influence. He was also salvaging what he could of the formal history he had contemplated and abandoned when the younger Cecil refused him access to state papers. The larger portion of the digressive book—and this no doubt is what repels readers, in spite of the frequently noble matter and style—is taken up with detailed analysis of the political, religious, and commercial forces that had kept Europe in turmoil. This analysis is given partly as Sidney's, since he had laboured and died for his ideal of England as the militant champion of European Protestantism. The sections dealing with Sidney himself narrate only a few episodes and are rather a *laudatio* than a life. Sidney appears in dim or dazzling outline as the perfect hero of a tragic drama, a statesman-saint, one of God's elect. Whatever we deduct for retrospective idealization, it is a testimony to both men that Sidney, fine as he was, should have inspired such deep devotion in a nature so toughly critical as Greville's. But the survivor of a great friendship is not erecting a mere private monument; it is to be 'a Sea-mark' for the nation. A dis-illusioned statesman whose world seems out of joint, Greville turns to the past and holds up Sidney as the image of England's ancient vigour, the symbol of a great epoch and a great race that are gone. He repeatedly contrasts 'those active times', 'the ancient greatness of hearts', with the 'decrepit', 'effeminate', corrupt, and self-seeking age in which he lives. Such pessimism is more than sentimental nostalgia. Elizabeth, as Greville de-scribes her, had faults along with her lustrous virtues, but she made England a great power, she did not lavish money on favourites, she did not scheme to enlarge her prerogative, she did not resort to new taxes, impositions, and proclamations without the consent of Parliament. It was just as well that Greville's history was incomplete and posthumous.

At the opposite pole from Greville's are two other famous and smaller and livelier memorials. They contain only one element of biography, but that element is the quintessence, for the books are Drummond's *Conversations with Ben Jonson* and Selden's *Table Talk*. Drummond's notes were recorded in 1619 and first printed in full in 1833. Since almost every sentence has been quoted again and again, perhaps one general observation will be enough. We recognize Ben's aggressive critical mind, in the candour of dishabille, and yet, without setting up a Jonsonian image akin to the Stratford bust, we may at moments almost wish the notes unwritten. The visit Jonson paid in 1618–19 to the 'widowed' recluse of Hawthornden must have been some-thing like that of Heracles at the house of Admetus—or possibly that remark is proof of the unfortunate effect the book has had. While his host's character and cellar may have tempted Jonson to throw his considerable weight about, the *Conversations*, for all their objectivity, must be a selection conditioned and heightened by Drummond's reaction to a more robust personality. Many spicy items, along with the final comments on Jonson's egoism and infinite thirst, linger in memories that have forgotten the more truly Jonsonian wisdom of the *Discoveries* and the plays and poems. Although we are thankful that Jonson was not Goethe and Drummond not Eckermann, we must acknowledge that the book has contributed more than anything else to estab-lish, in place of the magnanimous Renaissance humanist and poet, the popular picture of a burly, arrogant, swashbuck-ling toper and scabrous gossip. If Jonson were only the man

Drummond saw and heard, he would scarcely be the commanding figure in English literature that he is. To say that is not to
say that his prime virtues were humility and abstemiousness.

The hard-headed John Selden (1584–1654) was a friend of
Jonson's and in some ways not unlike him. His *Table Talk*,
a record made by his secretary during the last twenty years
of his life, was published in 1689, the year in which his principles triumphed. Apart from his acquaintance with the wits
and his notes on *Poly-Olbion*, this is his one title to admission
into a history of English literature. 'The chief of learned men
reputed in this Land' (in Milton's phrase) enjoyed European
fame, but only the most resolute investigator now looks into
his numerous important works on constitutional, ecclesiastical,
and oriental law and antiquities. It is both the special praise
and the partial limitation of the *Table Talk* that it records, in
crisp, colloquial English, the interests and the clear workings of
a great legal and political mind. What we call 'life' comes in
abundantly, but through the back door, in the homely simili-
tudes and racy anecdotes employed to elucidate knotty political
and ecclesiastical problems. In spite of its contemporary focus
the book is a shrewd and pregnant commentary on the unchanging motives and attitudes of men, particularly of those
men who will not let well enough alone but must upset ordered
liberty, peace, and learning. But the *Table Talk* can only be
mentioned here; some pungent quotations appear in other
places.

Thomas Fuller's best-known books, *The Holy State* (1642),
The Church History of Britain (1655), and *The History of the
Worthies of England* (1662), all show him as biographer, historian, and antiquary, and in these congenial roles he does
not cease to be a preacher and essayist. Something was said
of *The Holy State* in the last chapter. The biographical sketches
with which Fuller seasoned his moral counsels in that book are
what appeal to the modern reader, who, like Aguecheek, cares
not for good life. One needs no great knowledge of St. Hilde-
gard to relish such a phrase as 'God who denied her legs, gave
her wings'. The biographies are didactic examples of the
various social and vocational types, and they are also the expanded anecdotes of a talker who is happier with actual persons
than with ideal abstractions. And didacticism might be strained
in justifying the account of Paracelsus. Even scholars shun the

works of Fuller's admired Perkins, but that faithful minister's emphasis on the word 'damn' has left a doleful echo in every ear. The author's normal charity does not extend to Joan of Arc, who, along with the woman of Endor, exemplifies 'the Witch'. And, as a lifelong devotee of John Foxe, he takes Milton to task for some harsh words about the Marian martyrs.

In the two larger works, for which Fuller gathered material over many years, 'the true Church Antiquary' had full scope for his talents. The *Worthies* is among other things a dictionary of national biography, a series of county histories, a topographical and historical gazetteer, a guide-book, and a dictionary of proverbs. Fuller's house of many gables is built on the foundations laid by Camden, Speed, Stow, and others. Portions of his subject had been treated by such antiquarian topographers as Norden, Richard Carew, William Burton, and Fuller's friend Dugdale. Foxe supplied Protestant martyrs and Bishop Godwin bishops. Fuller was conscientious, according to his light, in trying to check authorities. Besides, he jogged indefatigably about the country to inspect public records, manuscripts, places, and buildings, and to question natives and surviving relatives. As he remarked of one of his creditors, John Pits, 'It is hard to say whether his hands took more pains in writing, or feet in travelling . . .'. Considering the difficulties of research at the time, and the vicissitudes of Fuller's life, we can respect as well as enjoy his monumental labour of love. He had five objects before him: the glory of God, the preservation of dead men's memories, the furnishing of examples for the living, the entertainment of readers, and some honest profit for himself. Not all these objects have been sought by the austere makers of modern biographical dictionaries, nor could they avow that they had 'purposely interlaced (not as meat, but as condiment) many delightful stories'. The *Worthies* is a lineal descendant of the medieval encyclopaedias. Apart from the lists of sheriffs and gentry, we skip at our own risk, for Fuller's best goods may be under the counter. Thus we read, to the greater glory of God, about the Vicar of Bray; the use of malt to make drink in Derbyshire ('a master-piece indeed'); the marriage customs of Lapland; Devonshire strawberries and cream; the Dunmow flitch; a volume of treatises found in the belly of a cod at Cambridge on Midsummer Eve, 1626; the bones of the carp, which are as dichotomous as Peter Ramus. . . . It mars our image of Fuller to have him leaving the virtues of tobacco to those who know them.

But such random items, which give a pleasant unexpectedness to all his works, are 'the Leakage and Superfluities of his Study'. His chief labour went into the biographies, and these display the honesty, humanity, individuality, and 'quick Jocundity of style' that are not unexpected. Many of Fuller's phrases and anecdotes—the preaching of Hooker and Travers, the wit-combats of Shakespeare and Jonson—have long done service for the literary historian; so has the tale of Ralegh's cloak, though it has been honourably retired. Yet the combination of preacher, antiquarian, and essayist is not enough to make a good biographer. We can excuse the omission of many modern writers (for early ones Fuller had the help of 'bilious Bale' and others) and even of some eminent divines; and, knowing his deep sense of the 'long Winter of woe and misery' brought on by the civil war, we do not wonder at the absence of parliamentary leaders. Fuller's prime limitation, which is also a prime source of his peculiar charm, is intellectual immaturity. It is this which separates him from most of the great divines of his age; and it is perhaps not irrelevant to observe that Fuller does not possess the classics in anything like the same degree as his fellows. We justly praise his moderation in a time of strife, but we may feel that his comprehension of the issues involved is not quite adequate. In the *Worthies*, while he can apply common sense, Protestant common sense, to saints' legends, he has small understanding of literature or philosophy. As a rule he hastens, like the modern popular biographer, from perfunctory comment to biographical fact, character, and anecdote; and if he is often amusing, even illuminating, he can also be exasperatingly trivial. His concern is with men, not ideas, and his heterogeneous learning remains an external, unphilosophical, antiquarian hobby. Our staunch royalist may be called a biographical Leveller. Bacon gets little more space than Charles I's dwarf, and Shakespeare a third as much as the unicorn's horn. Fuller appreciates piety or oddity better than genius, and one of his very best sketches is that of Thomas Coryate.

He says, disarmingly, that if he has overlooked any public benefactors, their names are written in the Book of Life. A similar broad plea must extenuate brief mention of the *Church History*. Fuller's best writings are only slices of Fuller, and what has been said of him already would be repeated with slight variations and a fresh store of choice phrases. The *Church History* begins with the Druids and ends in 1649. The closing account of the death and burial of King Charles is a fine example of the simple eloquence Fuller can command when deeply moved. In the earlier part of the book the antiquarian holds sway, in the latter we have a moderate Anglican's picture of his own troubled age. In 1651 he had traversed part of the ground in editing and writing some sketches for the first important collection of lives in English, *Abel Redevivus: The Lives and Deaths of the Modern Divines*. Though Fuller is a rambling annalist, not a philosophic historian, and though he sees churchmen more clearly than the Church, he does a good deal, between the lines as well as in them, to explain the hold of the Anglican tradition. Incidentally, Peter Heylyn would not have been pleased to know that he would live in common memory, not as a learned author, but as the man who censured Fuller—and was eventually seduced into friendship by his victim's indomitable good humour.

Ecclesiastical biography in the seventeenth century began with a work of distinction, Sir George Paule's *John Whitgift* (1612), but the quality and the fivefold achievement of Izaak Walton (1593–1683) have given him undisputed pre-eminence.[1] Accident, seconded by modest inclination and a genius for friendship, turned Walton into a semi-professional biographer. When Sir Henry Wotton died in 1639, leaving unwritten the life of Donne he was to have prepared for a collection of Donne's sermons, Walton, who had been gathering material, fulfilled the task. The memoir of 1640, composed in haste under pressure, was revised, enlarged, and issued separately in 1658. The projected publication of *Reliquiae Wottonianae* 'begot a like necessity' for a commemorative biography of Wotton (1651; enlarged

---

[1] Walton was the son of an alehouse-keeper in Stafford. He was apprenticed to a London sempster, a relative, and, though a dabbler in verse, he prospered in business. His life was as uneventful as that of his companion in Winchester Cathedral, Jane Austen; his one adventure was the transmitting of a jewel of Prince Charles's after the battle of Worcester. Walton was acquainted with a number of literary men, from Jonson and Drayton to the angler-poet Charles Cotton. His ecclesiastical connexions were multiplied through his two marriages (1626 and 1647) and through the friendships he cherished. After the Restoration Walton lived chiefly with his friend George Morley, Bishop of Worcester (where Walton was his steward, 1661–2) and later of Winchester, and during his last years with his clerical son-in-law in and near Winchester.

1654). Subsequent revisions in this life were much less important than those made, in 1658 and later, in the life of the more sanctified Donne. Personal interest in Hooker had led Walton to begin collecting notes on him and, at the request of Archbishop Sheldon, he produced a life (1665) as a corrective to Dr. John Gauden, whose life and edition (1662) contained matter disturbing to High Churchmen. Walton's life of Herbert (1670) was a freewill offering, written mainly to please himself. There was further revision when the four lives were printed together in 1670 and 1675. At a still more advanced age Walton wrote a life of Bishop Morley's friend, Bishop Sanderson (1678; revised 1681). We can only lament that his notes for William Fulman's life of Hales remained notes—though the peace-loving spirit of Hales breathes through the life of Wotton and the *Angler*.

Walton was Donne's parishioner, in some degree a friend, and he was a friend of Wotton, and his were the earliest lives of these men. Herbert he had seen once; Hooker, of course, he had never seen; Sanderson he knew well. For Herbert he had the accounts of Nicholas Ferrar (1633) and Barnabas Oley (1652); for Hooker the materials in Fuller's *Church History* and *Worthies*, Paule's *Whitgift*, and Gauden's vague and inaccurate sketch. But biographical data in print were not of much use and Walton was indebted mainly to his own conscientious research. His most valuable sources were his episcopal friends, Thomas Morton, Henry King, Ussher, George Morley, and others. First-hand or oral information was fortified by general reading and by increasing examination of records and documents. When Walton felt uncertain of his facts he said so (though his feeling was not always reliable), and mistakes in detail were seldom the result of negligence. His desire for accuracy, in contrast with the usual vagueness of his predecessors and contemporaries, is exemplified in his use, and his increasing use, of dates; at times he could go wrong. Then his subjects were all authors and he drew upon their writings, notably Herbert's. He quoted letters and, while he might telescope passages in a way not endorsed by modern scholarship, he rather heightened than falsified the essential impression. Significant incidents were sometimes dramatized through speeches remembered (perhaps with the aid of a diary), reported, or invented in accordance with the biographer's understanding of the situation. On the other hand, along with qualifications already registered, expert analysis has shown that, for the achievement of a preconceived effect, Walton's selective and shaping emphasis could now and then amount to distortion. Finally, the successive editions give proof of his zeal, both biographical and literary, in their continual alterations, especially enlargements, and in continual minute changes in expression for the sake of artistry or greater exactness; one result of revision is the enhancement of his subjects' dignity and, partly through more formal wording, of his own. His 'artless Pensil' laboured for perfection of phrase and rhythm and, though his sentences can be awkwardly involved or modestly rhetorical, even his faults are in keeping with the total effect of decorous, old-fashioned simplicity and honesty.

Of Walton's heroes Wotton alone was a man of the world and even he, who had been studious and religious, took orders on becoming Provost of Eton. In treating his five clerics Walton is always didactic—and digressive—but not always in the same way. The life of Donne, originally a preface to his sermons, in its fullest form continued to stress the preacher, his ascetic later years, and his saintly death. The predominance of either private or semi-official intentions explains the purely biographical handling of Donne and Wotton as individual worthies; the devoutly elaborate picture of the aristocratic Herbert as the ideal country parson, intended, like Oley's, as a 'serious call' to Restoration clergymen; and the historical sketches, in the lives of Hooker and Sanderson, of the Church's increasingly difficult struggles with Puritan nonconformity. The tragicomic story of Hooker's marriage and of Mrs. Hooker and her family has been shown to be a tissue of error and prejudice—probably because the aged biographer's High Church sponsors wished to discredit the authenticity of the last books of the *Ecclesiastical Polity* and thought it needful to discredit Mrs. Hooker first. Even if this persuasive argument is true, Tory churchmen may have accepted old and unfounded gossip in good faith; at any rate Walton did not question it. In all his writings he appears as one of those staunch and simple-minded Anglicans who saw history with the eyes of a bishop and could not regard other views as much better than perverse wickedness. But if he be accused of uncritical bias, or of 'an holy Lethargy' of memory, he also helps us to appreciate in their best purity the power and the beauty of the feelings he shared.

Modern readers are less disposed to quarrel with Walton the historian than with Walton the hagiographer or 'sentimental churchwarden'. He is charged with excessive idealization and with re-creating five different men in the likeness of that placid primitive Christian, Izaak Walton. But the charges must be qualified. It is true that Walton's prime virtue is his own personality, which irradiates every page. No English biographer invests his heroes with Walton's peculiar aura of dignity, piety, and peace, a kind of unearthliness which makes the biblical parallels seem quite natural—and there is abundant evidence outside of Walton that the stormy century contained many such persons and havens of quietude. But the path to heaven lies through this world, and Walton has not a little of the gift of Fuller and Aubrey, the eye for picturesque and apparently trivial detail. And Walton's reverence for the beauty of holiness is not incompatible with a very individual compound of wit, humour, and irony; at times, as in the account of Mrs. George Herbert's widowhood and remarriage, he is so blandly innocent that we are not quite sure how to take him. Then it must be an inattentive reader to whom the courtly and cosmopolitan Wotton and the 'timorous and bashful' Sanderson look alike, or the spiritually serene Hooker and such spiritual wrestlers as Donne and Herbert. In venerating the men he wrote about, in dwelling on their strength rather than their weakness, Walton was in the tradition of Plutarch—whom he knew—as well as the authors of saints' lives. At the same time, even if it is to enhance their later glory, he does not let us forget the youthful sins of Donne, the aristocratic pride of Herbert, and the worldly ambitions of both; and the most candid biographer could hardly find serious faults in Hooker and Sanderson, or perhaps many in the more worldly Wotton. As a mere friend of Dr. Donne, Walton may not have grasped the complexities of his nature so fully as we do nowadays, but he tried to see men as God would see them at the day of judgement.

We may glide from biography into autobiography by way of *The Complete Angler* (1653), since Walton avows that 'the whole Discourse is, or rather was, a picture of my own disposition'. (There is a poignant nostalgia in that parenthetical phrase, added in 1661.) But the historian falters in trying to say something of a book which has been second only to the Bible in popular fame. Against a rural background and in a partly holiday mood Walton fills in the portrait of the artist which the reader of the *Lives* can draw in outline. A love of angling is an outward and visible sign of an inward and spiritual grace, of a gentle, contemplative benignity of soul which abhors dissension and loves good old ways, whether in the choice of bait or ballads or barley-wine or the worship of the Creator. We may remember that this prose hymn of contentment in simple and eternal things appeared a few weeks after Cromwell expelled the Long Parliament. Walton's motto is 'Study to be quiet', and in his mind the piety of primitive Christians is linked both with angling and with 'the happy days of the Nations and the Churches peace' before the clergy were ousted. It would hardly have strained seventeenth-century etymology to identify 'angler' and 'Anglican'. If at times the nature of his theme betrays him into unctuousness, we still feel, to echo Dr. Butler's praise of the strawberry, that doubtless God could have made a better man than Walton, but doubtless God never did. Of piscatory lore, practical and theoretical, he was of course a devoted if not always reliable master (he borrowed in the usual way from earlier writers), and he proves the honourable estate and antiquity of angling with a brave show of frequently Brownesque learning and logic. Was it not the vocation of four of the Apostles and the avocation of Perkins, Whitaker, Nowell, and Wotton? Are not fish-hooks mentioned in Amos and Job? Walton's colloquial and poetic pastoral is the most homespun of idyllic day-dreams, the most substantial of poems of escape. He is as conscious, and as sincere, an artist as Theocritus or Virgil; only such an artist could have given the lyrics of Marlowe and Ralegh their perfect and foreordained setting. There was a mass of country literature before Walton and there has been a great mass since, yet he may be said to have had no predecessors and no successors. His mellow vision of field and stream, of lambs frisking and children gathering lilies and cowslips, of anglers thanking God for the 'Sweet day, so cool, so calm, so bright', or making good cheer in clean inns with lavendered sheets—the vision that is for ever England—is Walton's own creation.

Along with the universal and timeless autobiographical impulse, such special motives as an accentuated self-consciousness (which on the religious plane was expressed in many Puritan diaries), the antiquarian spirit, the habit of the commonplace book, and the practice of writing 'advice to my son', these inspired a multitude of records compiled for private or public perusal which contain the most varied kinds of material. Among these always valuable and nearly always very readable documents we have, for instance, the hodge-podge jotted down in 1602–3 by that lover of sermons and gossip, the lawyer John Manningham; Lady Hoby's chronicle (1599–1605) of domestic duties and pieties; the little sketch, written in 1609 and printed in 1647, by the typical Tudor humanist and diplomat, Sir Thomas Bodley (1545–1613), who could well afford to be brief, since the Bodleian Library 'will testifie so truly and aboundantly for me, as I neede not be the publisher of the dignitie and worthe of mine owne Institution'; the record of Oxford life (1626–40) by Thomas Crosfield; the diary (1625–43) of the clerical collector of satires, John Rous; the fragmentary journal of the masterful *grande dame* and master-builder, Lady Anne Clifford (1590–1676); the journals of those two fine specimens of the royalist country gentleman, Sir John Oglander (1585–1655) and Sir Henry Slingsby, who was executed in 1658; the memorials of his family and himself by a third admirable representative of the type, Gervase Holles (1607–75), whose life was for the most part 'nothing els but a varied scene of infelicity'; the diary (1647–9) of the devout and thrifty Yorkshire yeoman, Adam Eyre; the laconic diary of Sir William Drummond, the poet's son, which pictures the life of a young Scottish laird in 1657–9; and, to make an end, the diaries of the Puritan Nehemiah Wallington (1598–1658) and of Archbishop Laud. Wallington incorporated a pamphlet of thirty pages on the sufferings of Prynne, Burton, and Bastwick, an affair to which Laud gave less than thirty lines. In Laud's diary, and in the history of his troubles written in the Tower, we can read the tragedy of a high-minded but legally minded ecclesiastical dictator.

The more formal autobiographies, whatever their historical value, seldom approach those of seventeenth-century France. In the *Memoirs* (published in 1683) of Sir James Melville (1535–1617) the brightest bit is the famous picture of the rival queens and rival women. There is more flavour in the autobiography and diary of that wise, sturdy, and scholarly servant of God and the kirk, James Melville (1556–1614). The learned and upright antiquarian, Sir Simonds D'Ewes (1602–50), contributed much to our knowledge in his annalistic review of his life, his 'sweet and satisfying studies', his family, and current history. One might find parallels to the memoirs of Blaise de Monluc in the *Commentaries* (printed in 1657) of Sir Francis Vere (1560–1609), chief of 'the fighting Veres' and schoolmaster of military leaders, and in the narrative (printed in 1637) of Colonel Robert Monro, a follower of the great Gustavus more modest, pious, and intelligent than Dugald Dalgetty. Captain John Smith's autobiography has been noticed among books of travel, though some sour critics would put it with fiction. As an obvious if not very literary text around which to group some other autobiographies one might take the degree of their authors' consciousness of God's special favour. The royal shipbuilder, Phineas Pett (1570–1647), was sustained by the belief or the hope that what Fulke Greville and commissions of inquiry regarded as graft would be rightly understood in heaven. Arthur Wilson (1595–1652), servant of the Earls of Essex and Warwick, minor dramatist and historian, wrote *Observations of God's Providence in the Tract of my Life*, which is a much more mundane, active, and robust chronicle than the title might suggest. Better known than these men is Robert Carey, first Earl of Monmouth (1560?–1639), whose memoirs were written about 1627 and printed in 1759. Whether in pursuit of the Armada or of thieves on the Scottish border or of preferment at court, he was always happily aware of God's help, though he relied more upon his horse in the most notorious action of his life—posting from the death-bed of his queen and kinswoman to be the first to salute King James. Carey's book gives a candid, complacent, varied, and vivid picture of himself and his 'stirring world'.

All of these adjectives except the first may be applied to a much more famous book, the autobiography of Lord Herbert of Cherbury (1582–1648), written when he was past sixty and first printed by Horace Walpole in 1764. It ends in 1624, with the end of the author's public career. If Carey was a sort of Rosencrantz-Hotspur, Herbert deserves Sir Leslie Stephen's appellation of Bobadil-Kant. He carried the satisfying assurance of divine protection even into a street brawl. Herbert rationalized or romanticized his martial, duellistic, and amatory bravado by a naïve appeal to the traditional code of chivalry. His swashbuckling vanity would hardly suggest that he could make important contributions to philosophy, poetry, and history, not to mention his diplomatic and military services. But he does now and then betray his intellectual interests in his plea for more practical and scientific education, in his outline of natural theology, and in the notable account of the divine sanction invoked and bestowed upon the publication of *De Veritate*.

A less solid philosopher than Herbert, but a much finer knight-errant, was the handsome, charming, versatile, and unique Sir Kenelm Digby (1603–65), a planet whose orbit one crosses at every turn in the period. Digby's *Private Memoirs*, first printed in 1827, were written in 1628 to vindicate the clouded reputation of his beautiful wife, Venetia Stanley, and to celebrate an 'heroical' love ordained by the stars. He tells, in the form of a *roman à clef*, the truly romantic story of their attachment and their individual adventures from the time they were playmates until Sir Kenelm showed that love had not sapped his energies by winning in 1628 'a glorious victory' over a French and Venetian fleet at Scanderoon. Whatever gossip might say, and it said a good deal, about the bride's experience —her situation may have furnished the plot for Shirley's *The Wedding*—the marriage in 1625 proved to both lovers a reward for all their misfortunes. Lady Digby's death in 1633 was lamented in a shower of poems by Jonson, Felltham, Habington, and others. The *Memoirs* end of course before the period of Sir Kenelm's philosophic, scientific, and political activity, though 'Theagenes' is a student throughout his wanderings.

It is perhaps the stars that bring together here the autobiography of the high-souled, speculative, and eccentric inventor of the powder of sympathy and that of 'the thrice noble, chaste, and virtuous,—but again somewhat fantastical, and original-brain'd, generous Margaret Newcastle'. The two might have made a good match, but the duchess had an idol, whose *Life* she was to write. In it and in the earlier and briefer account of herself in *Nature's Pictures* (1656), she appears in her most lucid and attractive mood, and whatever we think, with Bridget Elia, of her 'intellectuals', we respect the qualities of her heart. Besides the analysis of her own character the duchess gives a picture of the aristocratic woman's breeding and mode of life.

Personal letters, mostly printed in modern times, have survived in sufficient bulk and variety to illustrate intimately every aspect of human nature and manners in a period of colour and candour. There are such shrewd and racy gossips as that disappointed but invincibly witty seeker after court preferment,

Sir John Harington, whose masterpiece is his account of the entertainment given the King of Denmark, and John Chamberlain, whose letters (1597–1626) afford the best single panorama of a grasping and violent age. We have the official or private correspondence of such public men as Bacon, Sir Henry Wotton, whose letter about *Comus* everyone knows, and Cromwell, whose despairing appeal to his infallible Scottish brethren almost everyone knows. And we have the 'conceited' reflections of Donne, the tortured farewells of Ralegh, and the manly and sometimes moving simplicity of a later inhabitant of the Tower, Sir John Eliot. Then there are such letters as those of the Verneys, the Oxindens, and the Peytons, and of the Norfolk squire Thomas Knyvett to his wife, which, like contemporary diaries, reveal both the apparently unshakable solidarity of old county families and the disintegrating effect of the civil war; the letters of Lady Paston to her son William at Cambridge (1624–7) and of Lady Harley to her 'Deare Ned' at Oxford and in London (1638 ff.), full of winning motherly solicitude in regard to temporal and eternal welfare; the voluminous exchanges between Lady Conway and Henry More, with their tale of bodily and spiritual pains and consolations; and the scientific and medical bulletins from the philanthropist and 'general artist', Samuel Hartlib, to Robert Boyle. In both of these last series, by the way, we have glimpses of the ubiquitous and mercurial Digby. The correspondence of Hartlib and John Worthington, the minor Cambridge Platonist, is another mirror of philosophic interests; it includes much praise of the angelic Dr. More, and some attempts at settling the question whether good angels appear with beards.

But, since we have noticed elsewhere the dubious 'letters' of James Howell and can linger with only a single exponent of the informal art, we may take an unpretentious woman, one who thought the noble authoress of Newcastle overbold and a little distracted. At Christmas, 1654, Dorothy Osborne (1627–95), daughter of a gallant and impoverished royalist and niece of Francis Osborn, married William Temple, the future statesman and author. Nearly all her extant letters, first printed in full in 1888, were written during 1653–4. Both families had objected and urged more advantageous matches—one of Dorothy's suitors was a son of the Protector—and marriage seemed remote or even hopeless; meetings were few and correspondence was surreptitious. At times Dorothy confessed herself 'a walking misery' and begged Temple to break off the engagement; at the best she could only preach stoic patience to herself and her lover and repeat her assurances of eternal loyalty. When obstacles were finally overcome, smallpox marred her beauty just before the wedding, but this Argalus and Parthenia lived happily ever after. There was ample time to fulfil that early wish which sounds so much like Donne: 'ffor god sake when wee meet let us designe one day to remember old story's in, to aske one another by what degree's our friendship grew to this height tis at. . . .'

Dorothy's letters live as a picture of provincial life, as a 'Romance Story' less artificial than her beloved and inexhaustible *Cléopâtre* and *Grand Cyrus*, and as the unaffected, wise, sad, and humorous revelation of one of the most loving and lovable feminine characters in English history. 'All Letters mee thinks should bee free and Easy as ones discourse, not studdyed, as an Oration, nor made up of hard words like a Charme.' We see her waylaying the carrier in the hope of a letter from her lover; escaping from tedious visitors and managing relatives to write to him and hit off their characters with shrewd strokes; playing shuttlecock with her companion, Jane; sitting up with her sick father; exchanging horticultural courtesies with Sir Samuel Luke; going out in the evening—this is a few weeks after the publication of *The Complete Angler*—to listen to the girls on the common as they sit and sing ballads, until they dash off after straying cows. Most of the time Dorothy is 'buried alive' in Bedfordshire, but she takes the waters at Epsom—though her 'spleen' is of the heart—and on a rare visit to London she has her picture drawn by 'Mr. Lilly', calls on the other Mr. Lilly, the astrologer, and even, duly masked, frequents the park and the new Spring Garden. 'Are not you in some fear what will become on mee? these are dangerous Courses.' We may look far to find another such individual mixture of Juliet, Rosalind, and Jane Austen.

While the sixteenth century was far from barren, it is in the seventeenth, through its multitude of autobiographies, diaries, and collections of letters, that we first become really and fully acquainted with the character, life, and background of many men and women both eminent and ordinary. It is axiomatic that no autobiography can be dull and, incomparably rich as the period is in more formal literature, this large body of informal records of actual experience, exciting or humdrum, is perhaps the most fascinating portion of its legacy. Formal works of history for the most part are naturally much less attractive, though parts of Ralegh are familiar and parts of Knolles and some other authors ought to be. In the field of biography and memoirs, a good many books were written in a modern manner by men conversant with court life and with Tacitus and Suetonius, Comines and Machiavelli, but the biographer whom we chiefly read was at least as typical of his century, and much closer to the supreme biographies of the world, in his naïve faith in God, virtue, and great men.

VIII

POLITICAL THOUGHT

THE political revolution gave birth to Gilberts and Harveys—
and Fludds—but it found no Bacon; and, on the royalist
side, Clarendon was no Hooker or Burke. Much of the
most vital thinking was done in the courts of law, in Pym's
lodgings, and on the floor of the House of Commons, or, later,
in the quarters of Ireton and Cromwell, and at all times by
multitudes of known or nameless people in manor and shop,
church and conventicle. As we observed in the last chapter, the
parliamentary leaders, like their opponents, appealed to constitutional theory and precedent, but their own instincts and the
exigencies of circumstance made their procedure more empirical
than doctrinaire; though speeches and remonstrances might
contain political wisdom, they had a special and practical purpose. On the other hand, the great literary champions of republicanism and absolutism, Milton and Harrington and Hobbes,
were more or less academic theorists, and the Levellers and
Diggers and other groups were more intent upon building ideal
states in the immediate future than upon philosophic analysis of
the immediate past. Yet if the revolution brought forth no single
author to whom we might turn for a view of the whole movement (and only an omniscient Deity could have filled that role),
there is, in the writers mentioned and in the innumerable tracts
of many less famous but important men, so large and diverse
a body of active thinking that the historian of political philosophy is almost overwhelmed, and an historian of literature,
with a chapter at his disposal, is reduced to the merest outline of some main currents in monarchical and revolutionary
writings. Three general facts may be noticed at the outset. Up
to about 1640–2 political thought, with relatively few exceptions,
may be said to follow a pattern of constitutional monarchism
more or less akin to that of Bodin; the next decade brings forth
with startling rapidity every kind of parliamentary, popular,
and radical opposition. Secondly, while personal factors on both
sides hastened the revolution, its seeds had been dormant in all
English constitutional history, in a vaguely legal conception of

royal government which endangered the subject's legal rights. Thirdly, political thinking was conditioned at every turn by religion; to the very complex problem of the 'two kingdoms' of Church and Crown were added the further complications which followed the overthrow of both.

King James, and England, would have been happier if he, the most learned of English sovereigns, had been a professor at Oxford, uttering words that did not matter, instead of ruling in one of the most critical periods in modern European history. The bases of political thought had been altered by the Renaissance, Reformation, and Counter-Reformation, and by economic and social change, and Protestant England was the inevitable laboratory for the test of democratic theory. James, who had early learned that a Scottish presbytery agreed as well with monarchy as God and the devil, and whose methods had been fairly successful in Scotland, was not aware that in crossing the border he was entering not only another country but another era. He had set down his theory of kingship in black and white before he came to the English throne. The theory appeared in its most attractive form in *Basilikon Doron* (1599), a book of advice for Prince Henry. This picture of the benevolent despot, the father and shepherd of his people, was in the tradition of the ideal prince perpetuated by many Christian humanists before and after Erasmus, a tradition which satisfied Shakespeare and was upheld by Bacon, Filmer, and others, including the fiery Eliot. But the theory, even if James had lived up to it, did not commend itself to the new generation of common lawyers and business-men and many country gentlemen. Besides, James acted rather in the spirit of a more realistic treatise, *The True Law of Free Monarchies* (1598). Here, and in later homilies to Parliament, he enunciated an Hebraic, Roman, and—in a one-sided sense—feudal doctrine of sovereignty such as no Tudor would have dreamed of asserting. James always stresses a ruler's obligations, but the degree of their fulfilment is to be judged by God alone. The crown is inherited as a piece of family property; the king is the absolute master of the lives and possessions of his subjects; his acts are not open to inquiry or dispute, and no misdeeds can ever justify resistance. James had moved far from his quondam tutor, Buchanan, and beyond Bodin. The ultimate sanction for this doctrine was the general conception of order and degree and the theory of divine right revived as an answer to the Catholic claim that the Pope had the right to depose heretical monarchs and release subjects from their allegiance. More important than any treatise of James's was the oath of allegiance (1606), which broke Catholic power in England by dividing Catholics against themselves and which offered the first effective challenge to the renewed claims of Rome. To this question, which for many years embroiled all learned Europe, James devoted three-fourths of his own political writing (1608–15), and he enlisted such distinguished helpers as Andrewes, Donne, and Casaubon. Whatever the subtle casuistry of Catholic apologists, the plain fact was that treason and assassination could be justified by good authority, and Protestants could only go one better and appeal to God Himself as the sole maker and breaker of kings. Yet Englishmen might be justly alarmed when such a supra-mundane theory was invoked in domestic affairs, when God's lieutenant claimed to be above Parliament and the law, above all restraints except his own inspired will. The public temper was indicated by the outcry over the definitions of sovereignty in Dr. Cowell's *Interpreter* (1607), but James, though he suppressed the indiscreet book, remained much more ready to suppress free speech in Parliament.

Representatives of royalism in its largely Elizabethan form are Bacon, Ralegh, and Fulke Greville; since the philosophical Greville's chief writings in this area were not in print, we may glance at Bacon, the active statesman. Because of both general monarchical tradition and his own family background, Bacon carried the 'father image' into his political thinking. He shared King James's theory of the powers and duties of the ideal prince and did not share the Commons' new notions of their powers and duties or his great rival's notions of the powers and duties of the common-law courts. Yet Bacon had once been bold enough to oppose Elizabeth and he was not unaware of a changing climate, and if James had listened to his counsels of compromise as well as to his endorsements of the prerogative the later crises might have been less violent. In regard to the Church, Bacon had long seen the necessity of internal reform and conciliation of the Puritans, and his ecclesiastical tracts were in demand in 1640–1. His insight was perhaps the clearer because he was 'a sincere if unenthusiastic Christian of that sensible school which regards the Church of England as a branch of the Civil Service, and the Archbishop of Canterbury as the British Minister for Divine Affairs'. Bacon's ideas on the general problems of politics are familiar, thanks to the *Essays*, and they are in the main more shrewd than exalted. A successful nation is a successful individual writ large. The humanist's traditional view of the State as an harmonious organism of divine institution is almost lost in the political physician's scientific knowledge of that body's chemistry and diseases and of useful prescriptions, such as foreign war, for continued good health. If Bacon sometimes appears a little old-fashioned in his Machiavellian nationalism as well as in his royalism, he is modern enough when, in the twenty-ninth essay and elsewhere, he gives hints of the economic basis of political power which Harrington was to take over and develop.

As later supporters of constitutional monarchy and a reformed episcopacy we might name Hyde, Falkland, and Selden. Hyde belongs to the next age, and Falkland's political faith was expressed in the House and in the field. John Selden (1584–1654), of whom we had a glimpse in the last chapter, was an anti-clerical whose Erastianism merits, still more than Bacon's, C. D. Broad's witty judgement quoted in the last paragraph. He early aroused ecclesiastical ire with his *History of Tithes* (1618), yet episcopacy was bound up with monarchy, tradition, and culture, and Selden's chief abhorrence was reserved for upstart sectaries and the Presbyterians whom he tormented in the Westminster Assembly with his learned barbs. The two words *Scrutamini Scripturas* 'have undone the World'. 'The Puretan would be judged by the Word of God: If he would speak clearly, he means himself, but he is ashamed to say so.' Selden was religious, after a fashion, but true Anglican light without heat has often been suspect, and more fervent contemporaries may be excused for seeing Hobbesian infidelity in the play of his cool, mundane intelligence. 'They talk (but blasphemously enough) that the Holy Ghost is President of their General-Councils, when the truth is, the odd man is still the Holy-Ghost.' Selden was rather an emancipated liberal than a high-souled patriot, though in his early reply to Grotius, *Mare Clausum* (printed in 1635), he interpreted the freedom of the seas in terms of 'Rule, Britannia'. The first article of his creed, if not anti-clericalism, was the contract between sovereign and people, but his understanding of that stopped far short of

the Puritans'. While his profound knowledge of the common
law was enlisted in the struggle to curb the prerogative, and
he went to prison along with other parliamentary leaders,
Selden was at times regarded, not without reason, as a friend
of the court. 'The Parliament-men are as great Princes as any
in the World, when whatsoever they please is Priviledge of
Parliament.' Selden was too detached and judicial to be a
partisan, and he withdrew from the public stage before Charles's
execution. 'The wisest way for men in these times is to say
nothing.' By temperament a scholar and man of the world, a
martyr 'unto the fire *exclusivè*', he served the difficult cause of
rational moderation with energy and honesty. His latitudinarian position in the midst of warring parties is typified in the
conflicting accounts of his death. According to one (Aubrey's),
Selden dismissed a clergyman on being rebuked by his friend
Hobbes for his feminine courage; according to another, he
denied admission to Hobbes and received the ministrations of
his friend Archbishop Ussher.

We have a further example of the difficulties of a moderate
constitutionalist in Philip Hunton (1604?–82), a country parson
who published *A Treatise of Monarchy* in 1643 and in 1657
became Provost of Cromwell's short-lived college at Durham.
Hunton sees the English monarchy as fundamentally limited and
mixed, a masterpiece, in fact, of architectural wisdom. There is
an avowed gap in the chain of argument whenever the question
of resistance comes up, since the frame of government provides
no constituted judge of a monarch's excesses, which involve a
private and moral rather than a legal verdict. (Seventeenth-
century notions of a competent judge ranged from the Deity of
King James and Hobbes to Lilburne's common jury.) Although
nothing can justify violence against a king's person, his agents
may be justly opposed by Parliament in the defence of its own
rights and the community. Hunton ends by proposing concessions on both sides which, he optimistically thinks, would
heal 'the wofull dissention of the Kingdome' and reunite the
three estates. But Hunton's distinctive merit is not merely his
lucid analysis of past and present theory, it is his prophetic
recognition of the corporate character of sovereignty, in England
'the king in Parliament', and the supremacy of legislative power.
The tract was fittingly reprinted, twice, in 1689.

It was the misfortune of the cultivated country gentleman,

Sir Robert Filmer (*c.* 1588–1653), to have his *Patriarcha: or The Natural Power of Kings* (1680) ridiculed by Locke and to be viewed thenceforth through a distorting lens. But he was, after Hobbes, the ablest defender of absolutism or rather, perhaps, the most acute critic of the logical bases of the democratic doctrines of freedom, popular sovereignty, the contract, in short, all merely man-made sanctions and natural rights. Apart from the brief *Directions for Obedience to Governors* (1652), Filmer's best expositions of his ideas were given in critiques of other writers, Hunton (*The Anarchy of a Limited or Mixed Monarchy*, 1648), Aristotle (1652), and Hobbes, Milton, and Grotius (*Observations concerning the Original of Government*, 1652). Filmer sees democrats as the heirs of the temporal claims of the papacy: 'Monarchy hath bin crucified (as it were) between two Theeves, the Pope and the People.' The corner-stone of his own theory is the moral obligation of obedience. The State is the macrocosm of the family. All government is arbitrary; the only question is who shall exercise it, and God and scriptural history, reason and nature have once for all established the absolute monarch, the magnified *paterfamilias*, as the only real sovereign. No group has the moral authority of a sovereign, and representative government, strictly considered, is only a legal fiction. Naturally Filmer finds anarchy in Hunton's limited and mixed monarchy and in his final appeal to private judgement. Milton makes a king a tyrant or a mere executive of the law instead of the agent of equity, and makes 'the people' only 'the sounder and better part', the judge of that part being apparently the army. Naturally, too, Filmer admires Bodin and rejoices in Hobbes's view of the rights of sovereignty, but he deplores the artificial theory of an original state of nature and a contract.

What hope of compromise there was in ideas of constitutional monarchy became more and more unreal as tension increased, and only extreme views on both sides could win a hearing. Hobbes's *Elements of Law* was circulating in 1640, the year of the impeachment of Strafford and Laud.[1] In 1642, the year

---

[1] In an autobiographical Latin poem of 1672 the bold thinker and timorous man said that his mother's alarm over the Armada had brought on the twin birth of himself and fear. At Oxford (1603–8) Hobbes, like Bacon, did not enjoy the scholastic curriculum (though his psychology and ethics were to bear the marks of Aristotle's *Rhetoric*), and he found solace in maps and books of travel. He was forty or more when he chanced upon Euclid and fell in love with the method of demonstration. After leaving Magdalen Hall, Hobbes entered, as tutor and companion,

of the outbreak of war, the first Latin edition of *De Cive* was printed at Paris. In 1651, two years after the king's execution, came the much less cool and much more famous *Leviathan*. All three books were developments of the same central ideas. Some malicious contemporaries said that Hobbes's absolutist doctrine could be used to justify a Cromwell as well as a Stuart, and doubtless it could, though hardly in 1640 or even 1651. That the real menace was much larger than any immediate problem Hobbes's best critics in his own time discerned, whatever their partial misconceptions of the man and his thought. The apostle of absolute sovereignty—and of an absolute law of duty—has been called not only a father of both the *laissez-faire* and the totalitarian State but, in a still deeper and broader

upon a fortunate connexion with the Cavendish family which, with interludes (1629-30, 1641-53), lasted for the rest of his life. At some time between 1621 and 1626 he was a sort of philosophic secretary to Bacon. As a tutor Hobbes made three continental tours (1610, 1629-30, 1634-6). His modernist thinking was stimulated by intercourse with Galileo and with Father Mersenne, whose cell was the nerve-centre of European philosophy, and Hobbes himself began 'to be numbered among the philosophers'. He led the royalist migration to Paris (1640) and lived there for eleven years, in renewed association with the French intellectuals. For a time he was mathematical tutor to Prince Charles. When Paris became uncomfortable for an anti-clerical, Hobbes returned to England (1651) and submitted to the government. After the Restoration his pregnant wit made him a favourite at court. In addition to the Cavendishes, Bacon, Mersenne, and Gassendi, Hobbes had many more or less close friends, such as Jonson, Lord Herbert, Petty, Hyde, Selden, members of Lord Falkland's circle, Sidney Godolphin, Waller, Davenant, Cowley, Dr. Harvey, Sir Kenelm Digby, and Aubrey. This last incomparable authority reports among other things that the philosopher was not drunk more than a hundred times in his long life, and that he was accustomed to shut himself up and sing for the good of his health. During his last twenty-five years Hobbes was embroiled, for the most part unhappily, in controversies with Bishop Bramhall, Seth Ward, John Wallis, and Boyle. He was in bad odour and, he thought, for a time in real danger on account of his religious opinions. Hobbes had begun his career with a translation of Thucydides (1629), and one of the tireless old man's latest works was a translation of Homer (1673-6). He died in 1679.

Hobbes had arrived at some of his main scientific notions in the 'Short Tract on First Principles' written probably in 1630 and certainly before 1636, but first printed in 1889. In 1641 he wrote *Objectiones* to Descartes's *Meditationes* which indicated the fundamental antithesis between the two chief thinkers of the age. The *Elements of Law, Natural and Politic*, after circulating in manuscript for ten years, was printed (1650) in imperfect form in two parts, *Human Nature* and *De Corpore Politico*. Hobbes's other principal works were: *De Cive*, 1642 (enlarged 1647; translated as *Philosophical Rudiments concerning Government and Society*, 1651); *Leviathan*, 1651 (Latin version, 1668); *De Corpore*, begun about 1642 and printed in 1655 (English version, *Elements of Philosophy, the first Section, concerning Body*, 1656); two replies to Bramhall, *Of Liberty and Necessity* (pirated 1654) and *Questions concerning Liberty, Necessity, and Chance* (1656), and a third published in *Tracts* (1682); and *De Homine* (1658). *Behemoth*, on the causes of the civil war, was finished about 1668 and published in *Tracts* (1682); surreptitious editions had appeared in 1679.

way, an author and symbol of the disintegrating individualism which has been as much as anything the definition of the modern world.

Necessity—in the common if not the Hobbesian sense—compels us to postpone to the next chapter Hobbes's scientific and ethical thought, which deals with body or matter and with the human body, man. The third part of his *Summa* comprised the science of the artificial body politic. In its outlines Hobbes's political theory is or seems to be very lucid and yet, even on some central doctrines (not to mention assumptions and implications), it is not always easy to distinguish between what the philosopher meant and what early and modern critics have taken him to mean, and to attempt a brief summary is to draw out leviathan with a hook.

In the state of nature, when all men are roughly equal in ability and power, and self-preservation is the only law, they are, from a desire for gain, safety, or glory, perpetually at war, every man against every man. Every man has a right to everything, and force and fraud are the cardinal virtues, so that life is 'solitary, poore, nasty, brutish, and short'. Nothing, however, can be unjust, for 'Where there is no common Power, there is no Law: where no Law, no Injustice'. But nature and reason lead men, from self-interest, to seek peace and for the sake of peace to surrender natural rights by making a contract among themselves. Since self-interest, however, may dictate the breaking of covenants, there must be

some coërcive Power, to compell men equally to the performance of their Covenants, by the terrour of some punishment, greater than the benefit they expect by the breach of their Covenant; and to make good that Propriety, which by mutuall Contract men acquire, in recompence of the universall Right they abandon: and such power there is none before the erection of a Common-wealth.

Men's only way of attaining peace and security, therefore,

is, to conferre all their power and strength upon one Man, or upon one Assembly of men, that may reduce all their Wills, by plurality of voices, unto one Will: which is as much as to say, to appoint one Man, or Assembly of men, to beare their Person; and every one to owne, and acknowledge himselfe to be Author of whatsoever he that so beareth their Person, shall Act, or cause to be Acted, in those things which concerne the Common Peace and Safetie; and therein to submit their Wills, every one to his Will, and their Judgements, to his Judgment. This is more than Consent, or Concord; it is a reall Unitie of them all, in one and the same Person, made by Covenant of every man with every man, in such manner, as if every man should say to every man, *I Authorise and give up my Right of Governing my selfe, to this Man, or to this Assembly of men, on this condition, that thou give up thy Right to him, and Authorise all his Actions in like manner.* This done, the Multitude so united in one Person, is called a COMMON-WEALTH, in latine CIVITAS. This is the Generation of that great LEVIATHAN, or rather (to speake more reverently) of that *Mortall God*, to which wee owe under the *Immortall God,* our peace and defence.

Having established his State (the case of conquest we may leave out), Hobbes proceeds to define the rights and obligations of sovereign and subjects. The basis of sovereignty is not divine right but mundane utility and security. The covenant by which men surrender their rights to the sovereign is made among themselves and not between them and him, so that they are the authors of all his actions and nothing that he does, however iniquitous in itself, can be called injustice or a breach of the covenant. While answerable to God, the sovereign cannot justly be opposed or called to account by his subjects. Nor may anyone resist him on the ground of a superior covenant with God, 'for there is no Covenant with God, but by mediation of some body that representeth Gods Person', and that is the sovereign, 'Gods Lieutenant'. The sovereign controls foreign policy, the means of peace and defence, the laws governing property, legislation, the judicature, the choice of administrative officers, rewards and punishments, censorship, in fact everything. If, says Hobbes, the notion had not prevailed in England that sovereign power was properly divided among the King, Lords, and Commons, there would have been no civil war. Since sovereign power is unlimited power (for otherwise the power imposing limitations would be sovereign), it follows that Hobbes cannot find much to say of the liberty of subjects. Their welfare depends upon the sovereign's recognition that it is bound up with his own. Although sovereignty comes originally from the people it never reverts to them, and the obligation of complete obedience lapses only when the sovereign becomes incapable of affording protection.

Hobbes's conception of sovereignty was born of a troubled time, and the war and its aftermath only intensified his passionate desire for peace and order. The measure of that desire is the measure of the sacrifices his theory entails. The sovereign power he creates 'is as great, as possibly men can be imagined to make it. And though of so unlimited a Power, men may fancy many evill consequences, yet the consequences of the want of it, which is perpetuall warre of every man against his neighbour, are much worse.' Thus in the lines, and often between them, the apparently detached theorist issues a realistic invitation to unwind the thread of argument and consider how quickly, with the overthrow of central authority, civilization may revert to barbarous anarchy. Contemplation of chaos led Machiavelli to believe that only a despot could establish order, but that artificial order was a stepping-stone to his ideal of organic order, a republic on the Roman model. Hobbes begins with a kind of democracy, created by fear, in order to establish a despotism maintained by coercion. He does praise the moral virtues, and allows almost involuntary glimpses of some faith in human goodness, but normally he builds upon the egoistic passions, above all the desire for power, of the natural man, and these passions can be restrained only by the public sword. The philosopher who sees man as a mechanism must perforce create a greater machine to control him. Or, to put the case in another way, the philosopher who, like Augustine and Calvin, has little confidence in man's character and reason, has to create an absolute and arbitrary deity, a human one.

Hobbes's picture of the state of nature and the evolution of society and government was not offered as historical anthropology but as logical theory, 'an imaginary state', in the language of Stillingfleet's *Irenicum*, 'for better understanding the nature and obligation of Laws'. In politics Hobbes's method was a mixture of the deductive and the empirical. While parliamentary speakers and writers, and many royalists, constantly invoked history and custom in support of their first principles, Hobbes—after his early Aristotelian and Thucydidean period—was temperamentally and prudentially disinclined to take an historical view. When he did come to analyse the causes of the war in *Behemoth* (finished about 1668 and published in 1682), he showed more prejudiced acuteness than historical breadth and insight. Like the theocratic foe of his impious *Leviathan*, Richard Baxter, Hobbes abhorred the ideas of republican liberty nourished by the study of ancient history. He

had translated Thucydides (1629) in order, he said, to show his
fellow citizens the folly of democracy. 'And by reading of these
Greek, and Latine Authors', he declares in *Leviathan*, with
unwonted warmth of feeling,

men from their childhood have gotten a habit (under a false shew of
Liberty,) of favouring tumults, and of licentious controlling the
actions of their Soveraigns; and again of controlling those con-
trollers, with the effusion of so much blood; as I think I may truly
say, there was never any thing so deerly bought, as these Western
parts have bought the learning of the Greek and Latine tongues.

Hobbes returns to the charge repeatedly in *Behemoth* and, since
his censure of the intellectual deadness of Oxford and Cambridge
is well known, it is of some interest to find him, especially in
the later and less familiar book, making hostile acknowledgement of the rebellious ideas developed there: 'The Universities
have been to this Nation, as the Wooden Horse was to the
Trojans.' When he inveighs against admirers of the ancient
republics Hobbes is doubtless thinking not only of the dissenting
clergy whom he loathed but of such men as Milton (who is
named in *Behemoth*, along with Salmasius, as an exponent of
good Latin and ill reasoning) and Harrington.

Harrington, the historical student, remarked that 'Leviathan
affirms the Politicks to be no ancienter then his Book *De Cive*'.
Although Hobbes regarded himself as an independent pioneer,
commentators have pointed out affinities and roots all the way
back to Aristotle's *Rhetoric*. What made Hobbes such an original
and formidable force was, first, the coherent clarity of his total
philosophic design; secondly, the utilitarian, secular, and scientific spirit of his selective reinterpretation of old ideas, even the
golden rule; and, thirdly, the relentless logic with which he
broke through tradition in pushing principles to their conclusions. Like all parties and individuals, he professed to derive
his doctrines from reason and Scripture (and he could quote the
Bible as profusely and aptly as any Puritan), but much of the
strongest opposition came from men whose appeal to the same
complementary authorities was in the tradition of Christian
humanism. Hobbes, like them, defined 'the Law of Nature' as
'the Dictate of right Reason', but at the same time nullified the
traditional conception by making right reason 'not, as many
doe, an infallible faculty, but the act of reasoning'—and no

philosopher was ever more devoted to reasoning than Hobbes, or more distrustful of human reason in general. Hobbes's view of the contract and of the State as an artificial construction, his complete subordination of the individual to the State (or, one might also say, his complete individualism), his equating (as it appeared) of justice and truth not with right reason but with *de facto* civil authority, his whole pragmatic and legalistic scale of values and motives, his philosophical determinism (which, when he did not ignore it, was an inconvenient factor in his own political thought), all this was nearly as abhorrent to royalists as to parliamentarians and republicans. Though Milton did not join in the hue and cry, his widow told Aubrey that he had disliked Hobbes and said that 'their interests and tenets did run counter to each other'. The corner-stone of Christian humanism was the 'true liberty' that Bramhall defined as 'the elective power of the rational will'. On all counts many men for generations shared Bramhall's vehement opinion that Hobbes's doctrines were 'pernicious both to piety and policy, and destructive to all relations of mankind, between Prince and Subject, Father and Child, Master and Servant, Husband and Wife; And that they who maintain them obstinately, are fitter to live in hollow trees among wild beasts, than in any Christian or political Society'. To mention only some notable names which come into this book, there were, besides Bramhall and Baxter, such diverse opponents of Hobbes's political and ethical theory as Filmer and Harrington, Cudworth and Traherne—and of course Alexander Ross. But Hobbes's impact upon the Restoration mind, and upon European thought at large, is beyond our limits.

Two much-quoted items, however, emphasize an especially provocative side of Hobbes's doctrine, his undisguised anticlericalism and what appeared to be disguised atheism. One is Warburton's martial picture: 'The Philosopher of Malmsbury was the Terror of the last Age, as Tindal and Collins are of this. The Press sweat with Controversy: and every young Churchman militant would try his Arms in thundering upon Hobbes's Steel Cap.' The other is Pepys's quietly impressive jotting of 3 September 1668: *Leviathan* 'is now mightily called for', and the price has quadrupled, 'it being a book the Bishops will not let be printed again'. A reader vaguely aware of Hobbes's outlook may be surprised to find that half of *Leviathan*, and parts of his other political works, are concerned with religious and ecclesiastical matters. Yet it can be argued that the problem of Church and State is really the central problem of Hobbes's political philosophy. In his theory subjects are excused from obedience to the sovereign only when obedience is 'repugnant to the Lawes of God', and, since his view of that exception differs widely from post-Reformation thought, he is bound to complete his survey of civil duty by showing what the laws of God are. He grants that the truths of faith are above the reason, and that that may be a sin which is not a crime; yet the kingdom of Christ is not of this world and, though Hobbes calmly decides what is necessary for salvation, it is this world that concerns him. For the individual, since thought is free, the question is one of outward conformity. The civil law is the public conscience and the measure of good and evil actions. In brief, as Selden put it (and as Henry Parker had been urging in his Erastian tracts), 'All is as the State pleases'. In Hobbes's words,

Temporall and Spirituall Government, are but two words brought into the world, to make men see double, and mistake their Lawfull Soveraign. . . . There is therefore no other Government in this life, neither of State, nor Religion, but Temporall; nor teaching of any doctrine, lawfull to any Subject, which the Governour both of the State, and of the Religion, forbiddeth to be taught.

As for Hobbes's own religious opinions, he may have been a conforming atheist or a deist, or he may have regarded himself as a sufficiently good Christian, according to his own peculiar definition.

Whatever the storm raised by Hobbes's ideas, his intellectual powers were acknowledged by such hostile judges as Bramhall, Milton, and Harrington. While condemning his political theory, Harrington avowed his firm belief 'that Mr. Hobbs is, and will in future Ages be accounted the best Writer, at this day, in the World: And for his Treatises of Humane Nature, and of Liberty and Necessity, they are the greatest of New Lights, and those which I have followed and shall follow'. The root of Hobbes's style is of course his scientific and materialistic thought; his doctrines could hardly have assumed the vesture of Milton or Browne. No member of the Royal Society achieved a plainer, stronger, clearer texture of exposition and argument than Hobbes brought to perfection in *Leviathan*. In the last paragraphs of that book he indicates how deliberately he has avoided ornament and cultivated the bare, athletic, and often epigrammatically homely style of a rational man talking to men; at the same time he is a thinker preoccupied with the discrimination of meanings. For a man of his cool intelligence, irony is a potent weapon; witness the Swiftian comparison of bees and ants with men, or the more than ironic exposure of the religious 'Kingdom of Darkness'. And we still enjoy the sight and sound of Hobbes's dichotomizing blade as it shears through layer after layer of illusory idealism:

The force of Words, being (as I have formerly noted) too weak to hold men to the performance of their Covenants; there are in mans nature, but two imaginable helps to strengthen it. And those are either a Feare of the consequence of breaking their word; or a Glory, or Pride in appearing not to need to breake it. This later is a Generosity too rarely found to be presumed on, especially in the pursuers of Wealth, Command, or sensuall Pleasure; which are the greatest part of Mankind. The Passion to be reckoned upon, is Fear; whereof there be two very generall Objects: one, The Power of Spirits Invisible; the other, The Power of those men they shall therein Offend. Of these two, though the former be the greater Power, yet the feare of the later is commonly the greater Feare.

If we grant that Hobbes's style was the easier of attainment because he was not burdened with a very complex or imaginative mind, we must grant also that he was not merely a thinking-machine, that his emotions, however seldom revealed, were deeply involved.

The Puritan revolution proceeded without taking as much account of Hobbes as he took of it. Whatever the force of economic factors, the mother of the movement, and of modern democracy, was the Reformation, with its evolving principles of free inquiry and the priesthood and equality of all believers. Its unacknowledged grandmother was Catholic, since farther back were the medieval principles of the popular origin of sovereignty, the contract between ruler and people, and the right of resistance or even of tyrannicide; and the third of these had lately been given a special prominence by such Jesuits as Cardinal Bellarmine, Mariana, and Robert Parsons. But the immediate background was the powerful re-expression of popular rights by the monarchist Huguenots and others who had the added impetus of Protestant individualism. The English Puritans of the seventeenth century, with their intense religious, millenarian, and iconoclastic zeal, their conviction of God's guidance of His chosen people, went far beyond their predecessors in both word and deed and in both religious and political spheres. The story in all its stages and aspects is much too complex to be simplified. The logical jurist Calvin could be quoted in support of submission to an absolutism like that of King James or Hobbes, and also in support of resistance on the part of the people's legal representatives (witness the plea of Milton's Samson that he had not rebelled as a mere private person), and of any individual's resistance to commands contrary to the law of God. The course of Protestant thought made these large exceptions stronger than the general rule. That development had been epitomized in the writings of John Knox and the result summed up in Buchanan's *De Jure Regni apud Scotos* (1579), a book odious to English royalists throughout the seventeenth century.

The period 1646–60, the second and more difficult phase of the revolution, witnessed the efforts of the victors, increasingly disunited by faction, sect, and theory, to decide what was to be done with the king, with Parliament, with the army, and with the Church, and to establish a working form of government. In the prolonged struggle between Parliament and the army, which may be roughly, but only roughly, equated with Presbyterianism and Independency, the old ideal of legality was kept alive chiefly by the Levellers. Colonel Pride delivered Cromwell from parliamentary opposition in 1648, and in 1653 the Lord, after a fashion, delivered him from Sir Henry Vane. But Presbyterian and parliamentary, royalist and Leveller theories were only drawn closer together and driven underground, and Vane, though he retired, was not subdued. To a chaotic nation ruled by force he offered the brief *Healing Question* (1656), a plea that men of goodwill should be assembled for the planning of a new constitution. The tract is a link between Leveller proposals and Milton's *Ready and Easy Way*.

Similarly the abolition of episcopacy and the Church of England, if it put an end to some troubles, introduced many others. Puritans hopelessly divided among themselves had to find new answers to insoluble questions both new and old. On the general problem of Church and State, logic and history suggested three possibilities: the direct or indirect subordination of civil to religious authority; the Erastian subordination of religious to civil authority; and the coexistence of civil and religious powers with separate jurisdictions. Here we touch upon the Puritan version of a paradox fundamental in Christian and Catholic thought from the gospels and Augustine to Suarez, the instinct of people who live and think in religious terms to segregate the spiritual and the secular. There was a practical necessity for reconciling membership in the realm of grace with membership in the realm of nature and man, and the tendency both to fuse and to separate which appears in the Puritan espousal of business, Baconian science, and all kinds of progressive reform, is conspicuous in political thinking. Then, too, from 1640 onward, Puritans of all colours were compelled to face what had been the Anglican problem, the fact of Nonconformity, of aggressively antagonistic diversity. Was there to be a Presbyterian establishment without toleration for dissent, a Puritan national Church with limited or unlimited toleration, or entire liberty of conscience without an establishment?

The origins, motives, and problems of religious and political democracy were so complicated and so closely interwoven that it would need a volume of this size to outline the history of even the last third of our period, and to try in a few pages of a literary history to notice a few of the many writers, ideas, and parties which might be called representative is to suggest a set tableau of a simple pattern. In fact, not only was it a time of kaleidoscopic multiplicity, but the labels, platforms, and alinements of individuals and parties, while retaining a basic consistency, were continually shifting under the pressure of events. As a microcosmic individual illustration of the historian's difficulties, though happily not of the prevailing quality of political ethics, there is the career of the astute journalist, Marchamont Needham (whose newspaper, *Mercurius Politicus*, was officially censored by Milton at least from March 1651 to January 1652). Needham was a political Vicar of Bray who wrote in turn for Parliament, for the king, for the Commonwealth, and, long after 1660, for the government against Shaftesbury. Incidentally, two of his substantial works, *The Case of the Commonwealth* (1650) and *The Excellency of a Free State* (1656), Needham ran as editorial serials in his paper in 1650–1 and 1651–2.

Before outlining the main movements of revolutionary thought we may take account of Milton, who is both representative and unrepresentative. The articles of his political creed were in the main no more original than most other men's, but, because of his personality, the course of his growth, and the nature and consistency of his first principles, the significance of his theory is greater than the sum of the parts. After his initial monarchism he was diverted to other problems, and the early stages of his political evolution can only be inferred. In the *Tenure of Kings and Magistrates* (February 1649), following Buchanan and the rest, Milton arrived at the doctrine of popular sovereignty and the revocable contract between king and people. The *Tenure* and *Eikonoklastes* (1649) were steps towards the thorough republicanism which Milton maintained, in tones ranging from exultation to despair, in the two *Defences* (1651, 1654) and *The Ready and Easy Way to Establish a Free Commonwealth* (1660). He shared the common attachment to a 'mixed' government, but painful experience, his loss of faith in bishops, monarch, Parliament, army, people, and even Cromwell, led him through progressive modification of the relative power to be given to the component parts of the mixture, so that he emerged with a republic predominantly 'aristocratic', an oligarchy of the wise and good. For the republican framework was only a means towards the holy community that inspired the hopes of Milton and other Puritans. And in his campaign on diverse fronts Milton was the chief exponent of the dynamic idea of Christian liberty inherited from Luther and Calvin and much enlarged in the process of transmission, much enlarged, indeed, in the process of Milton's own development. As he showed most fully in the *Christian Doctrine*, Christian liberty meant, in brief, the advance of the regenerate man from restrictive, external subjection under the Mosaic law to the positive, inward, and voluntary freedom of service and self-direction attained through faith in the gospel of Christ. The more or less revolutionary impulses in that idea were manifested by a number of progressive thinkers, such as Milton himself (who gave up Calvinism) and another uncompromising idealist, Roger Williams (who never gave it up). Milton and Williams were led—Williams in a more radical and unqualified degree—to the separation of Church and State and the freedom of the private conscience from civil jurisdiction. For the classically minded Milton, however, the aristocratic distinction between regenerate and unregenerate coalesced with the aristocratic principle of ancient republicanism and Renaissance humanism, so that he saw the rule of the saints as the rule of philosopher-kings—an attitude reinforced by his deepening distrust of the mass of mankind. Thus he could not accompany more radical Puritanism into complete democracy with its secular doctrine of natural rights.

From 1640 onward a swarm of tracts made clear the strength and intelligence of the popular party and also, very quickly, the wide divergences of political and religious opinion within its ranks. During 1603–40 the battle had been waged for the authority of the common law and the curbing of the prerogative, but it could not stop there. The traditional 'high court of Parliament' was changing, half unconsciously, into the supreme law-maker. The theory of parliamentary sovereignty was first set forth by the bold and able Henry Parker, notably in his *Observations upon Some of His Majesty's Late Answers and Expresses* (1642). In the interest of public safety Parker not only endorsed the recall of authority delegated to the king, when that authority was abused, but went on to claim for Parliament the supreme and final interpretation of law, even an arbitrary power above the law. Among the many vigorous replies was Bishop Bramhall's *Serpent Salve* (1643). An influential Presbyterian statement of 1643 was Prynne's *Sovereign Power of Parliaments*, which, with the author's usual barrage of documentation, enforced a view similar to Parker's. But Presbyterianism, though now entering upon its period of predominance, was the rightist party of the revolution, and in the next few years it showed itself too intolerant in its religious policy, too *bourgeois* in its economics, too much attached to parliamentary power (and to the Scotch), and, finally, too royalist, to satisfy or control the liberal and progressive Independents and the radical Levellers.

The Presbyterian plan for regimented uniformity was soon disturbed by the five Independent divines who wished to continue their congregational practice, and whose plea, carried from the Westminster Assembly into print early in 1644, focused debate upon the first principles of toleration and liberty. The religious side of the controversy is noticed later in this book; on the political side it was no less significant. The Leveller leaders, Lilburne, Walwyn, and Richard Overton, were predestined spokesmen for the political radicalism latent in the doctrine of Christian liberty. It was to be expected that the Reformation idea of the priesthood and equality of believers, which had been strong enough to overthrow an ancient ecclesiastical hierarchy and establishment, should be extended to the civil sphere as well. Despite a primary concern for the regenerate, the doctrine of Christian liberty was bound to lead Milton and Williams and the Levellers in their several ways and degrees to recognize the necessity of natural liberty for all. And such concepts as reason and the law of nature, which for men like Hooker and Bishop Bramhall were bulwarks of established authority, could be used by revolutionists—as they could be by Hobbes—in their religious or rational hostility to custom and the dead weight of antiquitarian tradition.

The Levellers, a left wing or temporary ally of Independency, were the one genuinely democratic party that played an important part in the revolution. Their intellectual and literary strength was embodied in such men as the scholarly merchant, William Walwyn, an antinomian in whom critical rationalism was warmed by spiritual and humanitarian charity; the tough libertarian and satirist Richard Overton, whose 'mortalist' heresy gave him some kinship with Milton and more with Hobbes; and the army officer Edward Sexby, later notorious as a plotter against Cromwell and as the author of *Killing No Murder* (1657). But the popular and picturesque Leveller hero was the stalwart, fearless, and irrepressible Lieutenant-Colonel John Lilburne (1614?–57).[1] If Walwyn was the keen and ironic (and prolific) Socrates of the party, and Overton its Thomas Paine, Lilburne might be called a religious Wilkes-Mirabeau. His power came from the merits of his cause, his personality and challenging martyrdoms, and his journalistic gift for making abstract questions concrete and dramatic. 'With Coke's "Institutes" in his hand', says Sir Charles Firth, 'he was willing to tackle any tribunal.' The hold that 'Honest John' and 'Freeborn John' had over the public was shown in the petitions on his behalf and the demonstrations at more than one acquittal. It was said that his writings were quoted 'as statute law' in the

---

[1] Lilburne, a younger son of a country gentleman, was apprenticed to a London clothier. During 1638–40 he was in prison for circulating such 'seditious' pamphlets as those of Bastwick and Prynne. He fought well in the parliamentary army, 1642–5, but refused to subscribe to the Solemn League and Covenant and gave up his commission. Thenceforth, throughout a career punctuated by imprisonments, Lilburne battled for popular rights, and his own, against vested interest and authority. Unlike some of his Leveller associates, he had always been religious, and in his last years he became a Quaker.

army. Lilburne was the champion of the lower middle class against bishops, king, Lords, Commons, lawyers, Presbyterians, Independents, and Cromwell. He abhorred arbitrary power whether it was held by an individual or a group.

In opposition to the claims of king, Parliament, and army the Levellers stood for the supremacy of law, a written constitution, and the rights of man. During 1647 their adherents multiplied in and outside of the army. The army as a whole was at odds with Parliament, and the soldiers, already discontented over arrears in pay, grew more and more restive and suspicious while their generals as well as Parliament negotiated with the captive king and delayed the settlement of a constitution. One highlight in the picture is the army debates of 1647–9 between the 'grandees', Cromwell, Ireton, and others, and the Leveller 'agitators' or delegates who represented the rank and file of the army. In the discussion of the franchise, for example, Ireton spoke for the substantial classes, and vaguely anticipated Harrington, in his insistence upon a property qualification. And, though the individualistic Levellers had no quarrel with private property, Colonel Rainborough put the doctrine of natural rights into the famous statement that 'the poorest he that is in England hath a life to live, as the greatest he'. The Leveller platform, set forth with variations and qualifications in successive *Agreements of the People* (1647–9) and other documents, included widened suffrage, biennial or annual Parliaments, re-apportionment of constituencies and other electoral changes, legal, judicial, and penal reforms, the abolition of commercial monopolies, the substitution for tithes and indirect taxes of a direct tax on real and personal property, the restoration of enclosed lands, free schools, maintenance for the poor and infirm, and of course liberty of conscience. Most of these proposals were destined to be adopted sooner or later. We may in fact wonder how the Levellers' appeals to reason and principle could arouse opposition; but we may remember that these democratic doctrinaires, being ahead of their time, did not always face the actualities of national dissension which Cromwell did see and had to meet. Also, the Levellers, after curing sores that Parliament had neglected or avoided, would have established a *laissez-faire* government with explicitly limited powers. Although the movement failed, its principles were to remain or reappear in English and American political thought. But we must turn to some less realistic programmes engendered in various quarters, in particular those of the 'True Levellers' or Diggers and of James Harrington.

In the sixteenth and seventeenth centuries manifold causes brought about a European revival of ancient utopian writings and gave birth to many new ones, from More's to the *Christianopolis* (1619) of J. V. Andreae and Campanella's *Civitas Solis* (1623). In revolutionary England, when so many imaginations were kindled by millenarian dreams, a great mass of political, social, religious, educational, and scientific literature was more or less utopian in spirit, even if it usually lacked an exotic costume. Before the revolutionary yeast had fermented two very different Utopias appeared, the strongly practical scheme of social reform incorporated in Burton's preface to his *Anatomy*, and the *New Atlantis* of Bacon, whose technological paradise had a setting of romantic geography and courtly pomp. Without unduly stretching the word 'utopian', we might include next the exuberant seventh Prolusion of the young Milton, possibly Bacon's first great disciple. In 1641 the full-fledged Baconian, Samuel Hartlib, addressed his *Description of Macaria* to Parliament. Macaria was a kind of prismatic mirage which shone before the zealous projector to the end of his life. In that welfare state co-operative planning improves production, develops trade and plantations, and encourages medical research. As the titles of many of his tracts indicate, Hartlib wanted to reform everything, education, religion, husbandry, the Virginian silk-worm, and the commonwealth of bees. One bee that buzzed in his bonnet was the notion of a central clearing-house which would co-ordinate every branch of human activity, from odd jobs to matrimony. In connexion with Hartlib it may be observed that the influence of J. V. Andreae was felt in England at least through the work of his friends Comenius and John Dury, and in the educational and religious Utopia, *Nova Solyma* (1648), of Samuel Gott.

The evolution of political theory outlined in the preceding part of this chapter might be epitomized in two titles. The sixteenth century ended with Thomas Floyd's *Picture of a Perfect Commonwealth* (1600), which, as its large debt to Elyot's *Governor* implies, was in the old humanistic tradition of the ideal prince; and our period ends with *The Ready and Easy Way to Establish a Free Commonwealth*, the bitterly disillusioned outcry of the greatest of all the Christian humanists and utopian idealists who had taken part in the revolution. But a significant change in the scope of political thought became conspicuous after the war and may be illustrated through two representative and individually important figures, Gerrard Winstanley (1609–*post* 1660) and James Harrington. Winstanley was the spokesman and active leader of the 'True Levellers' who in 1649–50 tried to assert the rights of the rural populace against the lords of the manors by tilling common ground in Surrey and elsewhere. The Digger movement failed, but some of Winstanley's ideas were to be revived by such men as Robert Owen and Henry George, and in recent years he has been honoured as the champion of the forgotten man. Magna Carta had been a victory for the barons, and in the late civil war the middle classes had made good their economic, political, and religious claims against the feudal, royalist, and Anglican régime. The lower classes, however, were not sharing the fruits of the revolution, and Winstanley insistently proclaimed that fact. Like some contemporaries, such as the Levellers, he dated economic, legal, and ecclesiastical tyranny from the Norman conquest. In the dedication of *The Law of Freedom in a Platform* (1652) he puts two alternatives before Cromwell, either to 'set the Land free to the oppressed Commoners, who assisted you, and payd the Army their wages', or merely to 'remove the Conquerors Power out of the Kings hand into other mens, maintaining the old Laws still'. If Cromwell follows the latter course, then his wisdom and honour are blasted for ever and he will either lose himself 'or lay the Foundation of greater Slavery to posterity' than he ever knew. Winstanley has been called Marxist in his economic reading of history and the class war, but he would have preferred to be placed in the long line of Christian communists who had pleaded for the under-dog since the Middle Ages. Quiet, happy, and unswerving obedience to the inner light led Winstanley from private mystical ecstasies to humanitarian effort. He was of course unrealistic in dreaming of a society rooted in equality, reason, and brotherly love, not corrupted by property and the possessive instinct, and enjoying freedom of conscience and free practical education.

The proletarian and mystical Winstanley and the high-born and rational author of *Oceana* (1656) have some affinity in their emphasis upon economic and agrarian problems and the principle of rotation in public office.[1] Harrington is a feudal land-owner with a touch of the Leveller and Digger about him, and a Renaissance amateur who has caught the spirit of the scientific lawgivers of his age and who in fact invokes the name of Harvey. He has the humanistic conception of the State as an organism like the individual man, with its passions similarly ruled by reason, an 'Empire of Lawes, and not of Men'; he seems to pay more than lip-service to the Christian view of a divine pattern for human society, and in his frequent appeals 'Unto God in the Fabrick of the Common-wealth of Israel' he evidently accepts the special authority of the Bible; yet he is commonly credited with a very secular outlook. As a hard-headed realist he writes in the inductive tradition of Bacon and especially Machiavelli, 'the onely Polititian of later Ages', 'the sole retreiver' of 'ancient Prudence': Bacon and Machiavelli had harped upon a string which they had not perfectly tuned, 'the ballance of Dominion or Propriety'. Harrington's aim is to demonstrate the working of economic law, to analyse the economic dislocation which had caused the civil war, and, since the commonwealth is still in a plastic state, to provide an economic and political constitution that will prevent such violent disturbances in the future. Like Hobbes, whose theories he opposes, Harrington is a master of clear logic and of a plain and sometimes lively style. But while Hobbes largely ignored history (except in *Behemoth*), Harrington, like Machiavelli and many men of his own time, used the historical method in com-bination with abstract principles. He draws constant examples

[1] James Harrington (1611–77) was the eldest son of Sir Sapcotes Harrington. In 1629 he entered Trinity College, Oxford, where he is said to have had Chilling-worth as his tutor, but the period of instruction must have been brief. Harrington left without a degree, was admitted to the Middle Temple in 1631, and spent some time in foreign travel. His observations, especially in Holland and Venice, made him a political scientist and a republican. Except for his attendance upon Charles in the Scottish expedition of 1639 and during most of the king's captivity, Harring-ton led a private life. *Oceana* appeared in 1656 after being held up, it seems, by Cromwell, and quickly provoked controversy. Harrington actively reiterated his views in print and, during the winter of 1659–60, at the much publicized Rota Club. He even dragged his agrarian theory into translations of Virgil (1658–9). With the Restoration Harrington's status altered. Imprisonment (1661) caused both physical and mental derangement from which he never entirely recovered. Among the friends of his later years were Aubrey, Marvell, and Henry Neville, author of the Harringtonian *Plato Redivivus* (1681). The first collected edition of his works was that of the notable John Toland (1700), who had edited Milton's prose in 1698. Toland printed for the first time Harrington's most compact statement of his doctrine, *A System of Politics*.

from Roman and Greek history because his heart, like Machiavelli's, is in the ancient city-state, which he tries in countless ways to reproduce (his model, it has been suggested, was Plato's *Laws*); the only modern government that approaches perfection is that of Venice. Whether his inspiration be philosophy or only tact, Harrington has his republic created by a strong man, 'Olphaus Megaletor', otherwise Cromwell. The imaginative title and framework of his Utopia, in addition to their protective value, unite romantic suggestions of fortunate isles with the imperialistic optimism of a citizen of a self-consciously maritime nation.

Harrington's most fundamental idea has already been touched upon. Ignoring the social contract employed by both republicans and royalists, he defines types of government not in purely political terms but according to the distribution of property among the several classes of people. For him, in his age, property consists chiefly in land, and one of the stable blessings of Oceana is its rural and agricultural economy. When the nobility and clergy possess most of the land, as they did in the Middle Ages, monarchy is possible. But the early Tudors imposed checks upon the old nobility and enabled the gentry and middle class to acquire land and grow strong, so that 'the dissolution of the late Monarchy was as natural as the death of a man'. Equality of estates causes equality of power, and equality of power means a commonwealth; a republican government is now the only kind that squares with economic facts. The main fact, the altered centre of economic gravity, Harrington was not the first to recognize, but he was the first thorough diagnostician. (Against the orthodox modern view, here meagrely summarized, it has been argued that Harrington was more of an historian of feudalism than an economic analyst.) The constitution proposed in *Oceana* is to further and preserve the harmony achieved by organizing the political power of the natural aristocracy of country gentlemen. Thus Harrington was by no means a complete democrat; and, though he touched upon commercialism, his personal and historical instincts tied him to the land. However, what he understands as 'popular government' comes nearest to the interest of mankind, and the reason of popular government comes nearest to right reason. A perfect government is that which affords no cause or means of sedition, and a popular government alone satisfies that need. It rests on two

principles, an agrarian law that ensures the perpetual distribution of land and prevents it from being inherited and accumulated by the few, and reform of the electoral and parliamentary
system that keeps new blood circulating through the body
politic. 'An equal Common-wealth', then, '. . . is a Government
established upon an equall Agrarian, arising into the super-
structures or three orders, the Senate debating and proposing,
the people resolving, and the Magistracy executing by an equal
Rotation through the suffrage of the people given by the
Ballot.' When he comes to religion Harrington, like Hobbes,
puts ecclesiastical laws in the power of the magistrate and sees
in papal and Puritan claims the cause of endless disorder and
war. Like Hobbes, too, he would have a national Church,
since 'a Common-wealth is nothing else but the National
Conscience'. His Church, however, is organized on a voluntary
basis, with an elected (but learned) ministry, and he insists
that liberty of conscience is bound up with civil liberty, though
he would exclude Jews, papists, and idolaters from toleration.

While Harrington acquired supporters in Parliament and
outside, both his theoretical and his practical ideas were
vigorously attacked and satirized. Among his critics were
Cromwell, Marchamont Needham, Dr. Henry Stubbe (who
later assailed the Royal Society), the younger Matthew Wren,
Richard Baxter in his *Holy Commonwealth* (1659), and Milton
in the *Ready and Easy Way* (though Milton's aristocratic republicanism—and his view of Cromwell—had something in common
with Harrington's). But Harrington's basic doctrines became
generally accepted commonplaces; the roll of his admirers
included Locke, Hume, and, in the nineteenth century,
Coleridge and Wordsworth and the Utilitarians and Radicals.
Yet his main influence, direct and indirect, was felt most
strongly in the American colonies, first in leaders like Penn and
in the constitutions of Carolina, New Jersey, and Pennsylvania,
and then, more effectually, in the movement for independence
and the formation of the union. Harrington's theory of the
economic balance of power had led him to predict the American
Revolution and, along with that inspiring prophecy, such men
as John Adams made much of the property qualification,
written constitutions, a double-chamber system with checks
and balances, rotation of office, and the ballot. To the French
Revolution and its aftermath Harrington also contributed,

partly through his own writings and partly through English and American applications of his doctrines. If *Oceana* is not now one of the living classics, probably the essential reason is that Harrington's Utopia is not only doctrinaire but somewhat drab and dusty; he wrote, not unnaturally, with a passion for external peace and order, but the greatest political thinkers have had a broader, more positive, and more humane vision of life.

In no kind of writing of our period, naturally, does the clash of old and new appear in such bold relief as in political thought. Yet nowhere is the difference between old and new harder to define, and both terms may be applied at once to the ideas and the individual writers on all sides of the great controversial questions. Of the many paradoxical phenomena of the age the only one that can be emphasized here is the change, accomplished in the course of a Puritan revolution, from a religious to a secular view of the State and society. However secular the outlook of men like Bacon, Selden, and Hobbes, they had no great influence. The Bible was the common source which linked together King James and Filmer, Milton and all the Puritans, the millenarian and antinomian sects, the more or less secular Harrington, and even Hobbes, who is in his way the best of all proofs of the power of Scripture. But though the ideals of Christian liberty and the holy community provided the religious dynamic of the political revolution (and had their most logical issue in Winstanley's religious communism), some Puritan parties stood for the complete separation of Church and State, and the most thoroughly democratic, secular, and modern theories of government came not only from the Levellers but from the intensely religious Roger Williams.

Finally, since this is a history of literature, it may be observed that this large body of political writing, though it dealt so much with abstract ideas, was mostly addressed to the middle classes and displayed as a whole a steadily increasing power of popular appeal. And though much of what was most effective has paid for its effectiveness by dropping below our horizon, there probably never was a period in English history when the heterogeneous battalion of minor political authors wrote so ably—and there again we may think of the Bible.

IX

SCIENCE AND SCIENTIFIC THOUGHT

ALTHOUGH science had been advancing steadily for many centuries, we think of the seventeenth as having given birth to the modern world. And in that age Englishmen made even larger contributions to the European movement than they had in the period from 1200 to 1600. The greatest single discovery, that of William Harvey (1578–1657), was described in lectures in the year of Shakespeare's death and in print in 1628. The result of his revolutionary demonstration was, he told Aubrey, 'that he fell mightily in his practize, and that 'twas beleeved by the vulgar that he was crack-brained; and all the physitians were against his opinion, and envyed him.' However, as his friend Hobbes said, he lived to see his doctrine established. While Harvey's chief debt was to continental anatomists, in mathematics and astronomy Englishmen of the seventeenth century had behind them the distinguished work of Recorde, Dee, Thomas Digges, and William Gilbert (1544–1603). In his *De Magnete* (1600) Gilbert, by experiment, laid a solidly scientific foundation, and more than a foundation, for the study of terrestrial magnetism. Thomas Harriot (1560–1621), the friend of Ralegh and the scientific sun of a notable circle, was an eminent mathematician and made telescopic observations contemporaneously with Galileo. John Napier's invention of logarithms (1614), in the famous phrase of Laplace, doubled the lifetime of astronomers. From the end of the sixteenth century onward Gresham College was a centre of practical and theoretical science. The two universities, whose scholastic darkness drew complaints from Bacon, Milton, Hobbes, and many lesser men, produced, if they seldom trained, a multitude of mathematicians and scientists. Among them, to add some more names, were Edward Wright, Henry Briggs, William Oughtred, Edmund Gunter, John Pell, and Jeremiah Horrocks. The Savilian professorships in geometry and astronomy, founded at Oxford in 1619, provided a stimulating current, and with the arrival thirty years later of her own John Wilkins and some illustrious Cantabrigians, for once Oxford became, involuntarily, the home of a winning cause. Throughout our period English and continental men of science followed one another's work closely, and between some there was personal acquaintance or correspondence.

These are only a few out of the scores of scientists who, in England as in Europe at large, made the seventeenth century one of unparalleled achievement. From being a cultural outcast science became a respectable and finally a dominant interest which attracted hosts of amateurs, including aristocrats and obscure business men. Ralegh, Bacon, and, when he first turned to science, Sir Kenelm Digby, were relatively isolated figures; by the time of Evelyn science was a major preoccupation of the virtuoso. The most various causes contributed to the scientific movement: the accident of genius; the critical impetus and the body of new knowledge inherited from the sixteenth century; Bacon's eloquent and timely propagation of new ideals; the middle-class and Puritan reaction against traditional academic learning and in favour of useful studies; the general Protestant approval of scientific research for the glory of God and the service of man; the popular appeal of experiment and invention to both utility and curiosity; and the pressure of countless technological problems created by the growth of an urban population, of industry and manufacturing, of a coal-burning economy, and of domestic and foreign commerce and transportation. The debt of navigators to science, for example, received quaint acknowledgement from Captain Luke Fox, who named some north-western islands, after his friend and patron, 'Brigges his Mathematickes'.

Along with this great forward movement in the sciences, and sometimes represented by the same persons, we have the old pseudo-sciences which, with or without the help of occult mysticism, were flourishing with unabated vigour. Sufficient reminders of this often murky penumbra of science are the names of Robert Fludd (1574–1637), William Lilly (1602–81), Nicholas Culpeper (1616—64), Elias Ashmole (1617–92), and Thomas Vaughan (1621/2–66). As we noted earlier, judicial astrology, though sometimes defended, was increasingly attacked; but critical minds like Ralegh and Bacon, even if they dismissed vulgar prognostications, could retain some belief in the influence of the stars, which, as Burton said, 'do incline, but not compel'. Medicine, biology, and chemistry were still more or less mixed with astrology, fantastic pharmacology (the royal touch retained its virtue far beyond our period), animism, and alchemy. Ancient or Paracelsian notions of primary elements and principles, and the qualitative conception of matter, stood in the way of scientific analysis, though experiment and 'Hooke's microscope' were soon to sweep away many cobwebs. Since Bacon is so often made the scapegoat of credulity, we may remember that Gilbert, Kepler, Descartes, and others were not immune from unscientific ideas. Boyle, for instance, stopped the bleeding of his nose with 'some moss of a dead man's skull'. After Harvey's, doubtless the most celebrated if not the most valuable medical discovery was Sir Kenelm Digby's 'powder of sympathy'; its miraculous efficacy was first publicly proclaimed in 1658. That versatile dilettante showed his really scientific capacity in his treatise on bodies (1644) and his lecture to the Royal Society on the vegetation of plants (1661). In general, the mixture of the fabulous or occult with the scientific was in part a natural legacy from medieval science, in part it was sustained by the persistent conviction, rational or mystical, of the unity between God and all His works. The dying bodies of alchemy and astrology, we may add, yielded—in Paracelsian fashion—an abundance of living metaphors and symbols for imaginative writers from Donne to Milton; and the music of the spheres could still bless some human ears.

In the sixteenth and seventeenth centuries, while science was extending man's knowledge of nature and the heavens more rapidly and radically than exploration had been extending his knowledge of the globe, there ran, side by side with enthusiastic optimism, a deep current of disillusionment. One early and long-lived manifesto of 'obscurantism' was Agrippa's *De Incertitudine et Vanitate Scientiarum et Artium atque Excellentia Verbi Dei* (1530). Bacon, in a defence of learning which was by no means otiose, put first 'the zeale and jealousie of Divines', and he constantly sought to guard himself and science against the charge of atheism. (On the other hand, it was a not insignificant fact that many English men of science were clerics.) In all ages any ray of scientific light may alter the focus of religious and humanistic vision, or enlarge the area of enveloping darkness, and in the seventeenth century the most disturbing light was astronomical. New observations and deductions, combined with old and new speculations, slowly effected a great change in the traditional picture of the universe and of man's place in it; some of the various literary repercussions we have met already.

The subject is difficult to handle briefly, since in recent years no part of the background of English literature has been more fully investigated; our attention shall be given primarily to three men who are conspicuously great writers. Bacon, though he touched everything, may represent study of the outer world, Burton study of the inner, and Hobbes a new and alarming approach to both. Sir Thomas Browne, though a genuine scientist and perhaps for many of us the supreme writer, must here realize, in a sense, his modest ambition 'to be but the last man, and bring up the Rere in Heaven'.

I

While Bacon has always occupied a throne, the extent of his realm and authority has been subject to many mutations. He outshines the normal scientific recluse by virtue of his literary, legal, and political eminence, the dramatic quality of his career, and the real or apparent puzzles in his character which have attracted so many biographers. Then when we look at the philosopher and his monumental collected works Bacon seems to bestride his age like a Colossus. Standing between the medieval and the modern world, he pointed along the road civilization was to take in the following centuries. His scientific ideals had been proclaimed and practised by other Englishmen, of whom Gilbert was the most influential, but they did not stand in the Baconian pulpit under the Baconian soundingboard. If he himself was the father of no important specific contributions to science, he was the godfather of many, and his strictly scientific thought has more significance than the conventional estimate allows.

While Bacon's predominant passion was natural science, he was a man of the Renaissance who, unlike many of his critics, never lost sight of the whole range of knowledge. *The Advancement of Learning* (1605) is the most attractive of his philosophic works because it is the most broadly comprehensive and humane, because its strength and vision are least impaired by dead technicalities, and because it is, with the *Essays*, the great example of his English prose. The other major work, the *Novum Organum* (1620), though confined to the philosophy and methods of science, embodies, like the *Advancement*, a criticism of the past and a programme for the future, and we may consider Bacon's ideas under these two headings rather than in relation to particular books or to his own elaborate classification of knowledge. The *Instauratio Magna*, as he outlined it in the *Distributio Operis* prefixed to the *Novum Organum*, was to comprise six parts. The first was fulfilled with relative adequacy in *De Augmentis Scientiarum* (1623), the enlarged Latin version of the *Advancement*. The *Novum Organum*, though incomplete, represents the second part, which was to teach the right method of investigating nature, a combination of the empirical and the rational; the title was a challenge to the Aristotelian tradition. For the rest we turn from torsos to *disjecta membra*. In the third part, which includes the natural histories and the *Sylva Sylvarum*, observations of natural phenomena were to be assembled as material for the new method of study. The fourth part, represented by a preface, was to give examples of its operation. In the fifth part, again represented by a preface, Bacon intended to report what he had himself discovered by more conventional methods, without the help of his special induction. This fifth part would lose its value with the completion of the sixth, which was to expound the new philosophy and methodology in full and describe the results of its application to all the natural phenomena of the universe. The fulfilment of this part Bacon left to posterity. Thus the *Instauratio Magna* is linked with *The Fairy Queen* and *The History of the World* as the partial accomplishment of an impossibly vast design.

As a destructive critic, a mouthpiece for the modern world's declaration of independence, Bacon has only one rival, Descartes (1596–1650), and Bacon, in addition to his priority, is more compendious and arresting. The *loci classici* are, next to the *Essays*, probably the best-known parts of Bacon's writings. The first is the discussion, in the first book of the *Advancement*, of the three principal vanities or distempers of learning (along with a series of 'peccant humours'). Bacon arraigns in turn the rhetorical discipline of medieval and Renaissance humanism, the study of words instead of matter; the medieval scholastic discipline, still dominant in the universities, which has also ignored nature and kept mankind in a desert of barren rationalism; and, thirdly, fallacious pseudo-sciences like astrology and alchemy. Then in the first book of the *Novum Organum*

present or absent with heat, always increases or decreases with it, and is a particular case of a more general nature. By progressive elimination of false alternatives from his tables Bacon arrives at the one remaining *sine qua non* which must be the form desired, that is, motion. The more difficult part of the inductive process, the establishment of exact scientific criteria for the method of exclusions, he recognized but never described. In general, he is not always clear or explicit and, since his views changed on some points, not altogether consistent. The experimental method in itself was of course very old and Bacon's elaborate superstructure, it is customary to say, was to prove more significant in the history of inductive logic than in the history of science, and was not of much value for Bacon's own end, the discovery of forms. Modern philosophic critics stress the fallacious ideas of card-indexing all nature, of uncontrolled experimentation, of co-operative research that can be carried out by mechanical industry and leaves no room for individual inspirations, inspirations, moreover, which have generally sprung from a very few experiments or even deductions. But many working scientists of Bacon's century, like Robert Hooke, praised the intellectual 'Engine' of 'the incomparable Verulam', and thought, as some men of science do now, that he had made a notable statement of the principles of scientific method. The reading of his works is enough to qualify the conventional charges. Bacon does not ignore hypothesis, for example, in the 'First Vintage concerning the Form of Heat' (his imaginative labels reveal both the scholastic and the poet), and elsewhere he frequently suggests experiments for the testing of hypotheses. And these facts with others—such as his consciousness that his method must be perfected as discovery advanced, or his very effort to guard the scientific mind from idols—imply allowance for the work of individual genius.

Blanket dismissals of Bacon's positive scientific thought are in part the result of misplaced emphasis, in part they are reactions against the panegyrical tradition of the French Encyclopaedists, Macaulay, and other laymen, and in part they are inherited from an age which accepted a strictly mechanical and materialistic view of the universe as the *ne plus ultra* of scientific philosophy. Tried, rather hastily, by this standard, Bacon seemed to belong to another world than Galileo and Descartes and to deserve banishment to the medieval lumber-room. More recent scientific thought has retreated, or advanced, from that mechanical absolutism, and some eminent philosophers of our time, including Whitehead, who have given Bacon serious and unprejudiced study, treat him with respect. This renewed but more intelligent admiration does not rest merely on the innumerable soundly scientific precepts scattered through Bacon's works, but on the scientifically prophetic penetration exhibited in his doctrine of forms and simple natures. The conception is not nullified by errors in the inductive method. A form is both an essence and a structural law, the mechanical condition or means of producing the physical property. Hence to discover forms is to understand the unity underlying diverse aspects of matter and also to have the power of intelligently producing the simple natures corresponding to the forms. Then by different combinations of simple natures, based on a knowledge of forms and latent structure, the scientist can transmute one substance into another, can ultimately control all the phenomena of nature. Bacon condemns the theories and methods of the alchemists but not their object, and modern science, with truer knowledge, has gone far in the same direction. If, as some writers say, the control of phenomenal recurrence is the only concern, the very definition, of the scientist, Bacon, whatever his particular shortcomings, is one of the pioneers of modernism. Further, as these summary remarks have indicated, Bacon represents a transitional phase of escape from the medieval qualitative conception of matter, and from the teleological animism of Renaissance thinkers, to something like the kinematical view. At the same time, whether from 'Aristotelian' insight or want of mathematical capacity, he generally stops short of the chief pitfall of 'classical' mechanism, the identification of reality with a kinematical pattern. If Bacon was not altogether in the direct line that led from Kepler and Galileo to Newton, he did fuse a limited mechanism with dynamism; and his conception of form and matter and motion was worked out by Boyle and others.

Bacon is not, then, historically negligible as a scientific thinker, but his great claims upon us are more familiar. His scientific deficiencies did not essentially weaken the force of his message for his time, the substitution of humble, critical interrogation of nature for the arbitrary concepts of traditional authority, abstract reason, and the unaided senses. It was not an insignificant thing that a great lawyer, judge, and statesman should take up the cause of natural science, and Bacon did more than any other individual except Descartes to create a favourable intellectual climate. He not only summoned men to research, he brought the Cinderella of science out of her partial obscurity and enthroned her as the queen of the world. No one any longer could be deaf to the scientific and humanitarian gospel of experiment, invention, utility, and progress. The traditional view of human history was static or deteriorationist; Bacon made it dynamic and optimistic. He transferred the Golden Age from the mythical infancy of man to an attainable future. He was the chorus of the scientific drama, the Moses, in Cowley's great image, who led his people to the edge of the promised land. If we say that such changes would have occurred without Bacon, we must say also that the discoveries of Galileo and Newton would have been made if those men had never lived.

And the office of spokesman required gifts no less distinctive than the practical discoverer's. The works of Gilbert and Harvey, if we read them, may make some of Bacon's technical discussions look immature, but to whom other than Bacon can we go for a comparable synthesis of the forces and motives that were changing the character of civilization? His voice, moreover, would have lost much of its power if he had not been one of the great masters of the language whose permanence he doubted. His deliberate aim, set forth in the *Parasceve* and elsewhere, Dr. Rawley summed up when he said that Bacon 'did rather drive, at a Masculine, and clear, Expression, than at any Finenes, or Affectation, of Phrases'. But if on this point we compare his chief works with those of Gilbert and Harvey, we find less bareness than plenitude, and a strongly figurative, even a poetic, strain. In English (and his Latin is not dissimilar) he was able to combine the homely and plthy stock of native idiom and diction with the pointed pregnancy of Tacitus without losing the massive dignity of the Ciceronian period. His virtues are not of course a mere matter of word and rhythm. Shelley, who manifested his devotion from *The Necessity of Atheism* to *The Triumph of Life*, coupled Bacon and Plato as poet-philosophers, citing especially the *Filum Labyrinthi* and the essay 'Of Death'; and he might have added such passages as the conclusion of the first book of the *Advancement*. Bacon is a scholar and a poet, a thinker and a wit, a realist and a dreamer. His

noble eulogies of learning and the quest of truth, his infinite
faith in the power of man, his vision of a new era and of himself as the torch-bearer, these things still quicken even the unsympathetic reader's pulse.

We may be unsympathetic because three centuries of progress
have made it clear that the conquest of external nature is
an inadequate goal, that, as Shelley said in one of his un-
Baconian moods, 'man, having enslaved the elements, remains
himself a slave'. Not that Bacon contemplated such an end.
'Only let the human race recover that right over nature which
belongs to it by divine bequest, and let power be given it; the
exercise thereof will be governed by sound reason and true
religion.' Such words fall on our ear as a piece of tragic irony.
But if scientific power was to override the assumed safeguards,
Bacon himself cannot be cleared of all responsibility. His personal religion, whatever its limitations, inspired some beautiful
and sincere utterances, and he would have been shocked at a
hint that he was less than a good Christian, but the whole drift
of his scientific and ethical thought was towards empirical
naturalism. He wished, with a reverent acknowledgement of
faith, to exclude theological and intuitional idols from the
temple of science (which of course was a scientific necessity),
but in doing so he virtually denied the validity of a religious
view of the world; if religion was outside the sphere of knowledge, it was outside the sphere of reality. Thus, while not
condemning inquiry into first causes, Bacon left such problems
to be settled by revelation and applied himself to the study of
things. Even if we grant that the material condition of mankind had long suffered from neglect, Bacon's aims and attitudes remain open to question. To machinery and material
progress he sacrificed, in a large and noble way, to be sure, that
scale of spiritual and ethical values which the best minds of
antiquity, the Middle Ages, and the Renaissance had striven to
make prevail. He not only brought philosophy down to earth,
he confined it within the four walls of a laboratory in which
Plato and Aquinas, and Shakespeare and Milton, would have
suffocated. That is why, though we recognize Bacon's intellectual power and our vast debt to him, we do not go back to his
works for vital nourishment.

2

Bacon's successors and disciples, however, had no such feeling. His eloquent statement of the claims and methods of experimental science received the praises not merely of his own countrymen but of continental thinkers and scientists from Descartes, Mersenne, and Gassendi to Huygens, Leibniz, and Vico. Bacon did 'ring a bell to call other wits together', and the bell was heard outside the domain of science. Within that domain we can notice only two illustrations of his influence. The first is the birth of what in 1662 became the Royal Society. Co-operative research, one of Bacon's feasible dreams, had its most sumptuously imaginative, and staggering, presentation in *The New Atlantis* (1627). Apart from general tributes to Bacon, before and after the formal inception of the Society, we have the familiar testimony of such men as Cowley, Sprat, Glanvill, Wallis, and Oldenburg to the potent inspiration of the Baconian ideal; the founders were, to be sure, aware of academies that had been multiplying on the Continent. The Society may be said to have been born in or about 1645, during the war, with the meetings at Gresham College of a group of professional and amateur scientists interested in experiment; divinity, state affairs, and news were barred from discussion. But 1645 is a nominal date, since these meetings grew out of the earlier activities of the scientific professors of Gresham College; they for years had been co-operating with one another and with men concerned in practical and especially nautical enterprise, and when Bacon's influence was felt, it furnished a grandiose sanction for a movement already vigorous and fruitful. With the migration of some leading members to Oxford (1648 ff.), the centre of gravity shifted. At Oxford the group developed in numbers, organization, and éclat. Including the ex-Londoners and new and future members, there were John Wilkins, John Wallis, Jonathan Goddard, William Petty, Robert Boyle, Seth Ward, Robert Hooke, Thomas Willis, Lawrence Rooke, Christopher Wren, and others. It was a constellation of varied scientific genius. By 1660 the centre of gravity had moved back to London and Gresham College, and towards the end of that year the Society was formally established.

The Society was a concrete symptom not only of the rising spirit of scientific inquiry but of the practical ideals of an

especially Puritan middle class conscious of the new needs of a
new world, ideals which were finding simultaneous expression
in pamphlets on educational reform. Most of the ten original
members of the London group whom we know—Wilkins, Wallis,
Goddard, and others—were moderate Puritans and parliamentarians. Theodore Haak, whom Wallis later credited with
having suggested the London meetings, was employed by the
Westminster Assembly. Wallis was a secretary to the Assembly,
and, as Hobbes did not fail to remind him after the Restoration, used his mathematical skill in deciphering royalist code-
messages during the civil war. Wilkins, Wallis, Ward, Petty,
and Goddard were appointed by Parliament, during the years
of Independent domination, to administrative or professorial
posts at Oxford (1648-51). There were general affinities between
Baconian science and rational Puritanism: impatience of traditional authority and useless learning; the critical and empirical
instinct; the ideal of action rather than contemplation; belief
in utility, progress, and reform, in the study of God's creation
and in 'works' as a religious and humanitarian duty and
pleasure; and—what is not really inconsistent with that—the
disposition to segregate the religious and the secular, the divine
and the 'natural'. The minutes of the Royal Society amply
attest its utilitarian consciousness of the multiplying technological and economic problems of an age of expansion. It goes
without saying that this active Puritan and middle-class sympathy with science contained no suspicion of the irreligious
philosophy associated with Hobbes. Lest this paragraph seem
to say too much, it may be added that, when the Society was
formally established and enlarged in 1660, most of the new
fellows were royalists; but, as we have seen, the leading pioneers,
who were still members, had been on the other side.

As a lively and literary representative of the manifold interests
of the Royal Society we may take John Wilkins (1614-72), probably the chief moving spirit in its development—'a working
head', Aubrey called him.[1] His first book (1638) was one of the

---

[1] Wilkins was a grandson of the noted Puritan divine, John Dod, and was
educated in the strongly Puritan Magdalen Hall. After a few years as an Oxford
tutor and country vicar, he held several chaplaincies. In 1648 he was made
Warden of Wadham College, in place of an ejected royalist. In the Oxford phase
of the Royal Society's growth Wilkins's enthusiastic leadership was the prime
factor. In 1656 he married Cromwell's sister. In 1659 he was appointed Master of
Trinity College, Cambridge. On losing this post shortly after the Restoration,

seventeenth century's numerous speculations regarding the moon as an inhabited globe; the notion of a plurality of worlds had been in men's minds since antiquity, but it gained new life with the new astronomy. In the preface Wilkins twice invoked the learned and judicious Verulam as the champion of observed fact against ancient authority. For particular ideas, though he was well read in the literature of astronomy, he was especially indebted to Campanella's *Apologia pro Galileo*. In his *Discourse concerning a New Planet* (1640) Wilkins was replying in part to the stout Aristotelian 'fundamentalist' of the age, Alexander Ross, who in a life of multifarious controversy made up in thunder what he lacked in lightning. Whatever Wilkins's deficiencies, by modern standards, he did more than any other Englishman of his time to popularize the Copernican doctrine, and perhaps did something to undermine the scientific authority of Scripture. We cannot follow his many ideas, original or borrowed, which include mechanics and microscopy, a chariot for flying to the moon and 'an Ark for submarine Navigations', but even this meagre notice may serve to register the new type of curious, forward-looking, scientific amateur and also the spirit of co-operative inquiry that drew such men together.

Wilkins's *Ecclesiastes* (1646) was one of the signposts in the history of plain preaching, and a signpost in another area was his *Essay towards a Real Character and a Philosophical Language* (1668), which was sponsored by the Royal Society. In the quest for a universal language the chief continental pioneer was Comenius, whose great aim of religious unity included a Baconian concern with things and the belief that linguistic differences and inexactness promoted sectarian divisions. In the three decades before Wilkins's *Essay* a number of progressive Englishmen, Hartlib of course in the van, were stirred by Comenian or more purely scientific motives to interest in the creating of a new medium of precise communication. Even if scientists were or became sceptical about a universal language, the motives behind the effort were significant. For—witness the modern preoccupation with semantics—there was a growing consciousness of the idols of the market-place and theatre, of the

---

Wilkins achieved a second and ecclesiastical career which ended with the bishopric of Chester (1668–72). He was a friend of Whichcote and other Cambridge Platonists, and of Evelyn. He died 'ready for the Great Experiment'.

dangerous ambiguities latent in words. Thus Thomas Sprat, in his *History of the Royal Society* (1667), enunciated both religious and scientific motives. And the Cambridge Platonists, along with smaller men, were accused of dealing in nothing but words—by a scientific bishop, Samuel Parker, who wished for an act of Parliament 'to abridge Preachers the use of fulsom and lushious Metaphors'. Although Bacon had been a leader in the movement towards precision, his own English is far from Hobbes's bareness. But science, as we have seen, was only one of many forces at work. We must reckon with the general advance of rationalism, the growth of the middle-class public and of utilitarian writing, Puritanism and religious and political controversy, and, within the province of style, the anti-Ciceronian movement and the neoclassical consciousness of Elizabethan aberrations.

3

Our other example of the Baconian spirit, if not of such direct influence or of baldly scientific prose, is *Pseudodoxia Epidemica* (1646), commonly known from its running title as *Vulgar Errors*, though the errors it scrutinized were not merely vulgar. Sir Thomas Browne (1605–82) was still more curious, versatile, and learned than Wilkins, but he looked backward and upward more often than forward;[1] one link with Wilkins is the fact that

[1] Browne was born in London and educated at Winchester (1616–23) and Oxford (1623–9). He pursued medical studies at Montpellier, Padua, and Leyden (1630?–3); at Leyden he took his degree. According to Anthony Wood, he practised for some time near Oxford. He wrote the first draft of *Religio Medici* in 1634–5. In 1637 he was incorporated M.D. at Oxford and settled in Norwich. In spite of his wish that mankind might procreate like trees—a wish not endorsed by Sir Kenelm Digby and James Howell—Browne married (1641) and had ten or twelve children (authorities differ). The publication of the *Religio* (1642–3) and of Digby's *Observations* brought rapid fame both in England and abroad, and it grew with later books. During and after the war Browne, though an open royalist, quietly busied himself with his profession and private studies. He was the physician and friend of Joseph Hall in Hall's late years (1641 f.). He corresponded with Henry Power, Evelyn, Ashmole, Lilly, Dugdale, Oldenburg, Aubrey, and others. Why he did not become a member of the Royal Society we do not know. He followed with paternal and scientific interest the travels and medical researches of his son Edward, and upon 'honest Tom', who sojourned in France and then entered the navy, he lavished advice ranging from underwear to the heroic examples 'in your beloved Plutark'. In 1664 he testified at a trial of witches, but, while we may regret the beliefs that he shared with other notable minds, the often-repeated charge that his evidence was decisive in this case has been repeatedly shown to be unwarranted. In 1671 Browne was knighted, on the occasion of a royal visit to Norwich, the

Browne's first two books were successively opposed by Alexander Ross. Since the Romantic Age the *Pseudodoxia* has acquired a reputation not in accord with the author's design or with the respect in which he was held by his scientific contemporaries. In the seventeenth century as in other periods we find critical and uncritical attitudes side by side and often in the same person, but there is a difference between mere compilations of the marvellous intended to entertain or edify and the cautious sifting of traditional lore. Bacon had repeatedly desiderated, and attempted to supply, 'a Kalender of popular Errors . . . chiefly, in naturall Historie', and he had called likewise for a 'Kalender of doubts or problemes'. Browne's book was a scientific treatise addressed to the learned and challenging 'the Goliah and Giant of Authority'. His introductory survey of the causes of error is, to be sure, antiquarian and Brownesque and only loosely akin to Bacon's dynamic analysis of the 'Idols', yet it is also a protest against credulous and passive acceptance of tradition. If we are especially conscious of passing from Bacon to Browne when we reach 'the last and common Promoter of false Opinions, the endeavours of Satan', on the other hand Browne is more scientific and sceptical than Bacon when he discusses some notions already touched in *Sylva Sylvarum*: for instance, that coral is soft under water and hardens in the air; that a salamander can live in and extinguish fire (if ancient tradition is true, says Bacon, the creature has a very close skin and some very cold 'virtue'); that the chameleon lives on air (Bacon makes air its 'principall Sustenance' but admits flies as well). In the examination of these and other arresting items in his encyclopaedia, Browne appeals to critical authority, reason, and experience; of these criteria only the last is strictly Baconian. But Browne was in fact a tireless observer and experimenter. And when a whale was thrown upon the coast of Norfolk he verified his notion of spermaceti; in later years he was able, through his son, to test the belief that 'the Ostridge digesteth Iron'—after swallowing a nugget the bird died 'of a soden'. But in the settling of a more commonplace problem, the reputed inequality of the badger's legs, the mere report of the senses appears, happily for readers, to count less than abstract and almost metaphysical logic. Many exotic and 'occult' traditions were less readily verifiable by

mayor effacing himself in favour of the town's most illustrious citizen. His other works are discussed in Chapter X.

experience, and in this un-Baconian realm Browne of necessity relied upon reason and the weighing of authorities. Over many years he had gathered bits of strange learning from countless books, both the standard ones and, preferably, the remote and unfamiliar, and his antiquarian instinct could enjoy what his scientific reason denied. In regard to the great astronomical problem Browne had natural Ptolemaic velleities, but his real position was a not unscientific agnosticism. In general, he tried to keep his mind and his book abreast of modern science. He admired Gilbert and Harvey and Galileo, and knew something of Descartes, even if he did not always comprehend their methods and significance. So far as he reveals uncritical credulity, he is in the company of such supposedly more critical minds as Gassendi, Walter Charleton, Henry More, and Joseph Glanvill (and Descartes himself).

The modern reader cares less for Browne's critical intentions than for his uncritical lapses, the variety and oddity of his matter, the piquant contrast between most of the topics and the polysyllabic arguments woven about them, and the continual revelation, even in this factual and impersonal book, of the author's temperament. Browne wished that the huge project had been undertaken by 'some co-operating advancers', but we rejoice that the stream of learning wound through his mind and not a committee's. He is a wit and a humorist in every sense of the words. We are not accustomed in modern books of science to an unobtrusive irony which can make jokes with quiet solemnity and touch religious mysteries with a reverent smile. 'We shall not, I hope, disparage the Resurrection of our Redeemer, if we say the Sun doth not dance on Easter day.' In the qualified recommendation of Oppian, which many critics have quoted, Browne may be wholly serious; we cannot be sure. One predominant and medieval strain in the book is certainly serious. Unlike Bacon, Browne does not bow to the Deity and pass on. For him science and religion are inseparable, or rather, science is still a part of religion. He looks with scientific detachment for scientific facts, but those facts have a divine aura, not of utility, about them. Although in the *Pseudodoxia* Browne is moving on the level of sober exposition and argument, his characteristic overtones are often heard, or seem to be heard. Even the badger's legs, we feel, illustrate the rational symmetry of the Creator's work, and the dance of the elephants at Germanicus's show—after which they 'laid them down in the Tricliniums, or places of festival Recumbency'—not only proves their possession of joints but touches a chord, in some ears, of the universal harmony.

This sketch of the Baconian tradition may end with a reminder of the optimism it embodied. In the quarrel of the ancients and moderns science, especially applied science, led the van of modernism and progress. Bacon even minimized the difficulties of his own induction in his earnest efforts to banish despair and all the other obstacles that stood between man and the conquest of nature, and his message owed something of its emotional force to his sense of man's actual misery as well as of his potential grandeur. For Spenser undiscovered America had been an imaginative justification of his medieval fairyland; for the young Donne, it was a woman's body, for Donne the preacher, heaven; for Bacon, and for Browne in his Baconian moods, America is the symbol of the unknown world to be revealed by science. The present and not the classical past is the ripe maturity of the race. Bacon, Browne, and Milton, in their several ways, are expressly seeking to repair the ruins of Adam, to restore man's forfeited heritage, and Bacon and the earlier Milton, along with the scientists, may stand as representatives of unbounded faith in the power of man and in the future.

4

When we turn from the possibilities of applied science to the facts and speculations of pure science, from the relief of man's estate to the state of his soul, the picture is less uniformly bright. The doctrine of progress was indeed one answer to scientific and other kinds of pessimism, but, though it was to prove victorious in the long run, it did not in the years 1600–60 win immediate and universal acceptance. At the same time the cautions registered in the first chapter, against the exaggeration of melancholy, may be reaffirmed here. We must not read back into the seventeenth century the cosmic shudders of later ages.

Within the field of astronomy proper, educated people were confronted by three major theories (all ancient in germ) of the solar system: the so-called Ptolemaic theory of a central earth around which the heavens turned, a system much patched with 'Cycle and Epicycle, Orb in Orb'; the more economical hypothesis of Copernicus, as corrected by the telescope and the

orbital laws of Kepler; and, thirdly, the popular compromise of
Kepler's master, Tycho Brahe, who made the earth the centre
of the universe and of the orbits of the moon, sun, and sphere of
fixed stars, the sun being the centre of the orbits of the five
planets. The difficulty was that all three theories 'saved the
phenomena' and that a critical decision required exceptional
command of mathematical science; most of us would have the
same difficulty to-day if we did not take the facts on trust.
Modern writers have often classified men of the period as sheep
or goats on the strength of their attitude towards the Copernican
doctrine, but some men's dissent or agnosticism might be based
on sounder knowledge of the conditions of the problem than
some other men's conventional acceptance. In any case the
matter cannot be thought of as a simple choice between two
alternatives; and, if it could, the common alternatives would be
the Copernican and Tychonic systems, since the Ptolemaic lost
ground steadily in the seventeenth century. Then came Descartes's theory of vortices which, though purely speculative,
won great favour. In addition to these general cosmic theories
there were particular problems, above all that of the diurnal
rotation of the earth. This idea was accepted in England earlier
than on the Continent, by Gilbertian Tychonists as well as
Copernicans. Conservatives might dismiss one, two, or all three
of the motions Copernicus ascribed to the earth, but even they
could hardly get over some facts of observation, the appearance
of new stars in 1572 and 1604 and other phenomena which
demolished for ever the Aristotelian and Christian conception
of changeless and incorruptible heavens. In obvious ways the
new astronomy might disturb traditional beliefs and habits of
mind. It contradicted the testimony of the senses, the authority of Aristotle and Ptolemy, and the still more authoritative
assumptions of the Bible and Christian doctrine. On the other
hand, it was supported by the scientific principles of simplicity
and harmony and, with telescopic aid, by the senses; classical
authority was no longer sacrosanct, and ingenuity could explain
away apparent conflict with the Bible.

But what we call the new astronomy, with reference to
strictly scientific theory and observation, was only one factor
in shaking traditional orthodoxies. There was the revival of
ideas which, though of ancient origin and largely theoretical,
were generally linked with the results of astronomy—a world

extending through infinite space; not merely our one solar system but others like it; not one but possibly many inhabited planets. Such speculations, of which Bruno was the best-known exponent, might be more damaging to theological and humanistic doctrine than astronomical science proper. For a philosophic layman's reaction we may take a passage from Drummond's *A Cypress Grove* (1623), a passage which contains some of his numerous echoes of Donne:

The Element of Fire is quite put out, the Aire is but Water rarified, the Earth is found to move, and is no more the Center of the Universe, is turned into a Magnes; Starres are not fixed, but swimme in the etheriall Spaces, Cometes are mounted above the Planetes; Some affirme there is another World of men and sensitive Creatures, with Cities and Palaces in the Moone; the Sunne is lost, for, it is but a Light made of the conjunction of manie shining Bodies together, a Clift in the lower Heavens, through which the Rayes of the highest defuse themselves, is observed to have Spots; Thus, Sciences by the diverse Motiones of this Globe of the Braine of Man, are become Opiniones, nay, Errores, and leave the Imagination in a thousand Labyrinthes. What is all wee knowe compared with what wee knowe not?

Yet modern writers have often exaggerated the supposed shock of the Copernican theory in a way that R. G. Collingwood pronounced 'philosophically foolish and historically false'. Copernicus did not disturb the mass of people, or even most of the educated, any more than Einstein disturbed us. And the earth was not dislodged from a prime position in a comfortably small world; since antiquity the earth had been regarded as a mere point in space and, for Christians, it was the basest part of creation. Donne, in his earliest extant sermon, declared that one drop of Christ's blood would be 'sufficient for all the souls of 1000 worlds', and he and Drummond only turned from cosmic ignorance and 'opinion' to hold the more firmly to religion and the revelation of true knowledge in heaven. And in general—for the relatively few concerned with the question— the telescopic or speculative picture of vast space might induce more optimism than pessimism. In 1576 Thomas Digges, contrasting an infinite universe with 'this litle darcke starre wherein we live', did not proceed in the vein of, say, Thomas Hardy; instead he could not sufficiently admire the wonderful frame of God's work. And his attitude was typical of the scientist and

Christian in the seventeenth century. Then on the metaphysical plane there might be additional support for optimism. Bruno and his fellows were only making an astronomical extension of what a distinguished philosopher of our day has described as the 'principle of plenitude'. This complex of ideas was very old. Along with the conception of God as the One, the absolute, transcendental, self-sufficient Idea of the Good, there was the conception, also Platonic, of the fecund Demiurge who could not but manifest Himself to the fullest extent by creating the visible and temporal world of the Many. The latter conception, always present but continually repressed or evaded in the medieval period, asserted its strength during the Renaissance. And if our earth was, by dialectical necessity, the best of possible worlds, then, since existence and diversity were good in themselves, a world of worlds was still better. But what intoxicated Bruno, and later Henry More, overwhelmed Pascal.

Another phase of the conflict between pessimism and optimism is illustrated in another set of theological and philosophical ideas of equal antiquity. Primitive man had lost his first innocence and happiness, and the Hebraic and Christian conception of the Fall had early coalesced with the pagan idea of progressive degeneration from the Golden Age. Christian humanists might celebrate man's dignity and his divine gift of reason, but the whole history of the human race and the physical world was one of increasing exhaustion and corruption. Wherever man looked, he could see nothing constant except the remote and incorruptible heavens—and then came astronomy to report that the heavens themselves were subject to mutation and decay. Two significant continental treatments of the great theme were Loys Le Roy's *De la vicissitude ou variété des choses en l'univers* (first edition dated 1575, 1576; translated into English 1594) and Justus Lipsius's *De Constantia* (1584; translated 1595, 1653, 1654, 1670). Le Roy, however, found in change the inspiring evidence of God and human progress, and to the distresses of war and circumstance Lipsius opposed the precepts of Christian Stoicism. In England, John Norden gave a picture of change and decay in his poem *Vicissitudo Rerum* (1600), but did not follow his model, Le Roy, to the optimistic conclusion. The most elaborate argument for progressive deterioration was *The Fall of Man, Or the Corruption of Nature Proved by the Light of our Natural Reason* (1616), by Godfrey Goodman (later a bishop who perhaps died a secret Catholic). The St. Cyprian of his age sees a microcosm and macrocosm alike succumbing to decay, and miserable man's only hope is in turning from the contemplation of external things to God. Allied with this belief in decay was the belief that the world, having had its two thousand years of nature and two thousand of Mosaic law, would end with the two thousand years of the Christian dispensation. In the sixteenth and seventeenth centuries men could say, with Donne, that of this 'last houre we have heard three quarters strike, more then fifteen hundred of this last two thousand spent'. By 1658 scientific optimism had risen high, but Dr. Browne the scientist could meditate in his richest style on the vainglorious ambition of modern men, born in this setting part of time, to raise a lasting monument. Izaak Walton, in 1665, thinks of Hooker as one of the saints grown rare 'in this weak and declining Age of the World'.

But the thought of a dying universe was only one distant cloud in the sky and for Christians—which nearly all men were—it was not necessarily a dark cloud. Nor, as we have seen, was the new astronomy commonly felt as a paralysing menace. The false modern emphasis on the bold confidence and rebellious energy of the Renaissance, and the modern tendency to carry nineteenth-century ideas back into the seventeenth century, have often combined to distort the picture. The prime cause of melancholy in the period—and all periods have had their full share—was the religious or the naturalistic pessimism inherent in life itself, the private and public troubles that in some form afflict all men (in this case religious and civil strife especially), and to some degree the results of age-old philosophies of scepticism. The greatest strains in Renaissance literature come from universal themes treated by the last generations of men who can contemplate the human condition with both the faith of real Christians and the natural feelings of 'natural men'. From Sackville to Spenser, from Shakespeare, Ralegh, and Donne to Browne and Shirley, men are haunted by the spectres of devouring time and change, the brevity, misery, and vanity of life, the littleness of man in the cosmic panorama. Even Alexander, in his vast and unreadable Dooms-day, can achieve one grand line, 'To scorne Corruption, and to mocke the Dust'.

This body of great writing, whether immediately affected by science or not, was more or less in the medieval and classical tradition, and to old pessimism old answers could still be made. Spenser tried to convince himself that the apparent sway of mutability was really a divinely ordered evolution towards the changeless stability his heart desired. Du Bartas, in Sylvester's very popular translation, combined old-fashioned science with a fervent faith in the providential beneficence of God and the universal harmony of His creation. In a world of flux Shakespeare saw at least the heroic individual as something more than the quintessence of dust. Donne and Drummond, as we observed, found the antidote to despair in the Christian-Platonic vision of death as rebirth. Concerning the specific problem of human deterioration or progress other men spoke with conviction on the modern side. Ben Jonson, following Vives, declared that nature was not exhausted, that she could still equal or surpass her former productions. The great answer to pessimists like Goodman was George Hakewill's *Apology of the Power and Providence of God in the Government of the World. Or an Examination and Censure of the Common Error Touching Nature's Perpetual and Universal Decay* (1627). This comprehensive and reassuring work was welcomed to the extent of two more enlarged editions in 1630 and 1635. Surveying the physical world, human attributes and powers, and the fruits of civilization, Hakewill finds no proof that either nature or man is suffering from decrepitude. His argument is a mixture of old and new, of the religious and the scientific, and his witnesses range from Lucretius, Ovid, Philo, and Boethius to Du Bartas, Bodin, Lipsius, and Ralegh. Like Spenser, Hakewill sees behind mutability a divine order and constancy. Like Le Roy (whom he cites), he expounds a cyclical theory of progress, denies the essential superiority of ancient genius and achievement, attributes decline to human sloth, and calls upon his generation to work with courage and hope. Where Hakewill's assertion of religious and philosophic optimism left off, the Baconian gospel of scientific progress began, and men whose uncertainties were not insoluble might be cheered by one or other or both. Whether or not the young Milton had read Hakewill, he was on Hakewill's side in his *Naturam non pati senium* (1628?) and seventh *Prolusion* (1631-2?). A generation later came the Royal Society and the next phase of the quarrel over the ancients and moderns.

5

Since we have been concerned with astronomy we may approach Robert Burton's *Anatomy of Melancholy* by way of 'a digression of the Ayr', a section which, in the course of successive editions, doubled in length and proliferated references and questions.[1] Probably no passage in the literature of the time gives us a more vivid picture of the intellectual confusion caused by the new astronomy—for relatively few persons of course—than Burton's galloping survey of the multitudinous theories that were, in more than one sense, in the air: the substance and movements of the heavens and heavenly bodies, the appearance of new stars and the problem of change and decay, 'that main paradox, of the Earths motion, now so much in question', the plurality of worlds (the idea that especially attracted and repelled him), and related facts and theories. We are left, like the author, 'almost giddy with roving about'. Faced with such an array of opinions and authorities—and Burton knows them all— he quotes one against another but refuses to commit himself; he is more favourable to Tycho than to Copernicus, but cannot be given a positive label. His attitude is one of interrogative, ironical, Lucianic scepticism. Like the Deity of *Paradise Lost*, he is moved to laughter at quaint opinions wide, at the theorists' desperate efforts to save appearances. He does not feel much spiritual distress, yet his conclusion is more in the vein of Donne or Browne or Milton than of Lucian; these mysteries God will reveal in His own good time.

The popularity of the *Anatomy* lapsed during the eighteenth century, in spite of Sterne's notorious thefts and Dr. Johnson's notorious devotion. A strong revival began with the beginning

[1] The life of Robert Burton (1577–1640) was even more uneventful than that of Browne. He was born in Leicestershire (of which county his brother William wrote a *Description*, 1622), entered Brasenose College in 1593, and was elected a Student of Christ Church in 1599 (B.A., 1602; M.A., 1605). He lived at Christ Church for the rest of his life, never travelling 'but in Map or Card'. He took the degree of B.D. in 1614 and in 1616 became vicar of St. Thomas's in Oxford. He also held a Lincolnshire living (1624–31) and in 1632 received a benefice in his native county from his patron, Lord Berkeley. Burton's bust in Christ Church Cathedral, put up by his brother, bears the epitaph he had himself composed: 'Paucis notus, paucioribus ignotus, hic jacet Democritus Junior, cui vitam dedit et mortem Melancholia.' *The Anatomy of Melancholy*, first published at Oxford in 1621, won great popularity and was revised and enlarged by the author in five more editions, the last being posthumous. Burton contributed Latin verses to numerous Oxford anthologies and in 1606 wrote a Latin comedy, *Philosophaster*, which was acted at Christ Church in 1618; it was first printed in 1862.

of the nineteenth century and there has been no subsequent lapse. In the appreciative tradition of that period Burton's book, like Browne's *Pseudodoxia Epidemica*, was commonly regarded as a mine of amusing oddities. A more historical view received impetus from Sir William Osler. Burton was writing a serious scientific treatise on abnormal psychology, and though his large orbit includes many epicycles and eccentrics, he moves on steadily to his goal. His thousands of Latin tags, while sprinkled more thickly than in most contemporaries, were not quaint pedantry in a bilingual age, and they are an unceasing reminder that Burton was a Renaissance humanist for whom the ancients had given final expression to all the commonplaces of experience. The quotations from countless authorities, now mostly forgotten, on psychology and other sciences were of course no less relevant than a modern psychologist's citations from Freud or Pavlov. Yet the old view of the *Anatomy* was not wholly wrong. If Burton's intention and in part his execution warrant putting a traditional bedside book into a chapter on science, nevertheless, sitting between Bacon and Hobbes, he appears as a kind of gargoyle between the two spires of the cathedral of English scientific thought. He exemplifies, it has been said, all three of Bacon's classes of false philosophy, the sophistical, the empirical, and the superstitious. His attitude towards problems of the inner and outer world is that of the layman, a layman of infinite learning, zest, curiosity, and common sense. He has no integrated scientific and critical principles, no forward-looking philosophy, one might almost say no historical sense; ancients and moderns are all contemporaries, living together in the happy isle of Burton's study. But since we read Burton for fun, as we seldom read Bacon or Hobbes, these deficiencies cannot be fatal.

Nothing shows his quality better than the long 'Satyricall Preface' in which Democritus Junior explains his pseudonym and purpose and, from his college window, surveys the mad world as it reels or rushes by. Given an invincible sanity and clarity of vision—and Burton has affinities with Lucian, Chaucer, Erasmus, Rabelais, Montaigne, and Shakespeare—no satire can be more effective than the mere cataloguing of what men feel and do, their carnal and worldly lusts, the fantastic objects, public and private, that they pursue, the follies and crimes they commit in the pursuit, the whole topsy-turvy scale of values and motives that society disowns and maintains. 'If it be so that the Earth is a Moon, then are we also giddy, vertigenous and lunatick within this sublunary Maze.' From the panorama of life as it is Burton turns to consider what it might be, and it is characteristic of his common sense that his Utopia—more or less enlarged in later editions—is not a chimerical commonwealth but a practicable improvement on what already exists. His proposals range from broad streets to hospitals and pensions for the aged and infirm, from the thorough cultivation of all land to the abolition of monopolies, from the suppression of extravagance in building and dress to the curing of idleness, 'the *malus Genius* of our nation'.

But though Burton is here and everywhere a realistic satirist, a detached observer of the human comedy, he is much more than that. He does not, like some modern psychologists, worship a particular idol of the cave, nor does he start with the tacit invocation, 'Now, Muse, let's sing of rats'. His subject is the soul, body, and whole life of man, and he writes as both a divine and a physician. The *Anatomy* proper begins with a contrast between the original endowment and felicity of 'Man, the most excellent and noble creature of the World, the principal and mighty work of God', and the present miseries, inherited from Adam, of the wretched being who is in many ways inferior to the lower animals. That contrast is seldom absent from Burton's mind and, since he feels as well as thinks, it is tragic as well as comic. His fundamental postulate is 'that all the world is melancholy, or mad, dotes, and every member of it'. 'Being then it is a disease so grievous, so common, I know not wherein to do a more generall service, and spend my time better, then to prescribe means how to prevent and cure so universall a malady, an Epidemical disease, that so often, so much crucifies the body and minde.' Melancholy had been studied ever since Galen, and among Burton's English predecessors, medical and spiritual, were Timothy Bright (1586), Thomas Wright (1601), and the Puritan divine, Thomas Adams (1616). For us it matters not that Burton's technical knowledge was of a kind soon to be, or in some quarters already, outmoded—the four humours; natural, vital, and animal spirits; the vegetal, sensible, and rational soul; the two parts of the rational soul, understanding and will; and so on. Nor would any modern reader except a psychologist complain because Burton begins with 'God a cause' and proceeds through 'A Digression of the nature of Spirits, bad Angels, or Devils, and how they cause Melancholy', to sections on witches and magicians and the influence of the stars. Like Shakespeare's, Burton's wisdom, got 'by melancholizing', is not of the laboratory and transcends text-books. For him religion and science are mingled and both are interpenetrated with a profound sympathy for deluded, erring, suffering humanity.

If Burton sees man's headaches and hallucinations against a cosmic and divine background, it does not detract from the emotional power of his vision of life, and he is none the less realistic in his treatment of natural causes, old age, heredity, diet ('I finde Gourds, Cowcumbers, Coleworts, Mellons, disallowed, but especially Cabbage'), constipation, 'Venus omitted' ('Intemperate Venus is all out as bad in the other extream'), bad air, immoderate exercise, solitariness, and idleness. No topic recurs more often than the last, for no man knew better the torments of *accidia* than one who wrote 'of melancholy, by being busie to avoid melancholy'. Then come the irascible passions and perturbations of the mind, sorrow, fear, shame, and the rest. In all ranks of society discontents and cares may be so grievous that if we had foresight and choice 'we should rather refuse, then accept of this painful life'. The concupiscible passions include ambition, covetousness, self-love and pride (if the earth is but a little star, 'wher's our glory?'), excessive devotion to learning and study; here follows a gloomy and angry 'Digression of the misery of Scholars'. It would be hard to find in modern text-books any mental disorder that Burton does not touch, and nowhere does he forget, as the divine or the physician alone might forget, the interrelations of body and mind. As for the lawful cures of melancholy, described in the second part, they range from prayer and sober Christian and Stoic precepts through the study of everything from the fine arts to geography and down to cathartics, bleeding, and cordials (including, from Sandys's *Relation*, the Turkish 'drink called Coffa'). Although not himself a wine-drinker, Burton declares that there is no relief so powerful and apposite as 'a cup of strong drink, mirth, musick, and merry company'. The English scene comes to life in advice for trippers and in the recitals of traditional games and country pleasures. And we think of Justice Shallow as well as of Izaak Walton when we read of old companions sitting by the fire or in the sunshine, remembering ancient matters which happened in their younger years.

Doubtless the section on love-melancholy is the most famous, and doubtless not for its Platonic pages. The follies and torments of love, especially 'Heroical love', clearly belong to his subject, but our celibate divine apologizes for venturing upon such a theme. The length and the liveliness of this part, however, testify to the half-irresponsible exhilaration with which a born essayist and raconteur frisks 'in this delightsome field'. He still draws upon the doctors, but chiefly upon the whole body of historical and imaginative literature, the obscure along with the familiar ancients, medieval and modern authors in Latin and the vernaculars. Ovid and Montaigne, St. Augustine and Aretino, and hundreds more furnish grist for the capacious mill. Among English writers Chaucer is most often quoted; others are Sidney, Spenser, Marlowe, Shakespeare, Bacon, Jonson, Daniel, Drayton, Wither, even Samuel Rowlands—Burton's library was not dusty. There is no less variety in the endless catalogue of examples, from the story of the beautiful Lamia to the Rabelaisian or Skeltonic picture, joyously transcribed by Keats in a letter, of an idealized mistress as she really is. Burton understands every phase of 'this Trage-comedy of Love', but he remains as skittishly detached as in astronomical matters. Twelve unanswerable arguments for marriage are followed by twelve unanswerable arguments against it. ''Tis an hazard both waies I confess, to live single or to marry.' If all remedies for passion fail, 'the last and best cure of Love Melancholy, is, to let them have their desire'. Here as elsewhere Burton's descriptive analysis is frequently in line with modern psychology, but his case-histories are enveloped in a mixture of romance and realism, humour and wisdom, which is a world away from the technical jargon and narrowly physiological objectivity we are accustomed to.

So far Burton has been enlarging upon traditional branches of his complex subject, but his last one, religious melancholy, has not, he says, been generally recognized as a distinct species, and he has no pattern to follow. However, some authorities divide 'Love Melancholy into that whose object is women; and into the other whose object is God'. Throughout his study rational moderation has been Burton's criterion and prescription, and this last topic is dichotomized into 'Excess and Defect,

Impiety and Superstition, Idolatry and Atheisme'. The diagnosis of both enthusiasm and scepticism (including diatribes against Catholics and Puritans) has historical interest, but the last pages deepen our understanding of the author. When he contemplates the causes and cure of religious despair the assured and angry Anglican becomes the wise and compassionate physician of afflicted souls. The prime agency of the devil, particular griefs and misfortunes, much pondering on ominous biblical texts and on the doctrine of election and reprobation, the consciousness of sin, the fear of God's wrath, all reinforced by the thunders of the pulpit—these things work upon neurotic introverts until they hear the howls of the damned and smell the eternal fire. To such people, and there were many in old and New England, Burton addresses his sermon, an earnest appeal to shun whatever aggravates their terrors, to seek the counsel of good physicians and divines, enjoy honest recreations, and dwell on thoughts of God's infinite love and mercy.

I can say no more, or give better advice to such as are any way distressed in this kind, then what I have given and said. Only take this for a corollary and conclusion, as thou tendrest thine own welfare in this, and all other melancholy, thy good health of body and mind, observe this short precept, give not way to solitariness and idleness. Be not solitary, be not idle.

Even a summary sketch of Burton cannot fail to suggest his sanity of mind and largeness of heart, his love of life and of human beings, his capacity alike for robustious or bitter laughter and for sensitive exploration of the darker places of the soul. His matter is never dull, but more than half of our pleasure is in his manner, the revelation of himself. He would have written in the international language—as Browne intended to write the *Pseudodoxia*—if the mercenary stationers had not shied at a Latin treatise. While feeling grateful for that blessing, we may wonder how such a scholar happens to be conspicuous not only in his own period but in the whole range of English prose for colloquial naturalness, garrulous spontaneity, and juicy vigour. Burton has his moments of eloquence (and he wrote passable verses which Milton may have read), but he is not, like some famous contemporaries, a poet in prose. No English author, however, certainly no author of a long didactic work, has more variety of tone on the prose level. His flood of slangy, proverbial, and picturesque language is nearer to Nashe and Dekker than to Cicero or Seneca. Burton piles up all the critical complaints that might be brought against his irregular, homespun writing, but his self-depreciation is really a satire on other men's affectations, and he did not fail to revise his style in successive editions—though he did often fail to verify his references and to catch multiplying misprints. His book was 'writ with as small deliberation as I do ordinarily speak', he says, and to his own accounts of his prose style may be added Anthony Wood's report of his talk:

I have heard some of the Antients of Christ Church often say that his Company was very merry, facete and juvenile, and no Man in his time did surpass him for his ready and dextrous interlarding his common discourses among them with Verses from the Poets or Sentences from classical Authors. Which being then all the fashion in the University, made his Company more acceptable.

6

Burton represents, in his loose and eccentric fashion, the religious and ethical assumptions of Renaissance humanism. It is something of a shock to turn from him to his long-lived contemporary, Thomas Hobbes (1588–1679), the plain and orderly exponent of extreme materialism. In the last chapter we surveyed what was for his own age and posterity the most vital part of his philosophy, the political; here we are concerned with his scientific and ethical thought. These last two parts are related to each other and both, especially of course the ethical theory, condition Hobbes's political thinking. As we have partly seen, his contemporary reputation, before as well as after 1660, resembled that of Machiavelli or Nietzsche (though atheism and libertinism did not have to wait for the supposed sanction of the decorous philosopher); to traditional orthodoxy he appeared, in the words of an obituary broadside, as 'the Bugbear of the Nation'.

Since Bacon stands for concrete experimental induction and Hobbes for abstract deductive logic, the common view is that the ex-Chancellor's amanuensis was not, in Hobbesian language, moved by a contiguous mind. Yet, however different their normal methods, the two were not so far apart in their aims and principles, in their hostility to most Greek philosophy and to

Aristotelian scholasticism and in their debt to both; in their attempt to systematize all human knowledge; in their laying hold of science as the key to truth; in their ideal of utility and power as the end of knowledge; in their conception of reality as more or less mechanical and of sense-impressions as subjective; in their dismissal of final causes and separation of the realms of knowledge and faith; and in their extension of naturalistic principles from the physical to the moral and social worlds. It depends on which end of the telescope we look through whether we call them the first English apostles of modern empirical realism or the last of the scholastic nominalists. For both descendants of Ockham, and especially for Hobbes, the new science was at hand to serve the doctrine of the particular.

Although the problem of knowledge was the great problem of the seventeenth century, epistemology had not yet become the sacred cow of philosophy. The tyranny of authority, the deceitfulness of the senses, even the weakness of reason, had been made clear, notably by Bacon, but, apart from Lord Herbert, few men, however intent on finding a sure guide through the labyrinths of opinion and error, went behind the senses and reason—and revelation—to inquire into the processes and grounds of knowledge. (From our standpoint that is not altogether a loss, since it means that philosophy was still in the main a branch of literature and not written in technical language.) Bacon combined the old faculty psychology with some more scientific ideas. To his division between supernatural and natural knowledge corresponds the division, borrowed from Telesio, of the soul into rational and animal. The immaterial rational soul, a direct gift of God to man, has for its instrument the animal soul, a corporeal substance, which man shares with the beasts. This dualism approaches that of Descartes, and still more Cartesian is Bacon's repeated hint of the subjectivity of the sensible qualities of objects. But theoretical psychology was not a major interest for Bacon, it was for Descartes; and Hobbes, like Descartes, put the problem of knowledge in the forefront of his thinking. However plain its gaps and short-cuts, no philosophic system has been more closely integrated than Hobbes's around one central principle. That principle, as everyone knows, is motion, and the word transports us from the medieval to the modern world. In the dedication of De Corpore Hobbes paid tribute to Galileo as 'the first

SCIENCE AND SCIENTIFIC THOUGHT

that opened to us the gate of Natural Philosophy Universal, which is the knowledge of the Nature of Motion'. Hobbes—though a reasoner and no admirer or practitioner of experimental science—conceived of himself as effecting for psychology and moral and civil philosophy what Galileo had done for physics and Harvey for physiology, the substitution of realistic facts for speculative unrealities. A similar enterprise had been a part of the *Instauratio Magna*, but Hobbes's scientific and philosophic orientation was more advanced than Bacon's.

Hobbes was the founder of modern empirical psychology, and psychology was the foundation of his system. His chief accounts of it are contained in the 'Short Tract' of 1630 (?), *Human Nature* (1640; published in 1650), *Leviathan* (1651), and *De Corpore* (1655). Philosophic knowledge differs from empirical knowledge in having to do with concepts, propositions, and conclusions, but there is no conception in a man's mind which has not at first, totally or by parts, been begotten upon the organs of sense. All of the sensible qualities 'are in the object that causeth them, but so many several motions of the matter, by which it presseth our organs diversly. Neither in us that are pressed, are they any thing else, but divers motions; (for motion, produceth nothing but motion.)' Nor can there be any cause of motion except in a body contiguous and moved. Thus all of the sensible qualities are but phantasms of the observer, not properties of the object. When the phantasm remains after the object is removed, the decaying sense-impression is fancy or imagination or memory. Emotions are also motions. If the motion from without quickens and helps the vital motion of the heart, the result is pleasure; 'and when it hindereth, it is Pain, Trouble, Grief, &c.' The small beginnings of motion, not yet translated into action, are 'endeavour'. Endeavour towards or away from a particular object is appetite or aversion. All the passions of the mind consist of appetite or aversion except pure pleasure and pain, which are a certain fruition of good or evil. Since the appetites and aversions of either an individual or men in common are not uniform but fluctuate, men, and beasts also, have deliberation, an alternate succession of appetites, aversions, hopes, and fears. The last and decisive appetite in deliberation is the will. The act of appetite, however, could not but follow appetite and its cause, so that such a liberty as is free from necessity is not to be found in the will either of men or of beasts, though both have the liberty or power to do what they will.

The general principles by which Hobbes explains the inner world of man and the world of terrestrial nature hold good for the planetary system. He accepts and comments at length upon the ideas of Copernicus, Kepler, and Galileo, but he avoids trouble by limiting the sphere of inquiry as he had already limited psychology. Since our conceptions are necessarily finite, it makes no difference what we think about the magnitude, beginning, duration, and singleness or plurality of the world, or about the nature of God. Such questions must be left to the authorized ministers of God and that means, in England, to the king; thus, as Sir Leslie Stephen remarked, 'Charles II apparently was to decide whether the world had a beginning'. But Hobbes seems to be sincere and consistent rather than cynical, and in his attitude towards supernatural knowledge he resembles not only Bacon but less questionable metaphysicians. However different his premisses, aims, and sanctions, he is not altogether remote from Aquinas or from many religious thinkers of his own time, including his mighty opposite, Milton; for, like Milton and others, Hobbes does not wish men to be distracted by vain speculation from the performance of their duty here and now.

Despite his belated introduction to geometry Hobbes tried to give his system a scientific basis. One instance is the atomic or rather the corpuscular theory. Science had been moving in that direction since the fifteenth century, and our period opened with Nicholas Hill's *Philosophia Epicurea, Democritiana, Theophrastica* (Paris, 1601); near the end came Walter Charleton's *Physiologia Epicuro-Gassendo-Charltoniana* (1654). Bacon did not formally accept the atomic theory; in fact he expressly rejected it because it implied the existence of a vacuum and the unchangeableness of matter. Yet, as an anti-Aristotelian, he gave special and repeated praise to Democritus and his fellows who had 'removed God and Mind from the structure of things, and . . . assigned the causes of particular things to the necessity of matter'. And Bacon himself accepted a corpuscular motion somewhat akin to that of Descartes and the later Boyle. Hobbes ignored Democritus and had little to say of Lucretius, except in criticizing his argument for a vacuum, but he was in the mechanistic current of Galileo, Gassendi, the chief reviver of

Epicureanism, and Descartes, and corpuscular motion was essential to his system. Of course everyone knew ancient speculative atomism in its Lucretian form, and the more scientific recent theories were familiar to a number of men, including Digby and Browne. Even Cudworth, Hobbes's great antagonist, accepted atomism as 'unquestionably true', while he abhorred the atheism traditionally linked with it.

Another basic principle of modern science was the distinction between primary and secondary qualities. In the customary view, that of the philosopher as well as the layman, the sensible qualities of objects, colour and the like, were what they seemed to be, inherent properties possessed by those objects as the Creator made them. The new science changed all that. The senses and the Aristotelian categories no longer furnished accurate criteria. Primary qualities were those that could be scientifically measured, such as space, time, number, force, velocity. The ordinary world ceased to be intelligible to the layman. What had been the solid facts of external nature became sensations in the mind of the observer which could not be quantitatively measured and were therefore scientifically negligible. This conception had been adumbrated by Bacon, but its historical development was the work of Galileo, Descartes, and Hobbes; Hobbes seems to have reached his view independently. The real world, the world of science, was a mathematical mechanism of bodies, vast or minute, moving in space and time in accordance with natural laws. In such a world man himself, a mere aggregate of secondary qualities, was, logically, an insignificant stranger, a superfluous accident. His spiritual experience, like the beauty and diversity of nature, was reduced to the deterministic motion of bodies. Nor was there much room for God, except as the First Cause of motion—and only the initial cause. The celestial machine did not need the compelling hand of Providence, since Galileo and others had exploded the Aristotelian idea that motion required the continuous application of force. Aristotelian and Christian teleology gave way to a chain of physical causes and effects. But these conclusions take us beyond our period, indeed beyond Newton, for whom God's finger was a continuously active cause.

Descartes, like Galileo a mathematical genius in his own right, was concerned far more than Galileo with the general problems of philosophy, and he tried to keep God and mind from being drawn into the widening vortex of mechanistic thought. To material substance he assigned the mathematical properties of the world of bodies and to thinking substance the non-mathematical properties. But it was inevitable that the materialistic cat should swallow the spiritual canary, and in this operation Hobbes was the ruthlessly efficient cause. That uncompromising logician would have no Cartesian dualism, no admission of the immaterial and occult. As Copernicus had transformed the pattern of the universe by including the earth in the question Ptolemy had asked of the heavenly bodies, so Hobbes transformed the pattern of man's inner and outer world by including *res cogitans* within *res extensa*. Nothing exists except body, and its attributes are extension and motion. The mind, or nervous system, and the processes of mental experience are not separate from the physical world; they consist, like everything else, of bodies in motion. Man is, though not in the medieval sense, a microcosm. And for Hobbes even the primary qualities of mathematical science, space and time, are consequences of motion, phantasms in the mind of the percipient. Thus the wheel of subjectivity comes full circle. The world of sensible qualities, itself an illusion, is both the cause and the object of perception in an observer who is one of that world's aggregates of non-qualitative particles. Thanks to Hobbes's clarity and relentless consistency (of aim if not of method), one of his unintentional achievements was the exposure of the defects of pure materialism.

There is some initial difficulty in regarding a world emptied of everything but bodies in motion as the material for ethical and political philosophy, but the man who squared the circle was equal to that. Some ethical implications in his psychology have already appeared, and they can be only briefly supplemented here. Hobbes's individual and social ethics are founded on what he takes to be man's fundamental impulse, self-preservation. All men strive towards this end, and pleasures and pains arise from the satisfaction or frustration of this motive. Even 'altruistic' feelings and acts are prompted by and minister to the sense of power. While unceasing endeavour towards a goal may be conceived as a kind of motion, external and internal, there is little real connexion between Hobbes's physical psychology and his ethics. His materialism is chiefly useful in guarding his wholly naturalistic man from any intrusive religious and idealistic motives. But even the naturalistic ego seeks peace in the interest of security, and in moments of deliberation the creature of passions, appetites, and egocentric will recognizes the utility and practical necessity of reason. However, as we have seen, reason aims only at self-preservation and power, and deliberation is only a succession of conflicting appetites and aversions. The last and victorious one is the will, the victory being merely the inevitable effect of an inevitable cause. Hobbes, like Milton, views life as a race; instead, though, of Milton's 'immortall garland' he sees 'no other Goal, nor other Garland, but being formost'. The will, in Milton's tireless and passionate exposition, is an ethical faculty and entirely free; reason is the *recta ratio* planted by God in the individual soul which teaches man the divine will, the moral law, the absolute values of good and evil, the control of his own passions and appetites. Hobbes's scale of values is not absolute but relative; those things are good which man desires, they are good because he desires them. The beliefs and ideals of traditional religion and ethics are unreal 'universals'; nor can the consistent nominalist, despite his own strong conviction of duty, furnish philosophic support for the moral law as good in itself. Hobbes's doctrine is a mixture of bold realism and unrealistic dogmatism. In ethics and science, as in politics, he was a kind of secular Calvinist.

Thus within the half-century that saw promulgated the teaching of Bacon and Hobbes, there appears in high relief the contrast which was to be worked out at large in philosophy and literature in the following centuries, including our own. Bacon's natural man is an emancipated slave who is being inducted into the rule of a kingdom, who may rejoice as he contemplates the infinite potentialities of his dominion over nature. From this demigod we turn to the natural man of Hobbes, who is a slave to his own and others' passions and whose only hope of escape from the jungle is the establishment of an absolute external authority. Incidentally, Hobbes's picture of naturalistic egoism was in part a reply to persistent dreams of a mythical Golden Age, and it was to have a large share in evoking new pictures of a future Golden Age of natural benevolence.

In the same two generations the Elizabethan world-picture was fading. While nature, 'the Art of God', might still support the 'argument from design', the emblematic and hieroglyphic conception, the whole unified system of analogy and correspondence which had been the habitation of the religious and poetic mind —this was encountering scientific reason, law, and fact. Even this brief survey, in touching early stages of the process, has revealed scientific optimism and religious pessimism side by side. But the acceptance of both man's grandeur and his misery, the double vision of a god and a beast, had been a central fact in religious and ethical humanism ever since Plato and Cicero, and a temperate faith in the ethical reason and will was far too strong to be quickly overthrown. Indeed when we survey English thought during our period we see that the whole-sale mechanistic revolution was largely confined to the brain of Hobbes. Most of the English scientists of the middle and latter part of the century, Wallis, Wilkins, Charleton, Boyle, Ray, and others, were concerned about the growth of atheism and sought, directly or through 'natural religion' (a double-edged weapon), to sustain Christianity. But while Bacon's sincere tributes to the Creator's glory—the tributes, so to speak, of a junior partner—helped to keep him immune from attack, the more obviously dangerous Galileo, Descartes, and Hobbes, despite their sincere or prudential concessions to orthodoxy, were in their several countries vigorously assailed. The greatest champion of the eternal verities, if not an overt anti-Hobbesian, was Milton. Another, as we saw above, was Bishop Bramhall. Since his polemics receive one contemptuous sentence in the *Dictionary of National Biography*, it may not be amiss to observe that Hobbes's determinism (which the philosopher in his ordinary pragmatic thinking commonly and conveniently ignored) cracked under the bishop's formidable spear. Hobbes was driven to the virtual admission that he could give no reason or evidence for necessity, and he fell back upon a religious dogma, the assertion of God's foreknowledge, a dogma which of course Bramhall accepted, though he stoutly rejected the equating of foreknowledge with necessitarian decrees. The later Cambridge Platonists also saw that the new Democritean and Protagorean philosophy did not merely 'nibble at Moses' but was destructive of the whole religious and ethical order of antiquity and Christianity. If we consider what was at stake we may think twice before dismissing the 'obscurantist' defenders of traditional concepts, especially since mechanistic thought, however valuable for the immediate problems of science, did not prove to be an ultimate explanation of reality. Of the army of religious writers to be reviewed in the next chapter, some were concerned with piety and salvation and some with ecclesiastical and sectarian problems, and many were unaware that scientific reason was undermining the citadel of truth; but many of the best minds were striving, in the tradition of Christian humanism, to uphold a religious view of man and the world by reasserting the divinity of reason.

X

RELIGION AND RELIGIOUS THOUGHT

MORE than two-fifths of the books printed in England from 1480 to 1640 were religious, and for the years 1600–40 the percentage is still higher. In Jaggard's *Catalogue* of 1619 nearly three-fourths of the books are religious and moral; in William London's *Catalogue of the most Vendible Books in England* (1657–8) the space given to works of divinity equals that occupied by all other kinds together. About a quarter of Sir Edward Coke's library was religious. Grotius and Casaubon declared, in the middle of James's reign, that there was little or no literary scholarship in England, that theology was the only interest of educated men. Religion, it does not need to be said, was a main and often intense concern of greater multitudes of people during our period than in any other before or since, and in many ways it profoundly affected the lives of those who were not especially devout.

In an age in which God and Satan, heaven and hell, were radiant or lurid realities, there was a sincere and insatiable demand for devotional and hortatory works, and English Protestantism had to create a new religious literature or re-create the old. The endless repetition and application of the central truths of faith and practice corresponded to the endless re-expression of the commonplaces of ancient ethics, and in some authors the two roads ran together. The appetite for counsels of piety and warnings against sin grew with the middle-class and Puritan public, but churchwomen in castle and hall likewise meditated over such handbooks in the intervals between good works, finding them a support against the pangs of widowhood or of matrimony. The type of book and its individual variations hardly need to be described, and at any rate cannot be here, but some bald figures may suggest the extent of the spiritual awakening. Next to the Bible the best-sellers of our period were such books as John Norden's *Pensive Man's Practice* (1584), which had gone beyond forty impressions by 1627; Arthur Dent's *Plain Man's Pathway to Heaven* (twenty-five editions, 1601–40, and many later ones); John Dod's *Plain and*

Familiar Exposition of the Ten Commandments (nineteen editions, 1603–35); Lewis Bayly's *Practice of Piety* (1612?), which achieved some fifty reprints during the century (and a sixteenth French edition in 1684). The books of Dent and Bayly, by the way, were the meagre dowry of Bunyan's first wife, and the former's influence on Bunyan was strong. Sir John Hayward's historical works were less popular than his *Sanctuary of a Troubled Soul* (two parts, 1601?–7). Other books of the kind were Michael Sparke's *Crumbs of Comfort* (1623?), which had forty-one editions by the middle of the century; Richard Bernard's allegorical *Isle of Man* (nineteen editions, 1626–1700), one of the forerunners of *Pilgrim's Progress* and second only to it in popularity among works of fiction; Dr. Daniel Featley's *Ancilla Pietatis* (eight editions, 1626–56); and Dr. Cosin's *Collection of Private Devotions* (five editions, 1627–38; tenth edition, 1719), which aroused Puritan feeling. In the last decade of our period came a cluster of books destined for a long life, Jeremy Taylor's manuals, Richard Baxter's earnest exhortations, *The Saints' Everlasting Rest* (1650) and *A Call to the Unconverted* (1657), and the cooler handbook of Christian ethics, *The Whole Duty of Man* (1658), by Richard Allestree. The same decade brought the first writings of George Fox and Bunyan, and the *Sancta Sophia* (1657) compiled from the works of the Catholic mystic, Augustine Baker (1575–1641). Then there was a large body of translations, especially from Catholic sources old and new; literature reveals an abiding attachment to the Catholic saints. And when sermons were printed they made an immense supplement; people denied the privilege of hearing could be privately moved by discourses on *The Back-Parts of Jehovah* and *Bowels Opened*. The quantity and the popularity of such books are facts which speak for themselves. And, moreover, as direct appeals to the heart and conscience, they form a great mass of normally plain writing. To works of devotional and practical piety may be added the older and more militant *Acts and Monuments* of John Foxe, commonly called the *Book of Martyrs*; this, as a collection of Protestant saints' lives, continued to nourish hostility to the Roman Anti-Christ and patriotic and religious belief in England as the providential channel and champion of the true faith.

We must briefly observe one other branch of religious writing, a branch once large and heavily laden but now long withered— unless it can be said to have flowered again in psycho-analysis.

Many men recognized, with Fuller, that 'in Case-Divinity Protestants are defective. For (save that a Smith or two of late have built them forges, and set up shop) we go down to our enemies to sharpen all our instruments, and are beholden to them for offensive and defensive weapons in Cases of Conscience.' Hence Fuller's praise of the great William Perkins (1558–1602), who 'brought the schools into the Pulpit, and unshelling their controversies out of their hard school-terms, made thereof plain and wholsome meat for his people. . . . An excellent Chirurgeon he was at joynting of a broken soul, and at stating of a doubtfull conscience.' Almost every divine had his portion of the same impulse and, whatever learning might be invoked, a practical and popular aim dictated such works of casuistry as those of Perkins, Ames, Joseph Hall, Sanderson, Fuller, and Jeremy Taylor.

I

It is hardly possible to exaggerate the importance of the sermon in the seventeenth-century world. 'The Religion of England', wrote Evelyn in his satirical tract of 1659, 'is Preaching and sitting stil on Sundaies.' Queen Elizabeth, believing that wherever two or three were gathered together the devil of sedition was among them, had been content with a very limited supply of sermons for her people. But a preaching ministry was one of the Puritans' great ends and a similar zeal, with a sacerdotal emphasis, inspired the Anglo-Catholic movement. According to Selden, 'To preach long, loud, and Damnation is the way to be cry'd up', and the brimstone sermons that moved James Howell to gibes might, as Burton testifies, have distressing effects upon the neurotic. But hell was not the main theme of the amiable and popular Fuller, for instance, and from Andrewes onward the great preachers celebrate holy joy. Then what we mean by the power of the press was still largely concentrated in the pulpit, and did not vanish even after the press had become a potent force in controversy. People are governed by pulpits more than the sword in times of peace, said King Charles in 1646, and possession of the public ear was a prime necessity for both parties in the religious and constitutional struggle. One example is the stir caused by the order (1627) for printing the sermons of Sibthorp and Manwaring on passive obedience. Thus in addition to his office as a guide to salvation, a preacher of repute combined the attractions of a modern journalist, publicist, and lecturer. He was also akin to the modern actor. A London or university audience, even a village congregation, had its squad, large or small, of theological and dramatic critics; Baxter warned preachers against the insidious consciousness of that fact, and Taylor urged that men should not come to church 'as into a Theatre'. The critical attitude was quickened by the taking of notes on sermons, which was, as Brinsley, Hoole, and others indicate, an established educational practice—a practice which enabled the pious Sir Simonds D'Ewes to escape from the 'desperate atheism' of his childhood and become 'a rational hearer' in his teens. Girls like Lucy Apsley and Katherine Fowler also memorized or took down sermons, though Sir Ralph Verney thought it as indecent for women to scribble as to speak in church. For the persistence of the habit in later life there is the diary of John Manningham, or the less familiar journal of the unhappy Edward Wingfield in far-off Jamestown.

While the sermon had the unique character of a divine message, and carried the obligation of close scrutiny of the inspired text, it was also a highly developed literary form, the product of an unbroken oratorical tradition which went back to the ancients. Its own special traditions of rhetoric and logic —the open and the closed hand, according to a common phrase—had been revivified by the powerful influence of Ramus and codified in such books as Keckermann's *Rhetoricae Ecclesiasticae*. It was natural that the preaching of men of all religious categories except ranters—should have a generic likeness, but there were tribal and individual differences. Many great Puritan preachers from Perkins to Baxter, such men as Laurence Chaderton (1537/8–1640), the first Master of Emmanuel College, Arthur Hildersam (1563–1632), and 'Decalogue Dod' (1555–1645), were disposed, from choice, not ignorance, to favour the presentation of truth in her naked purity, not bedizened with human and profane learning (and some Anglicans shared that view). But there is just the opposite contrast between the Puritan Thomas Adams and the Anglo-Catholic Lancelot Andrewes; and Manningham complained that the Puritan John Reynolds quoted an author for every sentence, almost every syllable. Whatever his particular method, the preacher had scope for his whole range of gifts, spiritual, intellectual, literary, and histrionic. The sermon was at once a sophisticated and a popular kind of literature and on both accounts it was a sensitive index to changing fashions in homiletic technique and in prose style, so that the variety of sermon literature is commensurate with its bulk. In these pages we must ignore dozens of eminent preachers and shall look at only four men, Adams, Andrewes, Donne, and Taylor.

Thomas Adams, whose wit and fancy Southey praised, was an heir of the silver-tongued Henry Smith and the sulphur-tongued William Perkins, and he was touched by both Euphuism and Senecanism (he speaks of Lipsius's style and often quotes Seneca).[1] In his *Mystical Bedlam* (1615) and *Diseases of the Soul* (1616) Adams was a lively exponent of the 'character' as a homiletic device—and recreation. The latter piece (called *The Soul's Sickness* in the *Works*) is 'a discourse divine, morall, and physicall' which reminds us of Burton; Adams is akin to Burton too, and to Latimer, in his mixture of sympathy for the poor and satire upon their oppressors.

Almost any sermon exhibits Adams's mastery of all the popular resources of the City and Puritan preacher. *The City of Peace* opens with a figurative and biblical character of Peace. Then peace is likened to a city, to London. The city of peace has walls of unity and concord; four gates, innocence and patience, benefaction and satisfaction, which correspond to Bishopsgate, Ludgate, Aldgate, and Cripplegate; and so on. The body of the sermon consists in the realistic and hortatory amplification of the *exemplum*. The method is not strictly allegorical, but it springs from the allegorical habit of mind that produced Latimer's sermons on the card, Bernard's *Isle of Man* (Adams uses this phrase), and the poetical treatments of the castle of the body. Some other suggestive titles are *The Gallant's Burden*, *The White Devil or the Hypocrite Uncased* (1613), *The*

---

[1] After graduating from Cambridge (B.A., 1601/2; M.A., 1606) Adams became a preacher in Bedfordshire. Then he held a living in Buckinghamshire and, from 1618 to 1623, the preachership of St. Gregory's under St. Paul's Cathedral. By 1629 he was in charge of St. Benet's, Paul's Wharf. He was also an occasional preacher at Paul's Cross and Whitehall. Adams was chaplain to the Chief Justice of the King's Bench, Sir Henry Montagu (later the first Earl of Manchester), who himself compiled a moral, religious, and at times mystical volume, *Contemplatio Mortis, & Immortalitatis* (1631). It may be added that in dedications Adams addressed William Earl of Pembroke, Lord Ellesmere, and others rather as friends than as patrons. His voice is last heard in 1653, speaking of his 'necessitous and decrepit old age'. Many of his sermons appeared separately, and his *Works* in 1629.

Spiritual Navigator Bound for the Holy Land. Whether or not an
entire discourse rests upon an allegorical frame, the texture of
Adams's sermons is rich in vivid and usually homely metaphor
and pointed wit. But his sole and fervent aim is to rebuke sin
and preach the gospel, and his tricks, including the rhetorical
schemata of which he is one of the last exponents, are only means
of arousing the sluggish conscience: 'all our preaching is but
to beget your praying.' There is very little of the theological
erudition and argument that make so many contemporary
sermons crabbed reading, and Adams's secular quotations,
though they range from numerous classics to Montaigne, John
Owen, Chapman, and Sylvester, are handled discreetly—one
may say ingeniously when Ovid's lines about a woman's feigned
resistance are applied to the soul and the body. Adams is, then,
an earnest preacher, a cultivated scholar, a topical humorist
and satirist, and he can write of a summer morning and the
lark in a lyrical vein half-way between Breton and Taylor. But
for quotation we take two passages on death. The first, from
God's Bounty, may be set beside Browne:

It is a foolish dreame, to hope for immortalitie and a long-lasting
name, by a monument of brasse or stone. It is not dead stones, but
living men, that can redeeme thy good remembrance from oblivion.
. . . Onely thy noble and Christian life makes every mans heart thy
Tombe, and turnes every tongue into a pen, to write thy deathlesse
Epitaph.

The second passage comes from *The Sinner's Mourning Habit*:

Dust, the matter of our substance, the house of our soules, the
originall graines whereof we were made, the top of all our kinred.
The glory of the strongest man, the beautie of the fairest woman; all
is but dust. Dust; the onely compounder of differences, the absolver
of all distinctions: who can say, which was the Client, which the
Lawyer: which the borrower, which the lender: which the captive,
which the Conquerer; when they all lie together in blended dust?

Adams's schematic generalities may be set beside this characteristic elaboration of particulars in the fifteenth of Donne's *LXXX
Sermons*:

The dust of great persons graves is speechlesse too, it sayes nothing,
it distinguishes nothing: As soon the dust of a wretch whom thou
wouldest not, as of a Prince whom thou couldest not look upon, will

trouble thine eyes, if the winde blow it thither; and when a whirle-winde hath blowne the dust of the Church-yard into the Church, and the man sweeps out the dust of the Church into the Church-yard, who will undertake to sift those dusts again, and to pronounce, This is the Patrician, this is the noble flowre, and this the yeomanly, this the Plebeian bran?

It may be a shock to turn from Adams's moving common-places to a bit of Andrewes's Easter sermon (1617) on Matthew xii. 39–40:[1]

They [the Pharisees] would see a Signe. The answere is negative, but qualified. There is in it, a *Non*, and a *Nisi*: *Non dabitur*, none shalbe given them. Indeed none should: They were worthy of none. Yet saith He not, *Non* simply. His *Non*, is with a *Nisi*, *Non dabitur, nisi*; it is with a limitation, with a *but*: *None, but*, that. So, that: So, one shalbe. In the *Non*, is their desert: in the *Nisi*, His goodnesse: that, though they were worthy none, yet gives them one, though.

The quotations from Adams represent only a slight elevation above his normal manner, and the quotation from Andrewes, which represents no great exaggeration of his normal manner, reads like a parody of the Lipsian and Senecan 'hopping style'. In about two-thirds of the texture of his *XCVI Sermons* (1629) Andrewes is condensed, jerky, and difficult. The reasons are partly personal, partly not. Nearly all of Andrewes's extant sermons were delivered before the court, many of them in series on the great festivals of the Christian year, and 'the first great preacher of the English Catholic Church' was addressing an audience of theological connoisseurs. While Adams seeks always to awaken the sinner and arm the Christian warrior for combat

---

[1] Lancelot Andrewes (1555–1626) was born in London of middle-class parents. In 1571 he followed Spenser from Mulcaster's school, Merchant Taylors', to Pembroke Hall, Cambridge. He was ordained in 1580–1 and some years later was appointed chaplain to Archbishop Whitgift and to the queen. He became Master of Pembroke Hall (1589–1605), Dean of Westminster (1601), Bishop of Chichester (1605), of Ely (1609), and of Winchester (1618). Throughout James's reign Andrewes was a prominent figure at court, as preacher and in other capacities, though his private preoccupations were devotional and scholarly. He was revered for his learning, his sermons, and his genuine sanctity; at the same time he shared in the common clerical practices of pluralism and nepotism and—unlike Archbishop Abbot—bowed to the king's will in the unsavoury Essex divorce. Andrewes was a friend of Hooker, apparently, and of Bacon, Camden, George Herbert, and of Casaubon and other foreign scholars, and his beneficiaries were innumerable. He was lamented in verse by the young Milton and Crashaw. Andrewes's part in the making of the Authorized Version was mentioned earlier, and his role in the philosophic establishment of the Church of England is indicated below.

in a world of evil, Andrewes, the biblical and patristic scholar, devotes himself to acute, exact, learned, and impersonal exegesis of his text, squeezing out the last drop of meaning from every word. He declares that 'The onely true praise of a Sermon is, some evill left, or some good done, upon the hearing of it', and his discourses are not without practical piety, but in much of his preaching Andrewes seems to take for granted all that Adams makes the basis of his religious and moral appeal. Moreover, the profane literature that Adams so freely draws upon Andrewes almost completely avoids. We may conclude that the Jacobean *stella praedicantium* has sunk altogether below our horizon.

Yet the persevering reader, unless he is too hard, or too soft, for all religious exposition, may come to qualify his first impressions. If he is chilled by Andrewes's severe and 'witty' intellectualism, he must grant that the preacher's mind is always working, and that he demands the same close attention as a jurist or a metaphysical poet. If Andrewes seldom approaches the ecstasies of Donne—we may not enjoy his juggling with 'the seasons' (Christmas, 1623) after Donne's great rhapsody—he has nothing of Donne's extravagance. If he seems to lack fire, its frequent brief flashes, analytic or emotional, are all the brighter for habitual repression. Whatever his fame owed to his delivery, Andrewes explicitly disparages the arts of the pulpit, the 'blazes' that 'make us a little sermon-warme for the while' but later 'flitt and vanish': 'It is the evidence of the Spirit, in the soundnesse of the sense, that leaves the true impression.' We feel beneath the austere surface what is more apparent in the famous little book of *Devotions* or *Preces Privatae* (translated 1647–8), the sincerity, gentleness, and power born of a disciplined purity of soul, of a life devoted to the contemplation and forwarding of the Christian ideal and heritage. The sermons do not lend themselves to anthologizing but, to speak of the more obvious literary attractions, a hasty glance may miss the bits of vivid paraphrase and imaginative re-creation that light up rigorous exegesis. One passage, from a Christmas sermon at court, 1622, has become known in our day as the 'source' of T. S. Eliot's 'Journey of the Magi'. Witness also the account of Mary Magdalene at the tomb (Easter, 1620), or the religious masque made out of the eighty-fifth Psalm (Christmas, 1616), or the passages, like the following from the same sermon, in which Andrewes shares his visions of Christian joy, visions none the less intense for their logical articulation:

And even so then let there be. So, may our end be as the end of the First Verse in peace; and as the end of the Second, in Heaven. So, may all the blessings that came to mankind by this meeting, or by the birth of Christ (the cause of it) meet in us and remaine upon us: till, as we now meet together, at the Birth; So we may then meet in a perfect man, in the measure of the fulnesse of the age of Christ: As meet (now) at the Lambes yeaning; so meet then, at the Lambes marriage; be caught up in the cloudes (then) to meet Him, and there to reigne for ever with Him, in His Kingdome of Glorie.

2

In their own time John Donne (1572–1631) was a smaller figure than Lancelot Andrewes, but modern opinion—largely of course on account of Donne's poetry—has much more than reversed their positions. In obvious ways Donne's experience, character, and genius set him apart from other divines. While they were almost born churchmen, the saintly ascetic of St. Paul's was a lily that had risen out of red earth. Walton's parallel was St. Augustine, the brilliant rhetorician, worldling, and sinner transformed into a mighty champion of Christ and the Church. Donne may well have exaggerated the libertine stains of his youth, but at least it was not the youth of Andrewes or Taylor. He had been brought up a Roman Catholic, keenly conscious of his heritage and his semi-outlawry. He had been a wit and gallant, a sensual and cynical poet, a student of sceptical and naturalistic thought, a traveller, a soldier, a courtier, and a member of Parliament. Though 'undone' by his marriage, he continued to cherish hopes of worldly advancement; and after years of penurious dependence he could not trust his own motives if he yielded to persuasion and took orders. Walton's 'higher hand' which 'at last forced him' into 'this sacred service' was not God, as we might think, but King James, though we may believe that Donne did not become a priest until he was convinced of his own sincerity and vocation and of Providential guidance; in 1627 he said 'I date my life from my Ministery'. His early Romanist training left a permanent impress upon his mind and modes of thought. Like other divines, he went through the classical, patristic, and scholastic mould, but none perhaps absorbed so little from the classics, none so much from the Fathers and 'the School'. Of his unusual acquaintance with the new astronomy something will be said later. Finally, Donne remained a poet. There are many general and specific parallels in substance and manner between the sermons and both the religious and the secular verse—normal avoidance of flowing and balanced rhythms, realistic particularity of reference, dramatic instinct and power, analytic and eccentric wit, abstruse learning, casuistical argument, a strain of the morbid and macabre, and the personal involvement that gives such urgency to the best religious poems and some of the prose. So far as we know, Donne never at any time in his life had doubts of the Christian faith; and if his devious approach to his profession enlarged his understanding of worldly temptation and human weakness, it also heightened his zealous orthodoxy.

We may notice first the minor and mainly early works. In *Biathanatos* (1608?), for which Donne had a fondness, though he did not publish it, he offered a qualified apology for suicide which ran counter to the main tradition of Christian thought. Neither the subject nor the learned casuistry is now inviting, but the book grew out of both temperamental inclinations and concrete trials and it represents a stage in the evolution of Jack Donne into Dr. John Donne. (The author said it was written by the former, not the latter.) Donne's empirical questioning of the law of nature and right reason, his appeal to the conditional and relative, is not Hooker's assured position, and Jack Donne already sees the light of nature as the moon, or fires and tapers, compared with the sun of God's word. The same image, by the way, is grandly elaborated in Donne's first sermon at St. Paul's, on Christmas Day, 1621.

After *Pseudo-Martyr* (1610), a defence of the oath of allegiance made, says Walton, at the king's request, Donne relaxed in *Ignatius his Conclave* (1611), a satire on Loyola and the Jesuits in the tradition of the Senecan and Erasmian skits on Claudius and Pope Julius and of more recent things. In the eighth 'Problem' (1607?) and in *Biathanatos* Donne showed his awareness of Kepler, but *Ignatius* contains his first precisely datable reference to the new astronomy; Galileo's *Sidereus Nuncius* had appeared early in 1610 and Donne had doubtless learned of it through the prompt agency of his friend Wotton. His reactions were touched on in connexion with the *Anniversaries*, and a word more may be said here. Like many knowledgeable conservatives, Donne seems to have accepted Tycho's geocentric compromise. His few late poems and the huge body of prose make it clear that new astronomical discoveries did not cause him any central or continued disturbance. They were outside his religious faith, and what anxieties he felt were religious and personal, not cosmic. The very rare allusions to the 'new Philosophy' in the sermons only illustrate religious truth. And, along with his regular assumption of a geocentric world, Donne can say, with the Psalmist, that God appointed the earth to rest and stand still, and that Joshua's stopping of the sun (a favourite reference) was less wonderful than 'that so vast and immense a body as the Sun, should run so many miles, in a minute'.

A tincture of scientific interest, though it is subordinated to religious concerns, persists in the first book of *Essays in Divinity*, a two-part series of private reflections on the creation and the Creator of the world and on the deliverance of the Israelites from Egypt. This book, written perhaps in 1614 when Donne sat in Parliament, or earlier, furnishes a partial picture of his mind in the years that were leading him towards the Church. The interspersed prayers for the infusion of grace recall the more violent 'Holy Sonnets'. The melancholy disenchantment of the *First Anniversary* and the liberating vision of the *Second* give place to a less excited, more positive, and more conventional contemplation of God and His purpose in the world. Later, in that initial sermon at St. Paul's, Donne argued that 'a meere naturall man'—not that he was ever such—must be drawn to faith by being shown first 'That this World, a frame of so much harmony, . . . must necessarily have had a workeman'. But he is much nearer the main line of the sermons in his view of the God who leads men's minds out of Egyptian darkness; and the metaphor is applied in a summary of his own situation:

Thou hast delivered me, O God, from the Egypt of confidence and presumption, by interrupting my fortunes, and intercepting my hopes; And from the Egypt of despair by contemplation of thine abundant treasures, and my portion therein; from the Egypt of lust, by confining my affections; and from the monstrous and unnaturall Egypt of painfull and wearisome idleness, by the necessities of domestick and familiar cares and duties. Yet as an Eagle, though she enjoy her wing and beak, is wholly prisoner, if she be held by but one talon; so are we, though we could be delivered of all habit of sin, in bondage still, if Vanity hold us but by a silken thred.

But there are few attractions in the knotty matter and manner of these mainly impersonal essays.

A very directly personal document, also composed under affliction, though in a time of much greater worldly and spiritual security, is the *Devotions* (1624). This book, which can be read as a consecutive whole, is the best introduction to Donne's religious prose and religious temper. What Walton called 'a Sacred picture of Spiritual Extasies' was the product of a dangerous illness, the record of a journey through the valley of the shadow. Donne's thoughts and feelings, linked in a triple chain(with an intricate system of smaller links) of 'Meditations upon our Humane Condition', 'Expostulations, and Debate-ments with God', and 'Prayers, upon the severall Occasions, to him', constitute a kind of allegorical interweaving of physical and spiritual sickness as he sinks down towards the grave and then, not without fear of relapse, returns to health. The theme brings out all Donne's special characteristics, his preoccupation with sin and death, his acuteness of psychological analysis, his keen awareness of the tension between his soul and the world, the originality of his wit, the troubled and sometimes lurid power of his imagination, the essential simplicity, despite its complex and learned surface, of his religious faith—and, it may be added, a degree of monotony and repetitious expansiveness and an emphasis on his sinfulness which combines real humility with something of Puritan exhibitionism. If, allowing for the special circumstances of his book and his life, we compare the *Devotions* with, say, Andrewes's prayers, we feel at once Donne's brooding, agitated egoism and unrestraint.

Donne's earliest extant sermon was preached at Greenwich on 30 April 1615 (he had been ordained on 23 January); his last, *Death's Duel*, of which Walton gives such a dramatic account, was delivered on 25 February 1631. During his minis-try Donne enjoyed the admiration of his royal patrons, of the grave Benchers of Lincoln's Inn (once the frisky companions of his youth), of 'The Representative Body of the whole Clergy of this Nation', and of countless miscellaneous auditors like his worshipful biographer. Walton describes his method of prepar-ing for the pulpit:

The latter part of his life may be said to be a continued study; for as he usually preached once a week, if not oftner, so after his Sermon he never gave his eyes rest, till he had chosen out a new Text, and that night cast his Sermon into a form, and his Text into divisions; and the next day betook himself to consult the Fathers, and so commit his meditations to his memory, which was excellent.

Some enthusiastic ministers and their hearers preferred extempore or 'inspired' preaching, but sentiment in general, while opposed to the reading of sermons, put less faith in Pentecostal visitations, and most Puritans and Anglicans preached from a more or less memorized manuscript or from notes. Donne, who condemned extempore preaching and praying, though he regarded the preacher as the mouthpiece of the Holy Ghost, seems commonly to have written out his sermons sooner or later after their delivery.

While his command of oratorical resources grew with experience and with confidence in his calling, and of course varied with his themes, Donne's sermons more or less conform to established patterns. There are as a rule three main parts: invention, or analysis of the natural divisions of the text; disposition, or amplification of these divisions with arguments and illustrations from the Bible, the Fathers, and later theologians; and the drawing together of the several lines into a general or specific application. For example, on 29 January 1626—after the plague of 1625—Donne preached at St. Paul's from the sixty-third Psalm: 'Because thou hast been my helpe, Therefore in the shadow of thy wings will I rejoyce.' In these words he sees

the whole compasse of Time, Past, Present, and Future; and these three parts of Time, shall be at this time, the three parts of this Exercise; first, what Davids distresse put him upon for the present; and that lyes in the Context; secondly, how David built his assurance upon that which was past; (*Because thou hast been my help*) And thirdly, what he established to himselfe for the future, (*Therefore in the shadow of thy wings will I rejoyce*).

In a sermon at Lincoln's Inn, on Psalm xxxviii. 4, a more general pattern is outlined: the literal or historical sense; the moral application to us; and the figurative or typical reference to Christ; but the literal sense is primary. The groundwork of the sermons is sober exposition and good counsel, in prose that has affinities with the Senecan tradition. Matters of doctrine Donne expressly makes secondary to exhortation, edification, 'and a

holy stirring of religious affections', and by his definition most
of Andrewes's sermons would approach 'lectures'. We are not
surprised to find him telling the lawyers of Lincoln's Inn that
his favourite parts of the Bible are the Psalms and Paul's
epistles, or to see that next to the Bible he quotes St. Augustine;
and these count strongly in the moulding of his own prose, its
parallelisms and paradoxes. (Incidentally, Donne is given, like
Andrewes, to the repetition of key-words, such as 'joy' in the
sermon of 29 January 1626, a sermon of triumph over death.)
Reading scraps of Donne's sermons in anthologies, with our
modern indifference to homiletic art, we miss the total design.
Yet not very many sermons as wholes win and hold our interest,
and most readers may well be content with the intoxications of
Donne's purple passages, such as those on the infinite extent
of God's mercies or the infinite duration of eternity, where, as
in his poetry, he makes an abstract idea intelligibly and intensely
vivid through concrete particulars imaginatively realized, and
in a spiralling rhythm all his own.

No preacher was ever more earnestly 'against sin' than
Donne. In *Devotions* (*Expostulation* iii) St. Paul's fear takes hold
of him, that when he has preached to others, he himself should
be a castaway. Even though he speaks from apparent security,
and is seldom openly personal, we tend, perhaps wrongly, to
read the 'Hymn to God the Father' between many lines of
prose. As one of his best critics has said, we do not feel in Donne,
as we do in St. Paul, God speaking to man, but rather man
speaking to God. Walton saw him—and Lord Falkland gave a
similar account in verse—

preaching the Word so, as shewed his own heart was possest with
those very thoughts and joys that he laboured to distill into others:
A Preacher in earnest; weeping sometimes for his Auditory, sometimes with them: always preaching to himself, like an Angel from
a cloud, but in none; carrying some, as St. Paul was, to Heaven in
holy raptures, and inticing others by a sacred Art and Courtship to
amend their lives; here picturing a vice so as to make it ugly to those
that practised it; and a vertue so, as to make it be beloved even by
those that lov'd it not; and, all this with a most particular grace and
an unexpressible addition of comeliness.

The picture confirms our impression, which does not at all
reflect upon Donne's entire sincerity, that in the pulpit he was
by nature something of a theatrical spellbinder. He had his

spark of the peculiar burning intensity of Paul and Augustine, and he evidently shared with them 'a delight, and a complacency, and a holy melting of the bowels, when the congregation liked' his preaching. In his illness his sensitive conscience reproaches him with sinning 'in my ostentation, and the mingling a respect of my selfe, in preaching thy Word'.

One who has, several times, read the 160 sermons, and with a fair degree of historical sympathy, may perhaps be allowed the opinion that the reading is much more of a task than an experience, that Donne, with all his unique power, has liabilities, generic and individual. By far the heaviest is the bulk of minute and barren exegesis. Others are incidental but recurrent. If the great fundamentalist drama of sin and death and salvation kindled potent eloquence in Donne and other preachers (and in playwrights), it could also inspire less winning eloquence on the corruption and the resurrection of the body (both obsessions of Donne's), and such other themes as original sin and the blood of Christ. An infant at birth is an absolute sinner, under sentence of damnation, and parents who let it die unbaptized are guilty of spiritual murder, even if God should be merciful. And, when we recall the poet's celebrations of love, we may regret the preacher's Pauline stress on marriage as 'a remedy against burning'—a note not much sweetened by the epithalamia of 1613.

One attitude was too common in Donne's age to be cited as a liability if he were not so constantly singled out by modern scholars and critics as a rare example of religious liberalism, tolerance, and charity. The *locus classicus* (often a sufficient proof) is Donne's letter to 'Sir H. R.' (Sir Henry Goodere) in which he said that Rome, 'Wittemberg', and Geneva were 'all virtuall beams of one Sun'; and *Essays in Divinity* has a similar passage, Canterbury being nearest the ideal. Donne the preacher could speak in that vein, but normally he was much less magnanimous and much more rigid. His occasional pleas against strife over non-essentials lose force when we see what he regards as essentials, and when, in non-essentials, Englishmen are bidden to submit to the king's directions. Donne's court of appeal, 'the Catholique Church', is, concretely, the church of the Bible, the Creeds, and the Fathers as it is continued in the Church of England (though Luther and Calvin are treated with respect); 'for to that Heaven which belongs to the Catholique Church,

I shall never come, except I go by the way of the Catholique Church.' Donne incessantly attacks Rome, the Devil's 'instrument' that propagates 'the doctrine of Devils'; the blessed King James 'leads us' in the knowledge that 'the Pope is Antichrist'. When religion is involved with political allegiance, 'the temporal sword may be drawn as well as the spiritual'. The enemies of God and His Anglican Church are atheists, idolaters, Jews, Turks, Papists, and 'non-Conformitans' or 'seditious and schismaticall Separatists'. 'Sects are not bodies, they are but rotten boughes, gangrened limmes, fragmentary chips, blowne off by their owne spirit of turbulency, fallen off by the waight of their owne pride, or hewen off by the Excommunications and censures of the Church.' Nor, apparently, does Christ's kingdom have any room for 'those herds of vagabonds, and incorrigible rogues, that fill porches, and barnes in the Countrey', of whom a very great part were never baptized. Not to multiply quotations, it would seem that Dr. Donne's liberal charity is exaggerated.

Two more labels may be noticed, by way of further definition of Donne's religious temper and writings. In general, recent criticism seems to have agreed that he is not to be called a mystic, although, like other men, he could on occasion speak the mystical language that was in the air. In 'A Valediction: of the Book' and in one of the poems to the Countess of Bedford, Donne says, and his prose gives a larger meaning to the words, that 'all Divinity Is love or wonder' and that 'Reason is our Soules left hand, Faith her right'. We may also remember 'A Litany':

> Let not my minde be blinder by more light
> Nor Faith by Reason added, lose her sight.

Such utterances might be a prelude to mysticism, but there are elements in Donne's mind and temper which—in spite of foretastes of holy and heavenly joy—stand in the way of the mystic's journey. For one thing, there was the actuality, the pressure, and the fascination of life and the world which, as man and as poet, Donne felt intensely and sought, as a dedicated Christian, to resist and escape from. There was the assertive will, which he had striven to subdue and make receptive to grace. Then there was his reason. The young Donne had had the restless, inquiring reason of the instinctive sceptic (if this last word may be used in a very limited and quite unmodern sense); he had realized the craggy approach to truth; he had, with intellectual detachment, refused to commit himself until he had digested the whole body of controversy regarding Roman and Anglican claims. But his mature faith, if not quite anti-intellectual fideism, was less rational and less mystical than evangelical. The preacher was rather a Christian warrior than a contemplative. In view of the late 'Hymns', it is doubtful if, with all his fervour, Donne attained the love of God that casts out fear. Because of his own and others' guilt, he fixes his mind, and theirs, on the Cross. For all the theological learning with which he fortifies his sermons, his central faith is not much more complex than General Booth's. Whatever his nominal text, his invariable theme is 'inquietum est cor nostrum, donec requiescat in te'. Donne's vision is of sin, salvation, the earthly road thereto, and the heavenly reward; it is not the vision of the mystic who can leave self and the world behind, or of the religious philosopher who can gather the broken and dispersed images of the world into a harmonious unity.

Our second label has been partly considered already. Critics have seen Donne as one of the rational moderates who established the Anglican *via media*, and no doubt he was, but only in a very limited way. There is a gulf between *Pseudo-Martyr* and *Of the Laws of Ecclesiastical Polity*, and, despite Donne's admiration for Hooker, one cannot imagine him expounding Hooker's grand, all-embracing conception of reason, 'right reason', and law. Sermons, to be sure, are not treatises, but Donne the preacher, if he had been so minded, might have presented a philosophic case for Anglicanism; it would have been more welcome, then and now, than dredging from the commentaries. In a larger perspective, Donne stands outside the rational Christian-humanist tradition represented by Erasmus and Hooker and the Cambridge Platonists, by Spenser and Milton. While for such men, as for all Christians, Scripture alone contains the supreme truths, the hallmark of the tradition is a ready appeal to the light of nature, the moral wisdom and semi-religious insight of the ancient philosophers, as a buttress of Christian ethics and thought. Thomas Adams the Puritan and Joseph Hall and Jeremy Taylor habitually cite or echo 'profane' writers; Donne, in the majority of his relatively few classical references, disparages 'Morall' men, Seneca, Epictetus, Plutarch

(Plato fares better). His intense concern with religious righteous-ness and with salvation leaves small room for humanistic virtue, much less for humane culture.

To the modern mind, sceptical in a way that Donne never was, the churchman's evangelical emphasis, his complete ortho-doxy, his upholding of Erastian uniformity in the Church, might appear less admirable than Milton's independent, liberal, and unorthodox creed, though it is Milton who attracts all the mis-siles. Donne found what he believed to be full satisfaction in his ministry, but perhaps, being the kind of man he was, he obtained full satisfaction for parts of his nature by virtually suppressing other parts. In the seventy-ninth of his *LXXX Sermons* we read:

> Even in spirituall things, there may be a fulnesse, and no satis-faction, And there may be a satisfaction, and no fulnesse; I may have as much knowledge, as is presently necessary for my salvation, and yet have a restlesse and unsatisfied desire, to search into unprofitable curiosities, unrevealed mysteries, and inextricable perplexities: And, on the other side, a man may be satisfied, and thinke he knowes all, when, God knowes, he knowes nothing at all; for, I know nothing, if I know not Christ crucified, And I know not that, if I know not how to apply him to my selfe, Nor doe I know that, if I embrace him not in those meanes, which he hath afforded me in his Church, in his Word, and Sacraments; If I neglect this meanes, this place, these exercises, howsoever I may satisfie my selfe, with an over-valuing mine own knowledge at home, I am so far from fulnesse, as that vanity it selfe is not more empty.

These words contain much of the burden of Donne's preach-ing, and they imply some of the conflicting elements in him. He had always been at least intellectually religious, and mar-riage and circumstances altered his mode of life rather than his creed. He underwent no sudden 'conversion'; his spiritual evolution was a gradual process. Yet Donne's religious writings, taken along with his personal history, suggest something forced and unnatural, something that often marks the religiosity of the converted worldling and intellectual, in his eager acceptance of authority and his eager quest of salvation, in his narrowness and his note of excess. In reading Hooker, Taylor, Browne, the Cambridge Platonists, and Milton, we know, whatever their defects may be, that we are in contact with the whole man, the normally ripened man. In reading Donne we may feel that the preacher who is always earnest and sometimes impressive has gained satisfaction at the cost of fullness, and that our satisfaction in him remains incomplete.

3

The metaphysical style, which was so well adapted to the paradoxes of faith, was a European phenomenon. In England it ran throughout our period but was especially strong in the first half of it. Andrewes and Donne, the greatest Anglo-Catholic preachers of the age, were, though very different, the chief exemplars. In prose as in verse wit involved not merely verbal tricks and surprises but the linking together of dissimilar objects, symbols, and ideas philosophized and fused by intellectual and spiritual perceptions and emotions, weighted by frequently abstruse or scientific learning, and made arresting by pointed expression. Along with the general and philosophic causes behind this mode of thought and feeling, there were the general stylistic influences represented by Euphuism and Senecanism and, for preachers, the example of some of the Fathers and their scholastic and schematic successors. On the other hand, a host of Puritan preachers, and some Anglicans—such as Herbert, the young friend of Andrewes and Donne—preferred a 'Scriptural and Christian Plainness'. That quality, to be sure, was not a fixed absolute. For Donne 'the Holy Ghost is an eloquent Author', abundant though not luxuriant, and, far from being low and homely, outdoes all the figures and tropes of classical poetry and oratory. For most Puritans, as John Downame put it, 'the holie Ghost in penning the Scriptures hath used great simplicitie and wonderfull plainnesse, applying himselfe to the capacitie of the most unlearned'. But this view did not exclude imagery and other popular and effective devices.

The cult of plainness, then, did not begin after 1660. Preaching was affected by the general causes that nourished plain writing: the extension of the middle-class reading public, the rapid growth of the varied literature of knowledge, the still more rapid growth of popular controversy in politics and religion, and the antiquarianism of Camden, Richard Verstegan, and William Lisle, which carried on, with patriotic and primitivist zeal, the sixteenth-century campaign for Saxon purism and clarity. We have observed already the multitude of devotional books. Perkins's Ramist manual for preachers was frequently reprinted throughout the century. Sir William Vaughan's *Golden Grove*

(1600) included a plea for homiletic simplicity. Bacon's reverberating attack on Ciceronian rhetoric (1605) was aimed partly at the pulpit. Some twenty years later Owen Felltham, a notable Senecan, urged the cultivation of a 'pleasingly-plaine' pulpit style, 'kemb'd I wish it, not frizzled, nor curl'd'. When Ussher was in Oxford in 1642, his plain preaching 'quite put out of countenance that windy, affected sort of Oratory, which was then much in use, called *floride* preaching, or strong lines'. And with Ussher may be grouped Hall and Hammond and Sanderson, Hales and Chillingworth. John Wilkins, a moderate Puritan, urged plainness in his *Ecclesiastes* (1646), a popular handbook for preachers; and it might be taken as allegorical that this father of the Royal Society was the father-in-law of Tillotson. There were, then, many important champions and exponents of plain preaching, and their cause was destined to triumph. But our last pulpit orator, who shared with the witty preachers the censures of the Restoration, is the great representative of the decorative school and one of the greatest masters of English prose, Jeremy Taylor.[1] Like so many other writers of his age, he was rediscovered by Coleridge, Lamb, and Hazlitt, although, unlike some others, he had never been lost. But, for

---

[1] Jeremy Taylor (1613–67), the son of a Cambridge barber, went from the new Perse School to Gonville and Caius College (1626–35). We do not know if he was acquainted with such Cambridge contemporaries as Milton, Crashaw, George Herbert, Fuller, Whichcote, and Henry More; More at any rate he knew later. As a substitute preacher at St. Paul's (which had lost Donne in 1631), the young man attracted the interest of Laud, who sent him to Oxford, as a fellow of All Souls (1636), to ripen in a favourable climate. In 1638 he became rector of Uppingham in Rutlandshire and a royal chaplain (he was also a chaplain to Laud). He married in 1639. In 1642 he left his pastorate to join the king, whom he more or less attended for some time. In 1645 he was captured by parliamentary troops at Cardigan Castle in Wales. Soon after his release he found protection with the Earl and Countess of Carbery at Golden Grove in Carmarthenshire, and there, during the next decade, he did much of his best work. In 1655 and later he was imprisoned for a time, it is not clear why. Moving to London, Taylor ministered to royalists and enjoyed the friendship of John Evelyn. Another friend, Lord Conway, provided a chaplaincy in north Ireland (1658). Taylor welcomed the Restoration by dedicating to the king his large and long-incubated work on cases of conscience, *Ductor Dubitantium*. In 1660 he was appointed to the Irish see of Down and Connor (in some doctrines he was too 'unsafe' for English preferment). As bishop Taylor had to adapt himself to the different policies of successive archbishops towards Presbyterian ministers who would not qualify by episcopal ordination or were personally unfit. As Vice-Chancellor of the University of Dublin he accomplished a good deal of reorganization. Taylor's funeral sermon on Archbishop Bramhall (1663) was his oratorical swan-song. His own death was the occasion of a fine (and biographically valuable) sermon by his friend Dean Rust. He was buried in the cathedral he had built in Dromore.

obvious reasons, he has not shared in the modern revival which has made much of Donne and even (through T. S. Eliot) something of Andrewes.

Taylor's first publication (1638), an anti-Romanist sermon delivered at Oxford on the anniversary of the Gunpowder Plot, and dedicated to the archbishop, was a thorny argument which contained no budding roses. His second book (1642) was a defence of episcopacy such as might have been expected from a young divine nurtured in the school of Laud. His anonymous *Discourse concerning Prayer Ex tempore* (1646) was a bold criticism of the new *Directory for Public Worship* and, enlarged in 1649 as *An Apology for Authorized and Set Forms of Liturgy*, was boldly dedicated to the king just before his execution. In these, along with a deep loyalty to the Church of England, there are hints of a broadening mind. Taylor sees the unity of the Catholic communion being destroyed by the contentiousness that 'makes every schoole point, become our religion'. And he upholds 'a latitude of Theologie, much whereof is left to us, so without precise and cleere determination, that without breach either of faith or charity, men may differ in opinion'.

These words might stand as the text of his first vital book, *The Liberty of Prophesying* (1647), a book which offended his royal master, though its liberalism was not un-Laudian. In dedicating a collected edition of 1657, Taylor denied any inconsistency on the ground that his plea for liberty of conscience was based, like his plea for episcopacy, on Scripture and antiquity, but the natural development of his mind was quickened by the 'common calamity' and his 'private Troubles'. Although he lamented that, cast upon the shore of Wales by the storm that had wrecked the Church, he had written almost without books, he did bring a weight of learning to his account of the difficulties of scriptural interpretation and the errors and disputes of the councils, Fathers, and later theologians. As a whole the work is the best example of Taylor's earlier prose, lucid, sober, unadorned, and animated by deep and sad conviction. His argument is, in brief, that all Christians agree on the few fundamentals of faith which are plainly revealed in the Bible; that nothing is necessary to salvation except belief in the Apostles' Creed and a good life; that the endless disagreements which lead to persecution turn upon unnecessary points that cannot be solved; and that there is accordingly no real excuse for intolerance and strife if men will only seek God with their best reason, with humility, and with charity. Taylor may have owed something to talk with Chillingworth in Oxford days, or to *The Religion of Protestants*. Writing ten years later, when the Presbyterians and Independents are dominant, Taylor is less preoccupied with Rome and more conscious of sectarian divisions, but he stands with Chillingworth and others in his latitudinarian principles and in his appeal to Scripture and reason. Yet we should not make the liberal High Churchman too broadly or loosely Protestant. In the twenty-second of his *XXVIII Sermons* (1651) he says: 'The Church of England had reason to separate from the Confession and practises of Rome in many particulars, and yet if her children separate from her they may be unreasonable and impious.' And, like most other liberals, Taylor is not of course an advocate of freedom in the modern sense. 'Whatsoever is against the foundation of Faith, or contrary to good life and the lawes of obedience, or destructive to humane society, and the publick and just interests of bodies politick, is out of the limits of my Question, and does not pretend to complyance or toleration.' Finally, for Taylor as for Chillingworth, the operations of reason are circumscribed by the premiss that 'there is no greater probation in the world that a proposition is true, then because God hath commanded us to believe it'.

Holy Living (1650) is, with Fuller's *Holy State* (1642), the best-known example of the religious, moral, and domestic branch of the literature of conduct. Such books had a pedigree stretching back through writers like William Gouge, Joseph Hall, Sir William Vaughan, and William Perkins into the early Middle Ages. *Holy Living* was dedicated to Taylor's patron, Richard Vaughan, Earl of Carbery, nephew of the author of *The Golden Grove* (1600) and himself the author of a courtesy book. In the epistle Taylor pictures the desolation of the Church, which creates all the more need for private guidance, and repeats his constant plea, the sufficiency for membership in Christ of the essentials of faith and a holy life. In the text he covers the usual range of personal and social topics, the care of our time, the uses of prayer (prayers are furnished for every kind of person and occasion), sobriety and temperance, chastity (a subject on which Taylor is more candid than many divines), humility, modesty, contentedness in all estates, the duties of inferiors and superiors, the exercises of piety and charity. Such a table of contents explains modern neglect of the book; and the style, though not the plain, workmanlike instrument of *The Liberty of Prophesying*, has achieved the copious, limpid flow without much of the richness that we associate with Taylor.

A strain of melancholy other-worldliness runs through *Holy Living*, and its most sustained piece of eloquence is an incidental prelude to the full orchestration of *Holy Dying* (1651). Lady Carbery, for whom this book was written, and Taylor's wife had just died, so that personal grief entered keenly into his contemplation of mortality and his precepts of faith and patience. 'Death is nothing but the middle point between two lives.' To us *Holy Dying* makes a much stronger appeal than its predecessor. Its compelling theme awakens in Taylor the qualities he shares with Browne and Shakespeare and the rest, with the authors of the moralities and the many works *de contemptu mundi*. He could command, and know that he commanded in others, all the ideas and emotions that had gathered about the supreme fact in antiquity and in sixteen centuries of Christian faith, and the devout rhetorician rings the solemn changes on them all. His book has nothing of the subtle and individual intellectualism of Donne's *Devotions*. Taylor's power is his capacity for feeling and expressing the great commonplaces. Even his circling repetitiousness has the effect of heightening the physical and spiritual frailty, the inescapable misery, of puny man, of multiplying mirrors in a labyrinthine charnel-house, and, though we pay less heed to this, of multiplying the evidences of God's chastening love and mercy.

With the Christian and—for want of a better word—medieval elements in Taylor's imagination is fused the classical, in a distinctive manner and degree. He extols the ancient philosophers and poets, especially the Greeks, even in the preface to his life of Christ, *The Great Exemplar* (1649). In *Holy Dying*, Christ's command to Peter to walk on the water recalls a parallel in the *Tusculan Disputations*; a sentence on administering the eucharist to the sick contains an echo of the *Satyricon*. Whatever he owes to commonplace books, Taylor's mind dwells so willingly in the world of the Caesars and the East that casual images, involving no proper names, keep us in a half-ancient atmosphere. It was not in Wales that he thought in terms of consulships and saw 'a wilde boar destroy our vineyards', or orchards planted to 'feed our Nephews', a filleted beast bound to the altar, gladiators, pirates, labouring galley-slaves, the tents and triumphal chariots of conquerors. He describes maternal cares and coddling with what is surely first-hand domestic knowledge, and then turns to a father's pride in a son who has speared a lion. Taylor's occasional consciousness of something wrong—'I speak in the stile of the Roman greatnesse'—happily does not check his imaginative realization of the timeless facts of life and death and the vain ambitions of man. Further, the counsels of the Christian priest are continually philosophized by the ethical wisdom of the pagans—Seneca (whom Donne disparaged as the oracle of moral men), Plutarch, Cicero, and a host of others; high on Taylor's allusive list, if not on the conventional roll of moralists, are Petronius and Martial. (And his references are not all classical; he has some, chiefly in the sermons, to Montaigne.) This instinctive fusing of the two great bodies of truth, natural and revealed, is wholly in keeping with the tradition of Christian humanism. In Taylor as in other men, like Whichcote, it is based on the principle that, in his own words, the 'Christian Religion in all its moral parts is nothing else but the Law of Nature, and great Reason'. Taylor's religious 'rationalism' is of course, like other men's, strongly qualified by his faith, as indeed the phrase just quoted indicates. At the same time he counts as a systematic thinker—much more than Donne—in the history of moral theology; and his boldly liberal interpretation of original sin in *Unum Necessarium* (1655) greatly disturbed episcopal friends.

Like *The Fairy Queen* and *Paradise Lost*, *Holy Dying* may be viewed as an interwoven series of variations on contrasting themes, God and man, heaven and hell, good and evil, light and darkness, health and disease, life and death, and—when they are not united—Christianity and paganism. These contrasts are carried out in the rich imagery that has kept alive a book which, its author says, 'needs no Apology for being plain'. Much of it is plain, to be sure, and even the most ornate passages are pure and simple in diction and, however solemn, almost lightly fluid in rhythm. Taylor's mature prose is as remarkable for its natural and sensuous images as Donne's is for the lack of them. Though he is stirred by pomp and circumstance, his characteristic imagery is common and fresh as the morning—water, wind, flowers, birds, stars, and above all the light of the sun. Perhaps Taylor's closest affinity, temperamental and didactic as well as artistic, is with Spenser. When we compare Taylor's best-known purple patch—'But so have I seen a Rose newly springing from the clefts of its hood . . .'—with a parallel stanza in *The Fairy Queen* (II. xii. 74), we may think that it is the divine and not the lay poet whose visual and decorative sense obscures his serious intention.

Taylor's sermons (mostly published in 1651 and 1653) are similar in purpose and character to *Holy Living* and *Holy Dying*. He disclaims novel speculations in favour of 'the sincere milk of the word' and 'the greater lines of Dutie'. Even in the grand funeral orations on Lady Carbery and Archbishop Bramhall daily practice is not forgotten. And, since Taylor has been accused of ignoring all but the well-fed, it may be added that he often contrasts virtuous poverty with sinful wealth and is aware of the oppression and 'the needs of the poor man, his rent day, and the cryes of his children'. The material of his sermons grows out of the simple and all-embracing patterns of contrast that had served preachers ever since St. Paul. Like his fellows, Taylor makes much of the atonement, but his special emphasis is indicated by the title of his 'holy romance', *The Great Exemplar* (1649). The pulpit and hortatory fervour do not forbid classical illustration and embroidery. The subject of epicurean intemperance brings forth allusions in clusters, and even a summary of the central mysteries of faith (at the beginning of *The Spirit of Grace*) contains an Anacreontic phrase.

Classical quotations and references, of course, do not make classical writing. The simile of the river and the brook, from the sermon on Lady Carbery, was quoted by Arnold as an example of the genius of poetry rather than the intelligence of prose, and, to underline Taylor's provincial note, he cited Bossuet. Whether or not we endorse the verdict, we should remember that purple patches quoted by critics or assembled in anthologies give a distorted view of Taylor's pulpit style, as they do of Donne's. The figurative and poetical element—that which offended Restoration preachers and attracts us—is not large in proportion to the bulk of relatively plain discourse. In Taylor's prose in general, variations in style are determined by both his emotional involvement and the nature of his theme, purpose, and audience. His emotions are as certainly involved in the plain *Liberty of Prophesying* and *Unum Necessarium* as in the most ornate periods of *Holy Dying* and the sermons, but in the latter his appeal to the mind much oftener becomes an appeal to the heart and imagination. He may take wing from any of his common themes, life and death, time and eternity, sin, repentance, and inexhaustible mercy. We cherish him most in the typical quiet moods that reveal his love for the familiar things of nature, the phenomena of water, earth, and sky. Like Spenser, Taylor has a special tenderness for small creatures, for those 'little images and reflexes' of God, children, lambs, roses and 'the softest stalk of a violet', 'the little birds and laborious bees', the lark struggling bravely against the wind.

The Spenser of divines can be both homely and romantic: the stomach may be seen, in old allegorical terms, as a castle with ovens and cooks; faint prayers are laid aside in heaven 'like the buds of roses which a cold wind hath nip'd into death, and the discoloured tawny face of an Indian slave'. Taylor's sense of fleshly allurements gives birth to images in which strangeness is added to beauty. Men 'look after white and red, and the weaker beauties of the night'—

. . . but as the fires die and desires decay, so the mind steals away and walks abroad to see the little images of beauty and pleasure, which it beholds in the falling stars and little glow-wormes of the world.

And while Taylor, like Spenser, is firmly on the side of the resolved soul, some of his readers (like some romantic misinterpreters of Spenser in parallel cases) may—to borrow further examples from L. P. Smith—retain the picture of the libertine who, full of 'wine, and rage, and pleasure, and folly', goes 'singing to his grave', and forget 'the severities of a watchfull and a sober life'; may remember 'the harlots hands that build the fairy castle' and not 'the hands of reason and religion' that must pull it down.

4

We turn now to some aspects of religious controversy and to philosophic attempts to find a broad and solid *via media* in a world unsettled by both religious dissension and scientific thought. The general situation was outlined in the first chapter, and even here we cannot go very far into the complex problems and the mass of strong and sometimes noble writing they called forth. At any rate those problems all spring from one two-sided question, 'What are the grounds of inward faith and of external authority'?

The construction, or reconstruction, of the Church of England was the work of men like Whitgift, Bancroft, and Laud, who in their increasingly coercive policy received increasing support from their several sovereigns. On the side of apologetics it was Andrewes, the successor of Hooker and Jewel, who established for our period the Anglo-Catholic, High Church, or Arminian position. Earlier generations of Anglicans had naturally stressed their Protestant remoteness from Rome; now that the time of active revolt was past, a larger view was possible. The Church of England was defended as a true Catholic Church, purified from the accumulated inventions and abuses of Rome, perpetuating the apostolic succession and the doctrines, rites, and organization authorized by Scripture, by three creeds, by the first four general councils, and by the Fathers of the first five centuries. If that sounds uninspiring to the secular mind, it may be remembered that Anglo-Catholicism, though it lost some popular and international roots, meant nevertheless the restored vitality of a body of traditional thought and feeling, ecclesiastical, philosophic, and mystical, without which the great religious poetry and much great prose could not have been written. In maintaining the continuity and Catholicity of the Church of England against the great champion of Rome, Cardinal Bellarmine, Andrewes deployed his judgement of fundamentals, his powers of acute reasoning, his exact learning, and wit, edged or blunt, with such success that the task of later apologists was mainly amplification. Historical buttresses were to be erected by the learned Ussher, Sir Henry Spelman, Sir Roger Twysden, and others, who broadened the ecclesiastical impulse inherited from the nationalist and Protestant antiquarian movement of the sixteenth century.

In the controversies with Rome one particular question was forced to the front. The papal bull of 1570 had put both the English government and English Catholics in a dilemma, and that was sharpened a generation later by the Gunpowder Plot. In addition to the Englishman's inveterate dislike of foreign and ecclesiastical intervention and his well-founded fear of Catholic treason, more philosophic arguments were raised by King James, Andrewes, Donne, and others in defence of the oath of allegiance (1606). Defence of the oath was of course bound up with the divine right of kings, which was the only adequate theoretical answer to the papal claim of deposing and dispensing power. If we recoil from the frequent servility of Jacobean and Caroline churchmen, we should remember that they shared the common dread of civil disorder and the common reverence for the throne, and that in fact if not in theory the Church of England was a new institution, struggling to maintain itself against enemies abroad and multiplying enemies at home, and depending for support upon the Lord's Anointed. It was wholly natural that many churchmen should have deserved the tribute Sir John Harington paid to Andrewes, that his sermons tended 'to raise a joynt reverence to God and the Prince, to the spirituall and civile magistrate, by uniting and not severing them'.

In theology our period witnessed very important reactions to the Calvinism of the Elizabethan Church. Against Calvinistic rigours 'our late Arminians', to quote Robert Burton, 'have revived that plausible doctrine of universall grace, which many Fathers, our late Lutherans and modern Papists do still maintain, that we have free-will of our selves, and that grace is common to all that will beleeve'. According to Fuller, the Dalmatian Archbishop of Spalatro, who was in England during 1616–22, was the first to use 'Puritan' in a doctrinal sense, as opposed to Arminian. While the original meaning of 'Arminian' was theological (and in that sense Milton was the greatest of Arminians), the word became for Puritans the odious label of the High Church and royalist party. Stages in the Anglican movement towards Arminianism are represented by the effective opposition of the elderly Peter Baro and the younger clergy, notably Andrewes, to Whitgift's Calvinistic Lambeth Articles (1595); by the Synod of Dort (1618–19), where John Hales bade good night to John Calvin; and by the storm that arose over Richard Montagu's *Appello Caesarem* (1625). Although many Anglicans, from King James down, retained more or less of Genevan theology (and Hales, it has been said, did not bid good morning to Arminius), the Deity of Anglican thought became more benevolent and rational. One factor in the process was the influence of Grotius.

At the same time, in both old and New England, Calvinism itself was undergoing a change. Much of the emotional power of the creed had come from its dogmatic picture of God as Absolute Will, an inscrutable Jehovah of whom not even human reasonableness and justice could be predicated, since His will, as the almost omnipotent Perkins said, 'it selfe is an absolute rule both of justice and reason', and what He wills 'thereupon becomes reasonable and just'. The doctrine reminds us that Calvin was an heir of Scotus and Ockham. But a group of younger Calvinist theologians, of whom the chief was Perkins's pupil, William Ames (1576–1633), could no longer be content to prostrate themselves before a Deity whose decrees were so far beyond human understanding. In his *Medulla Sacrae Theologiae* (1623; translated 1642), a standard text-book on both sides of the Atlantic, Ames sought to give Calvinist dogma an intellectual and rational foundation. Perkins himself, following Reformation divines, had planted seeds which, watered by men of such influence as Ames, John Preston, and Richard Sibbes, flowered into the great doctrine of the covenant. According to that legalistic conception, mankind from Adam downwards had shared in contracts with God. The original covenant of works was the moral law of nature which should have enabled Adam to walk uprightly. But Adam fell, and with Abraham God made the covenant of grace, by which He undertook not only to save believers but to supply the grace or power of belief that would make salvation possible. That covenant still holds, and modern men have the additional surety of Christ the mediator. Thus God's willingness to be a partner with His creatures proved His essential rationality, benevolence, mercy, and forethought for the progressive capacity of man. The covenant helped to resolve the terrible uncertainties of election and reprobation and gave a reasonable basis and incentive for virtuous effort. Such a doctrine, in reinterpreting Calvinism (while trying to shun Arminianism), in enlarging man's powers and reducing the element of arbitrary grace, has affinities with the more liberal and amiable principles of the mainly Puritan group of Cambridge Platonists, with those of the Oxford latitudinarians, and even with the natural religion of Lord Herbert of Cherbury.

All these theological philosophies sprang from a faith in human reason (however that word might be understood) which sometimes almost threatened the supernatural premises of religion. In his *Sacred Philosophy of the Holy Scripture* (1635) Alexander Gill carried Christian rationalism to the extreme limits of orthodoxy, limits which his quondam pupil Milton was to overstep. Chillingworth, said the horrified Cheynell, 'was not ashamed to print and publish this destructive tenet, That there is no necessity of Church or Scripture to make men faithfull men'; and Chillingworth admitted that Scripture could not prove that there is a God or that it is the word of God. When good Christians could go so far, the natural light of reason might take others still farther. The current of rationalism had been rising for centuries, fed by many Christian writers and many ancient and modern sceptics. Chillingworth, for instance, knew Montaigne and, according to Aubrey, was devoted to Sextus Empiricus. The pestilent heresy of Socinianism was denounced by Donne and Chillingworth as well as by Cheynell, and the epithet 'Socinian' was readily flung at anyone who tried to link reason with religion. We may deplore the attitude of those narrow-minded ecclesiastics and fundamentalists who abused even the orthodox latitudinarians in the name of religion, but, like their modern counterparts, they knew that liberalism was not likely to stop within the confines of faith. In 1652 Walter Charleton, the disciple of Gassendi, declared that England had lately produced more swarms of 'Atheisticall monsters' than any age or nation had been infected with. In 1659 the sophisticated Francis Osborn, whose own *Advice to a Son* the Vice-Chancellor of Oxford tried to suppress, observed that 'God and the Magistrate lies blasphemed on every Stall'.

In addition to all the rational and mystical, sceptical and scientific ideas in the air, there was a marked interest in study of the various religious creeds, contemporary and historical. It fostered a spirit of tolerance and a desire for Christian unity in such men as Sir Edwin Sandys, Edward Brerewood, Sir Thomas Browne, the orientalist John Lightfoot, and that attractive Leveller and lover of Montaigne, William Walwyn. Donne, at rare moments, and Henry More (for whom, as for Ficino, Plato was 'Moses Atticus'), could see diverse faiths as virtual beams of one sun. Yet contemplation of religious and sectarian chaos might also lead, as it had already led in Italy and France, either to complete scepticism or to the natural theology of Lord Herbert.

Lord Herbert (1582–1648) has commonly been christened the father of deism, and through the century after him he was both echoed and attacked as such. But deism of a kind may be said to have been alive since thought began. Although its modern origins were as various as its manifestations, it was on the negative side the child of scepticism, on the positive of

Stoicism, that very malleable Stoicism which could also be fused with Arminianism and Puritanism. It was Lord Herbert who explicitly formulated the principles of natural religion, at the end of his *De Veritate* (1624); he expanded them in *De Religione Laici* (published with *De Causis Errorum* in 1645) and the post-humous *De Religione Gentilium* (1663). Herbert's five articles were these: that a supreme and providential Deity exists; that He ought to be worshipped; that virtue and piety are the essentials of worship; that men should repent of their sins; and that rewards and punishments are dispensed in a future life. These articles Herbert found among the ancient pagans, although, as in modern times, truth had been corrupted by the priesthood. Thus, like Anglicans and Puritans and Platonists, Herbert was trying in his way to strip off the adventitious wrappings of religion and lay bare the kernel of universal truth supplied by reason, or rather, by natural instinct or 'common notions' (his version of *recta ratio*). He reflected the controversies of his age in his anti-Calvinist assertion of free-will and in his plea for the one infallible catholic 'church' of his five articles. To scriptural revelation Herbert assigned the diminished value of an historical document subject to critical scrutiny, but he by no means excluded direct revelation or intuition; there was, therefore, no inconsistency in his appealing for divine sanction to publish *De Veritate*. Herbert's summary of common notions in religion, though it became his most notorious legacy, was only a particular application of his very eclectic theory of knowledge and analysis of the criteria of truth. He exemplifies the position of those men who, not satisfied by traditional religion and critical of its excesses, wished to mediate between irreligious scepticism and what was often the ultimate phase of scepticism, irrational fideism. Like other transitional pioneers, Herbert was partly modern and partly not. The Bacon of metaphysics and epistemology, he stood as it were between Cicero and Kant. He was pre-scientific in identifying the principles of reason and religion, and he stopped far short of the sceptical deism of the Augustan age.

5

Orthodox champions of rational religion naturally stopped far short of Lord Herbert. Men of goodwill in all parties who, like Erasmus and Acontius, held by the New Testament as the charter of Christian liberty, could only deplore unchristian strife over non-essentials. Miscellaneous Anglicans such as Bacon, Selden, Joseph Hall, Ussher, Fuller, Browne, Hammond, and Taylor, and some liberal and especially Independent Puritans, such as Milton, and various radical and antinomian groups sought in their different ways for a faith based on fundamentals with a margin for disagreement, so that latitudinarianism cannot be too precisely defined. But the term is associated particularly with two schools, and the leaders of the first were 'the ever Memorable Mr John Hales of Eton College', William Chillingworth, and Lord Falkland, three friends who happened to be of small stature. ('It was an Age', says Clarendon, 'in which ther were many greate and wounderfull men of that size.')

John Hales (1584–1656), the oldest member of Falkland's philosophic circle, lives in common memory by his inalienable label, his eulogy of Shakespeare, and his farewell to Calvin.[1] 'He was', in Clarendon's words, 'one of the least men in the kingdome, and one of the greatest schollers in Europe.' Hales's place in his age was out of proportion to his meagre physique and meagre writings. He had more genial humanity than Chillingworth, but his religious outlook was similar. He 'exceedingly detested the tyranny of the Church of Rome', which had caused so many religious brawls, but he could also lay bare, in letters to Sir Dudley Carleton, what Clarendon summed up as 'the ignorance and passyon and animosity and injustice' of the Dutch Synod. Hales had little more trust than Selden in church councils and the Holy Ghost's attendance upon majorities. In his sermons and tracts he is always pleading for 'the unity of the Spirit in the Bond of Peace', the true unity of

---

[1] Hales, a graduate of Corpus Christi College, Oxford, in 1605 became a fellow of Merton and took orders, in 1615–19 was Regius Professor of Greek, and from 1613 to 1649 held a fellowship at Eton. He assisted Savile, the Provost of Eton, in the editing of Chrysostom (Wotton was Provost, 1624–39). Hales was, said Clarendon, 'the most separated from the worlde of any man then livinge', though he had visitors like Falkland and himself visited the wits in London; he has his niche in Suckling's *Sessions of the Poets*. As chaplain to Sir Dudley Carleton, Hales attended and reported on the Synod of Dort (1618–19). His *Tract Concerning Schism and Schismatics*, written apparently for Chillingworth *c*. 1636, circulated in manuscript and was published in 1642; though it did not find entire favour with Laud, Hales received a canonry at Windsor (1639). He was deprived of his canonry in 1642, of his fellowship in 1649, and spent his last years in retirement; necessity compelled him to sell most of his fine library. His writings were partly collected in *Golden Remains* (1659), edited by John Pearson (whose famous *Exposition of the Creed* appeared in the same year).

individual men who follow the plain guidance of Scripture and avoid vain speculation and debate about things not fundamental in the warfare of life. 'It was never the Intent of the Holy Ghost, to make it a matter of Wit and Subtilty, to know how to be saved.' 'Christ is our Aristotle.' The natural reason of the 'Ethnick Philosophers' brought them close to Christianity, and a Fabricius or a Regulus belongs as much to the Church of Christ as a Christian whose life falls short of his beliefs. Hales's emphasis on simple goodness does not forbid his use of such relatively neglected or dubious classics as Aeschylus, Thucydides, Euripides, Petronius, and Lucian. Like Chillingworth and Falkland, Hales was charged with Socinianism. Apart from Socinian tracts wrongly attributed to him, there was, for some minds, sufficient ground in his breadth of charity and common sense, in his linking of 'God and good Reason', in his dislike of formulated articles of faith, in his doubtful veneration for ecclesiastical history and the vested interests of religion, and in what he calls the freedom and gaiety of his 'open and uncautelous' temper. For a taste of the man let us quote a bit of nobly plain writing from his exculpatory letter to Laud. After citing Galen's assertion that he had followed truth and knowledge, not the opinion of the many, Hales says:

Some Title, some Claim I may justly lay to the Words of this excellent Person; for the Pursuit of Truth hath been my only Care, ever since I first understood the Meaning of the Word. For this, I have forsaken all Hopes, all Friends, all Desires, which might biass me, and hinder me from driving right at what I aimed. For this, I have spent my Mony, my Means, my Youth, my Age, and all I have; that I might remove from my self that Censure of Tertullian,— *Suo vitio quis quid ignorat.* If with all this Cost and Pains, my Purchase is but Error; I may safely say, to err hath cost me more, than it has many to find the Truth: And Truth it self shall give me this Testimony at last, that if I have missed of her, it is not my Fault, but my Misfortune.

Among the frequenters of Lord Falkland's house in the sixteen-thirties were Chillingworth, John Earle, Henry Hammond, George Morley, and Gilbert Sheldon (a high percentage of future bishops!), Edward Hyde, later Earl of Clarendon, and possibly Selden and Hobbes. A friend and frequent neighbour was George Sandys, to whom Falkland wrote several poems. In a sea of passionate prejudice and conflict Great Tew was an island of informed and rational discussion, and Clarendon's pictures of the young poet-scholar and his friends convey a rare and gracious urbanity. There was, however, intellectual and spiritual distress in that semi-collegiate Arcadia. We think of Falkland as the example *par excellence* of the noble and philosophical cavalier, the moderate royalist and Anglican who saw faults on both sides, and whose heart was to be divided and broken by the civil war.[1] The personal charm and integrity of soul which kindled an unwonted glow in the memory of Clarendon was combined with a restless desire for truth and assured conviction. It was partly inborn but, like that of Donne (whose rational faith Falkland praised in verse), it was heightened by the circumstances of his life—the domestic discord in which he grew up, his dislike of the self-seeking world of his father, the religious satisfaction of his Catholic (and argumentative) mother and of his Anglican wife, his troubled contemplation of growing religious and political strife, his aristocratic and idealistic bias towards King and Church, his instincts for both thought and action, his consciousness of personal abilities not put to use, his reasonable and ineffectual devotion to a policy frustrated by extremists. But Falkland's *Of the Infallibility of the Church of Rome* (printed in 1645), while it testifies to his serious study, is less important than *The Religion of Protestants a Safe Way to Salvation* (1637), on which Chillingworth worked at Great Tew and in which he expounded views similar to his host's.

---

[1] Lucius Cary (1610?–43), who became the second Viscount Falkland in 1633, was the son of a successful courtier and unsuccessful Lord Deputy of Ireland and a devoutly Catholic mother of literary, masculine, and eccentric character. He spent his boyhood in Oxfordshire, studied at Cambridge for a short time, went to Ireland with his parents in 1622, graduated from Trinity College, Dublin, in 1625, was knighted by his father in 1626, and returned to England in 1628–9. His friendship with Sir Henry Morison (d. 1629), son of an official in Ireland and nephew of Fynes Moryson, was celebrated in Jonson's famous ode, and Cary himself paid tribute in elegies. Early in 1630 Cary married his friend's sister Lettice. Estranged thereby from his father, he tried military service in Holland, and then retired to the country to read Greek. His father's death (1633) took him to London, where he renewed his friendship with the wits and 'his Noble Father, Mr Jonson', but most of the time from 1631 to 1639 he lived at Great Tew, studying religious problems and discoursing with friends from Oxford and London. Falkland left this retreat to take part in the Bishops' War (1639), and in 1640 he entered Parliament. With Hyde he laboured in vain to preserve constitutional monarchy, a reformed Church of England, and peace. He was persuaded to become, in January 1642, a Privy Councillor and Secretary of State. When war broke out Falkland lost all desire to live, and he found a welcome death at the first battle of Newbury (20 September 1643).

In politics Chillingworth was an absolute royalist, though in a sermon to the court at Oxford he boldly condemned the sins of the cavaliers.¹ In religion he had even more cause than Falkland to seek authority, since he for a time had gone over to Rome. He was perhaps in part the victim of his own dialectical instinct and skill, yet his religious shifts were made, as the not wholly sympathetic Clarendon bore witness, with entire sincerity and candour; 'all his doubtes grew out of himselfe' and he was 'in all his Sallyes and retreits his owne converte'. As a philosophic theologian Chillingworth is no Hooker, but he brings earnest conviction, trenchant logic, and exemplary controversial fairness to a denial of Roman authority and infallibility and a plea for scriptural Christianity. 'The Bible, I say, The Bible only is the Religion of Protestants!' 'Universall Tradition directs you to the Word of God, and the Word of God directs you to Heaven.' The difference between a Papist and a Protestant is 'that the one judges his guide to be infallible, the other his way to be manifest', and the way to heaven is no narrower now than Christ left it. Like Andrewes, Laud (in his *Conference with Fisher*), and Hales, Chillingworth refuses an exact formulation of the fundamentals of faith, since

it is sufficient for any mans salvation, to beleeve that the Scripture is true, and containes all things necessary for salvation; and to doe his best endeavour to find and beleeve the true sense of it.

So Chillingworth is not a special apologist for the Church of England (though he later wrote in defence of episcopacy), and on his death-bed, tormented by the Presbyterian Cheynell, he would neither absolve nor condemn Turks, Papists, and

¹ William Chillingworth (1602–44) was the son of an Oxford citizen and the godson of Laud. He became a scholar and fellow of Trinity College, Oxford (1618, 1628). Under the persuasions of the Jesuit Fisher he turned Catholic and went to Douai (1630). Laud exerted tactful influence, and the next year Chillingworth returned to England and later to Protestantism, though he did not subscribe to the Articles until he accepted preferment at Salisbury in 1638. His book was written in defence of Christopher Potter of Queen's College, who had been in controversy with Edward Knott, a Jesuit. Chillingworth's change of heart, and his book, drew a number of Romanist attacks. In 1643 he was at the siege of Gloucester and invented 'an Engyne' with the pacifistic notion of hastening the end of the war. Then, like Fuller, he joined Hopton's army. He fell ill, was captured at Arundel Castle, and died at Chichester early in 1644. In his last days he was tended, and badgered, by the Presbyterian Francis Cheynell, who in a recent treatise had (like Knott) accused him of Socinianism; Cheynell threw a copy of *The Religion of Protestants* into Chillingworth's grave as a prelude to a polemical sermon. All this Cheynell himself recounted in a pamphlet.

Socinians. Against the tyrannous and specious unity of Rome he sets the flexible diversity of biblical Protestantism, 'For why should men be more rigid than God?' If we wonder at the charge of Socinianism, we must recognize that Knott and Cheynell alike were right in their sense of the dangers latent in Chillingworth's constant appeals to reason. While he thinks reason will convince all but the perverse that the Bible is God's word, we can imagine the perverse carrying beyond the author's premisses such dicta as these:

Now nothing is more repugnant, than that a man should be required to give most certain credit unto that which cannot be made appear most certainly credible. . . . And for you to require a strength of credit beyond the appearance of the objects credibilitie, is all one as if you should require me to goe ten miles an houre upon a horse that will goe but five.

In fact Hobbes, who admired Chillingworth's intellectual powers and doubtless his plain, vigorous prose, exclaimed to Aubrey: 'But by God, he is like some lusty fighters that will give a damnable back-blow now and then on their owne party.'

Tillotson saw in Chillingworth 'the glory of this Age and Nation', a martyr in the cause of reasonable religion against 'Fancy and Enthusiasm'. Although Chillingworth, Hales, and Falkland attacked Rome, they were not welcomed as allies by Puritans. The Puritan attitude towards the Church of England was parallel to that of orthodox Anglicans towards Rome. From the first the Puritans, whether conformists or not, also appealed to Scripture and antiquity and demanded a Church purified from the Roman abuses, the Roman ritual, the Roman hierarchy, and, in Laud's time, the Roman Inquisition, of the Establishment. Doubtless nothing could have averted the sectarian revolt, but its force and extent might have been lessened if the national genius for compromise, of which the *via media* has been on the whole an illustrious example, had been working sympathetically. Puritan zeal, whatever its errors, was a rebuke to the Anglican lethargy that Andrewes deplored. His friend Bacon, in the *Better Pacification of the Church of England* (1604; reprinted in 1641), the earlier *Advertisement* (published in 1640), and the essay 'Of Unity in Religion' (1612–25), urged internal reform of the Church and conciliation on both sides. But the gulf grew too wide to be bridged. It was not easy for

men who had inherited the idea of absolute truth and its corollary, uniformity, to think of the seamless robe as a coat of many
colours. Hence, as Taylor said, every sect damned all but itself
and it was damned by 499 other sects. Too many men in all
parties fell short of even that measure of tolerance attained by
the perhaps apocryphal modern clergyman who remarked to
the dissenting minister: 'After all, we both serve the same
Master, you in your way and I in His.' To Puritan extremists
the Anglican appeal to ecclesiastical tradition and the beauty
of order meant as little as the sacred abstractions of Burke meant
to Paine; and the view of the sectaries held by many Anglicans
(and Presbyterians) was the same as that of Donne quoted
earlier in this chapter. Yet not all 'enthusiasm' was dogmatical.
There was the leaven, especially potent from about 1640 onward, of more or less mystical or antinomian thought and feeling represented by some of the sects, notably the Quakers, by
the diffusion of Boehme's and kindred books, and by such
individuals as John Everard, John Saltmarsh, William Walwyn,
and Gerrard Winstanley; and theological and ecclesiastical
differences melted away before the inner light. But our concern
is with the more central line of argument. We have seen the
broad basis for toleration laid down by Chillingworth and his
fellows, and that of the Cambridge Platonists we shall soon see;
here we may observe the effect of the struggle to survive carried
on by two large minority groups, the Presbyterians and Independents.

The battle for religious freedom may be said to have become
a bitter and conspicuous fact in 1637, with the brutal punishment of John Bastwick, Henry Burton, and William Prynne.
Especially after 1640 there was a flood of pamphlets, from the
Smectymnuus group, Milton, Lord Brooke, Henry Parker,
Thomas Goodwin and his fellows, Henry Robinson, Roger
Williams, John Goodwin, John Lilburne, Richard Overton,
William Walwyn, Samuel Richardson, and others. Some of
these names have appeared in our chapter on political thought,
and they indicate how far the tide of agitation spread beyond
anti-prelacy. Whatever their particular and often conflicting
aims, Puritans in general were inspired by the vision of a
Christian society, and the first steps towards realization were
the purifying or abolishing of the Laudian Church. We must
skip the somewhat dusty conflict with the bishops, though its

larger implications were visible at least to Milton and Lord Brooke (who, by the way, seem to have echoed each other). A little later toleration, which, as distinguished from comprehensive unity, had had few proponents, appeared as a definite and prominent issue. There is irony in the fact that this battle was not against the Establishment but against the Presbyterians who had overthrown it. When the Westminster Assembly settled down, in the latter half of 1643, to consider the reorganization of the Church, the Presbyterians' confident plans for national uniformity received a jolt. Five 'dissenting brethren', who had conducted self-governing congregations abroad and had the prestige of religious exiles, asked, with no thought of starting trouble, that they be allowed to carry on their old ways under the new régime. Their leader was Thomas Goodwin, a notable disciple of John Preston and Richard Sibbes. Failing in the Assembly, the five Independent divines appealed to Parliament and public opinion in *An Apologetical Narration* (January 1644). Roger Williams, in his *Queries of Highest Consideration* (February), promptly opposed their admission of civil interference and their limited view of religious freedom. Henry Robinson, a friend of Hartlib and Walwyn, a travelled man of business, and an apostle of commercial expansion and free trade, in *Liberty of Conscience* (March) and other tracts urged the necessity of Christian liberty and peace and the wicked folly of coercion, whether Presbyterian or civil. In July Williams contributed his bold and famous plea, *The Bloody Tenent of Persecution*; his concern for liberty of conscience and the spirituality of religion had the effect of secularizing the State and of affirming the natural rights of man. The Presbyterians, including Milton's Adam Stewart, Rutherford, and 'shallow Edwards', and of course the heroic, indefatigable, and exasperating Prynne, busily defended their position, now and later; to most of them toleration meant anarchy and libertinism. One of the ablest pleas for Independent liberty and toleration was the *Theomachia* (October) of John Goodwin, 'the great Red Dragon of Coleman streete'. In proclaiming, like others, the right of discussion and inquiry, the right of divine truth to be heard, even at the risk of error, Goodwin approached a greater man who had been learning that new presbyter was but old priest writ large. In *Areopagitica* (November) Milton turned aside from his main theme, freedom of the press, to plead for charity

in matters of conscience. The relatively small effect of *Areopagitica*—and of most of Milton's other tracts—is one indication
of the popular style that paper warfare had as usual developed;
Milton, though he moved in that direction, was rather too
academic and isolated to catch the public ear. In 1645 Joshua
Sprigg (the admiring chronicler of Fairfax's generalship) published the anonymous *The Ancient Bounds, or Liberty of Conscience*,
a remarkably broad and humane argument for toleration. As
the debate went on it was given a stronger political and democratic turn by the Levellers, Lilburne, Walwyn, and Overton,
but that does not concern us here. The Independent campaign
for toleration, even if its early motive was only anti-Presby-
terian, soon resulted, through Cromwell, in more security for
various religious groups than they enjoyed until 1689. Despite
the setback after 1660, it may be said that by that date toleration had been firmly established as both a religious and a
secular principle, thanks to these writers and others from D'Ewes
to Jeremy Taylor, from Vane to Harrington.

6

During these turbulent years the mainly Puritan group of
Cambridge Platonists were trying to open a broad and solid
road of rational religion that would avoid the deserts or quick-
sands of controversial dogmatism, irrational 'enthusiasm', and,
later, mechanistic science. But before we come to them we may
look at a minor and a major Platonist who, as philosophic
essayists rather than philosophers, made no very positive contribution to the movement, although they are more familiar to
most of us than the Cambridge men. The first is William
Drummond of Hawthornden (1585–1649). *A Cypress Grove*
(1623), a much-revised version of *A Midnight's Trance* (published in 1619; written probably in 1612–14), was a half-poetical
meditation on death, a natural product of its author's religious
and melancholy temper. Among his late additions were half the
scientific items in the account (quoted in the preceding chapter)
of the bewilderment brought about by the new astronomy.
Being the work of Drummond, and an elaborate mosaic of the
great commonplaces of the theme, the essay is full of echoes—
Seneca, *Hamlet*, Bacon, Donne's *Anniversaries*, Hayward's *Sanctuary of a Troubled Soul*, Sylvester's *Memorials of Mortality* (and
its original, Pierre Matthieu's *Tablettes*), Guevara, Granada,

Montaigne, Charron, and others. Drummond finds relief from the weight of man's frailty and misery and fear of death in Christian Platonism, in rhapsodical contemplation of 'the Arts-master of the World' and the soul's return to its source, to 'a vision of the Divine essence' and a changeless eternity.

The second of our irregular Platonists, Sir Thomas Browne (1605–82), we have met before in his scientific capacity. He took a place in literature—even to the extent of receiving an immediate commentary, Sir Kenelm Digby's—with his first and central book, *Religio Medici*, which he wrote in 1634–5, when his pulse had not yet 'beate thirty yeares'. It circulated in manuscript and in 1642 was printed in two surreptitious editions; an authorized edition appeared in 1643. But for references to his age and a kind of winning *naïveté*, one might suppose the gravely reflective and rambling author to be near three-score and ten. While most young physicians would be absorbed in professional concerns, Browne is intent upon taking stock of his relations with God and man. Although he was not writing for publication, his antipathy to theological and sectarian strife links him with the liberals who were trying to bring men back to the fundamentals of faith. He warned his readers that his book was 'a private exercise directed to my selfe', not a guide for others nor 'an immutable law' even to his own advancing judgement; that many things in it were 'delivered Rhetorically' or 'meerely Tropical' and were 'not to be called unto the rigid test of reason'; and he affirmed his entire deference to the 'maturer discernments' of the learned. In *Pseudodoxia Epidemica* (1646) Browne was a scientist exploring his own domain and did not need to be so apologetic, but in the *Religio* he was making an amateur's contribution to the problem of the century, the problem of knowledge and ignorance, authority and faith. We might, however, still expect a religious and philosophic man of science, fresh from continental study and writing while the *Discours de la Méthode* was being incubated, to grapple directly with the primary questions which had long been coming to the front. But, apart from its atmosphere, there is little in the book that might not have been uttered generations, even centuries, before. There is, too, more caprice than systematic reasoning; allusions to science are relatively few and casual; and many of the questions Browne loves to raise are of the kind propounded by the village atheist. Yet the book remains not only a literary treasure but a religious and philosophic testimony far more truly alive than many works historians of philosophy discuss.

Browne is neither a village atheist nor, in any formidable sense, a philosophic sceptic. His reason is much too 'soft and flexible', too 'extravagant and irregular', to arrive anywhere; his favourite image is a circle. He has, nevertheless, breathed sceptical air, and his consciousness of the *Zeitgeist*, while it does not disturb his faith, is just strong enough to demand a positive statement of it. We are (to echo Bottom) put out of fear at the beginning, for we are assured that the *medicus* is not a Pyrrhonist but Browne the believer. Despite the general scandal of his profession and his own religious pacifism, he is a thoroughly orthodox Christian; a Protestant, though he would prefer a less belligerent name and though he can 'never heare the Ave-Marie Bell without an elevation'; an Englishman who feels at home in any foreign land—because he is 'in England every where'!—and an Anglican who feels completely at home in a church that seems to have been framed to his particular devotion. It is no wonder that he can let his reason 'play and expatiate' in the realm of 'opinion', boldly challenging windmills, while his soul goes its serene way. 'In Philosophy where truth seems double-faced, there is no man more paradoxicall then my self: but in Divinity I love to keepe the road. . . .' Far from falling into any modern scientific infidelities, Browne cannot charge his youth with anything worse than three old, innocent, and generous errors. Though he regards his reason as a highly critical instrument, one of its chief functions is to start birds for faith to shoot down, and they are mostly tame birds. One must quote the most familiar and illuminating passage in the book:

As for those wingy mysteries in Divinity, and ayery subtilties of Religion, which have unhing'd the braines of better heads, they never stretch the *Pia Mater* of mine; me thinkes there be not impossibilities enough in Religion for an active faith; the deepest mysteries ours containes have not only been illustrated, but maintained, by syllogisme, and the rule of reason: I love to lose my selfe in a mystery, to pursue my Reason to an *oh altitudo*. 'Tis my solitary recreation to pose my apprehension with those involved aenigma's and riddles of the Trinity, with Incarnation, and Resurrection. I can answer all the objections of Satan, and my rebellious reason with that odde resolution I learned of Tertullian, *Certum est, quia impossibile est.*

I desire to exercise my faith in the difficultest points, for to credit ordinary and visible objects is not faith but perswasion.

This is not quite Chillingworth's 'Religion of Protestants'. And Browne's 'Ultra-Fidianism' (as Coleridge called it) is the easier for him, and the more intelligible to us, because he is 'naturally inclined to that, which misguided zeale termes superstition'.

The modern rationalist may be disappointed when our man of science so willingly subdues his reason to the will of faith, and when he refuses 'to pry into the maze' of God's counsels and prefers to wait for the ultimate revelation of heaven. But in this 'obscurantist' attitude he is at one with most religious—and scientific—Englishmen from Donne to Milton. He differs, however, from many of these in the positive and even genial delight with which he faces mysteries just because they are mysteries. For Browne more truly than for Donne, all divinity is love or wonder. He is 'content to understand a mystery without a rigid definition, in an easie and Platonick description'. The word of God is both a final authority and a book of riddles, and Browne's religious meditations are both a sober confession of belief and a solemn game. He can speak, with the accent of experience, of the battle of Lepanto raging within him, but amorous impulses can hardly have been troublesome, and the conquest of his other passions has left him unheated and unscarred. His religious faith, though earnest, spacious, and exalted, is not itself an intense passion. He loves to contemplate things mystical, but he is not a mystic. The firmness of his faith and the limitations of his reason, his common sense and equanimity, perhaps also the consciousness of both his own merits and his own insignificance, forbid his moving into either extreme scepticism or extreme evangelicalism. So he does not perceive, or at any rate does not discuss philosophically, the central problems of reason and faith. And yet his instinctive intuitional idealism contains an all-embracing answer. What occasion for doubt, argument, agitation, or strife can offer itself to a placid but God-possessed scholar and scientist for whom man is a true microcosm, 'this visible World . . . but a picture of the invisible', the whole variegated universe a divine symphony, the scale of being a mighty diapason, and even vulgar tavern music a reminder of the First Composer? 'Nature is the Art of God' and God is both transcendent and immanent—in the Hermetic description that Browne cherishes, the circle whose centre is everywhere and whose circumference nowhere. He studies the Artist's works, great and small, but he is no pantheist; he can never 'so forget God, as to adore the name of Nature'. He does not need to be stirred by miraculous contraventions of nature when the whole normal order is a stupendous mystery and his own quiet life a miracle of thirty years. 'Wee carry with us the wonders we seeke without us: There is all Africa and her prodigies in us.' 'There is surely a peece of Divinity in us, something that was before the Elements, and owes no homage unto the Sun.' Yet the almost buoyant reverence with which Browne contemplates the mysteries of life does not lessen his sense of death as both fearful and desirable.

Phrases already quoted suggest the imaginative and symbolic quality of Browne's Platonism, and, however much he owes to Stoicism, scholasticism, and other sources, and to his study of comparative religion, it is the Platonic strain (with all its 'impurity') that broadens, deepens, and sweetens his religious thought and feeling. To an even greater degree than in other men, Christian Platonism fosters in him a charitable, undogmatic tolerance. It is man, not God, who has multiplied articles of belief and dispute. 'The Foundations of Religion are already established, and the principles of Salvation subscribed unto by all, there remaine not many controversies worth a passion.' Although the centre of Browne's religion is salvation through Christ, it is the Christian Platonist who sees hell not as a fiery gulf but as the heart of man when Lucifer inhabits it, and who sees heaven, not as a city of 'Emeralds, Chrysolites, and precious stones', but in the soul that is filled with God, 'though within the circle of this sensible world'. It is the Christian Platonist who thinks continually of the soul imprisoned in its earthy house. And Browne is very truly Platonic in seeing humanity as 'a composition of man and beast, wherein we must endeavour to be as the Poets faigne that wise man Chiron, that is, to have the Region of Man above that of Beast, and sense to sit but at the feete of reason'. This ethical seriousness unites with religious faith to give Browne the four-square solidity of traditional Christian humanism, so that, no matter where his faculty of wonder may lead him, he never loses himself in a cloud; 'there is an edge in all firme beliefe'.

Another element in Browne that prevents his mystical impulses from evaporating in mist is his wit, which ranges from

pregnant ingenuity to sublimity: 'for all this masse of flesh that
wee behold, came in at our mouths; this frame wee looke upon,
hath beene upon our trenchers; In briefe, we have devoured
our selves'; 'And in this sense, I say, the world was before the
Creation, and at an end before it had a beginning; and thus was
I dead before I was alive; though my grave be England, my
dying place was Paradise, and Eve miscarried of mee before
she conceiv'd of Cain.' Such metaphysical wit is by definition
an instinct for paradoxical contrasts, or rather for arresting
analogies, and, as in the poets, realistic particularity barbs the
imaginative and emotional arrow.

Finally, Browne's 'mystical' ecstasies are not merely intro-
spective expansiveness, they are conditioned by his immense
and eclectic reading. His originality is in the chemical, or
alchemical, results of his curious and loving assimilation. His
ideas may become 'important' when expounded by other men;
in him they are important as the revelation of a temperament,
a temperament both individual and typical. Browne seems to
be 'a masse of Antipathies'—love of life and disdain of life,
devout piety and innocent scepticism, encyclopaedic thirst and
obscurantist 'superstition', scientific exactness and figurative
vagueness, sublime imagination and eccentric fancy, cosmopolitan breadth and English insularity, unambitious modesty
and amiable egotism, bookish pedantry and bookish humour.
. . . But beneath the surface Browne is a completely harmonious
microcosm of an age of contradictions.

Religio Medici quickly won fame abroad as well as at home.
In 1646 Browne gave birth to his Colossus, *Pseudodoxia Epidemica*,
and then for a decade he forsook authorship. Those years at
Norwich, devoted to his profession and his wide-ranging private
studies, his family and his learned friends, were the years
of Cromwell's rise and reign, but the antiquary and poet
could always withdraw into a timeless world of his own. In
1658, the troubled year of the Protector's death, Browne
published *Hydriotaphia: Urn-Burial* together with *The Garden of
Cyrus*.

In *Hydriotaphia*, inspired by the discovery of some 'sad and
sepulchral Pitchers' in a field of old Walsingham, Browne
unrolled a tapestry of curious lore about the burial customs of
all times and countries; his exotic learning and prodigal imagination and fancy were ordered and solemnized by a greatly

traditional and uniquely congenial theme. Against a sumptuously ironic background of funeral pomps, Browne contemplates death, the vanity of the world and earthly monuments, and the glory of Christian immortality. The grand and magical note is sounded in the first words of the dedication, 'When the Funerall pyre was out, and the last valediction over . . .'. The second sentence—which proved to be a prophetic one—points clearly to one major influence on Browne's style, the Bible: 'But who knows the fate of his bones, or how often he is to be buried? who hath the Oracle of his ashes, or whether they are to be scattered?' The theme evokes the ripest thoughts and emotions of a Christian, a poet, and a doctor whose study was life and death and who daily beheld examples of mortality. Many men of Browne's century, to go no farther back, had written greatly of death, but the last chapter of this work is surely, as many readers have said, the most magnificent thing of its kind, outside the Bible, in English prose—the last great outcry, an impressionist might say, of the dying Renaissance against devouring Time. And yet, in yielding to the intoxication of Browne's words and music, we should not miss the profoundly Christian character of his prose poetry. De Quincey and Landor, for instance, weave romantic visions and elaborate harmonies about the theme of death, but Browne, like Shakespeare, Ralegh, and their fellows, has a far more robust, more religious, and, in a good sense, more prosaic heritage. He feels the pull of both earth and heaven, the greatness and the littleness of the sons of Adam: 'But man is a Noble Animal, splendid in ashes, and pompous in the grave, solemnizing Nativities and Deaths with equall lustre, nor omitting Ceremonies of bravery, in the infamy of his nature.'

The Garden of Cyrus has suffered much more than Hydriotaphia from our failure to understand the analogical and hieroglyphic modes of apprehension which Browne shared with notable thinkers (who did not share his imaginative and expressive power). In the Garden, starting from horticulture and observation, Browne traces the figure of the quincunx and the number five through all things artificial, natural, and mystical, from the 'elegant ordination of vegetables' to the 'mysticall Mathematicks of the City of Heaven'; and the modern reader is likely to skip to the last page and surrender, with no more comprehension, to the hypnotic climax of 'inexcusable Pythagorisme'.

But recent insights have defined Browne's Platonic theme and its close and contrasting relation with that of *Hydriotaphia*. At the end of the fourth chapter of the *Garden* Browne invoked the congenial image in the *Timaeus* of two intersecting circles, an image which suggests the nature and unity of the two works and of his total vision. The two are complementary meditations on death and life, body and soul, matter and form, time and space, and other parallel and opposed concepts which come together only in the mind of God, in Eternity and Unity, where darkness and light are one. The funeral urn has the shape of the womb, and death is 'the Lucina of life'. In *Hydriotaphia*, 'Pious spirits who passed their dayes in raptures of futurity, made little more of this world than the world that was before it, while they lay obscure in the Chaos of pre-ordination, and night of their fore-beings', and in this life they may anticipate heaven through 'the kisse of the Spouse, gustation of God, and ingression into the divine shadow'. So in the *Garden*, seeds that lie within their husks in perpetual shades will break forth into life under the sun, the light that is 'but the shadow of God'. Both meditations arrive, by different roads, at the same end, death giving birth to life, to the resurrection, the littleness of temporal being and vainglory to 'the extasie of being ever'. We might say that the two discourses, or poems, are parallel to Donne's *Anniversaries* (though more alive and potent); or, since the *Garden* is also a cosmology, that they form a seventeenth-century and Christian *Timaeus*.

Probably in 1656 Browne had composed another and less formal discourse on life and death, *A Letter to a Friend* (printed posthumously in 1690). This recorded the observations of a doctor at the bedside of a dying man (who was, according to a persuasive argument, the young Robert Loveday, a minor writer and translator of La Calprenède). It is unique as a medical report, and in its physical basis and metaphysical glosses it shows perhaps even more clearly than other works the amphibian character of the author, who passes so readily, half-unconsciously, between divided and distinguished worlds. Strands of Brownesque purple, the commonplaces of mortality, are set off with bits of 'strange Pathology' from Hippocrates, Pliny, Cardan, and the rest, and Dante. In style the *Letter* is far from the homeliness of Browne's correspondence; even the most professional statement may approach an incantation:

'Omnibonus Ferrarius in mortal Dysenteries of Children looks for a Spot behind the Ear.' The diction may be plain or heavily latinized, but the rhythm commonly moves on Browne's middle level. In the *Letter* he writes: 'The long habit of Living makes meer Men more hardly to part with Life, and all to be nothing, but what is to come'; in *Hydriotaphia* we get: 'But the long habit of living indisposeth us for dying; When Avarice makes us the sport of death; When even David grew politickly cruell; and Solomon could hardly be said to be the wisest of men.'

The injunctions of the second part of the *Letter* were incorporated in *Christian Morals* (printed in 1716). This book, put together we do not know when, seems to have been designed as a continuation of *Religio Medici*. The belated sequel offers the fruit of age and experience (and the commonplace book) in aphoristic, objective, and oracular wisdom, practical in aim and unpractical in effect; and, if we still find wit, we miss the intimate charm, the questionings, the imagination, emotion, and inlaid beauty of the early work. There Browne had remarked that 'truely there are singular pieces in the Philosophy of Zeno, and doctrine of the Stoickes, which I perceive, delivered in a Pulpit, pass for currant Divinity'. The didactic purpose of *Christian Morals* brings out the strain of Christian Stoicism that was strong in Browne as in many writers of his time. But the biblical and Senecan moralist and stylist largely obscure the metaphysical poet.

Even this sketch has indicated that Browne's style did not evolve from comparative plainness of rhythm and language to mature richness; it must be considered in terms of decorum rather than chronology. While we cannot go into the technicalities of his varied patterns of syntax and sound, which have been minutely studied, it can be said that his basic texture is Senecan and that it partakes of both the 'curt' and the loose or 'libertine' kinds. Thus *Christian Morals*, a sort of Christianized version of Proverbs, and in the tradition of Felltham's *Resolves* and Quarles's *Enchiridion*, is a sustained example of the curt style of clipped parallel and antithetical clauses. The scientific exposition of *Pseudodoxia Epidemica* and the personal reflections of *Religio Medici* are on Browne's more typical 'low' or 'middle' level; the normal texture, however deliberate in composition compared with the artless utterance of Browne's letters, has the libertine naturalness of man thinking aloud. But, in keeping with the variety of theme and emotional tone, the *Religio* ranges from the curt style—illustrated in the sentences quoted above as examples of 'wit'—to the exalted and metrical 'and groane in the expectation of that great Jubilee'. On Browne's highest level, in the fifth chapter of *Hydriotaphia* and the conclusion and other parts of *The Garden of Cyrus*, Senecan, Platonic, Hebraic, and Christian elements of style and feeling are fused in richly allusive and figurative patterns of phrase and sound. Thus a general paradox, 'But man is a Noble Animal', is amplified in several further paradoxes increasing in length, particularity, and inner complication of antitheses, and in a counterpoint of rising and falling rhythm. But neither adjectives nor analysis can go very far in explaining the sublimity of Browne's meditations on death and life and light and darkness. Who can speak of it without a solecism, or think thereof without an ecstasy?

One prime feature of Browne's diction and rhythm is the combining of Saxon and classical derivatives. Sometimes his classicized language is technical (one of his most useful coinages was 'electricity'). Sometimes it is only the product of bilingual habit, as in 'the Pensill or hanging gardens of Babylon', where he takes over the *pensiles* of Lipsius (book two of *De Constantia*) and other writers. When the language overtops the idea we have inflation and 'quaintness', 'Emphatically extending that Elegant expression of Scripture: Thou hast curiously embroydered me'—though even then Browne has his own vitality and colour. But the use of such doublets, which had begun with Caxton and others as a primitive way of enriching English, had attained a functional beauty in the *Book of Common Prayer*, and Browne's combinations are functional in the same way and often touch the same level. A very simple specimen is: 'Every man is not a proper Champion for Truth, nor fit to take up the Gantlet in the cause of Veritie.' The Saxon 'Truth' supplies the plain sense, which is complete in the first clause; but the second, ending in the Latin 'Veritie', contributes more than half of the total effect through its fulfilment of both rhythmic expectation and the chivalric metaphor. A more complex example is the sentence already cited from *Hydriotaphia*: most of the words that support the pretensions of little man are Latin, most of those that declare his mortality are English. In general, Browne's polysyllables carry an aura of tradition, of august remoteness and pomp; we are gathered with him into the artifice of eternity. Yet his most splendid effects owe much of their slow, weighted music to the homely strength of Saxon—'Grave-stones tell truth scarce fourty years'.

7

The manifestations of Platonism in our period, as in every other, were of a protean diversity and an essential similarity. Sir Thomas Browne and the Puritan Lord Brooke, Henry More and Milton were unwitting allies. There was a Platonic strain in Lord Herbert, in his conception of the universe as a harmonious organism and of the correspondences between it and man, and his 'common notions' are akin to the 'truths of natural inscription' of the Cambridge Platonists. But the main Platonist movement was strongly Christian and to a large degree Puritan. Some Puritan divines approached Platonism through their rationalistic adaptation of Ramist logic to Calvinist theology. The seventeenth century inherited an eclectic Platonic tradition which was generally more rational and ethical than mystical, and once again Platonism helped to fuse theology and philosophy, Christian faith and humanistic reason, and to uphold idealism against scepticism and 'enthusiasm', empiricism and dogmatism. In *The Nature of Truth* (1640), Lord Brooke (1608–43) found his way out of the apparent disunity and multiplicity of the soul and knowledge and the world through trust in right reason and comprehension of the single, all-embracing reality, God, and the divine unity and harmony of all being, which is but one emanation from Him. Brooke's range of reference is almost as broad as his theme—Galileo, Kepler, and Copernicus, the Bible, Plato, and Ficino, Bacon and Lord Herbert, Sir John Davies and Suckling, Thomas Goodwin and John Cotton. And, with such a spacious and unifying vision, Brooke could not be intolerant; he saw all spiritual rivers flowing towards the infinite sea.

A similar vision of divine unity was proclaimed by the more rhapsodical Peter Sterry (1613–72), Lord Brooke's chaplain and later Cromwell's, and a noted Independent preacher. Sterry has philosophic and latitudinarian affinities with the Cambridge Platonists and is commonly grouped with them. He was one of their generation at Emmanuel College, and he retained the esteem of Whichcote till his death; and he was named by Baxter as a representative of that 'mixture of Platonisme, Origenisme & Arianisme' which was more rational than scriptural. Yet Sterry stands somewhat apart. In his chief work he opposes free-will, and his argument is inspired much less by reason than by a Christian and Platonic passion for the reality and ideal beauty of the divine love and goodness which unifies all creation, which is the very principle of being, and in which 'liberty and necessity meet in one'. This doctrine leads him towards the Coleridgean view of the imagination as the faculty that 'espouseth in it self the spiritual and corporeal world to each other'; God Himself is the supreme Poet. Like some other men of his time, Sterry is on the borderland between mysticism and enthusiasm. He has a remarkably wide knowledge of literature and philosophy ancient and modern, religious and secular, and his central idea gives a kind of sanction for drawing his imagery not only from the Bible but from the classics and allegorized myth, from painting and other arts, and from nature. His luxuriantly figurative utterance is quite instinctive, as his letters show, and it has beauty, but it may become oppressive.

Whether or not we include Sterry among the Cambridge Platonists, Christian Platonism owed its characteristic temper and philosophic importance to the academic group—Benjamin Whichcote (1609–83), Henry More (1614–87), John Smith (1616?–52), Ralph Cudworth (1617–88), and Nathanael Culverwel (1618/19–51?); and such allied figures as John Worthington (1618–71), the editor of Joseph Mead and John Smith and a translator of Thomas à Kempis, and Jeremy Taylor's friend, George Rust (c. 1626?–70). Except More, who entered Christ's College just before Milton left it, and Rust, who graduated from St. Catharine's Hall and became a fellow of Christ's, all of these men were educated in the great nursery of Puritan thought, Emmanuel College. Like the scientists who formed the nucleus of the Royal Society, the Cambridge divines were brought into fuller personal association by the civil war; later the centre of gravity moved from Emmanuel to Christ's. These latitudinarian Platonists shared with Lord Falkland's Oxonian group the desire to find a peaceful *via media*, but the Cambridge men tried to lay a broader philosophic foundation in ground that was more and more dangerously undermined. Illuminated by belief in the unity of truth, the ordered harmony of God's universe, the active reality of spirit, and the 'deiform' nature and freedom of man, they found in these conceptions a fullness, strength, and inwardness of rational faith which raised them above bitter contention, above both enthusiasm and ritualism, above the hard determinism first of Calvin and later of Hobbes. Some of these ideas appeared in *A Greek in the Temple* (1641) by John Sherman, who preached at Trinity about 1635–40.

Whichcote, the seminal spirit if one can be named, was more of a scriptural latitudinarian than a positive Platonist.[1] The admiring Bishop Burnet recorded that Whichcote had sent his students to 'Plato, Tully, and Plotin', and in 1651 his former tutor, Tuckney, made such interests a ground of reproach. In reply Whichcote avowed his debt to the philosophers but declared that he had given much more time to Calvin, Perkins, and Beza. He stands, in fact, with Hales, in the line of Christian humanists that goes back through Hooker and Erasmus. Whichcote brings his own pure, strong, and winning spirituality to a rational, ethical, and practical religion, the knowledge, love, and imitation of God. He is typical of the main tradition of Christian humanism in expressly repudiating the 'Mystical, Symbolical, Ænigmatical, Emblematical'. Whichcote was fond, as Tuckney complained, of the phrase from Proverbs xx. 27, 'The spirit of man is the candle of the Lord', the phrase that became the hall-mark of the Cambridge Platonists. And the candle of the Lord is not simply the gift of divine grace arbitrarily bestowed upon the impotent elect, nor is it a private and uncertain inner light (still less is the whole verse what Bacon, at the beginning of the *Advancement of Learning*, had taken it to be, Solomon's inspired endorsement of free inquiry into nature). The candle of the Lord is the *recta ratio* of the humanistic tradition, and *recta ratio* is found, Whichcote says to Tuckney, where

---

[1] Benjamin Whichcote (1609–83) graduated from Emmanuel College in 1629–30 (M.A., 1633; B.D., 1640). He soon made his influence felt both as a college tutor and a preacher. In 1643 he retired to a country living, but in 1644 he accepted, reluctantly, a parliamentary appointment as Provost of King's College in place of a ejected royalist. Whichcote was not a party man and did not subscribe to the Covenant. In 1651 his former tutor, Anthony Tuckney, now Master of Emmanuel, who had long viewed his old pupil's liberalism with keen though loving anxiety, took him to task, and they exchanged letters which illustrate two types of religious thought. In 1660 Whichcote was deprived of his academic post, but he complied with the Act of Uniformity and held several cures. He died at Cudworth's house in Cambridge. Whichcote himself published nothing. The sermons printed in 1698 and later years were apparently delivered in the period after 1660.

vera fides is found. There is no conflict between reason and faith, because God is perfect reason and goodness and because reason and goodness are natural to man, whatever his unnatural lapses. Nothing truly religious is irrational and nothing truly rational is irreligious. The meanings of 'reason' in seventeenth-century thought 'admit a wide solution', but for Whichcote, as for Taylor and Milton and others, reason signifies not the mere logical and critical faculty but the Platonic capacity for attaining divine truth, the whole unified personality, the philosophic conscience, of the well-disposed man. Since man's fall, however, his natural reason and natural religion ('Truths of first Inscription') need to be fortified and restored through revelation, through Christ 'as a principle of divine life within us, as well as a Saviour without us', and through man's own earnest effort. Like Matthew Arnold, Whichcote was charged, in Tuckney's words, with 'A kinde of a Moral Divinitie minted; onlie with a little tincture of Christ added: nay, a Platonique faith unites to God'. It is easy to see that Whichcote's version of humanistic optimism, his natural supernaturalism, might well draw from the undiscriminating those horrid epithets, Arminian and Socinian—and later win the eulogies of Tillotson, Locke, Shaftesbury, and Burnet. With a view of religion based on 'Reason and Scripture', Whichcote has little to say of the Church and ecclesiastical tradition; he urges Christian liberty and agreement in the few and clear fundamentals of Protestant faith. He believes, to use a phrase of Taylor's, that 'Theologie is rather a Divine life than a Divine knowledge', but he insists, much more strongly than Taylor, that the mind must be convinced along with the heart. The modern religious reader may not find much spiritual nourishment in the evangelical eloquence of Donne; he will find a great deal in the quiet, forceful *Aphorisms* of Whichcote.

The younger Cambridge Platonists developed, with varying emphasis, the principles taught by Whichcote, but they all have their individual genius, and to try to characterize them briefly is to burn their wings, and our fingers, in the candle of the Lord. John Smith, by his own account, 'lived upon Dr. Whichcote', and he also harmonizes 'common notions' or 'Truths of Natural Inscription' with revelation and exalts the unity and beauty of undogmatic truth, the divinity of human reason, the soul's dominion over the body, the quest of divine knowledge and participation in the divine life.[1] But while his master avowed his preference for meditation over reading, Smith reveals himself on almost every page as a learned Platonist and Neoplatonist, and he has a more rich and ample style. He constantly and beautifully celebrates the living spirit of Christ, but his hungry imagination reaches out to the supramundane and the infinite, from the Many to the unstained and unchanging One. He is preoccupied with immortality as the great fact of religion, and he reminds us of Vaughan in his Plotinian visions of 'the land of Light', of the soul's escape from fleshly contagion to the Divine Essence.

Nathanael Culverwel bears the generic label of latitudinarian and Platonist, and he was also a Calvinist and an Aristotelian.[2] Indeed his eclectic and critical detachment evades any too precise appellation. In the *Discourse of the Light of Nature* (1652) his main object was to vindicate the harmony of reason and faith against both fideists and Socinians. His major premiss, of course, is that of other Christian 'rationalists', that reason is subordinate only 'to God himself, and those Revelations that come from God', and it is 'expresse blasphemy to say that either God, or the Word of God did ever, or ever will oppose Right Reason'. Along with philosophic sophistication Culverwel has a spiritual fire and figurative utterance which justify the phrase of his editor of 1652, 'cloth of gold . . . weaved of Sunne-beams', though for the most part the gold shines intermittently through a tissue of learned quotations. Indeed to all the Cambridge Platonists except Whichcote learning was a handicap as well as an inspiration; it hurt their influence with an age disposed to welcome the bareness of Hobbes and, in spite of their many passages of power and beauty, it has hurt them with posterity.

Henry More's difficult verse and voluminous prose come from a very earnest and subtle mind which faces more fundamental problems than most men perceive, and which in its search for proofs of the reality of spirit is apt to pursue spirits.[3] More's

[1] John Smith (1616?–52) was educated at Emmanuel College (B.A., 1640; M.A., 1644) and received a fellowship at Queens' College (1644). He was a pupil of Whichcote and a friend certainly of Cudworth and presumably of Culverwel. His *Select Discourses* were edited by Worthington in 1660.

[2] Nathanael Culverwel (1618/19–51?) entered Emmanuel College in 1633 (B.A., 1636; M.A., 1640). He received a fellowship at Emmanuel in 1642 and, like Smith, spent his brief maturity in study, teaching, preaching, and writing. The *Discourse* and other remains were printed in 1652.

[3] Henry More (1614–87) was the son of a prosperous and cultivated Calvinist

weakness for the occult, though common enough in the century, is a liability in a serious philosopher who has nothing of Browne's invincible charm and literary beauty, and it is conspicuous enough in More to repel the unsympathetic reader and evoke the hasty opinion that no true Platonic light can be reflected from such a muddy pool. But the quality of his mind and the direction of his thought are in a way independent of his particular ideas, whether fanciful or respectable. More's troubled quest began in childhood. At Eton, where he breathed the air of Hales (in the literal sense and perhaps in the metaphorical), he had already formed a conviction of 'the Divine Justice and Goodness', and rebelled against 'that hard Doctrine concerning Fate' which he had imbibed in his Calvinist home. The dry studies of Cambridge and his own eager explorations of 'natural' knowledge, far from bringing relief to his thirsty soul, seemed to lead to 'mere Scepticism'. But More found what he needed in Ficino, Plotinus, the Hermetic writings, and other mystical works, especially the *Theologia Germanica*. He now perceived the end of life to be not in the 'Knowledge of things' but in the merging of his will with the Divine. His first efforts to describe his illumination, struggle, and assurance were made in verse. Through the veil of sense More the poet could see, more clearly than his readers do, 'that bright Idee Of steddie Good' which irradiated his soul and the infinite world. His fusion of

(and cavalier) family in Lincolnshire. He went from Eton to Christ's College, Cambridge, in 1631. The renowned and well-loved Joseph Mead, author of *Clavis Apocalyptica* (1627), was an antidote to scholastic narrowness if not to darkly allegorical ways of thought. In Cambridge also were Whichcote and the younger Platonists. In 1639 More received his M.A. degree and a fellowship. When in 1643–5 Parliament ejected many masters and fellows, including Joseph Beaumont, Cowley, Crashaw, and Cleveland, Whichcote was installed at King's and Cudworth, a fellow of Emmanuel, was nominated to the mastership of Clare Hall. More, who was always attached to the Church of England and the monarchy, remained in his place; he did not sign the Covenant but apparently accepted the later Engagement. Although he took orders, he steadily declined preferment and devoted his life to study, writing, and conversation. Except for visits at Ragley, the Warwickshire seat of the Conways, More lived in his beloved Cambridge, nourishing his high speculations on 'the College Small Beer'. Among his many friends and correspondents were Cudworth and other Platonists, Lady Conway and her circle, Descartes, Jeremy Taylor, Hartlib, Joseph Glanvill (who shared his occult interests) and other fellow-members of the Royal Society, William Penn, and John Norris of Bemerton. More's early verse was noticed above, in Chapter III. His chief works in prose were: *An Antidote against Atheism* (1653), *Conjectura Cabbalistica* (1653), *Enthusiasmus Triumphatus* (1656), *The Immortality of the Soul* (1659), *An Explanation of the Grand Mystery of Godliness* (1660), *Enchiridion Ethicum* (1668), *Divine Dialogues* (1668), and *Enchiridion Metaphysicum* (1671).

Neoplatonism and Christianity enabled him to face the new science without misgiving.

As a religious thinker in prose, More feared two great enemies, enthusiasm and atheism, and from the central position of the rational Christian humanist he fought stoutly against both, not without results. Especially after the appearance of his bold and much-discussed book, *The Grand Mystery of Godliness* (1660), the term 'latitude-men' began to be used by some 'Cholerick gentlemen' as equivalent to 'heretics'. In 1664 More published an *Apology* in reply to the criticisms of Joseph Beaumont, author of *Psyche* (1648) and now Master of Peterhouse. Here More nobly reaffirmed the creed of his school, that 'there is no real clashing at all betwixt any genuine Point of Christianity and what true Philosophy and right Reason does determine or allow, but that . . . there is a perpetual peace and agreement betwixt Truth & Truth, be they of what nature or kind so ever'. The many eminent men named in this sketch of the problem of reason and faith have all been on the side of the angels, and almost all, from Hales to Sir Thomas Browne, are Christian humanists whose approach to the problem is prescientific. Others might be added to the same list, such as John Bramhall, whose dispute with Hobbes over liberty and necessity became a public affair in 1654, or the great poet of the age who was about that time beginning his justification of God's ways to men. In our special group Culverwel at least was aware of Galileo and Descartes as well as of Lord Herbert, but he died in 1650–1 without realizing that a philosophic revolution was in progress. More and Cudworth, though rooted in the same traditions, lived longer and saw further, and they laboured to bring scientific thought into line with Christian Platonism, to reinterpret in modern terms the nature of God, the soul of man, and the soul of the world. If the last phrase—or 'plastic nature'— sounds naïve, it needs no apology when it becomes *élan vital*; and if we regard More's thought as unimportant, Newton did not. The campaign required more scientific and philosophic equipment than had sufficed for earlier champions of rational faith and ethics. Edward Davenant, Fuller's cousin, could not endure, says Aubrey, to hear of the new philosophy, for if that was brought in, a new divinity would shortly follow. Davenant spoke more wisely than he knew. But More, like his fellow Platonists, believed with Whichcote that 'To go against Reason, is to go against God'. It is one of the ironies frequent in the age-old controversy that the defender of liberal religion began by seizing upon the two-edged sword of Cartesianism.

The influence of Descartes in England may be said to date from 1637, when Sir Kenelm Digby sent to Hobbes, from Paris, a copy of the *Discours*. Digby cited Descartes in his *Two Treatises* (1644). Hobbes's relations with Descartes are a familiar story. Browne quoted him in 1646. To the English translators of the *Discours* and the *Passions* (1649, 1650) the philosopher's universal fame was an established fact, and they, with More's young Cantabrigian friend John Hall (in his tract on education, 1649), saluted him as the great gaol-deliverer of the modern mind. John Smith, though attracted by Cartesian psychology and physiology, was far from Descartes in spirit. Cartesian ideas appeared in More's *Democritus Platonissans* (1646); in 1648 the disciple commenced writing to the master; and in 1650 he took up the defence of Descartes against the mystagogue Thomas Vaughan. At first Descartes appeared as a modern Plotinus or Plato who, like More himself, had found in conventional philosophy a blind alley, and had created a new synthesis of divine and natural knowledge in harmony with both religion and science. Thus in a battle against mechanistic materialism Descartes, the champion of God and the thinking mind with its innate ideas, might well seem a powerful and heaven-sent ally. To the end More expounded Cartesian physics; but as Cartesian metaphysics looked less and less Platonic and Christian, his early 'transported Admiration' gave way by degrees to doubt and distrust and, in his last books, to open antagonism. Descartes came to represent, as the Church of Rome had already decided, mere atheistic materialism—a verdict opposed by the religious Boyle. We cannot go into the complex technicalities of More's thought—though it is unjust to his philosophic power not to do so, and Hobbes himself, according to More's early biographer, declared that if his own philosophy was not true he would have liked More's next best!—but we can understand something of his evolution if we recall Wordsworth's changing reactions to a system no less fatal to a spiritual view of man and the world. The universe of Descartes, even if maintained by a mathematical Creator, depended too simply upon matter and motion, while More saw in such phenomena as gravity the evidence of a 'Spirit of Nature', the vicarious power of God exerted upon matter. In short, a cool intellectual, mechanical, and dualistic system could not satisfy the soul of a man like More, whose religious and ethical faith was a vital flame, who with all his rationalism had, as he confessed, a strain of 'enthusiasm', and whose profound intuition of the divine, coupled with a philosophic belief in the 'extension' of spirit, led him to find the omnipresence of God in infinite and indwelling space. (At this point we might remind ourselves that More's younger contemporary, Thomas Traherne, who was noticed in earlier pages among the religious poets, gloried in infinite space as the image of divine goodness and love.)

Ralph Cudworth (1617–88) was in some ways a more modern, systematic, and important thinker than his brother-in-arms. He seems to have coined the phrase 'philosophy of religion', but there is nothing of the coldness we associate with it in the famous sermon he delivered before the Parliament of 1647, one of the noblest and most eloquent of latitudinarian pleas for the religion of the heart, the 'inward Soul and Principle of Divine Life'. Thirty years later, in 1678, came his first great broadside against atheistic materialism, *The True Intellectual System of the Universe*. In this, and in the posthumous *Treatise concerning Eternal and Immutable Morality* (1731), Cudworth laboured, with a philosophic power somewhat blunted by encyclopaedic and digressive learning, to assert the existence and providential goodness of God, the reality of mind and its priority over things, and a rational, humanistic, and immutable standard of values. But these works, philosophically and chronologically, lie too far beyond our limits for discussion here. Cudworth might have been surprised to find his *System* (ed. 1820, i. 216–17) echoed in Fielding's *Amelia* (i. iii).

'Nature', said Ralegh, near the end of his first chapter, 'is nothing, but as Plato calleth it, *Dei artem, vel artificiosum Dei Organum*, The art, or artificiall Organ of God.' 'Nature is the Art of God' is Browne's text. And *Leviathan* opens with the words, 'Nature (the Art whereby God hath made and governes the World)'. But it was Hobbes, the new Protagoras, who made absolute Bacon's divorce between philosophy and religion, who finally severed the golden chain that bound nature and man to God. The attempt of the later Cambridge Platonists—and of Milton—to reunite them was made in the spirit of their ancient, medieval, and Renaissance heritage, the Christian and Platonic belief in the oneness of a divine world. Because the attempt failed, and scientific empiricism and mechanism continued their triumphal advance, Cambridge Platonism has often been dismissed as only an interesting eddy in the stream of modern thought. But, whatever their philosophic inadequacies, the Platonists were in the main stream. More specifically, they were the founders of British idealism. Their anticipations of later philosophy, British and continental, have been recognized and, since our concern is with literature, we may remember that, after the age of the egoistic human animal, sensationalist psychology, and a clock-like universe, the romantic poets returned, if not to Christian Platonism and right reason, at least to Platonic conceptions of participation in infinity and 'the one Spirit's plastic stress'; and in our own time Yeats, recoiling from the 'Grey Truth' of science, found light and life in Henry More's *Anima Mundi*.

XI

HEROIC VERSE

THIS heading may be for many readers an invitation to
'Turne over the leef and chese another tale'. Yet from
Petrarch to Milton—or the hapless Blackmore—almost all
the serious poets of Europe dreamed of writing the great modern
heroic poem, and many of them, like the orator in the House
of Lords, woke up to find that they were doing it. For three
centuries Europe was strewn with epics which, as Porson said
of Southey's, will be read when Homer and Virgil are forgotten.
In England the one great heroic poem between Spenser and
Milton was Chapman's *Homer*; the most popular was Sylvester's
version of Du Bartas. Most of our material is, except in bulk,
small beer, but even the bulk warrants some attention. And
when we think of the long life and potency of the heroic impulse,
not to mention the fact that Milton awaits us, the attenuation
and ultimate death of the heroic poem mark a change of general
significance. The causes include the decline of patriotic and
ethical fervour, in the Renaissance meaning of the terms, and
the rise of scientific and satirical rationalism.

Conceptions of the heroic poem in the Renaissance and later
were so elastic and comprehensive—Dryden referred to *Cooper's
Hill* as an epic—that one is driven back to the invulnerable
title of Du Bellay's chapter, 'Du long poëme francoys'. Most
of the poems we can afford to name may be roughly grouped
as historical, classical, romantic, and biblical.

For the Elizabethans 'historical' and 'heroic' were almost
synonyms. Our early historical narratives, such as those of
Drayton and Daniel which we have met before, were the last
offshoots of the Elizabethan patriotic chronicle—though Daniel's
philosophic *Civil Wars* has been ranked as the first English neoclassical epic. The *Mirror for Magistrates* and Warner's *Albion's
England* received their final enlargements in 1610 and 1612
respectively. In 1609 Thomas Heywood (1574?–1641), the very
active dramatist who was to be an active popularizer of history,
produced *Troia Britannica*, a vigorous and sometimes fine poem
of about 13,000 lines on the story of Troy, with digressions and

with glances at Elizabethan naval heroes, hypocritical Puritans, and Guy Fawkes. The last two of the seventeen cantos bring Brute to England and chronicle the English sovereigns down to James. The main source was Caxton's *Recuyell* (which had been revised by William Fiston in 1596), though Heywood preferred to cite Homer and Virgil, and did use them, and he took a good deal from Ovid. *Troia Britannica* may be called the last of the 'historical' leviathans; it stands apart from *Poly-Olbion* and is quite different from such short narratives as Sir John Beaumont's *Bosworth-Field* and from the versified histories of Henry II and Edward III (1633, 1635) by the translator of Lucan, Thomas May. In *Henry the Second* May combined the epic manner of Lucan with a conscious sense of the five-act structure of a tragedy.

The Italianate Ovidian genre continued to spawn mythological tales, generally in imitation of *Hero and Leander* or Shakespeare's poems; Marlowe especially was constantly echoed. The narratives of Drayton, Chapman, Francis Beaumont (?), Basse, Phineas Fletcher, and Shirley have been mentioned already, and many others cannot be mentioned at all. But if no single poem rivals those written before 1600, a few have some intrinsic or adventitious interest. Leonard Digges's decorative paraphrase, *The Rape of Proserpine* (1617), written 'as a Patterne for a piece of Needle-work', was given a threefold allegory borrowed from that printed with Bevilacqua's version of Claudian. Patrick Hannay's *The Nightingale* (1622), a poem of nearly seventeen hundred lines on Philomela, was 'to be sung (by those that please) to the tune set downe before in the frontispice'. Ten years later the same theme (in George Pettie's English) tempted Martin Parker, the balladist, to an unaccustomed flight. Henry Reynolds, the friend of Drayton and the exponent, in *Mythomystes*, of the allegorical-mystical theory of poetry, published tales of Ariadne and Narcissus (1628, 1632) taken from Anguillara's free version of Ovid; *Narcissus* was provided with a quadruple allegory. And we might mention the schoolboy Cowley's embellishment of Golding's tale of Pyramus and Thisbe (1633). The longest and best of these poems is the 'Epick', *Cupid and Psyche* (1637), by Shakerley Marmion (1603–39), the playwright and 'son of Ben'. This first of many poetical versions of the tale, in a style as loose as its couplets, does not suffer in comparison with the more refined luxuriance of William Morris or the preciousness of Bridges. Marmion used Adlington (and Heywood's masque, *Love's Mistress*, printed in 1636) as well as Apuleius, and his verse has a robust Elizabethan colour. With lapses of taste go felicities, such as the literal rendering of *Veneris inevitabiles oculos*:

> What darknesse can protect me? what disguise
> Hide me from her inevitable eyes?

Marmion gives an allegorical exposition, derived from Fulgentius and Heywood, but his heart is in expansive story-telling.

This Ovidian genre had been European and it shared in the European reaction against excessive veneration for things classical. Though ancient tales had received comic handling from Shakespeare and Jonson, and Nashe and Dekker, and though mythological poems had contained more or less humorous seasoning, the first real burlesque was the jovial James Smith's 'Innovation of Penelope and Ulysses. A Mock-Poem'. This was first printed in *Wit Restored* (1658), but was apparently written in or before 1640—before Scarron's famous *Typhon* (1644) and *Virgile travesti* (1648). Then came the very scurrilous *Loves of Hero and Leander* (1651). Thus a fashion which in England was signalized by Cotton's *Scarronides* (1664) did not have to wait for the Restoration.

The Ovidian tradition contributed something to the purely romantic narrative which grew out of Elizabethan courtly and pastoral romance. This type, like the other, developed sophisticated and sometimes mock-heroic humour—as in the *Albino and Bellama* (1637) of the eccentric Cambridge wit, Nathaniel Whiting, who became a Puritan divine—but, in spite of the rise of the psychological French romance in prose, it remained on the whole invincibly old-fashioned. William Bosworth's *Chaste and Lost Lovers*, published in 1651 but written about 1626, was a labyrinthine maze of tales contrived by a youth intoxicated with Ovid, Marlowe, Sidney, and Spenser. Sidney's *Arcadia* was the obvious source of Quarles's one, and very popular, venture into secular romance, *Argalus and Parthenia* (1629). *Thealma and Clearchus* (1683) by John Chalkhill (*c.* 1593?–1642), a diffuse 'Pastoral History' in irregular couplets, breaks off at line 3170, and one cannot respond as one could wish to the appended 'And here the author died, and I hope the reader will be sorry'. Sir Francis Kynaston, who could catch the note

of the half-metaphysical Caroline love lyric, was Spenserian and
Chaucerian (as became the latinizer of *Troilus and Criseyde*) in
Leoline and Sydanis (1642). The scene was ancient Wales and
Ireland, but the Irish court could produce an elaborate Caroline
masque. The plot, which includes mock-heroic elements, recalls
the plots of Shakespeare's comedy and Shakespeare's sources.
The structure is conceived in terms of a five-act play, an idea
that May had been aware of and that Davenant utilized. In
Pharonnida (1659), by the Dorsetshire physician, William Chamberlayne (1619–89), heroic romance outdid itself in bulk,
narrative complexity, and energetic exuberance of fancy and
metaphor. If Sidney's *Arcadia* had been versified by Chapman,
the result would have been something like *Pharonnida*; Saintsbury pronounced the huge poem 'a Sinbad's valley of poetic
jewels', but few readers have sought for them. The author's
service with the royalist army interrupted composition, and in
recasting and continuing he evidently had an eye to the formal
pattern of *Gondibert* and followed the potent example of Barclay's
Argenis as well as his original Heliodorian plot. He not only wove
in personal and topical matter, from the second battle of Newbury through the Protectorate, but made his principal characters
allegorical symbols of the recent political and constitutional
struggles.

Two heroic poems, Davenant's *Gondibert* (1650) and Cowley's
Davideis (1656), are scarcely more read nowadays than the
Caroline romances, but they are important in themselves and
in the critical theory they represented. They are among the
many foot-hills that lead up towards both *Paradise Lost* and
Religio Laici. The Reformation and the Counter-Reformation
had alike opposed the paganizing strain in the Renaissance
and had fostered the ideal of the Christian epic. In addition
to the poems of Du Bartas, Tasso, and Spenser, there were such
others as Marino's *La Strage degli Innocenti*, which Crashaw
partly translated, and Chapelain's *La Pucelle*, which appeared
in the year of *Davideis* and was one of twenty or more Christian
epics in French written in the third quarter of the century.
This more or less positive concern for religious and moral
edification and genuine truth was assisted at some points by
two parallel movements, the first sober maturing of neoclassicism and the rise of new critical conceptions of reality.
The two latter movements accomplished a great civilizing

process all over Europe, but Cartesian and Hobbesian acid was to eat at the roots as well as the rank growths of the imagination. Finally, the more immediate background of *Gondibert* was the array of heroic tapestries in prose, narrative verse, and drama produced in England and France.

Davenant's long, serious, and ambitious *Discourse upon Gondibert* and Hobbes's *Answer*, which were published together in 1650, some months before the poem appeared with them, are landmarks on the road from the Renaissance to the Augustan age.[1] Whatever may have been Davenant's debt to Hobbes, and the debt of both to English and continental writers, they set forth an eclectic, empirical, and unpedantic theory of the heroic poem. It should be, not an imitation of the ancients, but a courtly and martial work which holds up to courtly and martial readers ideal patterns of active Christian virtue, yet permits the display of love and ambition in their bad excess. Davenant sees heroic poetry (in Arnoldian phrase) as the great *magister vitae*, more needful than ever because the Church and other traditional agencies have failed. He is more intent than Hobbes upon didactic utility. (Davenant favours, by the way, what Hobbes rejects as epic indecorum, metaphors taken from the language of 'men of any science, as well mechanicall as liberall'.) On the whole, both men retain a good measure of orthodoxy, yet their prevailing tone, compared with that of Chapman or Greville or Jonson, shows as much as anything

---

[1] The versatile and enterprising Davenant (1606–68) was the son of an Oxford tavern-keeper of good family. Tradition made him the godson, and Aubrey the son, of Shakespeare. He became a page to the Duchess of Richmond and then to Fulke Greville. His marital career began in 1623–4, his theatrical and military careers in 1627. In various difficulties, from syphilis (which was to occasion endless jokes about his nose) to homicide, he had a good friend in Endymion Porter. Davenant's first court masque was produced in 1635. The year 1638 yielded two masques, two plays, a volume of poems called *Madagascar*, a pardon for homicide, and appointment as Jonson's successor to what was virtually the office of Poet Laureate. Davenant took part in the two Bishops' Wars, was involved in the Army Plot of 1641, and served on land and sea in the civil war. He was knighted in 1643. During 1646–50 he was mostly in Paris with Hobbes, Cowley, Waller, and the other exiles. In 1650 he sailed for Maryland, of which Charles II had made him governor, but was captured and imprisoned. Part of a third book of *Gondibert* was written in prison. He was given restricted liberty in 1652 and pardoned in 1654 (the story that Milton befriended him, if true, might refer to the obtaining of the pardon). Davenant managed to carry on theatrical performances and produced the famous 'opera', *The Siege of Rhodes*, in 1656. In 1660 he was granted one of the two theatrical patents and he became among other things the chief reviver of Shakespeare. He himself wrote two dozen dramatic works. He was buried in the Abbey.

how far the religious, ethical, and imaginative fire of the Renaissance has been cooled by critical rationalism, literary and scientific. Bacon had exalted 'poesy parabolical' because he liked to rationalize myth and, though capable of a larger vision, he had commonly revealed a scientist's matter-of-factness and a scientist's distrustful and escapist view of the imagination. Hobbes's account of the poetic faculties begins with a commonplace schematized in terms of his psychology, and he goes on with unusual eloquence to celebrate the workmanship of fancy guided by the precepts of true philosophy; Davenant seems to expound a similar conception of wit, with a generous rhapsodical vagueness. But while Hobbes desiderates the fruitful union of imagination and judgement, his whole manner of thinking proves the division between them. And the critics' banishment of the supernatural, and even of conceits, goes beyond the words of the proscription. The praise bestowed upon *Gondibert* by Cowley and Waller and, more oddly, by Vaughan underlines for us the new emphasis on the rationalistic presentation of human nature and 'the manners of men'. This standard of nature and truth, the simple clarity of style that it enjoins, and the dichotomy between wit and judgement, mark the end of the older poetry and herald the Augustan.

Davenant, who in his grander moments claimed Lombard ancestry, saw himself as an heroic bard modernizing the tradition that led from Homer to Spenser, and he was no less sanguine in hoping that his several thousand stanzas might be sung. Even if the story, for which he got a few hints from Belleforest, had been carried through its second half, it would have been, as a story, hardly less dull than long, 'Calme as Rose-leafes, and coole as Virgin-snow', to pervert the spirit of Vaughan's eulogy. Against a background of civil war and the court of medieval Lombardy—the scene of Davenant's early play, *Albovine*—move various warriors and women. The all-embracing motives of love and honour seem to affect even a hunted stag. The noble Gondibert, proclaimed the betrothed of the perfect Rhodalind, the heiress of a kingdom, loves the no less perfect Birtha, daughter of the philosophic scientist Astragon, and the dilemma remains unsolved. In the last canto Davenant finished, the seventh of the third book, we meet a variation on the well-worn plot most familiar through *Much Ado About Nothing*. Thus *Gondibert*, though written for the most part with a masculine, weighty, and level plainness of statement, is obviously related to the heroic romances in prose and verse and to the early and later heroic plays of which Davenant the playwright was a progenitor; indeed, the narrative in its full five books was planned, as we have observed, to follow dramatic structure. But though the poem has arresting episodes, the story was on the whole an encumbrance. If the author had been able to cut loose from the convention of heroic romance and rely upon his real gift for massive and dignified reflection, he would have remained a more vital link between Sir John Davies (whose *Nosce Teipsum* was the chief exemplar of the stanza of *Gondibert*) and his old patron Fulke Greville on the one hand and Dryden and Gray on the other. One passage which shows Davenant's philosophic and poetic power is the account of Astragon's house, a scientific—and religious—college partly derived from *The New Atlantis* (an institution Cowley was to set in ancient Judaea). Another is the fragment first published in 1673, 'The Philosopher's Disquisition directed to the Dying Christian' with 'The Christian's Reply', a noble treatment of the problem that exercised so many minds, the relations of knowledge, reason, and faith.

The paraphrase or elaboration of a biblical tale had a venerable tradition behind it, a tradition revivified by Du Bartas's large work and by his smaller epics like *Judith*. Sir William Alexander's unfinished 'Jonathan: An Heroic Poem Intended' was printed in his *Recreations with the Muses* (1637); this volume, by the way, included the much enlarged version of the early *Dooms-day* which, if it did not, like a later Scotsman's *Lives of the Chancellors*, add a new sting to death, at least shortens the life of the literary historian. Other works were Drummond's fragment, 'The Shadow of the Judgement' (1630), Drayton's several efforts (1604, 1630), Fuller's *David's Heinous Sin* (1631), and Quarles's stories of Jonah, Esther, Job, and Samson (1620–31). The veteran Thomas Heywood's *Hierarchy of the Blessed Angels* (1635) has much interest for the student both in its poetical survey of mystical theology and occult lore (and brief roll-call of English poets) and in the prose sections containing 'Theologicall, Philosophicall, Poeticall, Historicall, Apothegmaticall, Hierogliphicall and Emblematicall Observations'. Cowley was severe upon the last two writers: 'For if any man design to compose a Sacred Poem, by onely turning a story of the Scripture, like Mr. Quarles's, or some other godly matter, like Mr. Heywood of Angels, into Rhyme; He is so far from elevating of Poesie, that he onely abases Divinity.' Finally, George Sandys's 'Paraphrase Upon Job' (1638) was named by Pope as one of Waller's models, and the couplets have much of the antithetical balance displayed in his *Ovid*.

Cowley's *Davideis, a Sacred Poem of the Troubles of David* was published in 1656 as a fragment of four books instead of the projected twelve. According to the traditional account, which began with Sprat, Cowley had written much of the fragment at Cambridge and revised it later; a recent argument would put the whole composition within 1650–4. In the critical preface he was in agreement with many Puritans and others in vigorously condemning mythological fables and urging the claims of biblical history; and although in his miscellaneous verse he helped to bring back the exiled train of gods and goddesses, he excluded from *Davideis* what the Puritan Milton poured abundantly into *Paradise Lost*. Cowley's exaltation of sacred themes, as his elegy on Crashaw also shows, was mainly based on sincere religious feeling, but it included two other motives, a poet's desire for fresh material and what he emphasized in his praise of *Gondibert*, the realistic standards of truth and human life held by a modern rational mind. For a poet of Cowley's nature and inheritance, however, these several motives were not incompatible with one another or with devotion to ancient art. David could combine Christian virtues with those of Aeneas and could be likewise the agent of Providence, the precursor of Christ. Cowley's avowed model was the patron saint of the neoclassical epic, whom he calls 'the most judicious and divine Poet', 'Virgil the Wise, Whose Verse walks highest, but not flies'. So we have constant imitations of Virgil, from infernal and celestial agencies and a prophetic vision down to similes and half-lines; Cowley's learned notes attest his concern for heroic precedent and propriety in technique and style. He also owed a good deal to Sylvester and Tasso and something to Crashaw's translation from Marino. When he tells us that Goliath's

> Spear the Trunk was of a lofty Tree,
> Which Nature meant some tall ships Mast should be,

he carries a phrase of Sylvester's in the Miltonic direction. Milton's reported esteem for Cowley we may presume to have been built largely on *Davideis*, and even the literary, theological, historical, and scientific notes, on everything from inverted adjectives to Moloch and Dagon, would have been congenial.

Earlier narratives do not much weaken Cowley's claim that he had written the first neoclassical religious epic in English. *Davideis* was also, unless we except the translations of Du Bartas's large and smaller works, the first neoclassical epic in the heroic couplets which Milton so vehemently damned. Coming in the middle of a long line of practitioners from Sylvester onward, Cowley was a not unskilful master of the closed couplet, though he took no great pains to harmonize the metrical movement with the sense and tone. Nor do couplets check his hyperboles; the picture of Lucifer with his iron teeth and fire-darting eyes is only less bad than Tasso's and Marino's. And they encourage antithetical wit perhaps as much Ovidian and Augustan as metaphysical. Envy saw Cain

> fling the stone, as if he meant,
> At once his Murder, and his Monument.

Bits of nature and oriental life and of psychological analysis, and the ideal friendship of David and Jonathan which appealed to Dorothy Osborne, are not enough to give life to 'the Cold-meats of the Antients', and we are more attracted, as the poet was, by such peripheral matters of topical and philosophic interest as the ideal college and the question of monarchy or republic, physical phenomena and metaphysics. Though aware of modern views and of 'endless space', Cowley accepts the Ptolemaic system for his Hebrew story, and his cosmology is a mixture of old and new, of Neoplatonism and science. The world was created 'From Nothing' by the triune God of Christianity, who with His angels combats Lucifer and his demons. The primal elements ranged themselves in order under the compulsion of Music and Love. The universe is 'God's Poem', 'the æternal minds Poetick Thought'. It is also 'Great Natures well-set Clock', but a clock which, 'the Schoolmen all agree' (if not the law of inertia), requires the 'immediate concurse of God'. But, despite Cowley's broad horizons, his combination of traditional religious and Platonic thought with scientific modernism, he had neither the intellectual nor the poetic power for such a synthesis of science and imagination as the divided age was in need of.

XII

MILTON

WHOEVER the third of English poets may be, Milton's place has been next to the throne, and he still stands there, 'Like Teneriff or Atlas unremov'd'. Until our century, his poetry had few detractors, but it has always had dubious friends. Although Milton grew in stature while most of the metaphysical poets fell into disrepute or oblivion, he, like them, continued to suffer because readers quickly and progressively lost touch with Renaissance art and ideology, with the whole religious world-view and its symbolic language. Apart from political prejudice, Dr. Johnson's estimate was a mixture of insight and blindness. The admiration for the great rebel felt by Blake and Shelley went along with antipathy for the theology to which he was supposedly committed; and nineteenth-century critics in general were inclined to save the 'poetry' by casting overboard ideas they did not understand. In the period between the two world wars, when the revival of Donne was at its height, Milton's poetry as well as ideas came under censure. The supreme English artist, the only one to be matched with Virgil and Dante in what Arnold called 'the sure and flawless perfection of his rhythm and diction', became the rhetorician who had crushed the fruitful metaphysical movement, divorced thought and feeling, and imposed an artificial style and prosody upon English poetry for over 200 years, until it was freed from bondage by the 'metaphysical' poets of our time. But during these same years Milton's thought began to be seriously explored by historians of ideas; they invoked a broader formula to unify and save the artist and thinker, and the rigid son of the Reformation became the bold son of the Renaissance. The new Milton, however, though he embodied some significant and amiable features which had been lacking in the grim Puritan, looked decidedly too much like a nineteenth-century liberal. This brief and unqualified summary indicates at least that Milton's poetic and philosophic character is less simple and obvious than friends as well as foes have often assumed it to be. (Prejudice against his personal character has also often soured critical judgements,

although few men's lives have been less blameworthy.) Our
present view is not final or quite unanimous—a few Thomas
Rymers are still heard from—but, with a far better understanding of Milton's background, roots, and evolution, we have
struck a truer balance between the Renaissance humanist and
the Puritan crusader. He is seen, in the first place, as the last
great exponent of Christian humanism in its historical continuity, the tradition of classical reason and culture fused with
Christian faith which had been the main line of European
development; his beliefs and attitudes, intensified and somewhat
altered by the conditions of his age and country and by his own
temperament, became as he grew old a noble anachronism in
an alien world. In the second place, recent criticism has brought
fresh perceptiveness to the study of Milton's poetic art and
heritage and has done much to reanimate and enrich the
traditional conception of the great classical artist among modern
poets; it has been increasingly seen that his poetry has 'fullness
in the concise and depth in the clear', that its deceptively
smooth surface covers abundant and subtle complexity.

I

The most valuable insights into Milton's life and mental
growth are given at large in the whole body of his works and,
more specifically, in the autobiographical passages in the
Reason of Church Government (1642), the *Apology for Smectymnuus*
(1642), and the *Defensio Secunda* (1654). Here we can mention
only a few facts and dates. Milton was born in 1608, in London,
not far from the Mermaid tavern, and Shakespeare and Jonson
may have heard his infant cries, if such an infant did cry.
John Milton senior, the disinherited son of a Catholic recusant,
was a prosperous scrivener and a composer of some note even
in that Golden Age of English music. He transmitted to his
namesake independence of mind and a love of music, and gave
him the best preparation for a literary career that education,
travel, and leisure could supply. Voracious private study
accompanied Milton's formal training at St. Paul's School
(1615/16?–25?) and at Christ's College, Cambridge (1625–32).
Among his Cambridge contemporaries were Roger Williams,
Fuller, Randolph, and Jeremy Taylor; John Cleveland was
at Christ's during 1627–31 and Henry More entered in 1631.
Though Milton's early clash with a tutor led to rustication, he

passed his seven years at the University 'with the approbation of the good, and without any stain' upon his character. Most of the next six years (1632–8) he spent in his father's house at Hammersmith and then at Horton in Buckinghamshire. The Horton period was not a prolonged rural holiday but a voluntary postgraduate course of hard reading and thinking which gave historical background and critical direction to Milton's maturing views on all manner of civil and religious problems. One interlude was the writing of *Comus*, which was acted in 1634. In 1638–9 Milton enjoyed some fifteen months abroad, chiefly in Italy. That sojourn—which included a call on Galileo—remained a bright spot in Milton's memory; in English literary circles he was virtually unknown, and the cordial welcome he received from Italian men of letters gave him confidence in his poetic destiny. *Mansus*, addressed to his Neapolitan host, Baptista Manso, Marquis of Villa, was one of his best Latin poems; it contained the first announcement of his projected epic. Milton returned to set up in London as a private schoolmaster and to follow with eager interest the climactic stages in the struggle between King and Parliament, Anglican and Puritan.

Milton's refusal to 'subscribe slave' by taking holy orders had been combined with a growing consciousness of his literary genius and vocation. Now, with notable achievements in minor genres behind him (though his collected poems did not appear until 1645/6), and with plans for a major poem revolving in his mind, he felt compelled to put aside his craving for poetic fame. With mingled ardour and reluctance he devoted his energies from 1641 to 1660 largely to the prose tracts that form the great bulk of his works. *The Tenure of Kings and Magistrates*, which followed close upon the king's execution, was followed by Milton's appointment (March 1649) as Secretary for Foreign Tongues to the Council of State. The impairment of his eyesight had begun about 1644–5 and was aggravated by his fierce labour upon the *Pro Populo Anglicano Defensio* (1651). He became completely blind in the winter of 1651–2, when, as we are apt to forget, he was still in his prime; it needed all Milton's courage and faith in Providence to rally from such a blow. The *Defensio Secunda* was published in 1654, and Milton may have begun *Paradise Lost* about that time, in the same heroic mood. After the Restoration the apologist for the regicides, though imprisoned for a time, was spared, through the good offices, according to different stories, of Davenant or Marvell, or because he was regarded as harmless. *Paradise Lost* was offered to the town in 1667 and *Paradise Regained* and *Samson Agonistes* appeared together in 1671.

Milton had been married three times: in 1642 to Mary Powell, who died ten years later; in 1656 to Katherine Woodcock, who died in 1658, her husband's 'late espoused Saint'; and in 1663 to Elizabeth Minshull. In the lesser sonnets of his middle years we have glimpses of friendships untroubled by external stress. Apart from memories of the good old cause, loss of property, some friction with his daughters, blindness and the pains of gout, Milton seems to have had a fairly cheerful old age. We know his simple routine and can see him walking in his garden, playing on his organ and singing, or, often with one leg thrown over the arm of his chair, meditating, listening to readers, dictating, talking with English and foreign visitors who sought him out, and finishing the day, like the heroic poet he had pictured in his youth, with a glass of water—and the unheroic but genial addition of a pipe. In 1674 'he died by a quiet and silent expiration'.

2

From beginning to end Milton worked within traditional genres and conventions, and he more or less re-created these in the process. The larger part of his early writing was, after the university fashion, in Latin, and he was a master of Latin verse before he was of English—though he displayed a Miltonic amplitude of ambition and, at moments, of style in 'At a Vacation Exercise' (1628). Further, while the disciple of Ovid and many other ancients, and of such neo-Latinists as George Buchanan, could lament the death of bishops and celebrate the fifth of November in a miniature anti-Catholic epic, the obscurity of a learned language and friendship with Charles Diodati encouraged more spontaneous and sensuous self-revelation than he allowed himself in his native tongue. The beauty of girls in the parks dazzles him and the reawakening of nature in the spring kindles positive intoxication, an ecstasy—in a coherent pattern—of innocent neopaganism. But the young Christian Odysseus clings to the magical herb, moly, and in the sixth elegy he goes on from playful praise of vinous and amorous verse to extol the ascetic poet of truly heroic themes.

This aspiration had just become accomplishment in the same month, December 1629. 'On the Morning of Christ's Nativity' announced Milton's coming of age, literally, poetically, and religiously. Like Crashaw, he uses the paradoxes that belong to the subject, but, whereas the Catholic weaves them into the simple story of the nativity, the Protestant's concern is the incarnation of the Redeemer, the central event in world-history. In the first of the three movements, the historical setting is the universal peace of the Roman world; in larger 'mythic' terms (which are not those of the 'pathetic fallacy'), all nature, conscious of her imperfections, awaits the coming of her Creator. Then the outburst of angelic song, which is blended with the music of the spheres, proclaims the new bond of harmony between heaven and earth, and calls up, in musical images, the two other supreme events, the Creation and the Day of Judgement. The full and perfect bliss of eternity has its beginning in the birth of Christ, which puts to flight the old Dragon's instruments, the gods and local divinities of pagan idolatry; their glamour or beauty—so sympathetically celebrated in the fifth elegy—cannot redeem their falsity. And the poem ends, as Milton's later poems commonly end, with a quiet assertion of divine order—here a final paradox. Like the mature poems too, this one suggests innumerable 'sources'—a *canzone* of Tasso, Virgil's Messianic eclogue, and so on—and the texture is rich in traditional symbolic detail, above all in images of light and darkness and of music. It is already characteristic in its thematic and structural unity and in presenting its author's ardent vision of perfection. As a hymn of rejoicing, it surges forward in a relatively regular rhythm and with a sweet or clangorous volume of sound.

The extent of the young Milton's knowledge of Elizabethan and contemporary verse is a question. He offers open tributes to Shakespeare and Jonson and seems to pay allusive homage to Spenser, to whom he was to owe much, and these and almost every major and minor poet have yielded echoes and analogues to the commentators. At any rate the main line of his development is in the main line of the Renaissance tradition, and he is scarcely touched by the metaphysical current. A subdued Elizabethan and Jacobean sweetness and richness of colour and fancy give way rapidly to the disciplined classical sobriety and courtly urbanity of the Jonsonian lyrical style. The change is not of course unwavering, and at all times Milton is Milton. The clearest early evidence of a finer gift than Jonson's is in 'L'Allegro' and 'Il Penseroso', which were written probably in the summer of 1631, when Milton was twenty-two. The obvious and enduring charm of these companion poems flowers from the author's temperament and assured artistic competence. His subjects are two ideal abstractions, Mirth (in heaven Euphro-syne, one of the Graces) and that benign form of Melancholy which is exalted Contemplation. These personifications are broken down into states of mind embodied in the two actor-observers and rendered through landscapes and interiors with or without human figures; in such descriptions realistic par-ticularity would be quite out of place, and 'neat-handed Phillis' could not be 'greasy Joan'. The cheerful, social man and the meditative solitary are different but not incompatible, since they represent two sides of refined human nature. The structural backbone of the poems is provided by the themes and the temporal sequence of an ideal day and night. With perfect tact and economy, and in flowing melody, Milton weaves together native and pagan folk-lore and literature, civilized rusticity and courtly ceremonial, romance and religion; and, for the first and the last time, he celebrates 'Merry England' and the Anglican ritual. The substance partakes of the traditions of medieval 'debate', pastoral, 'character', 'encomium', academic prolusion, allegorical myth, and 'emblem', all fused with fresh, easy, and impersonal originality and in modes of lyrical decorum that maintain continual parallels and contrasts.

Perhaps in the spring of 1632 Milton wrote the brief, conven-tional, and wholly graceful masque, *Arcades*, which was pre-sented before the aged Countess Dowager of Derby (once the Amaryllis of Spenser). Here a monologue by a partly Jonsonian Genius of the Wood is flanked by lyrics which echo Jonson. The cosmic and Christian Platonism touched in the Genius's speech was to be enlarged and intensified in *Comus*, and several short poems explain Milton's growing seriousness. The sonnet 'How soon hath Time', written apparently on his twenty-fourth birthday (December 1632), may be called a record of Milton's 'conversion' in the entirely authentic sense of matured religious development and earnest submission to the divine will.

He had been a distinguished figure at Cambridge, and now, while his contemporaries are making visible progress, he is an obscure and solitary student at home, and he feels the contrast. But both friendly remonstrance and his own self-searching only strengthen the resolve to prepare himself as best he can for the unknown future and inspire a renewed and positive consecration of his powers to God's service. The sober resolution of the sestet—which seems to echo Pindar's fourth Nemean ode—is of the most direct simplicity, almost monosyllabic. Notable first-fruits of this self-consecration were 'On Time' and 'At a Solemn Music'. Each poem is in the form of an Italian madrigal, or one paragraph of a *canzone*: and the slow, irregular lines give weight to every word and cadence. The two poems contrast, in reverse order, the temporal flux and sinful dissonance of earth with the changeless purity and harmony of heaven.

The same contrast inspired the opening lines, indeed the whole, of the *Mask* later known as *Comus*. *Comus* was presented on 29 September 1634 at Ludlow Castle before the Earl of Bridgewater, Lord President of Wales (and stepson of the Countess of Derby who had been honoured in *Arcades*). It was produced by the musician Henry Lawes, who had been responsible for *Arcades*, and who took the role of the Attendant Spirit; the parts of the two Brothers and the Lady were acted by the Earl's three children, of whom the eldest, Lady Alice Egerton, was only fifteen. We cannot discuss such sources and analogues as Ovid, Peele's *Old Wife's Tale*, Spenser's story of Amoret and Busyrane, Fletcher's *Faithful Shepherdess*, and other things. In place of the Circe of Homer and Ovid, who had many sisters and cousins in Renaissance literature, Milton utilized and refined the Comus who had appeared in Jonson's *Pleasure Reconciled to Virtue* and in the Latin *Comus* of Erycius Puteanus. The conventional masque, based on some allegorical 'device', appealed to the eye and ear. Jonson, the chief practitioner in the form, had given it a frequent serious or didactic note, but Milton's vision went beyond his range; and of course Milton had no interest in the pseudo-Platonics of the Caroline court. The moral lesson of Circe and her spells, doubtless present to Homer himself, was a commonplace from Horace down to George Sandys's *Ovid* (1632), and it had been fully worked out by Milton's great exemplar in the poetic handling of ethical ideas, the sage and serious Spenser. The gospel of libertine naturalism which Spenser, Sidney, and others set forth and condemned was set forth with sympathy or levity by Marlowe, Donne, and such contemporaries of Milton as Randolph and Carew; Comus is in fact a cultivated gentleman, a cavalier poet, and his self-revelation may be called a first sketch in the ironic method that was to be used with Satan.

The best approach to *Comus*, to the Christian-Platonic idealism of the young Milton, is the retrospective account he gave in the *Apology for Smectymnuus* (1642) of the development of his conception of chastity. Captured at first by Ovid and the other Roman poets of love, he continued to admire their art while recoiling from their sensuality; and he found fuller satisfaction in the two famous renowners of Beatrice and Laura. There grew the belief that 'he who would not be frustrate of his hope to write well hereafter in laudable things, ought him selfe to bee a true Poem, that is, a composition, and patterne of the best and honourablest things'. From Dante and Petrarch he had turned to the fables and romances of knighthood (especially, no doubt, Tasso and Spenser), and such works proved, not the fuel of wantonness, but incitements to virtue. Next came 'the divine volumes of Plato', the Platonic conception of the true love of the good. 'Last of all not in time, but as perfection is last', there were the precepts of the Christian religion, the doctrine that 'the body is for the Lord and the Lord for the body'. And along with St. Paul Milton put that apocalyptic book of the Bible which sheds an unearthly light over so many of his pages from first to last. *Comus* ends, like 'Lycidas' (and the much inferior *Epitaphium Damonis*), with what is for the young Puritan the beatific vision, a vision that gives the final couplet the magic of incantation. It is temperance and chastity, not their opposites, that are rational and natural, and true chastity, beginning in the order of reason and nature, attains its fullness in the order of grace. This alone possesses the beauty, joy, and freedom which the blind and perverted Comus thinks are to be found in slavery to sense. And it is this religious motive, the heavenly marriage of the virgin soul, that adds a mystical glow of adoration to Milton's picture of the security of the virtuous mind. Perhaps the best proof of that appears not so much in the exposition of Christian and Platonic ethics as in the crystal purity of tone that irradiates the whole. No 'prolusion' from the Elder Brother or the Lady bears truer testimony than the opening lines to the author's apprehension of 'those chaste and high mysteries', his passionate faith in invisible things.

In the literary way those opening lines are very characteristic. The speech is a Euripidean prologue, delivered by a Neoplatonic *daemon* who is also a guardian angel, about angels and the souls of the good, who live on the Olympus of Homer and Lucretius, above the *fumum et opes strepitumque* of Horace's Rome, among the white-robed elders of Revelation seated round God's throne. But no part of Milton is more completely Miltonic; literary reminiscences are fused in a pure clear flame of religious and moral passion. After the fourth line of this speech there is, in the Trinity College manuscript, a passage of fourteen lines beginning:

amidst the Hesperian gardens, on whose bancks
bedew'd with nectar, and celestiall songs
aeternall roses grow, and hyacinth
and fruits of golden rind, on whose faire tree
the scalie-harnest dragon ever keeps
his uninchanted eye . . .

Milton's artistic conscience compelled the removal of this beautiful passage—though he salvaged bits of it later in the masque—apparently because its sensuous luxuriance blurred his main idea, the contrast between the purity of heaven and the 'Sin-worn mould' of earth. Even the Ovidian Echo, in the Lady's first song, is translated to the skies. The 'Dorique delicacy' that Sir Henry Wotton found in the songs and odes displays richer mastery of the cool, translucent, sophisticated art of *Arcades*. The triumphant and beautiful epilogue is difficult in a way that is of our time as well as the Renaissance; Milton relies on allusive symbols rather than statement. In *Comus* as a whole, underneath the Miltonic unity and harmony of feeling and style, we meet descriptive sensuousness and expository bareness, juvenile conceits and dramatic realism, Greek, Jonsonian, and Augustan classicism, and, in Comus's speech on the bounties of nature, something like Shakespearian complexity—a complexity that is not fortuitous but functional, since the picture of swarming life reflects the speaker's moral disorder.

So far, except for the self-questioning resolved in the seventh sonnet, Milton's poetry has embodied a studiously contemplative happiness, a youthful idealism, serene or fervent, unmarred by outward or inward trouble. The soul of the young poet-priest, and the natural and supernatural worlds he inhabits, have been a celestial harmony. If we have any fear that study and religious and moral zeal may dry up sensuous impulses, we may move on to Milton's letter, written to Diodati in 1637, declaring his God-given love of beauty in all the forms and appearances of things; the words—which include a phrase from Euripides—are both an aesthetic and a religious affirmation.

In this same year 1637, however, we have the first testimony of genuine spiritual disturbance. In 'Lycidas' the conflict that Keats discerned in Milton, between the pleasures and the ardours of song, appears as a bitter reality; the poem might have been called 'A Faith on Trial'. It is not to be read primarily as an elegy, and the degree of the author's sorrow for Edward King is quite irrelevant. 'Lycidas' achieves its emotional power because the drowning of a virtuous young man at once crystallizes and releases all Milton's thoughts and feelings about his own past, present, and future and about the great Task-Master's will. And this inexplicable event adds its heavy weight to the ennui, the paralysing doubts, which may attack the most zealous student after five long years of hard and outwardly unprofitable toil. What is the value of the laborious and consecrated life of learning if it is to be cut off before fame is won? The answer, that true fame can be assessed only by God and enjoyed only in heaven, is to be Milton's final answer, yet what we have at this point is half-conventional faith, the will to believe rather than emotional conviction, and doubt remains. God allows a blameless young cleric to die and hireling shepherds to infest His church, the church Milton had refused to enter. The lovely passage on flowers is a temporary escape, not a solution. The problem returns in the picture of the dead body washed beyond the stormy Hebrides or toward Namancos and Bayona's hold; here the volume of sound heightens the idea—which, like many of Milton's chief ideas, is conveyed indirectly—of the littleness of man in a world of forces that God does not seem to control. But the answer returns, the definition of true achievement and true fame, and now Milton rises above Apollo and Jove to the imagery of Revelation. The vision of the virgin soul of Lycidas received into heaven banishes the last shadow of doubt. Thus beneath the smooth surface of a conventional elegy, ebbing and flowing with the motives of the pastoral pattern, the waves of regret, anger, despair, and resolution roll upon one another.

The spiritual struggle goes on before our eyes, rising steadily in intensity, momentarily assuaged or aggravated by the irregularly sweet or thunderous music, until the last movement asserts the victory of faith in a triumphant glimpse of the sure glory of heaven. Life is vindicated and serenity is won.

There is no more miraculous example of the way in which a great theme, artistic power, and complete and impassioned sincerity can transform a supposedly dead convention. The pastoral device—here moulded in the form of a *canzone*—had from the beginning proved its value as a dramatic mask, and Milton found in it both a disguise for personal utterance and a pattern that imposed order upon his surging emotions. The account of carefree college life in pastoral terms, which offended Dr. Johnson's common sense, is an ironic picture of nature's normal peace and an oblique involvement of the poet's life and possible fate with that of the dead man. Even the strident attack on the clergy—our first evidence that the poet has taken sides in the national conflict—has pastoral precedents from Petrarch to Mantuan and Spenser. More important, and more subtle, is the pervasive interweaving of pagan pastoralism with the Christian motives that oppose, accept, or transcend it. The poem is infinitely complex in the associations it awakens, but all things, landscape and sea, Cambridge and Paradise, British lore and classical myth, Christian and pagan symbols, are wrought through partial dissonance into an harmonious whole, an almost epic whole. Through this complexity and objective solidity Milton's personal struggle becomes universal. The final paragraph, which may seem a mere pastoral flourish, throws that struggle into perspective. Nature, God's instrument, which had shown in fact its destructive violence, and also, in the analogy of the sun, had symbolized the promise of Christian rebirth, is seen once more in its normal, peaceful order; and in the simple but ambiguous last line the poet turns his back upon death to face life with renewed faith.

While he was still in Italy, Milton was informed of the death (August 1638) of Charles Diodati, his oldest and closest friend. When, at home again in familiar scenes, he sought to express his sorrow for his loss, he resorted not only to the pastoral convention but to Latin, the language of his early verse-letters. In the *Epitaphium Damonis*, which was written and privately printed in 1639/40, some main themes of 'Lycidas' reappear, but not with the same power—the questioning of Providence, the author's ambitions (here the British epic), and the reception of the virgin soul into the upper world 'where the festal orgies rage under the heavenly thyrsus'. There are touching moments, as when Milton recalls his friend's cultured wit and gaiety poured out in summer walks and by the winter fire, but as a whole the elegy moves, slowly, on a level of pastoral artifice and suggests the poet's falling back, in the apathy of grief and vague personal discontent, on literary habit. One may not share orthodox opinion, which has commonly put the *Epitaphium* at the head of Milton's Latin poems.

3

Milton settled in London at a time when it was reserved only for God and angels to be lookers-on. The lover of contemplation, with an heroic poem in his mind, shrank from embarking 'in a troubl'd sea of noises and hoars disputes'; but he had loved 'the honest liberty of free speech' from his youth and the trumpet-call of his great Task-Master left him no choice. He would not have been Milton if he had not been able to sacrifice his poetic hopes to the claims of public duty and his own broadening interests. He belongs to that tradition which stretches back through the Renaissance to antiquity, the tradition of the poet who not only writes what is doctrinal and exemplary to a nation but takes his place as an active citizen and leader. What course Milton would follow in the crisis of English liberty might not, perhaps, have been confidently predicted from his early poems, but it could have been from his seventh prolusion. It was partly as a young Baconian, partly as a young Platonist, that he had attacked the sterile Aristotelianism of Cambridge and had pleaded for real and fruitful examination of man's outer and inner world. That discourse, on the text that learning brings more blessings to men than ignorance, seems at first sight only a tissue of the commonplaces of Christian humanism. But it embodies an intensely personal faith, the boundless dreams of a young idealist of genius who feels himself standing on the threshold of a new era, who sees no obstacle in the way of man's conquest of nature and of all human problems. And he aspires, with a half-concealed but proud self-confidence, to be one of the makers of that new era, to be the oracle of many nations, whose home will be honoured as a shrine. We cannot measure the depth of Milton's later pessimism unless we appreciate the fervid and, as we say, unrealistic optimism of his youth and early manhood.

If Milton had not written a line of verse his prose works would be important as the commentary of a great and growing mind on momentous issues, and they are still more important as a commentary on his major poems. Passing by some late pieces, the *De Doctrina Christiana*, and such miscellaneous works as the *History of Britain* noticed in an earlier chapter, we have five pamphlets against prelacy (1641–2); four on divorce (1643–5), with the letter on education and *Areopagitica* coming respectively after the first and second; in the political field, the *Tenure of Kings and Magistrates* and *Eikonoklastes* (1649), the two Latin defences of the English people (1651, 1654), and the *Ready and Easy Way to Establish a Free Commonwealth* (1660). Of these works two or three stand among the great possessions of the race, two or three more are at least required reading, and the rest, except for scholars, are mostly dead. Writing in the heat of the moment, and with his own views in process of change, Milton too seldom rose to philosophic principles of enduring wisdom; but that is not to say that his breathless exhortations do not contain much judicious and liberal thought on the problems of his time. They contain also, along with inevitable wrangling and an equally inevitable excess of citation, spontaneous jets both of the prophetic sublimity that we expect and of satirical wit that we may not expect. Though his tracts are built on rhetorical canons, and develop systematic arguments, the loosely Ciceronian prose of the most disciplined of poets seems remarkably undisciplined. But the man who mocked at the 'spruce fastidious oratory' of the Senecan Joseph Hall is full of racy Saxon language and racy images; and on all levels, 'lofty, mean, or lowly', whether he is praying, arguing, or snorting down opponents, he gives the effect of the living voice. When we remember how amiable a quality in that turbulent age was the true-born Anglican's love of his Church and some royalists' devotion to their king, we may wish that Milton's zeal for purer spirituality in religion and truer liberty in civil affairs had carried less of the common harshness with it. But critics have often, and quite unfairly, singled out Milton as the great offender; they do not refer to the controversial violence of the saintly Andrewes and Donne. If Milton's manners were not above the average, and sometimes below, it is clear that, like other bookish idealists (and Church Fathers), he was moved by the enemies of a sacred cause to a kind of fury which left him honestly amazed and indignant when they returned the attack.

While special occasions called forth Milton's pamphlets, the first principles of his liberal creed, as we know from his Commonplace Book, developed out of prolonged study and reflection, and they developed most rapidly during his years of public activity. In the mode and substance of his thought, as in his poetic art, Milton owed much to the classics, but whereas traditional Christian humanism, Catholic or Protestant, had been in the main a bulwark of authority, the conflicts of Milton's age, the Puritan ideal of the holy community, and the impetus of Protestant individualism led him—he being what he was— from Anglicanism to Presbyterianism, from Presbyterianism to Independency, and from Independency to independence. It has been said that Milton himself '*was* a sect'. Yet it was the humanist in him who could neither stand still with the rigid Presbyterians nor accompany radical Puritans all the way. Facing his array of works on religious, domestic, and civil liberty, we cannot do more than recall a few familiar signposts.

In the anti-episcopal pamphlets of 1641–2, which we now cherish mainly for their personal passages, the author of 'Lycidas' naturally allied himself with the 'Smectymnuus' group of ministers (among them was his old tutor, Thomas Young) against Archbishop Ussher and Bishop Hall. But, despite his full assurance for the moment, Milton could be no more than a temporary fellow-traveller. In the light of his vision of a great regeneration, Presbyterianism *iure divino* quickly proved itself no less intolerable than episcopacy *iure divino*, and the Long Parliament seemed no nucleus for the holy community. Such disinterested disillusionment was not lessened, as some angry sonnets testify, by the Presbyterian reception of the pamphlets on divorce. These brought Milton his first real notoriety; even James Howell called him 'a poor shallow-brain'd puppy'. Comment on the divorce tracts must be limited to a miniature 'tetrachordon'. First, modern research has freed Milton from the odium of having begun the series during his honeymoon; he was married over a year before the first tract was printed. Secondly, while a personal grievance furnished a special motive and heightened the anguished pictures of an inexperienced man bound to an image of earth and phlegm, the subject, as Milton's citations amply indicate, had been of major interest to Reformation thinkers and continued to be their successors, and he might well have got around to it even if his own first marriage had been wholly happy. Thirdly, his appeal for easier divorce was based on a high ideal of marriage, of that marriage of minds which the Bible and the law did not recognize. Finally, notwithstanding the common prejudice against Milton's 'Turkish contempt of females', he did not ignore the right of women as well as men to release from unworthy mates. If he always gave man a higher rank in the scale of being, so did everyone else; and in exalting the husband Milton exalts the wife who is to be the true companion of such a man.

The wrestlings of Milton's individual reason with biblical pronouncements on divorce, and his violent reaction against a new tyranny, quickened the natural evolution of his progressive thinking and carried him out of the Presbyterian ranks into the van of liberalism. The testimony of his emancipation is his most famous and in some respects, though it embodied only a part of his final outlook, his most central work in prose. In *Areopagitica* (1644) we breathe the true, large Miltonic air, the air of his admired Lord Brooke and other Platonists and latitudinarians. The tract is a signal reminder of its author's double affiliations. In form it is a classical oration, and classical liberty is one of its themes, but its background was the Independent-Presbyterian controversy over religious toleration. It was largely ignored by the controversialists, and it was indeed off the main line of argument, since Milton concentrated upon the licensing ordinance revived by the predominantly Presbyterian Parliament in its effort to control the press. (He dealt more directly with the problem of toleration in later tracts and in the *Christian Doctrine*.) Since *Areopagitica* has often been loosely taken as a plea for complete freedom of speech, it should be observed that Milton does in fact accept the necessity of guarding fundamentals and hence of judicious censorship of dangerous books after publication. We need not be disappointed in recognizing that Milton, like his fellows, assumed the necessity of maintaining certain absolute values, that he was a liberal of the seventeenth century, not of the nineteenth or twentieth—and even the modern liberal has to readjust his principles in war-time. But nowhere in Milton, or in English, have we a mightier plea for free discussion, a more splendid confidence in the invincible power of reason and truth, or a greater faith in England as the mansion house of liberty.

The brief sketch of Milton's political theory in an earlier chapter may be briefly amplified here. The hammer of bishops had been, or thought himself, a true monarchist, but the close of the civil war found him on the left. In the *Tenure of Kings and Magistrates* (February 1649) he condemned shallow sympathy for a tyrant and upheld the principles of popular sovereignty and resistance with an array of authorities from the Bible and the classics down to Reformation divines. Marked out as an able spokesman for the regicides, Milton was assigned the task of answering *Eikon Basilike*. *Eikonoklastes* (1649), though a forceful exposure, was inevitably ineffectual. Milton's next opponent was the great scholar Salmasius, who had been employed to state the royalist case. The Latin *Defence of the English People* (1651) discredited Salmasius but was hardly worth the remnants of Milton's sight. The *Second Defence* (1654), a reply to an anonymous and able royalist attack, included a drubbing of Alexander More (though the actual author was Peter Du Moulin), but Milton rose to a noble celebration of the liberty won, and the further liberty still to be won, by the Commonwealth, and gave a noble testimony to his own renewed faith and strength. Cromwell and Fairfax received the Miltonic praise of having proved their right to rule by ruling their own passions. It was a testimony also to the sincerity of Milton's convictions that even in eulogizing the Protector the staunch republican felt uneasy over symptoms of dictatorship.

Six years later, in the midst of general chaos, Milton made a last bold appeal for a free commonwealth. In the *Ready and Easy Way* (1660) he took account of ancient and modern republican constitutions and of political theorists from Plato to Bodin and Harrington, but with all its detailed plans the tract was an admission of defeat, how crushing a defeat we can understand if we realize what Milton had sacrificed to the cause of liberty. The sheltered idealist had believed that England was full of John Miltons who had only to be shown the right path to follow it. The early pamphlets had been aflame with hope of complete and immediate triumph:

Methinks I see in my mind a noble and puissant Nation rousing herself like a strong man after sleep, and shaking her invincible locks: Methinks I see her as an Eagle muing her mighty youth, and kindling her undazl'd eyes at the full midday beam; purging and unscaling her long abused sight at the fountain it self of heav'nly radiance. . . .

At times since 1640 that ecstatic vision of a noble and puissant nation had grown dim, but Milton's hopes had rallied in 1654. Now, in 1660, the vision has faded into the light of common day, and men worthy to be for ever slaves are rushing to put their heads under the yoke, 'choosing them a captain back for Egypt'. The good old cause is dead; God's new and greater Reformation is ending in the Restoration.

Yet Milton's career as a publicist was not wholly a loss, for him or for us. From the first he knew what he was giving up, since poetry was his right hand and prose his left, but he had always desired the fame of a great leader, an oracle of nations, and his work in prose, if in one sense a forced betrayal of his destiny, was also a large part of its fulfilment. It consoles him in his blindness to recall his defence of liberty, of which, he thinks, 'all Europe talks from side to side'. The monumental sonnets on public men and events, so different in theme and style from the mass of Elizabethan and later verse in that form, were soul-animating strains beyond the power of Tasso, and parallel rather to the exalted odes in which Horace reminded decadent Rome of the old Roman virtues—or, on the occasion of the massacre in Piedmont, to the comminatory thunders of a Hebrew prophet. The chief fruit of the author's experience in the arena was the strengthening and enrichment of the major poems. In addition to the heroic poet's 'insight into all seemly and generous arts and affaires', Milton gained the insight into less seemly arts which contributed to the human reality of the rebel angels; the Secretary to the Council (to echo Gibbon) was not useless to the historian of Pandemonium. But the great gain was on another level. If the British or biblical epic had been written when it was first planned, doubtless, as passages in the early prose suggest, it would have been a song of triumph; we cannot regret the endurance of dust and heat, the tragic frustration and disillusionment, which deepened and saddened its wisdom. However cheerful Milton's old age, the stress and stimulus of imaginative effort heightened his realization of heroic past and ignoble present. *Paradise Lost* is a divine comedy in which good grows out of evil, but the author's optimism is

far from facile; it must be measured by the strength of the
pessimism it has to overcome. Milton can declare himself still
able to sing with voice unchanged,

> though fall'n on evil dayes,
> On evil dayes though fall'n, and evil tongues;
> In darkness, and with dangers compast round,
> And solitude,

but his voice is changed, even in these very lines. He tries to
find ground for hope in the vision of future history revealed to
Adam, but Adam hears no such story of national courage and
high destiny as Aeneas heard from Anchises:

> Truth shall retire
> Bestuck with slandrous darts, and works of Faith
> Rarely be found: so shall the World goe on,
> To good malignant, to bad men benigne,
> Under her own waight groaning, till the day
> Appeer of respiration to the just,
> And vengeance to the wicked. . . .

Pessimism reaches its depth in *Samson*. God's chosen hero is
'Eyeless in Gaza at the Mill with slaves', and of all the temptations he has to conquer the greatest is that of despair. Yet—and
this is Milton's last message, the indestructible remnant of his
once boundless dreams of a new age—if his faith in men and
action has proved vain, there is still hope for individual man;
he can at least, with divine grace, rule himself. The kingdom of
Christ is not of this world. So when Adam has learned the
Christian way of life, he has no need of an earthly paradise, he
has a paradise within him, happier far. So Christ, man's perfect
model, maintains His integrity against the allurements of ambition. So Samson, resisting selfish and sensual temptations, wins
a new strength and internal peace which make his outward fate
of no account.

4

The central articles of Milton's ethical and religious creed
were developed in his prose, and we may here take both a
backward and a forward glance, remembering that that creed
was always growing under the pressure of thought and experience, and that some of the most significant developments, at
least in tone and emphasis, appeared only in the late poems.

If the first article was liberty, it was the liberty achieved through religious discipline, through education in the fullest sense of the word. In his letter (1644) to Hartlib, the Baconian and Comenian reformer, Milton showed, as he had in his prolusions, some affinity with Baconian critics of the prescribed methods and materials of education, both scholastic and linguistic, and—partly perhaps because of the demands of war— he gave a larger importance to the study of science than many of the older humanists had given. In the main, however, he wrote in the orthodox tradition of Renaissance humanism and his own St. Paul's School. His view is aristocratic (later he was to feel more strongly the need of popular education); he aims at the production of useful and cultivated citizens and leaders, not scholars; and he assumes that the classics are the fundamental literature of knowledge as well as of power. In stressing religion and virtue, the training of the moral judgement and the will, he only adds a personal earnestness to what had been the chief object of Christian humanism in all ages and countries. Of the two definitions of education in the tract, what might be called the 'modern' one is constantly quoted, but the 'medieval' one is even more truly Miltonic:

The end then of learning is to repair the ruins of our first parents by regaining to know God aright, and out of that knowledge to love him, to imitate him, to be like him, as we may the neerest by possessing our souls of true vertue, which being united to the heavenly grace of faith makes up the highest perfection.

That is the substance of the last words between Michael and Adam, and by that time the author had gained a fuller comprehension of their meaning.

It was inevitable that Milton—though he considered himself a Calvinist as late as 1644—should break with Calvinism as Erasmus had broken with Luther. A humanist believing in human and divine reason could not uphold the depravity of man and the arbitrary will of an inscrutable God. No ordinance, human or from heaven, Milton declared in *Tetrachordon*, can bind against the good of man. And in the tracts on divorce, in *Areopagitica*, and most fully and explicitly in the *Christian Doctrine*, Milton evolved that enlarged conception of Christian liberty of which he was in his day the great exponent. That conception of the self-directing independence of the regenerate man, of his freedom from external prescription, could be both aristocratic and revolutionary; it was, of course, far removed from the licence of the unregenerate and irresponsible. Man's guide is not the letter of civil or biblical law but the law of the Spirit written in the hearts of believers; for Milton as for Hooker and Taylor and others the law of God is the law of right reason and of nature. With Christian values and motives are fused ancient, aristocratic, and rational ideals of private and republican freedom. Both the right reason of the individual and the saving remnant of the regenerate are, like the created universe, worlds of divine order in the midst of chaos.

A good deal, though not all, of the purpose and substance of Milton's chief works is crystallized in some eloquent and familiar sentences of *Areopagitica*:

I cannot praise a fugitive and cloister'd vertue, unexercis'd & unbreath'd, that never sallies out and sees her adversary, but slinks out of the race, where that immortall garland is to be run for, not without dust and heat. Assuredly we bring not innocence into the world, we bring impurity much rather: that which purifies us is triall, and triall is by what is contrary. That vertue therefore which is but a youngling in the contemplation of evill, and knows not the utmost that vice promises to her followers, and rejects it, is but a blank vertue, not a pure; her whitenesse is but an excrementall whitenesse; Which was the reason why our sage and serious Poet Spencer, whom I dare be known to think a better teacher then Scotus or Aquinas, describing true temperance under the person of Guion, brings him in with his palmer through the cave of Mammon, and the bowr of earthly blisse that he might see and know, and yet abstain. . . .

Many there be that complain of divin Providence for suffering Adam to transgresse, foolish tongues! when God gave him reason, he gave him freedom to choose, for reason is but choosing; he had bin else a meer artificiall Adam, such an Adam as he is in the motions. We our selves esteem not of that obedience, or love, or gift, which is of force: God therefore left him free, set before him a provoking object, ever almost in his eyes; herein consisted his merit, herein the right of his reward, the praise of his abstinence. Wherefore did he creat passions within us, pleasures round about us, but that these rightly temper'd are the very ingredients of vertu? . . .

This justifies the high providence of God, who though he command us temperance, justice, continence, yet powrs out before us ev'n to a profusenes all desirable things, and gives us minds that can wander beyond all limit and satiety.

This last sentence, with its verbal anticipations of *Paradise Lost*, is a particular reminder of Milton's method of justifying God's ways to men, his emphasis on human freedom of choice and human responsibility (and that true freedom must include the freedom to do wrong is still a philosophical axiom of unimpaired force). The unwary Eve falls through 'pride And wandring vanitie', the credulous and mistaken desire for an apparent good, which mislead her reason, and Adam, whose reason is not deceived, allows uxorious idolatry to sway his will and break his higher tie with God. In putting the simple biblical story on a partly humanistic and rational basis, in making it a many-sided conflict between reason and unreason, 'knowledge' and 'ignorance', temperance and excess, hierarchic order and anarchic disorder, Milton had behind him the whole tradition of Christian humanism; two contemporary examples are the first chapter of Browne's *Pseudodoxia Epidemica* and Henry More's *Conjectura Cabbalistica*. But Milton has also risen above —some might say he had fallen below—the bold confidence of *Areopagitica* and *Tetrachordon*. If the zealous pamphleteer had not quite fully realized that reason and rectitude could partake of self-sufficient human pride, the ageing poet has had the lesson proved on his pulses. He has not abandoned the principles of Christian liberty and right reason, for these are religious and fundamental, but he has a new understanding of the prime need of humility and obedience. Irreligious pride and religious humility are indeed the one great theme of his major poems.

In *Paradise Lost*, even in exalting human reason and freedom, Milton stresses human weakness and the dangers of pride, which ruin Eve and Adam as well as Satan. The fallen angels lose themselves in the mazes of philosophic debate. The whole temptation of Eve is an appeal to the desire for godlike knowledge and power. In the long astronomical discussion of the eighth book, and with reiterated emphasis at the end of the poem, Adam is warned to check his roving fancy and to learn that the sum of wisdom is not scientific learning but everyday Christian goodness. We may be surprised at such 'obscurantism' in the man who had been kindled by Baconian ideas, who had given science a large place in his educational scheme, and who had written the great defence of free inquiry. But Milton is not condemning science in itself (he pays tribute to Galileo in the epic as well as in *Areopagitica*), he is only taking scientific knowledge and speculation as a cardinal example of the pride and presumption that obscure the true ends and values of life. In this view he recalls Chapman and Greville and Donne's *Anniversaries*. Like all Christian humanists from Petrarch to Matthew Arnold, he feared the confusing of wisdom and knowledge, law for man and law for thing. In the *Reason of Church Government* (1642) he had distinguished between the lower wisdom of natural science and the only high valuable wisdom of religion, and in the following decades it might well seem that the rising tide of scientific thought threatened to sweep away religious and ethical values altogether. For Milton as for the Cambridge Platonists, the physical and metaphysical worlds were a divine order with a divine purpose, and man was made in the image of God, with a spark of divine reason and divine will.

We may notice here a parallel case in *Paradise Regained*. Many readers, knowing Milton's lifelong devotion and infinite debt to classical literature and thought, feel a shock when they come upon Christ's repudiation of the philosophy, poetry, and oratory of Greece, which has just received through Satan the poet's beautiful and heart-felt praise. The shock is unwarranted. Like other Christian humanists, Milton had always set the Bible above all other writings, and he gave still higher authority to 'the Spirit and the unwritten word'. It is only in comparison with the divine light of humble Christian faith and virtue that Greek philosophy, like science, appears as the product and instrument of arrogant human pride. In itself, so far as it goes, it is good; Christ Himself, earlier in the poem, had ranked Socrates next to Job. Milton's favourite secular authors up to the end were ancients, and this very poem—not to mention its companion, *Samson Agonistes*—owes much to them. His condemnation is relative rather than absolute. At the same time his vehemence here is a mark of the growing inwardness of his thought; in his age he turns more and more from a degenerate world and secondary aids to cling to ultimate truth. He is saying, as his old opponent Bishop Hall, the Christian Stoic, had said, that true light and peace of mind are to be won not at Athens but at Jerusalem.

5

To speak briefly, as we must, of Milton's theological thought is to recognize his essential orthodoxy and to slight particular heresies (heresies which he derived from the Bible). The explicit statement of his views, ethical and social as well as theological, is the *De Doctrina Christiana* (first printed in 1825) which, however early it originated, had reached virtually final form by about 1658–60 and was later amplified only in some details. Starting from such models as Ames and Wollebius, and taking account of a mass of commentary, Milton was at great pains to draw up a body of strictly biblical teaching that would systematize his own beliefs and also, apparently, furnish an acceptable basis for Protestantism. Such rigorous exegesis of biblical doctrine provides chapter and verse for the theological concepts of *Paradise Lost*, though it leaves small room for the humanistic Milton, much less for the imaginative action and insights of his poetic fable. The several following paragraphs, while based partly on the treatise, are pointed towards the poem. It will be convenient, if not precisely correct, to use 'Christ' for 'the Son'.

Christ is the Logos, the Creative Word, God's executive agent in the heavenly war and in the creation and judgement of man. In contrast with Satan, He is the incarnation of divine love and right reason, the Mediator and Redeemer through whom man becomes regenerate. In all these roles Christ is the heavenly protagonist of the poem (the earthly one is Adam, whose defeat and loss are repaired by 'the second Adam'). Milton not only accepts but glorifies the Atonement in both verse and prose, though his more instinctive emphasis seems to be, like that of the Cambridge Platonists, on the imitation of Christ, the divine life. His final belief in the progressive subordination of the Son and the Holy Spirit to the Father, which in part resembles that of Cudworth and More, may be called Arian or merely anti-Trinitarian; its roots are in Neoplatonic traditions older than the Council of Nicaea. This belief, while clearly set forth in the treatise, is less distinct and obvious in *Paradise Lost* (which did not disturb generations of orthodox readers), but no doctrinal passage in the poem is inconsistent with it.

Like Christ, but on a higher, absolute level, God embodies divine love, and much more; He is—in the religious, not the naturalistic, sense—the total nature of things. He has been a stumbling-block to unsympathetic readers. One cause is that He speaks in bare, 'unpoetical' language; for the reverent, God-intoxicated poet, divine speech must have the naked simplicity

of truth itself. Then, if to some He appears to resemble an
almighty cat watching a human mouse, most of the trouble lies
in a conception of justice from which many modern minds
recoil:

> Die hee or Justice must; unless for him
> Som other able, and as willing, pay
> The rigid satisfaction, death for death.

On this grand point Bishop Andrewes (*XCVI Sermons*, p. 101)
may serve as spokesman for Milton and tradition:

Fond men! If He would quit His Justice, or waive His truth, He
could: But, His justice and truth are to Him as essentiall, as intrinsec-
ally essentiall, as His Mercie: of æquall regard, every way as deere
to Him. Justice otherwise remaines unsatisfied: and, satisfied it must
be, either on Him, or on us.

A third cause of trouble is the effect of dramatization: God and
Christ become, not two aspects of Deity, Justice and Love, but
two persons, one severe, the other merciful. And God suffers,
paradoxically, through being the mouthpiece for the very
doctrines that clear Him of arbitrary cruelty and justify His ways
to men, the Arminian and Miltonic doctrines of free grace
extended to all believers and of the right reason, free will, and
responsibility of man. Against the Absolute Will of Calvinism
Milton sets up Absolute Reason, the ultimate source and
guarantee of life, order, justice, all the values comprehended by
the reason that is man's divine endowment. There may be artistic
defects in the presentation—though God can speak like a
Deity—but there is nothing thin or cold in the conception. In
the great words of Hooker,

of lawe there can be no lesse acknowledged, then that her seate is the
bosome of God, her voyce the harmony of the world, all thinges in
heaven and earth doe her homage, the very least as feeling her care,
and the greatest as not exempted from her power, but Angels and
men and creatures of what condition so ever, though ech in different
sort and maner, yet all with uniforme consent, admiring her as the
mother of their peace and joy.

That is the divine and natural harmony, the hierarchical order,
which Satan seeks to overthrow in the universe and in the soul
of man.

To enlarge a little upon Milton's metaphysics, his conception

of the infinity, omnipresence, and omnipotence of God lies
behind some ideas which may seem to approach pantheism,
though Milton is no pantheist; he does not confound the Creator
with Creation. God includes all causes, even the material. God
did not create the world out of nothing, as orthodox tradition
maintained, but out of the eternal substance which is a part of
Himself. Uncircumscribed by necessity or chance, God com-
municates His goodness by manifesting Himself throughout the
great scale of being which descends from Christ and the angels
through the creatures and things of earth. All things proceed
from God and, unless depraved by evil, return to Him. Chaos
is Chaos because He has not chosen to put forth His creative
virtue upon it. (The germ of this idea is perhaps what in the
Timaeus is called 'the absence of God'.) Milton affirms the
reality and the goodness of matter; matter is not distinct from
spirit but is for ever passing into it. The optimism inherent in
such metaphysical monism receives characteristic expression
from the poet-musician in half-mystical celebrations of cosmic
harmony. It is obviously related to the ethical optimism that
Milton shared also with the Cambridge Platonists, and for him
it is a partial bulwark against the pessimism of experience. This
metaphysical monism is not incompatible with the ethical
dualism that is Christian and Platonic. What God is in the
universe the divine faculty of reason is in man, and when man's
reason is not in active control his nature becomes a chaos of
passions. An ethical corollary of Milton's belief in the essential
oneness of matter and spirit is his mature conception of human
love, a conception which retains his early Christian and Platonic
idealism without his early asceticism. Another logical consequence is the belief that man dies wholly until the day of
resurrection; in this Milton is allied with contemporary
'mortalists'.

If this outline of some of Milton's central ideas has taken
space which should have been given to 'the poetry', it is still the
merest sketch of the creed he devoted his life and art to proclaiming. If the fundamental part of the creed be dismissed as
elementary and commonplace, it was for Milton as for other
great men and great writers the armour of a Christian soldier.
And, it may be added, there is in *Paradise Lost* (as in the whole
body of Milton's poetry) very little that is specifically Puritan;
in essentials the so-called 'Puritan epic' is simply a poem of

traditional Christianity, Catholic as well as Protestant. Finally, what we think of as Milton's theology belongs mainly to the *Christian Doctrine* and *Paradise Lost*, and his particular and changing beliefs are less significant than his progress towards belief, in a deeper sense of the word. His earlier pamphlets had been largely directed towards militant action; the decline and collapse of that external hope left him feeling the need of a closer walk with God. In his late poems, in place of the old ardent confidence in public reform, we find an 'un-Miltonic' emphasis on private experience, on humility, obedience, faith, and divine grace. And *Paradise Lost*, while it has some metaphysical passages, is not a metaphysical effort to explain the origin of evil; it is a 'myth' in which evil is a fact of life.

6

We have had incidental hints of the epic ambitions that no Renaissance poet cherished more ardently than Milton. He had long contemplated the British theme that critical theory and poetic example prescribed, and his final choice was evidently determined by various causes, the scepticism induced by his own and others' study of early history, the cleavage in sentiment between 'Saxon' parliamentarians and 'British' royalists, the general European reaction in favour of biblical subjects, and chiefly, no doubt, his desire for a fable which would carry all that he now wished to say about God and man. The British and biblical subjects listed in the Cambridge manuscript (*c.* 1639–42) were planned as dramas, and Milton made four dramatic outlines of Adam's fall; indeed, the tale of Adam and Eve is in its very nature the pattern of a morality play. However, Milton did not give up his original and more satisfying project of an heroic poem. Having elected his subject and form, he still faced a problem which had existed in a smaller degree for Virgil and not at all for Homer, that is, the treatment of abstract spiritual ideas in the concrete terms of the heroic epic. As occasional apologies in the text indicate, Milton was conscious of the problem, quite as much as the modern reader who may feel that he has outgrown the epic as well as biblical religion and is unaware of traditional typology. We have touched already on the anthropomorphic presentation of God, which Milton's subject made almost unavoidable, and which has misled many modern readers and critics into seeing the trappings of a tyrant and not the religious and metaphysical conceptions He embodies (the tyrant of the poem is of course Satan). The battles in heaven, the account of Creation, and the concluding survey of Hebrew and western history are often thought to be too protracted and too realistic for their symbolic function; yet they do dramatize the contrast between chaotic passions and divine order, between destruction and the creative works of peace, between man's sinfulness and God's providence. Uniquely Miltonic power, imaginative, visual, and rhythmical, animates the climactic ending of the war by the Son, the irresistible force of good, and the pictures of His leaving and returning to heaven before and after the Creation; the whole account of the Creation is alive with movement and growth; and the historical survey is an essential link between Genesis and the modern world, between the primal sin and universal experience.

In the elaboration of his narrative and drama Milton had two main resources, the plastic materials of classical story and, more directly, the whole Bible and the body of extra-biblical lore accumulated in commentaries and in imaginative treatments of the Creation and the fall of Lucifer and of man. How many works of this last kind Milton had read we do not know; the *Adamus Exul* (1601) of Grotius and the *Adamo* (1613) of Andreini are perhaps the closest to *Paradise Lost*. Milton's poem is the great surviving monument of the immense mass of Renaissance writing, exegetical and poetical, that dealt with the matter of Genesis. God Himself hardly knew more about the beginnings of the world than the Du Bartas whom the young Milton had admired in Sylvester's popular translation and whose Protestant epic his own superseded. Imaginative versions of religious 'history' were bound to keep within the limits of orthodoxy (a flexible orthodoxy, to be sure), so that they all have a degree of family resemblance, and very many items, large and small, in Milton's fable are inevitably conventional. A Renaissance poet, like a Greek dramatist, was expected to show his originality in the reworking of traditional themes.

To appreciate the re-creative power of Milton's imagination we have only to think of Satan, who had for ages been an archetypal actuality and who now became one of the great figures of world literature. One need only refer to the romantic idea, which has been thoroughly pulverized by modern criticism, that Milton was of the devil's party without knowing it, that Satan was his real hero. It is a matter of course that Shakespeare, though devoted to order, could create heroic villains; why it should have been a wonder and a problem that Milton could is not clear. In his first speech, no less than later, Satan shows himself in every word a mighty outlaw, a great embodiment of egocentric pride and passion and a false ideal of liberty, and the intelligent reader—who hardly needs the poet's guiding comments—reacts as he does to the lawless speeches of Iago, Edmund, and Macbeth; Milton was, of course, a doctrinal poet as the dramatist was not, but they belong to the same traditions. It is not Milton's fault if the naïve or the flippant are incapable of responding to the old conceptions of pride and sin and order and grace (we may remember the modern definition of a romantic as one who does not believe in the fall of man).

Milton was daring enough to give his first two books, books of unexampled poetic splendour, to his epic villain, who was endowed, moreover, with the great qualities of the traditional epic hero. These qualities are none the less real for being wholly corrupted. But since Milton could, like Shakespeare, rely on the moral and religious reactions of his early audience, he could, like Shakespeare, use dramatic objectivity and irony. Satan, after the manner of Elizabethan villains, may tell the truth in soliloquies, but his public speeches and actions are enveloped in irony; he and his fellows—like fallen man—speak and scheme and act in blind unawareness or defiance of invincible good. Satan's magnificent vitality inspires an artistically necessary degree of imaginative response while, as a being dedicated to evil, he inspires profound aversion. Because he has a conscience (like Macbeth), he contains tragic potentialities, but these, in a conflict with absolute good, are not allowed fulfilment. Satan's epic role is somewhat like Dido's, though his deliberate aim succeeds, as her tragic passion does not, in deflecting the hero and the divine purpose; and the comparison is a reminder that the 'sympathy' he evokes is very limited indeed.

In his classical adaptations, though *Paradise Lost* has many incidental echoes of Homer, Milton followed especially Virgil, the great model of epic structure and decorum, and, like Virgil, he gave new meanings to the particular devices he imitated—celestial machinery, the roll-call and council of leaders, epic games, the flash-back narrative after the plunge *in medias res*, and the unfolding of future events. This last item suggests one of the larger affinities: the subject of both poems is a 'world destroy'd and world restor'd'. To mention a few adaptations from various sources, the revolt of the angels blends theological tradition with the wars of giants and Titans and gods; the rebel army in hell marches like the Spartans in Plutarch's *Lycurgus*; the mythical monster Scylla—and the epistle of James i. 15—inspired the unique allegory of Sin and Death, who, with Satan, make up a ghastly parody of the Trinity and are a potent reminder of the real nature of Satan's 'heroism'; Satan and Gabriel confront each other like Turnus and Aeneas in their last combat; Eve gives the first hint of her 'wandring vanitie' by innocently admiring her reflection in a pool, like Narcissus; the fall of Adam and Eve from love to lust is rendered partly in terms of Homer's Paris and Helen and Zeus and Hera; the biblical description of the flood invites expansion from Ovid and Du Bartas.... But all these things have gone through Milton's own imagination and been moulded, often with ironic effect, into a unified though infinitely complex whole.

Milton's great elaboration of his material went along with organization both massive and minute. The main lines of action and changes of scene have a logical coherence that no one can miss—and also depths of significance that can be missed. Parallels and contrasts range from the large and obvious to details and overtones—the fall of Satan and the fall of man, the 'merit' of Satan and of Christ, the infernal and celestial assemblies and the single volunteer in each, Satan's apostrophe to the sun in Book iv and his midnight soliloquy in Book ix, and so on. Milton greatly developed a kind of metaphor and symbol that was conspicuous in Spenser, that is, continual variations on the antitheses between natural simplicity, goodness, love, light, and life on the one hand and artificial luxury, evil, hate, darkness, and death on the other. One is always discovering more of the tiny threads that bind together and enrich the texture. As in the universe of Renaissance ideology, everything in *Paradise Lost* is related to everything else. Also, everything in this Miltonic world is not only described or revealed but is also judged.

While Homeric similes in the main keep us aware of a normal pastoral life beyond the roar of battle and the waves, Milton's allusiveness takes, of course, a much wider range, from the Gorgons to Galileo, from Orpheus to the London burglar. His geographical names are not merely incantation but an economical way of calling up great events and great tracts of space and time. In becoming less familiar some allusions have become less realistic than they were in Milton's own age. The investing of Satan, 'thir great Sultan', with oriental pomp and power was not glamorous tinsel for men whose grandfathers had feared the mighty Turk and coveted 'the wealth of Ormus and of Ind'. But if allusions are commonly prompted by substantial reasons, they may also be vague enough to sustain and heighten our sense of remoteness or mystery or grandeur or horror. And that is in keeping with Milton's fable and purpose. His vast stage and superhuman action demand, not the minute realism of Dante, but the constant use of the general and suggestive, whether in the pictures of hell or of the 'enormous bliss' of Eden. But that goes with and is controlled by a fundamental concreteness of thought and vision. Keats observed Milton's habit of 'stationing' characters in relation to solid objects; we see Adam 'under a Platan' and Satan disfigured 'on th'Assyrian mount'. Unlike the true romantic, Milton never surrenders to the vague and unearthly. One remarkable instance is that magnificently romantic island salt and bare, 'The haunt of Seales and Orcs, and Seamews clang', which disproves the special sanctity of what George Fox called steeple-houses.

Classical generality and romantic suggestion are never more perfectly fused than in Milton's images from ancient myth. They are the culmination of Renaissance art. They are, too, an index to Milton's own artistic and spiritual evolution; his successive allusions to Orpheus, for instance, reflect the lyrical serenity of 'L'Allegro' and 'Il Penseroso', the troubled disenchantment of 'Lycidas', the religious fortitude of the invocation to light, and the bitterness of the strident outburst against Bacchus and his revellers. While Milton's classical mythology shared in his general evolution from Elizabethan luxuriance through a chastened splendour to bare severity, and while the later books of *Paradise Lost* and the two last poems largely forbade the use of myth, this more than any other element in his writing retained the old sensuous warmth. In Milton generally, as in the Renaissance tradition, the unique value of the mythological symbol is its ideal beauty. Like such moderns as Arnold and T. S. Eliot, Milton instinctively turns away from the ugly present to the freshness and fecundity of the early world. The finest of all his similes, 'Not that faire field Of Enna', owes its complex magic to the musical and structural pattern, to the pathos of familiarity in the phrase 'all that pain', and to the implication that another innocent and lovely Proserpine is about to be gathered by the prince of darkness. Both the myth and the image of the flower are recalled, with a mixture of tragic irony and pity, in the description of Eve just before the temptation, when she goes forth like Ceres in her prime and when she is tying up the drooping stalks

> Her self, though fairest unsupported Flour,
> From her best prop so farr, and storm so nigh.

The various pictures of the 'Silvan Scene', in which Milton lets himself go, though not beyond control, in the evocation of an earthly paradise, are not merely a gorgeous exercise in a Renaissance convention (still less an attempt to render the sensation of being in a garden); they spring from the poet's half-unconscious desire to believe in some ideal perfection unmarred by evil. Yet Milton is no poet of escape and he never loses his hold upon reality; the idyllic beauty of Eden is seen from the first only under the ironic shadow of the tempter.

Milton's classical mythology may, in his most solemn moods, be blended with Hebraic or Christian feeling, as in the allusion to Proserpine and the prayers into which he transformed addresses to the epic Muse, or in the sonnet on his dead wife. But although tradition had reconciled classical and Hebrew story, and although the mature Milton could still link myth with religious and moral truth, he always claimed Christian superiority to 'th'Orphean Lyre' and he could feel, as Spenser did not, a conflict. His anti-pagan scruples, so often incorporated in the text of *Paradise Lost*, illustrate the dilemma of a sacred poet and a Puritan bred in the congenial air of Renaissance classicism. For one example, the lines about Mulciber's fall from heaven—which are, incidentally, a romantic transmutation of Homeric humour and embody an un-Homeric sense of space—begin and end with expressions of hostile disbelief, yet they contain a suggestiveness of picture and sound notable even in Milton.

When various cosmological theories were current it was natural for a layman and a poet to follow what is called the Ptolemaic system. Milton knew enough science to discuss the old and familiar notions of the diurnal rotation of the earth and the plurality of worlds, and to treat Copernican ideas with respect, but the actual universe of *Paradise Lost* was a Miltonic mixture of the traditional and the imaginative, and was modern chiefly in its immensity. He was, as we have seen, too much of a Christian humanist to let scientific speculation divert him from the problems of direct importance to man and society. It has been said that Shakespeare lived in a world of time, Milton in a world of space, but for Milton space is no parallel to the spectre of devouring Time which haunted so many minds of the Renaissance. In his traditional scale of values, science, so far as it is a description of God's works, is a branch of theology and as such he, like Du Bartas, can make use of it. Hence too, unlike some men of his century, Milton was apparently at no time bewildered and dismayed by the silence of infinite space. The axis of his faith rested on God and the soul of man, and if that faith was sometimes shaken, the cause was not any trepidation of the spheres. Without misgiving he accepts the universe as his scene and his imagination triumphantly expands to fill it. No other English poet has such a God-like vision of the world, a vision revealed in the great pictures of boundless chaos and warring elements and in the constant suggestion of vast distances. Such imperial command of space doubtless belongs to the age of the telescope, yet we may remember that no poet of the same age rivals the blind Milton and, further, that a sense of space was not wholly lacking in earlier men, among them such ancients as Lucretius, Ovid, and Manilius.

The use of blank verse for an heroic poem was a signal innovation and Milton's handling of it added, not a new province, but a new world, to English versification. Nothing can be said here about his prosodic inheritance, native, classical, and Italian; and only a few general remarks can be made on the actual operation of his system. First, in the sonnets Milton had been moving towards the massive blank-verse paragraph; even where rhymes were emphatic (as in the Piedmont sonnet), the formal pattern could almost disappear because of run-on lines and strong medial pauses. In the epic verse these two principles, working through long sentences, contribute greatly to the continuous flow. Secondly, as Edward Weismiller has shown, it is an error to regard Milton's basic unit as the iambic pentameter line with innumerable 'substitutions'. The unit is the line of ten syllables, grouped commonly in pairs; the commonest 'foot' is the iambic, but other 'feet' are more or less common too. The number of stresses varies in general from four to seven (though some lines have less than four or more than seven), and variations in weight and tempo are endless. Thus, while our ear should be conditioned to the count of syllables, there are characteristic underlying movements, based on accent, which give the pleasure of fulfilled expectation; at the same time departures from the expected are also common and are not merely 'licentious'. Further, as the initial comment on the sonnets partly indicated, the internal structure of the decasyllabic line and combinations of run-on lines create a sort of simultaneous second pattern of rhythmical units, those that flow from the natural pause or caesura in one line to the pause in the next; and the place and weight of such pauses are infinitely variable. For instance, in the lines quoted in the second paragraph below, the monosyllabic 'Day' is poised, abnormally and powerfully, at the beginning of a line. This is only one reminder of the expressive and emotional effects which mere descriptions of mechanics cannot begin to explain but which Milton's readers cannot slide over without loss; his rhythms are an active and essential part of what he is saying, a main element in his creative and moving power.

Milton's versification is inseparable from his style and tone. More or less hostile critics, old and new, have charged him with un-English diction and syntax, a charge which is not strengthened by irrelevant comparisons with Donne, with Shakespeare's dramatic speech, and with Dante's totally different kind of epic. Milton's poetic and critical heritage and his own purpose prescribed a long poem, and in such a long poem the reader must be made to feel the continuity, 'the enormous onward pressure of the great stream' on which he is embarked. In short, epic style must be stylized, and Milton's style is surely no more remote from popular English than Virgil's is from popular Latin or Homer's from popular Greek. Like the ancients, Milton wore his singing robes; a ritualistic elevation of style and movement was essential to a heroic and religious theme of cosmic dimensions. Classical theory and practice had been restated for the Renaissance by such a poet-critic as Tasso, and his precepts for the attaining of epic elevation are illustrated in *Paradise Lost*. One essential function of stylized elevation is

the preserving of aesthetic distance, in the depiction of hell,
heaven, chaos, and most of all Eden; presented realistically,
Adam and Eve would be a pair of suburban nudists.

But, granted the elevated and fitting stylization, the poem is
no stiff brocade; it has far more simplicity and variety than
stereotyped prejudice has recognized. Milton's syntax never
troubles those who leave it alone. Much of what has been loosely
condemned as classical idiom is rather forceful condensation,
such as the omission of connectives (which is not condemned
in the ultra-English Hopkins). Milton may place words and
phrases with something of the freedom of an inflected language,
but the result is a continual gain in emphasis and expressiveness.
And while the texture is full of suggestive overtones and ambiguities, the main meaning is always clear—as it often is not in
Shakespeare. Poetry, Milton conceived, should be 'lesse suttle
and fine, but more simple, sensuous and passionate' than logic
and rhetoric. For one example of sensuous and passionate writing which is far from 'simple' in the derogatory sense, an
example of the purest classical art and one of the most moving
things in English poetry, there is the invocation to Light:

> Thus with the Year
> Seasons return, but not to me returns
> Day, or the sweet approach of Ev'n or Morn,
> Or sight of vernal bloom, or Summers Rose,
> Or flocks, or heards, or human face divine. . . .

The last phrase is not disposed of when we say that the placing
of a noun between two adjectives is a Miltonic mannerism; in
that poignant paradox we feel the blind poet's loss of the everyday sight of other men and the miracle of ordinary human
existence and of man's being made in the image of God. It may
be added that, in the lines just quoted and the six that follow,
the percentage of classical words is 23·7, that of Anglo-Saxon
73·7, which, according to E. M. Clark's careful study, are
almost exactly the norm for the poem as a whole, though proportions vary from one kind of passage to another.

The length and general clarity of *Paradise Lost* encourage
the uncritical assumption that Milton splashes at a ten-league
canvas with brushes of comets' hair, that his smallest unit is the
paragraph with its planetary wheel, that his art is too simply
rhetorical for the subtler effects of phrase and rhythm. The

sensitive reader may discover for himself what there is no space to illustrate, the perpetual and significant variations, both broad and minute, in narrative of action, in description, in exposition, in oratory; and, within these categories, the further variations in manner between, say, the speeches of Moloch and Belial, or between the description of hell (a symbol of spiritual anarchy) and the description of Eden (a symbol of earthly perfection). One large contrast sets off the intimate drama of the garden from the epic narrative and drama of the opening books. The archangel who had opposed the Almighty becomes a sardonic Richard III or malignant Iago; the mother of mankind is a very feminine Everywoman, more concerned—after as well as before the fall—about Adam's reactions than about God's. He and she begin in ideal harmony with each other, with nature, and with God (though successive hints of potential weakness prepare for the outcome), and they pass through the phases of sinful disobedience, callous levity, sensual passion, shame, fear, mutual recrimination, despair, reunited love and loyalty to each other, and finally true penitence; and the stately speech that had been appropriate for regal innocence gives place to the broken, realistic accents of experience. Readers carried away by the heroic energy, spaciousness, and colour of the epic books neglect the story of the fall, yet the one achievement is hardly less remarkable in its way than the other. If Milton's 'unhuman' fable and vast setting invite austere grandeur of treatment, he achieves passionate warmth and organic unity through his profound concern with 'man, the heart of man, and human life'; all his epic machinery and decoration are subservient to that. Because of their partial ignorance and blindness Adam and Eve, like Satan, are enveloped in irony, but compassionate irony. The compassion Milton feels culminates in the closing picture of two human beings who, though 'with Providence thir guide', are commencing life anew and alone in the grim world of history; the last lines, in the simplest words and rhythms, carry an indescribable blend of emotions. Whether or not Milton justified the ways of God, his belief in a divine order, in the true heroism of Christian humility and love, did not impose a superficial unity and harmony upon his human and imaginative sense of division and conflict, evil strength and evil weakness. If some readers are prejudiced against a poet's assumption that the essence of his fable is absolute truth (an assumption Milton shares with Dante), they can read *Paradise Lost* as a re-created 'archetypal myth'—as indeed all readers must. It is a unique poem, and we can hardly imagine the gap there would be in English poetry and in our experience if it were not there.

7

Paradise Regained and *Samson Agonistes* were published together in 1671; we do not know when they were conceived or composed. *Paradise Regained* must of course have followed *Paradise Lost*, which was apparently finished by 1665; it seems equally certain that *Samson* must have been done after the Restoration, whether immediately or later, before or after *Paradise Regained*.

In the *Reason of Church Government* (1642), in setting forth his conception of poetry as the teacher of religion and virtue, Milton had specified three principal forms, epic, drama, and ode or hymn. He had stressed biblical along with classical models and for the epic, in addition to Homer, Virgil, and Tasso, had named the book of Job. Among many general subjects were 'the victorious agonies of Martyrs and Saints'. Much later, in the proem to the ninth book of *Paradise Lost*, Milton contrasted traditional epic themes with 'the better fortitude Of Patience and Heroic Martyrdom'. *Paradise Regained* and *Samson Agonistes* may be called the fulfilment of some of these aspirations. The 'Eden rais'd in the wast Wilderness' by the second Adam is the supreme type of the 'paradise within' partly regained by the first. It is in keeping with epic theory, as enunciated in the *Second Defence*, that Milton treats one 'particular action' in the life of his hero, and in keeping with his conception of poetry that the subject should be the temptation, not the crucifixion, a uniquely tragic story remote from normal experience. The book of Job makes its contribution to the brief epic (and to *Samson* also). Unlike Job, however, the sinless divine protagonist of *Paradise Regained* cannot falter, much less fall, and the loss of dramatic tension means some loss of human appeal. But a considerable measure of tension is supplied in two ways, by Satan's increasingly desperate efforts to ascertain if his adversary is the being he thinks He is, and by Christ's own lack of full knowledge concerning Himself and what lies before

Him (it is an essential part of Milton's conception that Christ is content with what knowledge God reveals).

Though Milton was far from Socinianism, his general view of Christ encouraged what his special aim required, the presentation of his hero not as a Deity untouched by common trials but as a man facing such trials with man's resources, chief among them 'Light from above'. His virtues may be superhuman in degree, but they are not in kind; they may be attained in some proportion by every Christian soul. Further, the conception of a perfect hero was not repugnant to writers of the Renaissance, and for not unworthy reasons. The names of Sidney and Spenser and Chapman sufficiently attest the humanistic belief in both the didactic value of ethical models and the ethical intentions of the long line of heroic authors. Milton's Christ is the last great figure in a procession which includes Arthur and Guyon, Rinaldo and Godfrey, Orlando and Ruggiero, Aeneas, Ulysses, Agamemnon, and Achilles. If the perfection of Christ is more complete than that of these heroes, it is not at all the perfection of Shelley's Prometheus and other products of romantic and sentimental idealism. Milton's hero sternly resists evil through the power of conscious reason guided and strengthened by humble and obedient trust in God. Modern readers, indifferent to the exalted didacticism, the heroic ideal of Christian 'magnanimity', developed by Renaissance poetry and criticism, have often seen in *Paradise Regained* the faults without the grand beauties of *Paradise Lost*. But if ever any artist knew what he was doing, it was Milton, and he was writing a very different kind of poem. Even in the long epic the major action had gone on in the souls of Adam and Eve, and *Paradise Regained*, like the book of Job, may be called a closet drama with a prologue and stage directions. The theme and the form dictate the elimination of much that attracts us in *Paradise Lost*; in interior drama—almost interior monologue with an objectified tempter—everything, including rhythm, must be pitched in a more subdued key. Milton follows the order of temptations as it is given in Luke (where the pinnacle of the temple is the climax), and makes some use of standard commentary, notably in his expansion of 'the kingdoms of the world' into a graduated series of tests. The poem is among other things a masterpiece of artistic form.

When we first see Him, Christ has already gained one

Miltonic victory: His view of His mission has changed from
patriotic action to preaching and now, with no thought of self
or glory, He awaits God's guidance. The young and disillusioned Shelley withdrew from active reform to dream of the
millennium; the old and disillusioned Milton fortified his citadel, the upright heart and pure, in the midst of this world of
evil. His *contemptus mundi* has purged away all hopes except in
man's religious humility and his reign over himself. The trials
embraced in the second temptation go beyond those of Spenser's
book of temperance, which made so deep an impression upon
his greatest disciple. Christ cannot be touched by a luxurious
feast or the promise of wealth or glory or empire, but the noblest
spirit might be swayed by Satan's appeal to the duty of rescuing
Israel from servitude and the need of the wisdom of Greece. Of
this last, the climax of the second temptation (and apparently
Milton's original addition to the canonical set), something was
said in the fourth section of this chapter. One moving element
in the poem is Christ's isolation, of which the outward symbol is
the wilderness. It is not merely Satan who misconceives Christ's
nature and purposes; even His followers look for the establishment of an earthly kingdom, even His mother's confidence is
troubled. Christ's stay is His complete trust in God's providence.
Both the first and the third temptations are calculated to create
distrust of that, distrust and presumption. If Christ has not
proved His divinity by superhuman resistance to unrighteous-
ness, proof is swiftly given, to both Satan and Himself, by the
third temptation, a challenge which evokes both a miracle and
the hero's first declaration that He is 'the Lord thy God'.

The poem has its purple patches, which are functional and
ironic, not merely decorative. We may forget the modicum of
epic machinery—apart from Belial's leering suggestion—but
not the great panorama of the Roman Empire or the eulogy of
Athenian culture. Nor has Milton entirely curbed his sensuous
instincts; the magical banquet inspires the last and one of the
loveliest of his evocations of myth and romance. But the characteristic beauty of *Paradise Regained*, a kind of beauty present
in *Paradise Lost* though obscured by surrounding splendours, is
that of simple and perfect statement, the style almost of the
gospels themselves, or, as Louis Martz sees it, the 'middle style'
of a meditative georgic. An occasional touch of the old sublimity,
or an occasional lapse, only heightens our sense of the normal

texture of speech and rhythm. A Miltonic and therefore a decorous nakedness of thought and emotional force make the prosaic poetic. It was not a 'tired' Milton who wrote 'For in the Inn was left no better room', or the image that Donne anticipated and Newton perhaps echoed, 'As Children gathering pibles on the shore', or the final quiet assertion of the triumph of solitary inward strength over the glories of the world—'hee unobserv'd Home to his Mothers house private return'd'.

8

If *Paradise Regained* expressed the settled faith and fortitude of Milton's old age, *Samson Agonistes* expressed the moods in which faith and fortitude contended with defiance and bitterness. Episodes in Samson's career were among the biblical subjects in the Cambridge manuscript; the *Reason of Church Government* contained a parallel between the Hebrew leader and King Charles; in *Areopagitica* the militant England of Milton's hopes was 'rousing herself like a strong man after sleep, and shaking her invincible locks'; and in *Paradise Lost* the sensual indulgence of Adam and Eve was likened to that of 'Herculean Samson'. When Milton came at last to write a tragedy he was naturally led to the Greek pattern by a scholar's admiration, by a strong feeling for decorum, and by indifference to the popular stage. His method, whatever his degree of consciousness, resulted in an eclectic and original adaptation both of the common elements of Greek tragedy and of various special features characteristic of the several dramatists. The opening soliloquy, the pervasive strain of philosophic ratiocination, and the characterization of Dalila, remind us of Euripides. The constant use of dramatic irony (which begins with the title and the suggestion of the whole theme in the simple first line, 'A little onward lend thy guiding hand'), the treatment of the chorus and of the denouement, and the subjecting of the hero's will to a series of tests, are mainly Sophoclean. The limitation of actors and plot, the dominance of the protagonist, and the prophetic fervour and passion for righteousness which animate the whole, are in the vein of Aeschylus. Among particular plays the nearest to *Samson* are *Oedipus at Colonus* and, in a lesser way, *Prometheus Bound*. Yet all such parallels spring, not from *ad hoc* imitation, but from lifelong saturation and essential affinity of temper—affinity conditioned, though in no sense impaired, by

Milton's Christian faith. Also, as his preface reminds us, he was aware of Italian drama.

Until the final catastrophe reported by the messenger *Samson* has no physical action, and some critics from Dr. Johnson down have complained that it is almost static. But the drama takes place in the soul of Samson—who is not, of course, the mere Hebrew Hercules of the book of Judges—and a brief outline of the psychological movement may be better than comment. At first, though he admits his own guilt, Samson laments chiefly the immediate torments of captivity, degradation, and blindness, and his pride is bitterly hurt by the manner of his fall. As the drama proceeds these motives recur, but self-pity and self-assertion give way to penitence and a single-hearted conviction of his own responsibility for his lot. However, the upward movement, if unbroken, might seem artificial, and Manoa's reference to the feast of Dagon enlarges the consequences of Samson's sin. With a new access of contrition he sinks the thought of his own fate in the contest between God and Dagon, a contest which, he vaguely feels, must end with him, and soon. Manoa's eagerness to arrange a ransom evokes the captive's further emphasis on his pride and sensuality. Every 'act', indeed, has an effect on Samson contrary to that expected by his successive interlocutors. And spiritual isolation grows with self-knowledge; even his father does not understand the real nature of his present anguish. Tortured by his own thoughts, and by the sense of Heaven's desertion, he longs for the release of death. The chorus—an average, not an ideal, spectator—strongly questions the ways of God to men: 'Just or unjust, alike seem miserable.' The approach of Dalila in her finery rouses Samson from his apathy. In vehemently repelling her specious excuses and hints of sensual invitation Samson proves that he has conquered his former weakness; he has still to conquer despair. In the fourth act his responses to the taunts of the Philistine giant proclaim a new and fearless confidence, and humility, born of inward peace. He can now affirm 'My trust is in the living God', and he challenges Dagon's champion to combat. The chorus rejoices in this outward proof of the renewed strength of Israel's defender and still more in the patient fortitude he has displayed as a man. Samson refuses a summons to entertain the Philistines, but then, impelled by divine prompting, he goes of his own accord. A major instance of tragic irony, the 'false dawn' before the denouement, is furnished by Manoa's joy over his success in ransoming his son. When the messenger bursts in and describes the scene at the feast, the chorus exults in Samson's heroic martyrdom and the father pronounces a eulogy of quieter nobility—though neither chorus nor father understands Samson's real victory. The quiet tone is continued in the last words of the chorus, which, beginning on the Euripidean note, turn into an assertion of God's oft-hidden but unwavering support of His faithful champion.

Samson Agonistes could not be purely Greek (if it were it would be only another museum piece), but Milton does not force his material into a theologically Christian mould. He preserves not only Greek but Hebrew decorum. The hero, compared with Adam and Christ, is wholly and merely human, and, if his sense of Heaven's desertion and his recovery are Hebraic and Christian, we still feel ourselves in the atmosphere of ancient rather than of modern tragedy. For the catharsis is attained not only through the triumph of character over circumstance and death; there is also, as in Aeschylus and Sophocles, a vindication of divine law and justice, though the Christian poet, like the ancients, does not offer an easy formula in solution of the mystery of pain and evil. These things occur within the providential order in which Milton believes, and, while *Samson* issues in death, it is, like *Paradise Lost*, a divine comedy in which the tragic is dominant. Samson is given no promise of heavenly immortality (there may be an ambiguous overtone in 'Home to his Fathers house'), no flights of angels sing him to his rest. As A. S. P. Woodhouse has said, Samson and Hamlet 'are on the side of the power—the overruling power—which destroys them'; 'they perish at last in giving effect to it'.

One obvious reason for the dynamic inspiration of the drama is that it was the retrospective and prophetic utterance, perhaps the last, of a great soul to an ignoble nation which he had laboured in vain to serve and save. Yet in his grand testament Milton remains a classical artist who sublimates and generalizes his private and public emotions. Samson may be, in his sins, the English people; he is—and is not—John Milton. Knowing what we do, we see autobiography in the whole picture of Israel in willing subjection to a godless race and of the great rebel and deliverer now blind, helpless, racked by physical and mental pains, while the bodies of other heroes are a prey to dogs and fowls, unjust tribunals, and the ungrateful mob; in the reasoned defence of rebellion; in the condemnation of the oppressors' idolatry, levity, and *hubris*; and, some would add, in the hero's fatal marriage to a Philistine woman and the censure of her sex. Such knowledge, if not pressed too far, may at times heighten the poignancy of the drama, yet all that material is dramatically logical and relevant. In any case *Samson* far transcends personal and particular facts. Its living power is in its direct and searching treatment of human experience, the hard struggle of humility, integrity, and faith against pride, sin, misery, and despair.

The difficulty and the doubtful issue of that battle are reflected in the rugged irregularities of rhythm and rugged strength of style. The irregular lines are not free verse, they are patterns, new in their abundance and variety, of the syllabic metre Milton had always used. In the realistic licences of *Samson* Milton's dramatic evolution reaches full maturity. But in plain statement and broken, colloquial rhythms there is still Miltonic grandeur and sublimity, a new kind of 'classical' writing:

> Nothing is here for tears, nothing to wail
> Or knock the breast, no weakness, no contempt,
> Dispraise, or blame, nothing but well and fair,
> And what may quiet us in a death so noble.

In general, the massive and sinewy dramatic idiom is the instrument not merely of thought but of thinking. In style as in form and spirit *Samson* gives the non-Grecian reader a truer feeling for Greek tragedy than most English translations of Greek plays. Verbal beauty is not lacking, but the real beauty is in the full yet bare statement of a noble theme. The touch of stiffness is not un-Greek, not even the 'tame villatic Fowl'. One phrase which has been termed sharply Dantesque, 'whence Gaza mourns', is rather Aeschylean—'ὡς στένειν πόλιν Περσῶν'.

9

To survey Milton's work from the beginning to *Samson* is to be impressed by both the uniformity and the variety of style. Always sensitively aware of critical theory and poetic practice, he was a disciple of Ovid, of the Elizabethans, of Jonson, and in those early stages he showed himself a more and more independent master of his craft. *Comus* looked both backward and forward. In 'Lycidas' and the heroic sonnets began the forging of the grand style, which was to be the medium of *Paradise Lost*. That grandeur, however uncommon, is not un-English. In Milton as in Bacon, Browne, and other representatives of ornate sublimity, the main texture is pure English. It would be odd if it were not, since in all the essential features of his personality and work Milton was one of the most thoroughly English of English authors. What is more important is that he was a man, and 'So far from being granite, his verse is a continual spring of beauty, of goodness, of tenderness, of humility'. The word 'Miltonic', commonly applied to *Paradise Lost* or to the three major works of the poet's last phase, really includes three very different styles, and within *Paradise Lost* itself there are large variations. Those several styles were dictated by the principle of decorum, which was for Milton the artist what religious and philosophic principles were for the man and the thinker, and the principle of decorum, like the others, united liberty and discipline. But in Milton's general movement away from epic grandeur towards plain, undecorated, dramatic speech it is not altogether fanciful—after we have given decorum its large due—to see a parallel to his inward evolution, his arrival at a deeper and more personal understanding of God and human experience.

Milton's style was the natural accompaniment of his view of the function of poetry. He was the last English poet whose unified mastery of learning might fairly justify the claim of the *vates* to be a teacher of his age. For him as for Spenser poetry embraced learning on the one side and action on the other. But Milton's knowledge, though much greater than Spenser's, was essentially of the same kind. During his lifetime the mere widening of knowledge, especially in science, had gone beyond the grasp of any one man, and through the division of labour the unacknowledged legislators of mankind were losing their leadership. Milton was a poet; Dryden was a man of letters. The inspiration and purposes of knowledge had changed also. While the humanistic values of the classical tradition were united with the religious and ethical force of medieval and re-formed Christianity, Milton was still possible. But the philosophy of the seventeenth century had been steadily undermining the ground on which Milton stood, had been destroying the soul of

Christian humanism and of poetry. Milton's partial consciousness of that movement only fortified his religious and ethical
faith. In spite of his public career, his immersion in the problems
of his time, he became more and more an isolated figure, like
Abdiel, Christ, and Samson.

The militant prophet of the revolution rallied from defeat

> With plain Heroic magnitude of mind
> And celestial vigour arm'd,

with a purer and humbler need of God. If the spirit of the
revolutionary Milton partook of Constantine's vision, 'τούτῳ
νίκα', the theme of his major poems is 'E la sua volontate è
nostra pace'. Unless our faculties have been vitiated by gross
and violent stimulants, or by ultra-sophisticated negations, we
cannot open Milton without an access of both strength and
humility, a feeling that we are greater, and weaker, than we
know. And that tonic power comes not merely from beauty of
phrase and rhythm but from Milton's magnanimous concern
with the highest issues and values in life, from his recognition
of intellectual and irreligious pride, and from his positive and
passionate faith in God and goodness. In the twentieth century
many men have undergone a kind of Miltonic disillusionment;
Milton himself did not stop there.

CONCLUSION

MILTON's major poems were less typical of the thought and feeling of a large part of the nation than, say, the popular *Satire Against Hypocrites* (1655) by his nephew John Phillips. Milton might have relished Phillips's anti-sectarian wit, but not his use of the great phrase 'Christian Liberty' as a mocking gloss on the picture of a Commonwealth Stiggins kissing his 'sisters'. To the country as a whole the restoration of Church and King and Parliament did not bring religious unity or even toleration, nor did it bring full measure of political unity, yet things moved towards the order and security of 1689. Throughout our period order of some sort had been a main object of such various men as King James and King Charles, Strafford and Cromwell, Laud and Prynne and Selden and Winstanley, Bacon and Jonson, Hobbes and Milton. The desire for order comprehended the civil and ecclesiastical spheres, the soul and the sentence, the cosmos and the couplet. That order, of course, had not been achieved, at least in public affairs, and the great body of great literature was the product of an age of unceasing controversy and conflict. The first sentence of Clarendon's *History of the Rebellion* echoes the first sentence of Hooker's preface to the *Ecclesiastical Polity*; it is almost as if the intervening time had appeared as a bad dream, a unique outbreak of feverous passions. In the latter part of the century, with all its disturbances, we breathe the cool air of Harrington and Locke, the air of modern secular liberalism. The State is not the feudal or humanistic or paternal hierarchy of 'degrees' bound by mutual obligations, still less the holy community of Puritan dreams, but an oligarchy of property-owners whose activities and privileges government exists to protect, and whose service is perfect freedom.

In other domains, from literature and thought to music and gardening, there is a similar movement towards rational and ordered regularity. All the tendencies that we call Augustan were at work before 1600, some of them before 1600, but during the years 1600–60 individuality of spiritual vision and expression was not reduced to decorous uniformity by a highly civilized ideal of restraint. There were many signs of vigorous

health. The age was the most erudite in English history, yet in
no age has literature been at once so close to learning and philosophy on the one hand and to life and action on the other. The
English language and idiom had attained its first disciplined
maturity without losing its youthful freshness and colour. The
diction of both prose and verse was a free and flexible mixture
of the plain and the purple, the learned and the colloquial. It
was only after 1660 that critical rationalism got definitely
rid of individual eccentricity and excess. 'Spend no time',
advised Francis Osborn, 'in reading, much less writing *Strong-
lines*: which like tough meat, aske more paines and time in
chewing, then can be recompensed by all the nourishment they
bring.' And having achieved in prose and verse an urbane
and mundane directness and clarity, free from metaphorical
thought and feeling, the reformers did not boggle at the price
they paid. There were of course great gains, but our concern
is with the loss. When we think of the dynamic humanism of
most serious writers from Chapman and Jonson to Milton,
Augustan classicism appears, with some notable exceptions, as
a pretty thinly diluted ideal of order. It would not be easy to
name a major or even a minor writer of the earlier period who
has received or deserved the verdict of thinking justly but faintly.

In the process of dilution an attenuated classicism was largely
assisted by scientific rationalism, so that some might prefer the
word 'enlightenment' to 'dilution'. To the thoroughly modern
mind the period 1600–60 may seem to have belonged to the
kingdom of darkness. Yet it was a period of conflict over great
issues in the abstract as well as the national sphere, over the
nature of reality and of God and man, the very foundations of
knowledge and faith. For the first time in England many men
were compelled to go behind the rubrics and formulas and work
out their own philosophy. The results ranged from various types
of mystical thought to sceptical naturalism. These philosophies
were in the main outgrowths of, or—very rarely—reactions
against, the all-embracing tradition of Christian humanism
which the age inherited, the tradition of the rational wisdom
and culture of antiquity purified and exalted and intensified
by the Middle Ages, the Renaissance, the Reformation, and the
Counter-Reformation. For the last time in England all these
forces, in differing degrees but in climactic concentration, made
up the basic texture of men's thinking. The consequence was

rich variety and strength, almost wholly within the Christian frame. Around 1600 the traditional patterns of thought and belief encountered little or no opposition; by 1700 the traditionalist could take little or nothing for granted. It could be increasingly taken for granted that the traditions of two thousand years did not provide adequate answers for the problems of the modern world and the modern mind. The types of 'truth' which satisfied Milton, More, Cudworth, Browne, Vaughan, Traherne, Baxter, and George Fox (to name a few men who lived into the Restoration period) did not appeal to thoughtful or thoughtless disciples of Descartes and Hobbes and Charles II. The 'rationalism' of Milton and the Cambridge Platonists was no longer rationalism. Reason was not *recta ratio*, the candle of the Lord, but a much drier light.

In the decade of *Leviathan* it was still possible for the researches of Lightfoot, Ussher, and Pearson to establish the date of Creation as Sunday, 23 October 4004 B.C. (and the year at least remained an article of popular faith well through the nineteenth century), but, in general, science had begun its slow eradication of all things irrational, supernatural, and intangible from the world and the mind of man. As the star of Bethlehem had put to flight the pagan gods, science—though its full victory was long delayed—banished fairies and witches, angels and devils. With superstition went the mythic and symbolic imagination, the capacity for 'an *O altitudo*'. Nature was not a 'mystick Book', the art of God, an object of contemplation, but a complex of forces to be measured and exploited. With superstition, too, went the active belief in human life enveloped by divine power, and the whole traditional conception, in its old dynamic form, of man as a creature between the beasts and the angels, of man's relations with himself, with society, with the universe, and with God. The year after Vaughan's death appeared Toland's *Christianity Not Mysterious*. Men had fought and died for their way of worshipping God; no one was called upon, or was ready, to die for deism. Nor did confident deism and mechanistic cosmology nourish the religious conviction of man's inescapable weakness and sin which, in times past, had sobered Platonic humanists as well as biblical Calvinists.

These paragraphs are not, it need hardly be said, a rounded estimate of the Augustan age; they are only a brief, exaggerated, and foreshortened statement of some general contrasts and tendencies and a reminder of some values and qualities of vision which grew dimmer after 1600. The poets and critics of the Romantic age, rebelling against effete classicism and mechanistic philosophies, rediscovered many neglected writers of the earlier seventeenth century, but that revival on the whole took too little account of those writers' religious and philosophic seriousness and made too much of literary 'quaintness'. While the number of readers and scholarly students multiplied throughout the nineteenth century, our own time has witnessed a second great revival, rich in interpretative learning and rich in its effects upon contemporary literature. This revival may be said to have been inaugurated, if a starting-point can be named, by Sir Herbert Grierson's edition of Donne's poems (1912); whatever changes in taste the future may bring, it can hardly be supposed that such a body of great writing will be dislodged from its present high place. Modern readers have found in it an artistic and spiritual health, a civilized and complex sensibility, a strength and rightness of style and tone, that have made it a principal criterion by which other modes are judged. And, if the age and its literature are enviable on the artistic level, they are still more so on the level of belief and outlook. Since the nature of literary art was bound up with and dependent upon the nature of belief, only some particular elements of the former can be recaptured by modern writers. But modern readers can at least live part of their lives in a finer air than their own.

CHRONOLOGICAL TABLES
AND
BIBLIOGRAPHY

Date	Public Events	Literary History	Verse
1600	Disgrace of Essex. Mountjoy in Ireland. Battle of Nieuport. Charles I b. East India Company founded.	Thomas Deloney d. Richard Hooker d. Thomas Nashe d.? John Earle b.? Thomas Goodwin b. John Ogilby b. William Prynne b.? William Walwyn b. Hayward in prison for his *Henry IV*.	Marlowe (d. 1593), *Lucan's First Book*, tr. Breton, *Melancholic Humours*; *Pasquil* pieces. Fairfax, *Godfrey of Bulloigne*, tr. Tasso. Middleton, *Ghost of Lucrece.* Rowlands, *Letting of Humour's Blood.* Song-books by Dowland, Jones, Morley, Weelkes. Miscellanies: *Belvedere*; *England's Helicon*; *England's Parnassus.*
1601	Rising and execution of Essex. Parliament attacks monopolies; Elizabeth revokes many patents but asserts prerogative. Poor Law.	William Lambarde d. Sir Thomas North d.? Donne married.	Breton, *Divine Poem*; *No Whipping, Nor Tripping.* Daniel, *Works* (enlar.). Rosseter and Campion, *Book of Airs.* R. Chester et al., *Love's Martyr* (incl. 'Phoenix and Turtle'). T. Morley, ed., *Triumphs of Oriana.*
1602	Irish campaign. B. Gosnold's voyage to New England. Sir J. Lancaster at Sumatra and Java. Bodleian Library opened.	William Perkins d. Edward Benlowes b. William Chillingworth b. Sir Simonds D'Ewes b. Mildmay Fane b. Owen Felltham b.? William Lilly b. William Strode b.	Basse, *Sword and Buckler*; *Three Pastoral Elegies.* F. Beaumont (?), *Salmacis and Hermaphroditus.* Breton, *Soul's Harmony.* Davies of Hereford, *Mirum in Modum.* Rowlands, *'Tis Merry when Gossips Meet.* F. Davison, ed., *Poetical Rhapsody.*
1603	Mountjoy completes conquest of Ireland. Elizabeth d. (March 24). Accession of James. Cecil chief minister. Millenary Petition. Monopolies revoked. Watson's plot. Recusancy fines remitted. Cobham's plot. Plague.	Thomas Cartwright d. William Gilbert d. Thomas Morley d. Sir Kenelm Digby b. Shakerley Marmion b. Roger Williams b.? Sir John Davies in Ireland (1603-19). Ralegh imprisoned, sentenced for treason.	Daniel, *Panegyric . . . Certain Epistles.* Davies of Hereford, *Microcosmos.* Dowland, *Third Book of Songs.* Drayton, *Barons' Wars* (rev. from *Mortimeriados*).

Prose	*Drama (date of acting)* [1]
Barclay, W. *De Regno et Regali Potestate.* Coke, *Reports* (1600 ff.). Cornwallis, *Essays*, i (ii, 1601). Gilbert, *De Magnete.* Hakluyt, *Principal Navigations*, iii (2nd ed.). Holland, *Roman History*, tr. Livy. Kemp, W., *Kemp's Nine Days' Wonder*, Perkins, *Golden Chain* (works). Vaughan, Sir W., *Golden Grove.*	Anon., 1 *Return from Parnassus.* Dekker et al., *Patient Grissill.* Jonson, *Cynthia's Revels.* Shakespeare, *Merry Wives of Windsor* (1601?).
Bacon, *Practices and Treasons Committed by late Earl of Essex.* Chamber, J., *Treatise against Judicial Astrology.* Dent, *Plain Man's Pathway to Heaven.* Dolman, R., *French Academy*, iii, tr. La Primaudaye. Holland, *History of the World*, tr. Pliny. Johnson, R., *Essays.* Wright, T., *Passions of the Mind.*	Dekker and Marston, *Satiromastix.* Jonson, *Poetaster.* Marston, *What You Will.* Shakespeare, *Hamlet* (1600?); *Twelfth Night* (1602?).
Brereton, J., *Discovery of the North Part of Virginia.* Breton, *Post with a Mad Packet of Letters.* Campion, *Observations in the Art of English Poesy.* Carew, R., *Survey of Cornwall.* Lodge, *Works of Josephus*, tr. Patericke, S., *Means of Well Governing against N. Machiavel*, tr. Gentillet.	Lindsay, Sir D. (d. 1555), *Satire of the Three Estates* pr. Anon., 2 *Return from Parnassus.* Chapman, *Gentleman Usher*; *May-Day.* Middleton, *Family of Love.* Shakespeare, *Troilus and Cressida*; *All's Well That Ends Well* (1602/4).
Perkins (d. 1602), *Treatise of the Vocations.* Barclay, J., *Euphormionis Satyricon*, i (ii, 1607). Daniel, *Defence of Rhyme.* Dekker, *Wonderful Year.* Florio, *Essays of Montaigne*, tr. Holland, *Morals*, tr. Plutarch. James, King, *Basilikon Doron* (public ed.). Knolles, *General History of the Turks.* Lodge, *Treatise of the Plague.* Tofte (?), *Bachelor's Banquet*, tr.	Anon., *Merry Devil of Edmonton.* Heywood, *Woman Killed with Kindness.* Jonson, *Sejanus.* Marston, *Dutch Courtesan.* Shakespeare, Q1 of *Hamlet* pr.

[1] The question-mark used after titles of uncertain date is ordinarily omitted in the Drama column, since so many of the dates of acting are conjectural and disputed. The latest and fullest guide in this area is G. E. Bentley (*infra*, I). A. Harbage's *Annals of English Drama* (1940) is being revised by S. Schoenbaum (forthcoming, 1961–2).

Date	Public Events	Literary History	Verse
1604	Hampton Court Conference. Whitgift d. Bancroft Archbishop. Commons claim right to deal with Church and State. Investigation of monopolies. Acts against priests and recusants. Anglican canons; enforcement of conformity. Peace with Spain.	Thomas Churchyard d. Edward de Vere, Earl of Oxford, d. Philip Hunton b.? Jasper Mayne b. Henry Parker b. Edward Pococke b.	Alexander, *Aurora*. Bateson, *First Set of English Madrigals*. Breton, *Passionate Shepherd*. Dekker, *News from Gravesend*. Drayton, *Moses*; *Owl*; *Paean Triumphal*. M. East, *Madrigals*. Rowlands, *Look to It, for I'll Stab Ye*.
1605	Some Puritan clergy ejected. Repression of Puritans and Catholics. Amnesty for Irish rebels. King tries to stifle Scottish General Assembly. Gunpowder Plot.	John Stow d. Sir Thomas Browne b. Sir William Dugdale b. John Gauden b. William Habington b. Henry Hammond b. Thomas Randolph b. Henry Robinson b. Bulstrode Whitelocke b.	Breton, *Soul's Immortal Crown*; *Honour of Valour*. Daniel, *Certain Small Poems, with Philotas*. Davies of Hereford, *Wit's Pilgrimage* (?). Drayton, *Poems* (coll.). Rowlands, *Hell's Broke Loose*; &c. Sylvester, *Divine Weeks and Works*, tr. Du Bartas.
1606	Penal legislation against recusants, with new oath of allegiance. Judges support king's right to levy impositions. Coke Chief Justice of Common Pleas. Common-law judges appeal to Parliament against ecclesiastical courts. Charter for Virginia.	Arthur Golding d. John Lyly d. Sir William Davenant b. Sir Thomas Herbert b. Sir William Killigrew b. Edmund Waller b.	J. Barclay, *Sylvae*. Dekker, *Double PP.* Drayton, *Poems Lyric and Pastoral*. Owen, *Epigrammata*. H. Parrot, *Mouse-Trap*. Rowlands, *Terrible Battle between . . . Time and Death*. Warner, *Albion's England* (books 14–16 added).
1607	King forces bishops upon Scottish Church. Flight of Tyrone and Tyrconnell. Conflicts between Coke and Bancroft. Jamestown founded.	Henry Chettle d. (1603/7?). Sir Edward Dyer d. Thomas Legge d. John Reynolds (Rainolds) d. William Bosworth b. Bacon Solicitor-General.	Daniel, *Certain Small Works* (rev. and enlar.). Davies of Hereford, *Summa Totalis*. Drayton, *Legend of Great Cromwell*. Rowlands, *Democritus*.

Prose

Bacon, *Better Pacification of the Church of England*; *Apology concerning the late Earl of Essex*. Breton, *Grimello's Fortunes*; *Fantastics* (?). Dallington, *View of France*. King James, *Counterblast to Tobacco*. Middleton, *Ant and the Nightingale: or Father Hubburd's Tales*; *Black Book*. Rich, *Soldier's Wish to Britain's Welfare*.

Drama (date of acting)

Alexander, *Monarchic Tragedies* pr. (enlar. 1607). Chapman, *All Fools* (rev.?); *Bussy D'Ambois*. Daniel, *Vision of the Twelve Goddesses*. Dekker and Middleton, 1 *Honest Whore*. Marston, *Malcontent*. Shakespeare, *Measure for Measure*; *Othello*; Q2 of *Hamlet* pr.

Bacon, *Advancement of Learning*. Camden, *Remains concerning Britain*. Hall, *Meditations and Vows*; *Mundus Alter et Idem* (?). Sir E. Sandys, *Relation of the State of Religion*. Verstegan, *Restitution of Decayed Intelligence*.

Chapman, Jonson, and Marston, *Eastward Ho*. Daniel, *Philotas*; *Queen's Arcadia*. Dekker, 2 *Honest Whore*. Jonson, *Masque of Blackness*. Marston, *Sophonisba*. Middleton, *Trick to Catch the Old One*. Shakespeare, *King Lear*.

Perkins (d. 1602), *Whole Treatise of Cases of Conscience*. Bryskett, *Discourse of Civil Life*, tr. Giraldi. Dekker, *Seven Deadly Sins of London*. Hall, *Heaven upon Earth*. Holland, *Twelve Caesars*, tr. Suetonius. Knolles, *Six Books of a Commonweal*, tr. Bodin. Rich, *Faults, Faults*.

Anon., *Yorkshire Tragedy*. Anon. (Tourneur? Middleton?), *Revenger's Tragedy*. Jonson, *Hymenaei*; *Volpone*. Middleton, *A Mad World my Masters*. Shakespeare, *Macbeth*.

Anon., *Dobson's Dry Bobs*. Cleland, J., *Institution of a Young Noble Man*. Cowell, *Interpreter*. Dekker, *Knight's Conjuring* (rev. from *News from Hell*, 1606). Lennard, *Of Wisdom* (1607/12), tr. Charron. Markham, *Cavelarice*; *English Arcadia*, i (ii, 1613). Topsell, *Four-footed Beasts*, tr. Gesner.

Beaumont, *Knight of the Burning Pestle*. Campion, *Lord Hay's Masque*. Day et al., *Travels of the Three English Brothers*. Dekker and Middleton, *Roaring Girl* (1608?). Shakespeare, *Antony and Cleopatra* (1606?); *Timon of Athens* (1605/8?).

Date	Public Events	Literary History	Verse
1608	Failure of plan for union with Scotland. *Post-nati* naturalized. Deficit reduced by new impositions. League with Dutch. O'Dogherty's rebellion crushed. Separatist congregation moves to Holland.	John Dee d. Sir Geoffrey Fenton d. Thomas Sackville, Earl of Dorset, d. Sir Aston Cokayne b. Sir Richard Fanshawe b. Thomas Fuller b. Robert Greville, Lord Brooke, b. John Milton b. Captain John Smith President of Virginia.	H. Parrot, *Epigrams.* H. Peacham, *The More the Merrier.* Sylvester, *Divine Weeks and Works,* tr. Du Bartas (1st complete ed.). R. Tofte, *Ariosto's Satires.*
1609	Continued conflicts over ecclesiastical jurisdiction. King entails Crown lands. New charter for Virginia. Virginian commissioners wrecked at Bermuda.	Barnabe Barnes d. William Warner d. Sir Matthew Hale b. Edward Hyde, Earl of Clarendon, b. Sir John Suckling b. Benjamin Whichcote b. Gerrard Winstanley b.	Spenser (d. 1599), *Fairy Queen* (1st folio ed., with 1st ed. of *Mutability*). Chapman, *Tears of Peace*; *Iliad*, i–xii, tr. (?). Daniel, *Civil Wars* (8 bks.). Heywood, *Troia Britannica.* Rowlands, *Knave of Clubs.* Shakespeare, *Sonnets*; *Lover's Complaint.* Wilbye, *Second Set of Madrigals.*
1610	Commons' Petition of Right and Petition of Grievances. Great Contract falls through. Judicial decision against royal proclamations. Scottish General Assembly approves episcopacy. Bancroft d. Plantation of Ulster. Hudson's last voyage. Cowell's *Interpreter* (1607) suppressed by the king.	Alexander Montgomerie d.? Robert Parsons d. Lucius Cary, Lord Falkland, b.? Henry Glapthorne b. Sidney Godolphin b. Casaubon in England (1610–14). Shakespeare retires to Stratford (1611?).	Davies of Hereford, *Scourge of Folly* (1611?). G. Fletcher, *Christ's Victory and Triumph.* J. Heath, *Epigrams.* R. Niccols, ed., *Mirror for Magistrates* (last enlar. ed.).
1611	Abbot Archbishop. Parliament dissolved.	Giles Fletcher the elder d.	Spenser (d. 1599), 1st folio of coll. works.

Prose

Perkins (d. 1602), *Damned Art of Witch-craft.* Dekker, *Bellman of London*; *Lanthorn and Candlelight.* Hall, *Characters of Virtues and Vices*; *Epistles* (1608–11). Heywood, *Two Notable Histories* (1608–9), tr. Sallust. James, King, *Apology for the Oath of Allegiance.* Smith, Captain J., *True Relation of Virginia.* Topsell, *History of Serpents.* Tuvill, D., *Essays Politic and Moral.*

Drama (date of acting)

Chapman, *Charles Duke of Byron.* Fletcher, *Faithful Shepherdess.* Jonson, *Lord Haddington's Masque*; *Masque of Beauty.* Shakespeare, *Coriolanus.* Shakespeare (reviser? collaborator?), *Pericles.*

Jewel (d. 1571), *Works.* Bible (R. C. version of O.T., 1609–10). Bacon, *De Sapientia Veterum.* Dekker, *Four Birds of Noah's Ark*; *Gull's Hornbook.* Healey, *Discovery of a New World* (?), tr. Hall's *Mundus.* Holland, *Roman History*, tr. Ammianus Marcellinus. T., I., *Philosophical Comfort*, tr. Boethius. Tuvill, D., *Essays Moral and Theological.*

Beaumont and Fletcher, *Philaster.* Greville, *Mustapha* pr. Jonson. *Epicoene*; *Masque of Queens.* Shakespeare, *Cymbeline* (1610?). Tourneur, *Atheist's Tragedy* (1610/11?).

Donne, *Pseudo-Martyr.* Guillim, *Display of Heraldry.* Healey, *City of God*, tr. Augustine; *Epictetus.* Cebes, tr. Holland, *Britain*, tr. Camden. Jourdain, *Discovery of the Bermudas.* Strachey, *True Reportory of the Wreck upon the Bermudas* (pr. 1625).

Chapman, *Revenge of Bussy D'Ambois.* Daniel, *Tethys' Festival.* Jonson, *Alchemist.* Webster, *Devil's Law-Case* (?).

King James Bible. Cartwright, J., *Preacher's Travels.* Coryate, *Coryate's*

Beaumont and Fletcher, *King and No King*; *Maid's Tragedy.* Fletcher,

Date	Public Events	Literary History	Verse
	Activity against recusants. Sale of baronetcies. Robert Carr advanced. Enlarged powers given Court of High Commission. Friction with Dutch over spice trade.	Richard Mulcaster d. William Cartwright b. James Harrington b. Robert Leighton b. Sir Thomas Urquhart b.	Brathwait, *Golden Fleece*. Byrd, *Psalms, Songs and Sonnets*. Chapman, *Iliad*, i–xxiv, tr. Daniel, *Certain Small Works* (rev. and enlar.). Donne, *Anatomy of the World*.
1612	Legate and Wightman burned for heresy. Lancashire witches hanged. Alliance with German Protestant princes. Salibury and Prince Henry d. Scottish Parliament ratifies episcopacy. Improved charter for Virginia.	Lodowick Bryskett d.? Sir John Harington d. Samuel Butler b. Richard Crashaw b. (1613?). James Graham, Marquis of Montrose, b. Thomas Killigrew the elder b.	Davies of Hereford, *Muse's Sacrifice*. Donne, *Second Anniversary*. Drayton, *Poly-Olbion* (Songs 1–18). O. Gibbons, *First Set of Madrigals and Motets*. Owen, *Epigrammata*. Peacham, *Minerva Britanna*. John Taylor, *The Sculler*.
1613	Princess Elizabeth married to Elector Palatine. Coke Chief Justice of King's Bench. Countess of Essex divorced, married to Somerset. Sarmiento (later Gondomar) Spanish ambassador.	Sir Thomas Bodley d. Henry Constable d. Overbury d. in the Tower. John Cleveland b. John Pearson b. Peter Sterry b. Jeremy Taylor b. Sir Henry Vane b. Dekker in debtors' prison (1613–19). Wither imprisoned for satires.	Browne, *Britannia's Pastorals*, i. Campion, *Two Books of Airs* (?). Wither, *Abuses Stript and Whipt*. Elegies on Prince Henry by Campion, Chapman, Donne, Drummond, Herbert, Heywood, Sylvester, Tourneur, Webster, Wither, et al. (1612–13).
1614	Parliament protests against impositions. Dissolved without grant of supply. Some members imprisoned. Benevolence imposed. Somerset at height of power. Villiers at court. Renewed proposals for Spanish marriage. Discontent in Ireland.	Sir William Cornwallis d. William Hammond b. John Lilburne b.? Henry More b. John Wilkins b. Fulke Greville Chancellor of Exchequer (1614–21).	Overbury (d. 1613), *A Wife*. Alexander, *Doomsday*. Browne, C. Brooke, Wither, and Davies of Hereford, *Shepherd's Pipe*. Chapman, *Andromeda Liberata*. Drummond, *Poems* (?). Sir A. Gorges, *Lucan's Pharsalia*, tr.

Prose

Crudities. Cotgrave, *Dictionary of French and English Tongues*. Donne, *Ignatius his Conclave*. Florio, *Queen Anna's New World of Words*. Speed, *Theatre* and *History of Great Britain*.

Drama (date of acting)

Valentinian. Jonson, *Catiline*; *Oberon*. Middleton, *Chaste Maid in Cheapside*; Middleton (?), *Second Maiden's Tragedy*. Shakespeare, *Winter's Tale* (1610?); *Tempest*.

Bacon, *Essays* (enlar. from 1597). Bayly, *Practice of Piety* (?). Brinsley, *Ludus Literarius*. Daniel, *History of England*, i. Davies, Sir J., *Discovery* . . . *Why Ireland Was Never* . . . *Subdued*. Heywood, *Apology for Actors*. Lok, *De Novo Orbe*, tr. P. Martyr (contin. of R. Eden). Shelton, *Don Quixote*, i, tr. Smith, Captain J., *Map of Virginia*.

Webster, *White Devil*.

Dallington, *Aphorisms*. Dekker, *Strange Horse-Race*. Hayward, *Lives of the Three Normans*. Purchas, *Purchas his Pilgrimage*. Savile, ed., *Chrysostomi Opera* (1610–13). Spelman, *De non temerandis Ecclesiis*. Whitaker, A., *Good News from Virginia*.

Beaumont, *Inner Temple Masque*. Campion, *Lords' Masque*; *Masque at Marriage of Somerset*. Cary, Elizabeth, Lady *Mariam* pr. Shakespeare and Fletcher, *Henry VIII*; *Two Noble Kinsmen*.

Overbury (d. 1613) et al., *Characters*. Barclay, J., *Icon Animorum*. Busher, L., *Religious Peace*. Lodge, *Works of Seneca*, tr. Napier, *Mirifici Logarithmorum Canonis Descriptio*. Ralegh, *History of the World*. Rich, *Honesty of this Age*. Selden, *Titles of Honour*.

Daniel, *Hymen's Triumph*. Jonson, *Bartholomew Fair*. Webster, *Duchess of Malfi* (1613?).

Date	Public Events	Literary History	Verse
1615	King at Cambridge. Roe sent to India to investigate commercial situation. Failure of negotiations with Dutch for sharing spice trade. Trial of Overbury's murderers.	Robert Armin d. Richard Baxter b. Sir John Denham b. John Donne ordained.	Barclay, J., *Poemata.* Harington (d. 1612), *Epigrams.* Brathwait, *Strappado for the Devil.* Chapman, *Odyssey* (1614-15). Rowlands, *Melancholy Knight.* Wither, *Fidelia*; *Shepherd's Hunting.*
1616	Cautionary towns surrendered to Dutch for cash. Trial of Earl and Countess of Somerset. Advancement of Villiers. Sale of peerages. Coke dismissed.	Francis Beaumont d. Richard Hakluyt d. Shakespeare d. Joseph Beaumont b. Nicholas Culpeper b. George Daniel b. Sir Roger L'Estrange b. Sir Edward Sherburne b. John Smith b.? John Wallis b. Jonson given royal pension.	Browne, *Britannia's Pastorals*, ii. Chapman, *Whole Works of Homer*; *Divine Poem of Musaeus*, tr. Drummond, *Poems.* Jonson, *Epigrams*; *Forest* (in *Works*).
1617	Pocahontas presented at court. Negotiations for Spanish marriage. King in Scotland. Conflicts with Dutch in East Indies.	Thomas Coryate d. Barnabe Rich d. Elias Ashmole b. Ralph Cudworth b. Seth Ward b. Bacon Lord Keeper. Ralegh sails for Orinoco.	Campion, *Third and Fourth Book of Airs* (?). Davies of Hereford, *Wit's Bedlam.* L. Digges, *Rape of Proserpine*, tr. Claudian. Drummond, *Forth Feasting.* Rowlands, *The Bride.*
1618	Cranfield's financial reforms. *Declaration of Sports.* Clerical opposition to it and to Selden's *History of Tithes.* King's Articles pressed on Scottish Assembly. Beginning of Thirty Years War. Reforms by Virginia Company.	Thomas Bastard d. John Davies of Hereford d. Ralegh executed. Josuah Sylvester d. Abraham Cowley b. Nathanael Culverwel b. (1619?). Richard Lovelace b. Bacon Lord Chancellor and Baron Verulam. Jonson in Scotland (1618-19).	Harington (d. 1612), *Epigrams* (enlar.). Chapman, *Georgics of Hesiod*, tr. H. Fitzgeffrey et al., *Certain Elegies. With Satires and Epigrams.*

Prose

Adams, T., *Mystical Bedlam*. Breton, *Characters upon Essays*. Camden, *Annales*, i. Markham, *Country Contentments*. Sandys, G., *Relation of a Journey*. Stephens, J., *Satirical Essays*, *Characters*. Swetnam, J., *Arraignment of Lewd Women*.

Drama (date of acting)

Browne, W., *Inner Temple Masque*. Fletcher, P., *Sicelides*. Jonson, *Mercury Vindicated*. Ruggle, *Ignoramus*. Tomkis, *Albumazar*.

Cornwallis (d. 1614), *Essays or Encomions*; *Essays of Certain Paradoxes*. Healey (d.?), *Characters*, tr. Theophrastus. Breton, *Good and the Bad*. Cotta, *Trial of Witchcraft*. Goodman, *Fall of Man*. King James, *Works*. Selden, ed., Fortescue's *De Laudibus Legum Angliae*. Smith, Captain J., *Description of New England*.

Jonson, *Golden Age Restored*; *Devil is an Ass*; *Works* pr.

Brathwait, *Law of Drinking*. Fennor, *Compter's Commonwealth*. Hall, J., *Quo Vadis?* Minsheu, J., *Guide into the Tongues*. Moryson, *Itinerary*. Selden, *De Diis Syris*.

Jonson, *Vision of Delight*; *Lovers Made Men*. Middleton and W. Rowley, *Fair Quarrel*.

Breton, *Court and Country*. Daniel, *History of England*, ii. Munday, *Amadis de Gaule*, iii–iv, tr. Mynshul, *Characters and Essays*. Selden, *History of Tithes*. Taylor, J., *Penniless Pilgrimage*.

Anon., *Swetnam the Woman-Hater* (?). Burton, R., *Philosophaster*. Fletcher et al., *Knight of Malta*. Jonson, *Pleasure Reconciled to Virtue*.

Date	Public Events	Literary History	Verse
1619	Queen Anne d. Calvinism triumphs at Synod of Dort. Agreement with Dutch for one-third of spice monopoly. Virginia Assembly. Elector Frederick chosen king of Bohemia. James's prestige high. Buckingham all-powerful.	Samuel Daniel d. Nathan Field d.? Richard Allestree b. Walter Charleton b. William Chamberlayne b. Sir Edward Herbert ambassador to France.	Campion, *Epigrammata,* &c. Drayton, *Poems* (coll. folio ed.). J. Vicars, *Epigrams of John Owen,* tr.
1620	Spinola invades Palatinate. Frederick loses Bohemia. English feeling against Spain. King vacillates. Proclamation forbids discussion of State affairs. 'New England' officially named. Voyage of *Mayflower.* Economic depression, 1620–4.	Thomas Campion d. Richard Carew d. Robert Tofte d. (1619?) Alexander Brome b. John Evelyn b. Lucy (Apsley) Hutchinson b. Marchamont Needham b. George Herbert Public Orator at Cambridge (1620–7).	Overbury (d. 1613), *Remedy of Love,* tr. Ovid. Dekker, *Dekker his Dream.* Peacham, *Thalia's Banquet.* Quarles, *Feast for Worms.* Rowlands, *Night Raven.* Wither, *Works* (pirated?).
1621	First Parliament since 1614. Impeachment of monopolists and of Bacon. Commons oppose king's continental policy. Williams Bishop of London and Lord Keeper. Sir William Alexander given charter for Nova Scotia. Protestation on liberties of the House.	John Barclay d. Thomas Harriot d. Mary Herbert, Countess of Pembroke, d. William Strachey d. Roger Boyle, Earl of Orrery, b. Andrew Marvell b. Donne Dean of St. Paul's (1621–31).	Brathwait, *Nature's Embassy.* Quarles, *Hadassa.* Sandys, *First Five Books of Ovid's Metamorphosis,* tr. Wither, *Songs of the Old Testament; Wither's Motto.*
1622	Parliament dissolved. Impositions and Benevolence. King treats with Spain for marriage and recovery of Palatinate. Popular zeal for Protestant cause. Gondomar recalled. King restricts preaching. Banqueting House at Whitehall completed.	William Gager d. John Owen d. Sir Henry Savile d. Algernon Sidney b. Henry Vaughan b. (1621?) Thomas Vaughan b. (1621?)	Drayton, *Poly-Olbion,* ii. P. Hannay, *Nightingale,* &c. Rowlands, *Good News and Bad News.* T. Tomkins, *Songs.* Wither, *Fair Virtue; Juvenilia.*

Prose	Drama (date of acting)
Napier (d. 1617), *Mirifici Logarithmorum Canonis Constructio*. Drummond, *Midnight's Trance*. Gill, A., *Logonomia Anglica*. Gorges, Sir A., *Wisdom of the Ancients*, tr. Bacon's *De Sapientia Veterum*. Purchas, *Purchas his Pilgrim*.	Shakespeare (d. 1616): quartos of 10 authentic and ascribed plays pr. by Jaggard, mainly with false dates and all but two in corrupt or apocryphal texts. Fletcher, *Humorous Lieutenant*; (and Massinger?), *Sir John Barnavelt*. Massinger and Field, *Fatal Dowry*.
Anon.: *Astrea*, i, tr. D'Urfé; *Decameron*, tr.; *Westward for Smelts*. Bacon, *Novum Organum*. Brent, *History of the Council of Trent*, tr. Sarpi. Cavendish, Sir W., *Horae Subsecivae*. Scott, T., *Vox Populi*. Shelton, *Don Quixote*, ii, tr. Smith, Captain J., *New England's Trials*. Earliest English newsbooks pr. in Holland.	Dekker and Massinger, *Virgin Martyr* (?). Fletcher and Massinger, *Custom of the Country*. Jonson, *News from the New World Discovered in the Moon*; *Pan's Anniversary*. Massinger, *Maid of Honour*. May, *Heir*. Middleton, *Women Beware Women* (?).
Barclay, J., *Argenis*. Bolton, E., *Hypercritica* (written?). Burton, *Anatomy of Melancholy*. Carpenter, N., *Philosophia Libera*. Heylyn, *Microcosmus*. Mun, *Discourse of Trade unto the East Indies*. Wroth, Lady M., *Urania*. Newsbooks pr. in London.	Fletcher, *Island Princess* ; *Wild Goose Chase*. Jonson, *Gipsies Metamorphosed*.
Bacon, *Henry VII*; *Historia Naturalis et Experimentalis*. Brinsley, *Consolation for our Grammar Schools*. Hawkins, Sir R., *Observations in his Voyage into the South Sea*. Mabbe, *Rogue*, tr. Alemán. Misselden, *Free Trade*. Peacham, *Complete Gentleman*.	Carlell, *Osmond the Great Turk*. Fletcher (and Massinger?), *Spanish Curate*. Jonson, *Masque of Augurs*. Massinger, *Duke of Milan*; *New Way to Pay Old Debts*. Middleton and W. Rowley, *Changeling*.

Date	Public Events	Literary History	Verse
1623	Charles and Buckingham in Madrid. Failure of Spanish negotiations. Massacre of Amboyna. Calvert receives grant in Newfoundland.	William Byrd d. William Camden d. Giles Fletcher the younger d. Thomas Weelkes d. Margaret (Lucas) Cavendish, Duchess of Newcastle, b. Sir William Petty b. Jonson's MSS. lost in fire.	Daniel (d. 1619), *Whole Works*. Drummond, *Flowers of Sion*. Wither, *Hymns and Songs of the Church*.
1624	New Parliament set on war with Spain, king on recovery of Palatinate. Treaties with Spain cancelled. Marriage arranged between Charles and Henrietta Maria. Recusancy laws suspended. Monopolies Act.	Stephen Gosson d. Patrick Cary b. George Fox b. Samuel Sheppard b.? Sir Edward Herbert recalled from France.	Chapman, *Crown of All Homer's Works* (?). Quarles, *Job Militant*; *Sion's Elegies*.
1625	James d. Accession and marriage of Charles. Plague. Failure of Mansfield's expedition. Parliament hostile to Buckingham's continental projects. War with Spain. Failure of Cadiz expedition. Alliance with Holland and Denmark. King re-annexes Crown and Church lands in Scotland.	John Fletcher d. John Florio d.? Orlando Gibbons d. Thomas Lodge d. John Norden d.? Thomas Stanley b. Nicholas Ferrar retires to Little Gidding. Commons censure R. Montagu's High Church writings.	Bacon, *Certain Psalms*. Quarles, *Sion's Sonnets*.
1626	Second Parliament, led by Eliot, impeaches Buckingham, declares tonnage and poundage illegal. Dissolved. King resumes non-parliamentary levies.	Lancelot Andrewes d. Francis Bacon d. Nicholas Breton d.? Sir John Davies d. John Dowland d. Samuel Purchas d. William Rowley d. Cyril Tourneur d. John Aubrey b. Sir Robert Howard b.	Parrot, *Cures for the Itch*. Sandys, *Ovid's Metamorphoses*, tr.

Prose	*Drama (date of acting)*
Ames, *Medulla Sacrae Theologiae*. Bacon, *De Dignitate et Augmentis Scientiarum*; *Historia Vitae et Mortis*. Drummond, *Cypress Grove*. Felltham, *Resolves* (?). Lisle, *Saxon Treatise*.	Shakespeare (d. 1616), First Folio pr. Jonson, *Time Vindicated*. Massinger, *Bondman*.
Alexander, *Encouragement to Colonies*. Donne, *Devotions*. Herbert, Lord, *De Veritate*. Heywood, *Gunaikeion*. Montagu, R., *New Gag for an Old Goose*. Smith, Captain J., *General History of Virginia*. Wotton, *Elements of Architecture*.	Davenport, *City Nightcap*. Fletcher, *Rule a Wife and Have a Wife*. Heywood, *Captives*. Massinger, *Renegado*. Middleton, *Game at Chess*.
Barclay (d. 1621), *Argenis*, tr. K. Long. Camden (d. 1623), *Annales*, ii. Bacon, *Essays* (enlar.); *Apophthegms*. Carpenter, N., *Geography*. Dekker, *Rod for Runaways*. Montagu, R., *Appello Caesarem*. Purchas, *Purchas his Pilgrims*. Wither, *Scholar's Purgatory* (?).	Beaumont, Sir J., *Theatre of Apollo* (written). Jonson, *Fortunate Isles*. Randolph, *Aristippus* (1626?). Shirley, *Grateful Servant*.
Bacon (d. 1626), *Sylva Sylvarum*; *New Atlantis* (1627?). Overbury (d. 1613), *Observations*. Roper (d. 1578), *Life of Sir T. More*. Bernard, *Isle of Man*. Donne, *Five Sermons*. Prynne, *Perpetuity of a Regenerate Man's Estate*. Spelman, *Archaeologus*, i. Vaughan, Sir W., *Golden Fleece*.	Jonson, *Staple of News*. Massinger, *Roman Actor*. Shirley, *Wedding*.

Date	Public Events	Literary History	Verse
1627	Resistance to forced loans. Passive obedience preached by Sibthorp and Manwaring. Archbishop Abbot sequestered for refusing to license Sibthorp's sermon for the press. Expedition to Isle of Rhé.	Richard Barnfield d. Sir John Beaumont d. Lucy Russell, Countess of Bedford, d. Sir John Hayward d. Thomas Middleton d. Robert Boyle b. John Hall b. Dorothy Osborne b. John Ray b.	Drayton, *Battle of Agincourt*, *Nymphidia*, &c. P. Fletcher, *Locustae*. May, *Lucan's Pharsalia*, tr. R. Niccols, *Beggar's Ape*.
1628	Third Parliament. Petition of Right becomes law. Laud Bishop of London. Buckingham assassinated. Failure of second expedition to Rochelle. Laudian *Articles of Religion*.	John Chamberlain d. Fulke Greville murdered. John Preston d. John Bunyan b. Sir William Temple b. George Villiers, second Duke of Buckingham, b. Sir K. Digby's victory at Scanderoon. Richard Montagu Bishop of Chichester.	P. Fletcher, *Britain's Ida*. May, *Virgil's Georgics*, tr. Wither, *Britain's Remembrancer*.
1629	Commons' resolutions against popery, Arminianism, impositions. Parliament dissolved. Eliot et al. imprisoned. Impositions exacted. Peace with France. Laudian censorship of press and restriction of lecturers. Charter to Company of Massachusetts Bay.	Sir Edwin Sandys d. Thomas Shelton d. ? John Speed d. Montagu's *Appello Caesarem* called in.	Sir John Beaumont (d. 1627), *Bosworth-Field*. Chapman, *Fifth Satire of Juvenal*, tr. May, *Selected Epigrams of Martial*, tr. Milton, 'Nativity' (written). Quarles, *Argalus and Parthenia*.
1630	Knighthood fines and impositions. Plague. Laud Chancellor of Oxford. Charles II b. Peace with Spain. Commission for relief of debtors. Drainage of fens (1630 ff.). 'Great Migration' to New England (1630 ff.).	Thomas Bateson d. Fynes Moryson d. Samuel Rowlands d. ? Isaac Barrow b. Charles Cotton b. John Tillotson b. George Herbert rector of Bemerton. Alexander Leighton punished for attacking prelacy. Roger Williams sails for America.	Drayton, *Muses' Elysium*, &c. Quarles, *Divine Poems*. John Taylor, *Works* (verse and prose).

Prose	Drama (date of acting)
Cosin, *Devotions*. Cotton, Sir R., *Henry III*. Hakewill, *Apology*. Mead, *Clavis Apocalyptica*. Sanderson, *Ten Sermons*.	Davenant, *Cruel Brother*. Heywood, *English Traveller* (?). Massinger, *Great Duke of Florence*.
Barclay (d. 1621), *Argenis*, tr. Le Grys. Ralegh (d. 1618), *Prerogative of Parliaments*. Coke, *Institutes*, i. Earle, *Microcosmography*. Drake the younger, Sir F., ed., *World Encompassed by Sir Francis Drake*. Harvey, *De Motu Cordis et Sanguinis*. Leighton, A., *Appeal to the Parliament*. Selden, *Marmora Arundelliana*.	Ford, *Lover's Melancholy*. Shirley, *Witty Fair One*.
Andrewes (d. 1626), *XCVI Sermons*; *Opuscula*. Bacon (d. 1626), *Certain Miscellany Works*. Adams, T., *Works*. Godwin, F., *Nuncius Inanimatus*. Hobbes, *Thucydides*, tr. Parkinson, *Paradisi in Sole*.	Brome, R., *City Wit* (?); *Northern Lass*. Davenant, *Just Italian*. Ford, *Broken Heart* (?); '*Tis Pity She's a Whore* (1629?/33). Jonson, *New Inn*. Massinger, *Picture*.
Hayward (d. 1627), *Edward VI*. Ames, *De Conscientia*. Brathwait, *English Gentleman*. Norton, R., *History of Elizabeth*, tr. Camden's *Annales*. Sibbes, *Bruised Reed*. Smith, Captain J., *True Travels*.	Randolph, *Amyntas*; *Muses' Looking Glass*. Wilson, A., *Inconstant Lady*.

Date	Public Events	Literary History	Verse
1631	Commission for poor relief. King vacillates between Spain and Gustavus Adolphus. Laud enforces conformity at Oxford and elsewhere. Wentworth subdues northern gentry.	Lewis Bayly d. Sir Robert Cotton d. John Donne d. Michael Drayton d. Gabriel Harvey d. Captain John Smith d. Richard Cumberland b. John Dryden b. John Phillips b. Falkland at Great Tew (1631–9).	Fuller, *David's Heinous Sin.* W. Lisle, *Fair Ethiopian,* tr. Heliodorus. Milton, 'L'Allegro' and 'Il Penseroso' (written?). Quarles, *History of Samson.*
1632	King's offers rejected by Gustavus. Futile negotiations with Holland, Spain, and France. Gustavus and Elector Frederick d. Van Dyck settles in England. Maryland charter.	Thomas Dekker d. Sir John Eliot d. (in the Tower). John Locke b. Katherine (Fowler) Philips b. Anthony Wood b. Sir Christopher Wren b. Milton at home (1632–8).	Quarles, *Divine Fancies.* Sandys, *Ovid's Metamorphoses* (with allegorical commentary) and *Aeneid* i, tr. J. Vicars, *Aeneid,* tr. Wither, *Psalms of David.*
1633	King in Scotland. Wentworth begins administration in Ireland. Abbot d. Laud Archbishop. Ordination of lecturers forbidden, chaplaincies restricted. Paul's Walk purified. *Declaration of Sports* reissued. James II b. Large migration to New England.	William Ames d. Francis Godwin d. George Herbert d. Anthony Munday d. Samuel Rowley d.? Samuel Pepys b. George Savile, Marquis of Halifax, b. Lady Douglas (Davies) imprisoned for prophecies.	Donne (d. 1631), *Poems.* Greville (d. 1628), *Works.* G. Herbert (d. 1633), *The Temple.* Cowley, *Poetical Blossoms.* P. Fletcher, *Purple Island,* &c. May, *Henry II.*
1634	Laud enforces conformity, revives visitations. Witch trials in Lancashire. Crown's forest claims revived. King secretly negotiates with Spain for naval alliance against Dutch. Ship-money levied on maritime districts. Anglican canons forced upon Irish Convocation. Massachusetts Bay establishes self-government.	George Chapman d. Sir Edward Coke d. John Marston d. Robert South b. Nathaniel Wanley b. Prynne pilloried, imprisoned (till 1637).	Crashaw, *Epigrammatum Sacrorum Liber.* Habington, *Castara.*

Prose

Brathwait, *English Gentlewoman*; *Whimsies*. Dekker, *Penny-Wise Pound-Foolish*. Lenton, *Characterismi*. Mabbe, *Spanish Bawd*, tr. de Rojas. More, Cresacre, *Sir Thomas More* (?). Powell, T., *Tom of All Trades*. Saltonstall, W., *Picturae Loquentes*. Smith, Captain J., *Advertisements for Unexperienced Planters*.

Drama (date of acting)

Ford (and Dekker?), *Perkin Warbeck*. Jonson, *Chloridia*; *Love's Triumph through Callipolis*. Marmion, *Holland's Leaguer*. Massinger, *Emperor of the East*; *Believe As You List*. Shirley, *Traitor*. Wilson, A., *Swisser*.

Donne (d. 1631), *Death's Duel*. Ralegh (d. 1618), *Instructions to his Son*. Holland, *Cyropaedia*, tr. Xenophon. Lithgow, *Rare Adventures*. Lupton, *London and the Country Carbonadoed*. Prynne, *Histriomastix*. Reynolds, H., *Mythomystes*.

Lyly (d. 1606), *Six Court Comedies* pr. Shakespeare (d.1616), Second Folio pr. Jonson, *Magnetic Lady*. Massinger, *City Madam*. Milton, *Arcades* (1630/3?). Randolph, *Jealous Lovers*. Shirley, *Hyde Park*. Townshend, *Albion's Triumph*; *Tempe Restored*.

Donne (d. 1631), *Juvenilia*. Gerard (d. 1612), *Herbal*, enlar. by T. Johnson. Spenser (d. 1599), *View of Ireland*. Fludd, *Clavis Philosophiae et Alchymiae*. Grimeston, *History of Polybius*, tr. James, T., *Voyage*.

Jonson, *Tale of a Tub* (rev.). Marston, *Tragedies and Comedies* pr. Massinger, *Guardian*. Montagu, W., *Shepherd's Paradise*. Nabbes, *Covent Garden* (?); *Tottenham Court*. Shirley, *Bird in a Cage*; *Young Admiral*; *Gamester*.

Donne (d. 1631), *Six Sermons*. Anon., *Strange Metamorphosis of Man*. Casaubon, M., *Marcus Aurelius his Meditations*, tr. Herbert, Sir T., *Description of the Persian Monarchy*. Hickes, F., *Certain Dialogues . . . True History*, tr. Lucian. Ross, A., *Commentum de Terrae Motu Circulari*.

Brome, R., and Heywood, *Late Lancashire Witches*. Carew, *Coelum Britannicum*. Davenant, *Wits*; *Love and Honour*. Heywood, *Love's Mistress*. Milton, *Masque* [*Comus*]. Shirley, *Triumph of Peace*.

Date	Public Events	Literary History	Verse
1635	Diplomatic relations with Vatican. Ship-money extended to inland counties and approved by judges.	Richard Corbett d. Edward Fairfax d. Sir Robert Naunton d. Thomas Randolph d. Richard Sibbes d. Thomas Burnet b.? Sir George Etherege b.? Thomas Flatman b. Thomas Sprat b. Edward Stillingfleet b. Roger Williams banished from Massachusetts.	Donne (d. 1631), *Poems* (2nd ed., rev.). Heywood, *Hierarchy of the Blessed Angels.* Kynaston, *Amorum Troili et Creseidae*, tr. Chaucer, i–ii. May, *Edward III.* Quarles, *Emblems.* Wither, *Collection of Emblems.*
1636	Failure of negotiations regarding Palatinate. Judges affirm king's superiority to law. Royal charter for Oxford Press. Laudian Statutes for Oxford. King and Laud at Oxford. Third writ of ship-money. Plague.	John Eachard b.? Joseph Glanvill b. Sir George Mackenzie b.?	Cowley, *Sylva* (in *Poetical Blossoms*, 2nd ed.). W. Saltonstall, *Ovid's Heroical Epistles*, tr. (2nd ed.). Sandys, *Psalms of David.* Drayton, Jonson, et al., *Annalia Dubrensia.*
1637	Catholic proselytizing at Court. Judges reaffirm king's right to levy ship-money at discretion. Censorship of press re-enforced. Scottish resistance to new Service Book and new canons. Trial of Hampden.	Nicholas Ferrar d. Robert Fludd d. Philemon Holland d. Ben Jonson d. Gervase Markham d. Wentworth Dillon, Earl of Roscommon, b. Thomas Ken b. Thomas Traherne b. Dr. Thomas Browne settles at Norwich. Star Chamber sentences Prynne, Bastwick, and Burton.	Drayton (d. 1631), *Poems.* Alexander, *Recreations with the Muses.* Heywood, *Pleasant Dialogues and Dramas.* Marmion, *Cupid and Psyche.* Whiting, *Albino and Bellama.*
1638	Scottish Covenant. General resentment over royal exactions and Laudian policy. Seven of twelve judges decide against Hampden.	Sir Robert Aytoun d. John Hoskyns d. Joseph Mead d. John Webster d.? John Wilbye d. Philip Ayres b. Davenant pensioned as virtual laureate. Lilburne imprisoned. Milton abroad (1638–9).	Randolph (d. 1635), *Poems.* Brathwait, *Barnabe's Journal* (enlar.). Davenant, *Madagasgar.* Quarles, *Hieroglyphics of the Life of Man.* Sandys, *Divine Poems.* B. Duppa, ed., *Jonsonus Virbius.* *Justa Edouardo King* (incl. 'Lycidas').

Prose	Drama (date of acting)
a m barde, W. (d. 1601), *Archeion*. Fox, Luke, *North-West Fox*. Scott, W., *Essay of Drapery*. Selden, *Mare Clausum*. Swan, J., *Speculum Mundi*.	Brome, R. *Sparagus Garden*. Cartwright, *Ordinary*. Chapman (d. 1634) and Shirley, *Chabot* (rev.). Davenant, *Temple of Love*; *News from Plymouth*; *Platonic Lovers*. Marmion, *Antiquary*. Shirley, *Lady of Pleasure*.
Blount, *Voyage into the Levant*. Burton, H., *For God, and the King*. Dacres, *Machiavel's Discourses*, tr. Heylyn, *History of the Sabbath*. Peacham, *Coach and Sedan*. Prynne, *News from Ipswich*.	Cartwright, *Royal Slave*. Davenant, *Triumphs of the Prince d'Amour*. Glapthorne, *Hollander*. Kynaston, *Corona Minervae*. May, *Old Couple*. Strode, *Floating Island*.
Bastwick, J., *Litany*. Chillingworth, *Religion of Protestants*. Hartlib, S., ed., *Conatuum Comenianorum Praeludia*. Morton, T., *New English Canaan*.	Mayne, *City Match*. Milton, *Masque* [*Comus*] pr. (1638?). Suckling, *Goblins*.
Bacon (d. 1626), *Operum Moralium et Civilium Tomus*. Fludd (d. 1637), *Philosophia Moysaica*. Godwin, F. (d. 1633), *Man in the Moon*. Lilburne, *Christian Man's Trial*; *Work of the Beast*. Peacham, *Truth of our Times*. Wilkins, *Discovery of a World in the Moon*.	Brome, A., *Cunning Lovers* (?). Brome, R., *Antipodes*. Cowley, *Loves's Riddle* pr.; *Naufragium Joculare*. Davenant, *Luminalia*; *Unfortunate Lovers*; *Fair Favourite*. Suckling, *Aglaura* (rev.).

Date	Public Events	Literary History	Verse
1639	War with Scotland (First Bishops' War). Treaty of Berwick. King pursues his old Scottish policy. Wentworth becomes king's adviser.	Shakerley Marmion d. Sir Henry Wotton d. Sir Charles Sedley b. Davenant, Falkland, Lord Herbert, Lovelace, Earl of Newcastle, Suckling, Wither, et al., in Bishops' War.	Glapthorne, *Poems*.
1640	Refractory 'Short Parliament'. Convocation grants Benevolence, issues Laudian canons. London refuses loans and shipmoney. Second Bishops' War. Long Parliament impeaches Strafford and Laud, declares ship-money and canons illegal. Root and Branch Petition.	William Alabaster d. William Alexander, Earl of Stirling, d. Robert Burton d. Thomas Carew d. John Day d.? Philip Massinger d. Richard Verstegan d. Aphra (Johnson) Behn b. Bastwick, Burton, Prynne, Lilburne, and Leighton released from prison.	F. Beaumont (d. 1616), *Poems*. Carew (d. 1640), *Poems*. Jonson (d. 1637), *Underwoods* (in *Works*, 1640–1). C. Harvey, *Synagogue*. R. Mather et al.,' Bay Psalm Book'. Miscellanies: *Academy of Complements*; *Wit's Recreations*.
1641	Laud imprisoned. Army Plot. Princess Mary married to William of Orange. Strafford executed. Sweeping reforms by Parliament. Scottish army withdrawn from England. Irish rising. Grand Remonstrance.	Augustine Baker d. Thomas Heywood d. Thomas Mun d. Sir Henry Spelman d. Thomas Rymer b. William Sherlock b.? William Wycherley b. Baxter called to Kidderminster. Comenius in England. Davenant arrested for Army Plot; Suckling escapes to France. Hobbes in Paris (1641–51).	Beedome (d. 1640/1), *Poems*. Quarles, *Threnodes*. Sandys, *Paraphrase upon the Song of Solomon*. Urquhart, *Epigrams*. Wither, *Hallelujah*.

Prose

Ponet (d. 1556), *Short Treatise of Politic Power* repr. (also 1642). Sibbes (d. 1635), *Beams of Divine Light*. Fuller, *Holy War*. Hurst, R., *Endimion*, tr. Gombauld. Laud, *Conference with Fisher*. Spelman, *Concilia, Decreta*, i. Ussher, *Britannicarum Ecclesiarum Antiquitates*.

Drama (date of acting)

Davenant, *Spanish Lovers* (or *Distresses*). Glapthorne, *Wit in a Constable* (rev.). Shirley, *Politician*. Suckling, *Brennoralt*.

Bacon (d. 1626). *Advertisement touching Controversies of the Church of England*. Donne (d. 1631), *LXXX Sermons*, with Walton's *Life* (rev. 1658 ff.). Jonson (d. 1637), *Timber; English Grammar*. Brooke, Lord, *Nature of Truth*. Dacres, *Prince*, tr. Machiavelli. Hall, *Episcopacy by Divine Right*. Howell, *Dodona's Grove*. Quarles, *Enchiridion*. Wilkins, *Discourse concerning a New Planet*.

Jonson (d. 1637), *Works* (1640–1), vols. ii, iii (cf. 1616), incl. later plays, masques, verse, and prose. Fane, M., *Raguaillo d'Oceano*. Habington, *Queen of Aragon*. Sandys, *Christ's Passion*, tr. Grotius, pr.

Cavendish, G. (d. 1561?), *Thomas Wolsey*. Naunton (d. 1635), *Fragmenta Regalia*. Brooke, Lord, *Discourse of Episcopacy*. Hall, *Humble Remonstrance*; &c. Hartlib, *Description of Macaria*. Milton, *Reformation touching Church Discipline; Prelatical Episcopacy; Animadversions upon Remonstrant's Defence*. Robinson, H., *England's Safety in Trade's Increase*. 'Smectymnuus', *Answer to Humble Remonstrance; Vindication*. Ussher, *Judgement of Dr. Rainolds; Original of Bishops and Metropolitans*.

Brome, R., *Jovial Crew*. Denham, *Sophy*. Fane, M., *Candy Restored*. Quarles, *Virgin Widow* (1641/2?). Shirley, *Cardinal*.

Date	Public Events	Literary History	Verse
1642	King tries to arrest five members, leaves London. Bishops' Exclusion Bill passed. Parliament's militia ordinances. Suppression of Irish; Adventurers' Act. King refused admission to Hull. Nineteen Propositions. Navy declares for Parliament. Essex parliamentary general. King raises standard (22 August). Edgehill. Turnham Green. Oxford the king's headquarters (1642–6).	Richard Bernard d. John Chalkhill d. Sir Francis Kynaston d. Henry Peacham d.? Sir John Suckling d. George Hickes b. Sir Isaac Newton b. Thomas Shadwell b. Davenant, Denham, Falkland, Wither, et al., in war. Howell in prison (1642–50). Lovelace in prison. Marvell abroad (1642–6). Milton's first marriage.	Denham, *Cooper's Hill*. Kynaston, *Leoline and Sydanis*, &c. More, *Psychodia Platonica*.
1643	Episcopacy abolished. Cromwell in eastern counties. Waller's plot. Ordinance for licensing the press. Hampden dies of wounds. Royalist victories. Westminster Assembly; controversy over toleration. Solemn League and Covenant. Irish cessation; troops sent to king. Pym d.	Lord Brooke killed. William Browne d.? William Cartwright d. Lord Falkland killed. Sidney Godolphin killed. Gilbert Burnet b. Charles Sackville, 6th Earl of Dorset, b. John Strype b. Chillingworth, Cleveland, Cowley, et al., at Oxford. Evelyn and Lovelace abroad (1643 ff.). George Fox begins his wanderings. Waller imprisoned.	Cowley, *The Puritan and the Papist*. Martin Parker, 'When the King Enjoys His Own Again'.
1644	Scots enter England. Ordinance imposes Covenant on all adults. Royalists ejected from Cambridge.	William Chillingworth d. Peter Hausted d. Francis Quarles d. George Sandys d.	Quarles, *Shepherd's Oracle*.

Prose

Ames (d. 1633), *Marrow of Sacred Divinity*, tr. *Medulla*. Coke (d. 1634), *Institutes*, ii. Ralegh (d. 1618), *Prince*. Browne, *Religio Medici* (unauth.). Fuller, *Holy State*. Goodwin, J., *Anti-Cavalierism*. Hales, *Schism and Schismatics*. Hartlib, *Reformation of Schools*, tr. Comenius. Hobbes, *De Cive*. Howell, *Instructions for Foreign Travel*. Milton, *Reason of Church Government*; *Apology for Smectymnuus*. Parker, H., *Observations upon his Majesty's Late Answers*. Many diurnals (1641–2 ff.).

Drama (date of acting)

Cowley, *Guardian*. Killigrew, T., *Parson's Wedding* (?). Shirley, *Sisters*. Theatres closed, 2 September.

Baker, Sir R., *Chronicle*. Browne, *Religio Medici* (auth. ed.). Digby, *Observations upon Religio Medici*. Hunton, *Treatise of Monarchy*. Milton, *Doctrine and Discipline of Divorce* (enlar. 1644). Overton, R., *Man's Mortality* (1643/4). Prynne, *Sovereign Power of Parliaments*. Walwyn, *Power of Love*.

Mercurius Aulicus (1643–5), *Mercurius Britanicus* (1643–6), *Mercurius Civicus* (1643–6), and many other newsbooks.

Coke (d. 1634), *Institutes*, iii, iv. Cleveland, *Character of a London Diurnal*. Digby, *Two Treatises*. Edwards, T., *Antapologia*. Goodwin, J., *Theomachia*. Goodwin, T., et al., *Apologetical Narration*. Milton, *Of Educa·*

Date	Public Events	Literary History	Verse
	Committee of Both Kingdoms. First decisive parliamentary victory at Marston Moor. Trial of Laud. Montrose's victories. Parliamentary army in Cornwall surrenders. Friction between Manchester and Cromwell. Oxford Propositions.	William Penn b. Bunyan in militia (1644–7). Cowley and Crashaw abroad (1644 ff.). L'Estrange condemned as royalist spy. Newcastle besieged in York; abroad (1644–60). Waller fined, banished; abroad (1644–51). Whichcote Provost of King's College.	
1645	Prayer Book abolished. Laud executed. New Model Army. Self-Denying Ordinance. Naseby (14 June) and other parliamentary victories. Montrose loses Philiphaugh. King tries to get Irish and foreign troops (1643–6). Witch-hunting (1645–7).	Sir Richard Baker d. William Lithgow d.? William Strode d. Baxter chaplain in parliamentary army. Sir K. Digby queen's agent in Rome. Lilburne in prison. Scientists meet at Gresham College (c. 1645).	Quarles (d. 1644,) *Solomon's Recantation*. Milton, *Poems* (1645/6). Waller, *Poems*. Wither, *Vox Pacifica*.
1646	Ordinance for Presbyterianism. Hopton surrenders to Fairfax. King takes refuge with Scots. Oxford surrenders. Virtual end of war. Newcastle Propositions. Friction between Presbyterians and Independents.	Anthony Hamilton b. Davenant in Paris (1646–50). Hyde begins *History of the Rebellion* in Scilly and Jersey. Lilburne in prison (1646–8).	Quarles (d. 1644), *Shepherd's Oracles*. Suckling (d. 1642), *Fragmenta Aurea*. Crashaw, *Steps to the Temple*. Lluelyn, *Men-Miracles*. Philipott, *Poems*. Sheppard, *Times Displayed*. Shirley, *Poems*. H. Vaughan, *Poems*.
1647	King given up to Parliament. Beginning of Presbyterian-royalist alliance. Army seizes King. *Heads of the Proposals*. Army occupies Lon-	Thomas Farnaby d. Francis Meres d. John Saltmarsh d. John Wilmot, Earl of Rochester, b. George Fox begins public ministry.	Corbett (d. 1635), *Poems*. Quarles (d. 1644), *Hosanna*. Cleveland, *Poems* (with *Character of a London Diurnal*). Cowley, *The Mistress*.

Prose

Drama (date of acting)

tion; *Judgement of Martin Bucer concerning Divorce*; *Areopagitica*. Prynne, *Independency Examined*. Robinson, H., *Liberty of Conscience*. Rutherford, S., *Rex, Lex*. Walwyn, *Compassionate Samaritan*. Williams, R., *Queries of Highest Consideration*; *Bloody Tenent of Persecution*.

Falkland, Lord (d. 1643), *Of the Infallibility of the Church of Rome*. Fuller, *Good Thoughts in Bad Times*. Herbert, Lord, *De Causis Errorum*. Howell, *Epistolae Ho-Elianae*, i. Lilburne, *England's Birth-Right Justified*. Milton, *Tetrachordon*; *Colasterion*. Overton, *Arraignment of Mr. Persecution*. Prynne, *Truth Triumphing*. Ross, A., *Medicus Medicatus*. Sparrow, J., et al., works of Boehme tr. (1645–62). Sprigg, J., *Ancient Bounds*.

Donne (d. 1631), *Biathanatos* (?). Browne, *Pseudodoxia Epidemica*. Edwards, T., *Gangraena*. Hall, John, *Horae Vacivae*. Lilburne, *London's Liberty*. Overton, *Remonstrance*. Ross, A., *New Planet No Planet*. Saltmarsh, *Smoke in the Temple*, Taylor, J., *Discourse concerning Prayer Ex tempore*. Walwyn, seven tracts on liberty of conscience. Wilkins, *Ecclesiastes*.

Robert Cox, drolls (1646–53).

Andrewes (d. 1626), *Private Devotions*. Bodley, Sir T. (d. 1613), *Life*. Browne, W., *Polexander*, tr. Gomberville. Cudworth, *Sermon before House of Commons*. Fuller, *Cause and Cure of a Wounded Conscience*; *Good Thoughts in Worse Times*. Howell, *Epistolae Ho-elianae*, ii. Lilburne, *Rash Oaths*. Lilly,

Beaumont (d. 1616) and Fletcher (d. 1625), *Comedies and Tragedies* pr. Fanshawe, *Pastor Fido*, tr. Guarini, pr.
Parliamentary ordinances (1647–8) for suppressing plays.

Date	Public Events	Literary History	Verse
	don. King treats with both Parliament and army. Putney debates. King escapes to Isle of Wight; makes secret engagement with Scots.	Joseph Hall expelled from bishopric of Norwich. Herrick ejected from Dean Prior.	John Hall, *Poems*. C. Harvey, *Schola Cordis*. More, *Philosophical Poems*. Stanley, *Poems and Translations*. Stapylton, *Juvenal*, tr.
1648	Second civil war. Battle of Preston. Surrender of Colchester. Parliament negotiates with king. Leveller Petition. *Remonstrance of the Army*. Army seizes king, enters London. Pride's Purge. End of Thirty Years War.	Lord Herbert of Cherbury d. Robert Barclay b. Elkanah Settle b. John Sheffield, Earl of Mulgrave, b. Lovelace in prison. Hammond, Sanderson, et al. ejected from Oxford. John Wilkins Warden of Wadham (1648–59).	Corbett (d. 1635), *Poetica Stromata*. Joseph Beaumont, *Psyche*. M. Fane, Earl of Westmorland, *Otia Sacra*. Herrick, *Hesperides*; *Noble Numbers*.
1649	King's trial and execution (30 January). Charles II proclaimed in Scotland. Rump abolishes House of Lords and monarchy, proclaims Commonwealth. Cromwell in Ireland. Act for relief of poor debtors. Diggers. End of Leveller movement. Act concerning Religion in Maryland.	Richard Crashaw d. William Drummond d. George Hakewill d. Sir Anthony Weldon d.? Evelyn abroad (1649–52). Lilburne tried, acquitted. Milton Secretary for Foreign Tongues to Council of State.	Lovelace, *Lucasta*. J. Ogilby, *Works of Virgil*, tr. R. B. [Richard Brome], ed., *Lachrymae Musarum* (elegies on Lord Hastings by Dryden, Marvell, Herrick et al.).
1650	Engagement imposed. Montrose executed. Charles accepts Scottish Covenant. Acts on Sunday observance, adultery, swearing, blasphemy. Battle of Dunbar. Recusancy penalties repealed. Trade with royalist colonies prohibited.	William Bosworth d.? Sir Simonds D'Ewes d. John Everard d.? Phineas Fletcher d. Thomas May d. Jeremy Collier b. Davenant in prison (1650–2).	Anne Bradstreet, *Tenth Muse*. Davenant, *Gondibert* (1650–1). R. Heath, *Clarastella*. Marvell, *Horatian Ode* (written). Vaughan, *Silex Scintillans*, i.

Prose   *Drama (date of acting)*

Christian Astrology. May, *History of the Parliament.* Overton, *An Appeal.* Taylor, J., *Liberty of Prophesying.* Wildman, *Case of the Army.*
Mercurius Melancholicus (1647–9), *Mercurius Pragmaticus* (1647–50), *Mercurius Elencticus* (1647–9), and other journals.

Bacon (d. 1626), *Remains.* Hooker (d. 1600), *Ecclesiastical Polity,* books vi, viii. Duncon, *Viscountess Falkland.* Filmer, *Anarchy of a Limited or Mixed Monarchy.* Gage, *New Survey of the West Indies.* Gott, *Nova Solyma.* Petty, *Advice to Hartlib.* Wilkins, *Mathematical Magic.*

Sherburne, *Medea,* tr. Seneca, pr.

Donne (d. 1631), *Fifty Sermons.* Herbert, Lord (d. 1648), *Henry VIII.* Dury, *Seasonable Discourse.* Gauden, *Eikon Basilike.* Goodwin, J., *Right and Might Well Met.* Hall, John, *Humble Motion concerning Advancement of Learning.* Lilburne, *England's New Chains Discovered*; *Legal Fundamental Liberties.* Milton, *Tenure of Kings and Magistrates*; *Eikonoklastes.* Taylor, J., *Great Exemplar.*

Baxter, *Saints' Everlasting Rest.* Davenant and Hobbes, *Discourse upon Gondibert. With an Answer.* Dury, *Reformed School* (?). Fuller, *Pisgah-Sight of Palestine.* Hobbes, *Human Nature*; *De Corpore Politico.* Howell, *Epistolae,* iii. Taylor, J., *Holy Living.* Ussher, *Annales Veteris Testamenti* (1650–4). Vaughan, T., *Anthroposophia Theomagica,* &c.
Mercurius Politicus (1650–60).

Date	Public Events	Literary History	Verse
1651	Charles crowned at Scone. Blake completes extermination of royalist privateers. Battle of Worcester. Charles a fugitive. Scotland subdued. Confiscation of royalist estates in England and Scotland. Navigation Act.	Nathanael Culverwel d.? Aurelian Townshend d.? Nathaniel Lee b.? Cowley in Jersey. Hobbes returns to England. Milton associated with *Mercurius Politicus*.	Bosworth (d. 1650?), *Chaste and Lost Lovers.* Cartwright (d. 1643), *Poems* (in *Comedies*, &c.). P. Cary, *Trivial Poems and Triolets* (written). Cleveland, *Poems.* Sherburne, *Salmacis*, &c. Stanley, *Poems.* Vaughan, *Olor Iscanus.*
1652	Commission for legal reforms. Proposals for national Church with toleration. Royalist colonies submit. Army petitions Parliament. End of twelve years' war in Ireland; confiscation of land and transplantation (1652–7). Dutch war.	Richard Brome d.? John Cotton d. Henry Parker d. Martin Parker d. John Smith d. William Dampier b. Thomas Otway b. Nahum Tate b. Milton's blindness complete.	Crashaw (d. 1649), *Carmen Deo Nostro.* Ashmole, ed., *Theatrum Chemicum Britannicum.* Benlowes, *Theophila.*
1653	Army seeks toleration, parliamentary and legal reforms. Parliament expelled by Cromwell. Nominated ('Barebones') Parliament. Dutch defeated by Blake and Monk. Instrument of Government establishes Protectorate.	Sir Robert Filmer d. John Taylor d. Thomas D'Urfey b. Roger North b. John Oldham b. Lilburne tried, acquitted; kept in prison (1653–7).	M. Cavendish, *Duchess of Newcastle, Poems and Fancies.* Cleveland, *Poems.* N. Hookes, *Amanda.* H. Lawes, *Airs and Dialogues.* Marvell, *Character of Holland* (written). Denham et al., *Certain Verses* (satires on *Gondibert*).
1654	Royalist and Leveller plots (1654 ff.). Reforms in law, manners, and education. Commission to examine clergy. Peace with Holland. Treaties with Sweden, Portugal, Denmark. French forts in Acadia seized. Parliament restricts power of Cromwell and Council.	William Basse d. Nicholas Culpeper d. William Habington d. Alexander Ross d. John Selden d. Sir Richard Blackmore b. Cowley returns to England.	

Prose

Donne (d. 1631), *Essays in Divinity; Letters to Several Persons of Honour.* Gilbert, W. (d. 1603), *De Mundo . . . Philosophia Nova.* Ralegh (d. 1618), *Sceptic.* Wotton, Sir H. (d. 1639), *Reliquiae Wottonianae,* with Walton's *Life.* Boyle, R., *Parthenissa* (1651 ff.). Harvey, *De Generatione Animalium.* Hobbes, *Leviathan; Philosophical Rudiments,* tr. *De Cive.* Milton, *Pro Populo Anglicano Defensio.* Taylor, J., *Holy Dying; XXVIII Sermons.*

Drama (date of acting)

Cartwright (d. 1643), *Comedies, Tragicomedies, With Other Poems* pr.

Culverwel (d. 1651?), *Light of Nature.* Donne (d. 1631), *Paradoxes, Problems, Essays, Characters.* Greville (d. 1628), *Life of Sidney.* Herbert, G. (d. 1633), *Remains.* Cogan, H., *Ibrahim,* tr. Scudéry. Cotterell, Sir C., *Cassandra,* tr. La Calprenède. Feltham, *Brief Character of the Low Countries* (unauth. ed., 1648). Filmer, *Aristotle's Politics; Original of Government.* Hall, John, *Longinus,* tr. Heylyn, *Cosmography.* Loveday, R., et al., *Hymen's Praeludia* (1652–9), tr. La Calprenède's *Cléopâtre.* Vaughan, H., *Mount of Olives.* Winstanley, *Law of Freedom.*

Bacon (d. 1626), *Scripta.* Cavendish, M., Duchess of Newcastle, *Philosophical Fancies.* Everard, J., *Some Gospel Treasures Opened.* G., F., *Artamenes or the Grand Cyrus* (1653–5), tr. Scudéry. More, *Antidote against Atheism; Conjectura Cabbalistica.* Ross, *Lethiathan Drawn out with a Hook; Pansebeia.* Taylor, J., *XXV Sermons.* Urquhart, *Rabelais,* i–ii, tr. Walton, *Complete Angler.*

Brome, R. (d. 1652?), *Five New Plays* pr. Shirley, *Six New Plays* pr.

Hobbes, *Of Liberty and Necessity.* Milton, *Defensio Secunda.* Vaughan, H., *Flores Solitudinis.* Ward, S., and Wilkins, J., *Vindiciae Academiarum.* Webster, J., *Examen Academiarum.* Worthington, *Christian's Pattern,* tr. à Kempis.

Governmental repression of plays.

Date	Public Events	Literary History	Verse
1655	Proclamation on religious liberty. Penruddock's rising. Blake subdues Algerian pirates. Massacre of Vaudois. Jamaica captured; West Indian colonies secured against Spain. Rule of major-generals. War with Spain. Treaty with France.	William Hammond d.? Samuel Sheppard d.? Andrew Fletcher b. Cleveland and Cowley in prison.	*Caedmonis Paraphrasis Poetica Genesios*, ed. F. Junius. Denham, *Cooper's Hill* (auth. ed.). Fanshawe, *Lusiad*, tr. Camoens. Marvell, *First Anniversary of . . . the Lord Protector*. J. Phillips, *Satire against Hypocrites*. Vaughan, *Silex Scintillans*, i–ii. Waller, *Panegyric to my Lord Protector*. Miscellanies: *Marrow of Complements*; *Musarum Deliciae*; *English Treasury of Wit and Language*, ed. J. Cotgrave; *Wit's Interpreter, The English Parnassus*, ed. Cotgrave.
1656	Blake blockades Spanish coast. Anglican and Catholic worship connived at. Virtual toleration of Jews. Second Protectorate Parliament; over 100 members excluded by government. Case of James Naylor. End of major-generals' rule.	Thomas Gage d. Godfrey Goodman d. John Hales d. John Hall d. Joseph Hall d. Robert Loveday d. James Ussher d. Gerard Langbaine the younger b. Jacob Tonson b.?	Drummond (d. 1649), *Poems*. Collop, *Poesis Rediviva*. Cowley, *Poems* (coll., with *Davideis* and odes). Denham, *Destruction of Troy*, tr. *Aeneid* ii. Evelyn, *First Book of Lucretius*, tr. Miscellanies: *Choice Drollery*; *Parnassus Biceps*, ed. A. Wright; *Sportive Wit; Wit and Drollery*.
1657	Alliance with France against Spain. Spain crippled by Blake. Humble Petition and Advice. Cromwell declines kingship; reinvested as Protector by parliamentary authority. New charter for East India Company. Quakers protected.	George Daniel d. William Harvey d. John Lilburne d. Richard Lovelace d. (1656?). John Dennis b. Thomas Killigrew the younger b. John Norris b. Matthew Tindal b.	King, *Poems*. J. Poole, ed., *English Parnassus*. T. Stanley, *Psalterium Carolinum*.

Prose

Bramhall, *Defence of True Liberty*. Davies, J., and Havers, G., *Clelia* (1655–61), tr. Scudéry. Dugdale, *Monasticon Anglicanum*, i. Fuller, *Church History of Britain*, &c. Hobbes, *De Corpore*. Howell, *Epistolae*, iv. Milton, *Pro Se Defensio*. Stanley, *History of Philosophy* (1655–62). Taylor, J., *Golden Grove*; *Unum Necessarium*. Vane, *Retired Man's Meditations*.

Seven independent newspapers suppressed; Needham's government papers, *Mercurius Politicus* and *Public Intelligencer*, excepted.

Drama (date of acting)

Lower, Sir W., *Polyeuctes*, tr. Corneille, pr.

Bunyan, *Some Gospel-Truths Opened*. Cavendish, M., Duchess of Newcastle, *Nature's Pictures*. Charleton, *Epicurus's Morals*. Dugdale, *Antiquities of Warwickshire*. Harrington, *Oceana*. Hobbes, *Questions concerning Liberty, Necessity, and Chance*. More, *Enthusiasmus Triumphatus*. Osborn, *Advice to a Son* (ii, 1658). Vane, *Healing Question*.

Davenant, *First Day's Entertainment at Rutland House*; 1 *Siege of Rhodes*. Lower, Sir W., *Horatius*, tr. Corneille, pr.

Bacon (d. 1626), *Resuscitatio*. Baker, A. (d. 1641), *Sancta Sophia*. Vere, Sir F. (d. 1609), *Commentaries*. Baxter, *Call to the Unconverted*. Bunyan, *Vindication*. Harrington, *Prerogative of Popular Government*. Howell, *Londinopolis*. Lawson, G., *Examination of Mr. Hobbes's Leviathan*. Sexby, *Killing No Murder*. Taylor, J., *Discourse of Friendship*. Thornley, *Daphnis and Chloe*, tr. Longus. Walton, B., et al., *Biblia Sacra Polyglotta*.

Date	Public Events	Literary History	Verse
1658	Republican opposition to Cromwell and second chamber. Parliament dissolved. Battle of the Dunes; England acquires Dunkirk. War increases public debt. Cromwell d. (3 September). Richard Cromwell Protector.	John Cleveland d. Gerard Langbaine the elder d. Edward Sexby d. Sir Henry Slingsby executed.	John Hall (d. 1656), *Emblems*. Cokayne, *Poems*. Harrington, tr. Virgil (enlarg. 1659). Waller and S. Godolphin (d. 1643), *Passion of Dido*, tr. *Aeneid* iv. Miscellanies: *Naps upon Parnassus*; *Wit Restored*; *Mysteries of Love and Eloquence*, ed. E. Phillips.
1659	Third Protectorate Parliament. Army officers force dissolution. End of Protectorate. Rump recalled, expelled by Lambert, again restored. Rota Club (1659-60).	Richard Johnson d.? Francis Osborn d. Thomas Creech b. John Dunton b.	Suckling (d. 1642), *Last Remains*. Chamberlayne, *Pharonnida*. Waller, Dryden, and Sprat, *Three Poems upon the Death of . . . Oliver Lord Protector*. E. Williamson, ed., *J. Cleveland Revived*.
1660	Monk leads army from Scotland, recalls Presbyterian members excluded in 1648. Dissolution. Declaration of Breda. New Parliament recalls Charles II. King enters London (29 May). Punishment of regicides living and dead. Legislation of Cromwell and Long Parliament regarded as void. Royal Society organized.	Henry Hammond d. Hugh Peter executed. Sir Thomas Urquhart d. Daniel Defoe b. Thomas Southerne b. Bunyan in prison. Return to England of Earle, Newcastle, et al. Pepys begins diary. Wither arrested.	Lovelace (d. 1656/7), *Lucasta. Posthume Poems* (dated 1659). Dryden, *Astraea Redux*. Pordage, *Poems*. Robert Wild, *Iter Boreale*. Poems on Restoration by Cowley, Davenant, Waller, et al. Miscellanies: *Rats Rhymed to Death*; B. Rudyerd et al., *Le Prince d'Amour*.

Prose

Drama (date of acting)

Bacon (d. 1626), *Opuscula. Cabinet Council* [wrongly attributed to Ralegh], ed. Milton. Allestree, R., *Whole Duty of Man*. Bramhall, *Castigations of Mr. Hobbes*. Browne, *Hydriotaphia*; *Garden of Cyrus*. Digby, *Powder of Sympathy*. Hobbes, *De Homine*. Phillips, E., *New World of English Words*.

Chamberlayne, *Love's Victory* pr. Davenant, *Cruelty of the Spaniards in Peru; Sir Francis Drake*.

Hales (d. 1656), *Golden Remains*. Loveday, R. (d. 1656), *Letters*. Baxter, *Holy Commonwealth*. Evelyn, *Character of England*. Fuller, *Appeal of Injured Innocence*. Milton, *Civil Power in Ecclesiastical Causes; Likeliest Means to Remove Hirelings out of the Church; Ruptures of the Commonwealth*. More, *Immortality of the Soul*. Pearson, *Exposition of the Creed*. Rushworth, *Historical Collections* (1659–1701). Somner, *Dictionarium Saxonico-Latino-Anglicum*.

Brome, R. (d. 1652?), *Five New Plays* pr. Davenant, 2 *Siege of Rhodes*. Shirley, *Contention of Ajax and Ulysses* pr.

Donne (d. 1631), *XXVI Sermons*. Smith, J. (d. 1652), *Select Discourses*. Boyle, *New Experiments Physico-Mechanical*. Fuller, *Mixed Contemplations in Better Times*. Hoole, *Old Art of Teaching School*. Milton, *Ready and Easy Way*. More, *Grand Mystery of Godliness*. Taylor, J., *Ductor Dubitantium*. Winstanley, W., *England's Worthies*.

Pordage, S., *Troades*, tr. Seneca, pr. Tatham, *Rump*. Theatre patents granted to Thomas Killigrew the elder and Davenant.

BIBLIOGRAPHY

This bibliography is arranged in six sections:

I. General Bibliographies and Works of Reference.

II. General Collections and Anthologies.

III. General Literary History and Criticism (general history and criticism; rhetorical theory and prose style; history and criticism of poetry; history of ideas).

IV. Special Literary Studies and Literary Forms (language; popular literature; journalism; fiction; essays and characters; historical and biographical literature; classical and foreign relations; translations; contemporary criticism; printing and bookselling).

V. The Background of Literature (political history and political thought; religion and religious thought; science and scientific thought; travel; social life; education and culture; music and the arts).

VI. Individual Authors.

Since the bibliography is to be 'selective and directive', a great deal of more or less important material is necessarily omitted; and a general reference to the bibliographies in the *BMC* and *CBEL* (*infra*) must suffice.

The following abbreviations are used in the citing of some works of reference and current periodicals:

Abbreviations

R. F. Brinkley   *Coleridge on the Seventeenth Century*, ed. R. F. Brinkley (Duke University, 1955)

BMC   *British Museum General Catalogue of Printed Books*

CBEL   *Cambridge Bibliography of English Literature*

CBS   *Transactions of the Cambridge Bibliographical Society*

DNB   *Dictionary of National Biography*

ELH   *English Literary History* (Johns Hopkins)

ESEA   *Essays and Studies by Members of the English Association* (including *English Studies*, 1948 and 1949)

HLB   *Huntington Library Bulletin*

HLQ   *Huntington Library Quarterly*

JEGP   *Journal of English and Germanic Philology*

JHI   *Journal of the History of Ideas*
Lewis   C. S. Lewis, *English Literature in the Sixteenth Century* (*O.H.E.L.*, vol. iii, 1954)
MLN   *Modern Language Notes*
MLQ   *Modern Language Quarterly*
MLR   *Modern Language Review*
MP   *Modern Philology*
NQ   *Notes and Queries*
OBS   *Oxford Bibliographical Society Proceedings & Papers*
PBSA   *Papers of the Bibliographical Society of America*
PMLA   *Publications of the Modern Language Association of America*
PQ   *Philological Quarterly*
Raysor   *Coleridge's Miscellaneous Criticism*, ed. T. M. Raysor (1936)
RES   *Review of English Studies*
Saintsbury   *Minor Poets of the Caroline Period*, ed. George Saintsbury (3 vols., 1905–21)
SP   *Studies in Philology*
STC   *Short-Title Catalogue . . . 1475–1640* (*infra*)
TLS   *London Times Literary Supplement*
UTQ   *University of Toronto Quarterly*
Wing   *Short-Title Catalogue . . . 1641–1700*, ed. Wing (*infra*)

In sections I–V the place of publication is ordinarily given for books published outside Great Britain, but not in VI if such books are there cited again.

I. GENERAL BIBLIOGRAPHIES AND WORKS OF REFERENCE

Some of the older and still useful bibliographical aids are the descriptive compilations of Sir Egerton Brydges and J. P. Collier and, for its subject-index, Robert Watt's *Bibliotheca Britannica* (4 vols., 1824); W. T. Lowndes, *Bibliographer's Manual of English Literature* (rev. ed. by H. G. Bohn, 6 vols., 1869); and such works by W. C. Hazlitt as the *Hand-Book to the Popular, Poetical, and Dramatic Literature of Great Britain* (1867) and *Collections and Notes* (6 vols., 1876–1903), with the *Index* to both by G. J. Gray (1893), these repr., 8 vols. (New York, 1961).

Other and mainly later works of reference for original texts are: *British Museum General Catalogue of Printed Books*; E. Arber, *Transcript of the Registers of the Company of Stationers of London, between 1554–1640 A.D.* (5 vols., 1875–94); the *Transcript* of the same (1640–1708) by G. E. B. Eyre and H. R. Plomer (3 vols., Roxburghe Club, 1913–14), this work and Arber repr., 8 vols. (New York, 1950); C. E. Sayle, *Early English Printed Books in the University Library Cambridge (1475 to 1640)* (4 vols., 1900–7); Grolier Club *Catalogue of Original and Early Editions*, &c. (3 vols., New York, 1905); *Catalogue of the Pamphlets, Books, Newspapers and Manuscripts . . . Collected by George Thomason, 1640–61*, ed. G. K. Fortescue (2 vols., 1908), a valuable guide to chronology; A. W. Pollard, G. R. Redgrave, et al., *Short-Title Catalogue of Books Printed in England, Scotland, & Ireland . . . 1475–1640* (1926; rev. cd. in preparation), supplemented by C. K. Edmonds, *HLB* (1933), W. W. Bishop, *A Checklist of American Copies* (2nd ed., University of Michigan, 1950), and P. G. Morrison, *Index of Printers, Publishers and Booksellers* (University of Virginia, 1950); C. R. Gillett, *Catalogue of the McAlpin Collection of British History and Theology* (5 vols., New York, 1927–30); *The Britwell Handlist* (2 vols., 1933); W. A. Jackson, *The Carl H. Pforzheimer Library: English Literature 1475–1700* (3 vols., New York, 1940); D. Wing, *Short-Title Catalogue of Books Printed in . . . 1641–1700* (3 vols., Columbia, 1945–51), with *Supplements* by M. I. Fry and G. Davies (*HLQ* xvi, 1953), W. G. Hiscock (1956) and J. Alden (University of Virginia, 1958), and an *Index of Printers*, &c. (*supra*), by P. G. Morrison (University of Virginia, 1955); D. Ramage, *A Finding-List of English Books to 1640 in Libraries in the British Isles* (1958); and items below in IV. 10.

The most essential work, the *CBEL*, ed. F. W. Bateson (4 vols., 1940), has had a *Supplement*, ed. G. Watson (1957), covering *c.* 1935–55, and a small abridgement, *The Concise Cambridge Bibliography of English Literature*, ed. Watson (1958). V. de S. Pinto's *The English Renaissance 1510–1688* (1938; rev. 1951) is a useful though sometimes inaccurate compendium. A comprehensive aid is A. G. Kennedy and D. B. Sands, *A Concise Bibliography for Students of English* (4th ed., Stanford, 1960). Here may be put Rudolf Stamm's *Englische Literatur* (Bern, 1957), a critical review of scholarship, roughly 1935–55, on English literature, 1500–1900.

Indispensable annual bibliographies are: *The Year's Work in English Studies* (English Association, since 1919–20); *Annual Bibliography of English Language and Literature* (Modern Humanities Research Association, since 1920); the bibliography included in *PMLA* since 1922; the Renaissance bibliography in *SP* since 1922, which includes the period 1600–60; the bibliography for 1660–1800 in *PQ* since 1926; *Dissertation Abstracts: Abstracts of Dissertations and Monographs in Microfilm* (University Microfilms, Ann Arbor, since 1938); *Abstracts of English Studies*, 1958 ff. (University of Colorado). To these must be added *Seventeenth-Century News*, edited since 1950 by J. M. Patrick (New York University).

Some miscellaneous works of reference are: Sir W. W. Greg, *English Literary Autographs 1550–1650* (3 vols., 1925–32); S. Halkett and J. Laing, *Dictionary of Anonymous and Pseudonymous English Literature*, rev. by J. Kennedy et al. (8 vols., 1926–56); *Annals of English Literature 1475–1950*, ed. W. Davin and R. W. Chapman (2nd ed., rev., 1962); Sir Paul Harvey, *Oxford Companion to English Literature* (3rd ed., rev., 1946), and the abridgement, the *Concise Oxford Dictionary of English Literature* (1939); A. Brett-James, *The Triple Stream: Four Centuries of English, French and German Literature 1531–1930* (1954), containing parallel chronological tables; C. L. Barnhart, *New Century Handbook of English Literature* (New York, 1956); D. C. Browning, *Everyman's Dictionary of Literary Biography* (1958).

Almost all the authors mentioned in the text are in the *DNB* and a few in the later *Dictionary of American Biography*. Many have a niche in G. E. Bentley's *Jacobean and Caroline Stage* (5 vols., 1941–56). Among early biographers of varying authority are Thomas Fuller, Samuel Clarke, who compiled several works of ecclesiastical biography, William Winstanley, and the unique John Aubrey (1626–97). The standard edition of Aubrey's *Brief Lives* is that of A. Clark (2 vols., 1898); a later edition is by O. L. Dick (1949; University of Michigan, 1957). *Athenae Oxonienses* (2 vols., 1691–2), by the less genial Anthony (à) Wood (1632–95), is quoted in this book from the revised and enlarged edition of 1721. J. M. French (*PMLA* lxxv, 1960) examined Wood's reliability in regard to a number of our authors.

II. GENERAL COLLECTIONS AND ANTHOLOGIES

1. PROSE

Special collections and anthologies are cited in appropriate places. Some general ones are: H. Craik, *English Prose*, vols. i–iii (1893–4); R. P. T. Coffin and A. M. Witherspoon, *A Book of Seventeenth-Century Prose* (New York, 1929); R. F. Brinkley, *English Prose of the XVII Century* (New York, 1951); H. C. White, R. C. Wallerstein, and R. B. Quintana, *Seventeenth-Century Verse and Prose*, vol. i, 1600–60 (New York, 1951); J. W. Hebel, H. H. Hudson, F. R. Johnson, and A. W. Green, *Prose of the English Renaissance* (New York, 1952), which covers our period; H. E. Rollins and H. Baker, *The Renaissance in England* (Boston, 1954), which includes some prose and verse beyond 1600; Roy Lamson and H. Smith, *Renaissance England* (New York, 1956), which includes prose and verse to 1660; M. A. Shaaber, *Seventeenth-Century English Prose* (New York, 1957). Smaller, more popular books are: W. Peacock, *English Prose*, i–ii (1921); K. Muir, *Elizabethan and Jacobean Prose* (Pelican, 1956); P. Ure, *Seventeenth Century Prose* (Pelican, 1956).

Two treasuries of rare pamphlets are *The Harleian Miscellany* (1744–6; ed. T. Park, 10 vols., 1808–13) and *Somers Tracts* (1748–52; enlarged ed. by Sir W. Scott, 13 vols., 1809–15). Some other collections are: W. C. Hazlitt, *Prefaces, Dedications and Epistles Selected from Early English Books, 1540–1701* (1874); Sir C. Firth, *Stuart Tracts* (1903); W. H. Dunham and S. Pargellis, *Complaint and Reform in England 1436–1714* (New York, 1938).

2. VERSE

This list comprises early miscellanies, modern collections and general anthologies, and anthologies of lyrical, pastoral, and religious verse. Collections of broadside ballads are listed below in IV. 2.

A. E. Case's *Bibliography of English Poetical Miscellanies 1521–1750* (1935), supplemented by the *CBEL*, is almost exhaustive. Some early miscellanies are: *Englands Helicon* (1600, 1614), ed. A. H. Bullen (1887, 1899), H. Macdonald (1925), H. E. Rollins (2 vols., Harvard, 1935), the standard edition, and H. Macdonald (Muses' Library, 1950); *Englands Parnassus* (1600), ed. T.

Park, *Heliconia*, iii (1815), C. Crawford (1913); *Bel-vedere* (1600), repr., Spenser Society (1875); *A Poetical Rapsody* (1602–21), ed. Bullen (2 vols., 1890–1), definitively by H. E. Rollins (2 vols., Harvard, 1931–2); *Witts Recreations* (1640), &c., ed. as *Musarum Deliciae* by T. Park (2 vols., 1817) and J. C. Hotten (2 vols., 1874); and *Parnassus Biceps* (1656), ed. G. Thorn-Drury (1927). Special collections are *Annalia Dubrensia* (1636), ed. A. B. Grosart (1877), E. R. Vyvyan (1878), C. Whitfield, as *Robert Dover and the Cotswold Games* (1962), and two cited in VI under Jonson and Milton, *Jonsonus Virbius* (1638) and *Justa Edouardo King* (1638).

Of the large, early modern collections the most useful is A. Chalmers's *Works of the English Poets* (21 vols., 1810). The first two volumes of T. H. Ward's once canonical *English Poets* (1880) are outmoded. Two standard volumes are the *Oxford Book Of Sixteenth Century Verse*, ed. Sir E. K. Chambers (1932), and the *Oxford Book Of Seventeenth Century Verse*, ed. Sir H. J. C. Grierson and G. Bullough (1934). Annotated anthologies for the student are: J. W. Hebel and H. H. Hudson, *Poetry of the English Renaissance 1509–1660* (New York, 1929); several books cited in II. 1; and R. C. Bald, *Seventeenth-Century English Poetry* (New York, 1959). A large gap was partly filled by Saintsbury's *Minor Poets of the Caroline Period* (3 vols., 1905–21). R. G. Howarth's *Minor Poets of the 17th Century* (Everyman's Library, 1931; rev. 1953) contains Lord Herbert, Carew, Suckling, and Lovelace.

Scottish poets are represented in the general anthologies. A special one is G. Eyre-Todd's *Scottish Poetry of the Seventeenth Century* (1895).

Wholly or mainly lyrical anthologies have been edited by H. J. Massingham (1919), A. C. Judson (University of Chicago, 1927), R. F. Brinkley (New York, 1936; rev. 1942), M. W. Black (Philadelphia, 1938), and W. H. Auden and N. H. Pearson (*Poets of the English Language*, 1950, vols. ii, iii). N. Ault's *Elizabethan Lyrics* (1925; 3rd ed., rev., 1949) and *Seventeenth Century Lyrics* (1928; rev. 1950) embody fresh work on the sources. Grierson's *Metaphysical Lyrics & Poems of the Seventeenth Century* (1921; repr. 1959) has done much to form modern taste. Two recent anthologies are H. Gardner's *Metaphysical Poets* (1957; 1961) and W. M. Merchant's *Metaphysical Poetry* (forthcoming). Two special books are L. B. Marshall's *Rare*

Poems of the Seventeenth Century (1936) and N. Ault's *Treasury of Unfamiliar Lyrics* (1938).

English Song-Books 1651–1702: A Bibliography (1940), by C. L. Day and E. B. Murrie, obviously covers only the end of our period. A. H. Bullen edited *Lyrics from the Song-books of the Elizabethan Age* (1887), *More Lyrics* (1888), a selection from the two volumes (1889), and the kindred *Shorter Elizabethan Poems* (1903). Other collections are: *Select English Songs and Dialogues of the 16th and 17th Centuries*, ed. A. Dolmetsch (2 parts, 1898–1912), with music; *English Madrigal Verse 1588–1632* (2nd ed., 1929), ed. E. H. Fellowes (see *infra*, V. 7); *An Elizabethan Song Book*, ed. N. Greenberg, W. H. Auden, and C. Kallman (New York, 1955), with music; and J. P. Cutts, *Seventeenth Century Songs and Lyrics Collected and edited from the original music manuscripts* (University of Missouri, 1959).

Englands Helicon (*supra*) was a pastoral anthology. Three modern ones are *English Pastorals*, ed. Sir E. K. Chambers (1895), *English Pastoral Poetry*, ed. F. Kermode (1952), and *The Pastoral Elegy*, ed. T. P. Harrison and H. J. Leon (University of Texas, 1939), which is especially useful for continental authors.

Some collections and anthologies of religious verse are: R. Cattermole, *Sacred Poets of the Seventeenth Century* (2 vols., 1835–6); E. Farr, *Select Poetry Chiefly Sacred of the Reign of King James the First* (1847); F. T. Palgrave, *The Treasury of Sacred Song* (1889); H. C. Beeching, *Lyra Sacra* (1895); D. H. S. Nicholson and A. H. E. Lee, *Oxford Book Of English Mystical Verse* (1917); Sir H. Newbolt, *Devotional Poets of the XVII Century* (1929); L. I. Guiney, *Recusant Poets* (1939); Lord D. Cecil, *Oxford Book Of Christian Verse* (1940).

III. GENERAL LITERARY HISTORY AND CRITICISM

This section comprises: (1) General literary history and criticism; (2) Rhetorical theory and prose style; (3) General and special history and criticism of poetry; (4) The history of ideas.

I. GENERAL LITERARY HISTORY AND CRITICISM

The fullest history is of course the *CHEL*, of which vols. iii–ix (1909–12) deal partly or wholly with the period 1600–60.

Smaller histories are those of E. Legouis and L. Cazamian (Paris, 1924; tr. 1926–7; last rev. ed., 1957); W. F. Schirmer (*Geschichte der englischen Literatur*, Halle, 1937; rev. ed., 2 vols., 1954); G. Sampson (*Concise Cambridge History of English Literature*, 1941); A. C. Baugh et al. (*A Literary History of England*, New York, 1948), Tucker Brooke being the historian of our period; H. Craig et al. (*History of English Literature*, New York, 1950), our period being handled by Craig; and D. Daiches, *A Critical History of English Literature* (2 vols., 1960). Sir H. J. C. Grierson's *First Half of the Seventeenth Century* (1906) has a European scope. C. V. Wedgwood's *Seventeenth-Century English Literature* (1950; repr. 1961) is a brisk if somewhat external survey. A number of writers who straddle 1600 are more or less discussed by Lewis. *From Donne to Marvell*, ed. B. Ford (Penguin, 1956), is an uneven but stimulating volume in the *Scrutiny* tradition; its predecessor, *The Age of Shakespeare* (1955), includes some of our authors.

Some selective interpretations are: E. Dowden, *Puritan and Anglican* (1900); Sir G. N. Clark (*infra*, V. 1); Grierson, *Cross Currents in English Literature of the XVIIth Century* (1929; repr., New York, 1958); *Seventeenth Century Studies Presented to Sir Herbert Grierson* (1938); F. P. Wilson's studies of transition, *Elizabethan and Jacobean* (1945); George Williamson's collected studies, *Seventeenth Century Contexts* (1960; University of Chicago, 1961); L. A. Sasek, *The Literary Temper of the English Puritans* (Louisiana State University, 1961); and some of the books cited below in III. 4 and V. 2 and 3. Two items that go together are Otto Funke, 'Probleme des englischen Literaturbarock' (*Wege und Ziele*, Bern, 1945), and Rudolf Stamm, 'Englischer Literaturbarock?' (*Die Kunstformen des Barockzeitalters*, ed. Stamm, Bern, 1956).

Histories of Scottish literature have less to say of the period 1600–60 than of the periods before and after. Some general works are: Hugh Walker, *Three Centuries of Scottish Literature* (2 vols., 1893); J. H. Millar, *Literary History of Scotland* (1903) and *Scottish Prose of the Seventeenth and Eighteenth Centuries* (1912); G. G. Smith, *Scottish Literature* (1919); A. M. Mackenzie, *Historical Survey of Scottish Literature to 1714* (1933); and J. Kinsley, *Scottish Poetry* (1955).

For Wales there are J. C. Morrice, *Wales in the Seventeenth Century: Its Literature and Men of Letters and Action* (1918), and

W. J. Hughes, *Wales and the Welsh in English Literature from Shakespeare to Scott* (1924).

2. RHETORICAL THEORY AND PROSE STYLE

Some studies of rhetorical theory and practice are: W. P. Sandford, on classicism, 1600–50 (*Quarterly Journal of Speech*, xv, 1929; *English Theories of Public Address, 1530–1828*, Columbus, Ohio, 1931); W. G. Crane, *Wit and Rhetoric in the Renaissance: The Formal Basis of Elizabethan Prose Style* (Columbia, 1937); K. R. Wallace, *Francis Bacon on Communication & Rhetoric* (University of North Carolina, 1943); and the standard broad survey, W. S. Howell's *Logic and Rhetoric in England, 1500-1700* (Princeton, 1956). On the nature and influence of Ramist logic and rhetoric there are Perry Miller, *The New England Mind: The Seventeenth Century* (New York, 1939); N. E. Nelson, 'Peter Ramus and the Confusion of Logic, Rhetoric, and Poetry', *University of Michigan Contributions in Modern Philology*, ii (1947); a long chapter in Howell (*supra*); W. J. Ong, *Peter Ramus, Method, and the Decay of Dialogue* and *Ramus and Talon Inventory* (both, Harvard, 1958); and V. Harris, *PQ* xxxvii (1958).

G. P. Krapp's *Rise of English Literary Prose* (New York, 1915) stops soon after 1600. F. P. Wilson's *Seventeenth Century Prose* (University of California, 1960) has five humane and delightful lectures. Anti-Ciceronian theory and practice were analysed by M. W. Croll in a series of important articles (which are being edited by P. W. London): *Revue du seizième siècle*, ii (1914), *SP* xvi, xviii (1919, 1921), *Schelling Anniversary Papers* (New York, 1923), *PMLA* xxxix (1924), *Studies in English Philology*, ed. K. Malone and M. B. Ruud (University of Minnesota, 1929), and *infra*. A sequel to these is G. Williamson's minutely discriminating *The Senecan Amble: A Study in Prose Form from Bacon to Collier* (1951); cf. Williamson's 'Restoration Revolt against Enthusiasm' (*SP* xxx, 1933; *supra*, III. 1). The scientific and homiletic quest of precise expression has been much studied by R. F. Jones, whose articles (*PMLA* xlv, 1930; *JEGP* xxx, xxxi, 1931, 1932; &c.) are collected in *The Seventeenth Century: Studies . . . by Richard Foster Jones and Others Writing in His Honor* (Stanford, 1951). An allied study by F. Christensen is cited under John Wilkins (*infra*, VI). Various aspects of style are discussed by J. Bennett (*RES* xvii, 1941), H. Macdonald (ibid. xix, 1943), F. P. Wilson (*supra*, III. 1), A. C. Howell (*ELH* xiii, 1946), D. C.

Allen (*ELH* xv, 1948), and H. Fisch (*infra*, V. 2). Studies of preaching are listed below in V. 2.

Among general studies of prose rhythm, of varying scope, are those of Saintsbury (1912), Albert C. Clark (1913), W. M. Patterson (Columbia, 1916), and N. R. Tempest (1930); articles by O. Elton (*ESEA* iv, 1913; *A Sheaf of Papers*, 1922) and M. W. Croll (*SP* xvi, 1919); and discussions of individual authors such as Browne (q.v.).

3. HISTORY AND CRITICISM OF POETRY

This section covers general history and criticism; odes; sonnets; lyrical, pastoral, metaphysical, religious, and heroic verse; diction; and prosody. Broadside ballads are noticed in IV. 2 below.

W. J. Courthope's *History of English Poetry* (ii and iii, 1897–1904, 1903), if somewhat outmoded, retains a spacious philosophic value. Some later general books are: H. W. Wells, *Poetic Imagery, Illustrated from Elizabethan Literature* (Columbia, 1924); E. Holmes, *Aspects of Elizabethan Imagery* (1929); W. Empson, *Seven Types of Ambiguity* (1930; rev. 1947); a chapter in F. P. Wilson (*supra*, III. 1); R. Tuve (*infra*); and two books that come up to or into our period, Hallett Smith's *Elizabethan Poetry* (Harvard, 1952) and M. Evans's *English Poetry in the Sixteenth Century* (1955). Essays on various poets are collected in *Seventeenth-Century English Poetry*, ed. W. R. Keast (New York, 1962). Two studies of poetry in relation to the graphic arts are W. Sypher's brilliant and baffling *Four Stages of Renaissance Style* (New York, 1955) and the first part of J. H. Hagstrum's *The Sister Arts: The Tradition of Literary Pictorialism from Dryden to Gray* (University of Chicago, 1958). H. V. S. Ogden had a related essay in *JHI* x (1949). J. Hollander's full study of ideas and poems about music is cited below in V. 7.

The chief studies of the ode are R. Shafer, *The English Ode to 1660* (Princeton, 1918), G. N. Shuster, *The English Ode from Milton to Keats* (Columbia, 1940), and C. Maddison, *Apollo and the Nine: A History of the Ode* (1960).

Some of our poets come into books on the Elizabethan sonnet: J. G. Scott, *Les Sonnets élisabéthains: les sources et l'apport personnel* (Paris, 1928); L. E. Pearson, *Elizabethan Love Conventions* (University of California, 1933); L. C. John, *Elizabethan Sonnet Sequences: Studies in Conventional Conceits* (Columbia, 1938); and

BIBLIOGRAPHY 471

J. W. Lever, *The Elizabethan Love Sonnet* (1956). C. B. Mitchell studied the mass of seventeenth-century sonnets (Harvard *Summaries of Theses 1939*). L. B. Salomon's *The Devil Take Her* (University of Pennsylvania, 1931) deals with 'the Rebellious Lover in English Poetry'.

Modern criticism has been less concerned with 'pure' than with 'metaphysical' lyrics. A substantial general study is W. P. Friederich's *Spiritualismus und Sensualismus in der englischen Barocklyrik* (*Wiener Beiträge*, lvii, 1932). More special is W. R. Bowden, *The English Dramatic Lyric, 1603–1642* (Yale, 1951). Some books focused on the preceding age touch on ours: G. Bontoux, *La Chanson en Angleterre au temps d'Élisabeth* (1936); F. Delattre and C. Chemin, *Les Chansons élizabéthaines* (Paris, 1948), an anthology with a 220-page introduction; B. Pattison, *Music and Poetry of the English Renaissance* (1948); and C. Ing, *Elizabethan Lyrics: A study in the development of English metres and their relation to poetic effect* (1951). There are also W. Mellers's chapter in *The Age of Shakespeare* (*supra*, III. 1), the special study of E. H. Scholl (*infra*, IV. 1), and items cited below in V. 7. A bibliographical article is E. F. Hart's 'Caroline Lyrics and Contemporary Song-Books' (*Library*, viii, 1953). R. Skelton's *Cavalier Poets* (British Council, 1960) is a pamphlet-essay with a bibliography.

Histories of pastoral literature are Sir W. W. Greg, *Pastoral Poetry and Pastoral Drama* (1906; repr., New York, 1959), and H. Genouy, *L'Élément pastoral dans la poésie narrative et le drame en Angleterre, de 1579 à 1640* (Paris, 1928). Other studies are: H. E. Cory, on the Spenserians (*PMLA* xxv, 1910); W. Empson's very individual *Some Versions of Pastoral* (1935; repr. 1950; U.S. title, *English Pastoral Poetry*, 1938); the introductory essays of Chambers and Kermode (*supra*, II. 2; the former repr. in *Sir Thomas Wyatt and Some Collected Studies*, 1933); a chapter in H. Smith (*supra*); the early part of J. E. Congleton, *Theories of Pastoral Poetry in England 1684–1798* (University of Florida, 1952). Of the poetic treatment of nature there are two old-fashioned studies, F. W. Moorman (under W. Browne, *infra*, VI) and A. von der Heide, *Das Naturgefühl in der englischen Dichtung im Zeitalter Miltons* (Heidelberg, 1915), and a recent, comprehensive, well-documented, and also discursive book by S. Korninger, *Die Naturauffassung in der englischen Dichtung des 17. Jahrhunderts* (*Wiener Beiträge*, lxiv, 1956). The same terms describe a kindred book, M.-S. Røstvig's *The Happy Man: Studies in the Metamorphoses of a Classical Ideal, 1600–1700* (Oslo and Oxford, 1954). The theme of rural retirement is treated also by M. C. Bradbrook (under Marvell, *infra*, VI) and H. G. Wright (*Etudes Anglaises*, vii, 1954). To these may be added G. R. Hibbard, 'The Country House Poem of the Seventeenth Century' (*Journal of the Warburg and Courtauld Institutes*, xix, 1956). R. C. Wallerstein's philosophic work is cited in the next paragraph.

The first and, with all its defects, the most seminal critique of metaphysical poetry was Dr. Johnson's 'Cowley' (*Lives of the Poets*, 1779). The modern vogue was stimulated by Grierson's edition of Donne (1912) and his anthology of 1921 (*supra*, II. 2) and by early essays of T. S. Eliot (*Selected Essays*, 1932). T. Spencer and M. Van Doren listed criticism of 1912–38 in *Studies in Metaphysical Poetry* (Columbia, 1939). The chief studies —along with others cited in following paragraphs and under individual poets in VI—are: George Williamson, *The Donne Tradition* (Harvard, 1930; repr., New York, 1958); Joan Bennett, *Four Metaphysical Poets* (1934; rev. 1953; repr., New York, 1960); J. B. Leishman, *Metaphysical Poets* (1934); Helen C. White, *The Metaphysical Poets* (New York, 1936; repr. 1956), on the religious writers; R. Tuve, *Elizabethan and Metaphysical Imagery* (University of Chicago, 1947; repr. 1961), a dynamic and corrective analysis of metaphysical poetry in relation to Elizabethan orthodoxy; M. M. Mahood, *Poetry and Humanism* (1950); R. C. Wallerstein, *Studies in Seventeenth Century Poetic* (University of Wisconsin, 1950), a learned exploration of the funeral elegy, Marvell, and the symbolism of the 'book of creatures'; O. de Mourgues (*infra*, IV. 7); J.-J. Denonain, *Thèmes et formes de la poesie "métaphysique"* (Paris, 1956), a very full description but not abreast of the newer scholarship and criticism; S. Gamberini, *Poeti metafisici e cavalieri in Inghilterra* (Florence, 1959), an introductory survey of twenty-one poets, from Chapman to Waller, which does not have much for English or American readers; R. Ellrodt, *Les Poètes métaphysiques anglais* (2 vols., Paris, 1959 [1960]), a magisterial analysis of eight poets, from Donne to Traherne, with full bibliographies (this is only one part of a five-part study of the poetry and the age); A. Alvarez, *The School of Donne* (1961); and F. J. Warnke, *European Metaphysical Poetry* (Yale, 1961), a critical anthology.

Among shorter discussions, by far the most potent have been T. S. Eliot's essays (*supra*), which dominated two decades but have come to seem more valid for his own poetry than for the metaphysicals'. Some others are: Grierson's introduction to his anthology (*supra*, II. 2); J. Smith (*Scrutiny*, ii, 1933–4; *Determinations*, ed. F. R. Leavis, 1934); F. R. Leavis (*Scrutiny*, iv, 1935–6; *Revaluation*, 1936); G. Williamson, 'Strong Lines' (*English Studies*, xviii, 1936; *supra*, III. 1); J. A. Mazzeo (*Romanic Review*, xlii, 1951; *MP* l, 1952–3; *JHI* xiv, 1953); chapters in *From Donne to Marvell* (*supra*, III. 1); H. Gardner's introductory essay (*supra*, II. 2); F. Kermode, 'Dissociation of Sensibility' (*Kenyon Review*, xix, 1957); R. M. Adams, in *Strains of Discord* (Cornell, 1958). Of the countless analyses of individual poems in the periodicals hardly any can be recorded in VI below, but one may mention D. C. Allen's *Image and Meaning* (Johns Hopkins, 1960), which has elaborate studies of poems by George Herbert, Lovelace, Marvell, and Vaughan.

The religious metaphysicals of course figure largely in many books named above, notably those of H. C. White and Ellrodt. Two substantial works are Louis L. Martz, *The Poetry of Meditation: A Study in English Religious Literature of the Seventeenth Century* (Yale, 1954), a fresh and important analysis of meditative techniques and poetic adaptations; and Arno Esch, *Englische religiöse Lyrik des 17. Jahrhunderts: Studien zu Donne, Herbert, Crashaw, Vaughan* (Halle, 1955). M. M. Ross's *Poetry & Dogma: The Transfiguration of Eucharistic Symbols in Seventeenth Century English Poetry* (Rutgers, 1954) is suggestive but extreme. Itrat-Husain's *Mystical Element in the Metaphysical Poets of the Seventeenth Century* (1948) is helpful but loose and discursive. Two valuable works on a distinctive strain are M. Praz, *Studies in Seventeenth-Century Imagery* (2 vols., 1939–47), and R. Freeman, *English Emblem Books* (1947); E. N. S. Thompson gave a short account of emblems in *Literary Bypaths of the Renaissance* (Yale, 1924). M. Willy's pamphlet, *Three Metaphysical Poets* (British Council, 1961), deals with Crashaw, Vaughan, and Traherne. Other books on religious verse are mentioned below under the heroic poem.

If psalmody, which attracted so many poets from Milton to Carew, may be noticed here, some items are: J. Holland, *Psalmists of Britain* (2 vols., 1843), which gives sketches of versifiers, with specimens; W. T. Brooke, *Old English Psalmody . . . 1557–1660* (1916), a good short history; P. von Rohr-Sauer, *English Metrical Psalms from 1600 to 1660* (Freiburg, 1938), the most scholarly account; H. Smith, on Elizabethan metrical psalms, *HLQ* ix (1945–6); M. Patrick, *Four Centuries of Scottish Psalmody* (1949); and M. Frost, *English & Scottish Psalm & Hymn Tunes, c. 1543–1677* (1953). The special significance and possible influence of the Sidney Psalter have been treated by L. L. Martz (*supra*) and J. C. A. Rathmell (*London Magazine*, vi, 1959), who is editing it.

Three books that move from metaphysical to later fashions are R. L. Sharp's *From Donne to Dryden: The Revolt Against Metaphysical Poetry* (University of North Carolina, 1940), G. Walton's *Metaphysical to Augustan: Studies in Tone and Sensibility in the Seventeenth Century* (1955), and G. Williamson's *The Proper Wit of Poetry* (University of Chicago, 1961). With these may be put P. Cruttwell's *The Shakespearean Moment and its Place in the Poetry of the 17th Century* (1954; repr., New York, 1960) and A. Alvarez (*supra*). Some essays on the transition are G. Williamson's 'Rhetorical Pattern of Neo-classical Wit' (*MP* xxxiii, 1935–6; *supra*, III. 1), L. I. Bredvold's 'Rise of English Classicism' (*Comparative Literature*, ii, 1950), and, on Johnson's criticism of the metaphysicals, W. R. Keast (*ELH* xvii, 1950) and D. D. Perkins (ibid. xx, 1953). The reputation of the metaphysicals down through the nineteenth century was traced by A. H. Nethercot (*MLN* xxxvii, 1922; *JEGP* xxiii, 1924; *PQ* iv and *SP* xxii, 1925; *MLR* xxv, 1930). The period from 1800 through recent years is covered with critical acumen by J. E. Duncan, *The Revival of Metaphysical Poetry: The History of a Style* (University of Minnesota, 1959). The later fortunes of pre-Restoration verse in general were followed by E. R. Wasserman (*MLN* lii, 1937; *MP* xxxvii, 1939–40; *Elizabethan Poetry in the Eighteenth Century*, University of Illinois Studies, xxxii, 1947).

The continental background of the heroic poem is sketched in the works of Spingarn (*infra*, IV. 9). Historical and heroic verse is discussed by L. F. Ball (*ELH* i, 1934), C. M. Dowlin (under Davenant, *infra*, VI), H. T. Swedenberg, *The Theory of the Epic in England 1650–1850* (University of California, 1944), H. Nearing, *English Historical Poetry 1599–1641* (University of Pennsylvania, 1945), R. H. Perkinson, 'The Epic in Five Acts' (*SP* xliii, 1946), and E. M. W. Tillyard, *The English Epic and its Background* (1954). The romances are discussed by N. T. Ting (Harvard *Summaries of Theses 1941*) and A. I. T. Higgins, *Secular Heroic Epic Poetry of the Caroline Period* (*Swiss Studies in*

English, xxxi, 1953). The problem of the religious epic in a scientific age is examined by B. Willey (*infra*, III. 4) and W. F. Schirmer (*Deutsche Vierteljahrsschrift*, xiv, 1936; *Kleine Schriften*, Tübingen, 1950). There are studies of the heroic poem and religious inspiration by L. B. Campbell (*HLB*, 1935, and *infra*) and C. D. Baker (*ELH* vi, 1939). Biblical narrative is treated by L. B. Campbell, *Divine Poetry and Drama in Sixteenth-Century England* (1959), and B. O. Kurth, *Milton and Christian Heroism: Biblical Epic Themes and Forms in Seventeenth-Century England* (University of California, 1959).

To the poetic qualities and uses of language there have been diverse approaches: H. C. Wyld, *Studies in English Rhymes from Surrey to Pope* (1923) and *Some Aspects of the Diction of English Poetry* (1933); O. Barfield, *Poetic Diction* (1928; rev. 1953); G. H. W. Rylands, *Words and Poetry* (1928); F. W. Bateson, *English Poetry and the English Language* (1934); V. L. Rubel, *Poetic Diction in the English Renaissance* (New York, 1941); Sister Miriam Joseph, *Shakespeare's Use of the Arts of Language* (Columbia, 1947); Josephine Miles, 'The Primary Language of Poetry in the 1640's' (*University of California Publications in English*, xix, 1948; incorporated in *The Continuity of Poetic Language*, University of California, 1951); and B. Groom, *The Diction of Poetry from Spenser to Bridges* (Toronto, 1955), which describes mainly the 'poetical' line. F. P. Wilson has a suggestive essay on Shakespeare's language (*Proceedings of the British Academy*, xxvii, 1941). The influence of Sylvester and Sandys in the moulding of Augustan poetic diction was touched by G. Tillotson (*On the Poetry of Pope*, 1938; 2nd ed., 1950) and treated fully by J. Arthos, *The Language of Natural Description in Eighteenth-Century Poetry* (University of Michigan, 1949).

The fullest account of metrics is Saintsbury's *History of English Prosody* (3 vols., 1906–10). Our period figures more or less in the smaller treatises and manuals, such as those of R. M. Alden (New York, 1903), Saintsbury (1910), P. F. Baum (Harvard, 1922), L. Abercrombie (1923 and 1932), William Thomson (1923), whose book is not small, J. C. Andersen (1928), E. Hamer (1930), and G. R. Stewart (New York, 1930). There are chapters in the *CHEL* vii and viii. The best study of the evolution of the heroic couplet is by R. C. Wallerstein (*PMLA* l, 1935), of blank verse by E. Weismiller (under Milton in VI). Lyric metres have been analysed by E. H. Scholl (*PMLA* lxiii,

1948) and C. Ing (*supra*). Recent metrical analyses have been concerned mainly with individual poets.

4. THE HISTORY OF IDEAS

Some books that might be put under this somewhat loose heading are cited elsewhere, especially in V. 1, 2, and 3, but a number may be grouped here: J. B. Bury, *The Idea of Progress* (1920); G. S. Brett, *History of Psychology*, ii (1921); Sir G. N. Clark (*infra*, V. 1); L. I. Bredvold, *The Intellectual Milieu of John Dryden* (University of Michigan, 1934; repr. 1956); P. Meissner, *Die geistesgeschichtlichen Grundlagen des englischen Literaturbarocks* (Munich, 1934), a too agile and facile analysis; B. Willey, *The Seventeenth Century Background* (1934; repr., New York, 1953), a standard and admirable account of philosophic cross-currents; G. Williamson, 'Mutability, Decay, and Seventeenth-Century Melancholy' (*ELH* ii, 1935; *supra*, III. 1); Hardin Craig, *The Enchanted Glass* (New York, 1936), a valuable analysis of the Elizabethan and Jacobean mind and its furniture; Richard F. Jones, *Ancients and Moderns* (Washington University, 1936; 2nd ed., 1961, with index and minor revisions), the fullest exploration of Baconian influence in various areas; A. O. Lovejoy, *The Great Chain of Being* (Harvard, 1936; repr., New York, 1960), a seminal work; *Seventeenth Century Studies Presented to Sir Herbert Grierson* (1938); Theodore Spencer, *Shakespeare and the Nature of Man* (New York, 1942); E. M. W. Tillyard, *The Elizabethan World Picture* (1943); L. Spitzer, 'Classical and Christian Ideas of World Harmony' (*Traditio*, ii–iii, 1944–5); F. P. Wilson (*supra*, III. 1); Victor Harris, *All Coherence Gone* (University of Chicago, 1949), on the controversy over the decay of nature; E. L. Tuveson, *Millennium and Utopia: A Study in the Background of the Idea of Progress* (University of California, 1949); Marjorie H. Nicolson, *The Breaking of the Circle: Studies in the Effect of the "New Science" upon Seventeenth Century Poetry* (Northwestern University, 1950; rev., Columbia, 1960); *Science and Imagination* (*infra*, V. 3), and *Mountain Gloom and Mountain Glory: The Development of the Aesthetics of the Infinite* (Cornell, 1959); L. Babb, *The Elizabethan Malady: A Study of Melancholia in English Literature from 1580 to 1642* (Michigan State University, 1951); S. L. Bethell, *The Cultural Revolution of the Seventeenth Century* (1951), a sketch of reason and faith; *The Seventeenth Century* . . . *Richard Foster Jones* (*supra*, III. 2); Herschel Baker, *The Wars of*

Truth: Studies in the Decay of Christian Humanism in the Earlier Seventeenth Century (Harvard, 1952), a comprehensive analysis of complex issues; J. B. Bamborough, *The Little World of Man* (1952), on Elizabethan psychology (cf. C. A. Patrides, *NQ* vii, 1960); Margaret L. Wiley, *The Subtle Knot: Creative Scepticism in Seventeenth-Century England* (Harvard, 1952); G. W. O'Brien, *Renaissance Poetics and the Problem of Power* (Chicago, 1956), a difficult but suggestive book; J. Winny, ed., *The Frame of Order: An Outline of Elizabethan Belief Taken from Treatises of the Late Sixteenth Century* (1957); M. Macklem, *The Anatomy of the World: Relations between Natural and Moral Law from Donne to Pope* (University of Minnesota, 1958); H. Baron, on the quarrel of the ancients and moderns (*JHI* xx, 1959); R. B. Hinman (under Cowley, *infra*, VI); R. Hoopes, *Right Reason in the English Renaissance* (Harvard, 1962); *Reason and the Imagination: Studies in the History of Ideas 1600-1800*, ed. J. A. Mazzeo (1962).

IV. SPECIAL LITERARY STUDIES AND LITERARY FORMS

This section comprises: (1) Language; (2) Popular literature; (3) Journalism; (4) Fiction; (5) Essays and Characters; (6) Historical and biographical literature; (7) Classical and foreign relations; (8) Translations; (9) Contemporary criticism; (10) Printing and bookselling.

I. THE LANGUAGE

A. G. Kennedy's *Bibliography of Writings on the English Language* (Harvard, 1927; repr., New York, 1961) is supplemented by his *Concise Bibliography* (*supra*, I). Some general histories are: O. Jespersen, *Growth and Structure of the English Language* (9th ed., 1948); H. C. Wyld, *History of Modern Colloquial English* (3rd ed., rev., 1953); G. H. McKnight, *Modern English in the Making* (New York, 1928); A. C. Baugh, *History of the English Language* (2nd ed., New York, 1957); C. L. Wrenn, *The English Language* (1949).

Some books more or less focused on 1600-60 are: Margaret Williamson, *Colloquial Language of the Commonwealth and Restoration*, an E.A. pamphlet (1929); M. Lehnert, *Die Grammatik des englischen Sprachmeisters John Wallis* (Breslau, 1936); O. Funke, *Die Frühzeit der englischen Grammatik . . . von Bullokar bis Wallis* (Berne, 1941); Sir W. Craigie, *The Critique of Pure English from Caxton to Smollett* (S.P.E. Tract lxv, 1946); Richard F. Jones,

The Triumph of the English Language: A Survey of Opinions Concerning the Vernacular from the Introduction of Printing to the Restoration (Stanford, 1953). Studies of pronunciation are: R. E. Zachrisson, *English Pronunciation at Shakespeare's Time as Taught by William Bullokar* (Upsala, 1927); E. H. Scholl, 'New Light on Seventeenth Century Pronunciation from the English School of Lutenist Song Writers', *PMLA* lix (1944); H. Kökeritz, *Shakespeare's Pronunciation* (Yale, 1953); E. J. Dobson, *English Pronunciation 1500–1700* (2 vols., 1957).

Efforts towards a universal language are described by O. Funke (*Anglistische Forschungen*, lxix, 1929) and B. DeMott (*PMLA* lxx, 1955); other items are cited under J. Wilkins in VI. Here may be mentioned D. C. Allen, 'Some Theories of the Growth and Origin of Language in Milton's Age' (*PQ* xxviii, 1949), and S. Korninger, 'Edward Brerewoods *Enquiries*: Ein Beitrag zur Sprachtheorie des frühen siebzehnten Jahrhunderts' (*Wiener Beiträge*, lxv, 1957).

The great treasury for diction and usage is, of course, the *New English Dictionary*, ed. Sir J. A. H. Murray et al. (1884–1928; corrected reissue, 13 vols., 1933). There is a *Glossary of Tudor and Stuart Words, Especially from the Dramatists* (1914) by W. W. Skeat and A. L. Mayhew. C. T. Onions's *Shakespeare Glossary* (1911; 2nd ed., rev., 1953) is valuable not only for Shakespeare. The standard survey of lexicography is D. T. Starnes and G. E. Noyes, *The English Dictionary from Cawdrey to Johnson, 1604-1755* (University of North Carolina, 1946).

2. POPULAR LITERATURE

This section covers London, the literature of roguery, broadside ballads, almanacs and prognostications, witchcraft, fairy lore, tobacco, jestbooks, and proverbs.

The best bibliographies are in the *CBEL*. The *CHEL* (iv and vii) has chapters on London and popular literature and on country pursuits. The most comprehensive survey of popular writing of all kinds is Louis B. Wright's *Middle-Class Culture in Elizabethan England* (University of North Carolina, 1935; repr., Cornell, 1958) which has much on the early seventeenth century.

London receives a section in the bibliographies of E. G. Cox (*infra*, V. 4) and M. T. Jones-Davies's *Thomas Dekker* (*infra*, VI). Stow's *Survay of London* is cited under Stow in VI. Some modern accounts, large and small, are: H. B. Wheatley, *London Past and*

Present (3 vols., 1891) and a chapter in *Shakespeare's England* (*infra*, V. 5); the *London County Council Survey of London* (1900 ff.); Sir W. Besant, *London in the Time of the Stuarts* (1903); W. Page, *Victoria History of London* (1909); N. Zwager, *Glimpses of Ben Jonson's London* (Amsterdam, 1926); N. G. Brett-James, *The Growth of Stuart London* (1935); R. J. Mitchell and M. D. R. Leys, *A History of London Life* (1958); and a full account of city and people in M. T. Jones-Davies (*supra*). Three studies of one grim topic are F. P. Wilson's *The Plague in Shakespeare's London* (1927), C. F. Mullett's *The Bubonic Plague and England* (University of Kentucky, 1956), and H. G. Wright's account of writers on the plague (*ESEA 1953*).

An excellent anthology of the literature of roguery is A. V. Judges, *The Elizabethan Underworld* (1930). The chief accounts are the chapters in the *CHEL* iv and *Shakespeare's England*; F. W. Chandler, *The Literature of Roguery* (2 vols., Boston, 1907; repr., New York, 1958); F. Aydelotte, *Elizabethan Rogues and Vagabonds* (1913); and Judges's introduction.

The best guide to balladry is H. E. Rollins's *Analytical Index* of registered ballads (*SP* xxi, 1924). Some collections are: *Political Ballads Published in England during the Commonwealth*, ed. T. Wright (Percy Society, iii, 1841): *Political Ballads of the Seventeenth and Eighteenth Centuries*, ed. W. W. Wilkins (2 vols., 1860); *Roxburghe Ballads*, ed. W. Chappell and J. W. Ebsworth (9 vols., 1871-97); *Shirburn Ballads 1585-1616*, ed. A. Clark (1907); and the long series expertly edited by H. E. Rollins—*Old English Ballads 1553-1625* (1920); *A Pepysian Garland . . . 1595-1639* (1922); *Cavalier and Puritan* (1923); *The Pack of Autolycus . . . 1624-1693* (1927); and *The Pepys Ballads* (8 vols., 1929-32); and V. de S. Pinto and A. E. Rodway, *The Common Muse: An Anthology of Popular British Ballad Poetry XVth–XXth Century* (1957). Two special anthologies are J. W. Draper's *Century of Broadside Elegies . . . of the seventeenth century* (1928) and J. Lindsay's *Loving Mad Tom. Bedlamite Verses Of the XVI and XVII Centuries* (1927).

Besides the introductions and notes in the volumes he edited, Rollins had a monograph on the broadside in *PMLA* xxxiv (1919). Other accounts, general and special, are: Sir C. Firth, on the ballad history of the reigns of James and Charles (*Transactions of the Royal Historical Society*, 3rd Series, vols. v, vi, 1911-12), and his chapter in *Shakespeare's England*; E. von Schaubert's long article in *Anglia*, l (1926); M. Austermann,

Die große englische Revolution im Spiegel der zeitgenössischen Lyrik (Düsseldorf, 1935); H. F. Brooks's index of 'Rump Songs' in *OBS*, vol. v, part iv, 1939 (1940); C. C. Smith, on late 'Drolleries' (*Harvard Library Bulletin*, vi, 1952); and C. V. Wedgwood's *Poetry and Politics under the Stuarts* (1960), a survey of both poetry and ballads, mainly satirical.

The bibliographical history of prognostications has been written by E. F. Bosanquet, *English Printed Almanacks and Prognostications* (1917). This, with additions and corrections in the *Library*, viii (1927–8) and xviii (1937–8), comes down to 1600, and is continued in the same journal, x (1929–30). Some other discussions are: C. Camden, *Library*, xii (1931–2); F. R. Johnson, *Astronomical Thought in Renaissance England* (Johns Hopkins, 1937); F. P. Wilson, 'Some English Mock-Prognostications', *Library*, xix (1938–9); M. Nicolson, 'English Almanacs and the "New Astronomy" ', *Annals of Science*, iv (1939); a chapter in D. C. Allen's *Star-Crossed Renaissance* (*infra*, V. 3); Allen's edition of *The Owles Almanacke* (Johns Hopkins, 1943); and J. Crow's account of Thomas Bretnor (*Elizabethan and Jacobean Studies Presented to Frank Percy Wilson*, 1959).

The most learned and massive studies of witchcraft are G. L. Kittredge, *Witchcraft in Old and New England* (Harvard, 1929), and H. C. Lea and A. C. Howland, *Materials Toward a History of Witchcraft* (3 vols., University of Pennsylvania, 1939). Some less formidable accounts, general and special, are: W. Notestein, *History of Witchcraft in England from 1558 to 1718* (Washington, 1911); sections in the *CHEL* vii and *Shakespeare's England*; several works by Montague Summers, such as *The Discovery of Witches: A Study of Master Matthew Hopkins* (1928), which includes a reprint of Hopkins's tract of 1647; C. L. Ewen, *Witch Hunting and Witch Trials* (1929) and the documentary *Witchcraft and Demonianism* (1933); *The Trial of the Lancaster Witches*, ed. G. B. Harrison (1929); C. Williams, *Witchcraft* (1941); C. Hole, *Witchcraft in England* (1945) and the documentary *Mirror of Witchcraft* (1957); R. T. Davies, *Four Centuries of Witch Beliefs: With special reference to the Great Rebellion* (1947), who argues that witch-beliefs provoked anti-Stuart feeling; and R. H. Robbins, *Encyclopedia of Witchcraft and Demonology* (New York, 1959).

Three books on fairy lore are F. Delattre, *English Fairy Poetry* (1912), M. W. Latham, *The Elizabethan Fairies* (Columbia,

1930), and K. M. Briggs, *The Anatomy of Puck: An Examination of Fairy Beliefs among Shakespeare's Contemporaries and Successors* (1959). The most sumptuous tribute ever paid to a fragrant theme is J. E. Brooks's *Tobacco. Its History Illustrated by The Books, Manuscripts and Engravings In the Library of George Arents, Jr.*, vol. i, 1507–1615, vol. ii, 1615–98 (New York, 1937, 1938); this work gives a facsimile of the title-page of every book described. The fullest studies are R. J. Kane's unpublished thesis, *Tobacco in English Literature to 1700* (Harvard *Summaries of Theses 1929*) and S. A. Dickson's *Panacea or Precious Bane* (New York, 1954; repr. from the *Bulletin of the New York Public Library*, lvii–lviii, 1953–4). There is also Count Corti, *A History of Smoking*, tr. P. England (1931).

John Ashton's *Humour, Wit, & Satire of the Seventeenth Century* (1883) is a miscellaneous anthology of jests and ballads. Some of the jestbooks named in the text are reprinted in vols. ii, vii, ix, and xxii of the Percy Society and in W. C. Hazlitt's *Shakespeare Jest-Books* (3 vols., 1864). Two scholarly studies of the genre are Ernst Schulz's *Die englischen Schwankbücher bis herab zu "Dobson's Drie Bobs"* (*1607*) (Berlin, 1912) and F. P. Wilson's article in *HLQ* ii (1938–9). The book named in Schulz's title is cited in VI below, under 'Anonymous'; see also Thomas Brewer.

For proverbs there are the *Oxford Dictionary of English Proverbs* (1935; 2nd ed., rev., 1948; new ed. forthcoming), M. P. Tilley's *Dictionary of the Proverbs in England in the Sixteenth and Seventeenth Centuries* (University of Michigan, 1950), F. P. Wilson, 'English Proverbs and Dictionaries of Proverbs', *Library*, xxvi (1945–6), and J. L. Lievsay (*infra*, V. 6).

3. JOURNALISM

W. P. Van Stockum edited *The First Newspapers of England Printed in Holland 1620–1621* (The Hague, 1914). F. J. Varley's *Mercurius Aulicus* (1948) summarizes and quotes from the royalist newspaper of 1643–5. The satirical *Great Assises Holden in Parnassus* (1645) was edited by H. Macdonald (1948).

The standard histories are M. A. Shaaber, *Some Forerunners of the Newspaper In England 1476–1622* (University of Pennsylvania, 1929), and Joseph Frank, *The Beginnings of the English Newspaper 1620–1660* (Harvard, 1961). Some bibliographies and descriptive accounts are: G. K. Fortescue's *Catalogue* of the Thomason collection (*supra*, I); J. G. Muddiman's *Tercentenary Handlist of English & Welsh Newspapers, Magazines & Reviews* (1920); E. N. S. Thompson's essay on war journalism (*Literary Bypaths of the Renaissance*, Yale, 1924); R. S. Crane et al., 'Census of British Newspapers and Periodicals, 1620–1800', *SP* xxiv (1927) and separately; A. J. Gabler, 'Check List of English Newspapers and Periodicals before 1801 in the Huntington Library', *HLB* (1931); chapter i in S. Morison, *The English Newspaper* (1932); M. A. Shaaber, 'The History of the First English Newspaper', *SP* xxix (1932); R. T. Mitford and D. M. Sutherland, 'A Catalogue of English Newspapers and Periodicals in the Bodleian Library 1622–1800', *OBS* iv, part ii, 1935 (1936), and separately; L. Hanson, 'English Newsbooks, 1620–1641', *Library*, xviii (1937–8); D. C. Collins, *A Handlist of News Pamphlets 1590–1610* (1943); K. K. Weed and R. P. Bond, 'Studies of British Newspapers and Periodicals from their Beginning to 1800: A Bibliography', *SP*, Extra Series, No. 2 (1946); F. Dahl, 'Amsterdam—Cradle of English Newspapers', *Library*, iv (1949–50); F. Dahl, *A Bibliography of English Corantos and Periodical Newsbooks, 1620–1642* (1952); L. Rostenberg's account of the publishers Butter and Bourne (*Library*, xii, 1957; *infra*, IV. 10); and P. M. Handover (*infra*, IV. 10).

Items on censorship, &c., are in IV. 10 below.

4. FICTION

C. Davies edited *Prefaces to Four Seventeenth-Century Romances: . . . Parthenissa; . . . Aretina*, &c. (Augustan Reprint Society, 1953).

Bibliographies are: A. Esdaile, *List of English Tales and Prose Romances Printed Before 1740* (1912); C. C. Mish, *English Prose Fiction 1600–1700: A Chronological Checklist* (University of Virginia, 1952); S. O'Dell, *A Chronological List of Prose Fiction in English Printed in England and Other Countries 1475–1640* (Cambridge, Mass., 1954).

The fullest history is E. A. Baker, *History of the English Novel*, ii and iii (1929; repr., New York, 1950, 1957). J. J. Jusserand's *English Novel in the Time of Shakespeare* (1890) goes on through our period. Some mainly special studies are: Charlotte E. Morgan, *Rise of the Novel of Manners* (Columbia, 1911); Sir Henry Thomas, *Spanish and Portuguese Romances of Chivalry* (1920); T. P. Haviland, *The Roman de Longue Haleine on English Soil* (University of

Pennsylvania, 1931); chapters in L. B. Wright (*supra*, IV. 2); C. W. Miller, on the influence of French romances (University of Virginia *Abstracts of Dissertations 1940*); V. Dupont's exhaustive *L'Utopie et le roman utopique dans la littérature anglaise* (Cahors, 1941); B. G. MacCarthy (*infra*, V. 5); M. Patchell, *The Palmerin Romances in Elizabethan Prose Fiction* (Columbia, 1947); K. Koller, 'The Puritan Preacher's Contribution to Fiction' (*HLQ* xi, 1947–8); C. C. Mish, 'Best Sellers in Seventeenth-Century Fiction' (*PBSA* xlvii, 1953), which is summarized in the text above; and items cited below in IV. 7 and 8.

5. ESSAYS AND CHARACTERS

In addition to the bibliographies of both genres in the *CBEL*, there are G. Murphy, *Bibliography of English Character-Books 1608–1700* (1925), and the larger *Bibliography of the Theophrastan Character in English*, by C. N. Greenough and J. M. French (Harvard, 1947).

Essays and characters are included in general anthologies (*supra*, II. 1). Special collections are: J. O. Halliwell [-Phillipps], *Books of Characters* (1857), devoted mainly to several rare works; H. Morley, *Character Writings of the Seventeenth Century* (1891); R. Aldington, *A Book of 'Characters'* (1924); G. Murphy, *A Cabinet of Characters* (1925); W. H. D. Rouse, *A Book of Characters* (1930); H. Osborne, *A Mirror of Charactery* (1933); R. Withington, *Essays and Characters: Montaigne to Goldsmith* (New York, 1933); I. Bowman, *A Theatre of Natures* (1955), a popular selection.

The most detailed studies of the essay are W. L. MacDonald's *Beginnings of the English Essay* (University of Toronto, 1914) and 'The Earliest English Essayists' (*Englische Studien*, lxiv, 1929), and E. N. S. Thompson's *Seventeenth-Century English Essay* (University of Iowa, 1926). To these may be added H. V. Routh's comparison of early English and French essays (*MLR* xv, 1920); some discussion in studies of style, e.g. W. G. Crane and G. Williamson (*supra*, III. 2); and studies of individual writers in VI below.

Paradoxes and problems may be approached through a chapter in Thompson (*supra*), A. E. Malloch (*SP* liii, 1956), and studies of Donne (E. M. Simpson, in *A Garland for John Donne*, 1931, her *Study of the Prose Works*, and P. N. Siegel, *PQ* xxviii, 1949) and Cornwallis (*infra*, VI), and D. C. Allen's edition of John Hall's *Paradoxes* (*infra*, VI). W. G. Rice described 'The *Paradossi* of Ortensio Lando' (*Essays and Studies in English*, University of Michigan, 1932). H. K. Miller has a full account of the paradoxical encomium in *MP* liii (1955–6).

The fullest and best studies of the character are B. Boyce's *The Theophrastan Character in England to 1642* (Harvard, 1947) and *The Polemic Character 1640–1661* (University of Nebraska, 1955). There is an essay in E. N. S. Thompson, *Literary Bypaths of the Renaissance* (Yale, 1924). The specific influence of Theophrastus has been treated also by E. C. Baldwin (*MLN* xvi, 1901; *PMLA* xviii, 1903); G. S. Gordon, *English Literature and the Classics* (1912); and most fully by K. Lichtenberg, *Der Einfluß des Theophrast*, &c. (Berlin, 1921). W. Clausen (*PQ* xxv, 1946) was sceptical about early Theophrastian influence.

6. HISTORICAL AND BIOGRAPHICAL LITERATURE

This section comprises historical writing, biography, autobiographies, diaries, and letters.

White Kennett's *Complete History of England* (3 vols., 1706) included Milton, Daniel, Habington, Sir George Buc, Bacon, Lord Herbert, Hayward, Francis Godwin, Camden, and Arthur Wilson. *Secret History of the Court of James the First*, ed. Scott (2 vols., 1811) included Francis Osborn, Sir Anthony Weldon, &c. Sir Thomas Wilson's *State of England . . . 1600* was edited by F. J. Fisher (*Camden Miscellany*, xvi, 1936). There is a bibliography of historical writings in E. G. Cox (*infra*, V. 4).

E. Fueter's *Geschichte der neueren Historiographie* (Munich, 1911; 3rd ed., 1936) and James W. Thompson's *History of Historical Writing* (2 vols., New York, 1942) are inevitably meagre on our period. There are discussions by C. Whibley and Sir A. W. Ward in the *CHEL* iii and vii; Sir G. N. Clark (*infra*, V. 1); L. B. Wright (*supra*, IV. 2); L. Strauss (under Hobbes in VI); and W. M. Merchant (under Lord Herbert in VI). Analyses of Elizabethan views of English history which touch some of our historians are in Lily B. Campbell, *Shakespeare's "Histories": Mirrors of Elizabethan Policy* (Huntington Library, 1947), E. M. W. Tillyard, *Shakespeare's History Plays* (1947), L. F. Dean's article in *University of Michigan Contributions in Modern Philology*, i (1947), and I. Ribner, *The English History Play in the Age of Shakespeare* (Princeton, 1957). Jean Bodin's ideas and influence have been treated by John L. Brown, *The Methodus ad Facilem*

Historiarum Cognitionem of Jean Bodin (Catholic University of America, 1939), by B. Reynolds in her translation of the *Methodus* (Columbia, 1945), and by L. F. Dean (*SP* xxxix, 1942).

The study of Old English and of English and British antiquities grew together. Some books and articles are: E. N. Adams, *Old English Scholarship in England from 1566–1800* (Yale, 1917); D. C. Douglas, *English Scholars 1660–1730* (1939; rev. 1951), which takes in the earlier age; J. Butt, 'Facilities for Antiquarian Study in the Seventeenth Century', *ESEA* xxiv (1939); L. Van Norden (under Spelman, *infra*, VI); R. F. Jones (*supra*, IV. 1); *English Historical Scholarship in the Sixteenth and Seventeenth Centuries*, ed. Levi Fox (1956); Joan Evans, *History of the Society of Antiquaries* (1956); and R. J. Schoeck, 'Early Anglo-Saxon Studies and Legal Scholarship in the Renaissance', *Studies in the Renaissance*, v (1958). This topic merges with legal and constitutional history. Some important books are : H. Arneke, *Kirchengeschichte und Rechtsgeschichte in England (von der Reformation bis zum frühen 18. Jahrhundert)* (Halle, 1937); H. Butterfield, *The Englishman and his History* (1944); J. G. A. Pocock, *The Ancient Constitution and the Feudal Law: A Study of English Historical Thought in the Seventeenth Century* (1957); and some books on law and political thought (*infra*, V. 1), such as that of S. Kliger. The relations of Camden, Cotton, Selden, and Spelman with a continental scholar are shown by L. Van Norden, *HLQ* xii (1948–9).

Full accounts of the growth and decay of the Trojan-Arthurian story are Sir T. D. Kendrick's *British Antiquity* (1950) and E. Jones's monograph, *Geoffrey of Monmouth 1640–1800* (*University of California Publications in English*, v, 1944). G. S. Gordon gave a short account of the Troy legend (*ESEA* ix, 1924; *The Discipline of Letters*, 1946). On the Arthurian and 'Saxon' side are A. E. Parsons (*MLR* xxiv, 1929); C. B. Millican, *Spenser and the Table Round* (Harvard, 1932); R. F. Brinkley, *Arthurian Legend in the Seventeenth Century* (Johns Hopkins, 1932); M. Schütt's long article (*Britannica*, xiii, 1936); R. Tuve, 'Ancients, Moderns, and Saxons' (*ELH* vi, 1939); and H. Nearing (*supra*, III. 3).

Two anthologies of biographical portraits are D. Nichol Smith's *Characters from the Histories & Memoirs of the Seventeenth Century* (1918) and V. de S. Pinto's more popular *English Biography in the Seventeenth Century* (1951), which includes chiefly

Aubrey and other late writers. The standard critical history is D. A. Stauffer's *English Biography before 1700* (Harvard, 1930), which has a full bibliography. One of F. P. Wilson's lectures (*supra*, III. 2) is on biography.

The *CBEL* has a long list of autobiographies, diaries, and letters. W. Matthews has compiled annotated bibliographies, *British Diaries* and *British Autobiographies* (University of California, 1950, 1955); H. M. Forbes a bibliography of *New England Diaries 1602–1800* (Topsfield, Mass., 1923). Extracts are given in A. Ponsonby's *English Diaries* (1923), *More English Diaries* (1927), and *Scottish and Irish Diaries* (1927), and in J. G. Fyfe's *Scottish Diaries and Memoirs 1550–1746* (1928). Approaches to a general survey are made by D. Hendrichs, *Geschichte der englischen Autobiographie von Chaucer bis Milton* (Leipzig, 1925), J. C. Major, *The Role of Personal Memoirs in English Biography and Novel* (University of Pennsylvania, 1935), and Stauffer. Our period is only touched in W. Shumaker, *English Autobiography: Its Emergence, Materials, and Form* (University of California, 1954). Browne, Lord Herbert, Bunyan, and Baxter are treated in M. Bottrall, *Every Man a Phoenix: Studies in seventeenth-century autobiography* (1958). The wealth of Puritan diaries is shown in W. Haller's *Rise of Puritanism* (Columbia, 1938).

Some collections of letters are: Sir Henry Ellis, *Original Letters, Illustrative of English History* (11 vols., 1824–46), and *Original Letters of Eminent Literary Men of the Sixteenth, Seventeenth, and Eighteenth Centuries* (Camden Society, 1843); J. O. Halliwell [-Phillipps], *A Collection of Letters Illustrative of the Progress of Science in England from the Reign of Queen Elizabeth to that of Charles the Second* (1841); S. J. Rigaud, *Correspondence of Scientific Men of the Seventeenth Century* (2 vols., 1841); two works compiled by T. Birch and edited by R. F. Williams, *The Court and Times of James the First* (2 vols., 1848) and *The Court and Times of Charles the First* (2 vols., 1848); and sections of such books as F. Bickley's *English Letter Book* (1925). Two short accounts of letter-writing are by E. N. S. Thompson (*supra*, IV. 5) and R. W. Ramsey (*Essays by Divers Hands*, xiv, 1935). Persons of our period come into W. H. Irving's *The Providence of Wit in the English Letter Writers* (Duke University, 1955). Studies of epistolary theory and formal practice are K. G. Hornbeak's *Complete Letter-Writer in English 1568–1800* (Smith College, 1934) and Jean Robertson's *Art of Letter Writing* (1942).

7. CLASSICAL AND FOREIGN RELATIONS

A comprehensive guide is F. Baldensperger and W. P. Friederich, *Bibliography of Comparative Literature* (University of North Carolina, 1950), with Friederich's annual *Yearbook of Comparative and General Literature* (ibid. 1952 ff.). Other bibliographies are cited below.

H. Brown's 'Classical Tradition in English Literature' (*Harvard Studies and Notes in Philology and Literature*, xviii, 1935) and the *CBEL* obviate the need of listing many titles here. Some important books appear above in III. 3 and below in IV. 8 and V. 6 and under individual authors in VI.

Sir J. E. Sandys's *History of Classical Scholarship*, ii (1908) is the standard work. F. Watson's chapter in the *CHEL* vii surveys classical and related fields of learning. M. Pattison's *Isaac Casaubon* (2nd ed., 1892) gives intimate pictures of scholarship in England and abroad.

The influence of many classical authors is sketched in the volumes of the series 'Our Debt to Greece and Rome', ed. G. D. Hadzits and D. M. Robinson (Boston, 1922 ff.). Some mainly general studies of themes and traditions are: J. S. Harrison, *Platonism in English Poetry of the Sixteenth and Seventeenth Centuries* (Columbia, 1903); E. Cassirer, *Die platonische Renaissance in England und die Schule von Cambridge* (Leipzig, 1932; tr. J. P. Pettegrove, *The Platonic Renaissance in England*, University of Texas, 1953); E. S. Duckett, *Catullus in English Poetry* (Smith College, 1925), J. B. Emperor, *Catullian Influence in English Lyric Poetry, Circa 1600–1650* (University of Missouri, 1928), and J. A. S. McPeek, *Catullus in Strange and Distant Britain* (Harvard, 1939); T. K. Whipple, *Martial and the English Epigram From Sir Thomas Wyatt to Ben Jonson* (University of California, 1925), and H. H. Hudson, *The Epigram in the English Renaissance* (Princeton, 1947), which just approaches our period; W. F. Schirmer, *Antike, Renaissance und Puritanismus* (rev. ed., Munich, 1933); D. Bush, *Mythology and the Renaissance Tradition in English Poetry* (University of Minnesota, 1932; repr., New York, 1957); K. A. McEuen, *Classical Influence upon the Tribe of Ben* (Cedar Rapids, 1939); D. T. Starnes and E. W. Talbert, *Classical Myth and Legend in Renaissance Dictionaries* (University of North Carolina, 1955), which has much fresh material but rides its thesis hard, Starnes has also done *Renaissance Dictionaries: English–Latin and*

488   BIBLIOGRAPHY

Latin–English (University of Texas, 1954). J. A. K. Thomson's *Classical Background of English Literature* (1948), *Classical Influences on English Poetry* (1951), and *Classical Influences on English Prose* (1956) are for the general reader. Neo-Latin writing is treated by F. A. Wright and T. A. Sinclair, *A History of Later Latin Literature* (1931), and L. Bradner, *Musae Anglicanae: A History of Anglo-Latin Poetry 1500–1925* (New York, 1940). The stylistic influence of Lipsius is discussed by Croll and Williamson (*supra*, III. 2). Some references for his and general Stoic thought and influence are: L. Zanta, *La Renaissance du stoïcisme au XVIe siècle* (Paris, 1914); B. Anderton, *Sketches from a Library Window* (1922); R. Kirk's editions of Stradling's translation of Lipsius, *Two Bookes Of Constancie*, and of *The Moral Philosophie of the Stoicks Written in French by Guillaume Du Vair Englished by Thomas James* (Rutgers, 1939, 1951); references under Joseph Hall (*infra*, VI); and J. L. Saunders, *Justus Lipsius: The Philosophy of Renaissance Stoicism* (New York, 1955). The influence on English-writing poets of 'the Polish Horace', Casimir Sarbiewski, is set forth by M.-S. Røstvig (*supra*, III. 3), who edited G. Hils's translation (1646) of his odes (Augustan Reprint Society, 1953). Since 1954 *Seventeenth-Century News* has included 'Neo-Latin News'.

Tudor-Jacobean Hebrew studies are surveyed by I. Baroway, *Jewish Social Studies*, xviii (1956). Hebrew scholarship comes more or less into books on biblical translation and interpretation, especially of Genesis: D. Daiches (*infra*, IV. 8); books cited under B. Walton (*infra*, VI); F. E. Robbins, *The Hexaemeral Literature, a Study of the Greek and Latin Commentaries on Genesis* (University of Chicago, 1912); H. F. Fletcher, *Milton's Semitic Studies* (University of Chicago, 1926) and *Milton's Rabbinical Readings* (University of Illinois, 1930); G. McColley, *Paradise Lost* (Chicago, 1940), on sources and traditions; Sister M. I. Corcoran, *Milton's Paradise with Reference to the Hexameral Background* (Catholic University of America, 1945); Arnold Williams, *The Common Expositor: An Account of the Commentaries on Genesis 1527–1633* (University of North Carolina, 1948); G. N. Conklin (under Milton, *infra*, VI), who in part controverts Fletcher; and D. C. Allen, *The Legend of Noah* (University of Illinois, 1949), which deals with 'Renaissance Rationalism in Art, Science, and Letters'. Allen has also investigated Donne's Hebraic learning (*ELH* x, 1943).

For continental literature and relations indispensable guides, in addition to those cited at the beginning of this section, are the current bibliographies in *SP*. In recent decades special studies have multiplied and comprehensive surveys have not; most of the latter are old, e.g. D. Hannay, *The Later Renaissance* (1898) and Grierson (*supra*, III. 1).

For France the fullest survey is A. H. Upham, *The French Influence in English Literature from the Accession of Elizabeth to the Restoration* (Columbia, 1908). The early part of our period is touched in Sir S. Lee's *French Renaissance in England* (1910), the later part in L. Charlanne's *L'Influence française en Angleterre au XVIIe siècle* (Paris, 1906). There is not much of literature proper in C. Bastide, *Anglais et français du XVIIe siècle* (Paris, 1912; tr. as *The Anglo-French Entente in the Seventeenth Century*, 1914), G. Ascoli, *La Grande-Bretagne devant l'opinion française au XVIIe siècle* (2 vols., Paris, 1930), or J. H. M. Salmon (*infra*, V. 1). O. de Mourgues's *Metaphysical, Baroque & Précieux Poetry* (1953) supplies a French perspective and touches on Crashaw et al. Among studies of particular authors (see Florio, Sylvester, et al. in VI) is H. Brown's *Rabelais in English Literature* (Harvard, 1933). References for P. Ramus were given above in III. 2. A solid special work is K. Lambley, *The Teaching and Cultivation of the French Language in England during Tudor and Stuart Times* (1920). R. Cotgrave's *Dictionarie of the French and English Tongues* (1611) has been reproduced in facsimile (University of North Carolina, 1950), and V. E. Smalley has studied his sources (Johns Hopkins, 1948). M. St. C. Byrne edited the 1609 edition of Holyband's *The French Littelton* (1953).

There is not much on our writers in F. Viglione, *L'Italia nel pensiero degli scrittori inglesi* (Milan, 1947). M. Praz's *The Flaming Heart* (New York, 1958) has half a dozen essays on Anglo-Italian relations. R. C. Simonini's *Italian Scholarship in Renaissance England* (University of North Carolina, 1952) touches on our period. A. L. Sells promised a sequel to his *Italian Influence in English Poetry from Chaucer to Southwell* (Indiana University, 1955). In addition to P. Toynbee's *Dante in English Literature from Chaucer to Cary* (2 vols., 1909), which was supplemented, for 1519–1610, by F. P. Wilson (*Italian Studies*, iii, 1946–8), there is W. P. Friederich, *Dante's Fame Abroad, 1350–1850* (Rome and University of North Carolina, 1950). Among special studies are H. M. Priest, 'Tasso in English Literature, 1575–1675'

(Northwestern University *Summaries of Dissertations*, i, 1933), and F. J. Warnke's sceptical account of Marino's influence (*Studies in the Renaissance*, ii, 1955; cf. his book, *supra*, III. 3). Some items are mentioned in IV. 8, V. 4, and under such authors as Crashaw, Fairfax, Florio, and Milton.

Our period is barely touched in J. G. Underhill's *Spanish Literature in the England of the Tudors* (Columbia, 1899) and M. Hume's *Spanish Influence on English Literature* (1905). The fullest account is E. G. Mathews's unpublished *Studies in Anglo-Spanish Cultural and Literary Relations, 1598–1700* (Harvard *Summaries of Theses 1938*). Special items are cited above in IV. 4 and under Mabbe, Munday, Shelton, et al. To E. A. Peers's study of Spanish mysticism (3 vols., 1930–60) may be added M. Hagedorn, *Reformation und spanische Andachtsliteratur. Luis de Granada in England* (Leipzig, 1934), and sections on Italian and Spanish sources in J. B. Collins (*infra*, V. 2) and L. L. Martz (*supra*, III. 3). E. M. Wilson discussed Spanish and English religious poetry in the *Journal of Ecclesiastical History*, ix (1958).

Some books facing in various directions are: G. Waterhouse, *The Literary Relations of England and Germany in the Seventeenth Century* (1914); T. de Vries, *Holland's Influence on English Language and Literature* (Chicago, 1916), with which may be linked R. L. Colie's account of English influence upon the early works of C. Huygens, '*Some Thankfulnesse to Constantine*' (The Hague, 1956), and A. G. H. Bachrach on Huygens (*UTQ* xxv, 1955–6); E. J. Simmons, *English Literature and Culture in Russia (1553–1840)* (Harvard, 1935); and Ethel Seaton, *Literary Relations of England and Scandinavia in the Seventeenth Century* (1935).

J. L. Rosier has studied 'The Sources and Methods of Minsheu's *Guide into the Tongues*' (*PQ* xl, 1961).

8. TRANSLATIONS

Many references in the preceding section are relevant here.

A number of our translators are reprinted in the large series of Tudor Translations. A. F. Clements's *Tudor Translations* (1940) includes, from our period, brief excerpts from Hobbes, Heywood, Holland, Shelton, Florio, and Urquhart. J. Winny's *Elizabethan Prose Translation* (1960) has passages from Holland and Florio. Further data are given under individual writers in VI.

Some critical studies are: introductions to the Tudor Translations; C. Whibley's chapter in the *CHEL* iv; F. R. Amos,

Early Theories of Translation (Columbia, 1920); F. O. Matthiessen, *Translation: An Elizabethan Art* (Harvard, 1931), which has full studies of Hoby, North, Florio, and Holland; and R. Sühnel (under Chapman in VI). The cultural importance of translations is shown by L. B. Wright (*supra*, IV. 2).

Bibliographical guides to translations from the ancient classics are: H. R. Palmer, *List of English Editions and Translations of Greek and Latin Classics Printed before 1641* (1911); F. M. K. Foster, *English Translations from the Greek* (Columbia, 1918); F. Seymour Smith, *The Classics in Translation* (1930); and H. Brown (*supra*, IV. 7). The fullest critical study, which stops early in our period, is H. B. Lathrop, *Translations from the Classics into English from Caxton to Chapman, 1477–1620* (University of Wisconsin, 1933). A full special study is L. Proudfoot, *Dryden's Aeneid and its Seventeenth Century Predecessors* (1960).

Translations from the French are listed and more or less discussed by A. H. Upham (*supra*, IV. 7). J. E. Tucker has an account, with a bibliography, of the prolific John Davies of Kidwelly (1627?–93) in *PBSA* xliv (1950).

For Italy the standard bibliography, which covers our period, is Mary A. Scott, *Elizabethan Translations from the Italian* (Boston, 1916).

For Spain the best guide is R. U. Pane, *English Translations From The Spanish 1484–1943: A Bibliography* (Rutgers, 1944), which was corrected and supplemented by E. G. Mathews, *JEGP* xliv (1945).

Some references for Hebrew scholarship are given in the preceding section. The standard bibliography of the English Bible is the *Historical Catalogue of the Printed Editions of Holy Scripture in the Library of the British and Foreign Bible Society* by T. H. Darlow and H. F. Moule (2 vols., 1903–11). Check-lists are in the *BMC*, *STC*, and Wing.

Editions especially useful to the literary student are Bagster's *English Hexapla Exhibiting the Six Important English Translations of the New Testament Scriptures* (1841), and the Authorized Version in the Tudor Translations (6 vols., 1903–4), the Cambridge English Classics, ed. W. A. Wright (5 vols., 1909), and the tercentenary edition, in reduced facsimile, with illustrative documents, ed. A. W. Pollard (1911).

Pollard also edited *Records of the English Bible: The Documents Relating to the Translation and Publication of the Bible in English,*

1525–1611 (1911). An early account of the prices of Bibles, M. Sparke's *Scintilla* (1641), is reprinted in Arber's *Transcript*, iv, and in Darlow and Moule.

Historical and critical accounts of the translating of the Bible are: chapters in G. P. Krapp (*supra*, III. 2) and F. R. Amos (*supra*); B. F. Westcott, *A General View of the History of the English Bible*, rev. by W. A. Wright (1905); J. Isaacs's two chapters in *The Bible in its Ancient and English Versions*, ed. H. W. Robinson (1940); C. C. Butterworth, *The Literary Lineage of the King James Bible 1340–1611* (University of Pennsylvania, 1941); D. Daiches, *The King James Version of the English Bible* (University of Chicago, 1941), which has special reference to the Hebrew tradition, and an essay in his *Literary Essays* (1956); some pages in Lewis; I. M. Price, *The Ancestry of Our English Bible* (1907; last ed., rev. by W. A. Irwin and A. P. Wikgren, New York, 1956); and G. S. Paine, *The Learned Men* (New York, 1959), a popular account of the 1611 translators and their methods. Two short, recent, and illustrated accounts are E. E. Willoughby's handsome *Making of the King James Bible* (Los Angeles, 1956), which has some new material on the work of the committee of revisers, and C. R. Thompson's *The Bible in English 1525–1611* (Folger Booklets, 1958). Two concrete special studies are J. G. Carleton, *The Part of Rheims in the Making of the English Bible* (1902), and R. Bridges and L. A. Weigle, *The Bible Word Book* (1960), on obsolete or archaic words.

No book could approach an adequate account of the literary influence of the English Bible. Among attempts are A. S. Cook's *The Bible and English Prose Style* (Boston, 1892) and his chapter in the *CHEL* iv, and *The Bible and Its Literary Associations*, ed. M. B. Crook (New York, 1937); and essays collected in V. F. Storr's *The English Bible* (1938). C. S. Lewis's pamphlet, *The Literary Impact of The Authorised Version* (1950), rather oddly slights the seventeenth century.

References for versification of the Psalms were given above in III. 3.

9. CONTEMPORARY CRITICISM

Standard collections are: G. G. Smith, *Elizabethan Critical Essays* (2 vols., 1904); J. E. Spingarn, *Critical Essays of the Seventeenth Century* (3 vols., 1908–9; repr., Indiana University, 1957); A. H. Gilbert, *Literary Criticism: Plato to Dryden* (New York,

1940), which is especially useful for continental writers; sections in the anthologies of K. Muir and P. Ure (*supra*, II. 1); and C. Gebert, *Anthology of Elizabethan Dedications and Prefaces* (University of Pennsylvania, 1933), which goes up to 1623. An early critical survey of special interest is Edward Phillips's *Theatrum Poetarum* (1675); S. Golding discussed its sources (*PMLA* lxxvi, 1961).

Many things cited above in III are relevant here, such as R. Tuve's analysis of poetic theory and practice and G. Williamson's study of prose style. Some general surveys, old and new, are: P. Hamelius, *Die Kritik in der englischen Literatur des 17. und 18. Jahrhunderts* (Leipzig, 1897); Saintsbury's comprehensive but unphilosophical *History of Criticism and Literary Taste in Europe* (3 vols., 1900–4) and *History of English Criticism* (1911); the introductions of Smith and Spingarn and the latter's *Literary Criticism in the Renaissance* (2nd ed., Columbia, 1908) and chapter in the *CHEL* vii; L. Jonas, *The Divine Science* (Columbia, 1940), an outline of poets' theories of poetry; and J. W. H. Atkins, *English Literary Criticism: The Renascence* (1947; 2nd ed., 1951) and *English Literary Criticism: 17th and 18th Centuries* (1951).

Many special studies are cited under individual authors in VI. Some others are: Donald L. Clark, *Rhetoric and Poetry in the Renaissance* (Columbia, 1922); H. O. White, *Plagiarism and Imitation during the English Renaissance* (Harvard, 1935); J. McClennen's sketch of allegory (*University of Michigan Contributions in Modern Philology*, vi, 1947). Theories of the imagination inherited by our period were discussed by M. W. Bundy (*JEGP* xxix and *SP* xxvii, 1930), and W. Rossky (*Studies in the Renaissance*, v, 1958). Neoclassical theories are viewed in different ways by G. Williamson (*SP* xxx, 1933; *supra*, III. 2), D. F. Bond (*PQ* xiv, 1935 and *ELH* iv, 1937), C. M. Dowlin and C. D. Thorpe (under Hobbes, in VI), and T. G. Steffan (*University of Texas Studies in English*, xxi, 1941); and some studies cited in III. 3 above. Here may be included L. Anceschi, *L'estetica dell' empirismo inglese, i: Da Bacone a Shaftesbury* (Bologna, 1959).

10. PRINTING AND BOOKSELLING

Many of the bibliographical works cited above in I are indispensable here. Two early items are Jaggard's *Catalogue of English Books* (1619), ed. O. M. Willard (*Stanford Studies in Language and Literature*, 1941), and William London's *Catalogue of*

The most vendible Books in England (1657–8). Some works of reference are: A. Growoll and W. Eames, *Three Centuries of English Booktrade Bibliography* (New York, 1903); R. B. McKerrow et al., *Dictionary of Printers and Booksellers . . . 1557–1640* (1910), and H. R. Plomer's *Dictionary* (1907), covering 1641–67; and P. G. Morrison (*supra*, I).

Some general and special studies are: chapters in the *CHEL* iv and xi (1909, 1914) and *Shakespeare's England* (1916); J. C. Reed, on Humphrey Moseley, *OBS* ii, part ii, 1928 (1929); F. A. Mumby, *Publishing and Bookselling* (1930; 4th ed., 1956); E. L. Klotz, 'A Subject Analysis of English Imprints . . . 1480 to 1640', *HLQ* i (1937–8); M. Plant, *The English Book Trade* (1939); F. S. Ferguson, 'English Books Before 1640', *The Bibliographical Society 1892–1942: Studies in Retrospect*, ed. F. C. Francis (1945); L. Kirschbaum, 'Author's Copyright in England before 1640', *PBSA* xl (1946); F. R. Johnson, 'Notes on English Retail Book-prices, 1550–1640', *Library*, v (1950-1); I. A. Shapiro, 'Publication Dates before 1640', *TLS*, 6 February 1953; Sir W. W. Greg, *Some Aspects and Problems of London Publishing between 1550 and 1650* (1956); W. A. Jackson, *Records of the Court of the Stationers' Company 1602 to 1640* (1957); C. Blagden, articles in the *Library*, xii and xiii (1957, 1958), and *The Stationers' Company: A History 1403–1959* (1960); L. Spencer's account of the inestimable George Thomason, *Library*, xiii and xiv (1958, 1959); P. M. Handover, *Printing in London from 1476 to Modern Times* (1960); and L. Rostenberg, *Seventeenth Century English Publishers and Booksellers* (New York, 1962).

For some of the chief publishing centres outside of London there are: F. Madan, *Oxford Books* (3 vols., 1895–1931); J. Johnson and S. Gibson, *Print and Privilege at Oxford to the Year 1700* (1946); R. Bowes, *Catalogue of Books Printed at or Relating to . . . Cambridge* (1894); Sir S. C. Roberts, *A History of the Cambridge University Press 1521–1921* (1921); C. Blagden, 'Early Cambridge Printers and the Stationers' Company' (*CBS* ii, part iv, 1957); H. G. Aldis, 'A List of Books Printed in Scotland before 1700' (*Edinburgh Bibliographical Society*, vii, 1904); and E. R. M. Dix, *Books Printed in Dublin in the 17th Century* (4 parts, Dublin, 1898–1912).

Guides to technical problems are McKerrow's *Introduction to Bibliography* (2nd ed., 1928), A. Esdaile's *Student's Manual of Bibliography* (3rd ed., rev. by R. Stokes, 1954), and F. T.

Bowers's *Principles of Bibliographical Description* (Princeton, 1949). With these may be put P. Simpson's *Proof-reading in the Sixteenth, Seventeenth, and Eighteenth Centuries* (1935). Aspects of fraudulent enterprise are described by C. B. Judge, *Elizabethan Book-Pirates* (Harvard, 1934); P. Simpson, 'Literary Piracy in the Elizabethan Age', *OBS*, N.S., i, 1947 (1948), enlarged as 'The Official Control of Tudor and Stuart Printing', *Studies in Elizabethan Drama* (1955); and P. M. Handover (*supra*).

On the relations of authors, patrons, and public there are: P. Sheavyn, *The Literary Profession in the Elizabethan Age* (1909); D. Nichol Smith, in *Shakespeare's England* (1916); E. C. Wilson, *England's Eliza* (Harvard, 1939) and *Prince Henry and English Literature* (Cornell, 1946); F. P. Wilson, 'Some Notes on Authors and Patrons in Tudor and Stuart Times', *Joseph Quincy Adams: Memorial Studies* (Washington, 1948); J. F. Danby, *Poets on Fortune's Hill* (1952); L. Parsons, on Prince Henry (*MLR* xlvii, 1952); P. Thomson, 'The Literature of Patronage, 1580–1630', *Essays in Criticism*, ii (1952); D. Taylor, 'The Third Earl of Pembroke as Patron of Poetry' (*Tulane Studies in English*, v, 1955); Edwin H. Miller, *The Professional Writer in Elizabethan England* (Harvard, 1959). V. B. Heltzel, who wrote on Sir Thomas Egerton as patron (*HLQ* xi, 1947–8), is publishing a book, *Elizabethan Patronage: 1550–1630*. F. B. Williams's comprehensive *Index of Dedications and Commendatory Verses in English Books before 1641* (Bibliographical Society) is promised shortly. The beginnings of subscription publication have been studied by S. L. Clapp (*MP* xxix, 1931–2) and, apropos of Minsheu's *Guide into the Tongues* (1617), by F. B. Williams (*Joseph Quincy Adams*, *supra*).

Some accounts of censorship (other than those concerned with the stage) are: C. R. Gillett, *Burned Books* (2 vols., Columbia, 1932); W. M. Clyde, *The Struggle for the Freedom of the Press from Caxton to Cromwell* (1934); H. Macdonald, 'The Law and Defamatory Biographies in the Seventeenth Century', *RES* xx (1944); F. S. Siebert, *Freedom of the Press in England, 1476–1776: the Rise and Decline of Government Controls* (University of Illinois, 1952); and E. Sirluck's introduction to *Areopagitica* in *Complete Prose Works of John Milton*, ii (Yale, 1959).

V. THE BACKGROUND OF LITERATURE

This section comprises: (1) Political history and political thought; (2) Religion and religious thought; (3) Science and scientific thought; (4) Travel; (5) Social life; (6) Education and culture; (7) Music and the arts.

I. POLITICAL HISTORY AND POLITICAL THOUGHT

Standard works of reference are Conyers Read, *Bibliography of British History, Tudor Period* (rev. ed., 1959) and Godfrey Davies, ditto, *Stuart Period, 1603–1714* (1928), and the bibliography (inadequately revised for the 2nd ed.) in Davies's *The Early Stuarts, 1603–1660* (*Oxford History of England*, 1937; rev. 1959).

Some collections are: S. R. Gardiner, *Constitutional Documents of the Puritan Revolution 1625–1660* (3rd ed., 1906); Sir C. Firth, *The Clarke Papers* (Camden Society, 4 vols., 1891–1901); J. R. Tanner, *Constitutional Documents of the Reign of James I* (1930; repr. 1960); W. Haller, *Tracts on Liberty in the Puritan Revolution 1638–1647* (3 vols., Columbia, 1934); M. James and M. Weinstock, *England During The Interregnum (1642–1660)* (1935); A. S. P. Woodhouse, *Puritanism and Liberty: Being the Army Debates (1647–9) from the Clarke Manuscripts with Supplementary Documents* (1938; 2nd ed., 1950); Don M. Wolfe, *Leveller Manifestoes of the Puritan Revolution* (New York, 1944); W. Haller and G. Davies, *The Leveller Tracts 1647–1653* (Columbia, 1944); G. Orwell and R. Reynolds, *British Pamphleteers*, i (1948); Christopher Hill and E. Dell, *The Good Old Cause* (1949), documents of 1640–60 illustrating the social significance of the revolution; V. Gabrieli, *Puritanesimo e libertà* (Turin, 1956), a translation (with an introduction) from the Putney debates and writings of Walwyn, Lilburne, and Winstanley. *English Historical Documents*, ed. D. C. Douglas, has not yet reached 1600–60.

Some surveys of Europe are: *Cambridge Modern History*, iii, iv (1904, 1906), and v (rev. 1961); D. Ogg, *Europe in the Seventeenth Century* (1925; 6th ed., 1952); Sir G. N. Clark, *The Seventeenth Century* (1929; rev. 1947; repr. 1961); C. J. Friedrich, *The Age of the Baroque, 1610–1660* (New York, 1952).

For the end of the Tudor period there are: J. B. Black, *The Reign of Elizabeth* (*Oxford History of England*, 1936; rev. 1959), with its bibliography; A. L. Rowse, *The England of Elizabeth: The Structure of Society* (1950); and Sir J. E. Neale, *Elizabeth I and her Parliaments 1584–1601* (1957). The best one-volume histories of our period are G. M. Trevelyan, *England under the Stuarts* (1904; 21st ed., 1949), and G. Davies (*supra*). The most detailed account of public affairs is in S. R. Gardiner's several works: *History of England from the Accession of James I. to the Outbreak of the Civil War* (1863–82 and later edns., 10 vols.); *History of the Great Civil War* (3 vols., 1886–91; 4 vols., 1893); and *History of the Commonwealth and Protectorate* (3 vols., 1894–1901; rev. ed., 4 vols., 1903). This last was continued in Sir C. Firth's *Last Years of the Protectorate* (2 vols., 1909), and in G. Davies's *The Restoration of Charles II 1658–1660* (Huntington Library, 1955). Abbott's work (under Cromwell, *infra*, VI) is very minute. C. V. Wedgwood's *The Great Rebellion: The King's Peace 1637–1641* (1955) and *The King's War 1641–1647* (1958), which are to have a sequel, have a narrative immediacy more reliable than the anti-Whig bias of E. Wingfield-Stratford's *Charles King of England, 1600–1637* and *King Charles and King Pym, 1637–1643* (1949) and *King Charles the Martyr, 1643–1649* (1950). C. Hill's stimulating *Century of Revolution, 1603–1714* (1961) has an economic and social emphasis. A recent special study is D. Underdown, *Royalist Conspiracy in England 1649–60* (Yale, 1960).

For commercial and colonial enterprise there are some books already named; the *Cambridge History of the British Empire*; A. D. Innes, *The Maritime and Colonial Expansion of England under the Stuarts (1603–1714)* (1932); Louis B. Wright, *Religion and Empire: The Alliance between Piety and Commerce in English Expansion 1558–1625* (University of North Carolina, 1943); A. L. Rowse, *The Expansion of Elizabethan England* (1955); and many items, especially concerning America, in V. 4 below.

There are general histories of Scotland by P. H. Brown (3 vols., 1899–1909) and Andrew Lang (4 vols., 1900–7), a shorter one by Brown (1924; rev. by H. W. Meikle, 1951). More special are C. V. Wedgwood, 'Anglo-Scottish Relations, 1603–40' (*Trans. Royal Historical Society*, xxxii, 1950; *Truth and Opinion*, 1960); D. Nobbs, *England and Scotland, 1560–1707* (1952); D. Mathew, *Scotland under Charles I* (1955); and books cited below in V. 2 and under James Graham (Montrose) in VI. P. H. Brown edited two collections, *Early Travellers in Scotland* (1891) and *Scotland Before 1700 from Contemporary Documents* (1893), and

A. M. Mackenzie *Scottish Pageant 1513–1625* (1948) and *Scottish Pageant 1625–1707* (1949).

For Wales there are Idris Jones, *Modern Welsh History from 1486 to the Present Day* (1934; 3rd ed., 1960), David Williams, *A History of Modern Wales* (1950), and A. H. Dodd, *Studies in Stuart Wales* (1952).

A history of Ireland is that of E. Curtis (1936; 5th ed., 1945). More special are R. Bagwell, *Ireland under the Stuarts and during the Interregnum* (3 vols., 1909–16); E. MacLysaght, *Irish Life in the Seventeenth Century* (1939; rev. 1950); T. L. Coonan, *The Irish Catholic Confederacy and the Puritan Revolution* (Columbia, 1954); and F. R. Bolton (under Jeremy Taylor in VI).

In economic history there are E. Lipson, J. Viner, E. F. Heckscher, J. U. Nef, P. W. Buck, et al. Some writings in economic and social history of more direct concern to the literary student are: R. H. Tawney, *The Agrarian Problem in the Sixteenth Century* (1912; repr., New York, 1961), which comes well into the seventeenth; *Religion and the Rise of Capitalism* (1926; Pelican repr., 1938), and *Business and Politics under James I: Lionel Cranfield as Merchant and Minister* (1958); M. James, *Social Problems and Policy During the Puritan Revolution 1640–1660* (1930); L. C. Knights, *Drama & Society in the Age of Jonson* (1937; repr. 1951); D. Mathew, *The Jacobean Age* (1938), *The Social Structure in Caroline England* (1948), and *The Age of Charles I* (1951); Mildred Campbell, *The English Yeoman Under Elizabeth and the Early Stuarts* (Yale, 1942; repr., New York, 1960); Sir G. N. Clark, *supra* and *The Wealth of England from 1496 to 1760* (1946); R. J. Mitchell and M. D. R. Leys, *A History of the English People* (1950); W. Notestein, *The English People on the Eve of Colonization 1603–1630* (New York, 1954); P. H. Hardacre, *The Royalists during the Puritan Revolution* (The Hague, 1956), and on royalist exiles (*HLQ* xvi, 1952–3); J. H. Hexter, 'Storm over the Gentry' (*Encounter*, x, 1958; *Reappraisals in History*, 1961); W. K. Jordan, *Philanthropy in England 1480–1660* (3 vols., 1959–61); B. E. Supple, *Commercial Crisis and Change in England 1600–1642* (1959); V. Pearl, *London and the Outbreak of the Puritan Revolution* (1961); A. Simpson, *The Wealth of the Gentry, 1540–1660* (1961); and books cited later in this section and in V. 5.

There is a *Bibliography of English Law* by W. H. and L. F. Maxwell (3 vols., 1925–33, with supplements). F. J. C. Hearnshaw described early legal writing in the *CHEL* viii. Sir W. S.

Holdsworth wrote the standard *History of English Law* (vols. iv-vi, 1924), *Sources and Literature of English Law* (1925), and *Some Makers of English Law* (1938). Some books on legal history, e.g. Arneke and Pocock, are cited above in IV. 6. Some others are McIlwain (*infra*), J. W. Gough, *Fundamental Law in English Constitutional History* (1955), Sir C. Ogilvie, *The King's Government and the Common Law* (1958), and C. J. Friedrich, *The Philosophy of Law in Historical Perspective* (University of Chicago, 1958). J. D. Eusden, in *Puritans, Lawyers, and Politics in Early Seventeenth-Century England* (Yale, 1958), seeks a parallel between Puritans and the common lawyers.

In the field of constitutional and parliamentary history some narrative and interpretative works, general and special, are: books cited just above; the constitutional histories of F. W. Maitland (1908) and Sir D. L. Keir (1938; 5th ed., 1955); Sir K. Feiling, *History of the Tory Party 1640–1714* (1924); J. R. Tanner, *English Constitutional Conflicts of the Seventeenth Century 1603–1689* (1928; repr. 1960); I. Deane Jones, *The English Revolution . . . 1603–1714* (1931); F. D. Wormuth, *The Royal Prerogative 1603–1649* (Cornell, 1939) and *The Origins of Modern Constitutionalism* (New York, 1949); G. L. Mosse, *The Struggle for Sovereignty in England From the Reign of Queen Elizabeth to the Petition of Right* (Michigan State University, 1950); Faith Thompson, *A Short History of Parliament 1295–1642* (University of Minnesota, 1953); W. M. Mitchell, *The Rise of the Revolutionary Party in the English House of Commons 1603–1629* (Columbia, 1957); Sir J. E. Neale (*supra*); *Conflict in Stuart England: Essays in honour of Wallace Notestein*, ed. W. A. Aiken and B. D. Henning (1960); and biographies of leaders, e.g. J. H. Hexter, *The Reign of King Pym* (Harvard, 1941).

Political thought comes more or less into books already cited and is the main subject of many others. Perhaps the most compendious survey, which has on our period the chapters of a specialist, is G. H. Sabine's *History of Political Theory* (New York, 1937; rev. 1950). Some other general works are: W. A. Dunning, *History of Political Theories from Luther to Montesquieu* (1905; repr. 1938); Sir R. W. and A. J. Carlyle, *History of Mediæval Political Theory in the West*, vol. vi (1936; repr. New York, 1950); and J. W. Gough, *The Social Contract* (1936; 2nd ed., 1957). Some books focused more or less on our period are: G. P. Gooch, *Political Thought in England from Bacon to Halifax* (1915) and *English*

Democratic Ideas in the Seventeenth Century (rev. by H. J. Laski, 1927; repr. 1954; New York, 1959); C. H. McIlwain, *The High Court of Parliament and Its Supremacy* (Yale, 1910), introduction to *Political Works of James I* (Harvard, 1918), and other writings; J. N. Figgis, *The Divine Right of Kings* (rev. ed., 1922); *Social & Political Ideas of Some Great Thinkers of the Sixteenth and Seventeenth Centuries*, ed. F. J. C. Hearnshaw (1926), and the companion volumes for the Renaissance and Reformation (1925) and the Augustan age (1928); Yung Chi Hoe, *The Origin of Parliamentary Sovereignty or 'Mixed' Monarchy* (Shanghai, 1935); J. W. Allen, *English Political Thought 1603–1660. Vol. I, 1603–44* (1938); Z. S. Fink, *The Classical Republicans* (Northwestern University, 1945); M. A. Judson, *The Crisis of the Constitution . . . 1603–1645* (Rutgers, 1949); S. Kliger, *The Goths in England: A Study in Seventeenth and Eighteenth Century Thought* (Harvard, 1952); P. Zagorin, *A History of Political Thought in the English Revolution* (1954); Paolo Treves, *Politici inglesi del Seicento* (Milan and Naples, 1958); and J. H. M. Salmon, *The French Religious Wars in English Political Thought* (1959).

Leftist parties and groups have been increasingly studied; special items are noted in VI below, under individual spokesmen. General surveys are D. M. Wolfe, *Milton in the Puritan Revolution* (1941), and W. Schenk, *The Concern for Social Justice in the Puritan Revolution* (1948); there are also introductions to some of the collections named above, and chapters in Sabine and Zagorin (*supra*). T. C. Pease's *Leveller Movement* (Washington, 1916) retains value, but has been largely superseded by J. Frank's *The Levellers* (Harvard, 1955); more special is D. B. Robertson's *The Religious Foundations of Leveller Democracy* (Columbia, 1951). M. Ashley's *John Wildman* (1947) is 'A Study of the English Republican Movement'. C. Hill stresses economic concerns in *The English Revolution 1640* (1940; 2nd ed., 1949) and *Puritanism and Revolution* (1958). J. F. MacLear discussed anticlericalism (*JHI* xvii, 1956). A phase of religious radicalism is treated in L. F. Solt's *Saints in Arms: Puritanism and Democracy in Cromwell's Army* (Stanford, 1959).

Some aspects of social thought are described in V. Dupont (*supra*, IV. 4) and G. Negley and J. M. Patrick, *The Quest for Utopia. An Anthology of Imaginary Societies* (New York, 1952). J. K. Fuz's *Welfare Economics in English Utopias from Francis Bacon to Adam Smith* (The Hague, 1952) is slight; A. L. Morton has a sketch in *The English Utopia* (1952). A very different approach to Utopia is analysed by E. L. Tuveson (*supra*, III. 4). Many of the books already cited necessarily mix politics with religion, and more will be named in the next section. Some studies of special importance for both are A. S. P. Woodhouse's introduction to his *Puritanism and Liberty* (*supra*) and his article in the *Philosophical Review*, lxi (1952), Arthur Barker (*infra*, V. 2), and W. Haller's *Liberty and Reformation in the Puritan Revolution* (Columbia, 1955).

2. RELIGION AND RELIGIOUS THOUGHT

This section covers Roman Catholicism; the Church of England; Puritanism and the sects; preaching; casuistry; toleration; Latitudinarianism and Cambridge Platonism; devotional literature and mysticism. Many books cited in V. 1 are relevant here. Items on biblical scholarship are given above in IV. 7, studies of translations of the Bible in IV. 8.

Hastings's *Encyclopaedia of Religion and Ethics* (13 vols., 1908–27) is invaluable. F. L. Cross's *Oxford Dictionary of the Christian Church* (1957) is recent and comprehensive. Other works of reference are cited in appropriate places. A handy collection is H. Bettenson's *Documents of the Christian Church* (1943). A classic historical work of broad scope is E. Troeltsch, *Social Teaching of the Christian Churches* (tr., 2 vols., 1931). A recent broad analysis is C. H. and K. George, *The Protestant Mind of the English Reformation 1570–1640* (Princeton, 1961).

For Roman Catholicism, in addition to the general histories of England, there are: *The Catholic Encyclopedia* (15 vols., New York, 1907–12); J. Gillow, *A Literary and Biographical History, or Bibliographical Dictionary of the English Catholics* (5 vols., 1885–1902; repr., New York, 1961); A. F. Allison and D. M. Rogers, *Biographical Studies, 1534–1829: Materials towards a biographical dictionary of Catholic history in the British Isles* (1951 ff.), which includes (iii, 1956) *A Catalogue of Catholic Books in English Printed Abroad or Secretly in England 1558–1640*; the old but still the best general account, *The Church History of England, From . . . 1500 to . . . 1688* (3 vols., Brussels, 1737–42), by 'Charles Dodd'; G. Albion (under Charles I, in VI, *infra*); D. Mathew, *Catholicism in England, 1535–1935* (1936); B. Magee, *The English Recusants* (1938), whose statistics are found unreliable by W. M. Wigfield

(*Theology*, xli, 1940); Philip Hughes, *Rome and the Counter-Reformation in England* (1942); and M. J. Havran, *Catholicism in Caroline England 1625–1640* (Stanford, 1962).

For the Church of England a standard work of reference is S. L. Ollard et al., *A Dictionary of English Church History* (3rd ed., rev., 1948). Some collections are: R. Cattermole, *Literature of the Church of England* (2 vols., 1844); H. Gee and W. J. Hardy, *Documents Illustrative of English Church History* (1896); P. E. More and F. L. Cross, *Anglicanism: The Thought and Practice of the Church of England, Illustrated from the Religious Literature of the Seventeenth Century* (Milwaukee, 1935).

Fuller's *Church-History of Britain* (1655) is of course a first-hand authority on our period. Some general histories are: W. H. Frere, *The English Church in the Reigns of Elizabeth and James I* (1904), and its sequel, *The English Church from the Accession of Charles I to the Death of Anne* (1903), by W. H. Hutton, who discussed Caroline divines in the *CHEL* vii; W. A. Shaw, *History of the English Church . . . 1640–1660* (2 vols., 1900); and G. B. Tatham, *The Puritans in Power* (1913). R. G. Usher's *Reconstruction of the English Church* (2 vols., 1910), an important study of the early Jacobean age, has a kind of sequel in R. S. Bosher's *Making of the Restoration Settlement: The Influence of the Laudians, 1649–1660* (1951). A good deal of N. Sykes's *Old Priest and New Presbyter* (1956) is relevant. A. G. Matthews's *Walker Revised* (1948) is authoritative on 'the sufferings of the clergy'. P. H. Hardacre (*supra*, V. 1) deals with churchmen (and Catholics) as well as the royalist laity. A novel and substantial work is C. Hill, *Economic Problems of the Church from Archbishop Whitgift to the Long Parliament* (1956). A number of churchmen, Laud et al., appear in VI below.

Most general accounts of Anglican thought are old: John Hunt, *Religious Thought in England*, i (1870); John Dowden, *Outlines of the History of the Theological Literature of the Church of England* (1897); H. H. Henson, *Studies in English Religion in the Seventeenth Century* (1903); A. W. Harrison, *Arminianism* (1937); and H. Baker (*supra*, III. 4). More special are G. W. O. Addleshaw's *High Church Tradition* (1941) and C. W. Dugmore's *Eucharistic Doctrine in England from Hooker to Waterland* (1942). Other books are cited in later paragraphs. J. K. Ryan (*New Scholasticism*, xxii, 1948) surveyed the reputation of Aquinas among English Protestant thinkers of the century. *Liturgy and*

Worship, ed. W. K. L. Clarke and C. Harris (1932), includes 'The History of the Book of Common Prayer down to 1662'.

The Puritans, ed. Perry Miller and T. H. Johnson (New York, 1938), is a large, fresh, and varied anthology of Puritan writing, hardly less valuable for England than for New England.

Of the older works on Puritanism the largest and most influential has been Daniel Neal's *History of the Puritans* (4 vols., 1732–8; later enlarged edns., e.g., 3 vols., 1837). Some representative modern works are: Douglas Campbell, *The Puritan in Holland, England, and America* (2 vols., New York, 1892; rev. 1902); H. M. and M. Dexter, *The England and Holland of the Pilgrims* (Boston, 1905), with an index of Separatist publications; Henry W. Clark, *History of English Nonconformity* (2 vols., 1911–13); C. Burrage, *The Early English Dissenters . . . (1550–1641)* (2 vols., 1912). Some smaller books are: James Heron, *Short History of Puritanism* (1908), John Brown, *The English Puritans* (1910), H. H. Henson, *Puritanism in England* (1912), and Alan Simpson's broad but lively and suggestive *Puritanism in Old and New England* (University of Chicago, 1955). The best introduction to our period is M. M. Knappen, *Tudor Puritanism* (University of Chicago, 1939). Two central books by W. Haller are *The Rise of Puritanism* (Columbia, 1938; repr., New York, 1957), which gives the best account of Puritan writing, and its sequel, *Liberty and Reformation* (*supra*, V. 1). The most solid and discriminating analyses of the attitudes of parties and persons are in A. S. P. Woodhouse's *Puritanism and Liberty* (*supra*, V. 1) and Arthur Barker, *Milton and the Puritan Dilemma* (University of Toronto, 1942; repr. 1955). Perry Miller's *Orthodoxy in Massachusetts 1630–1650* (Harvard, 1933; repr., Boston, 1959) and *The New England Mind: The Seventeenth Century* (New York, 1939; repr., Harvard, 1954) have institutional and intellectual emphasis respectively and are important for England as well as New England; so too is Miller's 'The Marrow of Puritan Divinity' (*Publications of The Colonial Society of Massachusetts*, xxxii, 1937; *Errand into the Wilderness*, Harvard, 1956). Puritan doctrine and practice, and Calvinism (which of course was not confined to Puritans), have been increasingly studied, in writings just cited and in such others as: H. D. Foster, 'Liberal Calvinism', on the Synod of Dort (*Harvard Theological Review*, xvi, 1923; *Collected Papers*, priv. pr., 1929); G. F. Nuttall, *The Holy Spirit in Puritan Faith and Experience* (1946); Horton

Davies, *The Worship of the English Puritans* (1948); G. S. Wakefield, *Puritan Devotion* (1957).

The character and origins of the sects are treated in some books already named and in the books by R. M. Jones and Robert Barclay cited near the end of this section. There are accounts in vols. ii and iii of Masson's *Milton* and in C. E. Whiting's *Studies in English Puritanism . . . 1660–1688* (1931). W. B. Selbie's *Nonconformity* (1912) is a brief and broad survey. There are many histories of the chief sects and biographies of leaders. Histories of Presbyterianism range from Heylyn's *Aerius Redivivus* (1670) to A. H. Drysdale (1889); a special study is S. W. Carruthers, *Everyday Work of the Westminster Assembly* (1943). A few bibliographical and historical works are: Joseph Smith, *Descriptive Catalogue of Friends' Books* (2 vols., 1867); W. C. Braithwaite, *The Beginnings of Quakerism* (1912; rev. by H. J. Cadbury, 1955); L. M. Wright, *Literary Life of the Early Friends 1650–1725* (Columbia, 1932); B. Hanbury, *Historical Memorials relating to the Independents* (3 vols., 1839–44); H. M. Dexter, *Congregationalism of the Last Three Hundred Years, As Seen In Its Literature* (New York, 1880); G. Yule, *The Independents in the English Civil War* (1958); W. T. Whitley, *Baptist Bibliography* (2 vols., 1916–22), which is being superseded by E. C. Starr, *A Baptist Bibliography*, in progress (Philadelphia and elsewhere, 1947 ff.); A. C. Underwood, *A History of the English Baptists* (1947); Louise Brown, *Political Activities of the Baptists and Fifth Monarchy Men In England During the Interregnum* (Washington, 1912); G. Huehns's *Antinomianism in English History With special reference to the period 1640–1660* (1951); and L. F. Solt (*supra*, V. 1).

An early work on Scottish religious history was the *History of the Church of Scotland* by David Calderwood (1575–1650), published in abridged form in 1678. Some modern books are: G. D. Henderson, *Religious Life in Seventeenth-Century Scotland* (1937); Duncan Anderson, *The Bible in Seventeenth-Century Scottish Life and Literature* (1936); Hugh Watt, *Recalling the Scottish Covenants* (1946); and W. M. Campbell, *The Triumph of Presbyterianism* (1958).

In addition to many sermons in Cattermole (*supra*), there are two small collections, *Selected English Sermons*, ed. H. H. Henson (1939), and the unscholarly *Wings of an Eagle: An Anthology of Caroline Preachers*, ed. G. L. May (1956). C. F. Richardson's

English Preachers and Preaching 1640–70 (New York, 1928) deals chiefly with the character and background of the clergy. Our preachers receive chapters in the *CHEL* iv, vii, and viii, some pages in C. Smyth's *Art of Preaching* (1940), and a lecture by F. P. Wilson (*supra*, III. 2). The fullest critical study is W. Fraser Mitchell, *English Pulpit Oratory from Andrewes to Tillotson* (1932). John Brown's *Puritan Preaching in England* (1900) has supplements in Haller's books of 1938 and 1955 and Miller's *New England Mind* (*supra*). The workings of an important popular institution are described by M. MacLure, *The Paul's Cross Sermons 1534–1642* (University of Toronto, 1958). Among articles are two on political sermons by E. W. Kirby (*American Historical Review*, xliv, 1938–9) and G. Davies (*HLQ* iii, 1939–40); one by R. F. Jones on the Restoration attack on pulpit eloquence (*JEGP* xxx, 1931; repr. in the Jones *Festschrift*, *supra*, III. 2); K. Koller (*supra*, IV. 4); H. Fisch, 'The Puritans and the Reform of Prose-style' (*ELH* xix, 1952). H. Caplan and H. H. King compiled 'Pulpit Eloquence: A List of Doctrinal and Historical Studies in English' (*Speech Monographs*, xxii, 1955).

Anglican casuistry has been studied by H. H. Henson (*supra*), H. R. McAdoo, *The Structure of Caroline Moral Theology* (1949), and T. Wood (under Jeremy Taylor in VI); and, on the Puritan and political side, by G. L. Mosse, *The Holy Pretence: A Study in Christianity and Reason of State from William Perkins to John Winthrop* (1957).

Many major documents in the controversy on toleration are reprinted and discussed in Haller's *Tracts on Liberty* and Woodhouse's *Puritanism and Liberty* (*supra*, V. 1). The standard and very comprehensive history is W. K. Jordan's *Development of Religious Toleration in England* (4 vols., 1932–40); vols. ii–iv cover 1603–60. Two shorter books are M. Freund, *Die Idee der Toleranz im England der Großen Revolution* (Halle, 1927), and T. Lyon, *The Theory of Religious Liberty in England 1603–39* (1937).

A current of heretical thought (with which liberals were likely to be associated by opponents) is traced by H. J. McLachlan, *Socinianism in Seventeenth-Century England* (1951); with this may be linked E. M. Wilbur's *History of Unitarianism In Transylvania, England, and America* (Harvard, 1952). One may refer here to philosophic and scientific books cited in III. 4 above and V. 3 below.

The fullest study of the religious outlook of Falkland and his circle is in John Tulloch, *Rational Theology and Christian Philosophy in England in the Seventeenth Century* (2 vols., 1872; rev. 1874). Among shorter accounts are E. A. George, *Seventeenth Century Men of Latitude* (New York, 1908); Kenneth B. Murdock's long essay, with a bibliography, in *The Sun at Noon* (New York, 1929); H. Baker (*supra*, III. 4); and items mentioned in VI under Lucius Cary (Falkland), Hales, and Chillingworth.

E. T. Campagnac's anthology, *The Cambridge Platonists* (1901), has selections from Whichcote, Smith, and Culverwel. The fullest study of the group is Tulloch's second volume; perhaps the best brief one is by J. A. Stewart in Hastings (*supra*), iii (1911). They are included in the 'shorter accounts' (except Murdock) mentioned just above, and in Mullinger, iii (*infra*, V. 6) and W. R. Sorley's *History of English Philosophy* (1920). A sketch of the later Platonists is in G. R. Cragg, *From Puritanism to the Age of Reason* (1950). In addition to Cassirer's distinctive work (*supra*, IV. 7), there are books on the whole group by F. J. Powicke (1926), G. P. H. Pawson (1930), and W. C. de Pauley (*The Candle of the Lord*, 1937). There are special studies by S. P. Lamprecht, on innate ideas (*Philosophical Review*, xxxv, 1926); M. Nicolson, 'Christ's College and the Latitude-Men' (*MP* xxvii, 1929–30); J. J. de Boer, *The Theory of Knowledge of the Cambridge Platonists* (Madras, 1931); E. M. Austin, *Ethics of the Cambridge Platonists* (Philadelphia, 1935); R. L. Colie (under More, in VI); and items listed below in V. 3 (e.g. W. B. Hunter and J. E. Saveson) and under individuals in VI.

On the character of mysticism the most familiar books are those of Evelyn Underhill and W. R. Inge. Some studies are: Robert Barclay, *The Inner Life of the Religious Societies of the Commonwealth* (1876); Rufus M. Jones, *Spiritual Reformers in the 16th and 17th Centuries* (1914; repr., Boston, 1959) and *Mysticism and Democracy in the English Commonwealth* (Harvard, 1932); E. N. S. Thompson, 'Mysticism in Seventeenth-Century Literature', *SP* xviii (1921); G. F. Hodgson, *English Mystics* (1922); Helen C. White, *English Devotional Literature (Prose) 1600–1640* (University of Wisconsin, 1931); Joseph B. Collins, *Christian Mysticism in the Elizabethan Age* (Johns Hopkins, 1940). For Boehme, there are Jones's *Spiritual Reformers* (*supra*), W. Struck, *Der Einfluß Jakob Boehmes auf die englische Literatur des 17. Jahrhunderts* (Berlin, 1936), and, in addition to lists of translations

in the *BMC* and *CBEL* ii, the very elaborate bibliography in
W. Buddecke, *Die Jakob-Böhme Ausgaben*, ii (Göttingen, 1957).

3. SCIENCE AND SCIENTIFIC THOUGHT

This section comprises anthologies and bibliographies;
general histories of science; guides to some sciences; alchemy
and astrology; origins of the Royal Society; scientific thought
and philosophy; the influence of Descartes.

A general anthology is H. Boynton's *Beginnings of Modern
Science: Scientific Writings of the 16th, 17th and 18th Centuries* (New
York, 1948). N. Davy's *British Scientific Literature in the Seventeenth
Century* (1953) barely touches our period. Collections of scientific
correspondence were cited above in IV. 6.

Bibliographies and references are given in many of the books
and articles cited below, and *Isis* has had annual bibliographies
since 1913. F. A. Dudley et al. compiled *The Relations of Literature and Science: A Selected Bibliography 1930–49* (State College of
Washington, 1949); K. Svendsen et al. have edited supplements of which a selection has appeared annually in *Symposium*
(1951 ff.).

Some general histories of varying scope are: H. T. Pledge,
Science since 1500 (1939; repr., New York, 1959); Sir W. C.
Dampier, *History of Science and its Relations with Philosophy &
Religion* (4th ed., rev., 1948); H. Butterfield, *Origins of Modern
Science* (1949; rev. 1957); A. C. Crombie, *Augustine to Galileo:
The History of Science A.D. 400–1650* (1952; 2nd ed., 2 vols., New
York, 1959; London and Harvard, 1961); S. F. Mason, *A History
of the Sciences* (1953); A. R. Hall, *The Scientific Revolution 1500–
1800: The Formation of the Modern Scientific Attitude* (1954; repr.,
Boston, 1956); L. W. Hull, *History and Philosophy of Science*
(1959); C. Singer, *A Short History of Scientific Ideas to 1900* (1959).

Some related and miscellaneous books and articles are: A.
Wolf, *History of Science, Technology, and Philosophy in the 16th &
17th Centuries* (1935; rev. D. McKie, 1950; repr., New York,
1959); *A History of Technology, Vol. III: From the Renaissance to the
Industrial Revolution c 1500–c 1750* (1957), ed. C. Singer et al.;
R. K. Merton, *Science, Technology and Society in Seventeenth Century
England* (*Osiris*, iv, 1938) and the last two chapters of his *Social
Theory and Social Structure* (rev. ed., New York, 1957); W. E.
Houghton, 'The History of Trades', *JHI* ii (1941); P. Allen,

'Scientific Studies in the English Universities of the Seventeenth Century', *JHI* x (1949); *Science, Medicine and History: Essays ... in honour of Charles Singer*, ed. E. A. Underwood (2 vols., 1953). Much varied material is in the many volumes of R. T. Gunther's *Early Science in Oxford* (1920 ff.) and in his *Early Science in Cambridge* (1937). Scientific relations between England and the Continent are illustrated in J. Jacquot's 'Sir Charles Cavendish and His Learned Friends', *Annals of Science*, viii (1952); cf. H. Hervey, *Osiris*, x (1952). The nature and sources of popular knowledge are described in K. Svendsen's *Milton and Science* (Harvard, 1956). R. L. Colie (*Bodleian Library Record*, vi, 1960) has recorded marginalia on Bacon and Browne by Dean Christopher Wren (1591–1658).

Such historians as Crombie and Hall (*supra*) have good classified bibliographies for the various sciences, and histories of these are mostly not cited here.

Some guides to theories of matter are: K. Laßwitz, *Geschichte der Atomistik vom Mittelalter bis Newton* (2 vols., Hamburg, 1890); G. B. Stones, *Isis*, x (1928); C. T. Harrison, *Harvard Studies and Notes in Philology and Literature*, xv (1933), and *Harvard Studies in Classical Philology*, xlv (1934); J. R. Partington, *Annals of Science*, iv (1939); M. Boas, 'The Establishment of the Mechanical Philosophy', *Osiris*, x (1952), and *Robert Boyle and Seventeenth-Century Chemistry* (1958).

Some books on mathematicians are: E. W. Hobson, *John Napier and the Invention of Logarithms* (1914); the *Napier Tercentenary Memorial Volume*, ed. C. G. Knott (1915); F. Cajori, *William Oughtred* (1916); J. F. Scott (under Wallis in VI); and E. G. R. Taylor, *The Mathematical Practitioners of Tudor & Stuart England* (1954).

A Source Book in Astronomy, ed. H. Shapley and H. E. Howarth (1929), has selections from Copernicus et al. Perhaps the best history is T. S. Kuhn, *The Copernican Revolution* (Harvard, 1957; repr., New York, 1959), which has a good bibliography. Francis R. Johnson's *Astronomical Thought in Renaissance England* (Johns Hopkins, 1937) is invaluable. G. McColley wrote many articles, e.g. on the plurality of worlds (*Annals of Science*, i, 1936), and some cited under J. Wilkins in VI. M. Nicolson collected six studies in *Science and Imagination* (Cornell, 1956): 'The Telescope and Imagination', *MP* xxxii (1934–5); 'The "New Astronomy" and English Imagination', *SP* xxxii (1935); 'Milton and the

Telescope', *ELH* ii (1935); &c. To her other books (*supra*, III. 4) may be added *A World in the Moon* (Smith College, 1936) and *Voyages to the Moon* (New York, 1948; repr. 1960). A short account of cosmic theories and reactions is a chapter in S. Korninger (*supra*, III. 3); a sketch of poetic responses is in D. Bush, *Science and English Poetry* (1950). This paragraph may include S. K. Heninger, *A Handbook of Renaissance Meteorology With Particular Reference to Elizabethan and Jacobean Literature* (Duke University, 1960).

A standard book is C. E. Raven, *English Naturalists from Neckam to Ray: A Study of the Making of the Modern World* (1947). R. T. Gunther (*Early Science in Oxford*, iii, 1925) gave an account of the Tradescants and their museum of natural history, the first in England.

For medicine one may cite articles by W. Pagel (*Bulletin of the Institute of the History of Medicine*, iii, 1935, and *Science, Medicine and History, supra*); P. Allen, 'Medical Education in 17th Century England', *Journal of the History of Medicine and Allied Sciences*, i (1946); P. H. Kocher, 'Paracelsan Medicine in England ... ca. 1570–1600', ibid. ii (1947); and items under Harvey in VI.

Lynn Thorndike's massive *History of Magic and Experimental Science*, Vols. *VII–VIII, The Seventeenth Century* (Columbia, 1958) is fuller on 'magic' than on science and oddly deficient on English writers. A. E. Waite wrote or edited books on alchemy and related matters (see Fludd and T. Vaughan in VI). The best history is F. Sherwood Taylor, *The Alchemists: Founders of Modern Chemistry* (1949); John Read had much material in *Prelude to Chemistry* (1936) and later books. A sketch of literary reactions is L. Nowak, *Die Alchemie und die Alchemisten in der englischen Literatur* (Breslau, 1934). H. Fisch had a shorter sketch in *Proceedings of the Leeds Philosophical Society*, vii (1953).

Full accounts of astrology are in Thorndike and Don C. Allen's *The Star-Crossed Renaissance* (Duke University, 1941), which covers the Jacobean age. J. Parr's *Tamburlaine's Malady* (University of Alabama, 1953), on astrology in Elizabethan drama, includes a bibliography of sources up to 1625. Some shorter studies are by H. G. Dick, in his edition of *Albumazar* (*University of California Publications in English*, xiii, 1944) and, on astrological medicine, in the *Journal of the History of Medicine*, i (1946); and W. D. Smith, *Shakespeare Quarterly*, ix (1958). Kocher (*infra*) has a good deal on both astrology and alchemy.

References for almanacs and prognostications are given above in IV. 2.

Scientific societies in general have been described by M. Ornstein, *The Rôle of Scientific Societies in the Seventeenth Century* (New York, 1913; University of Chicago, 1928), and Harcourt Brown, *Scientific Organizations in Seventeenth Century France* (Baltimore, 1934). Histories of the Royal Society began with Sprat's famous book (1667; ed. J. I. Cope and H. W. Jones, Washington University, 1958). R. H. Syfret, in 'The Origins of The Royal Society' (*Notes and Records of The Royal Society*, v, 1948), identifies the 'Invisible College' with Hartlib's Comenian group; this and other points are not accepted by G. H. Turnbull (ibid. x, 1953). The latest account is by D. McKie, in *The Royal Society: Its Origins and Founders*, ed. Sir Harold Hartley (1960). Some related studies are D. Stimson's 'Dr. Wilkins and the Royal Society' (*Journal of Modern History*, iii, 1931), 'Puritanism and the New Philosophy in 17th Century England' (*Bulletin of the Institute of the History of Medicine*, iii, 1935), and *Scientists and Amateurs* (New York, 1948), which is focused mainly beyond 1660; F. R. Johnson, 'Gresham College: Precursor of the Royal Society' (*JHI* i, 1940); J. B. Conant, 'The Advancement of Learning during the Puritan Commonwealth' (*Proceedings of the Massachusetts Historical Society*, lxvi, 1942); W. E. Houghton, 'The English Virtuoso in the Seventeenth Century' (*JHI* iii, 1942); C. C. Gillispie, on the role of the College of Physicians (*Journal of Modern History*, xix, 1947); and items cited under J. Wilkins in VI below. Of the Royal Society and its critics in the Restoration there are accounts in *Notes and Records*, e.g. R. H. Syfret and E. S. de Beer (vii, viii, 1950–1).

Important books on the history of ideas, some of them including scientific ideas, are cited above in III. 4. A few others are: A. N. Whitehead, *Science and the Modern World* (1925; many reprints); E. A. Burtt, *Metaphysical Foundations of Modern Physical Science* (New York, 1924; rev. 1932; repr. 1954); Preserved Smith, *History of Modern Culture. I. The Great Renewal 1543–1687* (New York, 1930); E. W. Strong, *Procedures and Metaphysics* (University of California, 1936), in part a reply to Burtt; J. H. Randall, *Making of the Modern Mind* (rev. ed., Boston, 1940); R. G. Collingwood, *The Idea of Nature* (1945), for a full perspective; M. Nicolson (*supra*); *Roots of Scientific Thought*, ed. P. P. Wiener and A. Noland (New York, 1957), a large selection of articles from the *JHI* of which a number are cited above. W. B. Hunter discussed the doctrine of 'Plastic Nature' in the *Harvard Theological Review*, xliii (1950).

A. D. White's *History of the Warfare of Science with Religion* (2 vols., 1896 and later edns.) is somewhat dated. Modern books are Dampier (*supra*); P. H. Kocher's substantial *Science and Religion in Elizabethan England* (Huntington Library, 1953); and R. S. Westfall's *Science and Religion in Seventeenth-Century England* (Yale, 1958), which deals with the scientists' views. S. F. Mason has an essay under the same title in *Past & Present*, iii (1953), M. H. Carré an essay in the *Church Quarterly Review*, clvi (1955). The conflict comes into other books cited in this section and in III. 4 above.

There is more or less on English thought in such histories of modern or seventeenth-century philosophy as those of H. Höffding (tr. Meyer, 2 vols., 1900; repr., New York, 1955), G. Sortais (2 vols., Paris, 1920–2), E. Bréhier, ii (Paris, 1929), A. Rivaud, iii (Paris, 1950) and F. Copleston, S.J., iii–v (1953–9). R. H. Popkin's *History of Scepticism from Erasmus to Descartes* (Assen, 1960) has a mainly continental scope. There are histories of English philosophy by C. de Rémusat (2 vols., Paris, 1875), who goes from Bacon to Locke; W. R. Sorley (1920), based on chapters in the *CHEL*; and M. H. Carré, *Phases of Thought in England* (1949). Other items are cited in VI under Bacon, Lord Herbert, Hobbes, et al.

Some studies of Cartesianism in England are: parts of A. J. Snow (under More in VI); M. Nicolson, 'The Early Stage of Cartesianism in England', *SP* xxvi (1929); S. P. Lamprecht, *Studies in the History of Ideas*, iii (Columbia, 1935); J. Laird, *Revue philosophique*, cxxiii (1937); C. Adam, on Descartes's English correspondents, *Revue de littérature comparée*, xvii (1937); H. Hervey (*supra*); A. Armitage, *Notes and Records of The Royal Society*, viii (1950–1); J. E. Saveson, 'Descartes and the Cambridge Platonists', *JHI* xxi (1960); and items cited in VI under Cudworth, More, and John Smith.

4. TRAVEL

This section covers general bibliographies, collections, and histories; England; the Continent; the East; and America.

The large standard bibliography is E. G. Cox, *Reference Guide to the Literature of Travel: i. The Old World; ii. The New World;*

iii. Great Britain (3 vols., University of Washington, 1935, 1938, 1949). There are extensive bibliographies in E. G. R. Taylor and B. Penrose (*infra*).

Purchas appears in VI below. Early modern collections which remain valuable are those of A. and John Churchill (4 vols., 1704; v and vi, 1732; 6 vols., 1744–6; vii and viii by Thomas Osborne, 1745, repr. 1747); John Harris (2 vols., 1705; 2nd ed., 1744–8); and John Pinkerton (17 vols., 1808–14). The records of many travellers and voyagers to East and West have been edited separately for the Hakluyt Society, for the Argonaut Press series, ed. N. M. Penzer (1925 ff.), and for the Broadway Travellers series, ed. Sir D. Ross and E. Power (1926 ff.). Much information about Hakluyt, Purchas, and the collections is in E. Lynam et al., *Richard Hakluyt & His Successors* (1946).

Some books of broad scope are: E. Heawood, *History of Geographical Discovery in the Seventeenth and Eighteenth Centuries* (1912); E. G. R. Taylor, *Late Tudor and Early Stuart Geography 1583–1650* (1934); and B. Penrose, *Travel and Discovery in the Renaissance 1420–1620* (Harvard, 1952). Among short surveys are chapters in Traill's *Social England*, iv; the *Cambridge Modern History*, iv; the *CHEL* iv; *Shakespeare's England*; and the *Cambridge History of the British Empire*.

For Great Britain the standard bibliography is Cox (*supra*), who includes many things from antiquities to agriculture. *Travel in England in the Seventeenth Century* (1925), by Joan Parkes, is authoritative and attractive. More special are *An Historical Geography of England before A.D. 1800*, ed. H. C. Darby (1936); G. E. Fussell, *Exploration of England* (1935), a bibliography of travel and topography, 1570–1815; and Sir H. G. Fordham's accounts of road-books (1924) and surveyors and map-makers (1929). For foreigners' impressions there are: W. B. Rye, *England as Seen by Foreigners in the Days of Elizabeth and James the First* (1865), M. Letts, *As the Foreigner Saw Us* (1935), W. D. Robson-Scott, *German Travellers in England 1400–1800* (1953), and such particular items as a German traveller's 'England in 1609', tr. G. P. V. Akrigg (*HLQ* xiv, 1950–1).

Some books on foreign travel are: E. S. Bates, *Touring in 1600* (Boston, 1911); Clare Howard, *English Travellers of the Renaissance* (New York, 1914); B. Penrose, *Urbane Travellers 1591–1635* (University of Pennsylvania, 1942), which has full sketches of

Moryson, Coryate, Sandys, and others; D. Carrington, *The Traveller's Eye* (1947), which has brief excerpts from and sketches of a dozen of our travellers; and J. W. Stoye, *English Travellers Abroad 1604–1667* (1952), a full, fresh, and scholarly account of travels in Europe. The second volume of G. B. Parks's *The English Traveller to Italy* will presumably cover our period. R. McCain listed 'English Travellers in Italy during the Renaissance' in the *Bulletin of Bibliography*, xix (1947–8).

For the East, of special interest to literary students are S. C. Chew's comprehensive *The Crescent and the Rose* (New York, 1937), W. G. Rice's 'Early English Travellers to Greece and the Levant' (*University of Michigan Publications*, x, 1933), and Terence Spencer's *Fair Greece Sad Relic: Literary Philhellenism from Shakespeare to Byron* (1954). O. Burian (*Oriens*, v, 1952) treated English interest in Turkey. Two popular books are E. F. Oaten, *European Travellers in India* (1909) and F. R. Dulles, *Eastward Ho!* (1931). Sir William Foster edited or wrote many volumes: *Letters Received by the East India Company From its Servants in the East* (with F. C. Danvers, 6 vols., 1896–1902), which covers 1602–17; *The English Factories in India* (1906 ff.); *Early Travels in India 1583–1619* (1921), a collection which includes Coryate; *England's Quest of Eastern Trade* (1933); and editions of individual narratives. For China there are the first part of W. W. Appleton, *A Cycle of Cathay* (Columbia, 1951), and Ch'ien Chung-shu, 'China in the English Literature of the Seventeenth Century', *Quarterly Bulletin of Chinese Bibliography*, i (1940).

For America the fullest bibliography is Cox, ii (*supra*). A full descriptive guide to early writings is Jarvis M. Morse, *American Beginnings* (Washington, 1952). A recent useful item is *A Selected Bibliography of Virginia, 1607–1699*, ed. E. G. Swem et al. (Williamsburg, 1957).

Some collections are: *Tracts*, ed. Peter Force (4 vols., Washington, 1836–46); *The Genesis of the United States*, ed. Alexander Brown (2 vols., Boston, 1890); *Original Narratives of Early American History*, ed. J. F. Jameson, a series which includes volumes like L. G. Tyler's *Narratives of Early Virginia 1606–1625* (New York, 1907); *Chronicles of the Pilgrim Fathers*, ed. J. Masefield (1910); *Forerunners and Competitors of the Pilgrims and Puritans*, ed. C. H. Levermore (2 vols., New York, 1912); *Colonising Expeditions to the West Indies and Guiana, 1623–1667*, ed. V. T. Harlow (1925); *The Puritans*, ed. Miller and Johnson (*supra*,

V. 2); *The Pilgrim Reader: The Story of the Pilgrims As Told by Themselves & Their Contemporaries*, ed. G. F. Willison (New York, 1953); *The Three Charters Of the Virginia Company Of London With Seven Related Documents; 1606–1621*, ed. S. M. Bemiss (Williamsburg, 1957). Two notable documents are William Bradford, *History of Plymouth Plantation 1620–1647*, ed. W. C. Ford (2 vols., Boston, 1912); *Of Plymouth Plantation 1620–1647*, ed. S. E. Morison (New York, 1952); and John Winthrop, *Winthrop's Journal: "History of New England" 1630–1649*, ed. J. K. Hosmer (2 vols., New York, 1908).

Some books on the expansion of England are cited above in V. 1. Some others, on early voyages, settlements, and colonial America, are: J. Winsor, *Narrative and Critical History of America*, iii (Boston, 1884); L. G. Tyler, *England in America 1580–1652* (New York, 1904); C. M. Gayley (under Strachey in VI); S. E. Morison, *Builders of the Bay Colony* (Boston, 1930); J. B. Brebner, *The Explorers of North America 1492–1806* (1933; repr., New York, 1955); C. M. Andrews, *The Colonial Period of American History*, i–ii (Yale, 1934–6); H. M. Jones, *The Literature of Virginia in the Seventeenth Century* (American Academy of Arts and Sciences, Boston, 1946), 'The Colonial Impulse. An Analysis of the "Promotion" Literature of Colonization' (*Proceedings of the American Philosophical Society*, xc, 1946), and 'The European Background', *Literary History of the United States*, ed. R. E. Spiller et al. (New York, 1948; rev. 1953); L. B. Wright, *supra*, V. 1, and *The Atlantic Frontier: Colonial Civilization 1607–1763* (New York, 1947); T. J. Wertenbaker, *The First Americans 1607–1690* (New York, 1927; repr. 1958), and three earlier books assembled as *The Shaping of Colonial Virginia* (New York, 1958); W. F. Craven, *The Southern Colonies in the Seventeenth Century 1607–1689* (Louisiana State University, 1949) and *The Virginia Company Of London, 1606–1624* (Williamsburg, 1957); P. Miller, books cited in V. 2 and 'Religion and Society in the Early Literature of Virginia' (*William and Mary Quarterly*, 3rd series, v–vi, 1948–9; *Errand into the Wilderness*, Harvard, 1956); K. B. Murdock, *Literature & Theology in Colonial New England* (Harvard, 1949); W. W. Abbot, *A Virginia Chronology 1585–1783* (Williamsburg, 1957), and other booklets by various authors in the Jamestown 350th Anniversary series; A. L. Rowse, *The Elizabethans and America* (1959); James M. Smith, ed., *Seventeenth-Century America: Essays in Colonial History* (University of North Carolina,

1959), which includes R. S. Dunn, 'Seventeenth-Century English Historians of America'.

The literary and cultural fruits of travel are more or less treated in a number of the books cited, and some may be added: J. E. Gillespie, *The Influence of Oversea Expansion on England to 1700* (Columbia, 1920); R. W. Frantz, *The English Traveller and the Movement of Ideas* (*University of Nebraska Studies*, 1932–3), which, though focused on 1660–1732, has suggestions for the preceding age: L. B. Wright (*supra*, IV. 2); R. R. Cawley, *The Voyagers and Elizabethan Drama* (Boston, 1938) and *Unpathed Waters: Studies in the Influence of the Voyagers on Elizabethan Literature* (Princeton, 1940); G. B. Parks, 'John Evelyn and the Art of Travel' (*HLQ* x, 1946–7) and 'Travel as Education' (*The Seventeenth Century . . . R. F. Jones, supra*, III. 2).

5. SOCIAL LIFE

Contemporary memoirs, diaries, and letters are touched upon in IV. 6 and in this section below. Some collections of original texts are: Andrew Lang, *Social England Illustrated. A Collection of XVIIth Century Tracts* (1903); R. B. Morgan, *Readings in English Social History from Contemporary Literature*, vol. iv, 1603–1688 (1922); M. St. C. Byrne, *The Elizabethan Home* (enlarged ed., 1949); G. B. Harrison, *England in Shakespeare's Day* (1928) and, if they may be included here, Harrison's unique series of *Elizabethan Journals* (1928 ff.; collected 1939) and *Jacobean Journals*, i, 1603–1606 (1941), ii, 1607–1610 (University of Michigan, 1958); D. Hartley and M. M. Elliot, *Life and Work of the People of England . . . The Seventeenth Century* (1928), an attractive pictorial record; A. V. Judges (*supra*, IV. 2); Dunham and Pargellis (*supra*, II. 1).

The massive *Victoria History of the Counties of England* (1900 ff.) is a rich mine. Some general works are: H. D. Traill and J. S. Mann, *Social England* (6 vols., 1893–7; rev. 1901–4); G. M. Trevelyan, *English Social History* (New York, 1942; 1944) and *Illustrated English Social History*, ii (1949); R. J. Mitchell and M. D. R. Leys (*supra*, IV. 2 and V. 1). Short surveys are given by Sir A. W. Ward (*CHEL* v) and Trevelyan and G. Davies (*supra*, V. 1). A number of books in economic and social history, listed above in V. 1, are relevant here. Some books touching or focused on our period are: *Shakespeare's England* (2 vols., 1916), ed. Sir Sidney Lee and C. T. Onions; E. Godfrey, *Home Life under the Stuarts 1603–1649* (1903; repr. 1925) and *Social Life under the Stuarts* (1904); E. Trotter, *Seventeenth Century Life in the Country Parish, with Special Reference to Local Government* (1919); M. Coate, *Social Life in Stuart England* (1924); M. St. C. Byrne, *Elizabethan Life in Town and Country* (1925; 7th ed., 1961); J. Parkes (*supra*, V. 4); R. Lennard et al., *Englishmen at Rest and at Play . . . 1558–1714* (1931); L. B. Wright (*supra*, IV. 2); C. Hole, *English Home-Life, 1500 to 1800* (1947); G. E. and K. R. Fussell, *The English Countryman, His Life and Work A.D. 1500–1900* (1955); W. Notestein (*supra*, V. 1); L. E. Pearson, *Elizabethans at Home* (Stanford, 1957). More special are: R. Withington, *English Pageantry* (2 vols., Harvard, 1918–20); M. and C. H. B. Quennell, *History of Everyday Things in England*, ii (3rd ed., 1937); Sir J. C. Drummond and A. Wilbraham, *The Englishman's Food. A History of Five Centuries of English Diet* (1939); and two companion items, Donald McDonald, *Agricultural Writers . . . 1200–1800* (1908), and G. E. Fussell, *Old English Farming Books . . . 1523–1730* (1947).

For the court there are items cited above in IV. 6 and V. 1 and in VI under James I and Charles I; Sir E. K. Chambers, *The Elizabethan Stage*, i (1923); G. P. V. Akrigg's *Jacobean Pageant* (Harvard, 1962), a very full and intimate picture of the court, society, &c.; and many biographies of courtiers, e.g. G. Huxley, *Endymion Porter* (1959). L. Stone (*Past & Present*, No. xiv, 1958) outlined the argument of a forthcoming book, *The Nobility of England, 1558–1642*. The country life of nobility and gentry is mirrored in G. S. Thomson's *Life in a Noble Household, 1641–1700* (1937; repr., University of Michigan, 1959) and in books cited in VI under Lady Anne Clifford, Lady Conway, Lady Harley, Thomas Knyvett, Lady Mildmay, Sir John Oglander, Dorothy Osborne, Henry Oxinden, Lady Paston, and the Verneys.

The strong religious colouring of social and family life may be seen best in diaries, letters, and (see V. 6) conduct books. Modern studies range from Troeltsch (*supra*, V. 2) to L. L. Schücking's *Die Familie im Puritanismus* (Leipzig, 1929) and H. Reinhold's *Puritanismus und Aristokratie* (Berlin, 1938). Here belongs W. P. Holden, *Anti-Puritan Satire 1572–1642* (Yale, 1954). That peculiarly English phenomenon, the Puritan Sunday, has evoked many books, e.g. R. Cox, *Literature of the Sabbath Question* (2 vols., 1865); a chapter in R. Lennard (*supra*); Max Levy,

Der Sabbath in England (Leipzig, 1933); and W. B. Whitaker, *Sunday in Tudor and Stuart Times* (1933). To general histories of Scotland (*supra*, V. 1) may be added books cited in V. 2.

In addition to books already named, there are many special studies, scholarly or popular, of the domestic and cultural status of women: C. L. Powell, *English Domestic Relations 1487-1653* (Columbia, 1917); Alice Clark, *Working Life of Women in the Seventeenth Century* (1919); Myra Reynolds, *The Learned Lady in England 1650-1760* (Boston, 1920); Violet Wilson, *Society Women of Shakespeare's Time* (1924); M. Phillips and W. S. Tomkinson, *English Women in Life & Letters* (1927); D. Gardiner, *English Girlhood at School* (1929); B. G. MacCarthy, *Women Writers: Their Contribution to the English Novel 1621-1744* (1945); C. Camden, *The Elizabethan Woman* (Houston, 1952); G. E. and K. R. Fussell, *The English Countrywoman: A Farmhouse Social History A.D. 1500-1900* (1953); C. Hole, *The English Housewife in the Seventeenth Century* (1953); W. Notestein, 'The English Woman, 1580 to 1650', *Studies in Social History: A Tribute to G. M. Trevelyan*, ed. J. H. Plumb (1955); R. Kelso, *Doctrine for the Lady of the Renaissance* (University of Illinois, 1956), which is focused on the period 1400-1600. Here may be included W. and M. Haller, 'The Puritan Art of Love' (*HLQ* v, 1941-2), pages in the former's *Liberty and Reformation* (*supra*, V. 1), and R. M. Frye's related discussion (*Studies in the Renaissance*, ii, 1955); and K. Thomas, 'Women and the Civil War Sects', *Past & Present*, No. xiii (1958).

6. EDUCATION AND CULTURE

This section comprises anthologies; general histories; universities; schools; the modernist movement and Comenius; books of conduct and courtesy; and libraries.

Henry Barnard's *English Pedagogy* (2 vols., 2nd ed., Hartford, 1876) has extracts from Bacon, Wotton, Milton, Hoole, Cowley, Hartlib, and Petty. Extracts from many writers are given in E. Rowland, *A Pedagogue's Commonplace Book* (1925).

Some histories of education that take more or less account of our period are those of S. S. Laurie (1903), J. W. Adamson (1919; and *infra*), R. Ulich (New York, 1945), and S. J. Curtis (1948; 4th ed., 1957). There are chapters by Woodward in the *CHEL* iii and by Sandys in *Shakespeare's England* (1916).

M. L. Clarke's *Classical Education in Britain 1500–1900* (1959) briefly surveys both schools and universities.

To Sir Charles Mallet's *History of the University of Oxford* (3 vols., 1924–7) and the histories of the colleges may be added the newer *Victoria History of the County of Oxford*, iii, *The University of Oxford* (1954), ed. H. E. Salter and M. D. Lobel. And to Anthony Wood's *Athenae Oxonienses* and *Fasti* (*supra*, I), which have more than Oxonian value, may be added his *History and Antiquities of the University of Oxford*, ed. J. Gutch (2 vols., 1792–6; see B. Twyne, *infra*, VI), and *The Life and Times of Anthony Wood . . . 1632–1695, described by Himself*, ed. A. Clark (5 vols., 1891–1900). A full account of academic disruption is given by M. Burrows, *The Register of the Visitors of the University of Oxford from A.D. 1647 to A.D. 1658* (Camden Society, 1881). Another side is presented in F. J. Varley's *The Siege of Oxford* (1932) and *A Supplement* (1935). Some works of reference are: C. W. Boase and A. Clark, *Register of the University of Oxford* (5 vols., 1885–9); John Griffiths, *Statutes of the University of Oxford Codified in the Year 1636* (1888); Joseph Foster, *Alumni Oxonienses 1500–1714* (4 vols., 1891–2); and Strickland Gibson, *Statuta Antiqua* (1931).

With J. B. Mullinger's *The University of Cambridge* (3 vols., 1873–1911), and the histories of the colleges, goes the *Victoria History of the County of Cambridge*, iii, *The City and University of Cambridge* (1959), ed. J. P. C. Roach. University organization around 1600 is well described in George Peacock, *Observations on the Statutes of the University of Cambridge* (1841). Some other histories and works of reference are: J. Heywood and T. Wright, *Cambridge University Transactions during the Puritan Controversies of the 16th and 17th Centuries* (2 vols., 1854); C. H. and T. Cooper, *Athenae Cantabrigienses* (3 vols., 1858–1913); D. Masson, *Milton*, i (1859; rev. 1881); John and J. A. Venn, *Alumni Cantabrigienses* (10 vols., 1922–54); F. J. Varley, *Cambridge During the Civil War* (1935); and H. F. Fletcher (*infra*), ii (1961). W. T. Costello's *Scholastic Curriculum at Early Seventeenth-Century Cambridge* (Harvard, 1958) is fresh, lively, and learned. Glimpses of religious debate are given in H. C. Porter (cited under Perkins in VI).

One of the best pictures of life and work at the English universities is given in S. E. Morison's *Founding of Harvard College* (Harvard, 1935). A valuable and corrective study is M. H. Curtis, *Oxford and Cambridge in Transition, 1558–1642: An Essay* on *Changing Relations between the English Universities and English Society* (1959). There is much material in contemporary memoirs, letters, and tracts, e.g. J. H. Marsden (under D'Ewes in VI).

Important documents on schools are the books of Brinsley and Hoole cited under their names in VI. Mullinger had a chapter in the *CHEL* vii. Larger accounts are F. Watson, *English Grammar Schools to 1660* (1908); T. W. Baldwin, *William Shakspere's Small Latine & Lesse Greeke* (2 vols., University of Illinois, 1944); D. L. Clark, *John Milton at St. Paul's School: A Study of Ancient Rhetoric in English Renaissance Education* (Columbia, 1948); H. F. Fletcher, *Intellectual Development of John Milton*, i (University of Illinois, 1956).

The modernist movement is surveyed, with varying focus, by J. W. Adamson, *Pioneers of Modern Education 1600–1700* (1905), and in the *CHEL* ix; F. Watson, *The Beginnings of the Teaching of Modern Subjects in England* (1909); and B. Dressler, *Die Entwicklung der englischen Erziehung im 17. Jahrhundert* (Leipzig, 1927). Baconian influence is fully analysed by R. F. Jones (*supra*, III. 4). A recent account of Puritan attacks on traditional education is by R. Schlatter, *Historical Magazine of the Protestant Episcopal Church*, xxiii (1954); cf. L. Solt, *supra*, V. 1. A related problem is treated in W. A. L. Vincent, *The State and Local Education 1640–1660 in England and Wales* (1950). Further items are noted in the next paragraph and, in VI, under Dell, Dury, John Hall, Hartlib, Petty, and Woodward.

Comenius's *Great Didactic* was translated and edited by M. W. Keatinge (1896; enlarged 1910), the *Analytic Didactic* by V. Jelinek (University of Chicago, 1953), with a full introduction. Of the many books on Comenius three are that of A. Heyberger (Paris, 1928), *The Teacher of Nations*, ed. J. Needham (1942), and M. Spinka, *John Amos Comenius* (University of Chicago, 1943); cf. Spinka's 'Comenian Pansophic Principles', *Church History*, xxii (1953). The subject of R. F. Young's *Comenius in England* (1932) has been further treated by G. H. Turnbull, *Hartlib, Dury and Comenius* (1947), in *NQ* cxcvi (1951), and *Acta Comeniana*, xvii (Prague, 1958), and in studies by R. H. Syfret and Turnbull cited above in V. 3. A corrective account of Comenius's ideas is given by E. Sirluck in Milton's *Complete Prose Works*, ii (Yale, 1959). H. R. Trevor-Roper (*Encounter*, xiv, 1960) sees Hartlib, Dury, and Comenius in a political setting.

For the literature of courtesy the fullest guides are G. E. Noyes, *Bibliography of Courtesy and Conduct Books in Seventeenth-Century England* (New Haven, 1937), and V. B. Heltzel, *Check List of Courtesy Books in the Newberry Library* (Chicago, 1942). The fullest study is J. E. Mason's *Gentlefolk in the Making* (University of Pennsylvania, 1935). Other studies, large and small, are: E. N. S. Thompson, *Literary Bypaths of the Renaissance* (Yale, 1924); Ruth Kelso, *The Doctrine of the English Gentleman in the Sixteenth Century*, with a bibliography to 1625 (University of Illinois, 1929); articles by W. L. Ustick, *SP* xxix (1932) and *MP* xxx (1932–3); sections of C. L. Powell (*supra*, V. 5), L. B. Wright (*supra*, IV. 2), and W. E. Houghton (under Fuller, in VI); R. Kelso (*supra*, V. 5); and J. L. Lievsay, *Stefano Guazzo and the English Renaissance 1575–1675* (University of North Carolina, 1961).

On libraries there are Mullinger's chapter in the *CHEL* iv and E. Edwards's *Memoirs of Libraries* (2 vols., 1859) and *Libraries and Founders of Libraries* (1865). For Oxford there are: W. D. Macray, *Annals of the Bodleian Library Oxford* (2nd ed., 1890); G. W. Wheeler, *The Earliest Catalogues of the Bodleian Library* (1928); items under Bodley in VI; and *infra*. For Cambridge there is C. Sayle, *Annals of Cambridge University Library* (1916). *The English Library before 1700*, ed. F. Wormald and C. E. Wright (1958), includes chapters on Oxford, Cambridge, and Sir Robert Cotton (q.v. in VI). The Lambeth Palace Library, 1610-64, was described by A. Cox-Johnson (*CBS* ii, 1955) and M. R. James (ibid. iii, 1959). S. Jayne compiled a bibliography, *Library Catalogues of the English Renaissance* (University of California, 1956).

7. MUSIC AND THE ARTS

This section covers collections and histories of music; the graphic arts; antiquities; architecture; decoration, furniture, and dress; and gardening. A survey of nearly all these and other arts is *The Stuart Period 1603–1714*, ed. L. G. G. Ramsey (Connoisseur Period Guides, 1957).

W. Chappell's *Popular Music of the Olden Time* (2 vols., 1855–9) was revised by H. E. Wooldridge as *Old English Popular Music* (2 vols., 1893). A facsimile of Chappell is forthcoming, with an introduction by Claude Simpson, who is also preparing a new edition. The great modern editions of Tudor and early Stuart music are: *The English Madrigal School*, ed. E. H. Fellowes

(36 vols., 1913–24); *The English School of Lutenist Song Writers*, ed. Fellowes (32 vols., 1920–32); and *Tudor Church Music*, ed. P. C. Buck, Fellowes, et al. (10 vols., 1923–9). 'Peter Warlock' and P. Wilson edited a selection, *English Ayres Elizabethan and Jacobean* (1927–31).

A standard bibliography is *The British Union-Catalogue of Early Music Printed before the Year 1801*, ed. E. B. Schnapper (2 vols., 1957). Two standard works of reference are *Grove's Dictionary of Music and Musicians* (5th ed., ed. E. Blom, 9 vols., 1954) and *Die Musik in Geschichte und Gegenwart*, ed. F. Blume (in progress, vols. 1–8, 1949–60, Kassel, Basel, London, New York). Historical accounts, long and short, general and special, are: W. B. Squire's chapter in *Shakespeare's England* (1916); the histories of Sir H. Parry, *Oxford History of Music*, vii (rev. by E. J. Dent, 1938), and Ernest Walker (3rd ed., rev. by J. A. Westrup, 1952); E. H. Fellowes, *The English Madrigal* (1925; repr. 1935, 1947), *The English Madrigal Composers* (2nd ed., 1948), *English Cathedral Music* (1941), *Orlando Gibbons* (2nd ed., 1951), and *William Byrd* (2nd ed., 1948); 'Peter Warlock', *The English Ayre* (1926); P. Scholes, *The Puritans and Music in England and New England* (1934), which was devoted to the destruction of 'a calumny'; E. Brennecke, *John Milton the Elder and His Music* (Columbia, 1938); M. C. Boyd, *Elizabethan Music and Musical Criticism* (University of Pennsylvania, 1940); W. M. Evans, *Henry Lawes* (New York, 1941); E. H. Meyer, *English Chamber Music* (1946; repr. 1952); A. Obertello, *Madrigali italiani in Inghilterra: Storia—Critica—Testi* (Milan, 1949); W. L. Woodfill, *Musicians in English Society from Elizabeth to Charles I* (Princeton, 1953); papers by J. A. Westrup, J. Jacquot, and W. Mellers in *Musique et poésie au XVIᵉ siècle* (Paris, 1954); D. Stevens, *Thomas Tomkins 1572–1656* (1957); J. Stevens, 'The English Madrigal' (*ESEA 1958*); M. Lefkowitz, *William Lawes* (1960); and some items cited above in III. 3, especially B. Pattison. J. Pulver compiled *A Biographical Dictionary of Old English Music* (1927); and Sir F. Bridge wrote a series of sketches, *Twelve Good Musicians from John Bull to Henry Purcell* (1920).

Some studies of the Renaissance philosophy and psychology of music are: Leo Spitzer (*supra*, III. 4); J. Hutton's monograph, 'Some English Poems in Praise of Music', *English Miscellany*, ed. M. Praz, ii (Rome, 1951); two articles by G. L. Finney in *JHI* viii (1947) and others in *ELH* xx (1953), *Studies in the Renaissance*, vi (1959), *Centennial Review*, iv (1960), &c., collected in *Musical Backgrounds for English Literature, 1580–1650* (Rutgers, 1962); and John Hollander's full study, *The Untuning of the Sky: Ideas of Music in English Poetry* (Princeton, 1961).

H. V. S. and M. S. Ogden had a bibliography of seventeenth-century English writings on the pictorial arts in *Art Bulletin*, xxix (1947), L. Salerno a descriptive analysis in the *Journal of the Warburg and Courtauld Institutes*, xiv (1951). A general survey is M. Whinney and O. Millar, *English Art 1625–1714 (Oxford History of English Art*, 1957). Some accounts of painting are: L. Cust's section in *Shakespeare's England*; C. H. C. Baker and W. G. Constable, *English Painting of the Sixteenth and Seventeenth Centuries* (Florence and New York, 1930); E. Waterhouse, *Painting in Britain 1530 to 1790 (Pelican History of Art*, 1953); J. R. Hale, *England and the Italian Renaissance: The Growth of Interest in its History and Art* (1954); Sir S. Colvin, *Early Engraving & Engravers in England (1545–1695)* (1905), and A. M. Hind, *Engraving in England in the Sixteenth & Seventeenth Centuries: A Descriptive Catalogue. Part I. The Tudor Period* (1952), *Part II. The Reign of James I* (1955), *Part III. The Reign of Charles I* (in preparation); H. V. S. and M. S. Ogden, *English Taste in Landscape in the Seventeenth Century* (University of Michigan, 1955) and the former's article cited above in III. 3.

Accounts of Charles I as a collector are cited under his name in VI; to these may be added G. Huxley's *Endymion Porter* (1959). The activities of another great collector are described in M. F. S. Hervey's *Life, Correspondence & Collections of Thomas Howard Earl of Arundel* (1921); to this may be added J. Hess's essay and bibliography (*English Miscellany*, ed. Praz, i, 1950). The chief descriptive catalogue of classical antiquities is A. Michaelis, *Ancient Marbles in Great Britain*, tr. C. A. M. Fennell (1882).

Perhaps the best book on architecture is Sir John Summerson, *Architecture in Britain 1530 to 1830* (1953; 2nd ed., 1958). Some other and related works are: books by J. A. Gotch, who had a section in *Shakespeare's England*; M. Whiffen, *An Introduction to Elizabethan and Jacobean Architecture* (1952); H. A. Tipping's sumptuous *English Homes*, Periods III and IV (1920–7); R. Dutton, *The English Interior 1500 to 1900* (1948); M. Jourdain, *English Interior Decoration 1500 to 1830* (1950); and J. Lees-Milne, *The Age of Inigo Jones* (1953). The standard *Dictionary of English Furniture* (3 vols., 1924–7) by P. Macquoid and R. Edwards was revised by the latter (3 vols., 1954). Among books on dress are: M. C. Linthicum, *Costume in the Drama of Shakespeare and his Contemporaries* (1936); G. Reynolds, *Costume of the World: Elizabethan and Jacobean, 1558–1625* (1951); and C. W. and P. Cunnington, *Handbook of English Costume in the Seventeenth Century* (1955).

B. S. Allen's *Tides in English Taste (1619–1800)* (2 vols., Harvard, 1937; repr., New York, 1958) covers architecture, interiors, gardens, &c. For contemporary writing on gardens there are: E. S. Rohde, *Old English Gardening Books* (1924), with a bibliography, and *The Old-World Pleasaunce* (1925); the two most famous early books, John Parkinson's *Paradisi In Sole Paradisus Terrestris* (1629), handsomely reproduced in 1904, and William Lawson's *New Orchard and Garden* (1618), edited by Mrs. Rohde (1927) from the 3rd edition; *The Garden Book of Sir Thomas Hanmer*, first printed from the manuscript of 1659 and edited by Mrs. Rohde (1933); and Sir Hugh Plat (*infra*, VI). Some modern accounts are: Sir Reginald Blomfield, *The Formal Garden in England* (1892; repr. 1936); Sir F. Crisp, *Mediæval Gardens* (2 vols.), which comes up into the Stuart period; E. S. Rohde, *The Story of the Garden* (1932); B. S. Allen (*supra*); and R. E. Clarkson, *Green Enchantment* (New York, 1940).

Accounts of herbals have been written by Agnes Arber (rev. ed., 1938) and Mrs. Rohde (1922). M. Woodward abridged Gerard's *Herball* from T. Johnson's 1636 edition (1927). Parkinson, Gerard, Johnson, and others are discussed by C. E. Raven (*supra*, V. 3).

VI. INDIVIDUAL AUTHORS

THOMAS ADAMS, *c.* 1583–*ante* 1660

Adams's sermons were collected in the *Workes* of 1629. The modern edition is that of J. Angus (3 vols., 1861–2). Twelve sermons were edited by John Brown (1909); one is in Henson's anthology (*supra*, V. 2). Some characters are in G. Murphy's *Cabinet* (*supra*, IV. 5). Adams's preaching is discussed in the books of J. Brown, C. Smyth, and especially W. F. Mitchell and M. MacLure (*supra*, V. 2), and by W. Mulder, *Harvard Theological Review*, xlviii (1955). C. Flanagan recorded Southey's references to Adams (*NQ* cxcvii, 1952). Webster's echoes of Adams (and some of Adams's echoes of others) are shown by R. W. Dent, *John Webster's Borrowing* (University of California, 1960).

SIR WILLIAM ALEXANDER, EARL OF STIRLING, 1577?–1640

The standard edition of the verse, with full apparatus, is by L. E. Kastner and H. B. Charlton (2 vols., 1921–9). *An Encouragement To Colonies* (1624) was reprinted in *Royal Letters, Charters, and Tracts* (Bannatyne Club, 1867) and in Slafter (*infra*). *Anacrisis*, an essay on poetry, first printed in the 1711 edition of Drummond's works, is in Spingarn (*supra*, IV. 9). E. L. Slafter's *Sir William Alexander and American Colonization* (Boston, 1873) remains useful; the standard biography is T. H. McGrail's *Sir William Alexander* (1940). Webster's debts to Alexander are shown by R. W. Dent (*MLN* lxv, 1950; and the book cited under Adams, *supra*). A. G. D. Wiles (*PBSA* l, 1956) discussed the date of Alexander's supplement to Sidney's *Arcadia*.

RICHARD ALLESTREE, 1619–81

The anonymous *Whole Duty of Man* (1658) was reprinted into the nineteenth century. The problem of authorship was reviewed by P. Elmen (*Library*, vi, 1951), whose unpublished Harvard thesis (1947) is the fullest study of the books. C. J. Stranks has a chapter in *Anglican Devotion* (1961).

WILLIAM AMES, 1576–1633

Ames's best-known books were *Medulla Sacræ Theologiæ* (Franeker, 1623), translated as *The Marrow of Sacred Divinity* (1642), and *De Conscientia, et Eius Iure, vel Casibus* (Amsterdam, 1630). In 1643 appeared his *Workes . . . Translated out of Latine for publike use*. The fullest and best account of his thought and influence is in P. Miller's *New England Mind* (*supra*, V. 2). His casuistry is discussed by G. L. Mosse, *Church History*, xxiii (1954), *HLQ* xvii (1953–4), and *The Holy Pretence* (1957).

LANCELOT ANDREWES, 1555–1626

XCVI. Sermons (1629) was edited by Bishops Laud and Buckeridge. An imperfect edition of *Preces Privatae* (1647) was issued by Moseley, who put out a better edition (1648) translated by R. Drake. The complete works, including early biographical material, were edited in the Library of Anglo-Catholic Theology (11 vols., 1841–54). Particular reprints are *Seventeen Sermons on the Nativity* (1898; repr., Grand Rapids, 1955) and *Two Sermons of the Resurrection* (1932). *Private Devotions* has had many editions, among them Newman's (1840); the standard one is by F. E. Brightman (1903). Andrewes has his place in general works on Church history (*supra*, V. 2). R. L. Ottley's *Lancelot Andrewes* (1894) remains valuable; there is a short account by F. Higham (1952), a full biography by P. A. Welsby (1958). *Bishop Lancelot Andrewes* (Chicago, 1955) by M. F. Reidy, S.J., is a study of his religious thought. His 'witty' preaching is discussed by W. F. Mitchell (*supra*, V. 2) and F. P. Wilson (*supra*, III. 1 and 2). Among essays are: W. H. Frere, *Lancelot Andrewes as a Representative of Anglican Principles* (1898); K. N. Colvile, *Fame's Twilight* (1923); T. S. Eliot, *For Lancelot Andrewes* (1928; title essay repr. in *Selected Essays*, 1932); and B. Blackstone, *Theology*, liii (1950).

ANONYMOUS

Dobsons Drie Bobbes (1607) has been edited by E. Schulz (*supra*, IV. 2) and E. A. Horsman (1955) and discussed also by F. P. Wilson (*supra*, IV. 2) and B. Colgrave (*Durham University Journal*, xii, 1951). Horsman also edited (1956) *The Pinder of Wakefield* (1632).

ANONYMOUS

The character book, *A Strange Metamorphosis of Man* (1634), has been edited by D. C. Allen (Johns Hopkins, 1949). The traditional attribution to the heavy-footed Brathwait (q.v.), doubted by M. Black and B. Boyce, is rejected by Allen.

ROBERT ARMIN, *c.* 1568–1615

Armin's *Works* were edited by Grosart (1880). Information about the actor-playwright is given in Sir E. K. Chambers's *Elizabethan Stage* (1923) and E. Nungezer's *Dictionary of Actors* (Yale, 1929), by A. K. Gray (*PMLA* xlii, 1927), F. P. Wilson (*HLQ* ii, 1938–9), and L. Hotson, *Shakespeare's Motley* (1952). The fullest account is C. S. Felver's monograph, *Robert Armin, Shakespeare's Fool* (*Kent State University Bulletin*, xlix, 1961).

ELIAS ASHMOLE, 1617–92

Ashmole's fame rests more solidly on the Oxford museum of natural history than on his antiquarian and occult labours, most of which belong to the Restoration. Two early books were *Theatrum Chemicum Britannicum*, which he edited in 1652 (see Nowak and other books on alchemy, *supra*, V. 3), and *The Way to Bliss* (1658). His *Diary* was edited in 1717 and 1774 and by R. T. Gunther (1927). Ashmole's translation of the *Prophecies of Merlin*, the first in English, was edited by C. B. Millican (*SP* xxviii, 1931). There are sketches of him by D. Wright (1924), A. L. Humphreys (1925; repr. from *Berks, Bucks & Oxon Archaeological Journal*, xxviii, 1924), and C. H. Josten (*The Royal Society*, ed. Hartley, *supra*, V. 3.) Josten's edition of the diaries, historical notes, and letters is forthcoming in 3 vols.

SIR ROBERT AYTOUN (AYTON), 1570?–1638

Most of Aytoun's verse was not printed in the seventeenth century. It was edited in the *Bannatyne Miscellany*, i (1827); by C. Roger in 1844 (rev. 1871); and also in *Transactions of the Royal Historical Society*, i (1875). Selections are in Eyre-Todd (*supra*, II. 2) and other anthologies. Aytoun's English and Latin verse is briefly discussed in J. Kinsley, *Scottish Poetry* (1955), and L. Bradner (*supra*, IV. 7). Some Scots versions are noted by M. P. McDiarmid, *NQ* iv (1957). C. B. Gullans (*MLR* lv, 1960) describes nine new poems, five English and four Latin. W. Roberts has a partial account of Aytoun in *MLR* liv (1959).

FRANCIS BACON, 1561–1626

Some of the writings published in Bacon's lifetime were: *Essayes. Religious Meditations. Places of perswasion and disswasion* (1597; enlarged 1612, 1625); *Certaine Considerations touching the better pacification and Edification of the Church of England* (1604); *The Twoo Bookes . . . Of the proficience and advancement of Learning, divine and humane* (1605); *De Sapientia Veterum* (1609; translated in 1619 as *The Wisedome of the Ancients*); *Instauratio Magna* (1620); *Historie of the Raigne of King Henry The Seventh* (1622); *De Dignitate & Augmentis Scientiarum* (1623), the enlarged Latin version of the *Advancement*; and *Apophthegmes* (1625). William Rawley edited an elegiac *Memoriae* (1626) and these volumes of remains: *Sylva Sylvarum or A Naturall History*, with *The New Atlantis* (1626/7); *Certaine Miscellany Works* (1629); *Operum Moralium et Civilium Tomus* (1638); *Resuscitatio* (1657; enlarged 1661, 1671); and *Opuscula Varia Posthuma* (1658). Some other early publications were: *A Collection of Some Principall Rules and Maximes of the*

Common Lawes (1630); *The Confession of Faith* (1641); *Remaines* (1648); *Scripta in Naturali et Universali Philosophia,* ed. I. Gruter (Amsterdam, 1653); *Baconiana,* ed. T. Tenison (1679); *Letters,* ed. R. Stephens (1702), *Letters and Remains* (1734).

A facsimile of the *Essayes* of 1597 was printed in *The Bibliographer,* ii (1903) and issued separately (New York, 1904).

The great modern edition of the works is by J. Spedding, R. L. Ellis, and D. D. Heath (7 vols., 1857–9), supplemented by Spedding's *The Letters and the Life* (7 vols., 1861–74), which includes the occasional writings. The whole edition is being reprinted.

Of volumes of selections the most substantial is that of J. M. Robertson (1905).

Bacon's poems, chiefly the *Translation Of Certaine Psalmes into English Verse* (1625), were edited by Grosart (*Miscellanies of The Fuller Worthies' Library,* i, 1870).

Arber's *Harmony of the Essays* (1871) facilitates comparison of the early editions. Some annotated editions of various works are: *Essays,* ed. W. A. Wright (1862 and rev. edns.), E. A. Abbott (2 vols., 1876), S. H. Reynolds (1890), M. A. Scott (New York, 1908); *Advancement of Learning,* ed. W. A. Wright (1868), F. G. Selby (2 vols., 1892–5); *Novum Organum,* ed. T. Fowler (1889); *Henry VII,* ed. J. R. Lumby (1876); *New Atlantis,* ed. G. C. M. Smith (1900), ed. A. B. Gough (1915).

Rawley's short *Life* (from *Resuscitatio,* 1657) is reprinted in Spedding's first volume of the *Works* and in Arber's *Harmony* (*supra*). Spedding's *Letters and Life,* which he himself abridged (*An Account of the Life and Times of Francis Bacon,* 1878), has been a main quarry for later biographers. Some modern biographies, semipopular or scholarly, are those of M. Sturt (1932), C. Williams (1933), A. W. Green (Syracuse University, 1948), J. G. Crowther (1960), and F. H. Anderson, *Francis Bacon: His Career and His Thought* (New York: University Publishers, 1962). R. C. Johnson (*HLQ* xxiii, 1959–60) traced the relations of Bacon and Lionel Cranfield.

Of early modern estimates of Bacon's philosophy the best known, Macaulay's essay (1837), is now of interest chiefly in regard to its author and his age. T. Fowler's *Bacon* (1881) and vol. ii of J. Nichol's *Francis Bacon: His Life and Philosophy* (1888–9) are still useful primers. Bacon's thought, in its scientific or its broader focus, has been examined from various standpoints by E. Wolff, *Francis Bacon und seine Quellen* (2 vols., Berlin, 1910–13);

A. Levi, *Il pensiero di Francesco Bacone* (Turin, 1925), perhaps the best analysis of his ideas in relation to their Renaissance background; C. D. Broad, *The Philosophy of Francis Bacon* (1926), a compendious review of the *Instauratio Magna*; F. H. Anderson, *The Philosophy of Francis Bacon* (University of Chicago, 1948), a full analysis of his ideas *per se*; B. Farrington, *Francis Bacon: Philosopher of Industrial Science* (1949) and an essay on the same theme in *Science, Medicine and History*, i (*supra*, V. 3); and Paolo Rossi, *Francesco Bacone: dalla magia alla scienza* (Bari, 1957), a selective but large study. Shorter discussions, focused on the *Novum Organum*, are those of A. N. Whitehead, *Science and the Modern World* (1925); A. E. Taylor, *Proceedings of the British Academy*, xii (1926); and C. J. Ducasse, in *Structure, Method, and Meaning*, ed. P. Henle et al. (New York, 1951), and also in *Theories of Scientific Method*, ed. E. H. Madden (University of Washington, 1960). The need for Bacon's defence of learning was shown by G. Bullough (*Seventeenth Century Studies Presented to Sir Herbert Grierson*, 1938). M. E. Prior discussed 'Bacon's Man of Science' in *JHI* xv (1954). Bacon's scientific influence has been treated from various angles by G. Sortais, *La Philosophie moderne depuis Bacon jusqu'à Leibniz* (2 vols., Paris, 1920–2), B. Willey and R. F. Jones (*supra*, III. 4), and many other writers, including H. Fisch and H. W. Jones (*MLQ* xii, 1951), R. C. Cochrane (*PQ* xxxvii, 1958), and H. Margenau et al. (*Proc. of the American Philosophical Society*, cv, 1961, no. 5). The *New Atlantis* figures in histories of utopian thought, notably Dupont (*supra*, IV. 4), and has been the special theme of E. D. Blodgett (*PMLA* xlvi, 1931), K. Sternberg (*Rivista di Filosofia*, xxv, 1934), and H. Minkowski (*Die Neu-Atlantis des Francis Bacon*, Jena, 1936). D. G. James's *The Dream of Learning* (1951) contrasts Baconian and Shakespearian 'knowledge'.

The essays of Bacon and Montaigne have often been contrasted, most solidly by J. Zeitlin (*JEGP* xxvii, 1928). R. S. Crane showed the relation of the *Essays* to Bacon's general programme (*Schelling Anniversary Papers*, New York, 1923); with that article belongs R. C. Cochrane's in *Studies in the Renaissance*, v (1958). The early influence of the *Essays* is treated by W. L. MacDonald and E. N. S. Thompson (*supra*, IV. 5). *De Sapientia Veterum* is analysed by C. W. Lemmi, *The Classic Deities in Bacon* (Johns Hopkins, 1933) and P. Rossi, *L'interpretazione baconiana delle favole antiche* (Milan, 1953; incorporated in Rossi's larger work cited above), and discussed in broad terms by E. Sewell, *The Orphic Voice* (1960).

Bacon's theory and practice of historical writing are discussed by F. J. C. Hearnshaw (*Contemporary Review*, cxxiii, 1923), in the *TLS*, 8 April 1926, most importantly by L. F. Dean (*ELH* viii, 1941), by T. Wheeler (*SP* liv, 1957), and, in relation to Guicciardini, by V. Luciani (*PMLA* lxii, 1947). The sources of *Henry VII* are set forth by W. Busch, *England under the Tudors. Vol. I. King Henry VII* (trans. 1895). A letter to Fulke Greville on methods of research, probably written by Bacon, is reprinted and discussed by V. E. Snow (*HLQ* xxiii, 1959–60).

Bacon's political outlook is assessed by such historians of political thought as G. P. Gooch and J. W. Allen (*supra*, V. 1), and more fully by W. Richter (*Bacon als Staatsdenker*, Berlin, 1928) and H. Bock (*Staat und Gesellschaft bei Francis Bacon*, Berlin, 1937). M. H. Carré has an essay in *History Today*, ix (1959). The fullest study of one affiliation is N. Orsini, *Bacone e Machiavelli* (Genoa, 1936), which is supplemented by V. Luciani (*Italica*, xxiv, 1947). P. H. Kocher has a suggestive article, 'Bacon and His Father' (*HLQ* xxi, 1958). Bacon's ecclesiastical policy is reviewed by W. K. Jordan, ii (*supra*, V. 2).

Bacon's legal theory and practice are treated in Holdsworth (*supra*, V. 1); Lord Birkenhead's *Fourteen English Judges* (1926); *Reports of Cases Decided by Francis Bacon . . . in the High Court of Chancery*, ed. J. Ritchie (1932); H. Cairns, *Legal Philosophy from Plato to Hegel* (Johns Hopkins, 1949); and P. H. Kocher, *JHI* xviii (1957).

Bacon's anti-Ciceronianism and theory of prose are discussed by M. W. Croll, K. R. Wallace, and W. S. Howell (*supra*, III. 2); his view of poetry and the imagination by Spingarn and in J. W. H. Atkins's 'Renascence' volume (*supra*, IV. 9), more fully by M. W. Bundy (*SP* xxvii, 1930), L. C. Knights (*Scrutiny*, xi, 1943; *Explorations*, 1946; queried, justly, by J. B. Leishman, *The Monarch of Wit*, 1951, and J. Andrews, *NQ* i, 1954), J. L. Harrison (*HLQ* xx, 1956–7), and L. Anceschi (*supra*, IV. 9). Bacon's poem, 'The World', is set in its background by Grierson (*MLR* vi, 1911; *Essays and Addresses*, 1940).

Bibliographical material on Bacon's works is scattered through Spedding's edition and summarized (along with criticism) in the *CBEL*. G. W. Steeves's *Francis Bacon* (1910), a small guide, is superseded by R. W. Gibson's *Francis Bacon: a*

Bibliography of his Works and of Baconiana to the year 1750 (1950; *Supplement*, 1959, issued by the author). References for philosophic criticism are supplied in books cited above and in V. 3. There is a pamphlet-essay with a bibliography by J. M. Patrick (British Council, 1961).

AUGUSTINE BAKER, 1575–1641

David (in religion Augustine) Baker, the chief Roman Catholic mystic of our period, is identified with the posthumous *Sancta Sophia. Or Directions for the Prayer of Contemplation, &c. Extracted out of more then XL. Treatises written by the late Ven. F. Augustin Baker . . . And Methodically digested by the R. F. Serenus Cressy* (2 vols., Douai, 1657). This was edited by J. N. Swceney (1876; rev. 1932 as *Holy Wisdom*; repr. 1950), who also wrote a *Life* (1861). Some other books by or about Baker are: volumes of selections, ed. B. Weld-Blundell (1907–33); *Confessions*, ed. J. McCann (1922); *The Cloud of Unknowing . . . With A Commentary on the Cloud by Father Augustine Baker*, ed. McCann (1924); *Memorials*, ed. McCann and H. Connolly (Catholic Record Society, xxxiii, 1933); the early lives by P. Salvin and S. Cressy, ed. McCann (1933), with a bibliography. There are essays by G. E. Hodgson (*supra*, V. 2), D. Knowles, *English Mystics* (1927; rewritten as *The English Mystical Tradition*, 1961), P. Cowley (*Theology*, xxxvii, 1938), P. Renaudin, *Quatre mystiques anglais* (Paris, 1945), and E. I. Watkin (*Great Catholics*, ed. C. Williamson, 1941; *Poets and Mystics*, 1953).

JOHN BARCLAY, 1582–1621

Barclay's chief works were: *Euphormionis Lusinini Satyricon* (Paris, 1603–7; the first part tr. by P. Turner, 1954) and *Euphormionis Satyrici Apologia pro se* (Paris, 1610); *Icon Animorum* (1614; tr. T. May, as *The Mirrour of Mindes*, 1631); *Poemata* (1615); and *Argenis* (Paris, 1621; London, 1622), tr. K. Long (1625), tr. Sir R. Le Grys (1628), with the verse rendered by May. Long was slightly revised by Clara Reeve (*The Phoenix*, 4 vols., 1772). The European fame of *Argenis* in its own century, long eclipsed among English-speaking readers (as Coleridge lamented), has inspired many monographs by continental scholars, such as A. Collignon (Paris, 1902), who wrote also *Notes sur l' "Euphormion"* (Nancy, 1901); K. F. Schmid (Berlin, 1904); P. Kettelhoit (Bottrop i. W., 1934); and L. Bardino

(Palermo, 1939). Among the few English accounts are those of E. Bensly (*CHEL* iv); G. Waterhouse (*supra*, IV. 7); K. N. Colvile, *Fame's Twilight* (1923); E. A. Baker, iii (*supra*, IV. 4); C. Smedley, London *Bookman*, lxxxi (1931–2); and, on the novel's influence, G. Langford, *University of Texas Studies in English* (1947).

WILLIAM BASSE, 1580?–1654

The *Poetical Works* were edited by R. W. Bond (1893). A five-page 'Abridgment' of E. V. Humphrey's *Study of William Basse* was issued by New York University (1953). A popular poem, 'A Memento for Mortalitie', in the popular *A Helpe to Discourse* . . . *By W.B. & E.P.* (1619) was, in shortened form, assigned to Francis Beaumont (*Poems*, 1653) under the title 'On the Tombes in Westminster'. N. Ault (*TLS*, 12 January 1933) assigned it to Basse. Miss Humphrey agrees with Bond that the *Helpe* was not Basse's work.

RICHARD BAXTER, 1615–91

Although some of Baxter's most famous works are *The Saints' Everlasting Rest* (1650; ed. W. Young, 1907), *A Call to the Unconverted* (1657), and the *Holy Commonwealth* (1659), he belongs rather to the next age and the next volume. For the general reader, at least, he lives in the memoir of his wife, the *Breviate* of 1681 (ed. J. T. Wilkinson, 1928), and the autobiography which, abridged from the *Reliquiæ Baxterianæ* (1696), was edited by J. M. Lloyd Thomas (1925; Everyman's Library, 1931). *The Reformed Pastor* (1656) was edited by Wilkinson (1939). The standard biography is by F. J. Powicke (2 vols., 1924–7). Two recent books are Hugh Martin, *Puritanism and Richard Baxter* (1954) and R. Schlatter, *Richard Baxter and Puritan Politics* (Rutgers, 1957). There are bibliographies by Grosart (1868) and A. G. Matthews (1932) and a checklist in Wing (*supra*, I).

LEWIS BAYLY, 1565–1631

The earliest extant edition of the immensely popular *Practise of Pietie* is the third (1613); it had been entered in January 1612. It was edited by G. Webster (1842). J. E. Bailey described the author and the book in *Papers of the Manchester Literary Club*, ix (1883). C. J. Stranks has a chapter in *Anglican Devotion* (1961).

FRANCIS BEAUMONT, 1584?–1616

Under Beaumont's name were published *Poems* (1640; enlarged, 1653), but a number were not his (cf. Basse, *supra*). *Poems* were reprinted in Chalmers's *English Poets*, vi, and in *Works of Beaumont and Fletcher*, ed. Dyce, xi (1846). *Salmacis and Hermaphroditus* (1602), attributed to Beaumont in 1640 and 1653 by the unreliable bookseller, was edited for the *Shakespeare Society's Papers*, iii (1847), and by G. Jones (1951); it is discussed by D. Bush (*supra*, IV. 7) and H. Smith (*supra*, III. 3). E. H. Fellowes edited *Songs & Lyrics, from the Plays . . . With Contemporary Musical Settings* (1928). Beaumont's mock 'Grammer Lecture', given at the Inner Temple revels (1601–5?), was edited by M. Eccles (*RES* xvi, 1940). Apart from studies of the dramatic partnership, there is C. M. Gayley's *Beaumont, the Dramatist* (New York, 1914). I. A. Shapiro's account of the 'Mermaid Club' led to debate with P. Simpson over Beaumont's verse-letter to Jonson (*MLR* xlv, xlvi, 1950–1). S. A. Tannenbaum's *Concise Bibliography* (New York, 1938) had a *Supplement* (1946).

SIR JOHN BEAUMONT, 1583?–1627

Much of Beaumont's verse, collected by his son (*Bosworth-field*, 1629), was reprinted in Chalmers's *English Poets*, vi, and edited, with additions, by Grosart (1869). Other works are the anonymous *Metamorphosis of Tabacco* (1602; repr. in Collier, *Illustrations of Early English Popular Literature*, i, 1863); the unprinted *Theatre of Apollo*, ed. Sir W. W. Greg (1926). The manuscript of the supposedly lost *Crowne of Thornes*, Beaumont's major work, was identified in the British Museum by B. H. Newdigate (*RES* xviii, 1942) and was given critical analysis by R. C. Wallerstein (*JEGP* liii, 1954). In addition to the standard histories, Beaumont is discussed by G. Williamson (*MP* xxxiii, 1935–6; *supra*, III. 1) and R. L. Sharp (*supra*, III. 3). M. Eccles gave a full biography in *HLQ* v (1941–2).

JOSEPH BEAUMONT, 1616–99

Psyche: or Loves Mysterie In XX. Canto's: Displaying the Intercourse Betwixt Christ, and the Soule (1648) had a 'second' edition (1702) which contained four new cantos and had received 'Corrections throughout'. This edition, with some minor poems, was edited by Grosart (2 vols., 1880). E. Robinson edited the *Minor Poems* (1914). Beaumont is discussed by his editors, by H. E. Cory (cited under P. Fletcher, *infra*), P. H. Osmond (*Mystical Poets of the English Church*, 1919), Austin Warren, *Richard Crashaw* (*infra*), R. C. Wallerstein and B. O. Kurth (*supra*, III. 3). *Memoirs* of Beaumont by John Gee (d. 1772) were edited from a manuscript by T. A. Walker (1934).

THOMAS BEEDOME, 1613–40/1?

Poems Divine, And Humane, edited by Henry Glapthorne (1641), has been edited with apparatus by M. Pagnini (Pisa, 1954), who urges Beedome's poetical claims. F. Meynell edited *Select Poems* (1928). C. L. Shaver gave some new biographical facts in *MLN* liii (1938).

EDWARD BENLOWES, 1602–76

Theophila (1652) was a handsome book which reflected its author's interest in the arts. The Harvard copy has an inscription from him to Mildmay Fane (q.v.). *Theophila* is reprinted in Saintsbury, i (1905). The standard biographical and critical work is H. Jenkins's *Edward Benlowes* (1952). There is criticism also by G. Williamson and R. L. Sharp (*supra*, III. 3), E. Roditi (*Comparative Literature*, ii, 1950), and C. Hill (*Essays in Criticism*, iii, 1953). To Benlowes's many borrowings from other poets, assembled by Jenkins, have been added those from the Polish Latinist Casimir (M.-S. Røstvig, *HLQ* xviii, 1954–5 and *supra*, III. 3) and George Herbert (E. Duncan-Jones, *RES* vi, 1955). Benlowes was a main model for Butler's character of 'A Small Poet'.

RICHARD BERNARD 1568–1642

Bernard's best-known book, *The Isle of Man: or, The Legall Proceeding in Man-shire against Sinne* (1626), is described, with other works, in W. Haller's *Rise of Puritanism* (1938), is studied most fully in Max Müller's *Richard Bernard: The Isle of Man* (Markneukirchen, 1933), and has a place in E. M. W. Tillyard's *The English Epic* (1954). J. I. Dredge compiled a bibliography, *The Writings of Richard Bernard* (priv. pr., 1890); also W. T. Freemantle in his *Bibliography of Sheffield and Vicinity, Section 1, To the end of 1700* (1911).

SIR HENRY BLOUNT, 1602–82

A Voyage into the Levant . . . With particular observations concerning the moderne condition of the Turkes, and other people under that Empire (1636 and later edns.) was reprinted in the collections of Churchill and Osborne and in the 10th volume of Pinkerton (supra, V. 4). Blount is discussed in the books (supra, V. 4) by S. C. Chew (1937), B. Penrose (1942), and T. Spencer (1954).

SIR THOMAS BODLEY, 1545–1613

The short Life, written in 1609 (printed in 1647), was included in Hearne's Reliquiæ Bodleianæ (1703), the Harleian Miscellany, ed. Park, iv (1809), and Trecentale Bodleianum (1913), and was reprinted by itself (1894; Chicago, 1906). Bodley's letters to Thomas James, the first Keeper, were mostly printed by Hearne and were edited (1926) by G. W. Wheeler, who also edited Letters of Sir Thomas Bodley to the University of Oxford, 1598–1611 (1927). H. R. Trevor-Roper edited five letters (Bodleian Library Record, ii, 1946). Bodley's draft of the statutes is in Hearne, the 1906 edition of the Life, and Trecentale Bodleianum. Pietas Oxoniensis (1902) contains much matter about Bodley and the Library. There are essays by J. D. Doty (Faculty Papers of Union College, i, 1930) and F. S. Boas (Essays by Divers Hands, xxiii, 1947; repr. in Queen Elizabeth in Drama and Related Studies, 1950). A letter of advice for the young traveller (Reliquiæ, ccxxxii) may have been written by Fulke Greville rather than Bodley (H. N. Maclean, Bodleian Library Record, vi, 1960). Other references for Bodley are given above in V. 6.

EDMUND BOLTON, 1575?–post 1634

Hypercritica; or A Rule of Judgment for writing, or reading our History's, apparently completed in or after 1621, was first printed in 1722 and is reprinted in Spingarn (supra, IV. 9). It is discussed in J. W. H. Atkins's first volume (supra, IV. 9). Bolton's proposal to King James for an English academy is described by E. M. Portal (Proceedings of the British Academy, vii, 1915–16), by Joan Evans (supra, IV. 6), and studied fully, with transcripts of all the documents, in an unpublished Harvard thesis by R. L. Dowling (2 vols., 1954).

WILLIAM BOSWORTH, 1607–50?

The Chast and Lost Lovers (1651; repr. in Saintsbury, ii, 1906) is discussed by D. Bush (*supra*, IV. 7) and A. I. T. Higgins (*supra*, III. 3).

ROGER BOYLE, BARON BROGHILL AND EARL OF ORRERY, 1621-79

Parthenissa was published in sections in 1651, 1654-6, and 1669, and 'Compleat' in 1676. C. W. Miller unravelled bibliographical tangles in *Studies in Bibliography* (University of Virginia), ii (1949-50). The romance is set in its background by E. A. Baker and Haviland (*supra*, IV. 4). Boyle's *Dramatic Works* were edited, with a full biographical and critical introduction, by W. S. Clark (2 vols., Harvard, 1937).

JOHN BRAMHALL, 1594-1663

The collected *Works* (Dublin, 1676) were reprinted in 5 vols. (1842-5). Jeremy Taylor's funeral sermon is of course in editions of Taylor. The fullest account is W. J. S. Simpson's *Archbishop Bramhall* (1927). There are essays by W. E. Collins, *Typical English Churchmen*, ed. Collins (1902); T. S. Eliot, *For Lancelot Andrewes* (1928; repr. in *Selected Essays*, 1932); C. Nye, *Church Quarterly Review*, cxvii (1933-4); and M. Taube's acute analysis of Bramhall's controversy with Hobbes in his *Causation, Freedom and Determinism* (1936), a topic treated also by J. Bowle (under Hobbes, *infra*). Other sides are discussed by W. K. Jordan, iv, and R. S. Bosher (*supra*, V. 2) and by F. R. Bolton (under Jeremy Taylor).

RICHARD BRATHWAIT, 1588?-1673

Only a few items from Brathwait's large and uncertain canon have been reprinted: *Barnabæ Itinerarium* (*c.* 1636, completed 1638), reprinted often in the eighteenth century, three times by J. Haslewood (1805, 1818, 1820; rev. by W. C. Hazlitt,1876), and again in 1932; *Essaies upon the Five Senses* (1620), ed. Sir E. Brydges, *Archaica*, ii (1815); *Whimzies: Or, A New Cast of Characters* (1631), ed. J. O. Halliwell[-Phillipps] (1859); *Natures Embassie* (1621) and *A Strappado for the Divell* (1615), ed. J. W. Ebsworth (1877, 1878); and *The Law of Drinking* (1617), ed. W. B. Hooker (New Haven, 1903). The one full study is M. W. Black, *Richard Brathwait* (Philadelphia, 1928). The *English Gentleman* (1630) and *English Gentlewoman* (1631) are discussed by J. E. Mason (*supra*, V. 6) and W. E. Houghton (under Fuller), Brathwait's characters by B. Boyce (*supra*, IV. 5), who has explained the *roman à clef* of 1659, *Panthalia* (*JEGP* lvii, 1958).

NICHOLAS BRETON, 1555?–c. 1626?

Grosart's *Works in Verse and Prose* (2 vols., 1879) is comprehensive but not complete. Breton's verse has appeared in many anthologies, especially since Bullen's *Poems, Chiefly Lyrical, from Romances and Prose-Tracts of the Elizabethan Age* (1890). Jean Robertson edited *Poems by Nicholas Breton* (*not hitherto reprinted*) in 1952, with a full study of the canon. Some reprinted works in verse and prose are: *The Passionate Shepheard* (1604), ed. F. Ouvry (1877); *Characters upon Essaies* (1615) and *The Good and the Badde* (1616), in H. Morley (*supra*, IV. 5); *Melancholike humours* (1600), ed. G. B. Harrison (1929); selected prose, *A Mad World My Masters*, ed. U. Kentish-Wright (2 vols., 1929); *Grimellos Fortunes* (1604) and *An Olde Mans Lesson* (1605), ed. E. G. Morice (1936); *The Court and Country* (1618), in Dunham and Pargellis (*supra*, II. 1); *The Whipper Pamphlets* (1601), ed. A. Davenport (1951). *Fantasticks* (1604?) has had a number of reprints.

There are appreciations by Bullen (*Elizabethans*, 1924) and E. Blunden (*TLS*, 22 August 1929; *Votive Tablets*, 1931). Comprehensive studies are E. M. Tappan, on the verse (*PMLA* xiii, 1898), N. E. Monroe, *Nicholas Breton as a Pamphleteer* (University of Pennsylvania, 1929), and F. H. McCloskey's unpublished thesis (Harvard *Summaries of Theses 1929*). Breton's essays, characters, letters, and fiction are noticed in the general accounts of those genres. The religious verse is discussed by J. B. Collins (*supra*, V. 2). There is a *Concise Bibliography* by S. A. and D. R. Tannenbaum (New York, 1947).

THOMAS BREWER, *fl.* 1624–36

The Life and Death of the merry Devill of Edmonton (entered 1608), by 'T.B.', was reprinted (1819) from the earliest extant edition (1631) and is included in W. A. Abrams's edition of the play, *The Merry Devill of Edmonton* (Duke University, 1942). While Abrams took 'T. B.' to be Anthony (Tony) Brewer, Sir W. W. Greg, in a review (*Library*, xxv, 1944–5), supported the authorship of Thomas Brewer; Greg also opposed the idea that the chap-book was based on the play, thinking that both drew on a body of tradition.

JOHN BRINSLEY, 1564/5?–1653/63?

Ludus Literarius (1612) was edited from the 1627 edition by E. T. Campagnac (1917), *A Consolation for our Grammar Schooles* (1622) by T. C. Pollock (Scholars' Facsimiles & Reprints, 1943). Brinsley's educational ideas are discussed in F. Watson's *English Grammar Schools to 1660* (1908), by G. W. McClelland in the *Schelling Anniversary Papers* (New York, 1923), and incidentally by W. F. Mitchell (*supra*, V. 2).

ALEXANDER BROME, 1620–66

Brome wrote a comedy, *The Cunning Lovers* (1654); *Songs and Other Poems* (1661; enlarged 1664, 1668; repr. in Chalmers's *English Poets*, vi; a selection, *Songs and Poems*, Louisville, 1924); and much of *The Poems of Horace . . . by Several Persons* (1666). Contributors to the *Horace* were identified by H. F. Brooks, *NQ* clxxiv (1938), and W. J. Cameron, ibid. iv (1957). A full study is J. L. Brooks, *Alexander Brome: Life and Works* (Harvard *Summaries of Theses 1934*).

SIR THOMAS BROWNE, 1605–82

The two unauthorized editions of *Religio Medici* (1642; see E. Cook, *Harvard Library Bulletin*, ii, 1948) were followed by an authorized, much-corrected, but imperfect edition (1643), and the nine later editions in the author's lifetime (the last in 1682) show progressive deterioration in the text. *Pseudodoxia Epidemica* (1646) reached its 6th edition, the last 'Corrected and Enlarged by the Author', in 1672. In 1658 appeared *Hydriotaphia, Urne-Buriall, Or, A Discourse of the Sepulchrall Urnes lately found in Norfolk. Together with The Garden of Cyrus.* After Browne's death came *Certain Miscellany Tracts*, ed. T. Tenison (1683); the folio *Works* (1686); *A Letter to a Friend, Upon occasion of the Death of his Intimate Friend* (1690); *Posthumous Works* (1712), with a *Life* and J. Whitefoot's personal portrait; and *Christian Morals*, ed. J. Jeffery (1716). The second edition of this last (1756; ed. Sir S. C. Roberts, 1927) contained the *Life* by Dr. Johnson.

There are facsimiles of the first 1642 *Religio* (ed. W. A. Greenhill, 1883) and of *Hydriotaphia* and *The Garden of Cyrus* (Noel Douglas Replicas, 1927).

S. Wilkin's pioneer edition of the works and letters (4 vols., 1835–6; Bohn ed., 3 vols., 1852) remains valuable. A commentary like Wilkin's was not attempted in C. Sayle's edition (3 vols., 1904–7) or in the standard edition of the works and correspondence by Sir G. Keynes (6 vols., 1928–31; vols. v and vi repr. with corrections, 1946; new edition forthcoming). L. C. Martin is preparing an edition with a commentary. Greenhill produced helpful annotated editions of the *Religio* (his text of this was based on the defective 1682 edition), *Christian Morals*, and *Letter to a Friend* (1881), and *Hydriotaphia* and *The Garden of Cyrus* (1896). J. Carter's edition (1958) of the two last-named works embodies autograph corrections by Browne and is now the standard text. The first thorough collation of the 8 MSS. and the printed editions of the *Religio* by J.-J. Denonain has greatly improved the accepted text, though his own (1953)—which is quoted in this book—is not quite a final one, nor his popular edition of 1955 (J. Sparrow, *RES* viii, 1957). Denonain has also edited the Pembroke College manuscript as *Une Version primitive de Religio Medici* (Paris, 1958). The *Religio* has been edited and translated with an elaborate commentary by V. Sanna, *Annali delle Facoltà di Lettere-Filosofia e Magistero dell' Università di Cagliari*, xxvi (1958).

Gosse's biography (1905) has been superseded by O. Leroy, *Le Chevalier Thomas Browne (1605–82), médecin, styliste & métaphysicien* (Paris, 1931), J. S. Finch, *Sir Thomas Browne: A Doctor's Life of Science & Faith* (New York, 1950), and F. L. Huntley, whose *Sir Thomas Browne* (University of Michigan, 1962) corrects some biographical traditions. Fresh material on Browne as 'orphan' and his stepfather is supplied by N. J. Endicott (*UTQ* xxx, 1961).

Criticism began with Sir Kenelm Digby's *Observations upon Religio Medici* (1643; repr. by Wilkin and in *Religio*, Oxford, 1909) and Alexander Ross's *Medicus Medicatus* (1645) and *Arcana Microcosmi* (1651); Joan Bennett has comments on their views in *Studies in the Renaissance*, iii (1956). Coleridge's remarks are in Raysor and R. F. Brinkley. Some of the older essays are by Sir Leslie Stephen (*Hours in a Library, Second Series*, 1876), W. Pater (*Appreciations*, 1889), E. Dowden (*Puritan and Anglican*, 1900), P. E. More (*Shelburne Essays, Sixth Series*, 1909), and L. Strachey (*Books and Characters*, 1922). Modern general criticism includes Leroy and Huntley (*supra*), J. Loiseau (*Revue Anglo-Américaine*, x, 1933), F. P. Wilson (*supra*, III. 2), and P. Green's pamphlet-essay with a bibliography (British Council, 1959). The best analyses of Browne's religious thought are in B. Willey (*supra*, III. 4) and W. P. Dunn, *Sir Thomas Browne* (University of Minnesota, 1950), and Huntley (*supra* and *infra*). Other discussions are in R. Sencourt, *Outflying Philosophy* (Hildesheim, 1924), D. K. Ziegler, *In Divided and Distinguished Worlds* (Harvard, 1943), a chapter in M. L. Wiley, *The Subtle Knot* (1952), and F. L. Huntley (*JHI* xiv, 1953). Some essays on *Hydriotaphia* and/or *The Garden of Cyrus* are: J. M. Cline, *University of California Publications in English*, viii (1940); J. S. Finch, *SP* xxxvii (1940), *PMLA* lv (1940); G. K. Chalmers, *Virginia Quarterly Review*, xxvi (1950); M. A. Heideman, *UTQ* xix (1949–50); and, most important, F. L. Huntley, *SP* liii (1956). There are articles by R. R. Cawley on Browne's reading (*PMLA* xlviii, 1933), by Huntley on the occasion and date (1656?) of *A Letter to a Friend* (*MP* xlviii, 1950–1; cf. *RES* ii, 1951), and on the publication and reception of *Religio Medici* (*Library Quarterly*, xxv, 1955). Discussions of Browne the scientist by A. C. Howell (*SP* xxii, 1925), A. Thaler (*SP* xxviii, 1931), and G. K. Chalmers (*Osiris*, ii, 1936; &c.) are taken account of in the fullest study, *Science and Imagination in Sir Thomas Browne* (Columbia, 1949) by E. S. Merton, who had further scientific studies in *Osiris*, ix and x (1950–2), *Isis*, xlvii (1956), &c.

Browne's style is discussed by many of the critics already named and in Saintsbury's *History of English Prose Rhythm* (1912). More concentrated analyses, general or technical, are those of B. Anderton, *Sketches from a Library Window* (1922); N. R. Tempest, *RES* iii (1927); the last article in Croll's series (*supra*, III. 2); E. L. Parker, *PMLA* liii (1938); D. Bischoff, *Sir Thomas Browne (1605–1682) als Stilkünstler* (Heidelberg, 1943); A. Warren, *Kenyon Review*, xiii (1951); G. Williamson (*supra*, III. 2); and M. F. Moloney, *JEGP* lviii (1959).

Sir G. Keynes compiled a *Bibliography* (1924), Leroy *A French Bibliography* (1931).

WILLIAM BROWNE, 1590/1?–1643/5?

The first book of *Britannia's Pastorals* appeared in 1613, the second, with a second edition of the first, in 1616, and the two books again in 1625; the unfinished third book was first printed for the Percy Society (xxx, 1852). *The Shepheards Pipe* (1614) included seven eclogues by Browne and four by C. Brooke, Wither, and Davies of Hereford. The *Inner Temple Masque*, first printed in the *Works* of 1772, was edited by G. Jones (1954). Modern editions of the works are those of W. C. Hazlitt (2 vols., 1868–9) and G. Goodwin (Muses' Library, 2 vols., 1894). It is uncertain whether the poet was the William Browne whose translation of *Polexandre* appeared in 1647.

The fullest studies are F. W. Moorman's *William Browne* (Strassburg, 1897) and E. S. Briggs's unpublished thesis (Harvard, 1956). There are shorter discussions in the books on pastoral literature (*supra*, III. 3) by Greg and Genouy, and by J. Grundy (*RES* iv, 1953 and also iii, 1952). More special discussions are in H. Ashton (*supra*, IV. 7) and L. Jonas (*supra*, IV. 9). The epitaph on the Countess of Pembroke has been treated by Philip Sidney (1907), Grierson (*MLR* vi, 1911), A. Holaday (*PQ* xxviii, 1949), and J. Grundy (*NQ* vii, 1960). G. Tillotson had bibliographical studies in *RES* vi and vii (1930–1) and the *Library*, xi (1930–1). Milton's annotations in his copy of *Britannia's Pastorals* are printed in the Columbia edition, xviii; some parallels with Milton were recorded by H. C. H. Candy (*NQ* clviii, 1930). Browne's influence on Keats was discussed by J. Grundy (*RES* vi, 1955).

ROBERT BURTON, 1577–1640

The Anatomy of Melancholy (Oxford, 1621) was more or less enlarged and revised in 1624, 1628, 1632, and 1638. The posthumous 6th edition (1651) included the author's few last revisions; he never corrected a number of slips and multiplying misprints. The 7th and 8th editions appeared in 1660 and 1676, the 9th not until 1800; then came a rapid succession of editions and reprints. In what has been the standard modern edition (3 vols., 1893, and various reprints), A. R. Shilleto did valuable pioneer work in tracing Burton's sources; he unfortunately based his text on the 7th edition, and numerous errors were pointed out by E. Bensly (*NQ*, Ser. 9, vols. xi and xii, Ser. 10, vols. i–vii and x). The Nonesuch edition (2 vols., 1925) is not complete or accurate. The two-volume edition of Floyd Dell and P. Jordan-Smith (New York, 1927; reissued in 1 vol., 1929) translates the Latin quotations and has a new index. The Everyman edition, ed. Holbrook Jackson (3 vols., 1932), is based on the 6th edition, collated with the 5th, and takes account of Shilleto and Bensly.

There is no extant manuscript of the *Anatomy* but there are two manuscripts, both now in America, of Burton's Latin play, *Philosophaster*. The play was first printed, along with Burton's Latin verses from Oxford anthologies, by W. E. Buckley (Roxburghe Club, 1862) and was re-edited, with a translation, by P. Jordan-Smith (Stanford, 1931).

Some general appreciations are: A. W. Fox, *A Book of Bachelors* (1899); C. Whibley, *Literary Portraits* (1904); E. Bensly, *CHEL* iv; Sir W. Osler, *Yale Review*, N.S., iii (1913–14), and *OBS* i, part iii, 1925 (1926); J. M. Murry, *TLS*, 28 April 1921; repr. in *Countries of the Mind* (1922); some pages in H. Craig (*supra*, III. 4); S. Prawer, *Cambridge Journal*, i (1947–8); and F. P. Wilson (*supra*, III. 2). The most fully rounded 'preface' is *Sanity in Bedlam* (Michigan State University, 1959) by L. Babb, the expert author of *The Elizabethan Malady* (*supra*, III. 4), in which Burton is prominent.

The first special study was J. Ferriar's *Illustrations of Sterne* (1798). Some modern ones are: B. Lake, *General Introduction to Charles Lamb* (Leipzig, 1903); H. J. Gottlieb's pamphlet, *Robert Burton's Knowledge of English Poetry* (New York University, 1937); S. B. Ewing, *Burtonian Melancholy in the Plays of John Ford* (Princeton, 1940); V. Dupont (*supra*, IV. 4); B. Evans, *The Psychiatry of Robert Burton* (Columbia, 1944); a chapter in J. W. Allen (*supra*, V. 1); J. M. Patrick, on Burton's 'Utopianism', *PQ* xxvii (1948); W. R. Mueller, articles in the *HLQ* xi (1947–8), *PMLA* lxiv (1949), and *MLQ* xv (1954), and *The Anatomy of Robert Burton's England* (University of California, 1952), the fullest study of his social and religious ideas; J. B. Bamborough (*supra*, III. 4); R. M. Browne (*MLQ* xiii, 1952) on Burton's attitudes, in his successive editions, towards the new cosmology. His style is discussed, e.g. by G. Williamson (*supra*, III. 2), Mueller (*Anatomy*), and L. Goldstein (*Journal of the Rutgers University Library*, xxi, 1958).

E. G. Duff had a bibliographical study of the 5th edition in the *Library*, iv (1923–4). The *OBS* volume already cited contains bibliographical pieces by Duff and Bensly, &c., including a list of the books Burton left to the Bodleian and Christ Church libraries. Much material about sources and editions is collected by P. Jordan-Smith, *Bibliographia Burtoniana* (Stanford, 1931), and some by him and M. Mulhauser in *Burton's Anatomy of Melancholy and Burtoniana* (1959).

WILLIAM BURTON, 1575–1645

Burton's translation of Achilles Tatius, *The Most Delectable and Plesant Historye of Clitophon and Leucippe* (1597), was handsomely edited by Sir S. Gaselee and H. F. B. Brett-Smith (1923). His *Description of Leicester Shire* appeared in 1622.

WILLIAM CAMDEN, 1551–1623

Camden's long-lived Greek grammar appeared in 1595. *Britannia . . . Chorographica descriptio* (1586) was enlarged in later editions and translated by Holland (1610); it was translated and enlarged by E. Gibson (1695) and had further editions. *Remaines of A Greater Worke, Concerning Britaine* (1605 and enlarged editions) was last reprinted in 1870. *Annales Rerum Anglicarum, et Hibernicarum, regnante Elizabetha, ad annum salutis M.D.LXXXIX* (1615) was revised and issued with a second part covering 1589–1603 (1625). The whole work was edited by T. Hearne (3 vols., 1717). The first three books (1558–88) were translated by A. Darcie, from a French version of Camden's Latin, as *Annales. The True and Royall History of the famous Empresse Elizabeth* (1625); the fourth book was done by T. Browne (1629). R. Norton made a complete translation (1630); selections are in Sir H. Newbolt's *Noble English*, ii (1925). A translation of the *Annales* and of Camden's notes on James's reign is in W. Kennett's *Complete History of England* (1706), ii. Camden's *Epistolæ* were printed in 1691. A manuscript 'Discourse Concerning the Prerogative of the Crown', written probably *c.* 1615–16, was first printed by F. S. Fussner, *Proceedings of the American Philosophical Society*, ci (1957). Camden is discussed in L. B. Wright (*supra*, IV. 2), Sir T. D. Kendrick (*supra*, IV. 6), and S. Kliger (*supra*, V. 1), and is the subject of papers by Sir M. Powicke (*ESEA 1948*) and S. Piggott, *Proceedings of the British Academy*, xxxvii (1951). R. B. Gottfried has studied the Irish side of Camden's scholarship (*ELH* x, 1943). H. S. Jones's 'The Foundation and History of the Camden Chair' (*Oxoniensia*, viii-ix, 1943–4) is of interest.

THOMAS CAMPION, 1567–1620

Campion's verse remained almost unknown after his own time until it was revived by Arber (*English Garner*, iii, 1880) and especially by Bullen in his anthologies of lyrics (*supra*, II. 2) and his editions of Campion (1889, 1903). P. Vivian edited the English poems and masques (Muses' Library, 1907) and the standard edition of the complete works (1909); the former edition is being revised by C. Ing. The *Observations* (1602) are in Bullen, in Vivian's large edition, and, with Daniel's reply, in G. G. Smith's *Elizabethan Critical Essays* (1904) and G. B. Harrison's Bodley Head Quartos (1925). Campion's music was edited by E. H. Fellowes in *The English School of Lutenist Song Writers* (1920 ff.). Apart from the Latin poems, the only book of Campion's reprinted in his own century was the treatise on counterpoint, which was included in the many editions of J. Playford's *Brief Introduction to the Skill of Musick* (1655 ff.).

The fullest critical study is M. M. Kastendieck's *England's Musical Poet: Thomas Campion* (Columbia, 1938). R. W. Short analysed Campion's metrics (*PMLA* lix, 1944). Later discussions are those of B. Pattison, C. Ing, H. Smith, W. Mellers (*supra*, III. 3), C. S. Lewis, and W. R. Davis (*MLQ* xxii, 1961). Among many studies of Elizabethan classical metres, G. D. Willcock's (*MLR* xxix, 1934) and G. L. Hendrickson's (*PQ* xxviii, 1949) are useful for the Campion–Daniel debate, which is treated briefly by Lewis and in J. W. H. Atkins's earlier volume (*supra*, IV. 9). Campion figures in books by J. A. S. McPeek and L. Bradner (*supra*, IV. 7). Rosseter's authorship of the second part of *A Booke of Ayres* (1601) was supported by R. W. Berringer (*PMLA* lviii, 1943). The use of Propertius in 'Lesbia' was noted by J. V. Cunningham (*PQ* xxxi, 1952); the record of Campion's medical degree by I. A. Shapiro (*NQ* cxcvii, 1952).

RICHARD CAREW, 1555–1620

Godfrey of Bulloigne (1594; ed. Grosart, 1881), Carew's version of Tasso's first five books, is examined by R. E. N. Dodge and W. L. Bullock (*PMLA* xliv and xlv, 1929–30). A translation from Spanish, by way of Italian, was *Examen de Ingenios. The Examination of mens Wits . . . By John Huarte* (1594; ed. C. Rogers, Scholars' Facsimiles & Reprints, 1959). Carew's *Excellencie of the English tongue* (1595–6?), an avowed imitation of tracts by H. Estienne and others, was printed in the 1614 edition of Camden's *Remaines* (repr. in G. G. Smith, *Elizabethan Critical Essays*, 1904).

The *Survey of Cornwall* (1602) has been edited, shorn of dead wood, by F. E. Halliday (1953), who includes parts of other works and gives an account of Carew. A. L. Rowse has a sketch of him in *Tudor Cornwall* (1941).

THOMAS CAREW, 1594/5–1640

The *Poems*, with the masque *Cælum Britanicum* (pr. 1634), were published in 1640 (enlarged 1642, 1651). The standard edition is that of R. Dunlap (1949). Handy small editions are those of A. Vincent (Muses' Library, 1899) and R. G. Howarth (*supra*, II. 2). Carew has had his place in anthologies from 1640 onward. He has received increasing recognition and increasingly precise criticism in Grierson, *Metaphysical Lyrics & Poems* (1921); G. Williamson, *The Donne Tradition* (1930); F. R. Leavis, *Revaluation* (1936); R. A. Blanshard's articles in *Trans. Wisconsin Academy of Sciences, Arts and Letters*, xliii (1954), *SP* lii (1955), and *Boston University Studies in English*, iii (1957); and E. I. Selig, *The Flourishing Wreath* (Yale, 1957). F. G. Schoff (*Discourse*, i, 1958) sees Carew as a 'son of Spenser'. One side of Carew is illustrated in K. A. McEuen (*supra*, IV. 7).

NATHANAEL CARPENTER, 1589–1628?

Carpenter's books were *Philosophia Libera* (Frankfort, 1621; Oxford, 1622; 2nd English ed., 1636) and *Geography Delineated* (1625; 2nd ed., 1635). The chief discussions are by F. Watson, *Beginnings of the Teaching of Modern Subjects* (1909); E. G. R. Taylor (*supra*, V. 4); W. S. Howell, 'Nathaniel Carpenter's Place in the Controversy between Dialectic and Rhetoric', *Speech Monographs*, i (1934); R. F. Jones (*supra*, III. 4); F. R. Johnson, *Astronomical Thought* (*supra*, V. 3); and G. McColley, *Popular Astronomy*, xlviii (1940).

WILLIAM CARTWRIGHT, 1611–43

In 1651 Moseley printed *Comedies, Tragi-Comedies. With other Poems . . . The Ayres and Songs set by Mr Henry Lawes*, with a great array of commendatory verses (omitted in Evans's edition, *infra*). The poems were edited by R. C. Goffin (1918). The standard edition is *The Plays and Poems of William Cartwright* (University of Wisconsin, 1951) by G. B. Evans, whose elaborate commentary gathers up previous discussions.

ELIZABETH CARY, VISCOUNTESS FALKLAND, 1585?–1639

The *Tragedie of Mariam* (1613) was edited by A. C. Dunstan (Malone Society, 1914). A *History* of Edward II, 'Written by E. F. in the year 1627', of which two versions appeared in 1680, is fully discussed by D. A. Stauffer (*Parrott Presentation Volume*, Princeton, 1935). The chief biographical source is *The Lady Falkland: Her Life* (1861). There is a substantial essay in K. B. Murdock, *The Sun at Noon* (New York, 1939).

LUCIUS CARY, VISCOUNT FALKLAND, 1610?–43

Of the Infallibilitie of the Church of Rome (1645) was reprinted with Henry Hammond's *View of Some Exceptions*, &c. (1646, 1650), and edited, with Thomas White's *Answer* and Falkland's *Reply*, by T. Triplet (1651; enlarged 1660). Biography began with Clarendon's two portraits (and the companion sketches of Falkland's friends), which are reprinted in D. Nichol Smith's *Characters* (*supra*, IV. 6). Two Victorian estimates are Arnold's (*Mixed Essays*, 1879) and Goldwin Smith's reply to Arnold (*Lectures and Essays*, New York, 1881). Sir John Marriott's *Life and Times* (1907) has a political emphasis. K. B. Murdock's elaborate study in *The Sun at Noon* (New York, 1939) combines public affairs with religious thought. Kurt Weber's *Lucius Cary, Second Viscount Falkland* (Columbia, 1940) stresses literary and philosophic interests. The fullest account of the Latitudinarianism of Great Tew is in Tulloch's *Rational Theology* (1872), i. Modern analyses, in addition to Murdock and Weber, are in W. K. Jordan, ii, and H. J. McLachlan (both *supra*, V. 2), and two chapters in B. H. G. Wormald, *Clarendon: Politics, History & Religion 1640–1660* (1951). To Grosart's edition of the poems (*Miscellanies of The Fuller Worthies' Library*, iii, 1871) should be added an appendix in Weber and the elegy on Morison edited by Murdock (*Harvard Studies and Notes in Philology and Literature*, xx, 1938). Murdock and Weber give full bibliographies.

PATRICK CARY, 1624–56

Cary, a younger brother of Lord Falkland, grew up abroad as a Catholic, led a disturbed and migratory life, religious and secular, and wrote *Trivial Poems, and Triolets* in 1651. These were first printed in 1771, edited by Scott in 1820, and again in Saintsbury, ii (1906). There is a full appendix given to him in Weber's *Lucius Cary* (*supra*).

MARGARET CAVENDISH, DUCHESS OF NEWCASTLE, 1623-73

There is no need of naming the prolific lady's publications, except *Natures Pictures* (1656), which included 'A true Relation of my Birth, Breeding, and Life', and *The Life of . . . William Cavendishe* (1667). M. A. Lower's edition of these two portraits was superseded by Sir Charles Firth's (1886; rev. 1906); the two texts are in an Everyman volume (1915). *The Cavalier and his Lady*, ed. E. Jenkins (1872), gives selections from the writings of the duke and duchess. D. Grant has edited *The Phanseys of William Cavendish Marquis of Newcastle* (1956), her suitor's poems and her letters in reply. There are sketches of her in C. Whibley's *Essays in Biography* (1913) and Virginia Woolf's *Common Reader* (1925), and a good account of the duke and her in A. S. Turberville's *History of Welbeck Abbey and its Owners*, i (1938). H. T. Perry's *The First Duchess of Newcastle and her Husband as Figures in Literary History* (Boston, 1918) retains its value; D. Grant's *Margaret the First* (1957) is a spirited account of the duchess and her books. Her writings are discussed also by B. G. Mac-Carthy (*supra*, V. 5), G. D. Meyer, *The Scientific Lady in England 1650-1760* (University of California, 1955), and J. Gagen (*SP* lvi, 1959).

WILLIAM CAVENDISH, SECOND EARL OF DEVONSHIRE, 1591?-1628

The volume of essays, *Horæ Subsecivæ* (1620), which has been assigned to either Grey Brydges, Lord Chandos, or Gilbert Lord Cavendish (see *DNB* on the former), was written by the William Cavendish whom Hobbes attended (to whom Malone and Park had attributed the work). The Stationers' Register (29 March 1619-20 and 1 July 1637) names '*A Discourse against flattery* and *of Rome*, with Essaies' and 'Lord Cavendishes Essaies'; and 'Discourse against flattery, by William Caven-dish Knight' is listed in Jaggard's *Catalogue* of 1619 (ed. O. M. Willard, *Stanford Studies in Language and Literature*, 1941). L. Strauss (*Political Philosophy of Hobbes*, 1936) described a Chats-worth manuscript, written between 1612 and 1620, apparently in Hobbes's hand, containing an earlier and shorter version of the published book. A full account of Fulgenzio Micanzio's letters to Cavendish is given by V. Gabrieli, *English Miscellany*, ed. Praz, viii (1957).

WILLIAM CECIL, LORD BURGHLEY, 1520–98

Burghley's *Certaine Precepts*, published anonymously in 1616–17 and often reprinted in the seventeenth, eighteenth, and early nineteenth centuries, is conveniently accessible in Craik's *English Prose*, i, G. B. Harrison's edition of *Henry Percy's Advice to his Son* (1930), and L. B. Wright's edition of Burghley, Ralegh's *Instructions*, and Osborn's *Advice* (Cornell, for The Folger Shakespeare Library, 1962).

JOHN CHALKHILL, c. 1593?–1642

Thealma and Clearchus. A Pastoral History was first printed in 1683, with a preface (dated 7 May 1678) by Izaak Walton, who had quoted two songs by Chalkhill in the *Angler*. It was reprinted by Singer (1820) and by Saintsbury, ii (1906). The author's identity was partly befogged by the phrase on the 1683 title-page, 'An Acquaintant and Friend of Edmund Spencer'. References for nineteenth-century discussions are in the *DNB* (along with many errors about Chalkhill). The mystery was cleared up by P. J. Croft (*TLS*, 27 June 1958), with the aid of eight newly discovered autograph manuscripts (with some new short poems also). Croft is preparing an edition. Chalkhill matriculated at Trinity College, Cambridge, in December 1610 (hence the guess at his birth-date, since Venn gives none). He had connexions with William Browne (Croft; and J. Grundy, *TLS*, 15 August 1958). The poem is discussed by A. I. T. Higgins (*supra*, III. 3).

JOHN CHAMBERLAIN, 1554–1628

The full and standard edition of the lively and indispensable letters is that of N. E. McClure (2 vols., Philadelphia, 1939). There is a long and attractive essay in W. Notestein, *Four Worthies* (1956).

WILLIAM CHAMBERLAYNE, 1619–89

Pharonnida: A Heroick Poem (1659) was reprinted in 1820 by Singer (along with the play of 1658, *Loves Victory*) and by Saintsbury, i (1905). The play was edited by C. K. Meschter (Bethlehem, Pa., 1914). Criticism includes the *Retrospective Review*, i (1820); Saintsbury; dissertations by E. Kilian (Königsberg, 1913) and A. J. Janssen (Münster, 1922: not seen); a fresh

548   BIBLIOGRAPHY

study by A. E. Parsons (*MLR* xlv, 1950); and A. I. T. Higgins (*supra*, III. 3).

GEORGE CHAPMAN, 1559?–1634

The defective *Poems and Minor Translations* (1875) has been replaced by P. B. Bartlett's edition of the *Poems* (New York, 1941). *Hero and Leander* is annotated also in Marlowe's *Poems*, ed. L. C. Martin (1931). Older reprints of the *Homer* have been superseded by A. Nicoll's fine edition (2 vols., 1956); a handy text is in the Temple Classics (4 vols., 1897–8). A sumptuous one is the Shakespeare Head edition (5 vols., 1930–1).

To the biographical sketch in R. L. Hine, *Hitchin Worthies* (1932), should be added the articles by J. Robertson (*MLR* xl, 1945), M. Eccles (*SP* xliii, 1946), and C. J. Sisson and R. Butman (*MLR* xlvi, 1951).

Swinburne's essay, prefixed to the *Poems* of 1875, was issued separately as *George Chapman* (1875). Chapman has come into his own in modern scholarly criticism. Of central importance is F. L. Schoell's display of his humanistic sources, *Études sur l'humanisme continental en Angleterre* (Paris, 1926), with which go his related studies in the *Revue Germanique*, ix (1913) and *MP* xiii (1915–16) and xvii (1919–20) and W. Schrickx's further account of Natalis Comes (*English Studies*, xxxii, 1951). The most comprehensive critical studies are J. Jacquot, *George Chapman (1559–1634), sa vie, sa poésie, son théâtre, sa pensée* (Paris, 1951), and M. Pagnini, *Forme e motivi nelle poesie e nelle tragedie di George Chapman* (Florence, 1957). The best analysis of Chapman's humanistic creed is in Ennis Rees, *The Tragedies of George Chapman* (Harvard, 1954). Some other discussions of Chapman's poetry and ideas are those of G. Williamson, *The Donne Tradition* (1930), and R. W. Battenhouse, 'Chapman's *The Shadow of Night*: An Interpretation' (*SP* xxxviii, 1941) and 'Chapman and the Nature of Man' (*ELH* xii, 1945). A special study is G. Lazarus, *Technik und Stil von Hero und Leander* (Bonn, 1915); D. J. Gordon's full, learned, and acute analysis of symbolism in that poem (*English Miscellany*, ed. Praz, v, 1954) is valuable for all Chapman's work.

Some notable comments on Chapman's *Homer* are those of Jonson (printed by P. Simpson, *TLS*, 3 March 1932, and in *Ben Jonson*, xi), Coleridge (Raysor, 1936; R. F. Brinkley, 1955), and Arnold, *On Translating Homer*. Chapman is discussed briefly in Lathrop (*supra*, IV. 8) and in valuable articles by P. B. Bartlett (*ELH* ii, 1935; *RES* xvii, 1941; *PMLA* lvii, 1942), D. Smalley (*SP* xxxvi, 1939), and H. C. Fay (*RES* ii, 1951; *Library*, vii, 1952; *RES* iv, 1953). G. de F. Lord's *Homeric Renaissance: The Odyssey of George Chapman* (Yale, 1956) is a freshly critical analysis of the *Odyssey* which also claims much for Chapman's insight. The most comprehensive study is R. Sühnel's *Homer und die englische Humanität: Chapmans und Popes Übersetzungskunst im Rahmen der humanistischen Tradition* (Tübingen, 1958). The *Concise Bibliography* by S. A. Tannenbaum (New York, 1938) had a *Supplement* (1946). There is a good bibliography in Pagnini.

KING CHARLES I, 1600–49

The *Εἰκὼν Βασιλικὴ* is noticed under Gauden. *Reliquiæ Sacræ Carolinæ* ('Hague', 1650), which included the *Εἰκὼν*, had many editions. Three modern collections are: *Charles I in 1646. Letters of King Charles the First to Queen Henrietta Maria*, ed. J. Bruce (Camden Society, lxiii, 1856); *Trial of King Charles the First*, ed. J. G. Muddiman (1928); and *The Letters, Speeches and Proclamations of King Charles I*, ed. Sir C. Petrie (1935). Of the countless contemporary pamphlets and memoirs listed in the *BMC*, a few are mentioned here under Sir Thomas Herbert, W. Lilly, Milton, H. Parker, and Sir A. Weldon. There are biographies by F. M. G. Higham (1932), Evan John (1933), et al.; G. M. Young's 'essay', *Charles I and Cromwell* (1935); and the general histories (*supra*, V. 1). Among special studies are: Sir Claude Phillips, *The Picture Gallery of Charles I* (1896); G. Albion, *Charles I and the Court of Rome* (1935); M. B. Pickel, *Charles I as Patron of Poetry and Drama* (1936); M. Jaffé and C. V. Wedgwood on Charles and Rubens, *History Today*, i (1951) and x (1960); *Abraham Van der Doort's Catalogue of the Collections of Charles I*, ed. O. Millar (Walpole Society, xxxvii, 1958–60). There are lives of the queen by Carola Oman (1936), Janet Mackay (1939), and Jane Oliver (1940).

WALTER CHARLETON, 1619–1707

Sir H. Rolleston had a general sketch in the *Bulletin of the History of Medicine*, viii (1940). Different sides of Charleton are discussed by F. Manning in his edition (1926) of *Epicurus's Morals* (1656) and T. F. Mayo, *Epicurus in England* (*1650–1725*)

(Dallas, 1934); G. Williamson, *SP* xxxii (1935) and *RES* xii (1936); C. D. Thorpe (under Hobbes, *infra*); and in two articles by W. Pagel and the books by L. Thorndike (vii) and R. S. Westfall, all cited above in V. 3. There are bibliographies in W. Munk, *Roll of the Royal College of Physicians* (rev. ed., 1878), i, and in Manning and Rolleston.

ROBERT CHESTER, *fl.* 1601

Loves Martyr: or, Rosalins Complaint. Allegorically shadowing the truth of Love, in the constant Fate of the Phœnix and Turtle (1601; ed. Grosart, 1878) contained an appendix of poems subscribed 'Vatum Chorus', 'Ignoto', 'William Shakes-peare', 'John Marston', 'George Chapman', and 'Ben Johnson'. These 'Poetical Essaies' have had separate editions, e.g. B. H. Newdigate (1937). Carleton Brown edited *Poems by Sir John Salusbury and Robert Chester* (E.E.T.S., Extra Series, cxiii, 1914). The endless discussion of Shakespeare's poem was summarized by H. E. Rollins in his variorum edition, *Shakespeare: The Poems* (1938). Some later studies are: T. W. Baldwin (under Shakespeare, *infra*); T. P. Harrison, *University of Texas Studies in English*, xxx (1951); J. V. Cunningham, *ELH* xix (1952); H. Straumann, *Phönix und Taube* (Zürich, 1953); C. S. Lewis, who has a bibliography; A. Alvarez, *Interpretations*, ed. J. Wain (1955); R. Bates, *Shakespeare Quarterly*, vi (1955); G. W. Knight, *The Mutual Flame* (1955); *Shakespeare: The Poems*, ed. F. T. Prince (1960); and D. Seltzer, *Shakespeare Quarterly*, xii (1961).

KATHERINE CHIDLEY, *fl.* 1641–5

This vigorous preacher, who failed of a place in the *DNB*, replied to Thomas Edwards in *The Justification Of The Independant Churches of Christ* (1641), which is summarized and excerpted in B. Hanbury's *Historical Memorials relating to the Independents*, ii (1841), and in *A New-Yeares-Gift* (1645). She is noticed in Masson's *Milton*; by E. M. Williams, 'Women Preachers in the Civil War', *Journal of Modern History*, i (1929); by W. Haller, *Tracts on Liberty* (1934), i; and A. Barker (*supra*, V. 2).

WILLIAM CHILLINGWORTH, 1602–44

The Religion Of Protestants A Safe Way To Salvation appeared at the end of 1637. The *Works* were edited in 3 vols. in 1820 and 1838. Cheynell's hostile tract was *Chillingworthi Novissima*

(1644); a happier early sketch was that of Clarendon. The first and only biography is the *Historical and Critical Account* of P. Des Maizeaux (1725). The fullest analysis of Chillingworth's thought is in J. Tulloch (*supra*, V. 2). Other discussions are: E. H. Plumptre, in *Masters in English Theology*, ed. A. Barry (1877); Sir James Stephen, *Horae Sabbaticae, First Series* (1892); H. Rashdall, in *Typical English Churchmen*, ed. W. E. Collins (1902); later accounts in the books on toleration by M. Freund, W. K. Jordan, ii, and T. Lyon, and in W. F. Mitchell and H. J. McLachlan, all cited above in V. 2; and in the studies of Falkland by Murdock, Weber, and Wormald (*supra*, Lucius Cary).

JAMES CLELAND, *c*. 1580–1627

The Scottish Cleland's *ΗΡΩ-ΠΑΙΔΕΙΑ, or The Institution of a Young Noble Man* (1607) is being edited by M. Molyneux (vol. i, Introduction and Text: Scholars' Facsimiles & Reprints, 1948). The book is discussed also by J. E. Mason and R. Kelso (*supra*, V. 6) and D. T. Starnes (*Texas Studies in English*, xxxvi, 1957).

JOHN CLEVELAND, 1613–58

Cleveland's several prose 'characters' (1644 ff.) are reprinted in H. Morley's and other anthologies and are discussed by B. Boyce (*supra*, IV. 5). *The Character Of A London-Diurnall: With severall select Poems* (1647) had many enlarged editions, especially as *Poems* (1651 ff.), and spurious pieces were mixed with authentic ones. The bibliographical problems are outlined in the edition of J. M. Berdan (New York, 1903; Yale, 1911). The poems are reprinted also in Saintsbury, iii (1921). S. V. Gapp supplied fresh biographical data in *PMLA* xlvi (1931). Rose Macaulay's novel is cited under Herrick below. For criticism, there are editorial prefaces, G. Williamson's *Donne Tradition* (1930), essays by H. Levin (*Criterion*, xiv, 1934–5) and C. V. Wedgwood (*The Listener*, lix, 1958; and *supra*, IV. 2); and J. L. Kimmey, on Cleveland's influence on the satiric couplet of the Restoration (*PQ* xxxvii, 1958).

LADY ANNE CLIFFORD, 1590–1676

Lives of Lady Anne Clifford . . . and of her Parents, Summarized by Herself, ed. J. P. Gilson (Roxburghe Club, 1916) was followed by V. Sackville-West's edition, from an eighteenth-century transcript, of *The Diary of the Lady Anne Clifford* (1923). The extant diary, which may be incomplete, covers, with gaps, the years 1603–19. Further information about Lady Anne and her background is given in G. C. Williamson's *George, Third Earl of Cumberland* (1920) and *Lady Anne Clifford* (1922), V. Sackville-West's *Knole and the Sackvilles* (1923), and a long essay in W. Notestein, *Four Worthies* (1956).

SIR EDWARD COKE, 1552–1634

The *Reports* appeared in 13 parts (1600–15 and later). The still more famous *First Part Of The Institutes Of The Lawes of England* ('Coke on Littleton') appeared in 1628 (rev. 1629), the second part in 1642, the third and fourth in 1644. The best biography is C. D. Bowen, *The Lion and the Throne: The Life and Times of Sir Edward Coke* (Boston, 1957). There are short studies by Lord Birkenhead (*Fourteen English Judges*, 1926), Sir William Holdsworth (*Some Makers of English Law*, 1938), S. E. Stumpf (*Vanderbilt Studies in the Humanities*, i, 1951), and S. E. Thorne (*Sir Edward Coke*, 1957). Coke figures in the political, legal, and constitutional histories and studies of political thought cited above in V. 1, and is treated in Arneke and Pocock (*supra*, IV. 6). A special item is D. O. Wagner's 'Coke and the Rise of Economic Liberalism', *Economic History Review*, vi (1935–6). W. O. Hassall edited *A Catalogue of the Library of Sir Edward Coke* (Yale, 1950).

JOHN COLLOP, 1625–*post* 1676

Poesis Rediviva (1656) was revived, with copious extracts, in an essay by John Drinkwater (*A Book for Bookmen*, 1926). Some poems are in L. B. Marshall's anthology (*supra*, II. 2). C. Hilberry edited the medical poems in the *Journal of the History of Medicine and Allied Sciences*, xi (1956) and *Poems*, with full apparatus (University of Wisconsin, 1962). F. N. L. Poynter discussed chiefly Collop's praise of Harvey (the same *Journal*, xi, 1956). The irenical *Medici Catholicon* (1656) is noticed by W. K. Jordan, iv (*supra*, V. 2).

LADY CONWAY, 1631–79

We meet many figures and ideas of the age in *Conway Letters: The Correspondence of Anne, Viscountess Conway, Henry More, and their Friends, 1642–1684*, edited from manuscripts by Marjorie

Nicolson (Yale, 1930). Lady Conway's notorious medical case is discussed by G. R. Owen, *Annals of Medical History*, N.S., ix (1937) and G. B. Sherrer, *Studies in the Renaissance*, v (1958).

RICHARD CORBETT (CORBET), 1582–1635

Two posthumous volumes were *Certain Elegant Poems, written By Dr. Corbet, Bishop of Norwich* (1647), edited by the younger John Donne, and the much better *Poëtica Stromata* (Holland? France? 1648). A 3rd impression (after 1648) of the former was enlarged with poems from *Poëtica Stromata*; this was reprinted (1672) as a 'Third Edition'. The 'fourth' and the first scholarly edition was that of O. Gilchrist (1807). Corbett was included in Chalmers's *English Poets*, v. The standard edition is that of J. A. W. Bennett and H. R. Trevor-Roper (1955), with a candid life and other apparatus (to which this note is indebted). J. E. V. Crofts has a biographical essay (*ESEA* x, 1924), corrected at points in the standard edition cited; and Cleanth Brooks an essay on 'The Fairies farewel' (*Twentieth Century English*, ed. W. S. Knickerbocker, New York, 1946).

SIR WILLIAM CORNWALLIS, 1579?–1614

Cornwallis wrote *Essayes* (two parts, 1600–1; ed. D. C. Allen, Johns Hopkins, 1946); *Discourses upon Seneca the Tragedian* (1601), included in the 1610 and 1632 editions of the *Essayes*, and edited by R. H. Bowers (Scholars' Facsimiles & Reprints, 1952); a tract on the union with Scotland (1604); and two posthumous volumes, *Essayes Or rather, Encomions* (1616) and *Essayes Of Certaine Paradoxes* (1616). The 'Praise of King Richard the Third' in this last volume was not by Cornwallis (W. G. Zeeveld, *PMLA* lv, 1940). R. E. Bennett edited 'Four Paradoxes', *Harvard Studies and Notes in Philology and Literature*, xiii (1931). A few essays are reprinted in some of the college anthologies (*supra*, II. 1). The essays are discussed in the monographs by W. L. MacDonald and E. N. S. Thompson (*supra*, IV. 5). A full study of Cornwallis's life and work was made by R. E. Bennett (Harvard *Summaries of Theses 1931*), who discussed the publication of the essays and paradoxes (*RES* ix, 1933) and the essayist's use of Montaigne (*PMLA* xlviii, 1933). Corrected biographical data were summarized by P. B. Whitt (*RES* viii, 1932) and in Allen's introduction.

THOMAS CORYATE, 1577?-1617.

Coryats Crudities Hastily gobled up in five Moneths travells (1611; repr. in 2 vols., 1905) was accompanied by two small pieces, also of 1611, *Coryats Crambe* and *The Odcombian Banquet. Thomas Coriate Traveller for the English Wits: Greeting. From the Court of the Great Mogul* (1616) was included, with other things, in the 1776 edition of the *Crudities* (3 vols.). Fragments on Coryate's eastern travels are also in *Purchas His Pilgrimes* and in Sir William Foster's *Early Travels in India* (1921); they are discussed by W. G. Rice and S. C. Chew (*supra*, V. 4). There are sketches of Coryate by A. W. Fox, *A Book of Bachelors* (1899) and B. Penrose, *Urbane Travellers* (1942), an account of his Swiss travels by J. Jacquot, *Revue Suisse d'Histoire*, i (1951).

JOHN COTTON, 1584-1642

For the writings of this Puritan divine one must refer to the *BMC*, Wing, and J. H. Tuttle's article in *Bibliographical Essays: A Tribute to Wilberforce Eames* (Harvard, 1924). E. H. Emerson has edited *Gods Mercie Mixed with His Justice* (1641) (Scholars' Facsimiles & Reprints, 1958). There is a brief account, with references, in the *Dictionary of American Biography* (1930), and discussion in Perry Miller's books (*supra*, V. 2), W. Haller's *Rise of Puritanism* (1938), and studies of Roger Williams (*infra*).

SIR ROBERT COTTON, 1571-1631

Cotton's writings were less important than his library, which is described in *Catalogus Librorum Manuscriptorum Bibliothecae Cottonianae*, ed. T. Smith (1696), *Catalogue of the Manuscripts in the Cottonian Library*, ed. J. Planta (1802), *A Guide to a Select Exhibition of Cottonian Manuscripts*, ed. H. I. Bell (1931), in E. Edwards's *Memoirs of Libraries* (1859), i, and Wormald and Wright (*supra*, V. 6); and in the books by E. N. Adams, D. C. Douglas, and J. Evans (*supra*, IV. 6). Many of Cotton's tracts were collected by James Howell in *Cottoni Posthuma* (1651; ed. E. Goldsmid, *Collectanea*, iii, 1884-8). Some pieces were reprinted in *Smeeton's Historical & Biographical Tracts* (1820), ii; *Harleian Miscellany*, ed. Park, ii (1809); and *Somers Tracts*, ed. Scott, iv (1810). W. A. Jackson described the editions of Cotton's *Henry the Third* (*Harvard Library Bulletin*, iv, 1950). Hope Mirrlees has done a biography, *A Fly in Amber* (1962).

ABRAHAM COWLEY, 1618–67

The collected though incomplete *Works* were edited in 1668 by Thomas Sprat, who edited the Latin poems in the same year. There was no complete edition after the 12th (1721)—though Cowley was included in the several large series of English poets—until that of Grosart (2 vols., 1881). This was in part superseded by A. R. Waller's edition of the English works (2 vols., 1905–6). The best modern anthology is J. Sparrow's *The Mistress With Other Select Poems* (1926). L. C. Martin edited a smaller selection of verse and prose (1949). Cowley's essays, which belong to the next volume, have been frequently edited. There are two standard biographies, by A. H. Nethercot (1931) and J. Loiseau (Paris, 1931).

The curve of Cowley's reputation, which has been traced by Nethercot (*supra* and *PMLA* xxxviii, 1923; cf. Duncan, *supra*, III. 3, and Hinman, *infra*) and in a monograph by Loiseau (Paris, 1931), is roughly parallel to the record of editions. The neoclassical reaction culminated in Johnson's 'Cowley' (*Lives of the Poets*, 1779), but the momentum of Cowley's early fame carried him along for a further century and a half. After fifty years of neglect came Gosse's essay (*Cornhill Magazine*, xxxiv, 1876; *Seventeenth-Century Studies*, 1883), a minor landmark but quite unreliable. Taking Courthope and the *CHEL* for granted, we may trace Cowley's modern return to modest repute through such items as these: K. N. Colvile, *Fame's Twilight* (1923); Sparrow's introduction; 'Cowley's Lyrics', *TLS*, 18 November 1926; an essay in H. W. Garrod, *The Profession of Poetry* (1929); G. Williamson, *The Donne Tradition* (1930); some criticism in Nethercot and much in Loiseau; R. C. Wallerstein's essay (*Trans. Wisconsin Academy of Sciences, Arts and Letters*, xxvii, 1932); T. S. Eliot (*infra*); J. C. Ghosh, *Sewanee Review*, lxi (1953); three chapters in G. Walton; a long essay in Ellrodt; and Alvarez (these three cited *supra*, III. 3). The latest and fullest studies, with stylistic and philosophic emphasis respectively, are Ulrich Suerbaum's *Die Lyrik der Korrespondenzen: Cowleys Bildkunst und die Tradition der englischen Renaissancedichtung* (Bochum-Langendreer, 1958) and Robert B. Hinman's *Abraham Cowley's World of Order* (Harvard, 1960). Hinman (who treated the theme in *ELH* xxiii, 1956) makes high claims for Cowley as the Christian poet of the new science.

With the full discussion of the odes by Shafer, Shuster, and C. Maddison (*supra*, III. 3) may be linked T. S. Eliot's 'Note' on two odes (*Seventeenth Century Studies Presented to Sir Herbert Grierson*, 1938), S. Elledge's account of one of them, 'Of Wit' (*MLQ* ix, 1948), and Suerbaum and Hinman. *Davideis* has been studied chiefly by J. M. McBryde (*JEGP* ii, 1899); Loiseau; H.-H. Krempien, *Der Stil der Davideis von Abraham Cowley im Kreise ihrer Vorläufer* (*Britannica*, xi, 1936); Tillyard, *The English Epic* and B. O. Kurth (*supra*, III. 3); Hinman (*supra*); F. Kermode (*RES* xxv, 1949), on the date of composition; and A. L. Korn (*HLQ* xiv, 1950–1), on the poem's utility for *MacFlecknoe*. Loiseau's full bibliography has been supplemented, for the years 1912–38, by T. Spencer and M. Van Doren (*supra*, III. 3), and, for later years, by Hinman.

RICHARD CRASHAW, 1612/13–49

Crashaw's published volumes were *Epigrammatum Sacrorum Liber* (1634), *Steps to the Temple* (1646; enlarged 1648), and *Carmen Deo Nostro* (Paris, 1652). While much less popular than Herbert in the seventeenth century, he did not in the eighteenth drop quite so much out of sight, thanks in part to Cowley's elegy and Pope's faint praise. He was edited in 1785 and included in several collections. The editions of Grosart (2 vols., 1872–3), A. R. Waller (1904), and J. R. Tutin (Muses' Library, 1905) were superseded by that of L. C. Martin (1927; 2nd ed., 1957).

Among critical essays are those of Francis Thompson, *Academy*, 20 November 1897, and *Works*, iii (1913); H. C. Beeching, in Tutin's edition; T. S. Eliot, *For Lancelot Andrewes* (1928); F. E. Hutchinson, *CHEL* vii and *Church Quarterly Review*, cvi (1928); E. I. Watkin, in *The English Way*, ed. M. Ward (1933), and *Poets and Mystics* (1953); sections in books on the metaphysical poets (*supra*, III. 3), especially H. C. White, A. Esch, and L. L. Martz; essays in the *TLS*, 1 June 1946 and 19 August 1949; M. Turnell, *Nineteenth Century*, cxlvi (1949); B. Willey, *Richard Crashaw* (1949); O. de Mourgues (*supra*, IV. 7); and sections in C. Maddison (*supra*, III. 3) and J. Hollander (*supra*, V. 7). M. Praz's important study in *Secentismo* (see Donne, *infra*) was revised as *Richard Crashaw* (Brescia, 1945); an abridged English version is in Praz's *The Flaming Heart* (New York, 1958). Ellrodt (*supra*, III. 3) has a long study. Two valuable books are R. C. Wallerstein's *Richard Crashaw: A Study in Style and Poetic Development* (University of Wisconsin, 1935; repr. 1959) and especially Austin Warren's *Richard Crashaw: A Study in Baroque Sensibility* (Louisiana State University, 1939; repr., University of Michigan, 1957). More special is M. E. Rickey's *Rhyme and Meaning in Richard Crashaw* (University of Kentucky, 1961). A number of explications of poems, e.g. by A. F. Allison (1947–8), R. G. Collmer (1956), A. Farnham (1956), J. Jacquot (1951), W. G. Madsen (1958), S. Manning (1955), K. Neill (1948), and J. Peter (1953), are recorded in the annual bibliographies. Two sceptics concerning Marino's influence are F. J. Warnke (*supra*, III. 3 and IV. 7) and L. Pettoello (*MLR* lii, 1957). The criticism of 1912–38 is listed by T. Spencer and M. Van Doren (*supra*, III. 3). J. E. Saveson supplied some biographical data in the *TLS*, 28 February 1958.

OLIVER CROMWELL, 1599–1658

While Carlyle's *Letters and Speeches of Oliver Cromwell* (2 vols., 1845; ed. S. C. Lomas, 3 vols., 1904) retains its special place, the standard collection, with a full narrative, is W. C. Abbott's *Writings and Speeches of Oliver Cromwell* (4 vols., Harvard, 1937–47). Abbott compiled a massive *Bibliography* (Harvard, 1929) and reviewed the course of Cromwell's fame in *Conflicts with Oblivion* (Yale, 1924; 2nd ed., Harvard, 1935; and *supra*, vol. iv); a recent review is C. Hill's pamphlet, *Oliver Cromwell 1658–1958* (1958). Among the many biographies, in addition to Abbott, are those of Sir C. Firth (1900), John Buchan (1934), C. V. Wedgwood (1939); R. S. Paul, *The Lord Protector: Religion and Politics in the Life of Oliver Cromwell* (1955); M. Ashley, *The Greatness of Oliver Cromwell* (1957) and the handbook *Oliver Cromwell and the Puritan Revolution* (1958). Two special studies are E. W. Kirby, 'The Cromwellian Establishment' (*Church History*, x, 1941), on problems of toleration, and F. G. Marcham, 'Oliver Cromwell, Orator', *The Rhetorical Idiom*, ed. D. C. Bryant (Cornell, 1958).

RALPH CUDWORTH, 1617–88

Cudworth's great *Sermon Preached before the Honourable House of Commons, At Westminster, March 31. 1647* was reproduced by the Facsimile Text Society (New York, 1930). His chief works were *The True Intellectual System of the Universe* (1678; ed. T. Birch, 2 vols., 1743; 4 vols., 1820; ed. J. Harrison, with full notes, 3 vols., 1845) and *A Treatise concerning Eternal and Immutable*

Morality (1731). Among the older critics are J. Tulloch (*supra,* V. 2), who remains of prime value, and C. de Rémusat (*supra,* V. 3). More recent are the books on the Cambridge Platonists, and M. Nicolson's article, cited above in V. 2; J. H. Muirhead's solid and acute analysis in his *Platonic Tradition in Anglo-Saxon Philosophy* (1931); J. C. Gregory, 'Cudworth and Descartes', *Philosophy,* viii (1933); B. Willey (*supra,* III. 4); J. Beyer, *Ralph Cudworth als Ethiker, Staatsphilosoph und Aesthetiker* (Bottrop, 1935); G. Aspelin, 'Ralph Cudworth's Interpretation of Greek Philosophy', *Göteborgs Högskolas Årsskrift,* xlix (1943); J. A. Passmore's close study, *Ralph Cudworth: An Interpretation* (1951), which takes account of manuscripts and includes a good bibliography; M. H. Carré, *Philosophical Quarterly,* iii (1953); R. L. Colie (under More, *infra*); and D. B. Sailor, 'Cudworth and Descartes', *JHI* xxiii (1962). The Fielding item in the text is from R. W. Rader, *MLN* lxxi (1956).

NICHOLAS CULPEPER, 1616–54

Among the works of the physician, herbalist, and astrologer were *A Physicall Directory* (1649), a translation of the College of Physicians' 'dispensatory' which outraged vested interests, and *The English Physician* (1652, unauthorized; enlarged and corrected, 1653). The latter has been issued, with more or less revision, ever since, up into the current decade (e.g. the volumes of Mrs. C. F. Leyel). The first two medical books published in British North America, in 1708 and 1720, were Culpeper's (D. L. Cowen, *Journal of the History of Medicine and Allied Sciences,* xi, 1956). His works were edited by G. A. Gordon (3 vols., 1802). There are accounts of him by W. H. Pollard (*Birmingham Medical Review,* v, 1930) and B. Chance (*Annals of Medical History,* N.S., iii, 1931). And there is the story in Kipling's *Rewards and Fairies.*

NATHANAEL CULVERWEL, 1618/19–51?

W. Dillingham edited *Spiritual Opticks* (1651) and *An Elegant And Learned Discourse Of the Light of Nature, With several other Treatises* (1652; other edns., 1654, 1661, 1669). The *Discourse,* edited by J. Brown and J. Cairns (1857), is abridged in E. T. Campagnac's *Cambridge Platonists* (1901). In addition to Rémusat (*supra,* V. 3), Culverwel is discussed in the books on the Cambridge Platonists by Powicke, Pawson, De Boer, and De Pauley, and by W. F. Mitchell (all cited above in V. 2), and in two articles by A. C. Scupholme (*Theology*, xxxviii, 1939). The fullest analysis is Margaret O'Brien's unpublished thesis (Radcliffe, 1951).

EDWARD DACRES, *fl.* 1636–40

Dacres did the first printed English translations of Machiavelli's chief works, *Machiavels Discourses. upon the first Decade of T. Livius* (1636) and *Nicholas Machiavel's Prince* (1640; Tudor Translations, 1905; ed. W. E. C. Baynes, 1929).

SIR ROBERT DALLINGTON, 1561–1637

The informative and entertaining *View of Fraunce*, written largely in 1598, was pirated in 1604 and reissued, with an introduction, by the author (in 1604–5?) as *A Method for Travell* (ed. W. P. Barrett, Shakespeare Association Facsimiles, 1936). Two other books were *A Survey of the Great Dukes State of Tuscany* (1605) and *Aphorismes Civill and Militarie: Amplified with Authorities, and exemplified with Historie, out of the first Quarterne of Fr. Guicciardine* (1613). Documents relating to the *Survey* were edited by A. M. Crinò (under Wotton, *infra*).

GEORGE DANIEL, 1616–57

Daniel's poems, first printed by Grosart (4 vols., 1878), are more attractively presented in *Selected Poems*, ed. T. B. Stroup (University of Kentucky, 1959). Along with intrinsic interest of substance and manner, the poems reflect the tastes of a cultivated country gentleman who admired Jonson, Donne, George Herbert, Sir Thomas Browne, et al. There is some discussion also in H. Nearing (*supra*, III. 3).

SAMUEL DANIEL, 1563?–1619

Daniel was included in Chalmers's *English Poets* (1810), iii. Grosart edited the complete works (5 vols., 1885–96). L. Michel has edited *Philotas* and *The Civil Wars* (Yale, 1949, 1958). J. Buxton is editing the poems, plays, and masques. A useful selection is *Poems and A Defence of Ryme*, ed. A. C. Sprague (Harvard, 1930). The *Defence* has had a number of reprints.

There are general essays by H. C. Beeching (*A Selection*, 1899), Sprague (*supra*), and A. H. Bullen (*Elizabethans*, 1924), comment in R. Tuve (*supra*, III. 3), discussions of the earlier poems in Lewis, a 'Reconsideration' by C. C. Seronsy (*MLR* lii, 1957). Coleridge's comments, chiefly on the *Civil Wars*, are in Raysor and, more fully, in R. F. Brinkley. This poem and its genre are studied by L. F. Ball, H. Nearing, and E. M. W. Tillyard (*supra*, III. 3), and Seronsy, whose articles are gathered up in Michel's full commentary. The prose *Historie* is discussed by M. Mac-Kisack (*RES* xxiii, 1947), R. B. Gottfried (*Studies in the Renaissance*, iii, 1956; *SP* liii, 1956), Daniel's general historical sense by W. Blissett (*English Studies*, xxxviii, 1957) and Seronsy (*SP* liv, 1957). M. H. Shackford has an essay on Daniel's epistles (*SP* xlv, 1948). His debt to Montaigne is treated by J. I. M. Stewart (*RES* ix, 1933) and R. Himelick (*NQ* iii, 1956; *PQ* xxxvi, 1957). M. Eccles dealt with his foreign travel (*SP* xxxiv, 1937). There is a *Bibliography* of Daniel's works by H. Sellers in *OBS* ii, part i, 1927 (1928), a *Concise Bibliography* (New York, 1942) by S. A. Tannenbaum.

SIR WILLIAM DAVENANT (D'AVENANT), 1606–68

This note ignores Davenant the playwright (see G. E. Bentley, *supra*, I, and below). *Madagascar*, a volume of poems (1638; repr. 1648), was followed by the *Discourse upon Gondibert* or *Preface to Gondibert* which, with Hobbes's *Answer*, appeared in two editions at Paris in 1650 (repr. in Spingarn's *Critical Essays*, ii). The unfinished poem, with these critical pieces, was issued in London in two editions dated 1651; one at least came out in 1650. Both old and unpublished poems were included in the folio *Works* (1673). *Gondibert* and some other poems were reprinted in Anderson's *British Poets* (1793), iv, and in Chalmers (1810), vi. Another canto of *Gondibert*, published in 1685, was edited by J. G. McManaway (*MLQ* i, 1940). H. Berry printed three new poems in *PQ* xxxi (1952). *Selected Poems* were printed by G. Bush (Cambridge, Mass., 1943). Davenant has a place in Aubrey's *Brief Lives*. There are standard biographies by Alfred Harbage (University of Pennsylvania, 1935), who has a chapter on *Gondibert*, and A. H. Nethercot (University of Chicago, 1938), whose longer work stresses biography and the theatre. There are theses on *Gondibert* by G. Gronauer (Erlangen, 1911) and C. M. Dowlin (University of Pennsylvania, 1934). Further discussion of the theory and the poem is in R. L. Sharp (*supra*, III. 3), C. D. Thorpe (under Hobbes, *infra*), and R. H. Perkinson (*supra*, III. 3). The suggestion about Milton, in the biographical note, was made by W. A. Turner (*MLN* lxiii, 1948).

LADY ELEANOR DAVIES, c. 1590–1652

Lady Davies is more commonly known by the name of her first husband, Sir John (*infra*), than by that of her second, Sir Archibald Douglas. Her prophetic instinct asserted itself in 1625. One specimen, *Strange and Wonderfull Prophesies* (1649), is reprinted in W. C. Hazlitt's *Fugitive Tracts, Second Series* (1875). T. Spencer had an amusing account of her in *Harvard Studies and Notes in Philology and Literature*, xx (1938). Briefer sketches are given by S. G. Wright (*Bodleian Quarterly Record*, vii, 1932) and by C. J. Hindle in his bibliography of her pamphlets in *Edinburgh Bibliographical Society Transactions*, vol. i, pt. i (1936). The 53 items run from 1625 to 1652.

SIR JOHN DAVIES, 1569–1626

Davies's poems are treated by Lewis, who gives a bibliography. *A Discoverie of the True Causes why Ireland was never entirely Subdued, nor brought under Obedience of the Crowne of England, untill the Beginning of his Majesties happie Raigne* (1612) was reprinted in *Works*, ed. Grosart (3 vols., 1869–76), and in *Ireland under Elizabeth and James the First*, ed. H. Morley (1890). The merits of Davies the historian are stressed by Pocock (*supra*, IV. 6).

JOHN DAVIES of Hereford, 1565?–1618

The complete works were edited by Grosart (2 vols., 1878). The chief studies are: H. Heidrich, *John Davies of Hereford* (Leipzig, 1924), which had a partly corrective review from R. B. McKerrow (*RES* i, 1925); R. L. Anderson, 'A French Source for John Davies of Hereford's System of Psychology' (*PQ* vi, 1927), and *Elizabethan Psychology and Shakespeare's Plays* (University of Iowa, 1927); and C. D. Murphy, *John Davies of Hereford* (Cornell *Abstracts of Theses 1940*), and an article on Davies's use of Mornay (*PQ* xxi, 1942). Davies's epigrams are discussed by T. K. Whipple (*supra*, IV. 7), and by L. Ennis in *HLB* (1937). R. J. Schoeck had some biographical data in *MLR* l (1955).

THOMAS DEKKER, 1572?–1632

The only comprehensive edition of Dekker's non-dramatic works, that of Grosart (5 vols., 1884–6), will be superseded by that of F. P. Wilson, who edited *Foure Birds of Noahs Arke* (1924) and *The Plague Pamphlets of Thomas Dekker* (1925). Some other reprints are: *A Knights Conjuring*, Percy Society, v (1842); *The Guls Horne-booke*, Temple Classics (1904) and ed. R. B. McKerrow (1904), the standard edition; *The Belman Of London* and *Lanthorne and Candle-light*, in the Temple Classics volume and, abridged, in A. V. Judges's *Elizabethan Underworld* (1930); *Penny-Wise Pound-Foolish*, ed. W. Bang, *Materialien*, xxiii (1908); *The Seven deadlie Sinns of London*, ed. H. F. B. Brett-Smith (1922); *The Wonderfull yeare*, ed. G. B. Harrison (Bodley Head Quartos, 1924), in Wilson's *Plague Pamphlets*, and in *Three Elizabethan Pamphlets*, ed. G. R. Hibbard (1951). His poem, *The Artillery Garden* (1616), was privately printed (1952) with a note by Wilson.

Besides the introductions of Wilson and other editors, there are essays in Swinburne's *Age of Shakespeare* (1908), A. H. Bullen's *Elizabethans* (1924), and H. H. Child's *Essays and Reflections* (1948; from *TLS*, 31 May, 1941). The fullest study is M. T. Jones-Davies, *Un Peintre de la vie londonienne: Thomas Dekker* (2 vols., Paris, 1958). Two monographs are: K. L. Gregg, *Thomas Dekker: A Study in Economic and Social Backgrounds* (University of Washington, 1924), and P. Shaw, 'Dekker's Position in Prison Literature', *PMLA* lxii (1947). The tracts on roguery are discussed by Chandler and Aydelotte (*supra*, IV. 2) and Judges (*supra*), and, with special reference to Dekker's sources, by E. H. Miller, *NQ* ii (1955). F. P. Wilson (*HLQ* xviii, 1954–5) showed Dekker's debt, in *The Double PP*, to W. Segar. Grobianism is described in C. H. Herford, *Studies in the Literary Relations of England and Germany* (1886) and E. Rühl, *Grobianus in England* (*Palaestra*, xxxviii, 1904). Dekker's 'characters' are discussed by W. J. Paylor (*MLR* xxxi, 1936; *The Overburian Characters*, 1936) and B. Boyce (*supra*, IV. 5). F. P. Wilson had biographical notes in *MLR* xv (1920). S. A. Tannenbaum's *Concise Bibliography* (New York, 1939) had a *Supplement* in 1945. There is a very full bibliography in M. T. Jones-Davies (*supra*).

WILLIAM DELL, *c.* 1607?–70

Several Sermons and Discourses (1652) was reprinted in 1709; *Select Works* appeared in 1773; and the *Works* in 1816 (Philadelphia) and 1817 (2 vols., London). *The Tryal of Spirits* (1653) included a discourse on 'The right Reformation of Learning,

Schools, and Universities, according to the state of the Gospel'. The same theme was touched in *The Stumbling-Stone* (1653). These pieces are included in the collections mentioned and in part in *A Collection of Devotional Tracts* (Philadelphia, 1760). A portion of *The Way of True Peace and Unity* (1649) is reprinted in A. S. P. Woodhouse, *Puritanism and Liberty* (1938). Dell receives more or less space in Mullinger (*supra*, V. 6); Rufus M. Jones, *Studies in Mystical Religion* (1909); R. F. Jones, *Ancients and Moderns* (1936); W. K. Jordan, iii (*supra*, V. 2); Woodhouse; W. A. L. Vincent (*supra*, V. 6); L. F. Solt (*Church Quarterly Review*, clv, 1954, and *supra*, V. 1). There is a biographical account in John Venn's *Caius College* (1901).

SIR JOHN DENHAM, 1615–69

The piratical first edition of *Coopers Hill* (1642) was reissued four times before the first authorized and enlarged text of 1655. Two other separate items were *The Destruction of Troy* (1656) and the *Version of the Psalms* (1714). The first collected edition, *Poems and Translations*, appeared in 1668, the tenth in 1780. The standard edition is that of T. H. Banks (Yale, 1928). Denham's life was done by Aubrey. His chief early critics were Dryden, in various essays, and Johnson (*Lives of the Poets*, 1779). B. Dobrée's *Sir John Denham* (1927; repr. in *As Their Friends Saw Them*, 1933) is a pleasant essay in the form of a dialogue between Bishop King and Waller. On the heroic couplet and neoclassical wit there are R. C. Wallerstein (*PMLA* l, 1935) and G. Williamson (*MP* xxxiii, 1935–6 and *supra*, III. 1). Fresh insight is brought to the theme of *Coopers Hill* by R. Putney (*University of Colorado Studies*, vi, 1957) and E. R. Wasserman (*The Subtler Language*, Johns Hopkins, 1959). The genre that this poem re-created is fully described in R. A. Aubin's *Topographical Poetry in XVIII-Century England* (New York, 1936). Denham's translation of Virgil is discussed by L. Proudfoot (*supra*, IV. 8).

ARTHUR DENT, 1553–1603

The enormously popular *Plaine Mans Path-way to Heaven* (1601) is discussed in H. C. White's *English Devotional Literature* (*supra*, V. 2) and L. B. Wright (*supra*, IV. 2), and is touched in Tillyard's *English Epic* (1954). M. Hussey had accounts of the man and the book respectively in the *Essex Review*, lvii (1948) and *MLR* xliv (1949).

SIR SIMONDS D'EWES, 1602–50

The *Journals of all the Parliaments During the Reign of Queen Elizabeth* was published in 1682. The *Journal . . . from the Beginning of the Long Parliament to the Opening of the Trial of the Earl of Strafford* has been edited by W. Notestein (Yale, 1923), the *Journal . . . from the First Recess of the Long Parliament to the Withdrawal of King Charles from London* by W. H. Coates (Yale, 1942). The *Autobiography and Correspondence* were edited by J. O. Halliwell[-Phillipps] (2 vols., 1845). J. H. Marsden's *College Life in the Time of James the First* (1851) was compiled from an unpublished diary.

SIR KENELM DIGBY, 1603–65

Some of Digby's writings were: *Observations upon Religio Medici* (1643); *Observations on the 22. Stanza in the 9th. Canto of the 2d. Book of Spencers Faery Queen* (1643); *Two Treatises . . . The Nature of Bodies . . . The Nature of Mans Soule* (Paris, 1644; London, 1645), his chief scientific and philosophic work; *A Late Discourse . . . Touching the Cure of Wounds by the Powder of Sympathy* (1658), translated from the French *Discours* of the same year; *A Discourse Concerning the Vegetation of Plants* (1661). The *Private Memoirs* were edited by Sir H. Nicolas (1827); the *Journal of a Voyage into the Mediterranean* by J. Bruce (Camden Society, xcvi, 1868); and *Poems from Sir Kenelm Digby's Papers* by H. A. Bright (Roxburghe Club, 1877); the cookery book attributed to Digby, *The Closet of . . . Sir Kenelm Digbie Kt. opened* (1669), by A. Macdonell (1910).

Criticism began with Alexander Ross's *Philosophicall Touch-Stone* (1645) and *Medicus Medicatus* (1645), and biography with Aubrey. Digby flits through contemporary memoirs and letters, such as the *Conway Letters*, ed. M. Nicolson (Yale, 1930). R. T. Petersson's *Sir Kenelm Digby* (Harvard, 1956) is a fully rounded biography which deals with the writings. V. Gabrieli's *Sir Kenelm Digby: un inglese italianato nell'età della Controriforma* (Rome, 1957) concentrates on episodes and on interpretation of Digby's mind and personality; he prints a number of letters in the book and in *The National Library of Wales Journal*, ix (1955–6) and x (1957–8). These recent and scholarly works obviate the need of many references, but one may mention E. W. Bligh's

Sir Kenelm Digby and his Venetia (1932) and J. F. Fulton's *Sir Kenelm Digby* (New York, 1937). Fulton has a short account in Hartley's *Royal Society* (*supra*, V. 3). The 'powder of sympathy' is discussed by W. G. A. Robertson (*Annals of Medical History*, vii, 1925) and L. Thorndike, vii (*supra*, V. 3), Digby's view of embryology by R. G. Grenell (*Bulletin of the History of Medicine*, x, 1941).

LEONARD DIGGES, 1588–1635

The Rape of Proserpine (1617; republished in 1628 as *Claudian Translated out of Latine into English Verse*) has been edited by H. H. Huxley (1959). Two poems in praise of Shakespeare are reprinted in Sir E. K. Chambers, *William Shakespeare* (1930), ii. Digges—a friend of Mabbe—translated a Spanish novel, *Gerardo* (1622); the translation is fully discussed by E. G. Mathews (*supra*, IV. 7). There is some account of Digges in L. Hotson's *I, William Shakespeare* (1937).

JOHN DONNE, 1572–1631

Donne's chief writings in prose were (in the order of publication, not of composition): *Pseudo-Martyr* (1610); *Ignatius his Conclave* (1611), in both Latin and English editions; *Devotions Upon Emergent Occasions* (1624); *Five Sermons* (1626); single sermons at various times, notably *Deaths Duell* (1632); *Juvenilia: or Certaine Paradoxes, and Problemes* (1633); *Six Sermons* (1634); *LXXX Sermons* (1640), with Walton's *Life*; *BIAΘANATOΣ* (1646?); *Fifty Sermons* (1649); *Essayes in Divinity* (1651); *Letters to Severall Persons of Honour* (1651); and *XXVI. Sermons* (1660/1).

Of the very few poems printed in Donne's lifetime the most important were *An Anatomy of the World* (1611) and *The Second Anniversarie. Of the Progres of the Soule* (1612), with which the *Anatomy* was reissued. The first collected edition was *Poems, By J. D. With Elegies On The Authors Death* (1633). Further editions, with variations, appeared in 1635, 1639, 1649, 1650, 1654, 1669, and 1719. The editions and manuscripts are described by Grierson and a fresh analysis, with reference to the divine poems, is made by H. Gardner (*infra*).

The Facsimile Text Society published facsimiles of *Biathanatos*, ed. J. W. Hebel (1930); *Juvenilia or Certain Paradoxes and Problems*, ed. R. E. Bennett (1936); and *Ignatius his Conclave*, ed. C. M. Coffin (1941). Noel Douglas Replicas included the two

Anniversaries (1926). *An Anatomy of the World* was reproduced for the Roxburghe Club (1951).

Donne's poems were included in the large collections from Bell (1779) onward. The editions of Grosart (2 vols., 1872–3), J. R. Lowell and C. E. Norton (Grolier Club, 2 vols., 1895), and Sir E. K. Chambers (Muses' Library, 2 vols., 1896) were superseded by that of Sir Herbert Grierson (2 vols., 1912), which opened a new era in Donne scholarship. Two complete small editions are Grierson's one-volume text (1929), which has a few textual changes from 1912 and a new introduction, and the modernized text of R. E. Bennett (Chicago, 1942; repr., New York, 1958), which embodied original work on the manuscripts. The importance of H. Gardner's edition of *The Divine Poems* (1952) has been indicated in the discussion of Donne. Miss Gardner is preparing an edition of the love poems.

H. Alford's edition of the sermons (*Works*, 6 vols., 1839) has been superseded by the *Sermons*, ed. G. R. Potter and E. M. Simpson (10 vols., University of California, 1953–62). Some volumes of selections are: *Donne's Sermons: Selected Passages*, ed. L. P. Smith (1919); *Ten Sermons*, ed. Sir G. Keynes (1923); Hayward and Coffin (*infra*); *Sermons*, ed. T. A. Gill (New York, 1958). Some other editions of prose are: *Letters to Severall Persons of Honour*, ed. C. E. Merrill (New York, 1910); *Paradoxes and Problemes*, ed. Keynes (1923); *Devotions*, ed. J. Sparrow (1923), ed. W. H. Draper (1925; repr., University of Michigan, 1959); *The Courtier's Library*, edited with a translation by E. M. Simpson (1930); *Essays in Divinity*, ed. E. M. Simpson (1952).

Anthologies of verse and prose are the standard *Complete Poetry and Selected Prose*, ed. J. Hayward (1929), a similar selection by C. M. Coffin (New York, 1952), and a small one, with the first version of Walton's *Life*, by H. W. Garrod (1946).

Walton's *Life* (prefixed to *LXXX Sermons*, 1640; enlarged 1658 ff.), though focused on Donne's later years, remains the foundation of biography; Walton's additions are recorded by J. Butt (*OBS*) and fully discussed by D. Novarr (both cited under Walton, *infra*). Gosse's *Life and Letters* (2 vols., 1899; repr., Gloucester, Mass., 1959), still the standard work though often inaccurate and out of date, will be superseded by the biography by R. C. Bald, who has published one segment, *Donne & the Drurys* (1959). I. A. Shapiro's long-awaited edition of the letters will be valuable for those who live to see it. The date of Donne's birth has been pinned down by W. Milgate (*NQ* cxci, 1946) and Shapiro (ibid. cxcvii, 1952). B. W. Whitlock summarized data on his heredity, childhood, and family (*NQ* vi, vii, 1959, 1960). Donne's relations with Mrs. Herbert and the Countess of Bedford were described by H. W. Garrod and P. Thomson respectively (*RES* xxi, 1945; *MLR* xliv, 1949); his interest in the Virginia Company by S. Johnson (*ELH* xiv, 1947).

Recorded criticism began with Jonson's remarks to Drummond. The most significant early estimate was Carew's 'Elegie'. Early references, collected by W. Milgate (*NQ* cxcv, 1950; cxcviii, 1953) and R. G. Howarth, are assembled in Keynes's *Bibliography* (*infra*; cf. F. Eldredge, *ELH* xix, 1952). Donne's poetic influence on his age has been treated most fully by G. Williamson, *The Donne Tradition* (1930), and R. C. Bald, *Donne's Influence in English Literature* (1932). His and other metaphysicals' fortunes have been traced down through the romantic age by A. H. Nethercot and from 1800 to the present by J. E. Duncan (*supra*, III. 3; cf. K. Tillotson, *Elizabethan and Jacobean Studies Presented to Frank Percy Wilson*, 1959).

The modern vogue of Donne's poetry was stimulated by Grierson's 1912 edition and especially his *Metaphysical Lyrics & Poems* (1921) and early essays of T. S. Eliot (*Selected Essays*, 1932); Mr. Eliot was cooler in *A Garland for John Donne*, ed. T. Spencer (1931; repr., Gloucester, Mass., 1958). General criticism includes: M. Praz, *Secentismo e Marinismo in Inghilterra* (Florence, 1925; the Donne part revised for college use in 1945 [Rome] and somewhat again as *John Donne* [Turin, 1958]); P. Legouis, *Donne the Craftsman* (Paris, 1928); books (1930–56) on the metaphysical poets by Williamson (*supra*), J. B. Leishman, J. Bennett, R. C. Wallerstein, and J.-J. Denonain (*supra*, III. 3); M. A. Rugoff, *Donne's Imagery* (New York, 1939); R. Tuve, *Elizabethan and Metaphysical Imagery* (1947), of radical importance for Donne's relation to Elizabethan convention; D. Louthan, *The Poetry of John Donne: A Study in Explication* (New York, 1951); J. B. Leishman, *The Monarch of Wit* (1951; rev. ed., 1962), a critique of all the poetry; Clay Hunt, *Donne's Poetry: Essays in Literary Analysis* (Yale, 1954); K. W. Gransden, *John Donne* (1954), a short survey of all the work; sections in *From Donne to Marvell* (*supra*, III. 3); two long essays in L. Unger, *The Man in the Name* (University of Minnesota, 1956); F. Kermode, *John*

Donne (1957; rev. 1961), an essay with a bibliography; a very full study in R. Ellrodt (*supra*, III. 3). Arnold Stein and H. C. White have books forthcoming.

The religious poems receive chapters in H. C. White, M. M. Mahood, and A. Esch (*supra*, III. 3). H. Gardner's revolutionary findings (1952) were stressed above. Irène Simon's *Some Problems of Donne Criticism* (Brussels, 1952) has much active analysis, especially of the religious poems. The *Anniversaries*, which of course figure in many studies already named, are prominent in M. Nicolson's *Breaking of the Circle* (*supra*, III. 4) and, with the other religious poems, in L. L. Martz's important book (*supra*, III. 3). E. M. Simpson discussed the date of the last 'Hymn' in *MLR* xli (1946). The latest attempt to date '*La Corona*' is by D. Novarr (*PQ* xxxvi, 1957). D. L. Peterson (*SP* lvi, 1959) sees the 'Holy Sonnets' as a unified sequence.

A few special studies of the poetry may be cited. Donne's use of alchemical figures has been explored by E. H. Duncan (*ELH* ix, 1942), W. A. Murray (*RES* xxv, 1949), and J. A. Mazzeo (*Isis*, xlviii, 1957). Murray's reinterpretation of *The Progresse of the Soule* (*RES* x, 1959) was utilized in the text. A. Stein's close analyses of Donne's metrics in various journals (1943, 1944, 1951) concentrated on the earlier poems; likewise M. F. Moloney (*PMLA* lxv, 1950). R. Ellrodt (*Etudes Anglaises*, xiii, 1960) summarized known and conjectural dates.

E. M. Simpson's standard *Study of the Prose Works of John Donne* (1924; rev. 1948) has been supplemented in her editions (*supra*). Donne the preacher, on whom Coleridge made extensive comments (in R. F. Brinkley), has been studied especially by J. Sparrow (*ESEA* xvi, 1931), W. F. Mitchell (*supra*, V. 2), H. H. Umbach (*PMLA* lii, 1937; *ELH* xii, 1945), M. M. Mahood (*supra*, III. 3), R. L. Hickey (*Tennessee Studies in Literature*, i, iii, 1956, 1958), and D. Quinn (*ELH* xxvii, 1960).

Studies of Donne's ideas, secular, scientific, and religious, include M. P. Ramsay's *Les Doctrines médiévales chez Donne* (1917; 2nd ed., 1924), an able pioneer work with an unwarranted Plotinian bias; L. I. Bredvold, *JEGP* xxii (1923) and *Studies in Shakespeare, Milton and Donne* (New York, 1925); M. Y. Hughes, in *Essays in Criticism, Second Series* (University of California, 1934); G. Williamson, on *Biathanatos* (*PQ* xiii, 1934; *supra*, III. 1); C. M. Coffin's *John Donne and the New Philosophy* (Columbia, 1937; repr., New York, 1958); I. Husain, *Dogmatic and Mystical*

Theology of John Donne (1938); M. F. Moloney, *John Donne: His Flight from Mediaevalism* (University of Illinois, 1944); Grierson, on Donne and the 'Via Media' (*MLR* xliii, 1948; *Criticism and Creation*, 1949); E. M. Simpson and M. Nicolson (*supra*); H. C. White, in *The Seventeenth Century . . . R. F. Jones* (*supra*, III. 2); J. C. Maxwell, 'Donne and the "New Philosophy" ', *Durham University Journal*, xii (1951); R. Ornstein, 'Donne, Montaigne, and Natural Law' (*JEGP* lv, 1956). W. R. Mueller has a study of Donne's theology in preparation.

This note necessarily omits a multitude of scholarly and critical discussions. For these there are T. Spencer and M. Van Doren (*supra*, III. 3), who list items of the years 1912–38; William White's *John Donne since 1900: A Bibliography of Periodical Articles* (Boston, 1942; repr. from *Bulletin of Bibliography*, xvii, 1941–2); M. Y. Hughes's survey of recent criticism in *Contemporary Literary Scholarship*, ed. L. Leary (New York, 1958); and the current bibliographies (*supra*, I). The *Bibliography* by Sir G. Keynes (3rd ed., rev., 1958) includes a list of books Donne owned and a checklist of biography and criticism, 1597–1957; cf. R. C. Bald, *Library*, xiv (1959) and W. White, *Bulletin* (*supra*), xxii (1959). H. C. Combs and Z. R. Sullens compiled a *Concordance* (Chicago, 1940).

MICHAEL DRAYTON, 1563–1631

Drayton's general eclipse is indicated by the lack of any full edition between 1637 and 1748; the 1748 folio was reprinted in 4 vols. in 1753. Signs of a slow return were his inclusion in the collections of Anderson (1793) and Chalmers (1810). The best modern selections are C. Brett's *Minor Poems* (1907) and J. Buxton's *Poems* (Muses' Library, 2 vols., 1953). The standard edition of the complete works is that of J. W. Hebel, K. Tillotson, and B. H. Newdigate (5 vols., 1931–41), which digested and augmented earlier scholarship and criticism, and which is being reprinted with a revised bibliography by B. Juel-Jensen. The best biographical account is Newdigate's *Michael Drayton and His Circle* (1941). Some critical discussions, in addition to the editors', are those of Courthope, iii (1903); O. Elton, *Michael Drayton* (1905); H. H. Child, *CHEL* iv; A. H. Bullen, *Elizabethans* (1924); E. Blunden's tribute to *Poly-Olbion* (*TLS*, 17 August 1922; *Votive Tablets*, 1931); R. L. Sharp and R. Tuve (*supra*, III. 3); F. P. Wilson (*supra*, III. 1); and C. S. Lewis.

More special studies are in the books on the pastoral by Greg and Genouy, on the ode by R. Shafer, on the sonneteers by J. G. Scott, L. E. Pearson, L. C. John, and J. W. Lever (all cited *supra*, III. 3); on the narrative poems, L. F. Ball and H. Nearing (*supra*, III. 3) and L. Zocca, *Elizabethan Narrative Poetry* (Rutgers, 1950); L. Jonas (*supra*, IV. 9); R. Noyes (*Indiana University Studies*, xxii, 1935), on Drayton's vogue since 1631. D. Taylor's 'Drayton and the Countess of Bedford' (*SP* xlix, 1952) is biographical and bibliographical. Bibliographies of the works are given in Elton, of works and scholarship in the Hebel edition; many data are assembled by B. Juel-Jensen, *Library*, viii (1953). There is a *Concise Bibliography* (New York, 1941) by S. A. Tannenbaum.

WILLIAM DRUMMOND of Hawthornden, 1585–1649

Drummond's *Poems* were edited by Milton's nephew, Edward Phillips, in 1656, his *Works* by Bishop Sage and T. Ruddiman in 1711. W. C. Ward's edition (Muses' Library, 2 vols., 1894) was superseded, for scholars, by that of L. E. Kastner (Scottish Text Society, 2 vols., 1913). Masson's book on the writer and his age has been mostly superseded by A. Joly, *William Drummond de Hawthornden* (Lille, 1934), and F. R. Fogle, *A Critical Study of William Drummond of Hawthornden* (Columbia, 1952). Kastner's notes, which gathered up his own numerous studies (chiefly in *MLR* iii–vi), emphasized the poet's lack of originality. The balance is righted by J. G. Scott (*Les Sonnets élisabéthains*, 1929), R. C. Wallerstein's critique (*PMLA* xlviii, 1933), and by Joly and Fogle. The *TLS* had a tercentenary essay (9 December 1949).

A Cypresse Grove was included in the editions of Ward and Kastner and reprinted separately by S. Clegg (1919). The earlier and shorter version, *A Midnight's Trance*, was discovered and edited (1951) by R. Ellrodt, who also noted revisions of 1630 (*MLR* xlvii, 1952). Drummond's borrowings have mounted through the notes of his editors, A. H. Upham (*French Influence*, 1908), G. S. Greene (*PQ* xi, 1932; *MLN* xlviii, 1933), M. A. Rugoff (*PQ* xvi, 1937), G. Smith (*PQ* xxvi, 1947), M. P. McDiarmid (*MLR* xliv, 1949), and Ellrodt (*HLQ* xvi, 1952–3). The *Conversations* with Jonson, since the first garbled text in the 1711 folio, have been printed with increasing accuracy by D. Laing (*Archaeologia Scotica*, iv, 1833; *Shakespeare Society Papers*,

1842); R. F. Patterson (1923); G. B. Harrison (1923); *Ben Jonson*, ed. Herford and Simpson, i (1925).

SIR WILLIAM DRUMMOND, 1636–1713

Drummond's *Diary* for 1657–9 was printed for the first time by H. W. Meikle, *Miscellany of The Scottish History Society*, vii (1941).

SIR WILLIAM DUGDALE, 1605–86

Some of the great antiquarian's chief works appeared before 1660: *Monasticon Anglicanum* (3 vols., 1655–73), for which a good deal had been compiled by Roger Dodsworth; *The Antiquities of Warwickshire* (1656); and *The History of St. Pauls Cathedral in London* (1658; ed. Sir H. Ellis, 1818). W. Hamper edited the *Life, Diary, and Correspondence* (1827). The best accounts of the man and his work are by D. C. Douglas (*History*, xx, 1935–6, and *supra*, IV. 6); E. S. Scroggs (*Journal of the British Archaeological Association*, 3rd Series, ii, 1937); and J. Evans and L. Fox (*supra*, IV. 6). *Sir William Dugdale* (1953), by F. Maddison et al., is a bibliography with other data.

JOHN DUNCON, 1603?–53/9?

Duncon's *The Holy Life and Death of the Lady Letice Vi-Countess Falkland* (1648) was edited by M. F. Howard (1908).

JOHN DURY (DURIE), 1596–1680

Dury's writings on religious and public questions were many and various; some were published by his friend Hartlib. His activities have been described by G. Westin, *Negotiations about Church Unity 1628–1634* (Uppsala, 1932), J. M. Batten, *John Dury Advocate of Christian Reunion* (University of Chicago, 1944), and G. H. Turnbull (under Hartlib, *infra*), who give bibliographies. Dury's educational writings are discussed by H. J. Scougal, *Die pädagogischen Schriften John Durys* (Jena, 1905), in the books by J. W. Adamson, R. F. Young, and R. F. Jones (*supra*, V. 6), and most recently by Turnbull (*supra*) and H. M. Knox (*infra*). *The Reformed Librarie-Keeper With a Supplement to the Reformed-School* (1650) was partly incorporated in an essay in A. W. Pollard's *Old Picture Books* (1902) and edited, without the *Supplement*, by R. S. Granniss (Chicago, 1906). H. M. Knox has edited *The Reformed School* (1649–50) with the *Supplement* (1958).

JOHN EARLE, 1600?–65

Micro-cosmographie. Or, A Peece of the World Discovered; In Essayes and Characters had three or four editions in 1628, the year of publication, and was enlarged in 1629 and 1633. The twelve editions of the seventeenth century were all issued anonymously. Bliss's edition (1811) includes Earle's occasional verse. The latest editions are by G. Murphy (1928), H. Osborne (1933), and A. S. West (1951). The work is also included in the anthologies of H. Morley and R. Aldington (*supra*, IV. 5). Clarendon's sketch of Earle is reprinted in Arber's edition and D. Nichol Smith's *Characters* (*supra*, IV. 6). Criticism and bibliographical data are provided by Earle's editors and the general studies cited above in IV. 5.

SIR JOHN ELIOT, 1592–1632

Grosart edited several works and letters, from manuscripts (6 vols., 1879–82). The view of Eliot represented by J. Forster's biography (2 vols., 1864) has been modified by modern scholarship. The standard *Life* is by H. Hulme (1957). There are essays by H. R. Williamson, *Four Stuart Portraits* (1949), and R. W. K. Hinton, *Cambridge Historical Journal*, xi (1953).

JOHN EVERARD, 1575?–1650?

Everard left a number of translations of mystical works in manuscript. Two published ones were *The Divine Pymander of Hermes Mercurius Trismegistus* (1650) and *The Single Eye* (1646), the latter (from Nicholas of Cusa's *De Visione Dei*) probably by Everard and Giles Randall. Extracts from translations were included with Everard's sermons in *Some Gospel-Treasures Opened* (1653). The fullest account of him (and of Randall) is in Rufus M. Jones, *Spiritual Reformers* (*supra*, V. 2). He is discussed also by Jones in *Mysticism and Democracy* (*supra*, V. 2) and by W. Haller, *The Rise of Puritanism* (1938) and W. K. Jordan, *HLQ* iii (1939–40).

ADAM EYRE, 1614–61

A Dyurnall, or Catalogue of all my Accions and Expences from the 1st of January, 1646 [i.e. 1647], which runs to 1649, was edited by H. J. Morehouse in Charles Jackson's *Yorkshire Diaries and Autobiographies in the Seventeenth and Eighteenth Centuries*, i (Surtees Society, lxv, 1877). Eyre receives an essay in W. Notestein's *English Folk* (1938) and is cited in Mildred Campbell's *English Yeoman* (1942).

EDWARD FAIRFAX, 1560/75–1635

Fairfax's Spenserian translation of Tasso's *Gerusalemme Liberata, Godfrey of Bulloigne* (1600; 1624; 1687; ed. H. Morley, 1890), has been edited by R. Weiss (Southern Illinois University, 1962). His tract on a case of witchcraft in his own family (1621) was printed in *Miscellanies of the Philobiblon Society*, v (1858–9) and edited, with two eclogues by Fairfax, by W. Grainge, as *Dæmonologia* (1882); Sir W. W. Greg edited the eighth eclogue in the English *Modern Language Quarterly*, iv (1901). The translation has been treated in the studies of Tasso in England by E. Koeppel, *Anglia*, xi–xiii (1888–90); Sir Sidney Lee, *Elizabethan and Other Essays* (1929); and A. Castelli, *La Gerusalemme Liberata nella Inghilterra di Spenser* (Milan, 1936). The best critique is by C. G. Bell, *Comparative Literature*, vi (1954). Fairfax and R. Carew (q.v.) are discussed by R. E. N. Dodge (*PMLA* xliv, 1929) and R. Nash (*Italica*, xxxiv, 1957); Fairfax's metrical technique and significance by R. C. Wallerstein (*PMLA* l, 1935). C. G. Bell has done 'A History of Fairfax Criticism' (*PMLA* lxii, 1947) and notes on Fairfax's illegitimacy and his lost eclogues (*MLN* lxii, 1947; *NQ* i, 1954).

MILDMAY FANE, EARL OF WESTMORLAND, 1602–66

Otia Sacra (1648) was edited by Grosart (1879). Selections are in Sir E. Brydges's *Restituta*, ii (1815) and L. B. Marshall's *Rare Poems* (*supra*, II. 2); a fugitive poem was printed in *Life and Letters*, li (1946). There is comment in M. C. Bradbrook's essay on Marvell (*RES* xvii, 1941) and M.-S. Røstvig (*supra*, III. 3). The fullest discussions are by E. Withington, *Harvard Library Bulletin*, ix (1955) and xi (1957). Two plays, *Raguaillo d'Oceano* (1640) and *Candy Restored* (1641), were edited from manuscripts, with a full introduction, by C. Leech (Louvain, 1938). Fane's dramatic work had been discussed by A. Harbage (*SP* xxxi, 1934).

SIR RICHARD FANSHAWE, 1608–66

Fanshawe's translations were: Guarini's *Pastor Fido* (1647), reissued in 1647–8 with original pieces and other translations, including that of the *Aeneid* iv (this last was edited by A. L. Irvine, 1924); *Selected Parts of Horace* (1652); Camoens's *Lusiad* (1655; ed. J. D. M. Ford, Harvard, 1940); and translations from Antonio Hurtado de Mendoza (1670). *Original Letters* appeared in 1701. The *Memoirs* of Fanshawe's widow, with some of his letters, first printed in 1829, were edited by B. Marshall (1905) and, more elaborately, by H. C. Fanshawe (1907). There are a general essay by J. W. Mackail, *Studies of English Poets* (1926), and articles on the Portuguese and Italian versions respectively by Sir H. Thomas, *Revue Hispanique*, xlviii (1920), and G. Bullough, *Studies . . . Presented to . . . Karl Brunner (Wiener Beiträge*, lxv, 1957). A thesis by W. E. Simeone is listed in *Dissertation Abstracts (supra*, I), xiii (1953). There is a bibliography in W. T. Freemantle (under R. Bernard, *supra*).

OWEN FELLTHAM, 1602?–68

The 1st edition of *Resolves* (1623?) contained a hundred essays; the 2nd (1628) had a second century; in the 3rd (1628–9) and later impressions the order of the two centuries was reversed. Further changes were made in number and content. The folio of 1661 contained, besides the 8th edition of the *Resolves*, 41 poems, some of which had been printed long before, letters, and the *Brief Character of the Low-Countries*. Of this last piece unauthorized editions had appeared in 1648 and 1652, an authorized one in 1652. The *Resolves* reached a 12th and last edition in 1709. Felltham's nineteenth-century revival can be partly traced in the *CBEL*. *Resolves* is in the Temple Classics (1904); selections are in anthologies (*supra*, II. 1). The chief critical discussions are by E. N. S. Thompson, *The Seventeenth-Century English Essay* (1926) and McC. Hazlett (*MP* li, 1953–4). The *DNB* has been supplemented by M. D. Cornu (University of Washington *Digests of Theses*, i, 1931), J. Robertson (*NQ* clxxiii, 1937), and F. S. Tupper (*MLN* liv, 1939). J. Robertson gave bibliographical data in *MLN* lviii (1943) and, on the plagiarizing of the *Resolves*, in *MLR* xxxix (1944); to the last topic C. A. Patrides added (*NQ* v, 1958). Echoes of Felltham in Henry Vaughan (see L. C. Martin's notes) are another matter.

NICHOLAS FERRAR, 1592–1637

Ferrar's translation, *The Hundred and Ten Considerations of Signior John Valdesso* (1638), was edited by F. Chapman (1905). J. E. B. Mayor edited *Nicholas Ferrar. Two Lives by his brother John and by Doctor Jebb* (1855). The first and part of the second of five manuscript books were edited by E. C. Sharland as *The Story Books of Little Gidding* (1899). Three standard books are A. L. Maycock's *Nicholas Ferrar of Little Gidding* (1938) and its sequel, *Chronicles of Little Gidding* (1954), and B. Blackstone's *The Ferrar Papers* (1938). C. L. Craig followed up 'The Earliest Little Gidding Concordance' (*Harvard Library Bulletin*, i, 1947; cf. N. G. Cabot, ibid. iii, 1949, xii, 1958) with *Nicholas Ferrar Junior* (1950). The tract, *The Arminian Nunnery* (1641), was edited by M. Hussey in the *Church Quarterly Review*, cxlviii (1949–50), and reprinted also in Maycock's *Chronicles*. There are sketches by H. Collett (1925) and M. Cropper (*Flame Touches Flame*, 1949). Reference is hardly needed to the picture in J. H. Shorthouse's *John Inglesant* (1880–1) and to T. S. Eliot's poem.

SIR ROBERT FILMER, c. 1588–1653

Filmer's chief works—which had six collected editions, 1679–96—were: *Patriarcha: or the Natural Power of Kings* (written between 1635 and 1642; pub. 1680); *The Free-holders Grand Inquest touching Our Soveraigne Lord the King and His Parliament* (1648), an expansion of the last part of *Patriarcha*; *The Anarchy of a Limited or Mixed Monarchy* (1648), a critique of Hunton (q.v.); *The Necessity of the Absolute Power of all Kings* (1648), compiled from Knolles's translation of Bodin; *Observations concerning the Originall of Government* (1652), which criticized Hobbes, Milton, and Grotius; *Observations upon Aristotles Politiques* (1652); and sensible tracts on usury (1653; repr., *Harleian Miscellany*, ed. Park, x, 1813) and witchcraft (1653). *Patriarcha* has been edited by H. Morley (1884), T. I. Cook (in *Two Treatises on Government By John Locke*, New York, 1947), and in a standard edition by P. Laslett, *Patriarcha and Other Political Works of Sir Robert Filmer* (1949). The critique of Milton was reprinted in W. R. Parker, *Milton's Contemporary Reputation* (Ohio State University, 1940). Filmer has been rehabilitated by J. W. Allen (*Social & Political Ideas of Some English Thinkers of the Augustan Age*, ed. F. J. C. Hearnshaw, 1928), by his recent editors (see also Laslett, *William and Mary Quarterly*, 3rd series, v, 1948), and by Zagorin and Treves (*supra*, V. 1) and Pocock (*supra*, IV. 6).

GILES FLETCHER, 1585/6–1623.

Christs Victorie, and Triumph (1610) reappeared in 1632 and 1640. A prose work, *The Reward of the Faithfull*, was printed in 1623. Grosart's edition of Giles's poems (1868; rev. 1876) was superseded by F. S. Boas's standard edition of the *Poetical Works* of the brothers (2 vols., 1908–9). The fullest critique is Arno Esch, *Giles Fletchers ,,Christs Victorie and Triumph``: Eine Studie zum Epenstil des englischen Barock* (Bottrop, 1937); Esch also had an article in *Anglia*, lxxviii (1960). Giles is discussed in relation to biblical narratives by B. O. Kurth (*supra*, III. 3), and in relation to Puritans and Catholics by A. Holaday (*JEGP* liv, 1955; *Studies in Honor of T. W. Baldwin*, ed. D. C. Allen, University of Illinois, 1958). He figures in accounts of the Spenserians and of English influences on Milton (see P. Fletcher, *infra*).

PHINEAS FLETCHER, 1582–1650

Besides the works named in the text Fletcher published two pieces of devotional prose, *The Way to Blessednes* and *Joy in Tribulation* (1632), and *Sylva Poetica* (1633). *A Fathers Testament*, a prose work containing verse, appeared in 1670. Grosart's edition of the poems (4 vols., 1869) was superseded by F. S. Boas's (see Giles Fletcher, *supra*). E. Seaton edited *Venus and Anchises* (*Brittain's Ida*) from a manuscript (1926). The standard book is A. B. Langdale, *Phineas Fletcher, Man of Letters, Science and Divinity* (Columbia, 1937); cf. L. E. Berry, *NQ* vii (1960). In addition to studies of pastoralism (*supra*, III. 3), there are H. E. Cory, 'Spenser, the School of the Fletchers, and Milton' (*University of California Publications in Modern Philology*, ii, 1912) and K. Waibel's study of Spenser and *The Purple Island* (*Englische Studien*, lviii, 1924). The Fletchers' influence on Milton is summarized in J. H. Hanford's *Milton Handbook* (4th ed., 1946).

JOHN FLORIO, 1553–1625?

Florio's works include a translation (1580), from the Italian, of Cartier's account of his first two voyages (repr. by Hakluyt, who had commissioned it, in the *Voyages*, 1600); the Italian phrase-books and readers, *Florio His firste Fruites* (1578; ed. A. del Re, Formosa, 1936) and *Florios Second Frutes* (1591; ed. R. C. Simonini, Scholars' Facsimiles & Reprints, 1953); the Italian-English dictionary, *A Worlde of Wordes* (1598), much enlarged as *Queen Anna's New World of Words* (1611); the translation of Montaigne's *Essayes* (licensed in 1600, printed in 1603). The last has had many popular editions: the text edited by J. I. M. Stewart (2 vols., 1931) was the first based on collation of the 1603, 1613, and 1632 editions. Florio had a share in the *Newfound Politicke* (1626) of Sir William Vaughan (q.v.). H. G. Wright, in *The First English Translation of the 'Decameron' (1620)* (Upsala, 1953), made an elaborate argument for Florio's authorship. The standard book is F. A. Yates, *John Florio* (1934). More special is Silvio Policardi, *John Florio e le relazioni culturali fra l'Inghilterra e l'Italia nel XVI secolo* (Venice, 1947). R. C. Simonini has an essay in *A Tribute to George Coffin Taylor*, ed. A. Williams (University of North Carolina, 1952), and in his *Italian Scholarship (supra, IV. 7)*. Among studies of the *Essayes* are Saintsbury's introduction (Tudor Translations, 3 vols., 1892–3), a solid chapter in F. O. Matthiessen (*supra*, IV. 8), and two articles on Florio's language by A. Koszul (*Revue Anglo-Américaine*, ix, 1931–2). F. Dieckow wrote a monograph on the influence of Montaigne and Florio on Bacon, Jonson, and Burton (Strassburg, 1903); their influence on Marston and Webster was treated by C. Crawford, *Collectanea, Second Series* (1907). The claims represented by G. C. Taylor's *Shakspere's Debt to Montaigne* (Harvard, 1925) are questioned by A. Harmon (*PMLA* lvii, 1942) and M. T. Hodgen (*HLQ* xvi, 1952–3); K. Muir cites further parallels in *NQ* cxcvii (1952).

THOMAS FLOYD, *c.* 1572?–?

Floyd's *Picture of a Perfit Common Wealth* (1600) is discussed by D. T. Starnes (*University of Texas Studies in English*, xi, 1931), who shows the author's large use of Elyot's *Governour* (1531) and N. Ling's *Politeuphuia Wits Common wealth* (1597).

ROBERT FLUDD, 1574–1637

'His Books written in Latine', said Fuller, 'are great, many and mystical', and there is no strong reason to recite titles. J. B. Craven's *Doctor Robert Fludd . . . The English Rosicrucian* (1902) may be supplemented by F. Freudenberg, *Paracelsus und*

Fludd (Berlin, 1918), and by parts of A. E. Waite's *Brotherhood of the Rosy Cross* (1924) and *Secret Tradition in Alchemy* (1926); D. Saurat, *Milton: Man and Thinker* (1925; section on Fludd enlarged in 1944 edition) and *Literature and Occult Tradition* (trans. 1930); K. B. Collier, *Cosmogonies of Our Fathers* (Columbia, 1934); the earlier of W. Pagel's medical articles (*supra*, V. 3); and H. G. Dick's article of 1946 (*supra*, V. 3).

EMANUEL FORD, *fl.* 1598 ff.

Parismus, The Renoumed Prince of Bohemia (1598), which had a sequel, *Parismenos* (1599), went through more than twenty reprints up to 1740; brief extracts are in R. B. Johnson's *Birth of Romance* (1928) and G. Bullough's *Narrative and Dramatic Sources of Shakespeare*, ii (1958). *Ornatus and Artesia* (first published in 1595?; extant in an edition of 1607) is reprinted in P. Henderson's *Shorter Novels*, ii (Everyman's Library, 1930). The earliest extant edition of *The Famous Historie of Montelyon, Knight of the Oracle* is that of 1633. Ford's works are listed in the bibliographies of Esdaile, Mish, and O'Dell and discussed in E. A. Baker, ii (1929) and M. Patchell (all cited *supra*, IV. 4).

THOMAS FULLER, 1608–61

Some of Fuller's works are: *Davids Hainous Sinne* (1631), edited, with his other verse, by A. B. Grosart (1868); *Historie of the Holy Warre* (1639; repr. 1840); *The Holy State* (1642), ed. J. Nichols (1841), ed. in facsimile, with elaborate apparatus, by M. G. Walten (2 vols., Columbia, 1938); *A Sermon of Reformation* (1643); *Good Thoughts in Bad Times* (1645); *Good Thoughts in Worse Times* (1647); *A Pisgah-Sight of Palestine* (1650); *Abel Redevivus* (1651; ed. W. Nichols, 2 vols., 1867), edited and partly written by Fuller; *The Church-History of Britain; . . . The History of the University of Cambridge* (1655), ed. J. S. Brewer (6 vols., 1845); *A Collection of Sermons* (1656); *The Appeal of Injured Innocence* (1659), Fuller's reply to Heylyn; *Mixt Contemplations in Better Times* (1660); and *The History of the Worthies of England* (1662), ed. P. A. Nuttall (3 vols., 1840) and, abridged, ed. J. Freeman (1952). There are also *Collected Sermons*, ed. J. E. Bailey and W. E. A. Axon (2 vols., 1891), and, among anthologies, that of E. K. Broadus (1928). J. O. Wood has argued (*HLQ* xvii, 1953–4) for an early and topical addition to the canon, *Andronicus: A Tragedy* (pub. 1661).

The anonymous *Life* (1661) is reprinted in Brewer's edition of the *Church-History* and in Broadus. The standard—though hardly readable—biography is by J. E. Bailey (1874). Good shorter ones are D. B. Lyman's *The Great Tom Fuller* (University of California, 1935) and W. Addison's more expansive *Worthy Dr. Fuller* (1951).

Coleridge's comments are given in Raysor and more fully in R. F. Brinkley. Broadus reprinted criticism from Lamb, J. Crossley (*Retrospective Review*, iii, 1821), and Sir Leslie Stephen (*Cornhill Magazine*, xxv, 1872). Among modern essays are those of E. N. S. Thompson (*Literary Bypaths of the Renaissance*, 1924), E. E. Kellett (*London Quarterly Review*, cxlv, 1926; *Reconsiderations*, 1928), and Sir S. C. Roberts (1953; repr. in *Doctor Johnson and Others*, 1958). The most substantial study of Fuller's mind and sources is W. E. Houghton's *The Formation of Thomas Fuller's Holy and Profane States* (Harvard, 1938). Fuller the writer of characters and essays figures in the studies of those genres (*supra*, IV. 5); the church historian and biographer in H. Arneke and D. A. Stauffer (*supra*, IV. 6); the preacher in W. F. Mitchell (*supra*, V. 2); the religious moderate in W. K. Jordan, iv (ibid.).

There is a full bibliography of Fuller's works by S. Gibson, with an introduction by Sir G. Keynes, in *OBS* iv, part i, ii, 1934 (1936); additions and corrections, *OBS*, n.s., i, 1947 (1948), p. 44.

THOMAS GAGE, 1602/3–56.

The English-American his Travail by Sea and Land: Or, A New Survey of the West India's (1648), which had a number of editions in English and in French, Dutch, and German translations, has been edited in abridged and modernized form by A. P. Newton (*A New Survey of the West Indies, 1648,* 1928) and J. E. S. Thompson (*Thomas Gage's Travels in the New World*, University of Oklahoma, 1958).

JOHN GAUDEN, 1605–62

Whatever small interest attaches to Gauden's religious and miscellaneous writings, or to his edition, with a *Life*, of Hooker (1662), his fame hangs on his connexion with Εἰκὼν Βασιλική. *The Pourtraicture of His Sacred Majestie in his Solitudes and Sufferings* (1649). F. F. Madan analysed the problem and its history in

A New Bibliography of the Eikon Basilike of King Charles the First (1950). His view, to which modern opinion had previously inclined, seems to be generally accepted. A hostile review (*TLS*, 9 February 1951) led to debate, which was followed up by Madan, ibid., 31 August 1956; cf. H. R. Trevor-Roper, *History Today*, i (1951); *Historical Essays* (1957). E. Sirluck (*MLN* lxix, 1954) showed that Gauden's authorship was apparently known or suspected from 1649 onward. Madan also dealt with the charge, elaborated by S. B. Liljegren, that Milton and Bradshaw had the prayer of Sidney's Pamela inserted in some editions in order to damage the book by the exposure of such an item. The charge was answered by J. S. Smart (*RES* i, 1925), revived by P. P. Morand (*The Effects of his Political Life upon John Milton*, Paris, 1939), and finally demolished by R. W. Chambers (*Proceedings of the British Academy*, xxvii, 1941), Madan, and M. Y. Hughes (*RES* iii, 1952; Milton's *Complete Prose Works*, iii, Yale, forthcoming, 1962–3).

SIR BALTHAZAR GERBIER, 1591?–1667

In addition to the *DNB*, there is a short account of the Academy by D. Wing (*To Doctor Rosenbach*, Philadelphia, 1946), a biographical essay in Hugh R. Williamson, *Four Stuart Portraits* (1949).

WILLIAM GILBERT, 1544–1603

Gilbert's great work was *De Magnete, Magneticisque Corporibus, et de magno magnete tellure, Physiologia nova, plurimis & argumentis, & experimentis, demonstrata* (1600; facsimile ed., Berlin, 1892; trans. P. F. Mottelay, New York, 1893; repr., Ann Arbor, 1941; New York, 1958; trans., with notes, by S. P. Thompson, 1900–1; ed. D. J. Price, New York, 1958). Gilbert also wrote *De Mundo nostro Sublunari Philosophia Nova* (Amsterdam, 1651). The standard biographical and scientific book is D. H. D. Roller, *The De Magnete of William Gilbert* (Amsterdam, 1959). Gilbert is discussed in general histories of science and astronomy (*supra*, V. 3), in Mottelay's *Bibliographical History of Electricity & Magnetism* (1922), in E. G. R. Taylor (*supra*, V. 4), F. R. Johnson, *Astronomical Thought* (*supra*, V. 3), and by E. Zilsel, 'The Origins of William Gilbert's Scientific Method' (*JHI* ii, 1941). R. Suter outlined his ideas in the *Scientific Monthly*, lxx (1950), his life in *Osiris*, x (1952). Roller gives a full bibliography.

ALEXANDER GILL the elder, 1564–1635

Gill is best known as Milton's headmaster at St. Paul's School and as the author of *Logonomia Anglica* (1619; rev. 1621; ed. O. L. Jiriczek, *Quellen und Forschungen*, xc, 1903; trans. and ed. by D. Dixon, University of Southern California *Abstracts of Dissertations . . . 1951*). His interest in the English language has been studied by Jiriczek (op. cit. and *Studien zur vergleichenden Literaturgeschichte*, ii, 1903), H. Kökeritz (*Studia Neophilologica*, xi, 1938–9), and R. F. Jones and E. J. Dobson (*supra*, IV. 1). *The Sacred Philosophie Of the Holy Scripture* (1635) was an attempt at a rational Christian theology (A. Barker, *MLR* xxxii, 1937). In addition to the *DNB* and Masson's *Milton*, D. L. Clark had a full account of the two Gills in *HLQ* ix (1945–6).

SIDNEY GODOLPHIN, 1610–43

Godolphin's poems, first collected in Saintsbury, ii (1906), were edited by W. Dighton (1931). His and Waller's translation of *Aeneid* iv is discussed by Dighton and by L. Proudfoot (*supra*, IV. 8). Clarendon's sketch of him is reprinted in D. Nichol Smith's *Characters* (*supra*, IV. 6).

FRANCIS GODWIN, 1562–1633

Bishop Godwin's solid works were *A Catalogue of the Bishops of England* (1601) and the Latin *Annales* (1616; trans. 1630) of the reigns of Henry VIII, Edward VI, and Mary. His much livelier *Man in the Moone* (1638) may have been written between 1601 and 1630, perhaps after 1620. The full text was first edited, along with Godwin's *Nuncius Inanimatus* (1629), by G. McColley (Smith College, 1937), who gave extracts in his *Literature and Science* (Chicago, 1940). Other discussions are: H. W. Lawton, *RES* vii (1931); McColley, *MP* xxxv, *Library*, xvii, and *PQ* xvi (all of 1937); F. R. Johnson, *Astronomical Thought* (*supra*, V. 3); M. Nicolson, *A World in the Moon* (Smith College, 1936), 'Cosmic Voyages' (*ELH* vii, 1940), and *Voyages to the Moon* (1948); V. Dupont (*supra*, IV. 4); and 'Bishop Francis Godwin, Historian and Novelist', *Journal of the Historical Society of the Church in Wales*, v (1955), by W. M. Merchant, who has a book in prospect. There is a popular sketch in P. Leighton, *Moon Travellers* (1960).

GODFREY GOODMAN, 1583–1656

Godfrey Goodman (1953) is a thorough biography (though prejudiced in religion and politics) by G. I. Soden, who had a sketch in the *Church Quarterly Review*, cxliv–v (1947) and cliv (1953). *The Fall of Man, Or the Corruption of Nature Proved by the light of our naturall Reason* (1616) is a rare book, but its argument can be followed in the 5th and 6th books of the 3rd edition (1635) of Hakewill's *Apologie*, in the full analysis of V. Harris (cited with others under Hakewill, *infra*), and in the short one by R. W. Hepburn (*Cambridge Journal*, vii, 1954). Goodman's *Court of King James the First*, written in reply to Weldon (q.v.), was first printed in 1839 (ed. J. S. Brewer, 2 vols.).

JOHN GOODWIN, 1594?–1665

Anti-Cavalierisme (1642) and *ΘΕΟΜΑΧΙΑ* (1644) are reproduced in W. Haller, *Tracts on Liberty* (1934), and parts of *Independencie Gods Veritie* (1647) and *Right and Might well met* (1649) are given in A. S. P. Woodhouse, *Puritanism and Liberty* (1938). One of Godwin's services to religious freedom was his sponsoring (with John Dury) a translation (1648) of part of Jacobus Acontius's *Stratagemata Satanae* (1565). There is an unsatisfactory life by T. Jackson (rev. ed., 1872). Goodwin's thought is discussed by Haller in his *Tracts* and two later books; by Woodhouse; by W. K. Jordan, iii; in books on Milton by D. M. Wolfe and A. Barker; and by P. Zagorin (all cited *supra*, V. 1 and 2).

THOMAS GOODWIN, 1600–80

The *Works* (5 vols., 1681–1704) were reprinted in 6 vols. (1861). The *Apologeticall Narration* (1644), by Goodwin and others, is reproduced in W. Haller, *Tracts on Liberty* (1934). Goodwin is discussed by John Brown, *Puritan Preaching in England* (1900), by Haller in his *Tracts* and two later books, by Jordan and Barker (all cited *supra*, V. 2), and by E. I. Watkin, *Poets and Mystics* (1953).

SAMUEL GOTT, 1614–71

Gott was a lawyer, M.P., country gentleman, and liberal Puritan. His chief work, the utopian romance *Novæ Solymæ Libri Sex* (1648), was translated by W. Begley (2 vols., 1902), who attributed it to Milton. The author was identified by S. K. Jones (*Library*, i, 1910). The book is discussed by F. E. Held in his edition of Andreae's *Christianopolis* (1916), fully by Dupont (*supra*, IV. 4), and by W. A. L. Vincent (*supra*, V. 6). J. M. Patrick gave an account of Gott and his writings in the *UTQ* viii (1938–9).

WILLIAM GOUGE, 1578–1653

The life and works of this Puritan divine are discussed in W. Haller's *Rise of Puritanism* (1938); his *Of Domesticall Duties* (1622) in C. L. Powell (*supra*, V. 5), L. B. Wright (*supra*, IV. 2), W. E. Houghton (under Fuller, *supra*), and G. S. Wakefield, *Puritan Devotion* (1957).

JAMES GRAHAM, MARQUIS OF MONTROSE, 1612–50

The two famous pieces, 'Montrose to his Mistress' and the lines on the dead Charles I, were printed as broadsides, the latter also in the 1653 edition of Cleveland's poems. These and the few others were edited (1938) by J. L. Weir, who had printed the texts in *NQ* clxxiii (1937) and early tributes to Montrose in *NQ* clxxiv (1938). The slender canon has been enlarged by 'This World's a Tennis-court', added in *The Green Garden*, ed. Sir James Fergusson (1946), and printed from another version in Miss Wedgwood's essay (*infra*). Montrose's letter on sovereignty, written in 1640–1, is printed in the standard biography by John Buchan (1928) and in Mark Napier's *Memorials* (2 vols., 1848–50) and *Memoirs* (2 vols., 1856). There is a short life (1958) by C. V. Wedgwood, who has an essay on the poems in *ESEA 1960*.

JOHN GREENE, 1616–59

Selections from Greene's diary (1635–57) were printed by E. M. Symonds, *English Historical Review,* xliii, xliv (1928–9).

FULKE GREVILLE, FIRST LORD BROOKE, 1554–1628

Apart from a few pieces from *Caelica* in anthologies and the unauthorized *Mustapha* of 1609, Greville's poems and minor prose were first printed in *Certaine Learned and Elegant Workes* (1633) and *Remains* (1670). *The Life of the Renowned Sir Philip Sidney* (1652) was edited by Nowell Smith (1907); a new manuscript is described by S. B. Ewing, *MLR* xlix (1954). Grosart's edition of the complete works (4 vols., 1870) has been partly superseded by G. Bullough's *Poems and Dramas* (2 vols., 1939).

Caelica was edited by U. Ellis-Fermor (1936). M. W. Croll's *The Works of Fulke Greville* (Philadelphia, 1903) remains a useful study. With Bullough's biographical account (*MLR* xxviii, 1933) and introduction to his edition may be joined N. Orsini's selective and succinct analysis, *Fulke Greville tra il mondo e Dio* (Milan, 1941). A special critique is W. Frost's *Fulke Greville's Caelica* (priv. pr., U.S.A., 1942). Studies of Greville's ideas, mainly political, are: H. W. Utz, *Die Anschauungen über Wissenschaft und Religion im Werke Fulke Grevilles* (Bern, 1948); P. Ure, *RES* i (1950); J. Jacquot, *Etudes Anglaises*, v (1952); H. N. Maclean, *HLQ* xvi (1952–3) and xxi (1957–8) and *NQ* iii (1956); and I. Morris, *Shakespeare Survey*, xiv (1961). G. A. Wilkes worked out the probable sequence of Greville's writings (*SP* lvi, 1959 and *NQ* v, 1958).

ROBERT GREVILLE, SECOND LORD BROOKE, 1608–43

Brooke wrote *The Nature of Truth Its Union and Unity with the Soule, Which is One in its Essence, Faculties, Acts; One with Truth* (1640) and *A Discourse opening the Nature of that Episcopacie, which is exercised in England* (1641; 2nd ed., 1642; ed. W. Haller, *Tracts on Liberty*, 1934). Brooke is discussed by C. de Rémusat (*supra*, V. 3); J. Freudenthal, *Archiv für Geschichte der Philosophie*, vi (1892–3); W. Haller, *Tracts* and *The Rise of Puritanism* (1938); W. K. Jordan, ii, and A. Barker (*supra*, V. 2). R. E. L. Strider's *Robert Greville Lord Brooke* (Harvard, 1958) gives a full analysis of the writings with a life. A mutual debt between Milton and Brooke is suggested in G. W. Whiting, *Milton's Literary Milieu* (University of North Carolina, 1939).

EDWARD GRIMESTON, ?–1640

There are articles on Grimeston by F. S. Boas (*MP* iii, 1905–6) and Sir G. N. Clark (*English Historical Review*, xliii, 1928), who gives a detailed bibliography. His work figures in discussions of Chapman's French sources, e.g. J. Jacquot (*supra*).

ELIZABETH GRYMESTON, *ante* 1563–1601/4

Miscelanea. Meditations. Memoratives, compiled for the guidance of the author's son, appeared in 1604 and was reissued in 1605–6, *c.* 1608, and *c.* 1618. A few pages are reprinted in Michael Roberts's *Elizabethan Prose* (1933). There is a full account of Mrs. Grymeston in the *Library*, xv (1934–5), by R.

Hughey and P. Hereford, who show among other things that all her bits of verse are taken from *Englands Parnassus*, Southwell, and R. Verstegan's *Odes* (Antwerp, 1601).

WILLIAM HABINGTON, 1605–54

Habington published a play, *The Queene of Arragon* (1640; repr. in Dodsley's *Collection*, ed. Hazlitt, xiii); two prose works, *The Historie of Edward the Fourth* (1640; repr. in W. Kennett, *supra*, IV. 6), in which his father had had a large share, and *Observations upon Historie* (1641); and *Castara* (1634), which was enlarged in 1635 and again, with a religious section that contains some of his best poems, in 1640. The 3rd edition was included in Chalmers, vi, and reprinted by C. A. Elton (1812) and Arber (1870). The standard edition is by K. Allott (1948). Habington is discussed by M.-S. Røstvig (*supra*, III. 3). H. C. Combs had a bibliographical study of *Castara* in Northwestern University *Summaries of Doctoral Dissertations*, vii (1939) and a note on the date of the poet's marriage (1633) in *MLN* lxiii (1948).

GEORGE HAKEWILL, 1578–1649

Hakewill's monument is *An Apologie of the Power and Providence of God in the Government of the World. Or an Examination and Censure of the Common Errour Touching Natures Perpetuall and Universall Decay* (1627; rev. and enlarged, 1630, 1635). His ideas are discussed by G. Williamson, R. F. Jones, and most fully by V. Harris (all *supra*, III. 4). R. W. Hepburn has a summary exposition in *JHI* xvi (1955). Hakewill and the great debate are partly reinterpreted by H. Baron (*supra*, III. 4). J. I. Dredge listed Hakewill's works and editions in *A Few Sheaves of Devon Bibliography . . . The Second Sheaf* (1890).

JOHN HALES, 1584–1656

Some publications, chiefly posthumous, were: *Oratio Funebris* on Sir Thomas Bodley (1613); *A Tract Concerning Schisme and Schismaticks* (1642); *Golden Remaines* (1659; enlarged 1673, 1688); *Several Tracts* (1677; enlarged, 1716, by the 'Letter to Archbishop Laud'); *Works*, ed. Lord Hailes (3 vols., 1765). There are large selections in Jared Sparks, *Collection of Essays and Tracts*, v (Boston, 1825), one sermon in Henson's anthology (*supra*, V. 2). Among early accounts are those of John Aubrey, Clarendon (repr. in D. Nichol Smith, *Characters*, *supra*, IV. 6), and Walton's notes (ed. J. Butt, *MLR* xxix, 1934). The standard book is J. H. Elson, *John Hales of Eton* (Columbia, 1948). Some other discussions are by J. Tulloch (i), W. F. Mitchell, H. J. McLachlan, and in the books on toleration by M. Freund, Jordan (ii), and Lyon (all cited above in V. 2); J. W. Allen (*supra*, V. 1); and J. J. Murray, 'John Hales on History' (*HLQ* xix, 1955–6).

JOHN HALL, 1627–56

Some of the many products of Hall's short and irregular life were his essays, *Horæ Vacivæ* (1646; extracts in Sir E. Brydges, *Restituta*, iii, 1815); *Poems* (1647; ed. Brydges, 1816; ed. Saintsbury, ii, 1906); *An Humble Motion To The Parliament Of England Concerning The Advancement of Learning: And Reformation of the Universities* (1649; ed. A. K. Croston, 1953); *Paradoxes* (1650; ed. D. C. Allen, Scholars' Facsimiles & Reprints, 1956); Περὶ ὕψους, *Or Dionysius Longinus of the Height of Eloquence* (1652); *A Letter written to a Gentleman in the Country* (1653), a piece of Cromwellian journalism which Thomason and Masson ascribed to Milton (P. S. Havens, *HLB* vi, 1934); *Hierocles upon the Golden Verses of Pythagoras* (1657), which contains an unusually concrete biographical sketch of Hall by John Davies of Kidwelly; and *Emblems* (1658), taken from Michael Hoyer's *Flammulae Amoris S. P. Augustini*. Hall's place in the educational debate is treated more or less by R. F. Jones (*supra*, III. 4), Croston, and E. Sirluck, *Complete Prose Works of John Milton*, ii (Yale, 1959). Besides the *DNB* and items cited above, there is some account of Hall in Mullinger (*supra*, V. 6). G. H. Turnbull summarized 'John Hall's Letters to Samuel Hartlib' in *RES* iv (1953).

JOSEPH HALL, 1574–1656

The works were edited by P. Wynter (10 vols., 1863). The standard edition of the poems is by A. Davenport (1949). Healey's translation of the *Mundus*, *The Discovery of A New World* (1609?), was edited by H. Brown (Harvard, 1937). The *Characters* are reprinted in the anthologies of H. Morley and R. Aldington and represented in others (*supra*, IV. 5), and were edited, with a full introduction, by R. Kirk, *Heaven upon Earth and Characters* (Rutgers, 1948). Hall's autobiographical writings are assembled in Wynter's first volume. There is a life by G. Lewis (1886), a sketch by R. W. Ketton-Cremer (*A Norfolk Gallery*, 1948), and glimpses are given in R. C. Bald, *Donne &*

the Drurys (1959). T. F. Kinloch's *Life and Works of Joseph Hall* (1951) is unsatisfactory. The early satires are discussed by C. S. Lewis, the characters by Kirk and in studies of the genre (*supra*, IV. 5), and other facets of Hall's work by W. F. Mitchell and H. R. McAdoo (*supra*, V. 2) and H. Fisch (*RES* xxv, 1949). The episcopal controversy is handled by W. Haller in his books of 1938 and 1955 (*supra*, V. 1 and 2); W. R. Parker, *Milton's Contemporary Reputation* (Ohio State University, 1940); A. Chew, *ELH* xvii (1950); and minutely in *Complete Prose Works of John Milton*, i, ed. D. M. Wolfe (Yale, 1953). Hall's Senecanism of thought and/or style is upheld or questioned by Kirk (*supra*), P. A. Smith (*PMLA* lxiii, 1948), A. Chew (ibid. lxv, 1950), H. Fisch (*Proceedings of the Leeds Philosophical Society*, vi, 1950), and G. Williamson, *The Senecan Amble* (1951). His popularity abroad is shown by G. Waterhouse (*supra*, IV. 7) and Kirk.

PATRICK HANNAY, *fl.* 1619–22.

Hannay's poems were reprinted by Saintsbury, i (1905). His *Sheretine and Mariana* is described by A. I. T. Higgins (*supra*, III. 3); its historical sources were traced by N. T. Ting (*JEGP* xliii, 1944).

SIR JOHN HARINGTON, 1560–1612

The early works are treated by C. S. Lewis. Some letters and papers were printed in *Nugæ Antiquæ* (2 vols., 1769–75; enlarged, 3 vols., 1779; ed. Park, 2 vols., 1804); other prose tracts have been edited separately. Two popular works were the translation, *The Englishmans Doctor. Or, the Schoole of Salerne* (1607; ed. F. R. Packard and F. H. Garrison, New York, 1920; London, 1922), and *Epigrams* (1613, 1615, 1618 ff.; ed. N. E. McClure, *Letters and Epigrams*, with a standard account of Harington, University of Pennsylvania, 1930); *The Prayse of Private Life*, which McClure includes, may be Daniel's. M. H. M. MacKinnon (*PQ* xxxvii, 1958) printed a letter to Bishop Hall in which Harington opposed Hall's views on marriage of the clergy. M. S. Goldman discovered and is editing 'Briefe notes upon the 6th booke of Virgils Æneads'. There are an essay by Sir Walter Raleigh (*Some Authors*, 1923) and popular sketches by D. Meadows (*Elizabethan Quintet*, 1956), D. McDonald (*History Today*, vi, 1956), and I. Grimble, *The Harington Family* (1957). The notorious *Metamorphosis of Ajax* (1596; repr. 1814, 1927;

ed. by E. S. Donno, 1962) and its sequels were discussed by A. E. M. Kirkwood (*Library*, xii, 1931–2); Harington's sanitary invention by H. E. Sigerist (*Bulletin of the History of Medicine*, xiii, 1943; repr. in *Henry E. Sigerist on the History of Medicine*, New York, 1960). Harington's Rabelaisian strain is treated in G. Rehfeld, *Sir John Harington* (Halle, 1914), and H. Brown, *Rabelais* (*supra*, IV. 7). M. S. Goldman discussed 'Sidney and Harington as Opponents of Superstition' (*JEGP* liv, 1955), K. E. Schmetzler manuscript versions of psalms (*PBSA*, liii, 1959). R. Hughey has followed up her article (*Library*, xv, 1934–5) with a very elaborate edition, *The Arundel Harington Manuscript of Tudor Poetry* (2 vols., Ohio State University Press, 1960), which includes poems by and information about Sir John.

BRILLIANA LADY HARLEY, 1600?–43

T. T. Lewis edited *Letters of the Lady Brilliana Harley* (Camden Society, 1854). They cover the years 1625–43.

JAMES HARRINGTON, 1611–77

The Common-Wealth of Oceana (1656) and smaller works were edited by Toland (1700). H. Morley's popular reprint of *Oceana* (1887) was superseded by S. B. Liljegren's elaborate edition (Heidelberg, 1924). *The Rota* (1660) is in Negley and Patrick (*supra*, V. 1). A useful selection is *The Political Writings of James Harrington*, ed. C. Blitzer (New York, 1955). The fullest studies of his thought and influence are Blitzer's *An Immortal Commonwealth* (Yale, 1960) and H. F. R. Smith's *Harrington and his Oceana* (1914). Some shorter studies are: V. Dupont (*supra*, IV. 4); R. H. Tawney, *Proceedings of the British Academy*, xxvii (1941); R. Polin, *Revue française de science politique*, ii (1952); C. Hill, *Puritanism and Revolution* (1958); J. N. Shklar, *American Political Science Review*, liii (1959); and C. B. Macpherson, *Past & Present*, No. xvii (1960). Harrington has his place in such studies of political thought as those of Gooch, Sabine, Fink, Kliger, Zagorin, and Treves (*supra*, V. 1); Pocock (*supra*, IV. 6) criticizes orthodox views. One of Liljegren's supplementary studies, on maritime and utopian ideas, is in *Festschrift Johannes Hoops* (Heidelberg, 1925); another is an edition of *A French Draft Constitution of 1792 modelled on . . . Oceana* (1932). The problem of

Church and State is discussed in the books on toleration by M. Freund and W. K. Jordan, iv (*supra*, V. 2).

THOMAS HARRIOT, 1560–1621

A briefe and true report of the new found land of Virginia (1588), the second original English book about America, was reprinted by Hakluyt and often later. There are several facsimiles (ed. L. S. Livingston, *Bibliographer*, i, 1902, and separately, New York, 1903; ed. R. G. Adams, Ann Arbor Facsimile Series, 1931). Henry Stevens edited the text (1900). T. de Bry's illustrated edition (Frankfort, 1590) has also been reproduced in various forms (New York, 1871; ed. W. H. Rylands, 1888; Quaritch, 1893; ed. S. Lorant, *The New World*, New York, 1946). The background of the book is supplied by the editors; by Stevens's *Thomas Harriot and his Associates* (1900); by G. P. Winship, *Cambridge History of American Literature*, i (1917); G. W. Cole, 'Elizabethan Americana', *Bibliographical Essays: A Tribute to Wilberforce Eames* (Harvard, 1924); and G. B. Parks, *Richard Hakluyt and the English Voyages* (New York, 1928). Harriot's friend Walter Warner edited a mathematical work (1631), and Harriot's 'Observations' of Halley's comet in 1607 are given as an appendix in James Bradley's *Miscellaneous Works and Correspondence* (1832); there are unpublished manuscripts in the British Museum. Stevens's account of Harriot, and the *DNB*, have been amplified by M. Nicolson (*SP* xxxii, 1935), F. R. Johnson, *Astronomical Thought* (*supra*, V. 3), and the historians of mathematics and science, including E. G. R. Taylor (*supra*, V. 3). J. Jacquot discussed Harriot's reputation for impiety in *Notes and Records of The Royal Society*, ix (1951–2).

SAMUEL HARTLIB, 1596/1600–1662

Some of the many and varied writings that Hartlib composed or sponsored or inspired are: *A Description of the famous Kingdome of Macaria* (1641; *Harleian Miscellany*, ed. Park, i, 1808); *A Further Discoverie of The Office of Publick Addresse For Accommodations* (1648; *Harleian Miscellany*, vi, 1810), probably by John Dury; *Londons Charity inlarged* (1650); *The Reformed Virginian Silk-Worm* (1655; P. Force, *Tracts*, iii, 1844). Hartlib's correspondence with Robert Boyle is in Boyle's *Works*, ed. Birch (1744), v or (1772), vi. His correspondence with Worthington is cited under the latter. G. H. Turnbull's *Samuel Hartlib: A Sketch of his*

Life and his Relations to J. A. Comenius (1920) has been largely supplemented by the same author's *Hartlib, Dury and Comenius* (1947), which has a full bibliography. Hartlib's scientific and educational interests are treated also by R. F. Jones (*supra*, III. 4), R. H. Syfret and Turnbull (*supra*, V. 3), and R. F. Young and Sirluck (*supra*, V. 6). *Macaria* is discussed by Dupont (*supra*, IV. 4), Negley and Patrick and Fuz (*supra*, V. 1), and R. H. Bowers, *NQ* iii (1956). The tracts on husbandry come into the books by D. McDonald and G. E. Fussell (*supra*, V. 5).

CHRISTOPHER HARVEY, 1597–1663

Harvey, a cleric and friend of Izaak Walton, wrote *The Synagogue* (1640), a small book of sacred poems in avowed imitation of Herbert (with whose *Temple* it was often bound up), and *Schola Cordis* (1647), a collection of emblems (based on Van Haeften's) which, up into the nineteenth century, was attributed to Quarles. Harvey's poems were edited by Grosart (1874). A. C. Howell had a full account of *The Synagogue* and its history in *SP* xlix (1952).

WILLIAM HARVEY, 1578–1657

Exercitatio Anatomica de Motu Cordis et Sanguinis in Animalibus (Frankfort, 1628) was printed in facsimile by G. Moreton (1894); had several tercentenary editions, a facsimile (Florence, 1928), *Anatomical Exercises . . . The first English text of 1653*, ed. Sir G. Keynes (1928), and a facsimile with a translation by C. D. Leake (Springfield, Illinois, and Baltimore, 1928; 3rd ed. of translation, 1941); a French translation by C. Laubry, with the Latin text and a full introduction (Paris, 1950); and a translation, *Movement of the Heart and Blood in Animals* (1957), by K. J. Franklin, who also translated *De Circulatione Sanguinis* (1649) as *The Circulation of the Blood* (1958). G. Whitteridge translated unpublished notes as *William Harvey De Motu Locali Animalium* (1959). Harvey's second major work was *Exercitationes de Generatione Animalium* (1651; tr. 1653). The *Works* were translated in 1847 by R. Willis, whose version of *De Motu* is reprinted, with letters, in Everyman's Library. The standard critical biography is Louis Chauvois, *William Harvey . . . sa vie et son temps, ses découvertes, sa méthode* (Paris, 1957; tr. 1957). Sir G. Keynes has a lecture on Harvey's 'Personality' (1949). C. J. Sisson (*ESEA 1960*) reported one of Harvey's case-histories. Among the many studies are: C. Singer, *The Discovery of the Circulation of the Blood* (1922); H. P. Bayon, *Annals of Science*, iii–iv (1938–9); sections in H. Butterfield and A. R. Hall (*supra*, V. 3); tercentenary articles in the *Journal of the History of Medicine and Allied Sciences*, xii (1957); and articles by W. Pagel, *Isis* xlii (1951) and *Science, Medicine and History* (*supra*, V. 3). Harvey's other major treatise is discussed by J. Needham, *History of Embryology* (1934), most fully by A. W. Meyer, *Analysis of the De Generatione Animalium of William Harvey* (Stanford, 1936), and by H. P. Bayon in the *Journal* cited above, ii (1947). Sir G. Keynes compiled a *Bibliography of the Writings of William Harvey* (1928; rev. 1953).

SIR JOHN HAYWARD, 1564?–1627

Hayward's histories were: *The First Part of The Life And raigne of King Henrie the IIII* (1599; repr., 1642, with Cotton's *Henry III*); *Lives of the III. Normans, Kings of England* (1613; repr. in *Harleian Miscellany*, ed. Park, ii and ix, 1809, 1812); *The Life and Raigne of King Edward the Sixt* (1630; repr. in W. Kennett, ii, *supra*, IV. 6); *Annals of the First Four Years of the Reign of Queen Elizabeth* (finished by 1612; ed. J. Bruce, Camden Society, 1840). The *DNB* is supplemented by data in *NQ* iv (1957). Hayward's troubles over *Henry IV* are described by M. Dowling, *Library*, xi (1930–1); cf. Greg, ibid. xi (1956). The fullest analysis of Hayward's historical methods is by S. L. Goldberg (*RES* vi, 1955), who has a postscript in *NQ* iv (1957). He is discussed also by E. M. W. Tillyard, *Shakespeare's History Plays* (1947). Debts to Savile's translations of Tacitus are noted by E. B. Benjamin, *RES* viii (1957).

JOHN HEALEY, *c.* 1585/6–*post* 1609

Healey translated Hall's *Mundus Alter et Idem* as *The Discovery of A New World* (1609?), which was elaborately edited by H. Brown (Harvard, 1937); *St. Augustine, of the Citie of God* (1610), which has had several modern editions (2 vols., 1890, repr. 1909; Temple Classics, 3 vols., 1903; ed. E. Barker, 1931; Everyman's Library, 2 vols., 1945); and *Epictetus his Manuall. And Cebes his Table* (1610), to which Healey's version of Theophrastus's *Characters* was added in 1616. The Theophrastian translation is reprinted in the Temple Classics edition of Earle's *Microcosmographie*.

ROBERT HEATH, *fl.* 1650

A few poems from *Clarastella* (1650) are in anthologies, e.g. the *Oxford Book Of Seventeenth Century Verse* and N. Ault (*supra*, II. 2). A selection was edited by W. G. Hutchinson (Orinda Booklets, 1905). The book was discussed in the *Retrospective Review*, ii (1820). Some poems attributed to Herrick may be Heath's (R. G. Howarth, *NQ* v, 1958). F. H. Candelaria has a study in preparation. Wing mistakenly telescopes the poet with the jurist, Sir Robert Heath (1575–1649).

EDWARD LORD HERBERT OF CHERBURY, 1582–1648

The standard edition of the autobiography (first printed by Horace Walpole, 1764) is that of Sir S. Lee (1886; rev. 1906). A handsome reprint (1928) has an introduction by C. H. Herford. There are essays by E. Blunden (*Votive Tablets*, 1931) and B. Willey (*ESEA* xxvii, 1942), and a bibliographical article by R. I. Aaron (*MLR* xxxvi, 1941).

The Life and Raigne of King Henry the Eighth (1649) is in W. Kennett, ii (*supra*, IV. 6). W. M. Merchant has a paper, 'Lord Herbert . . . and Seventeenth-Century Historical Writing', *Trans. of the Honourable Society of Cymmrodorion* (1956).

Occasional Verses (1665) was edited, badly, by J. C. Collins (1881). The standard edition of the English and Latin poems is by G. C. M. Smith (1923). A handy text of the English poems is in R. G. Howarth (*supra*, II. 2). There is discussion by G. Williamson, P. Cruttwell, and especially R. Ellrodt (all *supra*, III. 3), F. J. Warnke (*supra*, IV. 7), who had a bibliographical note in *NQ* i (1954), and M. E. Rickey (*JEGP* lvii, 1958).

De Veritate (Paris, 1624) was translated by M. H. Carré (1937). *De Causis Errorum* and *De Religione Laici* appeared in 1645; the latter was edited and translated by H. R. Hutcheson (Yale, 1944). An English manuscript in Herbert's hand, called *Religio Laici* but different from the published work, was edited by H. G. Wright (*MLR* xxviii, 1933); cf. S. E. Sprott, *Library*, xi (1956). Another work was *De Religione Gentilium* (Amsterdam, 1663; trans. W. Lewis, 1705). *A Dialogue between A Tutor and his Pupil* (1768) is not accepted as Herbert's by Rossi (*infra*). H. Scholz edited selections from *De Veritate* and *De Religione Gentilium* in *Studien zur Geschichte des neueren Protestantismus*, v (1914).

The standard biographical and critical study, exhaustive on

everything except the poetry, is Mario M. Rossi, *La vita, le opere, i tempi di Edoardo Herbert di Cherbury* (3 vols., Florence, 1947). Herbert was discussed (along with Hobbes) in Rossi's *Alle fonti del deismo e del materialismo moderno* (Florence, 1942). Besides editorial introductions, and Rossi, some accounts of Herbert's philosophy are: C. C. J. Webb, *Studies in the History of Natural Theology* (1915); W. R. Sorley, *CHEL* iv and his *History of English Philosophy* (1920); B. Willey (*supra*, III. 4); C. Lyttle, *Church History*, iv (1935); W. K. Jordan, ii (*supra*, V. 2); M. H. Carré, *Mind*, lvii (1948); and R. H. Popkin (*supra*, V. 3).

C. J. Fordyce and T. M. Knox listed the books Herbert bequeathed to Jesus College, Oxford, in *OBS* v, part ii, 1937 (1937). T. Dart described his lute-book in *Music and Letters*, xxxviii (1957).

There are full bibliographies in Hutcheson and Rossi.

GEORGE HERBERT, 1593–1633

The Temple was printed posthumously, under the supervision of Nicholas Ferrar (q.v.), in 1633 (facsimiles, ed. J. H. Shorthouse, 1883; ed. Grosart, 1885). There were 13 editions by 1709. *Herbert's Remains* (1652) contained *A Priest to the Temple, Jacula Prudentum* (an enlarged form of *Outlandish Proverbs*, 1640), &c., and a biographical discourse by B. Oley. From the early eighteenth century to the early nineteenth Herbert was pretty well ignored, except by John Wesley and Cowper. The first edition of *The Temple* after 1709 appeared at Bristol in 1799. In 1835–6 Pickering published the collected *Works* (2 vols.) with some notes from the hand of Coleridge, Herbert's critical rediscoverer. Grosart's edition (3 vols., 1874) was superseded by G. H. Palmer's edition of the English works (Boston, 3 vols., 1905; rev. 1907; 1 vol., 1916); Palmer's valuable work was marred by an arbitrary view of the poet's spiritual evolution. The standard edition of the *Works* is that of F. E. Hutchinson (1941; rev. 1945). H. Gardner has edited this text in popular form (1961).

Walton's *Life* (1670) has of course unique value, though modern scholars have somewhat readjusted his sights (see D. Novarr, under Walton, *infra*). There is a sketch in Hutchinson, a chapter in Summers (*infra*), and a full account in M. Chute, *Two Gentle Men* (New York, 1959).

Along with A. G. Hyde's *George Herbert and His Times* (1906), some of the older modern critics are E. Dowden (*Puritan and Anglican*, 1900), Palmer, and P. E. More (*Shelburne Essays, Fourth Series*, New York, 1906). Herbert has shared fully in the modern revival of the metaphysical poets and in the books on them by G. Williamson, J. B. Leishman, J. Bennett, H. C. White, A. Esch, and R. Ellrodt (*supra*, III. 3). Other essays and short studies are: T. S. Eliot (*Spectator*, 12 March 1932); *TLS*, 2 March 1933 and 12 July 1941; Austin Warren (*American Review*, vii, 1936; *Rage for Order*, Chicago, 1948; repr., University of Michigan, 1959); F. E. Hutchinson, in *Seventeenth Century Studies Presented to Sir Herbert Grierson* (1938) and in his edition; R. Freeman (*RES* xvii, 1941; *English Emblem Books*, 1947); L. C. Knights (*Scrutiny*, xii, 1943–4; *Explorations*, 1946); M. M. Ross (*UTQ* xvi, 1946–7; *Poetry and Dogma*, 1954); M. M. Mahood, *Poetry and Humanism* (1950); much valuable analysis in L. L. Martz (*supra*, III. 3); and R. L. Montgomery (*Texas Studies in Literature and Language*, i, 1959–60). The best full study is Joseph H. Summers, *George Herbert: His Religion and Art* (1954). For the general reader and the specialist respectively are M. Bottrall's *George Herbert* (1954) and R. Tuve's *A Reading of George Herbert* (1952), a selective analysis of biblical and liturgical symbolism. Miss Tuve had a full and fresh study of Herbert and *Caritas* in the *Journal of the Warburg and Courtauld Institutes*, xxii (1959). The many explications of individual poems cannot be recorded.

There are studies of the Latin verse by E. Blunden (*ESEA* xix, 1934), of *Jacula Prudentum* by H. G. Wright (*RES* xi, 1935) and J. L. Lievsay (*supra*, V. 6), of Herbert's metrical technique by A. Hayes (*SP* xxxv, 1938), of 'The First English Pattern Poems' by M. Church (*PMLA* lxi, 1946), of Wesley's use of Herbert by E. A. Leach (*HLQ* xvi, 1952–3). The Ovidian item in the text was noticed by A. Davenport (*NQ* ii, 1955).

G. H. Palmer's *Herbert Bibliography* (Cambridge, Mass., 1911) is a catalogue of the compiler's collection. In addition to the *CBEL* and its *Supplement* (1957), there are T. Spencer and M. Van Doren (*supra*, III. 3) and a *Concise Bibliography* (New York, 1946) by S. A. and D. R. Tannenbaum. There is a *Concordance* by C. Mann (Boston, 1927).

SIR THOMAS HERBERT, 1606–82

A Discription of the Persian Monarchy Now beinge, of which the inner title was *A Relation of Some Yeares Travaile, Begunne Anno*

1626, appeared in 1634. Later editions were increasingly swollen with second-hand material. From the 1677 edition Sir W. Foster edited the attractive original matter as *Thomas Herbert: Travels in Persia 1627–1629* (Broadway Travellers, 1928). Herbert receives a chapter in M. H. Braaksma, *Travel and Literature* (Groningen, 1938) and in B. Penrose, *Urbane Travellers* (1942). In his old age Herbert, who had attended Charles I in 1647–9, wrote *Memoirs of the Two last Years of . . . King Charles I*, which were first printed in full in 1702. They were edited, with contemporary documents, by Allan Fea, *Memoirs of the Martyr King* (1905), and G. S. Stevenson, *Charles I in Captivity* (1927); extracts are in R. Lockyer, *The Trial of Charles I* (1959).

ROBERT HERRICK, 1591–1674

The volume of 1648 was first reprinted as a whole by T. Maitland (2 vols., Edinburgh, 1823; London, 1825). Herrick had a very small place in nineteenth-century anthologies until H. Morley's *The King and the Commons* (1868) and Ward's *English Poets*, ii (1880). Among modern editions are that of A. W. Pollard (Muses' Library, 2 vols., 1891; rev. 1898), with a preface by Swinburne, and that of F. W. Moorman (1915; abridged, 1921). L. C. Martin's standard edition (1956) adds many poems (some admittedly doubtful; cf. R. G. Howarth, *NQ* v, 1958), letters from the young Herrick to his uncle, and full notes.

The meagre biographical data are set forth in Moorman's *Robert Herrick* (1910), F. Delattre's *Robert Herrick* (Paris, 1912), and M. Chute's attractive *Two Gentle Men* (New York, 1959). There is also Rose Macaulay's novel, *They Were Defeated* (1932; U.S. title, *The Shadow Flies*).

Among appreciations are those of Sir E. Gosse (*Seventeenth-Century Studies*, 1883), Swinburne (*supra*), Saintsbury (Aldine *Herrick*, 2 vols., 1893), E. Blunden (*Votive Tablets*, 1931), and B. Willey (*Church Quarterly Review*, clvi, 1955). The fullest scholarly criticism is Delattre's. Modern criticism includes C. Brooks's essay (*The Well Wrought Urn*, New York, 1947), comments in R. Tuve (*supra*, III. 3), S. Musgrove's pamphlet, *The Universe of Robert Herrick* (Auckland University, 1950), T. R. Whitaker's essay (*ELH* xxii, 1955), and M. K. Starkman on *Noble Numbers* (in Mazzes, *supra*, III. 4). Herrick's classical affinities ave been treated by Delattre, by Emperor, McPeek, and K. A. McEuen (*supra*, IV. 7), and C. Maddison (*supra*, III.

3); his Horatian quality in a monograph by P. Aiken (University of Maine, 1932) and by G. W. Regenos (*PQ* xxvi, 1947). Classical echoes are abundantly recorded in Martin's notes. Herrick's reputation is outlined by Delattre, E. M. Cox (*Library*, viii, 1917), and N. Roeckerath, *Der Nachruhm Herricks und Wallers* (Leipzig, 1931). Poems that appeared in miscellanies and song-books are listed in Delattre, in Moorman's 1915 edition, by N. Ault (*TLS*, 20 April 1933), and Martin. M. MacLeod compiled a *Concordance* (1936), S. A. and D. R. Tannenbaum a *Concise Bibliography* (New York, 1949). J. Press has a pamphlet-essay with a bibliography (British Council, 1961).

PETER HEYLYN, 1599–1662

Ecclesia Restaurata (1661) was edited by J. C. Robertson (2 vols., 1849), with the life by Heylyn's son-in-law, J. Barnard. Heylyn's geographical work is noticed by F. Watson, *Beginnings*, &c. (*supra*, V. 6), and E. G. R. Taylor (*supra*, V. 4). The fullest study is A. M. Kendall's unpublished thesis (Radcliffe, 1947).

THOMAS HEYWOOD, 1573/4?–1641

Some non-dramatic works were: *Oenone and Paris*, by T[homas?] H[eywood?] (1594; ed. J. Q. Adams, Folger Shakespeare Library, 1943); the translation of Sallust (1608–9; ed. C. Whibley, Tudor Translations, 1924); *Troia Britanica* (1609); *An Apology for Actors* (1612; ed. Shakespeare Society, 1841; ed. R. H. Perkinson, Scholars' Facsimiles & Reprints, 1941); *Englands Elizabeth* (1631; repr., *Harleian Miscellany*, ed. Park, x, 1813); *The Hierarchie of the blessed Angells* (1635); *Pleasant Dialogues and Dramma's* (1637; ed. W. Bang, *Materialien*, iii, 1903); *The Life of Merlin* (1641; repr. 1812; reissued 1813). The non-dramatic works are treated in A. M. Clark's *Thomas Heywood* (1931), in L. B. Wright (*supra*, IV. 2), and in F. S. Boas's small *Thomas Heywood* (1950). *Troia Britanica* is discussed by J. S. P. Tatlock (*PMLA* xxx, 1915), D. Bush (*supra*, IV. 7), H. Nearing (*supra*, III. 3), and A. Holaday (*JEGP* xlv, 1946). The *Hierarchie* is described by P. H. Osmond, *Mystical Poets of the English Church* (1919). The complexities of Heywood's quarrel with Jaggard over piracy are disentangled by H. E. Rollins in his edition (1940) of the 1612 edition of *The Passionate Pilgrime*. Clark has a full bibliography of Heywood's works in

OBS i, part ii, 1924 (1925). There is a *Concise Bibliography* by S. A. Tannenbaum (New York, 1939).

NICHOLAS HILL, 1570?–1610

Philosophia Epicurea, Democritiana, Theophrastica (Paris, 1601; Geneva, 1619) is noticed in T. F. Mayo, *Epicurus in England* (*1650–1725*) (Dallas, 1934) and discussed by F. R. Johnson, *Astronomical Thought* (*supra*, V. 3), and especially by G. McColley, *Annals of Science*, iv (1939). Jonson's copy of the first edition passed to Donne (J. Sparrow, *TLS*, 5 August 1955).

THOMAS HOBBES, 1588–1679

Hobbes's chief works are listed in the biographical note in Chapter viii. Sir W. Molesworth edited the complete works in Latin and English (16 vols., 1839–45). Some individual texts are: *Leviathan*, ed. A. R. Waller (1904; repr. 1935), ed. W. G. P. Smith (1909), ed. M. Oakeshott (1946; repr. 1957), and popular editions; *Behemoth*, ed. F. Tönnies (1889); *Elements of Law Natural & Politic*, ed. Tönnies (1889; 1928); *De Cive or The Citizen*, ed. S. P. Lamprecht (New York, 1949); *Thucydides*, ed. D. Grene (2 vols., University of Michigan, 1959). F. J. E. Woodbridge edited selections (New York, 1930).

John Aubrey (*supra*, I) is at his best in his portrait of Hobbes; their relations are described in A. Powell, *John Aubrey and his Friends* (1948). The books by G. C. Robertson (1886) and Sir Leslie Stephen (1904) are still good biographical and critical introductions. Hobbes is of course prominent in histories of philosophy (*supra*, V. 3) and in B. Willey (*supra*, III. 4). Some general studies are F. Tönnies, *Thomas Hobbes: Leben und Lehre* (3rd ed., Stuttgart, 1925); A. Levi, *La Filosofia di Tommaso Hobbes* (Milan, 1929), and John Laird's minutely documented *Hobbes* (1934). Two smaller accounts are D. G. James, *The Life of Reason: Hobbes, Locke, Bolingbroke* (1949), and R. Peters, *Hobbes* (Pelican, 1956). D. Krook analysed Hobbes's 'Doctrine of Meaning and Truth' in *Philosophy*, xxxi (1956), his ethics in a chapter in her *Three Traditions of Moral Thought* (1959).

Hobbes's scientific thought is placed in its setting by E. A. Burtt (*supra*, V. 3); its development is studied in F. Brandt, *Thomas Hobbes' Mechanical Conception of Nature* (Copenhagen, 1928). Hobbes's atomism is discussed by K. Lasswitz and C. T. Harrison (*supra*, V. 3).

Hobbes the political and ethical thinker figures largely in the general studies of him and in histories of political thought (*supra*, V. 1). Of the great mass of especially political commentary some representative items are: Sir J. F. Stephen, *Horae Sabbaticae, Second Series* (1892); G. S. Brett, *History of Psychology*, ii (1921); R. Hönigswald, *Hobbes und die Staatsphilosophie* (Munich, 1924); B. Landry, *Hobbes* (Paris, 1930); Leo Strauss, *The Political Philosophy of Hobbes* (tr. 1936; repr. 1952); M. Oakeshott's critique of Strauss (*Politica*, ii, 1936–7) and his introduction to *Leviathan* (*supra*); A. E. Taylor, in *Philosophy*, xiii (1938); G. P. Gooch's lecture (*Proceedings of the British Academy*, xxv, 1939; *Studies in Diplomacy and Statecraft*, 1942); W. K. Jordan, iv (*supra*, V. 2); H. Cairns, *Legal Philosophy from Plato to Hegel* (Johns Hopkins, 1949); J. Bowle, *Hobbes and his Critics: A Study in Seventeenth Century Constitutionalism* (1951); R. Polin, *Politique et philosophie chez Thomas Hobbes* (Paris, 1953); H. Warrender, *The Political Philosophy of Hobbes* (1957); J. B. Stewart, an analysis of recent criticism (*Political Science Quarterly*, lxxiii, 1958).

Hobbes's impact on thought and literature belongs chiefly to the Restoration, and is treated in some studies already named, but reference may be made to L. I. Bredvold (*supra*, III. 4); G. Williamson (*SP* xxx, 1933; *supra*, III. 1); L. Teeter (*ELH* iii, 1936); M. E. Hartsook (*Seventeenth Century Studies, Second Series*, ed. R. Shafer, Princeton, 1937); T. B. Stroup (*SP* xxxv, 1938); J. I. Cope and J. A. Winterbottom (*JEGP* lvii, 1958); M. Taube (under Bramhall, *supra*); studies of More and Cudworth (q.v.); and S. I. Mintz, *The Hunting of Leviathan* (1962), on early reactions to Hobbes's materialism and moral philosophy.

Hobbes's literary and aesthetic doctrines are discussed by Spingarn, who reprinted the *loci classici* (*supra*, IV. 9); C. M. Dowlin (under Davenant, *supra*; and *RES* xvii, 1941); D. F. Bond (*ELH* iv, 1937); C. D. Thorpe, *The Aesthetic Theory of Thomas Hobbes* (1940); M. Kallich (*ELH* xii, 1945); D. G. James (*supra*); and V. de S. Pinto (*Essays in Criticism*, vii, 1957). R. Schlatter discussed Hobbes and Thucydides (*JHI* vi, 1945). The confusion over Hobbes's actual and attributed books on rhetoric was cleared up by W. J. Ong (*CBS* i, part iii, 1951, and *supra*, III. 2) and M. C. Dodd (*MP* l, 1952–3). J. Jacquot described the manuscript of a Latin work by Hobbes directed against Thomas White (*Notes and Records of The Royal Society*, ix, 1951-2). In the same journal (vii, 1949–50) G. R. de Beer edited some hitherto unknown letters written in 1630 by Hobbes when abroad. There are convenient bibliographies in the *DNB* and *CBEL* and Laird, and the much more elaborate *Thomas Hobbes: A Bibliography* (1952) by H. Macdonald and M. Hargreaves. T. E. Jessop has a pamphlet-essay with a bibliography (British Council, 1960).

MARGARET LADY HOBY, 1571–1633

The *Diary of Lady Margaret Hoby 1599–1605*, the earliest extant diary by an Englishwoman, was edited from the British Museum manuscript by D. M. Meads (1930), with a full introduction.

PHILEMON HOLLAND, 1552–1637

Holland's major translations are listed in the text. Those that have been reprinted in part or as wholes are: Livy's *Romane Historie* (1600; selections in W. H. D. Rouse, *Hannibal in Italy*, 1905); Pliny's *Historie of the World* (1601; selections in H. N. Wethered's *Mind of the Ancient World*, 1937, and ed. P. Turner, Southern Illinois University, 1962); Plutarch's *Morals* (1603; selected essays, ed. F. B. Jevons, 1892; ed. E. H. Blakeney, Everyman's Library); Suetonius's *Historie of Twelve Cæsars* (1606; repr., Tudor Translations, 2 vols., 1899, Broadway Translations, 1923, Haslewood Books, 1931); *Cyrupaedia* (1632; repr., Gregynog Press, 1936). A. F. Clements (*supra*, IV. 8) has brief excerpts from the Livy, Pliny, and Suetonius, Winny (loc. cit.) from the first two. One of several medical pieces, *Regimen Sanitatis Salerni* (1617), was reprinted in Sir John Sinclair's *Code of Health and Longevity*, iii (1807).

The fullest study of Holland's workmanship is in F. O. Matthiessen and some discussion is in H. B. Lathrop (both *supra*, IV. 8). C. Whibley's *Literary Portraits* (1904) contains his appreciation reprinted from the Tudor Translations Suetonius. A. Shäfer made a detailed study of the Livy (Burgstädt, 1910). H. Silvette's *Catalogue of the Works of Philemon Holland . . . 1600–1940* (Charlottesville, 1940) is enlarged from his *Short-Title List* (1939). Some biographical details are furnished by Silvette and by C. L. Shaver (*Annals of Medical History, Third Series*, iv, 1942).

600 BIBLIOGRAPHY

CHARLES HOOLE, 1609–67

Hoole's translation (1659) of the famous illustrated textbook, Comenius's *Orbis Sensualium Pictus*, was reprinted even in the nineteenth century, was edited by C. W. Bardeen (Syracuse, 1887), and was described by A. W. Holland (*Contemporary Review*, cliv, 1938). Hoole's own treatise, *A New Discovery Of the old Art of Teaching Schoole* (1660; first written *c.* 1637), was edited by T. Mark (Syracuse, 1912) and E. T. Campagnac (1913). Hoole is discussed in F. Watson's two books and by W. A. L. Vincent (*supra*, V. 6). W. T. Freemantle (under R. Bernard, *supra*) gave a biographical sketch and full bibliography. P. J. Wallis had biographical notes in *NQ* i (1954).

JOHN HOSKYNS, 1566–1638

Full material by and about Hoskyns is contained in H. H. Hudson's *Directions for Speech and Style* (Princeton, 1935) and L. B. Osborn's *Life, Letters, and Writings of John Hoskyns* (Yale, 1937). He receives a good deal of comment in R. Tuve (*supra*, III. 3).

JAMES HOWELL, 1593/4–1666

Two well-known specimens of Howell's large and varied output were ΔΕΝΔΡΟΛΟΓΙΑ. *Dodona's Grove* (1640; second part, 1650), a political allegory which won rapid popularity, and *Instructions for forreine Travell* (1642; enlarged 1650; ed. Arber, 1869). The first two volumes of *Epistolæ Ho-Elianæ* appeared in 1645 and 1647. A 'second' edition, with a third volume of new letters, and with dates added, was issued in 1650; the 'third' edition (1655), the last in Howell's lifetime, had a fourth volume of new letters. Nine other editions appeared between 1673 and 1754. The next edition, the standard one, with full apparatus, was that of J. Jacobs (2 vols., 1890–2). Other modern editions are those of W. H. Bennett (2 vols., 1890) and Agnes Repplier (2 vols., Boston, 1907), and the one in the Temple Classics (3 vols., 1903).

Howell is discussed in some studies of familiar letters cited in IV. 6, and by Ward in the *CHEL* vii. There is a thesis on the *Epistolæ* by G. Jürgens (Marburg, 1900). Jacobs's notes were corrected and extended in a series of articles by E. Bensly, *Aberystwyth Studies*, iii–vi and viii–ix (1922–7). Howell's linguistic works and knowledge were discussed by E. H. Mensel

(*JEGP* xxv, 1926). V. M. Hirst (*MLR* liv, 1959) shows how he probably digested his epistolary material. W. H. Vann's *Notes on the Writings of James Howell* (Baylor University, 1924) gave a full bibliography with a biographical sketch.

PHILIP HUNTON, 1604?–82

Hunton published *A Treatise of Monarchie* in 1643, a *Vindication* (against Dr. Ferne) in 1644. The *Treatise* was reprinted twice in 1689; one edition contained most of the *Vindication*. The *Treatise* is in the *Harleian Miscellany*, ed. Park, vi (1810). The significance of Hunton's thought has been stressed by C. H. McIlwain in *Politica*, i (1934–5) and *Constitutionalism and the Changing World* (1939) and by Yung Chi Hoe, J. W. Allen, and M. A. Judson (*supra*, V. 1), and he receives a section in J. Bowle (under Hobbes, *supra*).

KING JAMES I, 1566–1625

Separate publications were collected in the *Workes* (1616). Some standard editions are: *Political Works*, ed. C. H. McIlwain (Harvard, 1918), with an introduction which has become classical; *Basilicon Doron*, ed. J. Craigie (Scottish Text Society, 2 vols., 1944–50); *Poems*, ed. J. Craigie (Scottish Text Society, 2 vols., 1955–8). Some tracts, e.g. *Daemonologie* (1597) and *A Counter-blaste to Tobacco* (1604), have had modern reprints.

Some of the contemporary histories are cited here under Camden, Goodman, Osborn, Weldon, and Wilson; and the letters of John Chamberlain (q.v.) are important. J. Nichols's *Progresses, &c. of King James the First* (4 vols., 1828) and *The Court and Times of James the First*, ed. R. F. Williams (2 vols., 1848), have documentary value. Some of the standard modern histories are cited above in V. 1. The most substantial biography is D. H. Willson, *King James VI and I* (1956). More special are H. G. Stafford, *James VI of Scotland and the Throne of England* (New York, 1940), and H. Witte, *Die Ansichten Jakobs I. von England über Kirche und Staat* (Berlin, 1940). There are essays by C. J. Sisson (*Seventeenth Century Studies Presented to Sir Herbert Grierson*, 1938), G. Davies (*HLQ* v, 1941–2), and W. H. Greenleaf (*Political Studies*, v, 1957), who relates James's doctrine of divine right to the large Elizabethan philosophy of order and degree.

Basilikon Doron is touched in studies of conduct books (*supra*,

V. 6), receives the last chapter in W. Kleineke, *Englische Fürstenspiegel* (Halle, 1937), and is most fully discussed by Craigie. For James's education and learning there are Craigie; T. W. Baldwin, *William Shakspere's Small Latine*, &c. (1944), i; and Sir G. F. Warner, 'The Library of James VI. 1573–1583', *Publications of the Scottish History Society*, xv (1893). His attitude towards witchcraft is assessed by W. Notestein and, more favourably, by G. L. Kittredge (*supra*, IV. 2).

RICHARD JOHNSON, 1573–1659?

Johnson's chief works were: *The nine Worthies of London* (1592; repr., *Harleian Miscellany*, ed. Park, viii, 1811); *The Seaven Champions of Christendome* (1596–7), which has had editions and abridgements even since 1800; *Tom a Lincolne* (1599, 1607; repr. by W. J. Thoms, *Early English Prose Romances*, 3 vols., 1828 and 1858, 1 vol., 1907); *The Pleasant Conceites of Old Hobson* (Percy Society, ix, 1844; Hazlitt, iii, *supra*, IV. 2); a book of ballads, *A Crowne-Garland of Goulden Roses* (Percy Society, vi, 1842, xv, 1845); two tracts on London life (repr. by Collier, *Illustrations of Early English Popular Literature*, ii, 1864); and *The History of Tom Thumbe* (1621), which is commonly assigned to Johnson. His writings are described by L. B. Wright (*supra*, IV. 2). His most famous romance was the subject of a thesis by H. W. Willkomm (Berlin, 1911) and is touched upon in G. E. Dawson's edition of *The Seven Champions of Christendome by John Kirke* (Western Reserve, 1929). Some romances are treated by M. Patchell (*supra*, IV. 4). *Old Hobson* comes into the studies of jestbooks by E. Schulz and F. P. Wilson (*supra*, IV. 2). A. G. Chester (*MLQ* x, 1949) described Johnson's compilation of ballads, &c., *The Golden Garland of Princely Pleasures* (1620).

ROBERT JOHNSON, *fl.* 1601 ff.

Essaies, Or, Rather Imperfect Offers (1601; repr. 1607, 1610, 1638) is edited by R. H. Bowers (Scholars' Facsimiles & Reprints, 1955), who suggests that the author was a fellow of King's College and was living in 1615. A Robert Johnson also produced *The Travellers Breviat* (1601; enlarged edns., 1601–16, and one in 1630 altered by an editor); this was abridged, with changes, from G. Botero's *Relationi Universali* and enlarged with further borrowings from Botero, Bodin's *Methodus*, Dallington (q.v.), and G. Sandys (R. Shackleton, *MLR* xliii, 1948;

J. Fellheimer, *English Miscellany*, ed. Praz, viii, 1957). If these books were by the same man, it was probably another Robert Johnson who wrote two pieces of American 'promotion' literature, *Nova Britannia* (1609) and *The New Life of Virginea* (1612), both reprinted in P. Force's *Tracts*, i (1836) and G. P. Humphrey's *American Colonial Tracts*, 6 and 7 (Rochester, N.Y., 1897). The essayist is discussed by E. N. S. Thompson (*supra*, IV. 5) and Bowers (*supra*).

BENJAMIN JONSON, 1572/3–1637

Epigrammes and *The Forrest*, and of course the lyrics in a number of plays and masques, appeared in the folio *Workes* (1616), which was reprinted as the first volume of the *Workes* of 1640–1. The third volume of this edition contained more plays and masques, *Under-woods* (properly *The Under-wood*), *Horace, His Art of Poetrie*, *The English Grammar*, and *Timber: or, Discoveries*. Some poems had been printed before and some appeared in two small volumes issued separately in 1640.

H. H. Hudson edited a facsimile of *Epigrammes*, *The Forrest*, and *Under-wood* (Facsimile Text Society, 1936). The standard edition of the complete works, with much the fullest commentary, is *Ben Jonson*, ed. C. H. Herford and P. and E. M. Simpson (11 vols., 1925–52). A few separate editions are: the complete *Poems*, ed. B. H. Newdigate (1936), 'the bulk' edited by G. B. Johnston (Muses' Library, 1954), a selection, ed. J. Hollander (New York, 1961); *Timber*, ed. M. Castelain (Paris, 1906), who gives some sources; ed. G. B. Harrison (1923); ed. R. Walker (Syracuse University, 1953), who had 'A New Analysis' in *ESEA 1952*.

Biography began with the *Conversations* recorded by Drummond (q.v.). Biographical and critical surveys are: M. Castelain, *Ben Jonson: l'homme et l'œuvre* (Paris, 1907); the slighter books of G. G. Smith (1919) and J. Palmer (1934); Herford and Simpson, i-ii; and M. Chute's *Ben Jonson of Westminster* (New York, 1953), which is both popular and scholarly. M. Eccles investigated Jonson's marriage and imprisonment (*RES* xii, xiii, 1936–7), F. T. Bowers his acting experience (*SP* xxxiv, 1937), D. J. Gordon the intellectual setting of his quarrel with Inigo Jones (*Journal of the Warburg and Courtauld Institutes*, xii, 1949), and C. J. Sisson his professorial role at Gresham College (*TLS*, 21 September 1951).

Formal criticism began with commendatory poems and the elegiac *Jonsonus Virbius* (1638; repr. in J. F. Bradley and J. Q. Adams, *The Jonson Allusion-Book*, Yale, 1922, and Herford and Simpson, xi; cf. Simpson, *TLS*, 27 November 1953). Jonson's early fame is traced in G. E. Bentley, *Shakespeare and Jonson* (2 vols., University of Chicago, 1945). Victorian criticism may be represented by J. A. Symonds, *Ben Jonson* (1886), and Swinburne's *Study of Ben Jonson* (1889). The fullest criticism of the non-dramatic writing is in Castelain, Herford and Simpson, ii, and G. B. Johnston, *Ben Jonson: Poet* (Columbia, 1945). W. Trimpi is preparing a full study of Jonson's plain style. Other discussions of the poetry are: parts of E. C. Dunn, *Ben Jonson's Art* (Northampton, Mass., 1925); W. M. Evans, *Ben Jonson and Elizabethan Music* (Lancaster, Pa., 1929); R. Walker (*Criterion*, xiii, 1933–4; abridged in *Timber, supra*); R. L. Sharp (*supra*, III. 3); H. H. Child (*TLS*, 4 July 1936; *Essays and Reflections*, 1948); *TLS*, 5 July 1947; L. J. Potts, on Jonson and his age (*ESEA 1949*); G. Walton and C. Maddison (*supra*, III. 3); P. M. Cubeta, on 'Charis' (*ELH* xxv, 1958); A. D. F. Brown, on 'Drink to me' (*MLR* liv, 1959). The problem of Jonson's or Donne's authorship of a group of elegies was discussed by E. M. Simpson (*RES* xv, 1939; and Herford and Simpson, xi, 66–70).

For Jonson's classical debts and affinities there are books on the ode (*supra*, III. 3) and those of Whipple, Emperor, McPeek, and K. A. McEuen (*supra*, IV. 7); W. D. Briggs, on sources of the poems (*MP* x, 1912–13, xv, 1917–18; *Classical Philology*, xi, 1916); C. B. Hilberry's pamphlet, *Ben Jonson's Ethics in Relation to Stoic and Humanistic Ethical Thought* (University of Chicago, 1933); J. E. Hankins, on the Pindaric ode and Seneca (*MLN* li, 1936). Though the masques are outside our purview, studies of their mythological sources and symbolism are not. C. F. Wheeler's *Classical Mythology in the Plays, Masques, and Poems of Ben Jonson* (Princeton, 1938) has been modified and enlarged through emphasis on Renaissance sources: E. W. Talbert (*SP* xl, 1943; *PQ* xxii, 1943; *SP* xliv, 1947); D. J. Gordon (*Journal of the Warburg and Courtauld Institutes*, vi, 1943, viii, 1945; *MLR* xlii, 1947); A. H. Gilbert, *The Symbolic Persons in the Masques of Ben Jonson* (Duke University, 1948); D. T. Starnes and E. W. Talbert (*supra*, IV. 7); and W. T. Furniss (et al.), *Three Studies in the Renaissance* (Yale, 1958). Jonson's classicist principles have been treated by F. E. Schelling (*PMLA* xiii, 1898; *Shakespeare and "Demi-Science"*, University of Pennsylvania, 1927); H. Reinsch, *Ben Jonsons Poetik und seine Beziehungen zu Horaz* (Leipzig, 1899); J. W. H. Atkins (*supra*, IV. 9); R. Walker (*English*, viii, 1951); L. I. Bredvold (*supra*, III. 3); W. K. Wimsatt and C. Brooks, *Literary Criticism* (New York, 1957); and some writers already listed.

Some miscellaneous items may be added. Jonson's use of Micanzio was noted by A. T. Shillinglaw (*TLS*, 18 April 1936; *Englische Studien*, lxxi, 1936–7; cf. Gabrieli, under W. Cavendish, *supra*). Jonson's English and the *English Grammar* have been studied by J. H. Neumann (*PMLA* liv, 1939) and O. Funke (*Anglia*, lxiv, 1940). The hallowed name of S. Pavy was corrected by G. E. Bentley (*TLS*, 30 May 1942). J. M. Osborn printed the scribblings of Charles Lord Stanhope (1595–1675) on Jonson et al. (*TLS*, 4 January 1957; cf. G. P. V. Akrigg, *Joseph Quincy Adams Memorial Studies*, Washington, 1948).

S. A. Tannenbaum's *Concise Bibliography* (New York, 1938) had a *Supplement* (1947).

SILVESTER JOURDAIN (JOURDAN), *d.* 1650

A Discovery of the Barmudas (1610) had a second edition, *A Plaine Description of the Barmudas* (1613), which was edited by 'W.C.', perhaps William Crashaw (father of the poet), who edited Alexander Whitaker's *Good Newes from Virginia* in the same year. The pamphlet of 1610 was included in the Aungervyle Society Reprints, Second Series (1884), and was edited by J. Q. Adams (Scholars' Facsimiles & Reprints, 1940). The *Plaine Description* is reprinted in P. Force, *Tracts*, iii (1844). The Shakespearian importance of the work is discussed by editors of *The Tempest*, by Adams, and by C. M. Gayley, *Shakespeare and the Founders of Liberty in America* (New York, 1917).

HENRY KING, 1592–1669

King's metrical version of the Psalms appeared in 1651, *Poems, Elegies, Paradoxes, and Sonnets* in 1657 (enlarged 1664, 1700). There was no other edition until J. Hannah's selection, *Poems and Psalms* (1843). Modern editions, which include poems from miscellanies and manuscripts, are those of L. Mason (Yale, 1914), Saintsbury, iii (1921), J. Sparrow (1925), and J. R. Baker (Denver, 1960). For criticism, there are editorial introductions, some pages in G. Williamson and R. Tuve (*supra*, III.

3) and F. Berry, *Poets' Grammar* (1958), and an essay by R. F. Gleckner, *Trans. Wisconsin Academy of Sciences, Arts and Letters*, xlv (1956). The fullest biographical and bibliographical account is L. Mason's 'Life and Works of Henry King', *Trans. Connecticut Academy of Arts and Sciences*, xviii (1913). R. Berman is preparing *Henry King and the Seventeenth Century*, a study of all the writings. Sparrow's edition includes a bibliography by Sir G. Keynes. P. Simpson described the Bodleian MSS. in the *Bodleian Quarterly Record*, v (1929) and *Bodleian Library Record*, iv (1952–3).

RALPH KNEVET(T), 1602–72

Knevet, a Norfolk cleric, wrote *ΣΤΡΑΤΙΩΤΙΚΟΝ or A Discourse of Militarie Discipline* (1628); *Rhodon and Iris. A Pastorall* (1631), which is discussed by H. Smith (*PMLA* xii, 1897), J. Laidler (*Englische Studien*, xxxv, 1905), and Greg (*supra*, III. 3); an unpublished *Supplement of the Faery Queene* ('finished . . . 1635'), first assigned to Knevet by C. B. Millican (*RES* xiv, 1938; cf. Millican and R. F. Brinkley, *supra*, IV. 6), and edited by A. Lavender, *Dissertation Abstracts* (*supra*, I), xviii (1958); *Funerall Elegies* (1637), on Katherine Lady Paston (d. 1636); and the unpublished *A Gallery to the Temple. Lyricall Poemes upon Sacred Occasions*, evidently written between 1633 and 1660. This last work, from which 14 poems were printed by L. B. Marshall (*supra*, II. 2), has been edited with apparatus by G. Pellegrini (Pisa, 1954). The fullest study is *The Poetry of Ralph Knevet*, summarized in *Dissertation Abstracts*, xii (1952), by A. M. Charles, who described the manuscript of the *Gallery* in *NQ* vi (1959). W. M. Merchant has an essay in *ESEA 1960*.

RICHARD KNOLLES, 1550?–1610

The *Generall Historie of the Turkes* (1603) was brought up to date in editions of 1610, 1621, &c. It is discussed by S. C. Chew (*supra*, V. 4). Knolles also translated Bodin's *Les six livres de la Republique* (1576) as *The Six Bookes of a Commonweale* (1606; ed. K. D. McRae, Harvard, 1962). O. Burian (*NQ* cxcvii, 1952) printed Knolles's appeal to Sir Robert Cotton for help.

THOMAS KNYVETT, 1596–1658

The *Knyvett Letters (1620–1644)* were edited by B. Schofield (1949). Schofield includes (p. 169) the dedication by Ralph Knevet (*supra*) of his first book of 1628.

SIR FRANCIS KYNASTON, 1587-1642

Kynaston's productions were: *Amorum Troili et Creseidæ Libri duo priores Anglico-Latini* (1635), the translation from Chaucer; *Leoline & Sydanis An Heroick Romance*, with amatory poems (1642; unsold copies reissued with a new inner title-page, 1646); and the account of his academy, *The Constitutions of the Musæum Minervæ* (1636). The English poems are reprinted in Saintsbury, ii (1906). The romance is discussed by R. H. Perkinson and A. I. T. Higgins (*supra*, III. 3). H. G. Seccombe had biographical and bibliographical notes in *RES* viii (1932). G. H. Turnbull described Hartlib's connexion with the Musaeum Minervae in *NQ* cxcvii (1952).

SIR JAMES LANCASTER, 1554/5-1618

The Voyages of Sir James Lancaster, Kt., to the East Indies were edited from Hakluyt and Purchas by Sir C. Markham (Hakluyt Society, 1877) and were augmented and re-edited by Sir W. Foster (1940).

WILLIAM LAUD, 1573-1645

The famous statement of Laud's Anglican position was *A Relation of The Conference betweene William Lawd . . . And Mr. Fisher the Jesuite* (1639; ed. C. H. Simpkinson, 1901). Laud's chaplain, Heylyn, wrote a eulogistic biography, *Cyprianus Anglicus* (1668). H. Wharton edited Laud's diary and *The History of the Troubles and Tryal of . . . William Laud*, written by himself in the Tower, in 1695, and a *Second Volume of the Remains* in 1700; the *Autobiography* (1839) was compiled from the diary, the *History*, and the history of Laud's chancellorship. The *Works* were edited in the Library of Anglo-Catholic Theology (7 vols. in 9, 1847-60). From his own time to the present Laud's character and work have evoked antithetical estimates. He figures of course in general political and church histories (*supra*, V. 1 and 2). Perhaps the best-balanced biography is still that of W. H. Hutton (1895). Two later books may balance each other, the biography, more political than ecclesiastical, by H. R. Trevor-Roper (1940), and a defensive interpretation, *The Anglicanism of William Laud* (1947), by E. C. E. Bourne. Among essays are those of J. B. Mozley (*Essays Historical and Theological*, i, 1878), E. R. Adair (*Church History*, v, 1936), and W. C. Costin's *William Laud* (1945), an account of his services to Oxford.

JOHN LILBURNE, 1615–57

A number of tracts are given in full or in part in the two collections of Leveller writings edited by W. Haller and G. Davies and by D. M. Wolfe, in Haller's *Tracts on Liberty*, in Woodhouse, and in D. M. Wolfe, *Milton* (*supra*, V. 1). Besides editorial matter in these books, there are T. C. Pease, Haller's two books of 1938 and 1955, and books by J. Frank, W. Schenk, and others (*supra*, V. 1). Most of these contain bibliographies of Lilburne's tracts. There are biographies by M. A. Gibb (1947) and P. Gregg (1961). H. W. Wolfram has a long account, stressing the trial of 1649, in the *Syracuse Law Review*, iii (1952). H. N. Brailsford's very full but unfinished *The Levellers and the English Revolution* (ed. C. Hill, 1961) must be called inadequate.

WILLIAM LILLY, 1602–81

Some of Lilly's many publications were: *Merlinus Anglicus Junior: The English Merlin revived* (1644); *A Collection Of Ancient And Moderne Prophesies Concerning these present Times* (1645); *The Starry Messenger* (1645); *Christian Astrology* (1647); and *Monarchy Or No Monarchy in England* (1651). This last included *Several Observations upon the Life and Death of Charles late King of England*. The very interesting *Mr. William Lilly's History of His Life and Times* (1715) was edited by C. Burman in *Lives of . . . Elias Ashmole . . . and William Lilly, Written by Themselves* (1774) and reprinted several times in the early nineteenth century. The *Several Observations* was reprinted with the autobiography in 1715 and some later editions, and is included in F. Maseres, *Select Tracts* (1815). A valuable bibliography of astrology is the catalogue of Lilly's library at the end of his *Easie and plain Method Teaching How to judge upon Nativities* (1658). An anonymous translation, *Pantagruel's Prognostication* (1659/60; ed. F. P. Wilson, 1947), includes some good-natured satire on Lilly. Modern accounts of astrology are cited above in V. 3.

WILLIAM LISLE (L'ISLE), 1569?–1637

The Faire Æthiopian (1631; 2nd ed., 1638) was a verse translation of Heliodorus. Lisle's chief work was *A Saxon Treatise Concerning The Old And New Testament* (1623), reissued as *Divers Ancient Monuments in the Saxon Tongue* (1638). His labours in Old English are discussed by E. N. Adams, R. Tuve, and R. F. Jones (*supra*, IV. 6).

609

WILLIAM LITHGOW, 1582?–1645?

A Most Delectable, And True Discourse, of an admired and painefull peregrination (1614; enlarged, 1623) was used by Purchas and by Lithgow in his larger work, *The Totall Discourse, Of the Rare Adventures, and painefull Peregrinations of long nineteene Yeares Travayles, from Scotland, to the most Famous Kingdomes in Europe, Asia, and Affrica* (1632 and later edns.; repr. 1906; abridged by B. I. Lawrence as *Rare Adventures and Painefull Peregrinations*, 1928). J. Maidment edited Lithgow's *Poetical Remains* (1863). There is a sketch in B. Penrose, *Urbane Travellers* (1942). Lithgow's eastern travels are discussed by S. C. Chew, W. G. Rice, and T. Spencer (*supra*, V. 4).

MARTIN LLUELYN, 1616–82

Lluelyn's chief book, *Men-Miracles. With other Poemes* (1646), was republished in 1656, 1661 (as *The Marrow of the Muses*), and 1679. He contributed a poem to the English translation (1653) of Harvey's *De Generatione Animalium*. Some poems are reprinted in Brydges, *Censura Literaria*, x (1809); Corser, *Collectanea Anglo-Poetica*, Part 8 (Chetham Society, cii, 1878); and the anthologies of N. Ault and L. B. Marshall (*supra*, II. 2). There is a critical study by R. C. Wallerstein (*JEGP* xxxv, 1936).

THOMAS LODGE, 1558–1625

Lodge's original works, which came before 1600, were collected for the Hunterian Club (4 vols., 1875–88), with an essay by Gosse (repr. in his *Seventeenth-Century Studies*, 1883); a number of things have had separate editions. The literary fruit of his medical degree (1598) was a *Treatise of the Plague* (1603). Other works of our period, and of the author's sober maturity, were: *The Flowers of Lodowicke of Granado* (1601); *The Famous And Memorable Workes of Josephus* (1602); *The Workes both Morrall and Natural of Lucius Annaeus Seneca* (1614; rev. 1620); and *A Learned Summary Upon the famous Poeme of William of Saluste Lord of Bar as* (1621), a version of Simon Goulart's commentary. The standard biographical and critical studies are by N. B. Paradise (Yale, 1931) and E. A. Tenney (Cornell, 1935). The earlier writings are treated by C. S. Lewis, some religious works by J. B. Collins (*supra*, V. 2). Much biographical matter was

812202 R r

brought forward by C. J. Sisson (*Thomas Lodge and Other Eliza-bethans*, Harvard, 1933) and A. Walker (*RES* ix and x, 1933-4). There is a *Concise Bibliography* (New York, 1940) by S. A. Tannenbaum, a full bibliography in P. M. Ryan, *Thomas Lodge, Gentleman* (Hamden, Conn., 1958).

RICHARD LOVELACE, 1618–56/57

Only the prologue and epilogue of Lovelace's Oxford comedy reached print. *Lucasta* (1649) was published by him; the inferior *Lucasta*. *Posthume Poems*, dated 1659 but issued in 1660, was edited by his brother and E. Revett. Except for 'To Althea, From Prison', Lovelace had no great fame in his century (though he received intelligent praise from Edward Phillips in 1675), and he was largely forgotten until a revival began with Percy's *Reliques* (1765). The original two volumes had no second edition until Singer's (1817-18). The standard edition is that of C. H. Wilkinson (1930; repr. 1953), based on his own edition of 1925. The handiest text is in R. G. Howarth (*supra*, II. 2). The fullest picture of the poet, C. H. Hartmann's *The Cavalier Spirit and its Influence on the Life and Work of Richard Lovelace* (1925), received some correction from Wilkinson (*supra*), who also contributed biographical and bibliographical data to the *TLS*, 14 August 1937. The question of Lucasta's actuality or identity was discussed by Hartmann, Wilkinson, A. C. Judson (*MP* xxiii, 1925-6), and H. M. Margoliouth (*RES* iii, 1927). W. M. Evans described newly attributed songs or variant versions in *PMLA* liv (1939) and lx (1945), *PQ* xxiii, xxiv (1944-5), *MLQ* vii (1946) and ix (1948), and a prison poem in *PQ* xxvi (1947). 'The Grasse-Hopper' is analysed by D. C. Allen (*MLQ* xviii, 1957; *Image and Meaning*, 1960). H. Berry and E. K. Timings recorded biographical and textual items in *MLN* lxix (1954).

JAMES MABBE, 1572–1642?

Mabbe translated *The Rogue: or The Life of Guzman de Alfarache. Written in Spanish by Matheo Aleman* (1622; ed. J. Fitzmaurice-Kelly, Tudor Translations, 4 vols., 1924); *The Spanish Bawd, Represented in Celestina: or, The Tragicke-Comedy of Calisto and Melibea* (1631), from F. de Rojas (ed. Fitzmaurice-Kelly, Tudor Translations, 1894; ed. H. W. Allen, 1908, and, in the Broadway Translations, 1923); and Cervantes's *Exemplarie Novells* (1640; ed. S. W. Orson, 2 vols., 1900; selections, *The*

Spanish Ladie and Two Other Stories, 1928). In addition to editorial introductions, H. P. Houck discussed 'Mabbe's Paganization of the *Celestina*' (*PMLA* liv, 1939), F. Pierce his alteration of one of the novels (*Revue de littérature comparée*, xxiii, 1949). A. W. Secord had Shakespearian and other data in *JEGP* xlvii (1948).

SIR GEORGE MACKENZIE, 1636?–91

The first part of *Aretina; Or, The Serious Romance* (1660) remained a fragment. Brief excerpts are in R. B. Johnson's *Birth of Romance* (1928); the preface is in C. Davies (*supra*, IV. 4). Mackenzie's legal and miscellaneous writings are beyond our limits; some are touched in M.-S. Røstvig (*supra*, III. 3). There is a biography by Andrew Lang (1909), a bibliography by F. S. Ferguson, *Edinburgh Bibliographical Society Transactions*, i, pt. i (1936).

GERVASE (JERVIS) MARKHAM, 1568?–1637

Among Markham's 'literary' works were religious poems (1600–1; ed. Grosart, *Miscellanies of The Fuller Worthies' Library*, ii, 1871), which are discussed by J. B. Collins (*supra*, V. 2). The lines 'I walkt along a streame', attributed to Marlowe since *Englands Parnassus* (1600), have been shown to be from Markham's *Devoreux* of 1597 (J. Crow, *TLS*, 4 January 1947); the author of the French original is described by F. N. L. Poynter (*ibid.*, 16 October 1959). *Devoreux* is one link in R. Gittings's argument (*Shakespeare's Rival*, 1960) for Markham as not only the victim of parody (Armado in a revised *Love's Labour's Lost*) but as the rival poet of the *Sonnets*. J. H. H. Lyon (*A Study of The Newe Metamorphosis Written by J. M., Gent, 1600*, Columbia, 1919) gave some account of Markham in arguing for his authorship of a long unpublished Ovidian poem. His many books on the arts of country life make a bibliographical tangle, which is more or less clarified in the *STC*, by G. E. Noyes (*supra*, V. 6), G. E. Fussell, *NQ* clxxv (1938) and his book (*infra*), and C. F. Mullett, *Isis*, xxxv (1944); a full bibliography by F. N. L. Poynter is promised by *OBS*. Markham gets some space in D. McDonald and G. E. Fussell (*supra*, V. 5) and Lord Ernle, *English Farming Past and Present* (1912 and later edns.). The repetitious author's agreement with the booksellers is printed in Arber's *Stationers' Register*, iii, 679.

612   BIBLIOGRAPHY

SHAKERLEY MARMION, 1603-39

Cupid and Psyche (1637; another issue, 1638, and, as Cupid's Courtship, 1666) was reprinted by Singer (1820) and in Saintsbury, ii (1906). It has been edited with a life and elaborate commentary by A.J. Nearing (University of Pennsylvania, 1944). The poem was studied in A. Hoffmann, Das Psyche-Märchen des Apuleius in der englischen Literatur (Strassburg, 1908), and touched in D. Bush (supra, IV. 7) and A. I. T. Higgins (supra, III. 3).

ANDREW MARVELL, 1621-78

The first collection, which did not include the late satires, was Miscellaneous Poems (1681; repr. 1923). Marvell's poems were edited by T. Cooke (2 vols., 1726, 1772) and his complete works by E. Thompson (3 vols., 1776), but he did not appear in the large collections down to and including Chalmers's (1810); for the eighteenth century—and for Landor in the Imaginary Conversations—Marvell was wholly or mainly a publicist. Appreciation of his lyrical verse is represented by Bowles, Hazlitt, Campbell, Lamb, Hartley Coleridge, Emerson, Poe, and Tennyson. Marvell first won recognition (without the aid of the 'Coy Mistress') in Palgrave's Golden Treasury (1861 ff.). Grosart edited the complete works (4 vols., 1872-5). The standard edition (without the prose) is Poems and Letters, ed. H. M. Margoliouth (2 vols., 1927; 2nd ed., 1952). Aitken's small edition (Muses' Library, 2 vols., 1892, 1901) has been in part superseded by H. Macdonald's edition (1952) of the Miscellaneous Poems in the same series. D. Davison edited Selected Poetry and Prose (1952), J. H. Summers an ample selection of the poetry (New York, 1961). The mystery of the 'Mary Marvell' who supposedly edited the 1681 volume was cleared up by F. S. Tupper (PMLA liii, 1938).

A. Birrell's Andrew Marvell (1905) and other books were superseded by P. Legouis, André Marvell, poète, puritain, patriote (Paris, 1928). Andrew Marvell (1940; corrected reprint, 1962), by M. C. Bradbrook and M. G. Lloyd Thomas, is fresh and suggestive. R. C. Wallerstein's and R. Ellrodt's elaborate studies are cited above in III. 3. Some short, more or less general, discussions are: T. S. Eliot (Tercentenary Tributes, ed. W. H. Bagguley, 1922; repr. in Homage to John Dryden, 1924; Selected Essays, 1932); G. Williamson, The Donne Tradition (1930); F. R. Leavis (Scrutiny, iv, 1935; Revaluation, 1936); M. C. Bradbrook,

'Marvell and the Poetry of Rural Solitude' (*RES* xvii, 1941); incidental comment in R. Tuve (*supra*, III. 3); J. H. Summers, 'Marvell's "Nature" ' (*ELH* xx, 1953; cf. J. Corder, *NQ* vi, 1959); M.-S. Røstvig, G. Walton, and S. Korninger (*supra*, III. 3); P. Legouis, a review of some critical aberrations (*RES* viii, 1957); J. Press, *Andrew Marvell* (British Council, 1958), an essay with a bibliography; A. Alvarez (*Hudson Review*, xiii, 1960; *supra*, III. 3); and P. Colaiacomo (*English Miscellany*, ed. Praz, xi, 1960).

Modern criticism has yielded multiplying critiques of individual poems, e.g. on 'The Garden': W. Empson (*Scrutiny*, i, 1932; repr. in *Determinations*, ed. F. R. Leavis, 1934, and *Some Versions of Pastoral*, *supra*, III. 3); M. C. Bradbrook and M. G. Lloyd Thomas (*Criterion*, xviii, 1939); and F. Kermode (*Essays in Criticism*, ii, 1952). Some articles that gather up more or less previous criticism are: D. Davison, on 'The Definition of Love' (*RES* vi, 1955); Von W. Iser, on the 'Coy Mistress' (*Die Neueren Sprachen*, xii, 1957); L. Spitzer (*MLQ* xix, 1958) and D. C. Allen (*Image and Meaning*, 1960), on the 'Nymph Complaining'; Allen (ibid.), on 'Upon Appleton House'; R. H. Syfret (*RES* xii, 1961) and J. M. Wallace (*PMLA* lxxvii, 1962), on the 'Horatian Ode'. C. E. Bain has a study of the Latin poems in *PQ* xxxviii (1959). Legouis's full bibliography must be supplemented, for 1912–38, by T. Spencer and M. Van Doren (*supra*, III. 3), for later years by the *CBEL Supplement* (1957), J. Press (*supra*), and the annual bibliographies (*supra*, I).

THOMAS MAY, 1595–1650

In addition to his plays May wrote a popular translation, *Lucan's Pharsalia* (3 books in 1626, the whole in 1627), an also popular *Continuation* of Lucan (1630), versions of *Virgil's Georgicks* (1628) and *Selected Epigrams of Martial* (1629), and two historical poems, *The Reigne Of King Henry the Second* (1633) and *The Victorious Reigne Of King Edward the Third* (1635). In prose he translated some of John Barclay (q.v.) and produced a *History of the Parliament Of England* (1647; repr. 1812, 1854). The standard book is A. G. Chester's *Thomas May: Man of Letters* (University of Pennsylvania, 1932). The historical poems have been discussed by H. Nearing and E. M. W. Tillyard (*supra*, III. 3), the *Continuation*, in its English and Latin versions, by R. T. Bruère (*Classical Philology*, xliv, 1949). G. W. Whiting argued for

Milton's use in *Eikonoklastes* of May's account of the Long Parliament (*Milton's Literary Milieu*, University of North Carolina, 1939; cf. Milton's *Complete Prose Works*, iii, Yale, forthcoming).

JOSEPH MEAD (MEDE), 1586–1638

Mead's chief work, *Clavis Apocalyptica* (1627), was translated in 1643 by R. More as *The Key of the Revelation*; there were translations also in 1831 and 1833. Mead's works were edited in 1664 and 1672 by John Worthington. Letters are printed in *The Court and Times of James the First* and *The Court and Times of Charles the First* (*supra*, IV. 6) and in Heywood and Wright (*supra*, V. 6). A *Life* was included in the *Works* of 1664–72; better accounts are in the *DNB* and Mullinger (*supra*, V. 6). M. Nicolson suggested Mead as the original of Milton's 'old Damoetas' and Henry More's Mnemon (*MLN* xli, 1926). The influence of his love of precise expression is noted by W. F. Mitchell (*supra*, V. 2). The influence of his biblical commentary is shown by E. L. Tuveson (*supra*, III. 4). H. F. Fletcher, ii (*supra*, V. 6) makes full and fruitful use of Mead's account books, 1614–37, in reconstructing Cambridge education.

SIR JAMES MELVILLE, 1535–1617

Melville's *Memoires* were first printed in 1683 by G. Scott, whose text, a translation from the original Scots, has been followed in subsequent editions, including that of A. F. Steuart (1929). The Scots text, which Steuart made some use of, was printed for the Bannatyne Club (1827) and reprinted for the Maitland Club (1833). There are selections in J. G. Fyfe (*supra*, IV. 6).

JAMES MELVILLE, 1556–1614

The *Diary* was printed for the Bannatyne Club (1829), the *Autobiography and Diary* for the Wodrow Society (2 vols., 1842). The diary proper ends in 1601; the *Continuation*, 1596–1610, is more heavily ecclesiastical and political. Melville's record was largely used by David Calderwood in his *True History of the Church of Scotland* (pr. 1678). There are selections in J. G. Fyfe (*supra*, IV. 6), who edited a separate *Selection* (1948). M. A. Bald had an essay on Melville in *MLR* xxi (1926), H. S. N. McFarland an account of his education in the *Aberdeen University Review*, xxxvi (1955–6).

Sir John Mennes, 1599–1671

The names of Mennes, a seaman and soldier, and of the unclerical divine, James Smith, appeared in the miscellanies *Musarum Deliciae* (1655), *Wit and Drollery* (1656), and *Wit Restor'd* (1658). The pair have also been associated with *Witts Recreations* (1640). These last two books, with *Musarum Delicae*, were edited by T. Park as *Musarum Deliciae* (2 vols., 1817) and reprinted by J. C. Hotten (2 vols., 1874). The numerous early editions are described by A. E. Case (*supra*, II. 2); cf. C. C. Smith (*supra*, IV. 2).

Grace Lady Mildmay, *c.* 1552–1620

Lady Mildmay was the wife of Sir Anthony, son of the well-known Sir Walter. Her unpublished diary was described, with excerpts, by R. Weigall (*Quarterly Review*, ccxv, 1911). Sir Anthony's nephew, Sir Humphrey (1592–*post* 1666), left a diary from which P. L. Ralph pictured the life of a country gentleman during 1633–52 (*Sir Humphrey Mildmay*, Rutgers, 1947). Mildmay's playgoing is recorded in G. E. Bentley, ii (*supra*, I).

John Milton, 1608–74

The chief poetical publications in Milton's lifetime were: *A Maske Presented At Ludlow Castle* (1637/8), now known as *Comus*; 'Lycidas', in *Justa Edouardo King naufrago* (1638); *Epitaphium Damonis*, privately printed in 1640 (?); *Poems* (1645/6), reprinted with additions in 1673; *Paradise lost* (1667; 2nd ed., 1674); *Paradise Regain'd* with *Samson Agonistes* (1671). Of the prose works published in his lifetime the most important are: *Of Reformation Touching Church-Discipline in England* (1641); *The Reason of Church-governement* (1642; dated 1641); the tract commonly cited as *An Apology for Smectymnuus* (1642); *The Doctrine and Discipline of Divorce* (1643; rev. ed., 1644); *Of Education* (1644); *Areopagitica* (1644); *The Tenure of Kings and Magistrates* (1649); *EIKONOKΛΑΣΤΗΣ* (1649); *Joannis Miltoni Angli Pro Populo Anglicano Defensio* (1651, the *Defensio Prima*); the *Defensio Secunda* (1654); *A Treatise of Civil power in Ecclesiastical causes* (1659); *The Readie & Easie Way to Establish a Free Commonwealth* (1660); *The History of Britain* (1670); *Epistolae Familiares* and *Prolusiones* (1674).

The most important surviving manuscript is that of the minor poems, mostly in Milton's own hand, in the library of Trinity

College, Cambridge (facsimile, ed. W. A. Wright, 1899; facsimile of part, ed. F. A. Patterson, Facsimile Text Society, 1933). Other valuable manuscripts, not autograph, are: the Bridgewater MS. of *Comus*, in the possession of the Egerton family (printed 1910); *De Doctrina Christiana*, in the Public Record Office, first published with a translation by C. Sumner (2 vols., 1825); the Pierpont Morgan MS. of *Paradise Lost*, Book I, ed. with facsimile by H. Darbishire (1931).

There are facsimiles of *Comus*, 1637 (ed. L. S. Livingston, New York, 1903); *Justa Edouardo King*, 1938 (Facsimile Text Society, 1939); *Areopagitica* (Noel Douglas, 1927); *Poems*, 1645 (Oxford, 1924; N. Douglas, 1926, omitting the Latin and Greek poems); *Paradise Lost*, 1667 (ed. R. H. Shepherd, 1873; ed. D. Masson, 1877); and the complete poetical works, with much apparatus, ed. H. F. Fletcher (4 vols., University of Illinois, 1943–8).

The Columbia University edition (18 vols., 1931–8) is the only complete edition in the original spelling with generally full collations; the Index (2 vols., 1940) is an invaluable work of reference. Five supplements to the edition were printed by T. O. Mabbott, J. M. French, and M. Kelley in *NQ* (1939–41, 1950–2).

Early editions of the poems—fully described by A. Oras, *Milton's Editors and Commentators . . . 1695–1801* (1931)—were: P. Hume's annotated *Paradise Lost* (1695), the first scholarly edition of an English poem; R. Bentley's eccentric edition of the same work (1732); T. Newton's edition of the poems (3 vols., 1749–52); T. Warton's edition of the minor poems (*Poems upon Several Occasions*, 1785; rev. 1791); complete poems, ed. H. J. Todd, with a variorum commentary (6 vols., 1801; 5th ed., 4 vols., 1852), which remains useful. Modern library editions are: D. Masson (3 vols., 1890), with full introductions and commentary; Sir H. J. C. Grierson (2 vols., 1925); H. Darbishire (2 vols., 1952–5), with a textual commentary. Of the many small editions some are: H. C. Beeching (1900; enlarged 1938; repr. 1952), with the old spelling; W. A. Wright (1903), with textual notes; W. V. Moody (Boston, 1899; rev. E. K. Rand, 1924); M. Y. Hughes (2 vols., New York, 1935–7; see also *infra*), with fresh notes; H. F. Fletcher (Boston, 1941); J. H. Hanford (New York, 1937; enlarged 1953); B. A. Wright (Everyman's Library, 1956), a text partly modernized with special care; H. Darbishire (1958), without the apparatus of her 1952–5 edition.

The standard editions of the prose works are the Columbia text and the *Complete Prose Works*, ed. D. M. Wolfe et al., with very full commentaries (8 vols., Yale; vols. i and ii, 1953, 1959); the latter is superseding earlier editions of individual prose works. Groups of prose works have had many small editions.

Useful collections of prose and verse in one volume are *The Student's Milton*, ed. F. A. Patterson (rev. ed., New York, 1933), which contains the poems and most of the prose, and *Complete Poems and Major Prose*, ed. M. Y. Hughes (New York, 1957), with notes. E. H. Visiak edited a smaller collection (1938).

Among many editions of particular works are those of most of the minor poems and *Paradise Lost* and *Samson Agonistes* by A. W. Verity, with full notes; *Sonnets*, ed. J. S. Smart (1921); *Latin Poems*, ed. W. MacKellar (Cornell, 1930); *Private Correspondence and Academic Exercises*, ed. P. B. and E. M. W. Tillyard (1932); *Areopagitica*, tr. and ed. O. Lutaud (Paris, 1956); and some items below.

Six lives written by men who knew Milton or who knew men who knew him (Aubrey, an anonymous writer, Anthony Wood, Edward Phillips, Toland, and J. Richardson) are collected as *Early Lives of Milton* (1932) by H. Darbishire; debate over the anonymous life is recorded under John Phillips (*infra*). Masson's *Life* (6 vols., 1859–80, with rev. edns. of vols. i–iii and an Index, 1881–96) remains indispensable, though now often out of date. Some biographical books are: J. S. Diekhoff, *Milton on Himself* (1939), an annotated collection of personal passages from the works; W. R. Parker, *Milton's Contemporary Reputation* (Ohio State University, 1940), which contains an essay, a list of allusions, and facsimiles of five pamphlets written in answer to Milton; J. M. French, *Life Records of John Milton* (5 vols., Rutgers, 1949–58), an annotated collection of all documents and allusions; J. H. Hanford, *John Milton, Englishman* (New York, 1949), a critical biography by the dean of Milton scholars; books on Milton's education and intellectual development by D. L. Clark and H. F. Fletcher (*supra*, V. 6; cf. A. Gill, *supra*); D. M. Dorian, *The English Diodatis* (Rutgers, 1950); E. Saillens, *John Milton poète combattant* (Paris, 1959). W. R. Parker has a biography in preparation.

Milton Criticism: Selections from Four Centuries, ed. J. Thorpe (New York, 1950), is a small anthology with modern emphasis. A mass of modern scholarship and criticism is digested in a 3-volume variorum commentary on all the poetry (the first since Todd) edited by M. Y. Hughes et al. (in preparation).

Eighteenth-century criticism, from Addison's *Spectator* papers onward, is mainly of historical interest, though Johnson's (*Lives of the Poets*, 1779) is, with all its prejudices, classical. Nineteenth-century criticism included the comments and essays of Hazlitt, Coleridge, Keats, Landor, Macaulay, Emerson, Arnold, Bagehot, and the books of M. Pattison (1879) and Sir W. Raleigh (1900). Much of this, focused likewise on *Paradise Lost*, is now also mainly of historical interest, since it tended either to follow the Blake–Shelley line or to ignore Milton's ideas for a purely (and hence inadequate) aesthetic approach. In our century conservative criticism may be represented by J. W. Mackail (*The Springs of Helicon*, 1909), J. Bailey (*Milton*, 1915), Grierson (*supra*, III. 1, and *Milton and Wordsworth*, 1937), and E. E. Stoll (*Poets and Playwrights*, University of Minnesota, 1930; *From Shakespeare to Joyce*, New York, 1944). Nineteenth-century views of Milton were carried on, with added negations, by T. S. Eliot (*Selected Essays*, 1932, *passim*; *ESEA* xxi, 1936), who later modified his position (*Proceedings of the British Academy*, xxxiii, 1947; *Sewanee Review*, lvi, 1948; repr., with the *ESEA* 'Note', in *On Poetry and Poets*, 1957), and by F. R. Leavis (*Revaluation*, 1936; *Sewanee Review*, lvii, 1949; *The Common Pursuit*, 1952).

Modern scholarship and criticism (*c.* 1917 ff.) sought to rescue Milton's personality, ideas, and poetry from the older traditions. Among pioneers were J. H. Hanford, in many articles, and D. Saurat in his stimulating if erratic *Milton: Man and Thinker* (1925; rev. 1944). The most compendious summary of modern scholarship, though it is increasingly in need of revision, is Hanford's *Milton Handbook* (4th ed., New York, 1946). Some general surveys, or general studies of the poetry, are: E. M. W. Tillyard, *Milton* (1930), *The Miltonic Setting* (1938), *Studies in Milton* (1951), and the British Council pamphlet, *Milton*, with a bibliography (1952); Rose Macaulay, *Milton* (1934; rev. 1957); C. Williams's essay in the World's Classics edition of the English poems (1940); T. H. Banks, *Milton's Imagery* (Columbia, 1950); D. C. Allen, *The Harmonious Vision; Studies in Milton's Poetry* (Johns Hopkins, 1954); K. Muir, *John*

Milton (1955; 2nd ed., 1960); W. B. C. Watkins, *An Anatomy of Milton's Verse* (Louisiana State University, 1955); A. S. P. Woodhouse's pamphlet, *Milton the Poet* (Toronto, 1955); R. M. Adams's robustious *Ikon: John Milton and the Modern Critics* (Cornell, 1955); D. Daiches, *Milton* (1957); essays in *The Living Milton*, ed. F. Kermode (1960).

There are surveys of recent criticism by F. Fogle (*HLQ* xv, 1951–2) and M. Y. Hughes (*Contemporary Literary Scholarship*, ed. L. Leary, New York, 1958).

Much recent criticism has focused on particular works and topics and much that has to be omitted here will be cited in the forthcoming variorum commentary (*supra*).

On the early poems there are important studies by Hanford ('The Youth of Milton', *Studies in Shakespeare, Milton and Donne*, New York, 1925); A. S. P. Woodhouse (on *Comus*, *UTQ* xi, 1941–2, and xix, 1949–50; on Milton's early development, ibid. xiii, 1943–4; on 'Lycidas' and the *Epitaphium Damonis*, *Studies in Honour of Gilbert Norwood*, University of Toronto, 1952); C. Brooks and J. E. Hardy, *Poems of Mr. John Milton* (New York, 1951), suggestive if not always reliable 'new criticism'; J. B. Leishman, on the twin poems (*ESEA 1951*); J. Arthos, *On a Mask Presented at Ludlow-Castle* (University of Michigan, 1954); R. Tuve's penetrating *Images & Themes in Five Poems by Milton* (Harvard, 1957). S. Jayne, in his Platonic reading of *Comus* (*PMLA* lxxiv, 1959), cites other recent discussions. C. A. Patrides's *Milton's Lycidas: The Tradition and the Poem* (New York, 1961) is a useful anthology of essays.

On *Paradise Lost* there are: C. S. Lewis, *A Preface to Paradise Lost* (1942; repr. 1960); Sir M. Bowra, *From Virgil to Milton* (1945); D. Bush, *Paradise Lost in Our Time* (Cornell, 1945; repr., New York, 1948); J. S. Diekhoff, *Paradise Lost: A Commentary on the Argument* (Columbia, 1946; repr., New York, 1958); B. Rajan, *Paradise Lost & the Seventeenth Century Reader* (1947); M. Mahood (*supra*, III. 3); A. Stein, *Answerable Style* (University of Minnesota, 1953); A. S. P. Woodhouse, 'Pattern in Paradise Lost' (*UTQ* xxii, 1952–3); F. T. Prince, *The Italian Element in Milton's Verse* (1954); I. G. MacCaffrey, *Paradise Lost as "Myth"* (Harvard, 1959); J. B. Broadbent, *Some Graver Subject* (1960); Books on *Paradise Lost* are forthcoming in 1962 from B. A. Wright, Jackson I. Cope (Johns Hopkins), and Joseph H. Summers (Harvard). A quite wrong-headed acuteness or obtuseness animates A. J. A. Waldock's *Paradise Lost and its Critics* (1947; repr., New York, 1959). John Peter (*A Critique of Paradise Lost*, 1960) has moments of discernment when he is not following Waldock. W. Empson's *Milton's God* (1961) is more Empsonian than Miltonic.

Of the many books for specialists, three are G. McColley's *Paradise Lost* (Chicago, 1940), on sources and literary patterns; A. H. Gilbert's speculative *On the Composition of Paradise Lost* (University of North Carolina, 1947), and W. Kirkconnell's collection and translation of analogues, *The Celestial Cycle* (University of Toronto, 1952); and items cited below.

On *Paradise Regained* there are: E. M. Pope, *Paradise Regained: The Tradition and the Poem* (Johns Hopkins, 1947); J. Blondel's full introduction to his edition (Paris, 1955); H. Schultz (*infra*); A. Stein, *Heroic Knowledge* (University of Minnesota, 1957); and, among multiplying short studies, those of F. Kermode (*RES* iv, 1953), N. Frye (*MP* liii, 1955–6), A. S. P. Woodhouse (*UTQ* xxv, 1955–6), B. K. Lewalski (*SP* lvii, 1960), L. L. Martz (*ELH* xxvii, 1960), and W. W. Robson's restatement of conventional strictures (*The Living Milton, supra*).

On *Samson* there are Hanford (*Studies, supra*); W. R. Parker, *Milton's Debt to Greek Tragedy in Samson Agonistes* (Johns Hopkins, 1937); F. M. Krouse's one-sided *Milton's Samson and the Christian Tradition* (Princeton, 1949); A. Stein, *Heroic Knowledge* (*supra*); and A. S. P. Woodhouse (*UTQ* xxviii, 1958–9).

Some studies of metrics are: Robert Bridges, *Milton's Prosody* (rev. ed., 1921; cf. G. E. Kellog, *PMLA* lxviii, 1953); S. E. Sprott, *Milton's Art of Prosody* (1953); F. T. Prince (*supra*); J. Whaler's fresh, acute, and sometimes esoteric *Counterpoint and Symbol: An Inquiry into the Rhythm of Milton's Epic Style* (Copenhagen: *Anglistica*, vi, 1956); and especially E. Weismiller, in the forthcoming variorum commentary (*supra*).

Some studies of Milton's poetic language, in addition to comment in writings already cited, are: E. Holmes, *ESEA* x (1924); L. P. Boone, *SAMLA Studies in Milton*, ed. J. M. Patrick (University of Florida, 1953); F. T. Prince and R. M. Adams (*supra*); W. B. Hunter, *Essays in Honor of W. C. Curry* (Vanderbilt, 1955); E. M. Clark, *SP* liii (1956); H. Darbishire, *ESEA* *1957*; C. L. Wrenn, *Wiener Beiträge*, lxv (1957).

Along with general studies of prose style (*supra*, III. 2) there are articles by E. N. S. Thompson (*PQ* xiv, 1935),

J. H. Neumann (*PMLA* lx, 1945), and F. E. Ekfelt (*PQ* xxv, 1946; xxviii, 1949).

Milton's doctrines and ideas come into many books and articles already cited. The fullest commentaries on the prose works are in the Yale edition (*supra*) and A. Barker (*supra*, V. 2). Milton figures more or less in the studies of political and religious thought by Sabine, Woodhouse, Haller, Wolfe, Fink, and Zagorin (*supra*, V. 1 and 2); a late phase is treated by B. K. Lewalski (*PMLA* lxxiv, 1959). Some studies, mainly of religious ideas, are: A. Sewell, *A Study in Milton's Christian Doctrine* (1939), which retains value though partly superseded by M. Kelley's standard *This Great Argument* (Princeton, 1941); I. Samuel, *Plato and Milton* (Cornell, 1947); books on Hebraic studies (*supra*, IV. 7) and G. N. Conklin, *Biblical Criticism and Heresy in Milton* (Columbia, 1949); Woodhouse, on Milton's view of the Creation (*PQ* xxviii, 1949); H. Schultz, *Milton and Forbidden Knowledge* (New York, 1955); W. C. Curry, *Milton's Ontology, Cosmogony, and Physics* (University of Kentucky, 1957); W. G. Madsen, on Milton's idea of nature (*Three Studies in the Renaissance*, Yale, 1958) and his typological symbolism in the epic (*PMLA* lxxv, 1960); C. A. Patrides, on the Atonement (*PMLA* lxxiv, 1959); J. Reesing on 'The Materiality of God' and W. B. Hunter, 'Milton's Arianism Reconsidered' (*Harvard Theological Review*, l, 1957 and lii, 1959; cf. J. H. Adamson, ibid. liii, 1960), and Hunter's related article (*JHI* xxi, 1960); R. M. Frye, *God, Man, and Satan* (Princeton, 1960), which links Milton with Christian existentialism.

Some miscellaneous special studies are: Sir C. Firth, 'Milton as an Historian' (*Proceedings of the British Academy*, iii, 1907–8; *Essays Historical & Literary*, 1938); R. D. Havens, *The Influence of Milton on English Poetry* (Harvard, 1922; repr., New York, 1960); J. Finley, 'Milton and Horace', on the sonnets (*Harvard Studies in Classical Philology*, xlviii, 1937); D. P. Harding, *Milton and the Renaissance Ovid* (University of Illinois, 1946); R. R. Cawley, *Milton and the Literature of Travel* (Princeton, 1951); K. Svendsen, *Milton and Science* (Harvard, 1956), which is comprehensive and critical; J. H. Sims, *Use of the Bible in Milton's Epic Poems* (University of Florida, 1962).

Among works of reference are the Columbia Index (*supra*); concordances to the English poems by J. Bradshaw (1894) and to the Latin, Greek, and Italian poems by L. Cooper (Halle,

1923); L. Lockwood, *Lexicon to the English Poetical Works* (New York, 1907); C. G. Osgood, *Classical Mythology of Milton's English Poems* (New York, 1900); A. H. Gilbert, *A Geographical Dictionary of Milton* (Yale, 1919); E. S. LeComte, *A Milton Dictionary* (New York, 1961).

Bibliographies of scholarship and criticism are D. H. Stevens, *Reference Guide to Milton from 1800 to the Present* (University of Chicago, 1930), with H. Fletcher's supplementary *Contributions* (University of Illinois, 1931), and C. Huckabay's *John Milton: A Bibliographical Supplement 1929–57* (Duquesne University, 1960). For books and countless articles of recent years there are also the *CBEL* (1940) with its *Supplement* (1957) and the current bibliographies (*supra*, I), of which the most up to date are those in *SP* and *PMLA*.

HENRY MORE, 1614–87

More's chief works were listed in the biographical note. Grosart's *Complete Poems* (1878) has been partly superseded by G. Bullough's *Philosophical Poems* (1931), which has large selections and a full critique. Two early collected editions of prose were *A Collection* (2nd ed., 1662; 4th ed., 1712) and *Theological Works* (1708). Two modern texts are the English translation (1690) of *Enchiridion Ethicum* (Facsimile Text Society, 1930) and F. I. MacKinnon's anthology, *Philosophical Writings of Henry More* (New York, 1925). More's letters to Descartes are in *Œuvres de Descartes*, ed. C. Adam and P. Tannery, v (Paris, 1903); they are partly translated by L. D. Cohen, *Annals of Science*, i (1936). R. Ward's vague *Life* (1710; ed. M. H. Howard, 1911) had a concrete supplement in M. Nicolson's *Conway Letters* (Yale, 1930). Coleridge's comments are in R. F. Brinkley. Short discussions are in the books on the Cambridge Platonists by Powicke, Pawson, and De Pauley (*supra*, V. 2). The fullest studies are by J. Tulloch, ii (*supra*, V. 2), Paul R. Anderson, *Science in Defense of Liberal Religion* (New York, 1933), Hugo Reimann, *Henry Mores Bedeutung für die Gegenwart* (Basel, 1941), and A. Lichtenstein's close analysis of 'rationalist theology', *Henry More* (Harvard, 1962). Some more or less special studies are M. Nicolson's articles on More and Milton (*SP* xxii, 1925; *PQ* vi, 1927) and early Cartesianism (*SP* xxvi, 1929), and her *Breaking of the Circle* (1950; rev. 1960) and *Mountain Gloom and Mountain Glory* (1959); E. A. Burtt (*supra*, V. 3); A. J. Snow,

Matter & Gravity in Newton's Physical Philosophy (1926); J. T. Baker, *Historical and Critical Examination of English Space and Time Theories* (Sarah Lawrence College, 1930) and 'Henry More and Kant' (*Philosophical Review*, xlvi, 1937); J. W. Beach, *The Concept of Nature in Nineteenth-Century English Poetry* (New York, 1936; repr. 1956); W. K. Jordan, iv (*supra*, V. 2); W. B. Hunter, on 'Plastic Nature' (*supra*, V. 3); E. L. Tuveson, 'Space, Deity, and "Natural Sublime" ' (*MLQ* xii, 1951); G. A. Panichas, on More's 'Mysticism' (*Greek Orthodox Theological Review*, 1956); and chapters in J. I. Cope, *Joseph Glanvill* (Washington University, 1956), and R. L. Colie, *Light and Enlightenment: A Study of the Cambridge Platonists and the Dutch Arminians* (1957). F. I. MacKinnon gives a bibliography.

FYNES MORYSON, 1566–1630

Moryson's big work was *An Itinerary Written . . . First in the Latin Tongue, and then translated By him into English: Containing His Ten Yeeres Travell Through . . . Germany, Bohmerland, Sweitzerland, Netherland, Denmarke, Poland, Italy, Turky, France, England, Scotland, and Ireland* (1617; repr., 4 vols., 1907–8). A small section was included in H. Morley, *Ireland under Elizabeth and James the First* (1890). Selections from an unprinted part of Moryson's manuscript were edited by C. Hughes, with a full account of the author, as *Shakespeare's Europe* (1903). Moryson receives a section in B. Penrose, *Urbane Travellers* (1942), and figures in the books by E. S. Bates, C. Howard, S. C. Chew, and T. Spencer (*supra*, V. 4). R. B. Gottfried (*PQ* xvii, 1938) showed his debt, for things Irish, to Spenser's *View*.

THOMAS MUN, 1571–1641

Mun's books were: *A Discourse of Trade, From England unto the East-Indies* (1621; repr., J. R. McCulloch, *Select Collection of Early English Tracts on Commerce*, 1856, repr. 1952; ed. Facsimile Text Society, 1930); *England's Treasure by Forraign Trade*, written 1626 ff. (1664; repr., McCulloch, *supra*, and A. E. Monroe, *Early Economic Thought*, Harvard, 1924; and in separate edns., 1895 ff. and 1928). Mun has a place in books on economic history and mercantilism, e.g. those of E. Lipson and E. F. Heckscher. The fullest study is R. Granchet, *L'Œuvre économique de Thomas Mun* (Angers, 1921). J. D. Gould has two discussions (*Journal of Economic History*, xv, 1955). Two others (*Bulletin of the*

Institute of Historical Research, xxvii, 1954, and xxx, 1957) are by B. E. Supple (also *supra*, V. 1) and R. de Roover; the latter deals with Mun in Italy.

ANTHONY MUNDAY (MUNDY), 1560–1633

The standard book is *Anthony Mundy, An Elizabethan Man of Letters* (University of California, 1928) by Celeste Turner, who has a fresh survey of his early career in *SP* lvi (1959). M. Eccles added biographical data in *Studies in The English Renaissance Drama*, ed. J. W. Bennett et al. (New York University, 1959). Munday's books are discussed by M. St. C. Byrne (*Library*, i, 1920–1), his romances by G. R. Hayes (ibid. vi and vii, 1925–7) and Sir H. Thomas and M. Patchell (*supra*, IV. 4). S. A. Tannenbaum compiled a *Concise Bibliography* (New York, 1942).

PETER MUNDY, *c.* 1596–1667?

The Travels of Peter Mundy in Europe and Asia, 1608–1667 were edited by Sir R. C. Temple and L. M. Anstey for the Hakluyt Society (5 vols., 1907–36).

GEFFRAY MYNSHUL, 1594?–1668

Certaine Characters and Essayes of Prison and Prisoners (1618) had another edition (1618) with altered title and contents; the latter was reprinted at Edinburgh in 1821. Specimens are in anthologies, e.g. G. Murphy and H. Osborne (*supra*, IV. 5). Mynshul is discussed in general studies of essays and characters (*supra*, IV. 5), by M. L. Hunt (*Thomas Dekker*, Columbia, 1911, and *JEGP* xi, 1912), and by P. Shaw and M. T. Jones-Davies (under Dekker, *supra*).

SIR ROBERT NAUNTON, 1563–1635

Fragmenta Regalia, or Observations on the late Q. Elizabeth, her times and favorites (1641) was reprinted from the 1653 ed. by Arber (1870) and is included in A. C. Ward's *Miscellany of Tracts and Pamphlets* (1927).

MARCHAMONT NEEDHAM (NEDHAM), 1620–78

Some of Needham's books were: *The Case of the Commonwealth of England, Stated* (1650); *Of the Dominion, Or, Ownership of the Sea* (1652), a translation of Selden's *Mare Clausum*; *The*

Excellencie of a Free-State (1656; repr. 1767); and the pamphlet, *A Discourse Concerning Schools And School-Masters* (1663; repr. in Dunham and Pargellis, *supra*, II. 1). C. V. Wedgwood (*supra*, IV. 2) quoted some of his sharpest verse. His tortuous career is described by Firth in the *DNB*, with a bibliography. One phase is illuminated by J. M. French, 'Milton, Needham, and *Mercurius Politicus*', *SP* xxxiii (1936), and E. A. Beller, *HLQ* v (1941–2). He comes into P. Zagorin (*supra*, V. 2), J. Frank (*supra*, IV. 3), and *Oxinden Letters 1642–1670* (*infra*).

JOHN NORDEN, 1548–1625/26

Of more than a dozen religious works the first and most popular was *A Pensive Mans Practise* (1584). Other books were: *A Progresse of Pietie* (1591?; repr., Parker Society, 1847); the poem *Vicissitudo rerum . . . The first Part* (1600; ed. D. C. Collins, Shakespeare Association Facsimiles, 1931); *The Surveyors Dialogue* (1607; repr. in *Architectural Publication Society. Detached Essays*, 1853); *The Labyrinth Of Mans Life* (1614). The division, made in the *DNB*, between the religious writer and the surveyor was closed in A. W. Pollard's 'The Unity of John Norden' (*Library*, vii, 1926–7). *Vicissitudo rerum* was studied in relation to its source by K. Koller (*SP* xxxv, 1938). Norden's 'historicall and topographicall' descriptions of English counties have been published over a long stretch of time, from 1593 to 1938, when C. M. Hood edited *Norfolk*, with an account of his work. H. B. Wheatley contributed 'Notes upon Norden and his Map of London, 1593' to the New Shakspere Society edition (1877) of William Harrison's *Description of England*. Norden has a place in books on English topography and in E. G. R. Taylor (*supra*, V. 4), in D. McDonald and in M. St. C. Byrne's *Elizabethan Life* (*supra*, V. 5), and in Sir T. D. Kendrick (*supra*, IV. 6). W. B. Gerish's *John Norden* (1903) has a biographical sketch and bibliography.

SIR JOHN OGLANDER, 1585–1655

Selections from Oglander's commonplace book were edited by W. H. Long (*The Oglander Memoirs*, 1888) and, better, by F. Bamford (*A Royalist's Notebook*, 1936); and he receives a good share of C. Aspinall-Oglander's *Nunwell Symphony* (1945). He provides a brief case history in H. R. Trevor-Roper's 'The Gentry 1540–1640', *Economic History Review Supplement* (1953).

FRANCIS OSBORN, 1593–1659

Osborn's chief writings were *Historical Memoires on the Reigns of Queen Elizabeth, and King James* (1658; repr. in *Secret History*, ed. Scott, *supra*, IV. 6) and *Advice to a Son* (1656, with 2nd part, 1658; ed. Sir E. A. Parry, 1896; see William Cecil, *supra*).The collected *Works* reached their 11th and last edition in 1722 (2 vols.). According to Sir William Petty (Pepys's *Diary*, 27 January 1664) the *Advice* was one of three works most esteemed for wit—the other two being *Religio Medici* and *Hudibras*. It is discussed by J. E. Mason (*supra*, V. 6) and, most fully, by S. A. E. Betz, *Seventeenth Century Studies, Second Series*, ed. R. Shafer (Princeton, 1937). Osborn's religious outlook is treated by W. K. Jordan, iv (*supra*, V. 2), his political outlook by Zagorin (*supra*, V. 1). F. F. Madan had bibliographical notes in *OBS*, N.S., iv, 1950 (1952).

DOROTHY OSBORNE, 1627–95

Temple (q.v.) probably destroyed his letters to Dorothy but he and his descendants preserved hers. Extracts in T. P. Courtenay's *Memoirs of . . . Sir William Temple* (1836) aroused Macaulay's enthusiasm, which inspired Judge Parry to edit them (1888; rev. 1903; repr. in Everyman and Wayfarer's Library). The letters were also edited by Gollancz (1903). The standard edition, with full apparatus, is by G. C. M. Smith (1928). The letters have 'a sequel' in J. G. Longe's *Martha Lady Giffard* (1911). Among essays on Dorothy are those of Maurice Hewlett (*Nineteenth Century*, xciii, 1923; *Last Essays*, 1924); L. L. Irvine, *Ten Letter-Writers* (1932); V. Woolf, *The Second Common Reader* (1932); F. L. Lucas, *Studies French and English* (1934); and Lord David Cecil's full and graceful account in *Two Quiet Lives* (1948).

SIR THOMAS OVERBURY, 1581–1613

The characters are given almost in full in the anthologies of H. Morley and R. Aldington and are represented in others (*supra*, IV. 5). The standard edition is W. J. Paylor's *The Overburian Characters* (1936). The thirty-two characters now assigned to John Webster are included in F. L. Lucas's edition of Webster (1927). The characters are discussed in studies of the genre cited above in IV. 5; and data are supplied in the bibliographies named there and by Paylor in his edition and in the *Library*, xvii (1936–7). Overbury's *Observations* of the Netherlands (1626) are in Arber's *English Garner*, iv (1882) and Firth's *Stuart Tracts* (1903), and, with other things, in the *Miscellaneous Works*, ed. E. F. Rimbault (1856).

Overbury's murder and the ensuing trials have been described and analysed by many writers from John Chamberlain and James Howell onward. The material in T. B. Howell's *State Trials* (ii, 1816) is included with other early documents in *Sir Thomas Overbury's Vision (1616) By Richard Niccols, and Other English Sources of Nathaniel Hawthorne's 'The Scarlet Letter'*, ed. A. S. Reid (Scholars' Facsimiles & Reprints, 1957). The fullest inquiry is W. McElwee's *The Murder of Sir Thomas Overbury* (1952). Some other accounts are: J. Spedding and J. Gairdner, *Studies in English History* (1881), S. R. Gardiner, ii (*supra*, V. 1), W. Roughead, *The Fatal Countess and Other Studies* (1924), and M. A. deFord's popular *Overbury Affair* (Philadelphia, 1960). Two Italian observers' reports of the Somerset trial were printed by A. M. Crinò, *English Miscellany*, ed. Praz, viii (1957).

RICHARD OVERTON, *fl.* 1642–63

Overton's political tracts are listed and studied in books cited in V. 2 and under Lilburne, especially those of Frank and Schenk. D. M. Wolfe discussed 'Unsigned Pamphlets of Richard Overton: 1641–1649', *HLQ* xxi (1957–8). *Mans Mortallitie* (1643; repr. almost exactly in 1644) is treated by Masson and Saurat in their books on Milton; by G. Williamson (*SP* xxxii, 1935; *supra*, III. 1); P. Zagorin (*Library*, v, 1950–1); and by Frank and Schenk.

JOHN OWEN, 1564–1622

Owen's Latin epigrams were published in four volumes, 1606–12; there were many editions and translations. Owen is discussed by E. Bensly, *CHEL* iv, and by Wright and Sinclair and Bradner (*supra*, IV. 7). His influence in Germany is described by E. Urban, *Owenus und die deutschen Epigrammatiker des XVII. Jahrhunderts* (Berlin, 1900), and more briefly by G. Waterhouse (*supra*, IV. 7). Bibliographical confusions in the *DNB*, *STC*, &c., were clarified by J. J. Enck, *Harvard Library Bulletin*, iii (1949).

HENRY OXINDEN (1608–70) et al.

Dorothy Gardiner edited two attractive volumes, *The Oxinden Letters 1607–1642* (1933) and *The Oxinden and Peyton Letters 1642–1670* (1937).

HENRY PARKER, 1604–52

One of the most important of Parker's score of pamphlets, *Observations upon some of his Majesties late Answers and Expresses* (1642), is reproduced in W. Haller, *Tracts on Liberty* (1934). He is discussed by Haller in his *Tracts* and his two books of 1938 and 1955 (*supra*, V. 2); by J. W. Allen (*supra*, V. 1); most fully by W. K. Jordan, *Men of Substance* (University of Chicago, 1942), who gives a bibliography; and by M. A. Judson (*supra*, V. 1).

MARTIN PARKER, *c*. 1600?–52

Parker's ballads may be found in the collections cited in IV. 2, especially the many volumes edited by H. E. Rollins, who gave the only authoritative account of him in *MP* xvi (1918–19) and xix (1921–2). Some ballads are given in the recent collection of Pinto and Rodway (*supra*, IV. 2). Parker used Pettie's *Petite Pallace* for one ambitious flight (D. Bush, *MLN* xl, 1925).

HENRY PARROT, *fl.* 1606–26

Parrot and his five books of epigrams have been studied by M. C. Pitman in *MLR* xxix (1934) and by F. B. Williams in *PMLA* lii (1937) and *Harvard Studies and Notes in Philology and Literature*, xx (1938).

KATHERINE LADY PASTON, 1578?–1629

The *Correspondence of Lady Katherine Paston 1603–1627* was edited by Ruth Hughey (Norfolk Record Society, xiv, 1941). Her son's wife, also Katherine (d. 1636), was lamented by Ralph Knevet (q.v.).

SIR GEORGE PAULE, 1563?–1637

Paule's *Life* of Whitgift (1612) was reprinted in Christopher Wordsworth's *Ecclesiastical Biography*, iii (3rd ed., 1839), and is noticed in D. A. Stauffer (*supra*, IV. 6).

HENRY PEACHAM, 1578?–1642?

Writings that have been reprinted are: *The Compleat Gentleman* (1622, enlarged 1627, 1634, and—not by Peacham—1661; 1634 text ed. G. S. Gordon, 1906); *Coach and Sedan* (1636; repr. 1925); *The Truth of Our Times* (1638; ed. R. R. Cawley, Facsimile Text Society, 1942); *The Worth Of A Peny* (1641?; Arber's *English Garner*, vi, 1883, and A. Lang's *Social England Illustrated*, 1903); *The Art of Living in London* (1642; *Harleian Miscellany*, ed. Park, ix, 1812). There are introductory essays by Gordon and Cawley and an essay in A. W. Fox's *Book of Bachelors* (1899). M. C. Pitman had a condensed and corrective survey of Peacham's life and work in the *Bulletin of the Institute of Historical Research*, xi (1934). He has a place in the studies of courtesy books by J. E. Mason (*supra*, V. 6) and of taste by H. S. V. and M. S. Ogden (*supra*, V. 7). His debt to Elyot was shown by D. T. Starnes (*MLR* xxii, 1927). In addition to the known volume of epigrams, *Thalias Banquet* (1620), Peacham's title to *The More the Merrier* (1608) was established by Miss Pitman (*MLR* xxix, 1934).

HENRY PERCY, EARL OF NORTHUMBERLAND, 1564–1632

The latter part of *Advice to his Son* was printed, in expurgated form, in *Archaeologia*, xxvii (1838); the whole tract was edited by G. B. Harrison (1930). G. R. Batho had a two-part popular account of the earl in *History Today*, vi (1956), and an account of his library in the *Library*, xv (1960). J. W. Shirley described the scientific experiments of the Tower prisoners, Ralegh and the earl (*Ambix*, iv, 1949).

WILLIAM PERKINS, 1558–1602

The enormous influence of Perkins's writings may be partly judged from the list of editions in the *STC*. The first folio edition of the collected works appeared in 1600. Fuller's sketch is a famous part of *The Holy State* (1642). A pioneer work, in Dutch, was J. J. van Baarsel, *William Perkins* ('s-Gravenhage, 1912). L. B. Wright had a general account in the *HLQ* iii (1939–40). The influence of Perkins's book on preaching is shown by W. F. Mitchell (*supra*, V. 2). This and other sides of his work are treated in W. Haller's *Rise of Puritanism* (1938). R. A. Sisson presented Perkins as a stylist and apologist for the Church

(*MLR* xlvii, 1952). His teaching on vocations, domestic duties, and casuistry was discussed in W. E. Houghton's book on Fuller (*supra*). His casuistry is treated also by G. L. Mosse (*HLQ* xvii, 1953–4; *The Holy Pretence, supra*, V. 2). Perkins's Calvinism and the reaction against it are analysed by P. Miller in *Publications of The Colonial Society of Massachusetts*, xxxii, 1937 (*Errand into the Wilderness*, Harvard, 1956) and his *New England Mind* (1939). His theology receives a chapter in H. C. Porter, *Reformation and Reaction in Tudor Cambridge* (1958). For his views on witchcraft there is G. L. Kittredge (*supra*, IV. 2). C. Hill discussed his attitude towards the poor (*Puritanism and Revolution*, 1958).

THOMAS PESTELL, 1585–1667

Though some pieces have appeared in modern anthologies (e.g. H. J. Massingham, *supra*, II. 2), much of Pestell's verse existed only in manuscript until it was edited by Hannah Buchan (1940).

HUGH PETER(S), 1598–1660

Peter counts as a man of action and a voice if not much as a writer. R. P. Stearns's full biography, *The Strenuous Puritan: Hugh Peter 1598–1660* (University of Illinois, 1954), pictures both England and New England. A more compendious study is by J. M. Patrick (*University of Buffalo Studies*, xvii, 1946), who had an account of Peter's arrest in *HLQ* xix (1955–6).

SIR WILLIAM PETTY, 1623–87

Petty's pioneer work in political economy lies beyond our limits. *The Advice of W. P. to Mr. Samuel Hartlib. For The Advancement of some particular Parts of Learning* (1648; repr., *Harleian Miscellany*, ed. Park, vi, 1810) is discussed by R. F. Jones and some other writers on education (*supra*, V. 6). Petty figures also in accounts of the origins of the Royal Society, most lately in *The Royal Society*, ed. Hartley (*supra*, V. 3). There is a biography by E. Strauss, *Sir William Petty: Portrait of a Genius* (1954).

THOMAS PHILIPOTT, c. 1616–82

Poems (1646), dedicated to Mildmay Fane (q.v.), were edited by L. C. Martin (1950).

KATHERINE PHILIPS, 1632–64

Mrs. Philips's most famous work was *Pompey* (Dublin and London, 1663), her translation from Corneille. Her unauthorized *Poems* (1664) were enlarged in 1667 with more poems and the tragedies *Pompey* and *Horace*; there were further editions in 1669, 1678, and 1710. Her *Letters from Orinda to Poliarchus* (1705; enlarged 1729) give a valuable picture of the author and her world. *Selected Poems* were published in 1904 by J. R. Tutin, with a preface by L. I. Guiney. Saintsbury (i, 1905) reprinted the poems from the 1678 text. P. Elmen printed some manuscript poems in *PQ* xxx (1951). The standard book is P. W. Souers, *The Matchless Orinda* (Harvard, 1931).

JOHN PHILLIPS, 1631–1706

The popular *Satyr Against Hypocrites* (1655; ed. L. Howard, Augustan Reprint Society, 1953) is discussed by F. L. Beaty (*Harvard Library Bulletin*, vi, 1952). Most of Phillips's writings came after 1660. He was credited by H. Darbishire (*Early Lives of Milton*, 1932) with the anonymous Life; her case was opposed by E. S. Parsons (*PMLA* l, 1935), who first edited the Life in the *English Historical Review*, xvii (1902). There was further debate by A. H. Gilbert (*SP* xxxiii, 1936) and A. R. Benham and Parsons (*ELH* vi, 1939 and ix, 1942). J. S. Smart's suggestion of Cyriack Skinner as the author has been supported by M. Kelley (*MP* liv, 1956–7) and W. R. Parker (*TLS*, 13 September 1957; cf. R. W. Hunt and M. Kelley, ibid., 11 October, 27 December; and Parker, *PBSA* lii, 1958).

SIR HUGH PLAT, 1552–1611?

Sir Hugh's *Delightes for Ladies* (1602) was reprinted by V. and W. H. Trovillion (Herrin, Illinois, 1939) and edited by G. E. and K. R. Fussell (1948). He figures in books on gardening and agriculture, e.g. D. McDonald (*supra*, V. 5). C. F. Mullett had a full account of his writings in *Studies in Honor of A. H. R. Fairchild* (University of Missouri, 1946). There is a bibliography by B. Juel-Jensen, *The Book Collector*, viii (1959).

JOSHUA POOLE, c. 1615–c. 1656

Poole's *English Parnassus: or, A Helpe to English Poesie* (1657), one of the books Hoole (q.v.) recommended for schools, is discussed by F. Watson (*Beginnings of the Teaching of Modern*

Subjects, 1909) and G. Williamson (*MP* xxxiii, 1935–6; *supra*, III. 1). Poole's quotations from Milton are collected by A. Farrell (*MLN* lviii, 1943). P. J. Wallis gives an account of him in *NQ* i (1954).

THOMAS POWELL, 1572?–1635?

Tom of All Trades. Or The Plaine Path-way to Preferment (1631) was reprinted, with an account of Powell, by F. J. Furnivall (New Shakspere Society, Series 6, 1876) and is in Dunham and Pargellis (*supra*, II. 1). *Tom* and another social piece are in the *Somers Tracts*, ed. Scott, vii (1812).

JOHN PRESTON, 1587–1628

Preston's sermons were mostly issued after his death by Thomas Goodwin, Richard Sibbes, John Davenport, and other friends. Some of the popular collections were *The New Covenant* (1629), *The Breast-Plate Of Faith And Love* (1630), and *Life Eternall* (1631). Preston's writings and influence are discussed in W. Haller's *Rise of Puritanism* (1938), P. Miller (under Perkins, *supra*), and G. S. Wakefield's *Puritan Devotion* (1957); his political sermons by C. Hill, *Puritanism and Revolution* (1958); his relations with Buckingham by J. F. Maclear, *HLQ* xxi (1957–8). There is a biography by I. Morgan, *Prince Charles's Puritan Chaplain* (1957).

WILLIAM PRYNNE, 1600?–69

Of Prynne's nearly 200 pamphlets and books probably the best known is *Histrio-mastix* (1632; dated 1633); it is discussed by E. N. S. Thompson, *The Controversy between the Puritans and the Stage* (New York, 1903), T. R. Lounsbury (*Yale Review*, xii, 1923), E. W. Kirby (*infra*), and J. W. Allen (*supra*, V. 1). A few of Prynne's pieces are in *Somers Tracts*, ed. Scott, iv–vi (1810–11); *Vox Populi* (1642) is in the *Harleian Miscellany*, ed. Park, vii (1811). S. R. Gardiner edited *Documents relating to the Proceedings against William Prynne in 1634 and 1637* (Camden Society, 1877). The *DNB* article is by Firth. The standard book, with a bibliography, is E. W. Kirby's *William Prynne* (Harvard, 1931). The Presbyterian pamphleteer gets more or less space in the general histories and in W. Haller's three works, J. W. Allen, and W. K. Jordan, iv (*supra*, V. 1 and 2); the historical scholar—who became an invaluable Keeper of the Records under Charles II —is discussed by E. W. Kirby and by J. G. A. Pocock (*supra*, IV. 6). Sir G. Hurst had a sketch in *Lincoln's Inn Essays* (1949). M. I. Fry and G. Davies gave a list of Prynne's writings in the *HLQ* xx (1956–7).

SAMUEL PURCHAS, 1577–1626

Purchas's works were: *Purchas his Pilgrimage. Or Relations Of the World And The Religions Observed In All Ages And places discovered, from the Creation unto this Present* (1613; enlarged 1614 ff.); the jeremiad *Purchas his Pilgrim. Microcosmus, or The Historie Of Man* (1619); and the great collection of voyages, *Hakluytus Posthumus or Purchas His Pilgrimes* (4 vols., 1625; repr., 20 vols., 1905–7). Two volumes of selections are H. G. Rawlinson's *Narratives from Purchas His Pilgrimes* (1931) and Cyril Wild's *Purchas His Pilgrimes in Japan* (1939). There are accounts of Purchas by G. B. Parks, *Richard Hakluyt and the English Voyages* (New York, 1928); E. G. R. Taylor (*supra*, V. 4); Sir W. Foster, in E. Lynam (*supra*, V. 4; rev. and expanded from article in *Geographical Journal*, lxviii, 1926); and, from a special angle, by L. B. Wright, *Religion and Empire* (*supra*, V. I).

FRANCIS QUARLES, 1592–1644

The only collected edition is Grosart's (3 vols., 1880–1). J. Horden edited *Hosanna . . . and Threnodes* (1960). Quarles figures in studies of emblems by Thompson, Praz, and R. Freeman (*supra*, III. 3); the fullest study of his emblem imagery is by E. James (*University of Texas Studies in English*, 1943). One side of Quarles is shown by W. K. Jordan, ii (*supra*, V. 2). His play, his debt to Bacon and Machiavelli, and his royalist tracts were discussed by G. S. Haight (*RES* xii, 1936). Quarles's biblical narratives are treated by B. O. Kurth (*supra*, III. 3). R. E. Tyner (*NQ* ii, 1955) gave a list of words first used by Quarles in addition to some 200 recorded in the *O.E.D.* Quarles's fame was traced by A. H. Nethercot (*MP* xx, 1922–3). Haight supplied biographical data (*TLS*, 11 April and 17 October 1935). J. Horden had a full bibliography in *OBS*, N.S., ii, 1948 (1953), with a biographical sketch (cf. Horden, *TLS*, 27 May, 1955); and an account of illustrations for *Argalus and Parthenia* in *CBS* ii (1958).

SIR WALTER RALEGH, 1552? 1554?–1618

Here, as in the text, early writings in prose and verse are slighted, since these are treated by C. S. Lewis. Later works in prose were: *The History of the World* (three issues in 1614 and later edns.); *The Prerogative of Parliaments in England* (1628); *Instructions to his Sonne* (1632; ed. C. Whibley, 1927; Roanoke Island Historical Association, 1939; see William Cecil, *supra*); *The Prince, or Maxims of State* (1642); *Judicious And Select Essayes And Observations* (1650); *Sir Walter Raleigh's Sceptick, or Speculations* (1651; in 1657 and later, enlarged as *Remains*). The *Cabinet-Council*, edited by Milton (1658), has been shown not to be Ralegh's (E. A. Strathmann, *TLS*, 13 April 1956). Miscellaneous works were edited by T. Birch (2 vols., 1751). The one complete edition, with biographies by Oldys and Birch, is in eight volumes (1829). The best anthology of prose is by G. E. Hadow (1917). The standard edition of the poems is by A. M. C. Latham (1929; rev., Muses' Library, 1951).

Early biographical portraits were in Naunton's *Fragmenta Regalia* (1641), Fuller's *Worthies* (1662), and Aubrey. The most substantial biographies are those of E. Edwards (2 vols., 1868), W. Stebbing (1891, 1899), E. Thompson (1935), and W. M. Wallace (Princeton, 1959). P. Edwards's compact survey (1953) includes literary criticism. Two books of special focus are V. T. Harlow's *Ralegh's Last Voyage* (1932; cf. A. M. C. Latham, *ESEA 1951*) and D. B. Quinn, *Raleigh and the British Empire* (1947). Miss Latham offered evidence for 1554 as Ralegh's birth-date (*Etudes Anglaises*, ix, 1956), and gave a full account of *Instructions to his Sonne* in *Elizabethan and Jacobean Studies Presented to Frank Percy Wilson* (1959); she is editing Ralegh's letters. A. L. Rowse has done *Ralegh and the Throckmortons* (1962).

An early critical item is Thoreau's *Sir Walter Raleigh*, ed. H. A. Metcalf (Boston, 1905). There is criticism of the poetry in E. C. Dunn, *Literature of Shakespeare's England* (New York, 1936); Tucker Brooke (*ELH* v, 1938; *Essays on Shakespeare and Other Elizabethans*, Yale, 1948); P. Edwards (*supra*); C. S. Lewis; J. Horner (*Essays in Criticism*, v, 1955); P. Ure, *The Age of Shakespeare* (*supra*, III. 1) and *Review of English Literature*, i (1960). W. Oakeshott's *The Poet and the Queen* (1960), a fresh study of Ralegh's personal and poetic relationship with Elizabeth, is a mixture of the solid and the nebulous (the latter word applies to all accounts of the so-called 'School of Night'); he adds some poems to the canon.

The fullest and best analysis of the *History* and of Ralegh's mind is E. A. Strathmann's *Sir Walter Ralegh: A Study in Elizabethan Skepticism* (Columbia, 1951). Shorter discussions of the *History* are by Sir C. Firth (*Proceedings of the British Academy*, viii, 1917–18; *Essays Historical & Literary*, 1938); L. B. Campbell and L. F. Dean's article of 1947 (*supra*, IV. 6); and P. Edwards. Ralegh's use of biblical commentaries was shown by A. Williams (*SP* xxxiv, 1937; *supra*, IV. 7). A useful study, modified by Strathmann, is N. Kempner, *Raleghs staatstheoretische Schriften: die Einführung des Machiavellismus in England* (Leipzig, 1928). V. Luciani dealt with Ralegh's *Discourse of War* and Machiavelli's *Discorsi* in *MP* xlvi (1948–9). P. Lefranc (*Etudes Anglaises*, xiii, 1960) edited a short early tract on the succession.

The fullest *Bibliography* of works and older biographies is by T. N. Brushfield (2nd ed., rev., 1908), who contributed much miscellaneous 'Raleghana' to *Trans. of the Devonshire Association*, xxviii–xlii (1896–1910). Strathmann (*HLQ* xx, 1956–7) showed that Ralegh's supposed *Discourse of Tenures* came from Sir Roger Owen.

THOMAS RANDOLPH, 1605–35

The bulk of Randolph's non-dramatic verse was first collected in *Poems With The Muses Looking-Glasse: And Amyntas* (1638; enlarged, 1640 ff.). W. C. Hazlitt's poor edition of the works (2 vols., 1875) was partly superseded by J. J. Parry's *Poems and Amyntas* (Yale, 1917) and G. Thorn-Drury's *Poems* (1929). C. L. Day reported new poems (*RES* viii, 1932). Theatrical data are summarized in G. E. Bentley, v (*supra*, I). There are essays by G. C. M. Smith (*Proceedings of the British Academy*, xiii, 1927) and E. Blunden (*Votive Tablets*, 1931), and a monograph by K. Kottas (*Wiener Beiträge*, xxix, 1909). S. A. and D. R. Tannenbaum compiled a *Concise Bibliography* (New York, 1947).

HENRY REYNOLDS, *fl.* 1628–32

The allegorical exposition of poetry, *Mythomystes* (1632), is in Spingarn and is discussed by him and J. W. H. Atkins (*supra*, IV. 9). Reynolds—to whom Drayton addressed his most attractive verse-epistle—also published *Torquato Tasso's Aminta Englisht. To this is added Ariadne's Complaint in imitation of Anguillara*

(1628) and, appended to *Mythomystes*, *The tale of Narcissus* (ed. J. S. Starkey, *Englische Studien*, xxxv, 1905; ed. J. R. Tutin, 1906). The latter was also a paraphrase of Anguillara's version of Ovid (D. Bush, *MLN* xli, 1926 and *supra*, IV. 7).

BARNABE RICH, 1542–1617

From Rich's large and varied output, 1574–1617, some pieces that have been reprinted are: *Riche his Farewell to Militarie profession* (1581; repr., Shakespeare Society, 1846; *Apolonius and Silla*, ed. M. Luce, Shakespeare Library, 1912; this and other extracts in G. Bullough, *Narrative and Dramatic Sources of Shakespeare*, ii, 1958; facsimile ed., with full apparatus, ed. T. M. Cranfill, University of Texas, 1959); *The Honestie of this Age* (1614; repr., Percy Society, xi, 1844); two Irish tracts edited by C. L. Falkiner (*Royal Irish Academy*, xxvi, 1906) and E. M. Hinton (*PMLA* lv, 1940). T. M. Cranfill and D. H. Bruce have done *Barnaby Rich: A Short Biography* (University of Texas, 1953). Some short studies are: D. T. Starnes, on the fiction (*SP* xxx, 1933); H. J. Webb, on the military tracts (*JEGP* xlii, 1943); T. M. Cranfill, a sequel to Starnes (*University of Texas Studies in English*, 1945–6) and 'Barnaby Rich and King James' (*ELH* xvi, 1949); J. L. Lievsay, *JEGP* lv (1956) and *supra*, V. 6; and F. Ferrara, *English Miscellany*, ed. M. Praz, viii (Rome, 1957).

HENRY ROBINSON, 1605–73?

Englands Safety, in Trades Encrease (1641) and *Certain Proposalls* (1652) are reprinted in W. A. Shaw, *Select Tracts and Documents Illustrative of English Monetary History 1626–1730* (1896). *Liberty of Conscience* (1644) is reproduced in W. Haller, *Tracts on Liberty* (1934). Robinson is discussed by Haller in *Tracts* and *Liberty and Reformation* (1955), by W. K. Jordan, iv (*supra*, V. 2), and most fully in Jordan's *Men of Substance* (University of Chicago, 1942).

SIR THOMAS ROE, 1580–1644

The standard book, Sir William Foster's *Embassy of Sir Thomas Roe to the Court of the Great Mogul, 1615–1619* (Hakluyt Society, 2 vols., 1899), was revised as *The Embassy of Sir Thomas Roe to India* (1926). Roe's parliamentary speech on the decay of trade (pub. 1641) is in the *Harleian Miscellany*, ed. Park, iv (1809) and Dunham and Pargellis (*supra*, II. 1). D. Hannay had a sketch of Roe in *Blackwood's*, ccxxi (1927). He figures in studies of things eastern by Foster, W. G. Rice, S. C. Chew, and T. Spencer (*supra*, V. 4), and in accounts of John Dury (q.v.).

ALEXANDER ROSS, 1591–1654

Among Ross's scientific and controversial works were: *Commentum de Terræ Motu Circulari* (1634), which led to debate with John Wilkins in *The New Planet no Planet* (1646); *The Philosophicall Touch-Stone* (1645), against Digby; *Medicus Medicatus* (1645), against *Religio Medici* and Digby's *Observations*; *Arcana Microcosmi* (1651; enlarged, 1652), against Browne's *Vulgar Errors*, Bacon, and Harvey's *De Generatione*; and *Leviathan drawn out with a Hook* (1653), against an obvious monster. Some other works were *Virgilius Evangelisans, sive Historia Jesu Christi* (1634), a poem in Virgilian language on the life of Christ; *Mel Heliconium* (1642) and *Mystagogus Poeticus* (1647), handbooks of allegorized mythology; and *ΠΑΝΣΕΒΕΙΑ: Or, A View of all Religions in the World* (1653). F. Watson had an account of Ross in the *Gentleman's Magazine*, cclxxix (1895). G. McColley's articles on Ross and Wilkins are cited below under the latter. The reply to Hobbes is discussed by J. Bowle (under Hobbes, *supra*); see also J. Bennett under Sir Thomas Browne (*supra*).

SAMUEL ROWLANDS, 1570?–1628/30?

The *Complete Works . . . 1598–1628* were first collected by the Hunterian Club (1880), with an essay by Gosse (repr. in his *Seventeenth-Century Studies*, 1883). The *Works* do not include *A Theater of Delightfull Recreation* (1605) or *The Bride* (1617; ed. A. C. Potter, Boston, 1905). Some pieces have been reprinted separately, such as the 'Knave' tracts (Percy Society, ix, 1844). The only full study is by J. R. Bowman (Harvard *Summaries of Theses 1933*). Some short discussions are in R. M. Alden, *The Rise of Formal Satire in England* (Philadelphia, 1899); *CHEL* iv, by H. V. Routh; the books on roguery by Chandler, Aydelotte, and Judges (*supra*, IV. 2); T. K. Whipple (*supra*, IV. 7); and L. B. Wright (*supra*, IV. 2). More special are articles, some of them on Rowlands's borrowings, by E. D. McDonald (*Indiana University Studies*, ix, 1911); E. M. Waith, on *Humors Antique Faces* (1605), &c. (*RES* xviii, 1942); A. Davenport (*NQ* clxxxiv, 1943); J. L. Lievsay, 'Newgate Penitents' (*HLQ* vii, 1943–4; cf. J. J. O'Connor, *PQ* xxx, 1951); and S. Dickson, on the 'Humours' (*PBSA* xliv, 1950) and on a plagiarism (1654) of *The Melancholy Knight* (1615), in *Studies in Bibliography* . . . *University of Virginia*, v (1952–3).

LUCY HARINGTON RUSSELL, COUNTESS OF BEDFORD, 1581–1627

Though the Countess's own writings are few and uncertain, so notable a patroness cannot be overlooked. A biographical summary is given by F. H. Morgan, University of Southern California *Abstracts of Dissertations . . . 1956*. There is a popular sketch in I. Grimble, *The Harington Family* (1957). Lord Braybrooke's *Private Correspondence of Jane Lady Cornwallis; 1613–1644* (1842) contained some letters. There are data in Grierson's edition of Donne (1912), in *Ben Jonson*, ed. Herford and Simpson, in F. A. Yates's *John Florio* (1934), in the *TLS*, 8 October 1938, where P. Simpson corrected the *DNB*, and in P. Thomson's account of her relations with Donne (*MLR* xliv, 1949). The linking of the Countess to 'The Phoenix and the Turtle' (*TLS*, 24 October, 28 November 1936; 13 and 20 February 1937) was dealt with by H. E. Rollins, *Shakespeare: The Poems* (1938).

JOHN SALTMARSH, c. 1610–47

Some reprints are: *Sparkles of Glory* (1647; repr. 1811, 1847); extracts from *The Smoke in the Temple* (1646) and a letter to the Council of War (1647) in Woodhouse (*supra*, V. 1); extracts from *Reasons For Unitie, Peace, and Love* (1646) in D. M. Wolfe, *Milton in the Puritan Revolution* (1941). Saltmarsh is discussed by R. M. Jones, *Studies in Mystical Religion* (1909) and *Mysticism and Democracy* (*supra*, V. 2); by Woodhouse and Wolfe; by W. K. Jordan, *HLQ* iii (1939–40); and by L. F. Solt, *Journal of Ecclesiastical History*, ii (1951) and *supra*, V. 1.

WYE SALTONSTALL, *fl.* 1630–40

Saltonstall translated *Ovids Tristia* (1633), *Ovids Heroicall Epistles* (1636), *Ovid De Ponto* (1639), and Gerard Mercator's *Historia Mundi* (1635), &c. His chief other work was a book of characters, *Picturæ Loquentes* (1631; enlarged 1635; ed. C. H. Wilkinson, 1946). This last is discussed by B. Boyce (*supra*, IV. 5).

ROBERT SANDERSON, 1587–1663

Sanderson's most popular work was *Logicæ Artis Compendium* (1615). *Ten Sermons* (1627) had by 1689 become *XXXVI. Sermons*. The works of casuistry to which he owed his special fame appeared in his later years and posthumously. The standard edition of the *Works* is that of W. Jacobson (6 vols., 1854). C. Wordsworth edited, in translation, *Bishop Sanderson's Lectures on Conscience and Human Law* (1877). Izaak Walton's *Life* (1678) receives important commentary in D. Novarr (under Walton, *infra*). G. Lewis's *Robert Sanderson* (1924) is supplemented by discussion of the sermons in W. F. Mitchell (*supra*, V. 2) and of the books on casuistry by H. R. McAdoo (*supra*, V. 2) and T. Wood (*Church Quarterly Review*, cxlvii, 1948–9, and under Jeremy Taylor, *infra*). There is a bibliography in W. T. Freemantle (under R. Bernard, *supra*).

SIR EDWIN SANDYS, 1561–1629

Sandys wrote a version of selected Psalms (1615) and *Europæ Speculum* (1629), which in 1605 had had three unauthorized and garbled editions as *A Relation Of The State Of Religion . . . in . . . these westerne parts of the world*. Revised accounts of Sandys's Virginian activities were given in W. F. Craven, *Dissolution of the Virginia Company* (New York, 1932), and C. M. Andrews (*supra*, V. 4); cf. R. B. Davis's *George Sandys* (*infra*). W. M. Wallace wrote a monograph, *Sir Edwin Sandys and the First Parliament of James I* (University of Pennsylvania, 1940). H. Craig discussed Sandys's concern with the publication of Hooker (*JHI* v, 1944).

GEORGE SANDYS, 1578–1644

Sandys's chief writings were: *A Relation of a Journey begun An: Dom: 1610* (1615); *Ovids Metamorphosis* (books i–v, 'edit: 2d', 1621; repr. 1623; complete, 1626; enlarged in 1632 with an allegorical commentary and a version of *Aeneid* i); *A Paraphrase upon the Psalmes of David* (1636); *A Paraphrase upon the Divine Poems* (1638); and the drama *Christs Passion* (1640), translated from Grotius. The last three works were edited by R. Hooper (2 vols., 1872). The University of Nebraska Press is reprinting the 1632 *Ovid*. The standard book, R. B. Davis's *George Sandys Poet-Adventurer* (1955), has a full bibliography. Extracts from the *Relation* are in Purchas and J. Harris (*supra*, V. 4); the book is discussed by Penrose, Rice, Chew, and T. Spencer (*supra*, V. 4). There is a thesis on the translation of Grotius by G. H. Grüninger (Tauberbischofsheim, 1927), an unpublished thesis on the *Ovid* by B. I. Ingalls (Radcliffe, 1950). Sandys's versification was analysed by R. C. Wallerstein (*PMLA* l, 1935), his diction by G. Tillotson and more fully by J. Arthos (*supra*, III. 3). The story of the composition and publication of the *Ovid*, traced by R. B. Davis (*PBSA*, xxxv, 1941), was completed by J. G. McManaway, who described the rediscovered 1621 edition (*Bibliographical Society: University of Virginia*, i, 1948–9), and by Davis (ibid. viii, 1956). F. T. Bowers and Davis compiled 'George Sandys: A Bibliographical Catalogue of Printed Editions in England to 1700' (*Bulletin of the New York Public Library*, liv, 1950). Davis also gave accounts of the *Song of Solomon* (*PBSA* l, 1956) and of 'Volumes from George Sandys's Library Now in America' (*Virginia Magazine of History and Biography*, lxv, 1957).

SIR HENRY SAVILE, 1549–1622

Savile translated parts of Tacitus (1591; 6th ed., 1640) and edited *Rerum Anglicarum Scriptores post Bedam* (1596), Xenophon's *Cyropaedia* (1613), and, his great achievement, the works of Chrysostom (8 vols., 1610–13). There is some comment on his translation in H. B. Lathrop (*supra*, IV. 8), a biographical essay by H. W. Garrod in the *TLS*, 27 January 1950. J. R. L. Highfield is to supply more biographical data in the *Bodleian Library Record*.

THOMAS SCOTT, 1580?–1626

The clerical author of a potent tract against Gondomar and the Spanish marriage, *Vox Populi* (1620; *Somers Tracts*, ed. Scott, ii, 1809), is placed in his setting by L. B. Wright, 'Propaganda against James I's "Appeasement" of Spain', *HLQ* vi (1942–3). Another item is noted under Sir William Vaughan (*infra*). Scott's writings are listed in the *DNB*.

JOHN SELDEN, 1584–1654

Without disturbing the dust on *Joannis Seldeni Jurisconsulti Opera Omnia*, ed. D. Wilkins (3 vols., 1726), one may mention *De Dis Syris* (1617), *The Historie of Tithes* (1618), *Marmora Arundelliana* (1628), *Mare Clausum* (1635; see M. Needham, *supra*), and *Table-Talk* (1689; ed. Arber, 1868; S. H. Reynolds, 1892; Sir F. Pollock, 1927; Everyman's Library, 1934). The standard text of Selden's annotations on *Poly-Olbion* is in Hebel's edition of Drayton. Among general accounts are Sir E. Fry's full article in the *DNB* and essays in Herbert Paul's *Men and Letters* (1901) and the *TLS*, 22 October 1925. Selden's legal work is analysed by H. D. Hazeltine in *Festschrift Heinrich Brunner* (Weimar, 1910) and the *Harvard Law Review*, xxiv (1910-11), by D. Ogg in his edition of *Ioannis Seldeni Ad Fletam Dissertatio* (1925), and by H. Arneke (*supra*, IV. 6). His position on Church and State is discussed in the general histories, such as Gardiner, in the books on political thought by G. P. Gooch and P. Treves (*supra*, V. 1), and in the books on toleration by M. Freund and W. K. Jordan, ii (*supra*, V. 2). The history of Selden's library has been told by J. Sparrow (*Bodleian Quarterly Record*, vi, 1931) and D. M. Barratt (*Bodleian Library Record*, iii, 1951).

EDWARD SEXBY, d. 1658

Killing No Murder, printed in Holland in 1657 as by 'William Allen', is reprinted in the *Harleian Miscellany*, ed. Park, iv (1809), H. Morley's *Famous Pamphlets* (1886), A. C. Ward's *Miscellany of Tracts and Pamphlets* (1927), and R. F. Brinkley's *English Prose* (*supra*, II. 1). In the *English Historical Review*, xvii (1902) Firth modified his *DNB* article and defined the probable extent of Silius Titus's collaboration. Sexby is noticed in some studies of the Levellers, e.g. M. Ashley's *John Wildman* (1947), and in W. C. Abbott (under Cromwell, *supra*).

WILLIAM SHAKESPEARE, 1564–1616

The *Sonnets*, though published in 1609, belong with the earlier sequences and, with 'The Phoenix and the Turtle', are discussed by Lewis, who has a bibliography. Some additions to it are: T. W. Baldwin, *On the Literary Genetics of Shakspere's Poems & Sonnets* (University of Illinois, 1950); G. W. Knight, *The Mutual Flame* (1955); J. W. Lever, *The Elizabethan Love Sonnet* (1956); C. Schaar, *An Elizabethan Sonnet Problem: Shakespeare's Sonnets, Daniel's Delia, and their Literary Background* (*Lund Studies in English*, xxviii, 1960); and J. B. Leishman, *Themes and Variations in Shakespeare's Sonnets* (1961). Some references for the 'Phoenix' are given above under Robert Chester.

THOMAS SHELTON, fl. 1597–1629?

The first part of *The History Of ... Don-Quixote* appeared in 1612; the second part, with a second edition of the first (revised, but perhaps not by Shelton), in 1620. The complete work was

reprinted in 1652 and 1675. Some modern editions are those of
J. Fitzmaurice-Kelly (Tudor Translations, 4 vols., 1896), A. W.
Pollard (3 vols., 1900), and F. J. H. Darton (Navarre Society,
2 vols., 1923). J. D. M. Ford and R. Lansing compiled *Cervantes:
A Tentative Bibliography* (Harvard, 1931). A detailed account of
the English reception of Cervantes is E. B. Knowles, *Four
Articles on Don Quixote in England* (New York University, 1941);
three of the articles were in *PQ* xx (1941), *Hispanic Review*, ix
(1941), and *Hispania*, xxiii (1940). Knowles had a textual study
in *PBSA* xxxvii (1943). E. M. Wilson discussed Cervantes's
influence in seventeenth-century England (*Bulletin Hispanique*, l,
1948), and E. A. Peers all the translators (*Bulletin of Spanish
Studies*, xxiv, 1947). The shadowy Irish translator was given
substance, with excerpts from letters, by Knowles (*Studies in the
Renaissance*, v, 1958) and J. George (*Bulletin of Hispanic Studies*,
xxxv, 1958).

SAMUEL SHEPPARD, 1624?-55?

The article on Sheppard in the *DNB* is quite unreliable. A
full and authoritative account, with copious excerpts, especially
from his roll-calls of English poets, and with valuable information about journalism and other matters, is given by H. E.
Rollins in *SP* xxiv (1927). Sheppard comes into J. Frank
(*supra*, IV. 3).

SIR EDWARD SHERBURNE, 1616-1702

Sherburne, a cousin and friend of Thomas Stanley, is neglected in the text because he was wholly a translator. A volume
issued in 1651 under two titles, *Salmacis, Lyrian & Sylvia*, &c.,
and *Poems And Translations. Amorous, Lusory, Morall, Divine*,
reprinted in Chalmers, vi, and as *Miscellaneous Poems* (1819),
has been edited by F. J. van Beeck (Assen, 1961); the
sources are set forth by M. Praz, *MLR* xx (1925). Sherburne's
other works were versions of Seneca's *Medea* (1648) and
Troades (1679) and *Tragedies of L. Annæus Seneca* (1701), containing these two and others; and *The Sphere of Marcus Manilius*
(1675). J. M. Osborn (under Stanley, *infra*) printed Stanley's
verses on their friendship. In the *TLS*, 14 March 1958, G. C.
Crump printed Sherburne's reply (1688) to queries from Anthony
Wood, in which he recalled early association with Carew, May,
Randolph, Shirley, Herrick, and other 'Witts'.

Sir Anthony Sherley (1565-*post* 1636), Sir Robert Sherley (1578/81?–1628), and Sir Thomas Sherley (1564?–1633?)

Of the abundant material produced by and about the renowned trio, only a few items can be mentioned. *Sir Antony Sherley His Relation of his Travels into Persia* (1613) was abridged in Purchas. W. Parry's *Travels of sir Anthony Sherley . . . to the Persian Empire* (1601), also abridged in Purchas, is reprinted in Collier's *Illustrations of Early English Popular Literature*, ii (1864), and, with other documents and with a full introduction and bibliography, in *Sir Anthony Sherley and his Persian Adventure*, ed. Sir Denison Ross (Broadway Travellers, 1933). *Sir Robert Sherley . . . His Royall entertainement into Cracovia* (1609) is reprinted in the *Harleian Miscellany*, ed. Park, v (1810), and in Bullen's ed. of Thomas Middleton (1885–6), viii. Sir Thomas's *Discours of the Turkes*, written in 1606–7, is edited from the manuscript by Ross in the *Camden Miscellany*, xvi (1936). Extracts from various narratives were given in the anonymous *The Three Brothers* (1825). Anthony Nixon's *The Three English Brothers* (1607) is discussed by Ross and by L. Ennis in his article on Nixon (*HLQ* iii, 1939–40). E. P. Shirley's *The Sherley Brothers* (Roxburghe Club, 1848) remains valuable. The most recent account is B. Penrose's *The Sherleian Odyssey* (1938). The brothers' activities are summarized in S. C. Chew, *The Crescent and the Rose* (1937). A special study of Sir Anthony is F. Babinger's *Sherleiana* (Berlin, 1932).

John Sherman, *c.* 1609/10–61

Sherman is sometimes associated with the Cambridge Platonists on the strength of *A Greek in the Temple; Some Common-places delivered in Trinity Colledge Chapell in Cambridge, upon Acts xvii, part of the 28. verse* (1641). He is noticed in Mullinger (*supra*, V. 6) and in the same writer's chapter in the *CHEL* viii.

James Shirley, 1596–1666

Poems &c. (1646) was reprinted in the *Dramatic Works*, ed. Gifford and Dyce (1833), vi. The standard edition is *The Poems of James Shirley*, ed. R. L. Armstrong (New York, 1941). Biographical and theatrical data are fully summarized in G. E. Bentley, v (*supra*, I). Biographical data are added by J. P. Feil (*RES* viii, 1957), J. M. Osborn (under Stanley, *infra*), and

A. M. Taylor (*NQ* vii, 1960). S. A. and D. R. Tannenbaum compiled a *Concise Bibliography* (New York, 1946).

RICHARD SIBBES, 1577–1635

Sibbes's influence was felt by many men, notably Baxter, John Cotton, and Hugh Peter. Among his many volumes (most of them posthumously edited by Thomas Goodwin and other friends) were *The Bruised Reede, and Smoaking Flax* (1630) and *Beames of Divine Light* (1639), both collections of sermons. His collected works were printed in 1809 and 1812 and were edited by Grosart (7 vols., 1862–4). Sibbes is discussed in W. Haller's *Rise of Puritanism* (1938) and by W. F. Mitchell (*supra*, V. 2) and R. F. Hudson, *Quarterly Journal of Speech*, xliv (1958).

JAMES SMITH, 1605–67. *See* SIR JOHN MENNES

CAPTAIN JOHN SMITH, 1579/80–1631

Some of Smith's chief publications are cited in the text. The standard collected edition is *Travels and Works of Captain John Smith*, ed. A. G. Bradley, with a bibliography by T. Seccombe (2 vols., 1910), a revision of Arber's edition (1884; 2 vols., 1895). Of the many reprints of one or more works, one is *The True Travels, Adventures, & Observations*, ed. J. G. Fletcher and L. C. Wroth (New York, 1930). J. M. Morse reviewed the attacks on Smith's veracity in the *Journal of Southern History*, i (1935). There are biographies by J. G. Fletcher (New York, 1928) and Bradford Smith (Philadelphia, 1953). L. P. Striker translated Henry Wharton's Latin *Life* (written 1685), with a full introduction (University of North Carolina, 1957). Smith has his place in many studies of the colonization of America, including H. M. Jones, 'The Literature of Virginia' (*supra*, V. 4). W. Eames compiled a *Bibliography* (New York, 1927).

JOHN SMITH, 1616?–52

Select Discourses, with Simon Patrick's funeral sermon, were edited by John Worthington (1660; 2nd ed., 1673; 3rd ed., 1821; 4th, ed. H. G. Williams, 1859). Lord Hailes had published an incomplete edition (1756) and John Wesley had put extracts into his *Christian Library*. W. M. Metcalfe edited selections as *The Natural Truth of Christianity* (1882; enlarged as *The Cambridge Platonists*, 1885). The most accessible selections are in

Campagnac (*supra*, V. 2). Coleridge's comments are reprinted in R. F. Brinkley; Arnold's are in 'A Psychological Parallel' (*Last Essays on Church and Religion*, 1877). Smith is discussed in J. Tulloch, in R. M. Jones, *Spiritual Reformers*, in the books on the Cambridge Platonists by Powicke, Pawson, De Boer, and De Pauley, and in W. F. Mitchell (all cited above in V. 2); in B. Willey (*supra*, III. 4); and by E. I. Watkin (*Catholic World*, cxlv, 1937; *Poets and Mystics*, 1953) and J. K. Ryan (*New Scholasticism*, xx, 1946). J. E. Saveson had a note on Smith's library in *NQ* v (1958), a discussion of Descartes's influence on him in *JHI* xx (1960). A bibliography of Smith's book is given in R. C. Christie's *Bibliography of . . . John Worthington* (Chetham Society, N.S., xiii, 1888).

MICHAEL SPARKE, d. 1653

The earliest extant edition of Sparke's very popular *Crums of Comfort* (1623?) is the 7th (1628). His *Scintilla* is cited above in IV. 8. The Puritan publisher and author is discussed by H. R. Plomer, *The Bibliographer*, i (New York, 1902), and by C. Blagden and P. M. Handover (*supra*, IV. 10).

JOHN SPEED, 1552?-1629

The topographical and antiquarian *Theatre Of The Empire Of Great Britaine* (1611) was continued in the large *History of Great Britaine* (1611), which came from the beginning to the reign of James. From the *Theatre* J. Arlott edited *John Speed's England. A Coloured Facsimile of the Maps and Text* (4 parts, 1953-4). E. G. R. Taylor edited *An Atlas of Tudor England and Wales: Forty Plates from John Speed's Pocket Atlas of 1627* (Penguin, 1951). Speed is discussed by C. Whibley (*CHEL* iii), L. B. Wright (*supra*, IV. 2), and Sir T. D. Kendrick (*supra*, IV. 6).

SIR HENRY SPELMAN, 1561?-1641

Some of Spelman's works were: *De non temerandis Ecclesiis* (1613); *Archæologus. In modum Glossarii* (2 vols., 1626-64); *Concilia, Decreta, Leges, Constitutiones, In Re Ecclesiarum Orbis Britannici* (2 vols., 1639-64); *Reliquiæ Spelmannianæ*, ed. E. Gibson (1698); *The English Works . . . Together with his Posthumous Works, Relating to the Laws and Antiquities of England* (1723). Spelman and the movement in which he had a notable part have been increasingly studied: Sir M. Powicke, *Proceedings of*

the British Academy, xvi (1930); H. Arneke and D. C. Douglas
(*supra*, IV. 6); R. L. Schuyler, 'The Antiquaries and Sir Henry
Spelman', *Proceedings of the American Philosophical Society*, xc
(1946); L. Van Norden, 'Sir Henry Spelman on the Chronology
of the Elizabethan College of Antiquaries', *HLQ* xiii (1949–50);
J. Evans, R. J. Schoeck, J. G. A. Pocock (especially), and L.
Van Norden (all cited *supra*, IV. 6).

JOSHUA SPRIGG(E), 1618–84

Sprigg, a devoted admirer of Sir Thomas Fairfax, has a place
in the *DNB* mainly because of *Anglia Rediviva* (1647; repr. 1854;
ed. H. T. Moore, Scholars' Facsimiles & Reprints, 1960). He
was identified by B. Kiefer (*Church History*, xxii, 1953) as the
author of *The ancient Bounds, or Liberty of Conscience* (1645), the
importance of which was shown by M. Freund (*supra*, V. 2)
and by A. S. P. Woodhouse in *Puritanism and Liberty* (1938),
where he gave an extract; cf. W. K. Jordan, iv, and A. Barker
(*supra*, V. 2).

THOMAS STANLEY, 1625–78

Stanley's poems and translations appeared in several volumes,
1647–52. Some reprinted works are: *Poems* (1651; ed. Brydges,
1814–15); *Anacreon*, ed. Bullen (1893, 1906); *Kisses*, from
Secundus (in the Bohn *Propertius*; repr. separately, 1923); the
translation from Pico, *A Platonick Discourse Upon Love* (in *Poems*,
1651), ed. E. G. Gardner (1914). The ostensibly original verse
and some of the shorter translations were reprinted in L. I.
Guiney's *Thomas Stanley* (1907) and Saintsbury, iii (1921). G. M.
Crump has done a new edition (1962). Stanley's large use of
Italian, Spanish, and French poets has been shown by M. Praz
(*MLR* xx, 1925), Sir H. Thomas (*Revue Hispanique*, xlviii, 1920),
and E. M. Wilson and E. R. Vincent (*Revue de littérature comparée*,
xxxii, 1958). His once famous *History of Philosophy* (1655–62)
was a good pioneer work of popularization. His notable edition
of Aeschylus (1663), in which he had much help from Bishop
Pearson, is judiciously assessed by E. D. M. Fraenkel in his own
edition of *Agamemnon* (1950), i. G. E. Bentley reprinted poems
by Shirley, Sherburne, and other friends on Stanley's wedding
(*HLQ* ii, 1938–9). J. M. Osborn (*Yale University Library Gazette*,
xxxii, 1958) describes and quotes from the hitherto lost 'Register
of Friends' containing 366 lines of verse. There are biographical

and bibliographical notes by G. M. Crump (*TLS*, 26 July 1957; *NQ* v, 1958; *CBS* ii, part v, 1958); and H. A. Roberts and G. Isham (*NQ* v, 1958). M. Flower had 'A Bibliography of His Writings in Prose and Verse (1647–1743)' in *CBS* i, part ii (1950).

GEORGE STARKEY (STIRK), 1628?–65

Starkey's life and alchemical and medical activities are described, with a bibliography, by G. H. Turnbull, *Publications of The Colonial Society of Massachusetts*, xxxviii (1959). *Natures Explication and Helmont's Vindication* (1657) was placed in its setting by R. F. Jones (*supra*, III. 4). In *The Dignity of Kingship Asserted* (1660) 'G. S.' inveighed against Milton's *Readie and Easie Way*, and in editing the tract (Facsimile Text Society, 1942) W. R. Parker argued for Starkey's authorship and gave some account of him.

JOHN STEPHENS, *fl.* 1615

Satyricall Essayes Characters And Others (1615) had a second enlarged edition in 1615. The book was reprinted in Halliwell [-Phillipps], *Books of Characters* (1857), and extracts are in modern anthologies. The characters are discussed by G. Murphy in her *Bibliography*, by W. J. Paylor, and, more generally, by B. Boyce (*supra*, IV. 5); the essays in E. N. S. Thompson's *Seventeenth-Century English Essay* (ibid.).

PETER STERRY, 1613–72

A number of sermons appeared separately. Of the larger (and posthumous) works the best known is *A Discourse of the Freedom of the Will* (1675). The standard book is V. de Sola Pinto's *Peter Sterry, Platonist and Puritan, 1613–1672: A Biographical and Critical Study with passages selected from his Writings* (1934). A somewhat lower estimate of Sterry's literary power is in W. F. Mitchell (*supra*, V. 2). Other accounts of his religious thought are in R. M. Jones, *Spiritual Reformers*, F. J. Powicke, and W. K. Jordan, iv (*supra*, V. 2).

JOHN STOW, 1525–1605

After Stow's edition of Chaucer (1561) came *A Summarie of Englyshe Chronicles* (1565), which had abridged and enlarged editions; *The Chronicles of England* (1580), from 1592 called *Annales* and in 1615 ff. continued by E. Howes; and his best work, *A Survay of London* (1598), enlarged by Stow in 1603 and from 1618 by Anthony Munday and others. The standard edition of the last by C. L. Kingsford (2 vols., 1908; *Additional Notes*, 1927) gives the text of 1603, with a full account of Stow and a bibliography. The book is included in Everyman's Library. J. Gairdner edited *Three Fifteenth-Century Chronicles* from Stow's collection (Camden Society, xxviii, 1880) and Kingsford *Two London Chronicles* (*Camden Miscellany*, xii, 1910). Stow is discussed by C. Whibley (*CHEL* iii and *Essays in Biography*, 1913), L. B. Wright (*supra*, IV. 2), Sir T. D. Kendrick (*supra*, IV. 6), C. S. Lewis, and T. S. Dorsch (*ESEA 1959*). J. A. Bryant (*MLR* xlv, 1950) showed E. Howes's probable authorship of the defence of Brute in the 1615 and 1631 editions of the *Chronicles*.

WILLIAM STRACHEY, 1572–1621

Strachey's account of Virginia, written 1609–12 but first printed in 1849, has had a new edition, based on the Percy Manuscript (written or finished in 1612), by L. B. Wright and V. Freund, *The Historie of Travell into Virginia Britania* (Hakluyt Society, 1953). The editors include fresh material on Strachey's life and sources from S. G. Culliford's University of London thesis (1950). Strachey's chief other writings were *For The Colony in Virginea Britannia. Lawes Divine, Morall and Martiall* (1612; repr., P. Force, *Tracts*, iii, 1844; facsimile, Massachusetts Historical Society, Boston, 1936) and *A true reportory of the wracke, and redemption of Sir Thomas Gates* (in Purchas, 1625). Shakespearian and other associations are discussed by C. M. Gayley (under Jourdain, *supra*); R. R. Cawley, *PMLA* xli (1926); L. Hotson, *I, William Shakespeare* (1937); H. M. Jones, 'The Literature of Virginia' (*supra*, V. 4); C. R. Sanders, *Virginia Magazine of History and Biography*, lvii (1949) and *The Strachey Family* (Duke University, 1953); and editors of *The Tempest*.

WILLIAM STRODE, 1602–45

Strode's poems were first collected, along with the tragicomedy *The Floating Island* (pr. 1655), by B. Dobell (1907). There is a study of the play by E. G. Hoffsten (St. Louis, 1908), an account of it in G. E. Bentley, v (*supra*, I). H. Morris had a critique of the poetry in *Tulane Studies in English*, vii (1957) and a note in *Renaissance News*, xii (1959), M. C. Crum an account of an autograph manuscript in the *Bodleian Library Record*, iv

(1952–3), and C. F. Main notes on attributed poems in *PQ* xxxiv (1955).

SIR JOHN SUCKLING, 1609–42

Aglaura (1638) and some other things were printed in Suckling's lifetime; for the plays, see G. E. Bentley, v (*supra,* I). *Fragmenta Aurea* (1646; repr. 1648, 1658) contained poems, letters, *An Account of Religion by Reason,* and plays. *Last Remains* appeared in 1658–9. W. C. Hazlitt's edition of the complete works (2 vols., 1874; rev. 1892) was superseded by that of A. H. Thompson (1910). The poems are in R. G. Howarth (*supra,* II. 2). H. Berry has edited new material in *Sir John Suckling's Poems and Letters From Manuscript* (University of Western Ontario, 1960). T. S. Clayton is preparing a critical edition. Suckling figures in accounts of the cavalier poets and in K. M. Lynch's *Social Mode of Restoration Comedy* (New York, 1926). Two critiques are F. O. Henderson, 'Traditions of *Précieux* and *Libertin* in Suckling's Poetry' (*ELH* iv, 1937), and an essay in the *TLS,* 9 May 1942. 'A Sessions of the Poets' was discussed by P. H. Gray (*SP* xxxvi, 1939; cf. W. Marquardt, *HLQ* xv, 1951–2) and A. R. Benham (*MLQ* vi, 1945). H. Berry gave a precise biography in University of Nebraska *Abstracts of Doctoral Dissertations 1953* (pp. 136–40); he has a book in prospect. T. S. Clayton recorded Thorn-Drury's marginalia on Suckling (*NQ* vi, 1959) and supplied fresh biographical data (*TLS,* 29 January 1960). In a close scrutiny of the canon (*SP* lvii, 1960), I. A. Beaurline accepted the *Fragmenta* but was sceptical about much of the *Last Remains* and all later attributions.

JOHN SWAN, *fl.* 1635

The encyclopaedic *Speculum Mundi. Or A Glasse Representing The Face Of The World* (1635) had further editions in 1643, 1665, and 1670. Swan's scientific ideas are discussed by F. Watson, *Beginnings* (*supra,* V. 6), L. B. Wright (*supra,* IV. 2), F. R. Johnson, *Astronomical Thought* (*supra,* V. 3), and K. Svendsen (under Milton, *supra*).

JOSUAH SYLVESTER, 1563–1618

Sylvester's miscellaneous publications must be skipped. Parts of his and other men's translations from Du Bartas appeared in 1584 ff. The first collected edition of Sylvester was *Bartas His*

Devine Weekes & Workes (1605; completed 1608). Editions included minor pieces translated from Du Bartas and others. Grosart edited the *Complete Works* (2 vols., 1880). An abridgement of the chief work was edited by T. W. Haight as *The Divine Weeks of Josuah Sylvester* (Waukesha, Wisconsin, 1908). Study of Du Bartas and Sylvester has been advanced by the critical edition of the former edited by U. T. Holmes, J. C. Lyons, and R. W. Linker (3 vols., University of North Carolina, 1935–40). To their critical matter, and French scholarship, may be added A. E. Creore's study of Du Bartas's style (*MLQ* i, 1940). The chief accounts of Du Bartas's influence in England are H. Ashton, *Du Bartas en Angleterre* (Paris, 1908), and A. H. Upham (*supra*, IV. 7). Other studies, of varying scope, are: P. Weller, *Joshuah Sylvesters englische Übersetzungen der religiösen Epen des Du Bartas* (Tübingen, 1902); G. C. Taylor, *Milton's Use of Du Bartas* (Harvard, 1934); L. B. Campbell, 'The Christian Muse' (*HLB*, 1935, and *Divine Poetry*, *supra*, III. 3); some pages in F. R. Johnson, *Astronomical Thought* (*supra*, V. 3); G. Tillotson and J. Arthos, on diction (*supra*, III. 3); W. B. Hunter, on prosody (*PQ* xxviii, 1949); V. L. Simonsen's study of 'The First Week' as a translation (*Orbis Litterarum*, viii, 1950); E. M. W. Tillyard, *The English Epic* (1954); and B. O. Kurth (*supra*, III. 3).

JEREMY TAYLOR, 1613–67

The standard edition of the complete works is that of R. Heber (15 vols., 1822) revised by C. P. Eden (10 vols., 1847–54). Grosart edited *Poems and Verse-Translations* (*Miscellanies of The Fuller Worthies' Library*, i, 1870). *Holy Living* and *Holy Dying* have had many modern reprints, e.g. Temple Classics (3 vols.). Three anthologies are *Jeremy Taylor*, ed. M. Armstrong (1923), *The Golden Grove*, ed. L. P. Smith (1930), and *The House of Understanding*, ed. M. Gest (Philadelphia, 1954).

Biography began with George Rust's funeral sermon, which is reprinted by Heber and Eden, who supplied the first scholarly life. Sir E. Gosse's biography (1903) has been superseded by C. J. Stranks, *The Life and Writings of Jeremy Taylor* (1952), to which, for the last phase, should be added F. R. Bolton's *The Caroline Tradition of the Church of Ireland* (1958). New material on Taylor's later life was furnished by M. Nicolson (*PQ* viii, 1929; *The Conway Letters*, Yale, 1930).

Coleridge's many comments are assembled in R. F. Brinkley; she discussed them in *HLQ* xiii (1949–50). Hazlitt's are in his *Dramatic Literature of the Age of Elizabeth* and elsewhere; Arnold's in 'The Literary Influence of Academies'. For later literary criticism there are Gosse and Smith (*supra*); W. F. Mitchell and briefer remarks in C. Smyth (*supra*, V. 2); J. R. King, *English Studies*, xxxvii (1956); F. P. Wilson (*supra*, III. 2). Sister M. S. Antoine's *The Rhetoric of Jeremy Taylor's Prose: Ornament of the Sunday Sermons* (Catholic University of America, 1946) is a technical compilation.

The fullest accounts of the divine and theologian are W. J. Brown, *Jeremy Taylor* (1925) and H. T. Hughes, *The Piety of Jeremy Taylor* (1960). General and special studies of his religious thought are: J. Tulloch (*supra*, V. 2); Sir James Stephen, *Horae Sabbaticae, First Series* (1892); E. Dowden (*supra*, III. 1); the books on toleration by M. Freund and W. K. Jordan, iv (*supra*, V. 2); T. G. Steffan, *University of Texas Studies in English* (1940); H. R. McAdoo (*supra*, V. 2); S. Herndon, summary of a thesis on Taylor's use of the Bible (New York University, 1949); R. G. Hoopes, *HLQ* xiii (1949–50); H. Baker and M. L. Wiley (*supra*, III. 4); Thomas Wood, *English Casuistical Divinity during the Seventeenth Century: With Special Reference to Jeremy Taylor* (1952); P. Elmen, *MLQ* xiv (1953); and a chapter in C. J. Stranks's *Anglican Devotion* (1961).

Smith's *Golden Grove* includes a bibliography by R. Gathorne-Hardy which was corrected and enlarged in the *TLS*, 25 September, 2 and 9 October 1930, and especially 15 September 1932. He had further notes and articles, ibid., 13 and 20 September 1947, 20 April 1951, 18 February 1955, and the *Library*, ii (1947–8), iii (1948–9).

John Taylor, 1578?–1653

Sixty of the pamphlets written up to 1630 were reprinted in the *Workes* of that year; this folio was reprinted (1869) by the Spenser Society, which reprinted Taylor's later pieces in 5 vols. (1870–8). C. Hindley reprinted many pieces in his *Old Book Collector's Miscellany*, ii and iii (1872–3), and 21 more, with an introduction and bibliography, in his *Works of John Taylor* (1872). *A Dog of War* was reprinted in 1927. Southey had a long account of Taylor in *Lives of the Uneducated Poets* (1831; ed. J. S. Childers, 1925). The one full study is the manuscript dissertation of R. B. Dow (Harvard *Summaries of Theses 1931*). There are essays by W. Thorp (*Texas Review*, viii, 1922–3) and W. Notestein, *Four Worthies* (1956). One side of Taylor's activity is discussed in E. G. R. Taylor (*supra*, V. 4). S. Williams described 'A Lord Mayor's Show' by Taylor (*Bulletin of the John Rylands Library*, xli, 1958–9).

'TOM TELL-TROATH'

Tom Tell-Troath: Or, A free Discourse touching the Manners of the Time was apparently written about 1622, though possibly not published until the beginning of Charles's reign. It is reprinted in the *Harleian Miscellany*, ed. Park, ii (1809), and *Somers Tracts*, ed. Scott, ii (1809), and abridged in Dunham and Pargellis (*supra*, II. 1).

SIR WILLIAM TEMPLE, 1628–99

The works of Temple's maturity lie beyond our limits. G. C. M. Smith edited *The Letters of Dorothy Osborne to William Temple* (1928) and his *Early Essays and Romances* (1930). There are biographical and critical books by Clara Marburg (Yale, 1932) and H. E. Woodbridge (New York, 1940).

ROBERT TOFTE, 1561/2–1619/20

Tofte was rather a translator than an original author. *The Batchelars Banquet* (1603; ed. F. P. Wilson, 1929) was tentatively ascribed to Tofte by its editor, whose introduction and F. B. Williams's full study (*RES* xiii, 1937, and ibid. vi, 1955) are the best accounts of him. Tofte's annotations in his *Blazon of Jealousie* (1615) were studied by G. M. Kahrl (*Harvard Studies and Notes in Philology and Literature*, xviii, 1935). R. W. Dent (*PQ* xxxv, 1956, and the book cited under T. Adams, *supra*) showed borrowings in Webster's *White Devil* from Tofte's translation, *Honours Academie* (1610).

EDWARD TOPSELL, 1572–1625

Topsell's *Historie of Foure-Footed Beastes* (1607) and *Historie of Serpents* (1608) were drawn largely from Conrad Gesner. Extracts are in M. St. C. Byrne's *Elizabethan Zoo* (1926). M. Doran discussed Topsell in relation to Elizabethan 'credulity' (*JHI* i, 1940), and C. E. Raven (*supra*, V. 3) placed him among the English naturalists. The *DNB* was corrected and enlarged by Miss Byrne and by V. B. Heltzel, who described the unpublished *Fowles of Heaven* (*HLQ* i, 1937–8).

AURELIAN TOWNSHEND, 1583?–1651?

Two masques, *Albions Triumph* and *Tempe Restord* (pr. 1632), along with poems from miscellanies and manuscripts, were edited by Sir E. K. Chambers (1912). This volume and the *DNB* received bibliographical and biographical supplements from G. C. M. Smith in *MLR* xii (1917) and the *TLS*, 23 October 1924. Dramatic data are given in G. E. Bentley, v (*supra*, I).

THOMAS TRAHERNE, 1637–74

Some works published in Traherne's century were: *Roman Forgeries* (1673); *Christian Ethicks* (1675; two chapters, *Of Magnanimity and Charity*, ed. J. R. Slater, Columbia, 1942); and *A serious and patheticall Contemplation of the Mercies of God* (1699; ed. R. Daniells, *University of Toronto Studies*, xii, 1941). *Poems*, first printed by B. Dobell (1903), was followed by *Poems of Felicity*, ed. H. I. Bell (1910) and *Poetical Works*, ed. G. I. Wade (1932). *Centuries of Meditations*, first printed by Dobell (1908), has been reprinted with introductions by J. Hayward (1950), H. Vaughan (1960), and J. Farrar (New York, 1960). The standard edition is *Thomas Traherne: Centuries, Poems, and Thanksgivings*, ed. H. M. Margoliouth (2 vols., 1958). This edition, along with much else, summarizes biographical material from G. I. Wade's critical biography (Princeton, 1944) and additions made by K. W. Salter and Margoliouth (*NQ* i, 1954) and A. Russell (*RES* vi, 1955).

Critical studies have multiplied: R. M. Jones, *Spiritual Reformers* (*supra*, V. 2); G. E. Willett, *Traherne* (*An Essay*) (1919); E. N. S. Thompson, *PQ* viii (1929); T. O. Beachcroft, *Criterion*, ix (1929–30) and *Dublin Review*, clxxxvi (1930); Q. Iredale, *Thomas Traherne* (1935); sections in the books on the metaphysical poets by J. B. Leishman and especially H. C. White (*supra*, III. 3); G. I. Wade (*supra*); A. H. Gilbert, 'Thomas Traherne as Artist', *MLQ* viii (1947); R. W. Hepburn, on 'The Nature and Dignity of Imagination', *Cambridge Journal*, vi (1952–3); K. W. Salter (*NQ* ii, 1955) and W. H. Marshall (*MLN* lxxiii, 1958) on original sin; R. L. Colie, on 'Traherne and the Infinite' (*HLQ* xxi, 1957–8); J. M. Wallace, on 'the

Structure of Meditation' (*ELH* xxv, 1958); M. Nicolson, *The Breaking of the Circle* (1950, 1960) and *Mountain Gloom and Mountain Glory* (1959); R. Ellrodt's full study (*supra*, III. 3); and a chapter in C. J. Stranks's *Anglican Devotion* (1961). M. Willy has a pamphlet essay and bibliography (*supra*, III. 3).

DANIEL TUVILL, c. 1584–1660

Tuvill, a clergyman (B.A., Cambridge, 1600–1; M.A., 1607), whose name appears in ten other forms, wrote *Essaies Politicke, and Morall* (1608), *Essayes, Morall and Theologicall* (1609; reissued 1629, 1631, 1638, as *Vade Mecum*), *The Dove and the Serpent* (1614), *Asylum Veneris, Or A Sanctuary for Ladies* (1616), *Christian Purposes and Resolutions* (1622), *St. Pauls Threefold Cord* (1635), and probably three poems in Overbury's *A Wife* (7th ed.). The essays are discussed by E. N. S. Thompson (*supra*, IV. 5) and, with other works, by J. L. Lievsay (*HLQ* ix, 1945–6; *MLN* lxiii, 1948; *JEGP* xlvii, 1948; *SP* xlvi, 1949; and *supra*, V. 6), who reported that he was editing the first two books.

BRIAN TWYNE, 1580–1644

As a young man Twyne wrote the first history of Oxford, *Antiquitatis Academiæ Oxoniensis Apologia* (1608), and he left large manuscript collections which were used by Wood. Some correspondence, 1596–1613, was printed in the *Bodleian Quarterly Record*, v (1927–8). S. Gibson had a full account of Twyne and his work in *Oxoniensia*, v (1940), and R. F. Ovenell of his library in *OBS*, n.s., iv, 1950 (1952).

SIR THOMAS URQUHART, 1611–60

After *Epigrams: Divine and Moral* (1641) Urquhart published (to omit his eccentric Greek titles) a mathematical treatise (1645), a work on chronology, including the famous Urquhart pedigree (1652), *The Discovery of A most exquisite Jewel* (1652), a tract on a universal language (1653), and the first two books of Rabelais (2 vols., 1653). Urquhart's version of the 3rd book was printed (dated 1693) in the 1694 edition of Rabelais of which the first two books were a reprint of Urquhart, the 4th and 5th translated by Motteux. The whole text of the translation by Urquhart and Motteux has been often reprinted, e.g. in the Tudor Translations, ed. C. Whibley (3 vols., 1900). Some miscellaneous works were collected in *Tracts* (1774) and all in the *Works* (Maitland Club, 1834). H. Miles edited *The Life and Death of the Admirable Crichtoun* (1927), from the *Jewel*; J. Purves a small volume of miscellaneous *Selections* (1942); and C. H. Wilkinson *A Challenge* (Luttrell Society, 1948), with a full introduction. There are a biography by J. Willcock (1899), essays by Whibley (repr. in *Studies in Frankness*, 1910) and other editors; a scholarly discussion by H. Brown, *Rabelais (supra, IV. 7)*; F. C. Roe's lecture, *Sir Thomas Urquhart and Rabelais* (1957), altered from his essay *(Aberdeen University Review, xxxv, 1953–4)*, and a note on a source of the *Epigrams* (ibid. xxxvii, 1957–8). K. B. Harder had notes in *NQ* i (1954), iii (1956), and iv (1957).

JAMES USSHER, 1581–1656

The standard edition of the works, with a life, is that of C. R. Elrington and J. H. Todd (17 vols., Dublin, 1847–64). Richard Parr's *Life* (1686) is valuable for the scholarly background of the age as well as for the man. The modern *Life and Times* is by J. A. Carr (1895); this may be supplemented by F. R. Bolton (under Jeremy Taylor, *supra*). In addition to the *DNB*, there is a sketch by E. W. Watson in *Typical English Churchmen*, ed. W. E. Collins (1902). An account of Ussher's historical work is in H. Arneke *(supra, IV. 6)*, of his preaching in W. F. Mitchell *(supra, V. 2)*. A group of studies appeared in *Hermathena*, lxxxviii (1956).

SIR HENRY VANE, 1613–62

Two of Vane's significant writings were *The Retired Mans Meditations, or the Mysterie and Power of Godliness* (1655) and *A Healing Question* (1656). The latter is reprinted in *Somers Tracts*, ed. Scott, vi (1811), in John Forster's *Sir Henry Vane* (D. Lardner's *Eminent British Statesmen*, iv, 1838), and in *Old South Leaflets*, General Series, vol. i, no. 6 (Boston, 1896). The *DNB* has a long article by Firth, the *Dictionary of American Biography* (1936) a short one by J. T. Adams. There are biographies by J. K. Hosmer (Boston, 1888), W. W. Ireland (1905), and John Willcock (1913). Vane's religious ideas are discussed by R. M. Jones, *Spiritual Reformers*, A. Barker, *Milton*, and in the books on toleration by M. Freund and W. K. Jordan, iv (all cited above in V. 2).

HENRY VAUGHAN, 1621/2–95

Vaughan's publications are listed in the biographical note. Apart from *Silex* i (1650, 1655), the only book reissued in his own century was *Olor Iscanus* (1679). After long oblivion— though Cowper owned and studied *Silex*—Vaughan crept into several anthologies in the early nineteenth century (E. L. Marilla, *MLQ* v, 1944); he was probably not known to Wordsworth (H. McMaster, *RES* xi, 1935). H. F. Lyte's *Sacred Poems* (1847) had a number of reprints and the text was included in the Temple Classics (1900). The complete works were edited by Grosart (4 vols., 1871), the complete *Poems* by Sir E. K. Chambers, with an introduction by H. C. Beeching (Muses' Library, 2 vols., 1896). The standard edition of the *Works* is that of L. C. Martin (2 vols., 1914; rev. and enlarged, 1957). The *Secular Poems* are elaborately edited by E. L. Marilla (Uppsala, Copenhagen, and Harvard, 1958). Among small editions are *The Mount of Olives*, &c., ed. L. I. Guiney (1902), *Silex Scintillans*, ed. W. A. L. Bettany (1905), and volumes of selections (Nonesuch Press, 1924 and Gregynog Press, 1924).

The standard biography is F. E. Hutchinson, *Henry Vaughan: A Life and Interpretation* (1947), though defects are noted (*JEGP* xlvii, 1948) by Marilla, who clarified some problems— Vaughan's military service (*JEGP* xli, 1942), the relations of Henry and his brother Thomas (*MLR* xxxix, 1944), the process of his 'conversion' (*RES* xxi, 1945; *MLN* lxiii, 1948).

The course of general criticism may be represented by L. I. Guiney, *A Little English Gallery* (New York, 1894); Lionel Johnson's essay of 1896 (repr. in *Post Liminium*, 1911); E. Dowden, *Puritan and Anglican* (1900); W. de la Mare's essay of 1915 (repr. in *Private View*, 1953); H. W. Wells, *Tercentenary of Henry Vaughan* (New York, 1922); E. Blunden, *On the Poems of Henry Vaughan* (1927); T. S. Eliot, *The Dial*, lxxxiii (1927); sections in the books on the metaphysical poets by G. Williamson, J. Bennett, J. B. Leishman, A. Esch, and especially H. C. White (*supra*, III. 3); F. Kermode, *RES* i (1950); M. M. Mahood and M.-S. Røstvig (*supra*, III. 3); S. L. Bethell (*supra*, III. 4); E. I. Watkin, *Poets and Mystics* (1953); H. J. Oliver's 'Reply' to Kermode, *JEGP* liii (1954); and Marilla's reply to Oliver, ibid. lvii (1958). Two recent books are Ross Garner's *Henry Vaughan: Experience and the Tradition* (University of Chicago,

1959), which, reacting against Hermetic preoccupations (*infra*), places Vaughan in the tradition of Christian devotion, and E. C. Pettet's general work, *Of Paradise and Light: A Study of Vaughan's Silex Scintillans* (1960). R. Ellrodt (*supra*, III. 3) has a full study. R. A. Durr has a book forthcoming (Harvard, 1962).

There have been many studies of philosophic and particularly Hermetic influence: R. Sencourt, *Outflying Philosophy* (Hildesheim, 1924); A. C. Judson, *SP* xxiv (1927); E. Holmes, *Henry Vaughan and the Hermetic Philosophy* (1932); W. O. Clough, *PMLA* xlviii (1933); A. J. M. Smith, *Papers of the Michigan Academy of Science, Arts and Letters*, xviii (1933); R. M. Wardle, *PMLA* li (1936); L. C. Martin, *Seventeenth Century Studies Presented to Sir Herbert Grierson* (1938) and *RES* xviii (1942); M. Y. Hughes, *Renaissance Studies in Honor of Hardin Craig* (Stanford, 1941); R. H. Walters, *RES* xxiii (1947); and S. L. Bethell, *Theology*, lvi (1953). Explications of particular poems cannot be recorded.

Some special studies are: on the problems of *Olor Iscanus*, W. R. Parker (*Library*, xx, 1939–40), H. R. Walley (*RES* xviii, 1942), and Marilla (*RES* xxiv, 1948, and *Secular Poems*, *supra*); R. P. Lehmann, on the contrast between Vaughan and Welsh poetry (*PQ* xxiv, 1946); P. M. Check, on the 'Latin Element' (*SP* xliv, 1947); notes by J. D. Simmonds and R. G. Howarth (*NQ* vii, 1960). E. Wolf listed books from Vaughan's library (*Book Collector*, ix, 1960).

Criticism of the years 1912–38 is listed in T. Spencer and M. Van Doren (*supra*, III. 3). Marilla compiled *A Comprehensive Bibliography* (*University of Alabama Studies*, 1948).

RICHARD VAUGHAN, EARL OF CARBERY, 1600?–86

Carbery was Jeremy Taylor's patron, and his third wife (1652) was the Lady Alice Egerton of *Comus*. *Advice to his Sonn*, written in 1651, was partly printed, in somewhat garbled form, in an anonymous anthology, *Practical Wisdom* (1824, 1901, 1907), where it was attributed to William, Earl of Bedford. A full and accurate text, from the Ellesmere MS., was printed by V. B. Heltzel, with a valuable introduction, in *HLB* (1937).

THOMAS VAUGHAN, 1621/2–66

Vaughan's alchemical and mystical writings (1650–5) were edited by A. E. Waite as *The Works of Thomas Vaughan: Eugenius*

Philalethes (1919). His poems were included in Grosart's edition of Henry's works (ii) and in Waite. For commentary there are Waite's introduction; E. Martin (*Fortnightly Review*, March 1924); and a number of the studies of Hermetic thought cited under Henry Vaughan.

SIR WILLIAM VAUGHAN, 1575–1641

Vaughan's writings belong rather to the documentary than to the literary domain, unless we except the conduct book, *The Golden-grove* (1600; ed. W. F. Marquardt, Northwestern University *Summaries of Doctoral Dissertations*, xvii, 1949). Others were *The Golden Fleece* (1626), *The Newlanders Cure* (1630), and *The Church Militant* (1640). Marquardt ('The First English Translators of Trajano Boccalini's *Ragguagli di Parnaso*', *HLQ* xv, 1951–2) shows that *The New-found Politicke* (1626) was the work of Florio, Thomas Scott (q.v.), and Vaughan. The *DNB* was corrected and amplified by M. Eccles (*HLQ* v, 1941–2) and Marquardt: e.g. Vaughan sent colonists to Newfoundland but did not go there himself. A. L. Rowse (*The Elizabethans and America*, 1959) follows the old accounts.

VERNEY FAMILY

We become acquainted with the Verneys through the following books: *Verney Papers. Notes of Proceedings in the Long Parliament, Temp. Charles I. Printed from original pencil memoranda taken in the House by Sir Ralph Verney, Knight*, ed. J. Bruce (Camden Society, xxxi, 1845); *Letters and Papers of the Verney Family down to the End of the Year 1639*, ed. Bruce (Camden Society, lvi, 1853); and especially *Memoirs of the Verney Family during the Civil War*, compiled by F. P. Verney (2 vols., 1892), and *Memoirs of the Verney Family During the Commonwealth 1650 to 1660*, by M. M. Verney (1894), who in a 4th volume (1899) carried the story up to 1696.

RICHARD (ROWLAND) VERSTEGAN, c. 1550–1640

The Catholic Verstegan, whose later life was spent abroad, produced an account of English and other martyrs, *Theatrum Crudelitatum Hæreticorum Nostri Temporis* (Antwerp, 1587; French trans., 1588, repr. Lille, 19–?), and *Odes. In Imitation of the Seaven Penitential Psalmes* ([Antwerp], 1601). There are selections from the latter, with a biographical sketch, in L. I. Guiney's *Recusant Poets* (1939). One side of Verstegan's activity is stressed in E. Rombauts, *Richard Verstegen, Een Polemist der Contra-Reformatie* (Brussels, 1933). S. C. Chew (*HLQ* viii, 1944–5) discussed his translation of O. van Veen's *Amorum Emblemata* (Antwerp, 1608). His best-known work is *A Restitution of Decayed Intelligence: In antiquities. Concerning the most noble and renowmed English nation* (Antwerp, 1605). He has been seen by S. Kliger (*supra*, V. 1) as 'The ancestor of the Gothicists in England' and he figures also in Kendrick (*supra*, IV. 6). On the linguistic side there are P. H. Goepp, *Philologica: The Malone Anniversary Studies* (Johns Hopkins, 1949) and R. F. Jones (*supra*, IV. 1). Verstegan's *Letters and Despatches* have been edited by A. G. Petti (Catholic Record Society, lii, 1959), who is preparing a critical biography.

EDMUND WALLER, 1606–87

The first issue of the *Poems* in 1645 may have been unauthorized, but Waller seems to have been associated with the second issue and the other two editions of 1645, although the 1664 edition claimed to be the first authorized one. The notorious *Instructions to a Painter* appeared in 1665 (enlarged 1666). The *Second Part of Mr. Waller's Poems* (1690) had a critical essay by Atterbury. The *Works* were edited by E. Fenton in 1729 and by P. Stockdale in 1772. Waller was included in the large collections of English poets. The standard modern edition is by G. Thorn-Drury (Muses' Library, 1893; 2 vols., 1905). Of the older critiques the most famous is Johnson's, in *Lives of the Poets* (1779). Among modern discussions, in addition to Thorn-Drury, Courthope (iii, 1903), and A. H. Thompson (*CHEL* vii), there are D. C. Tovey, *Reviews and Essays* (1879); H. C. Beeching, 'A Note upon Waller's Distich', in *An English Miscellany Presented to Dr. Furnivall* (1901), and 'Atterbury on Waller', in *Provincial Papers* (1906); a thesis by S. H. Werlein (MS., Harvard, 1919); important articles by R. C. Wallerstein on the heroic couplet (*PMLA* l, 1935) and G. Williamson, 'The Rhetorical Pattern of Neo-classical Wit' (*MP* xxxiii, 1935–6; *supra*, III. 1); and R. L. Sharp (*supra*, III. 3). F. W. Bateson had a brief rehabilitation in his *English Poetry* (1950). Discussions of Waller's Virgilian translation are cited under Godolphin (*supra*). Waller's reputation was traced by N. Roeckerath (under Herrick, *supra*). B. Chew's account of the first editions of the poems is in the *Bibliographer*, i (New York, 1902) and

Essays & Verses About Books (New York, 1926). P. H. Hardacre (*HLQ* xi, 1947–8) printed a letter of 1656 or 1657 from Waller to Hobbes.

JOHN WALLIS, 1616–1703

Wallis's mathematical and theological works cannot be itemized. With his *Defence Of the Royal Society* (1678) goes his account of his education and the beginnings of the Society (in *Peter Langtoft's Chronicle*, ed. T. Hearne, 2 vols., 1725). The standard book, J. F. Scott's *Mathematical Work of John Wallis* (1938), is for mathematicians, but the first two chapters deal with Wallis's life and the Royal Society. Scott also treats him in his *History of Mathematics* (1958) and gives a general sketch in Hartley's *The Royal Society* (*supra*, V. 3). Wallis figures in other accounts of the Society, and in some books on Hobbes. His *Grammatica Linguæ Anglicanæ* (1653) is studied by M. Lehnert and E. J. Dobson and discussed briefly by R. F. Jones (*supra*, IV. 1).

BRIAN WALTON, 1599/1600–61

The *Biblia Sacra Polyglotta*, the work of Walton and many collaborators, was published in six tomes dated 1657. Information about it and about the state of oriental learning is given in H. J. Todd's *Memoirs and Writings of . . . Brian Walton* (2 vols., 1821), in the biblical bibliography of Darlow and Moule (*supra*, IV. 8), in W. E. Barnes's essay in *In Memoriam Adolphus William Ward* (1924) and in Harris Fletcher's books on Milton's Semitic and biblical learning (*supra*, IV. 7).

IZAAK WALTON, 1593–1683

The Compleat Angler (1653; facsimile, 1928) was much enlarged and altered in 1655. The 3rd and 4th editions appeared in 1661 (repr. 1664) and 1668. The 5th (1676) included some new matter by Walton, Cotton's imitative supplement (which has often been printed with Walton's book), and Robert Venables's *Experienced Angler* (first printed in 1662). There were 10 editions and reprints in the eighteenth century, 164 in the nineteenth, and the twentieth will doubtless surpass that number if it has not done so already. The bibliographical history was set forth by Peter Oliver, *A New Chronicle of The Compleat Angler* (1936). H. J. Oliver analysed 'The Composition and Revisions' (*MLR* xlii, 1947). The place of the *Angler* in piscatory literature was treated by R. B. Marston, *Walton and Some Earlier Writers on Fish and Fishing* (1894). The question of Walton's debt to the recently discovered *Arte of Angling* (1577) is discussed by G. E. Bentley et al. in their edition (with a facsimile) of the *Arte* (Princeton, 1956) and fully by M. S. Goldman, *Studies in Honor of T. W. Baldwin*, ed. D. C. Allen (University of Illinois, 1958); T. P. Harrison (*NQ* vii, 1960) identifies the author of the *Arte* as Rev. William Samuel. To introductory essays on the *Angler* by a long line of editors may be added Sir Leslie Stephen's 'Country Books' (*Hours in a Library*, ed. 1907, iv) and B. D. Greenslade, '*The Compleat Angler* and the Sequestered Clergy' (*RES* v, 1954).

The *Lives* underwent continual revision in substance and style. The life of Donne, first printed with Donne's *LXXX Sermons* (1640), was much enlarged and printed separately in 1658. Further additions were made in the collected *Lives* of 1670 and 1675. The life of Wotton, in *Reliquiæ Wottonianæ* (1651), was enlarged in the 2nd edition (1654), in the *Lives* (1670), and in the 3rd edition of the *Reliquiæ* (1672). The life of Hooker (1665) was reprinted with a few changes in Hooker's *Works* (1666) and the *Lives* (1670). The life of Herbert was issued twice in 1670, by itself and in the *Lives*; a revised version was prefixed to the 10th edition of *The Temple* (1674), and slight changes were made in the *Lives* (1675). The life of Sanderson, prefixed to a volume of Sanderson's tracts (1678), was enlarged and added to the 7th and 8th editions of Sanderson's *Sermons* (1681, 1686). The first four lives were printed together in 1670; the chief additions in the 2nd edition (called the 4th) of 1675 were in the life of Donne. Among modern editions of the five biographies are those in the Temple Classics (2 vols.), the Scott Library, and the World's Classics, the last in the original spelling, with an essay by Saintsbury. John Butt edited Walton's notes on Hales (q.v.) and compiled a bibliography of the *Lives* in *OBS* ii, part iv (1930).

A. W. Pollard edited the *Angler* and the *Lives* (1901). *The Compleat Walton*, ed. Sir G. Keynes (1929), includes, with the major works, the anonymous tract *Love and Truth* (1680), miscellaneous notes, letters, verses, &c.

There are good short studies of Walton the biographer by D. A. Stauffer (*supra*, IV. 6) and J. Butt (*ESEA* xix, 1934). D. Novarr's *The Making of Walton's Lives* (Cornell, 1958) is an

exhaustive analysis of his sources, methods, revisions, and attitudes. Fresh material on one biography was given in C. J.
Sisson's *Judicious Marriage of Mr. Hooker* (1940); and F. E.
Pamp examined Walton's Anglican motives in the same life
(*Church History*, xvii, 1948). H. J. Oliver had a corrective
account of Walton's prose style in *RES* xxi (1945). Oliver's
argument for Walton's authorship of *Love and Truth* (*RES* xxv,
1949) was supported by D. Novarr (ibid. ii, 1951).

The standard life of Walton, Stapleton Martin's *Izaak Walton
and his Friends* (2nd ed., 1904) has been supplemented by Keynes
(*supra*); by A. M. Coon, in Cornell *Abstracts of Theses 1938* and
various journals (1937–41); and in Novarr's book. M. Bottrall's
Izaak Walton is a pamphlet-essay with a bibliography (British
Council, 1955).

WILLIAM WALWYN, 1600–80

To the references given under Lilburne (*supra*) should be
added W. K. Jordan, iv (*supra*, V. 2), W. Schenk (*Economic
History Review*, xiv, 1944), and O. Lutaud's account of Walwyn's
use of Montaigne (*Rivista di letterature moderne e comparate*, xii,
1959).

SETH WARD, 1617–89

Ward published sermons and theological and mathematical
treatises, but he is perhaps best known as co-author with John
Wilkins of *Vindiciæ Academiarum* (1654), a reply to John Webster,
Hobbes, and Dell. The fullest account of the controversy is in
R. F. Jones, *Ancients and Moderns* (1936). J. M. J. Fletcher has
a discursive biographical sketch, with a bibliography, in the
Wiltshire Archæological & Natural History Magazine, xlix (1940).
Walter Pope's *Life* (1697) has been edited by J. B. Bamborough
(Luttrell Society, 1961).

JOHN WEBSTER, 1610–82

For the background of Webster's *Academiarum Examen* (1654)
reference may be made to the note on Seth Ward just above.
In another realm, the limitations of Webster's supposed scepticism in *The Displaying of Supposed Witchcraft* (1677) are displayed
by G. L. Kittredge (*supra*, IV. 2).

SIR ANTHONY WELDON, d. 1649?

The Court and Character of King James (1650; enlarged in 1651 with 'The Court of King Charles') was reprinted in *Secret History of the Court of James the First*, ed. Scott (2 vols., 1811), and in *Smeeton's Historical & Biographical Tracts* (1820), i. Among critics of the work were Godfrey Goodman, Sir William Sanderson (*Aulicus Coquinariæ*, 1650; repr. in *Secret History*), and Heylyn. Weldon's *Perfect Description of Scotland* (pr. 1647), wrongly attributed to Howell, is reprinted in the *Secret History*, in Nichols's *Progresses* (1828), iii, and in P. H. Brown, *Early Travellers in Scotland* (1891).

ELIZABETH JANE WESTON, 1582–1612

Poemata appeared at Frankfort in 1602, *Parthenicon* at Prague in 1606. *Opuscula* were edited by J. C. Kalckhoff (Frankfort, 1723). There are accounts of the author in G. Ballard, *Memoirs of Several Ladies of Great Britain* (1752; *Memoirs of British Ladies*, 1775), the *DNB*, Myra Reynolds, *The Learned Lady in England* (1920), and A. Kolář, *Humanistická Básnířka Vestonia* (Bratislavě, 1926), which has a two-page summary in English.

BENJAMIN WHICHCOTE, 1609–83

Select Sermons, based on the author's and hearers' notes, were printed in 1698 with a preface by Shaftesbury, and re-edited by W. Wishart (1742). Larger collections were *Several Discourses*, ed. J. Jeffery (4 vols., 1701–7), and *Works* (4 vols., Aberdeen, 1751). *Moral and Religious Aphorisms*, ed. Jeffery (1703) was enlarged, with the Whichcote-Tuckney letters, by S. Salter (1753). Selections are in E. T. Campagnac's *Cambridge Platonists* (1901). The *Aphorisms* were reprinted in 1930 with a preface by W. R. Inge. Whichcote is discussed by J. Tulloch (*supra*, V. 2); B. F. Westcott, in two essays, *Masters in English Theology*, ed. A. Barry (1877) and *Essays in the History of Religious Thought in the West* (1891); R. M. Jones, *Spiritual Reformers*; in the books on Cambridge Platonism by Powicke, Pawson, and De Pauley; and by W. F. Mitchell and W. K. Jordan, iv (all these cited above in V. 2).

NATHANIEL WHITING, *c.* 1612–*post* 1662

Le hore di recreatione: Or, The Pleasant Historie Of Albino and Bellama (1637) is reprinted in Saintsbury, iii (1921). It is described by A. I. T. Higgins (*supra*, III. 3).

RICHARD WHITLOCK, *c.* 1616–*c.* 1672

Whitlock, who does not appear in the *DNB*, was an Oxonian who studied law and medicine and at the Restoration took orders. G. Williamson (*PQ* xv, 1936 and *supra*, III. 1; and his *Senecan Amble*) showed the significance of his rare and only work, *ZΩOTOMÍA, or, Observations on the Present Manners of the English* (1654). The preface has been edited in *Two Seventeenth-Century Prefaces* (1949) by A. K. Croston, who summarizes the meagre biographical data and Whitlock's open-minded defence of learning.

JOHN WILKINS, 1614–72

Apart from sermons, Wilkins's chief works were: *The Discovery of a World in the Moone* (1638), enlarged in 1640 with a *Discourse on the earth as a planet*; *Mercury* (1641), a book on ciphers; *Ecclesiastes* (1646), a book on preaching often reprinted; *Mathematicall Magick* (1648), of which one chapter, on 'an Ark for submarine Navigations', is reprinted in Sir Hubert Wilkins's *Under the North Pole* (1931); *Vindiciæ Academiarum* (1654), cited above under Seth Ward; *An Essay Towards a Real Character, And a Philosophical Language* (1668), a part of which is reprinted in F. Techmer, *Beiträge zur Geschichte der französischen und englischen Phonetik und Phonographie* (Heilbronn, 1889); and *Of the Principles and Duties of Natural Religion* (1675). The *Mathematical and Philosophical Works* were collected in 1708 (repr., 2 vols., 1802).

P. A. W. Henderson's *Life and Times* (1910) has been superseded by many special studies, e.g. R. F. Jones (*supra*, III. 4), D. Stimson and other writers on the Royal Society, and R. K. Merton and R. S. Westfall (all cited above in V. 3). The sketch in Hartley's *Royal Society* (*supra*, V. 3) makes no reference to modern scholarship; J. G. Crowther's chapter (*Founders of British Science*, 1960) is better. Wilkins's astronomical ideas have been treated by M. Nicolson and F. R. Johnson (*supra*, V. 3) and G. McColley (*Annals of Science*, i, iii, and iv, 1936–9; *PMLA* lii, 1937; and *SP* xxxv, 1938). Dr. Johnson's use of Wilkins's ideas for a flying-machine and a submarine was shown by G. J. Kolb (*MP* xlvii, 1949–50) and R. Fox (*NQ* v, 1958). His theory of preaching is discussed by W. F. Mitchell (*supra*, V. 2), his concern with the reform of prose style by F. Christensen (*MLQ* vii, 1946) and some writers listed above in III. 2. Wilkins's interest in a universal language has been much studied: E. N. Andrade (*Annals of Science*, i, 1936); L. Hogben, *Dangerous Thoughts* (1939); C. Emery (*Isis*, xxxviii, 1948; *MLQ* ix, 1948); B. F. DeMott (*Isis*, xlviii, 1957; *JEGP* lvii, 1958); O. Funke (*English Studies*, xl, 1959); and some of the writings listed above in IV. 1, e.g. E. J. Dobson. H. M. Lord compiled a full *Bibliography* (typescript: London?, 1957).

ROGER WILLIAMS, 1603?–83

The standard edition of Williams's chief works was issued by the Narragansett Club (6 vols., 1866–74). E. B. Underhill edited *The Bloudy Tenent, of Persecution, for cause of Conscience* of 1644 (Hanserd Knollys Society, 1848); large extracts are in A. S. P. Woodhouse, *Puritanism and Liberty* (1938). The latest biographies are by S. H. Brockunier (New York, 1940) and O. E. Winslow (New York, 1957). Experts in seventeenth-century thought have got away from the unhistorical 'liberal' stereotype established a generation ago. Some of the many discussions are: P. Miller, *Orthodoxy in Massachusetts* (1933); W. Haller, *Tracts on Liberty* (1934); W. K. Jordan, iii (*supra*, V. 2); Woodhouse (*supra*); A. Barker (*supra*, V. 2); R. H. Bainton, *The Travail of Religious Liberty* (Philadelphia, 1951); M. Calamandrei, *Church History*, xxi (1952); P. Miller, *Roger Williams* (Indianapolis, 1953), a volume of selections and commentary; and Haller, *Liberty and Reformation* (*supra*, V. 1).

ARTHUR WILSON, 1595–1652

The History of Great Britain, Being The Life and Reign of King James the First (1653) was reprinted in White Kennett, ii (*supra*, IV. 6). *Observations of God's Providence, in the Tract of my Life* is in Francis Peck's *Desiderata Curiosa* (2 vols., 1732–5; repr. 1779) and in Bliss's edition (1814) of Wilson's play, *The Inconstant Lady*. His dramatic work is summarized in G. E. Bentley, v (*supra*, I).

GERRARD WINSTANLEY, 1609–*post* 1660

G. H. Sabine edited Winstanley's *Works . . . with an appendix of Documents Relating to the Digger Movement* (Cornell, 1941); L. Hamilton a volume of selections (1944). Winstanley's ideas have been more or less misconstrued by Marxist interpreters, most of whom are omitted from this list: G. P. Gooch, *Political Thought in England* (1915); M. James and D. M. Wolfe (*supra*, V. 1); D. W. Petegorsky, *Left-Wing Democracy in the English Civil War* (1940); Sabine (*supra*); J. M. Patrick, *UTQ* xii (1942–3); W. S. Hudson, *Journal of Modern History*, xviii (1946); W. Schenk (*supra*, V. 1); P. Elmen, *Church History*, xxiii (1954); and P. Zagorin (*supra*, V. 1). P. H. Hardacre (*HLQ* xxii, 1958–9) printed a letter of 1650 from the needy Winstanley to Lady Eleanor Davies (q.v.).

GEORGE WITHER, 1588–1667

Wither was recalled from oblivion by Percy's *Reliques* and revived by Lamb, Brydges, et al. Nearly all his works were reprinted by the Spenser Society (1871–82) and several early ones in Arber's *English Garner*, iv and vi (1882–3). The best edition, chiefly of his pastoral verse, is by F. Sidgwick (2 vols., 1902). Besides Lamb's essay, remarks in his letters, and comments reproduced by Swinburne in his 'Charles Lamb and George Wither' (*Miscellanies*, 1886), there are essays by Sidgwick (*supra*), J. Fyvie, *Some Literary Eccentrics* (1906), and Gosse, *Selected Essays, Second Series* (1928); some pages in the general histories and in H. Genouy (*supra*, III. 3); and a chapter in L. Jonas (*supra*, IV. 9). The fullest study is the unpublished Harvard thesis (1928) of J. M. French, who has printed Witheriana in *PMLA* xlv (1930) and *HLB* (1931) and *Wither's History of the Pestilence* (Harvard, 1932). Other sides of his work are treated in books on psalmody (*supra*, III. 3); in I. Tramer, *Studien zu den Anfängen der puritanischen Emblemliteratur in England: Andrew Willet—George Wither* (Berlin, 1934); W. M. Clyde (*supra*, IV. 10); W. K. Jordan, ii (*supra*, V. 2); E. M. Clark, on Wither and Milton (*SP* lvi, 1959); C. V. Wedgwood (*supra*, IV. 2), on the war-time satirist. There are bibliographical articles on the *Workes* of 1620 by P. Simpson and L. Kirschbaum (*Library*, vi, 1925–6 and xix, 1938–9); and notes, chiefly on the canon, by L. H. Kendall (*NQ* cxcviii, 1953, ii, 1955, iii, 1956; *RES* v, 1954; *HLQ* xx, 1956–7). The attribution of *The Great Assises* (*supra*, IV. 3) to Wither is not accepted by its editor or J. M. French (*NQ* i, 1954); J. Frank (*supra*, IV. 3) thinks him 'almost certainly' the author. In *HLQ* xxiii (1959–60) French records and discusses Thorn-Drury's notes on Wither and reprints an attributed poem.

HEZEKIAH WOODWARD, 1590–1675

Woodward contributed tracts to the religious controversy; his use of some of Milton's anti-episcopal ideas was suggested by G. W. Whiting (*SP* xxxiii, 1936). He is best known as a friend of Hartlib (q.v.) and a fellow-supporter of Comenian education. Short extracts are in Edith Rowland, *A Pedagogue's Commonplace Book* (1925), and F. Watson, *Beginnings* (*supra*, V. 6). His views are discussed by Watson and by W. A. L. Vincent and E. Sirluck (*supra*, V. 6).

JOHN WORTHINGTON, 1618–71

The most popular of Worthington's publications was *The Christians Pattern* (1654), a translation of à Kempis or rather a revision of the one by B. F. (Anthony Hoskins) of 1613. He edited the works of John Smith (1660) and Joseph Mead (1664). His own *Miscellanies . . . Also A Collection of Epistles, Written to Mr Hartlib* appeared in 1704. The *Diary and Correspondence*, ed. J. Crossley and R. C. Christie (Chetham Society, 3 vols., 1847–86), gives a good picture of contemporary scholarship. Christie compiled a *Bibliography* (Chetham Society, 1888). Further information is in W. A. Copinger, *Bibliographiana No. 3. On the English Translations of the 'Imitatio Christi'* (1900).

SIR HENRY WOTTON, 1568–1639

The first collection of prose and verse, with Walton's *Life*, was *Reliquiæ Wottonianæ* (1651; enlarged, 1654, 1672, 1685). Reprinted pieces are: *The Elements of Architecture* (1624; in *Somers Tracts*, ed. Scott, iii, 1810, and Dunham and Pargellis, *supra*, II. 1; ed. G. Kirkham, Springfield, Mass., 1897, and S. Prideaux, 1903); *A Philosophical Survey of Education or Moral Architecture and The Aphorisms of Education*, ed. H. S. Kermode (1938). The poems were edited by Dyce (Percy Society, vi, 1842) and J. Hannah (1845 and later edns.). J. B. Leishman summarized the complicated history of 'You meaner Beauties of the Night' (*Library*, xxvi, 1945–6). The 'Character of a Happy Life' first appeared among the Overburian characters (4th ed., 1614); its bibliography was traced by C. F. Main (*Library*, x, 1955). Walton's *Life* was fully examined by D. Novarr (under Walton). The standard account of Wotton is L. P. Smith's *Life and Letters* (2 vols., 1907). Anna M. Crinò published unedited letters in her *Fatti e figure del Seicento Anglo-Toscano* (Florence, 1957). There are essays by A. W. Fox, *A Book of Bachelors* (1899), P. E. More, *Shelburne Essays, Fifth Series* (1908), and F. Hard, *Pacific Spectator*, vii (1953).

MARY LADY WROTH, *c.* 1586–*post* 1640

Sir Philip Sidney's niece, who married Sir Robert Wroth in 1604, was a literary patroness and author of *The Countess of Montgomeries Urania* (1621); the sale was stopped because of references to scandals (J. J. O'Connor, *NQ* ii, 1955). The romance is noticed by E. A. Baker (*supra*, IV. 4) and B. G. MacCarthy (*supra*, V. 5).

INDEX

Modern names, some minor names of the period, and many incidental references are omitted. Main entries are in bold figures. An asterisk indicates a biographical note. Topics and seventeenth-century authors in the bibliography are indexed.